THE HORIZON BOOK OF

# MAKERS
# OF
# MODERN
# THOUGHT

THE HORIZON BOOK OF

# MAKERS OF MODERN THOUGHT

With an introduction by BRUCE MAZLISH

Published by
AMERICAN HERITAGE PUBLISHING CO., INC.
New York

Several of these essays appeared originally in *Horizon* Magazine
and in *The Horizon Book of the Renaissance*. Two are adapted
from *The Western Intellectual Tradition* by J. Bronowski and
Bruce Mazlish. The rest were written expressly for this book.

Library of Congress Catalog Card Number: 75-190074
ISBN: 07–030339–8

# TABLE OF CONTENTS

# INTRODUCTION

"What is Man that Thou shouldst be mindful of him?" is a question that still resonates dramatically for us, even when deprived of its religious intonations. One of the most compelling answers is that "Man is the thinking animal"; he is that creature who has "thoughts." His thoughts are carried by language, which becomes a sort of social genetic code, transmitting the accumulated experience of generations in symbol form. As J. Bronowski, one of our authors included here, remarks elsewhere, "Human progress stems from the gift of fixing past experience in images which are moved in the mind to make imaginary experiences."

Animals other than man can be said also to have language, to communicate, and, in some sense, to "think." But they do not have "thoughts," in the sense we are attributing to human beings. Only man, it seems, can play out aspects of his life purely in his imagination, without committing himself physically to the projected experiences; or only in part, as he chooses. In this sense, while a cat may have nine lives, they are all basically repetitious; man has the potential for many lives, through his imagination, and all possibly different. Whatever the exact distinctions between man's thought and that of the other animals—the subject of lively debates by philosophers and scientists, as many of the articles included in this book will show—no one will deny the central importance for man of his ability to move images in his mind so as to make imaginary experiences, and to transmit these to his descendants.

This book deals with some of the great movers of images in the mind, the monumental thinkers of the modern period. These men have laid the imaginary mental rails along which our own thoughts now travel, though we are frequently unaware of how directed we are by these "Makers of Modern Thought." In spite of these men being dead, they live in our minds, in a most contemporary fashion.

In our choice of thinkers, we have decided to include no one before the Renaissance, though we realize that no Renaissance thinker emerges self-made and devoid of intellectual ancestors. We have made this choice on the grounds that the Renaissance is, by and large, the beginning of the modern age. Scholars argue heatedly over this point, but somewhere around 1450–1500 one senses an increasing interest in man as a creature capable of change, perhaps even progressive change; in man as a secular being, a scientist, Faustian in ambition, and not merely a fallen Adam seeking salvation; and in man as a unique personality, whose individuality expresses

*By* BRUCE MAZLISH

itself in new and changing works—artistic or technological, political or intellectual—and this perception of a total personality is a fitting corrective to any view that thought is merely an abstract entity rather than the vital product of developing men living in changing circumstances.

Next, we have arbitrarily decided to include no living persons, though some would surely qualify. We must also admit that we have not attempted to include all the makers of modern thought, but again, though somewhat less arbitrarily, have necessarily made a choice. As best we could, we have included undeniable giants—the Newtons, Darwins, and Marxes—but we have also included a number of those whose presence may surprise some readers: a George Perkins Marsh, a Mary Wollstonecraft, a Norbert Wiener. They were chosen not because they bulk very large in orthodox histories of modern thought, but because what they thought and said is of particular relevance to the ideas and problems of our own time.

Even with rigid selection, our list of thinkers is quite large. To fix their contribution luminously, we have called upon an almost equally long list of present-day scholars and writers, from numerous fields. Intellectual history has become so complex, and must deal with so many areas of special knowledge, that the single enterprise even of a resolute scholar may no longer be enough. Human thought is a collective endeavor, and seems to call for a collective effort to best capture its meaning and significance. We have sought, therefore, scholars whose expertise vis-à-vis a particular figure has allowed them to write pieces of unusual lucidity and readable thoughtfulness.

We have wished, also, to guard against narrowness, and our authors have responded with a constant attention to the interplay of ideas, both in the mind of a single thinker and among the various thinkers considered. The thought of Descartes, for example, looms large in the article on Wiener and Warren McCulloch, as well as in the article on Descartes. Necessarily, treating occasionally of the same ideas and thinkers from different perspectives, our authors have implicitly, if not explicitly, presented contradictory judgments. Is Luther a medieval mind, or the pioneer of the modern outlook? The authors of the pieces on Luther and Calvin seem implicitly to render different verdicts. Did Descartes mainly set man the knower off against nature the object, or primarily stress that man must, before examining the universe, examine his way of looking at it? The chapter on Wiener and McCulloch offers one emphasis; that on Descartes another. We think such colliding views and emphases healthy and instructive.

Our articles do not offer disembodied specters, ideas without a mind and body in back of them. We believe that the personality of the man forms part of the meaning and importance of his thought. Or, better still, that thought (in the broadest sense) is merely one, though one of the most important, embodiments of a man's personality and life. The two go together, and are separated only at the utmost risk. Modern philosophy, as with Wittgenstein, seems to support this "anthropological" view of thinking. As Professor Malcolm remarks, "An outstanding feature of Wittgenstein's second philosophy is his concern in showing how concepts are linked to actions and activities, to responses and reactions, to the expression of the concepts in human life. In a sense his conceptual investigations are anthropological studies; as he puts it, they are 'remarks on the nature history of human beings.' "

Science, too, appears increasingly to confirm the idea that thinker and thought are fundamentally connected and must be studied together. Moreover, with Freud, our attention can be directed to the unconscious elements of a man's thoughts, as well as to the conscious, and to the connection of both to his total personality. With such inspirations to guide us, our authors have mixed significant biographical accounts with intellectual history, and offer us, where possible, fascinating portraits of man and thought conjoined.

A re there overriding themes that emerge from this account of man's mental odyssey? A number of syntheses can be made of our various pieces, but each will merely highlight some aspects of the kaleidoscopic picture. It it hoped that each reader will make his own synthesis and constantly reshape it as he reads on. As a purely personal, and provisional, list of themes that intrigue me, I can offer the following. In the pieces that make up this book, I see the emergence of science into general thought as a persistent thread. In this process there is a constant cross-fertilization, or reverse effect as well, with, for example, the general ideas of a Malthus, derived from political economy, influencing a Darwin in his theory of evolution, and then the latter influencing political economy in terms of Social Darwinism. This is a blatant example; the reader will detect far subtler instances as he reads the various selections.

At the time of the Renaissance, and still in the sixteenth and seventeenth centuries, science was closely connected with religious thought and institutions. At times, the connection was stimulating; at other times, suffocating. Gradually, however, the two fields drew increasingly apart. While science might still shake religious belief in the nineteenth century, it no longer drew sustenance from it or ran the danger of being stifled by it. Secularization of thought, and life, pushed constantly outward from the scientific beachhead, eventually to dominate the entire landscape of man's thought and institutions.

Yet, such increasing secularization ought not to obscure the steady throb of the religious impulse. In the sixteenth century religion still dominated Western man by both its inspirations and its institutions. Men such as Erasmus, Luther, Calvin, and Loyola felt deeply not only about the nature of man and his moral obligations but about the authorities who might rightfully speak on these matters. Then, the Reformation and Counter Reformation divided the institutional world and left it increasingly open to tolerant attack. More and more the divided institutions lost their true vitality, though not their seeming strength. Religious notions became translated into secular concepts—for example, Providence became Adam Smith's "invisible hand" regulating the market place—and religious enthusiasm a private affair. In such a climate a Hegel and a Kierkegaard flourished rather than a Luther and a Pascal; and a Nietzsche with his "God is dead" voiced the negative affirmation of the religious commitment. The commitment, however, was still there.

Somewhere seemingly between science and religion stood philosophy. A dominant theme of the philosopher's endeavor, from the time of Hobbes and Locke to the present, has been the inquiry into the knower rather than the thing known. Even God, as in Hegel, was important primarily for His consciousness. A related main thrust of the philosophers was an inquiry into language, whether Hobbes's attack on ambiguity, Bentham's on fictions, or Wittgenstein's on nonempirical statements; for language was increasingly perceived as the tool by which we know, the probe by which we seek to discover the reality behind appearances. Mathematical or verbal, language (and logic) was the means by which man imagined experience in his mind and imagined new combinations not yet in actuality.

Another constant theme of modern thought has been the problem of rationality and irrationality, no simple matter to decide. Are only science and logic rational? Mystical and poetic means of "knowing" irrational? A glance at Rousseau's thought shows us how crucial this problem had become for late-eighteenth-century man, as he began to wrestle with the consequences of his increasingly scienticized and secularized world. Industrialized society posed the problem anew, and the question of what is a rational society joined the ancient question of what is a just society, both adding to the seriousness of the intellectual question of rationality-irrationality.

For me, two other themes are closely joined to the one just mentioned. The first is the problem of control versus chance, or the way in which man seeks to shape his own existence rather than be at the mercy of hazard. Machiavelli and Clausewitz, as much as Newton and Wiener–McCulloch, seek to control the phenomena—political, military, astronomical, computational—that they study. Or at least to explore the limits under which control is possible. The second theme is that our thinkers often seek to place their controlled phenomena in the service of constructing a more just and rational world for men—or, as Mary Wollstonecraft reminds us, men *and* women! Thus, many of our thinkers are also reformers, searching for economic order, an equitable social system, etc., and trying to inspire us, as well, with their particular vision.

Lastly, I would stress the theme of our thinkers moving us into the modern world at the same time that they are helping us to recapture the whole of our antiquity. Modernization, paradoxically, involves the deepest historical sense of what we have been before. Thus, a Darwin enables us to see how we evolved animally. A Hegel and a Marx, how we have developed religiously and economically. A Frazer, how we have moved as a mythmaking creature. A Freud, how we have evolved psychically. At this point in time, aided by our makers of modern thought, we have all become *anthropologists,* in the deepest and most extended sense of that word. In short, one cannot be modern without encapsulating all of man's varied past.

The articles that follow in this book touch on these themes and many, many more. Each reader will draw from the articles his own inspiration, for it is a rich legacy that they offer us. Contact with the minds, and men, introduced to us in what follows cannot be other than an exhilarating experience. In part taxing, nonetheless the reading ahead is constantly exciting. Whatever synthesis of themes and awareness of ideas each reader devises for himself, we shall all, I believe, emerge with a sense of sheer enjoyment of the individual contributions.

# LEONARDO
# DA VINCI
## 1452-1519

Leonardo was born outside the small town of Vinci, near Florence, in 1452; the traditional date of his birthday is April 15. The birthday is hardly worth remembering, but the year is, for its remoteness remains a constant surprise. Leonardo's gifts speak so directly, his imagination is so immediate to us, that we have to remind ourselves with an effort that he was born more than five hundred years ago. He lived long before William Shakespeare and Rembrandt and Isaac Newton. Leonardo was dead before Nicolaus Copernicus felt sure that the earth goes around the sun; he was an old man, unhappy and full of regrets, when Martin Luther began the Reformation; and he had already passed the turning point of middle life when Christopher Columbus discovered America.

Leonardo was the illegitimate son of a lawyer and a woman who may have been a servant in the house of Leonardo's grandparents. The boy's father did take several wives—each a member of a good Florentine family—but not for over twenty years were there any more children. Leonardo was thus his father's only child during those formative years.

Italians in the Renaissance were not outraged by the thought that a bright child had been conceived out of wedlock. Illegitimacy was a commonplace of the time; men were proud of making their own way; and Churchmen and *condottieri,* artists and statesmen, boasted that they were born out of wedlock. This was no stigma among the thrusting, self-made men of the Renaissance; indeed, as the historian Jakob Burckhardt wrote, "The fitness of the individual, his worth and ca-

*In this self-portrait Leonardo drew an old man with the fire of his genius dimmed.*

*By* J. BRONOWSKI

pacity, were of more weight than all the laws and usages which prevailed elsewhere in the West."

Nevertheless, we get the feeling that Leonardo never walked easily in the houses of the great, and that this wariness goes back to his childhood. There is something hooded and withdrawn about his character which calls up a picture of a child made much of and yet not at home in the house of his birth. All his life he hated to see suffering. The story is told of Leonardo buying birds in the market place, holding them in his hand for a moment, and then setting them free. It is evident that in that rough, insensitive time he was one of the few men who could not bear to give pain to animals.

When Leonardo was about fourteen, his father apprenticed him to Andrea del Verrocchio, one of the noted artists in Florence. At that time Florence was aflower with wealth and splendor; its tone was set, its taste was led, by the great family of the Medici. Here the display of riches was more than a reward for success—it was a public announcement of status and authority.

The *botteghe,* or workshops, of Verrocchio and other artists supplied this society with its beautiful treasures and trinkets. Verrocchio was a painter and sculptor, and was also a goldsmith and a decorator. His studio was, in an exact sense, a workshop, and it was Verrocchio's business to supply from it a picture or a chair, a statue or a goblet, a golden chafing dish or a ceremonial suit of armor. Verrocchio himself could turn his hand to all these things; however, he was a rather wooden painter, and he seems therefore to have turned more and more to sculpture.

One reason why Verrocchio could turn from painting was that his apprentice Leonardo was so good at it. The artist who ran his studio as a workshop had to conserve and to divide its labor intelligently and expediently; and when he had an apprentice who could paint, he gave him his head—and did something else himself. Tradition has it that Leonardo was still a boy when he painted an angel in one of Verrocchio's religious commissions, and made it more lifelike than his master could.

The story of the boy painter who outdoes his master is characteristic of the Renaissance; it is also told of Raphael and others. For this was an age in love with surprises, eager to discover genius, native and untaught. Yet the evidence is that the story is true of Leonardo. There is at least one picture by Verrocchio, *The Baptism of Christ,* in which one of the angels is unlike the rest, and has clearly been painted by a more sensitive and subtler hand. Moreover, the landscape of the *Baptism,* the detail of trees and grasses, has a vivid intimacy and an absorbed lucidness of vision which belong to no painter before Leonardo. There is at least one other painting by Verrocchio whose landscape shows the hand of Leonardo in the same way. Verrocchio must have known that the young Leonardo was not merely a better painter: he was a new painter.

Leonardo finished his training with Verrocchio about 1472, when he was twenty or so, and then went on working in Florence for another nine or ten years. He was good at other things besides painting. He is described as tall and handsome, graceful in all his actions, and apparently he had a fine singing voice, and the official records show that he was accused once of some homosexual scrape. (The evidence is that he lacked the usual sensual feelings for women, and tended rather to admire strong men.) He was interested in mathematics and mechanics, and particularly in the mechanics by which living things move: he constantly drew birds in flight, and he also made his first studies of human anatomy then.

These are odd interests in a painter, in the traditional sense; and yet they are inseparable from that desire to enter into the very structure of natural things which to Leonardo was the essence of painting. Later in life he wrote very simply about this:

And you who say that it is better to look at an anatomical demonstration than to see these drawings, you would be right, if it were possible to observe all the details shown in these drawings in a single figure, in which, with all your ability, you will not see nor acquire a knowledge of more than some few veins, while, in order to obtain an exact and complete knowledge of these, I have dissected more than ten human bodies, destroying all the various members, and removing even the very smallest particles of the flesh which surrounded these veins without causing any effusion of blood other than the imperceptible bleeding of the capillary veins. And, as one single body did not suffice for so long a time, it was necessary to proceed by stages with so many bodies as would render my knowledge complete; and this I repeated twice over in order to discover the differences.

*Leonardo's signature, above, in the mirror writing that fills his notebooks, is read from right to left.*

This is an account of work in anatomy, but it carries no hint of a medical interest. For Leonardo did not want to cure men: he wanted to know how their bodies are made and work. He distrusted the doctors of his time, and indeed the whole of medical and chemical science then, which saw nature as an interplay of occult qualities. Leonardo looked at nature directly, not through the mind but through the eye. And his was a wonderful eye, sharp and abrupt as a camera, which could stop a bird in flight and fix the muscled movement of its wing. He wanted no speculation about the soul of the bird, which scholars were still repeating from Pythagoras; he wanted to understand the harsh mechanics of its flight:

A bird is an instrument working according to mathematical law, which instrument it is within the capacity of man to reproduce with all its movements, but not with a corresponding degree of strength, though it is deficient only in the power of maintaining equilibrium. We may therefore say that such an instrument constructed by man is lacking in nothing except the life of the bird, and this life must needs be supplied from that of man.

These preoccupations with the structure of things, with the muscle under the skin and the bone under the muscle, seem to have grown on Leonardo from the time that he began to work for himself. They made him uninterested in, and perhaps unhappy with, the opportunities which Florence in the 1470's held out to artists who could display the warm beauty of the surface of things.

At this time Verrocchio was working on a statue of the great *condottiere* of Venice, Colleoni, and he left Florence to finish the work in Venice. Perhaps Leonardo felt that Florence was no longer the center of art it had once been. Or perhaps he could not resist the urge to create a statue better than Verrocchio's, for although he was not a sculptor, he wrote a long letter in 1482 to Lodovico Sforza in Milan, offering, among many other things, to make a statue of his father, the *condottiere* Francesco. In that same letter he described in detail his talents as a military engineer and inventor (two abilities likely to appeal to a Sforza), and soon after, at the age of thirty, he left Florence, carrying with him a silver lute that he had made in the shape of a horse's head, to spend nearly twenty years at the court of Milan.

Leonardo was in many respects self-taught, a self-willed man who did things almost truculently at times. Some of his paintings are lost as a result of bad luck, but others because of his insistence on mixing pigments with curious ingredients or on drying them in new and different ways. He was an innovator, an experimenter, a man never satisfied with the accepted or acceptable, and his decision to leave Florence was taken because Florence was a city of tradition, living on its golden dreams of the past.

We can only guess at the reasons for Leonardo's move from Florence to Milan. Yet if his reasons, intellectual and emotional, had any psychological coherence, it is clear enough what was the common strand in them. When Leonardo chose between Florence and Milan, he was not merely choosing between different cities: in a profound sense he was choosing between different cultures—between two different aspects of the Renaissance.

The Renaissance had begun, as its name implies, as a rebirth of a culture which had already been born once. It was, in the first place, a recovery of ancient learning, and the early Renaissance was not a revolution, but a revival.

Florence was above all the home of this classical revival. The medieval Church had leaned heavily on Aristotle, and had elevated him almost to the status of an honorary saint; now the Medici, in opposition, praised the work and the outlook of Plato. The pride of Florence was the Medici library of ancient manuscripts and commentaries on them, and the Platonic Academy. Florence in the 1470's, when Leonardo worked there, was dominated by the taste of the greatest of the Medici, Lorenzo the Magnificent, which was wholly classical and luxurious.

By contrast, Leonardo was one of the first men in whom the Renaissance expressed itself in a new way, not as a recovery but as a discovery. By the standards of Lorenzo, Leonardo was an unscholarly, unlettered painter: he did not even know Latin (he learned it later in Milan) and he never aspired to Greek. This is a subject to which he returned often and with heat in his notebooks:

I am fully aware that the fact of my not being a man of letters may cause certain arrogant persons to think that they may with reason censure me, alleging that I am ignorant of book-learning. Foolish folk! Do they not know that I might retort by saying, as did Marius to the Roman patricians, "They who themselves go about adorned in the labor of others will not permit me my own." They will say that because of my lack of book-learning, I cannot properly express what I desire to treat of. Do they not know that my subjects require for their exposition experience rather than the words of others? And since experience has been the mistress of whoever has written well, I take her as my mistress, and to her in all points make my appeal.

*Leonardo first hoped to devise wings that man could use like a bird's (above). When he realized this was impossible, he considered such schemes as the man-powered helicopter, shown in the original sketch and in a modern model below.*

In this and other passages Leonardo is making two points. First, he is expressing his contempt for the new aristocracy of Florence, the moneyed men who lean on the talents of others, and whose taste, however authoritative, shows no mind of its own: "Whoever in discussion adduces authority uses not his intellect but rather memory." And second, Leonardo is setting up a new standard for the creation of works of art: the standard of the original mind that goes directly to nature, without intermediaries:

The painter will produce pictures of little merit if he takes the works of others as his standard; but if he will apply himself to learn from the objects of nature he will produce good results. This we see was the case with the painters who came after the time of the Romans, for they continually imitated each other, and from age to age their art steadily declined. . . . it is safer to go direct to the works of nature than to those which have been imitated from her originals with great deterioration and thereby to acquire a bad method, for he who has access to the fountain does not go to the water-pot.

In these quotations we have the crux of principle which divided Leonardo from his predecessors in the Renaissance. The medieval Church had taught that the universe can be understood only spiritually, as a God-given and abstract order; that the beauty of man and of nature is a snare which tempts us away from that stark understanding. The Renaissance denied these morose dogmas, holding instead that fleshly and natural beauty is not sinful, that it is, on the contrary, an expression of the divine order. Yet the form which this humanistic belief took was different at different times. The pioneers of the Renaissance found their ideal of man and nature in the splendid texts of the classics and in the works of art of antiquity. But the new men of the Renaissance, the self-taught and self-willed men like Leonardo, were not content with anything at second hand. They wanted to see, to understand, to enter into nature for themselves. Leonardo above all wanted not to recover, but to discover, his own humanity.

When Leonardo left Florence, he was, therefore, turning his back on the classical Renaissance, and looking for the kinship of other men who shared his thirst for a more popular Renaissance. It was natural that he should look for such men in Milan. Here was a city larger than Florence, less dependent on its rich men, less self-satisfied, and with a more cosmopolitan outlook toward the rest of Europe—particularly toward France and toward Germany. Printing had been invented before Leonardo was born, but hitherto had spread little into Italy; now in the 1480's it became important in Milan. Mathematics and mechanics, too, were more highly regarded in Milan than they were in the Platonic climate of Florence. Leonardo all his life was deeply drawn toward mathematics, and in Milan he drew the pictures for a book, *The Divine Proportion,* which the mathematician Luca Pacioli wrote and later printed. The divine proportion is that geometric ratio which we now call the golden section, and it may be that this modern name was in fact first used for it by Leonardo da Vinci.

*"The Horse," above, a massive statue commissioned by Lodovico Sforza, was never executed, but a model won Leonardo more recognition than* The Last Supper. *The swimming aid that Leonardo thought up (below) is exactly like the lifesaver we use nowadays.*

Intellectually, Leonardo was drawn to Milan because he was seeking a more downright and popular expression of Renaissance humanism than Florence offered. Emotionally, also, we sense that there was something about the brutal power of the court of Milan which attracted him more than the classical air of Florence. Lodovico Sforza was hardly a gracious man; yet something in the sinister directness of such a man, his naked drive to power, his simple and single will, plainly fascinated Leonardo. Like other sensitive men of the mind, he seems to have found a satisfaction in watching other men impose themselves ruthlessly on a world in which he himself was so ill at ease. We catch a hint of the same regard for male power in Leonardo's feelings for his model Giacomo Salai, whom he picked up in the streets of Milan, and whose endless misdeeds he forgave year in and year out with a tender and tolerant contempt.

This is another side of the search for the simplest, most rudimentary forces in man and in nature which took Leonardo to Milan. It made him accept the whims of Lodovico in a way in which he would not have accepted those of Lorenzo. Whatever his other faults may have been, Lodovico was an admirable patron. The fact that his patronage lacked the literary overtones of the Medici made it more attractive to Leonardo, and the variety of the work which Leonardo was called upon to perform at once appealed to his ingenuity, his curiosity, and his interest in experiment. In Milan, Leonardo became a busybody bending his great powers of invention to the trivial mechanics of court entertainment. He painted portraits of Lodovico's mistresses. He designed the costumes and devised the trick surprises of scenery for the court masques. To celebrate a visit of the king of France, he made an automaton shaped like a lion, which spilled a shower of lilies from its breast. He drew maps and proposed schemes of irrigation, he founded cannon and installed central heating, he planned engines of war and palaces, he designed a dozen schemes that Lodovico disregarded. And he went on making countless sketches of the most stupendous surprise of all, the statue of a rearing horse on which should sit Francesco Sforza, the soldier who had created the Milan that Lodovico now ruled. (It is interesting that he considered the animal the center of the monument, and referred to the statue simply as "the horse.") But like everything that Leonardo did for his patron, this also came to nothing.

Yet the years Leonardo spent in Milan were not wasted. In an odd way, he could follow his bent here. The pageants and the plans expected of him can hardly have filled his time, and Lodovico was too busy with his ambitions to pester the court sculptor who had not finished his commission. In Milan, Leonardo did not have to work hard to earn his keep by doing the things that he knew how to do —above all, by painting. In one way this is a pity for us: we would have more great paintings, and fewer sketches, if Leonardo had had to deliver his work for cash during the years in Milan, when his gifts flowed most easily. But in another way we can be grateful that Leonardo in those years of his middle life did not have to do the things he could do so well, which somehow were becoming distasteful to him. Leonardo in Milan grew impatient with his own gifts; he did not care to paint, he disliked the likenesses that he could catch so swiftly, the tricks of light and shade, the surface appearances. His interest was more and more in the structure of things, and as a result his notebooks are now full of sketches which are always, as it were, taking nature to pieces. He did not want to copy: he wanted to understand.

An indication of how his mind was working during these years may be seen in the beautiful portrait of a mistress of Lodovico Sforza painted soon after Leonardo arrived in Milan. The sitter, who could have been no more than a girl when he painted her, was probably Cecilia Gallerani. The ermine which she holds in her arms was an emblem of Lodovico, and is probably also a pun on the girl's name. And in a sense the whole picture is a pun, for Leonardo has matched the ermine in the girl. In the skull under the long brow, in the lucid eyes, in the stately, beautiful, stupid head of the girl, he has rediscovered the animal nature; and done so without malice, almost as a matter of fact. The very carriage of the girl and the ermine, the gesture of the hand and the claw, explore the character with the anatomy. The painting is as much a research into man and animal, and a creation of unity, as is Darwin's *Origin of Species*.

The notebooks of Leonardo are as unexpected, and as personal, as everything about him. There are about five thousand pages of them which have been preserved. Each page is a wonderful jumble of drawings and notes, in which a piece of geometry, a horse's head, an astronomical conjecture, and a flower stand side by side. A photograph shows all this with Leonardo's transparent clarity, but it does not show the delicate scale on which Leonardo worked. Many of the pages in the notebooks, crowded with detail, are no bigger than a man's hand. This is perhaps another expression of Leonardo's withdrawn and indrawn character, and so, no doubt, is the mirror writing which Leonardo used, writing with his left hand. The shading in his drawings is left-handed also, but it is not certain that he painted with his left hand. It is possible that he had damaged his right hand in Florence and that thereafter he still used it, but only for the most delicate parts of his pictures. The pocket notebooks, the left-handed shading, the mirror writing, express something else, too, in Leonardo's character: a determination to do everything for himself, in his own way, down to the smallest detail. Witness, for example, his anatomical drawings showing the hollows and blood vessels in the head—drawings so exact that they have been compared point by point with photographs made by X ray or by radioactive tracers. It is not only the enormous scope of his researches that is impressive, it is the absorption, the meticulousness, and the intensity with which he looked for the mechanism behind what he saw. Leonardo was not merely an original man, in the sense that he had two or three profound and new ideas. He had a passion for looking afresh at everything that came into his life, no matter how trivial the occasion. In this sense, he was not merely an original but a perverse man; and perhaps all the oddities of his life reach back into the childhood of the lonely boy.

"Intellectual passion drives out sensuality," Leonardo wrote on a page of his notebooks. But perhaps his tragic and unfulfilled life proves that when the intellect becomes the subject of such a passion, it ends by being a kind of perversion.

Leonardo's notebooks from this time are full of the penetrating observation of nature, particularly in the anatomical drawings, and are full, too, of a springing invention which was fired by his observation. He had long been absorbed by the flight of birds, and now it led him to invent a parachute and a form of helicopter. The fact that the latter did not work may be blamed on the age in which he lived, which did

*These drawings of the pectoral muscles and the movements of the arm, which Leonardo made around 1510, cannot be bettered.*

not understand, and could not have commanded, the mechanical energy necessary for flight. He observed, one hundred years before Galileo, that the pendulum might be used to make a clockwork keep equal time. He saw that red light penetrates through mist and that blue light does not, and so devised practical rules for giving depth to the painting of landscapes. There are mechanisms on his pages here and there which he noted from others, but the bulk of what he outlined was original, and it included various types of bridges, a mechanical excavator, machines for grinding needles and mirrors, a rolling mill, an automatic file-cutter, an instrument for measuring wind speeds, and a self-centering chuck. Here is a characteristic invention, which characteristically goes into every essential detail:

#### A WAY OF SAVING ONESELF IN A TEMPEST OR SHIPWRECK AT SEA

It is necessary to have a coat made of leather with a double hem over the breast of the width of a finger, and double also from the girdle to the knee, and let the leather of which it is made be quite air-tight. And when you are obliged to jump into the sea, blow out the lappets of the coat through the hems of the breast, and then jump into the sea. And let yourself be carried by the waves, if there is no shore near at hand and you do not know the sea. And always keep in your mouth the end of the tube through which the air passes into the garment; and if once or twice it should become necessary for you to take a breath when the foam prevents you, draw it through the mouth of the tube from the air within the coat.

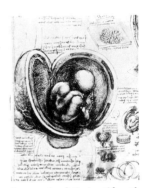

*Leonardo defied a Church ban on dissecting bodies to get material for these accurate drawings of the womb and the brain cavity.*

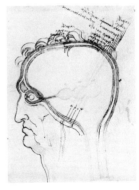

There is no wonder that, as Leonardo grew more absorbed in the mechanism of nature, the work which he had come to Milan to do was put off further and further. At last, in 1493, it could be put off no longer. Lodovico Sforza was arranging to marry his niece to the emperor Maximilian. Leonardo made a full-sized model of the statue of Francesco Sforza on horseback in clay. The bronze to cast the statue was gathered, too, but that had to be sent off next year to make cannon for Lodovico's allies. Lodovico was now deep in intrigue, trying to marshal one group of the city-states of Italy against another. Finally he invited the French to come into Italy on his side, and they, as treacherous as Lodovico, entered Milan in 1499. Lodovico fled, but a year later they took him prisoner.

Leonardo also fled from Milan in that year, a defeated man now nearing fifty, who had given the richest years of his life to a second-rate tyrant with a passion for power. The French archers had used the clay horse and its rider as a target, and there remained in Milan little to show for Leonardo's spent years except a painting of the Last Supper which began to molder on its damp convent wall even before the artist died. The prior had complained that Leonardo had been dilatory in finishing even that, and Leonardo in revenge had said that he would paint the prior for eternity into the figure of Judas. Yet, characteristically, when it came to the point, Leonardo had done something more profound with the figure of Judas: he had moved Judas out of the place that the Middle Ages had assigned to him and had put him on the same side of the table with Jesus.

Leonardo lived for twenty years after the fall of Milan, wandering irresolutely from one city to another, and from one commission to another, without ever again settling down to any one. In 1502 he served briefly in the train of Cesare Borgia as military engineer. This was the same treacherous campaign on which Niccolò Machiavelli was present —the one which provided the Florentine diplomat with a portrait of undeviating ambition for *The Prince*.

Soon after, Florence commissioned two patriotic pictures of battle scenes, one from Leonardo and one from Michelangelo. Leonardo's drafts of the picture survive, but the painting itself deteriorated almost immediately. During this time Leonardo painted a portrait of the third wife of a local merchant named Giocondo. This is the *Mona Lisa,* which in its day was admired for the warmth of its flesh tones, and which time and varnish have now turned to the faint green of ice in a landscape of rocks.

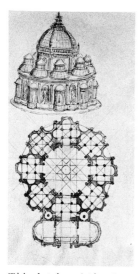

*This sketch and plan for a domed church, resembling St. Peter's in some ways, is one of the many unrealized ideas that fill Leonardo's incredible notebooks.*

Leonardo went back to Milan from time to time to make sketches, now, for another horse and rider. This time the rider was to be Gian Giacomo Trivulzio, that Italian *condottiere* who had fought on the side of the French in the battle for Milan and had overthrown his one-time master and Leonardo's patron, Lodovico. Once again, nothing came of this monument. Then, in 1513, the son of Lorenzo de' Medici became Pope Leo X, and Leonardo went to Rome, where Raphael and Michelangelo had been working for some years, and there received several papal commissions. The story goes that Leonardo began, upon his arrival, to make the varnish for one picture before he started to paint it, and that Leo X observed, sadly and wisely, "This man will never do anything, for he begins to think of the end before the beginning."

The king of France at last offered Leonardo a retreat without obligation near Amboise, and there he spent the remainder of his life, from 1516 until 1519. His self-portrait, drawn a few years earlier, shows him as a man looking much older than his sixty years, full-bearded and patriarchal, his eyes veiled against emotion and his mouth set bitterly, and the distress of an old age full of regrets for the wonderful things that he had planned and never finished now fills his notebooks. Once he had been so sure of his own gifts that there had seemed to be an infinity of time in which to fulfill them. In those confident young days he had written:

I wish to work miracles;—I may have less than other men who are more tranquil, or than those who aim at growing rich in a day.

Now he was conscious every day of the merciless erosion of time, which leaves nothing of the living vigor and beauty of a man if the man has not perpetuated them in his own creations. Leonardo is looking into his own face when he thinks of Helen of Troy and, borrowing from Ovid, writes:

O Time, thou that consumest all things! O envious age, thou destroyest all things and devourest all things with the hard teeth of the year, little by little, in slow death! Helen, when she looked into her mirror and saw the withered wrinkles which old age had made in her face, wept, and wondered to herself why ever she had twice been carried away. O Time, thou that consumest all things! O envious age, whereby all things are consumed!

The works of art Leonardo left behind are indeed sadly few— not a whole statue, about a dozen finished paintings, some fine anatomical and mechanical drawings, and the thousands of sketches. For some artists with one small gift, this might be enough; but when we consider the prodigious talent of Leonardo, the instant eye, the exact hand, and the penetrating mind, we understand why he scribbled desperately on page after page of his later notebooks: "Tell me if anything at all was done . . . Tell me if anything at all was done . . ."

And no doubt Leonardo was right to think that he had wasted his life; but he was wrong to think that he had wasted his gifts. At bottom, his true gifts were not those of a painter, for his painting, original as it was, was not out of the reach of his contemporaries. As a painter Leonardo was in the stream of the Renaissance tradition which Botticelli, Raphael, Michelangelo, and others were also helping to form. Leonardo's most profound gifts were of another kind, and make him seem modern to us today, five hundred years after he lived.

The first of the gifts which made Leonardo a pioneer was his absorbed interest in the structure and mechanism of nature. The science of his day has hardly a hint of this, because it was still dominated by a magical view of man. The alchemists of Leonardo's time believed that they would command nature only by breaking the natural order of things, by casting a spell over nature which made her function in a way contrary to her own laws. They wanted to bewitch the world, and to gain power by forcing it to obey them instead of the laws of nature. Leonardo realized, as his contemporaries did not, that we command nature only when we understand her, when we enter into her processes and give them scope to work naturally. He was full of contempt for those who wanted to force nature to do the impossible: "O speculators about perpetual motion, how many vain chimeras have you created in the like quest? Go and take your place with the seekers after gold."

Leonardo's second pioneering gift was to see that the structure of nature also reveals her processes, which are perpetually in movement and in development. The way a skeleton is hinged, the way a muscle is anchored, the way a leaf is veined—all such knowledge tells something about the functioning of the organism and therefore, in the end, about the whole cycle of its growth. Leonardo dismissed the easy appeals to vital forces and the spirits that inhabit living things with which his age fobbed off all questions; he looked for the strict mechanism by which living things move and act; and he saw that mechanism as something dynamic. This dynamic quality is present even in his simplest sketch of a machine, and in his old age it expressed itself in a growing preoccupation with the forms of plants and of flowing water. Leonardo did not think that a scientific analysis of the processes of nature deprived them of life; on the contrary, he wanted the analysis to express their changing and living movement.

Third, and most important, Leonardo understood that science is not a grand parade of a few cosmic theories, of the kind that Aristotle and Saint Thomas Aquinas had propounded. Until Leonardo's time a theory was expected to give a general explanation of some large phenomenon, such as the motion of the moon, and no one then asked whether the theory could also be made to match the precise times at which the moon rises and sets. The detail was not thought important and any discrepancy between theory and fact was shrugged off as a point of detail. Leonardo for the first time elevated the detail so that it became once and for all the crucial test of a scientific theory. He was seldom misled by what the classical medicine of Galen said in general about the functioning of the heart or the way that the eye sees; he drew what his dissection showed him, and then asked how it could be squared with the vague medical beliefs which were then accepted.

Here we are at the center of Leonardo's pioneering mind. Because he had an exact eye, because he was a painter for whom nature lived not in generalities but in the very shape of a flower or a waterfall, he was at the opposite pole from the theorizing scientists of his own age. Leonardo did not therefore lose interest in science: he transformed it. Only a painter could have forced science to change its outlook, and to become as dedicated as his art was to the discovery of the natural order in the minute detail of its structure. Leonardo *was* that painter, who is the true pioneer of science as we practice it.

His interest in what was new made him unwilling to look back; his gaze was outward and forward into nature. His passion for the exact turned him toward mathematics, his passion for the actual urged him to experiment, and it is significant that these two dominant themes— logic and experimentation—have remained, ever since Leonardo's time, at the base of scientific method.

It was natural that, with these gifts, Leonardo should have quarreled with the classical and literary Renaissance in which he was brought up and should have turned to a more popular and naturalistic Renaissance. It was natural that he should give up pictures for machines, and that his machines should have that subtle quality of human intelligence, of one operation controlling another, which today we call automation. It was natural that these interests should take him from the rich merchant culture of Florence to the brutal thrust for power of the Sforza and the Borgia. And it was natural and inevitable that a life spent at the courts of such men should have about it the modern ring of our own age, the pointless planning of pageants and machines of war, the aimless postponement of every constructive scheme, and the final despair of a great mind that from childhood has been baffled by an alien world. At the end of his life Leonardo wrote constantly of his visions of the cruelty of man to man, and what he foresaw links his gangster age to ours:

### OF THE CRUELTY OF MAN

Creatures shall be seen upon the earth who will always be fighting one with another with very great losses and frequent deaths on either side. These shall set no bounds to their malice; by their fierce limbs a great number of the trees in the immense forests of the world shall be laid level with the ground; and when they have crammed themselves with food it shall gratify their desire to deal out death, affliction, labors, terrors, and banishment to every living thing. And by reason of their boundless pride they shall wish to rise towards heaven, but the excessive weight of their limbs shall hold them down. There shall be nothing remaining on the earth or under the earth or in the waters that shall not be pursued and molested and destroyed, and that which is in one country taken away to another; and their own bodies shall be made the tomb and the means of transit of all the living bodies which they have slain. O Earth! what delays thee to open and hurl them headlong into the deep fissures of thy huge abysses and caverns, and no longer to display in the sight of heaven so savage and ruthless a monster?

*Leonardo's tank, circa 1485, anticipates those of World War I.*

# NICCOLÒ
# MACHIAVELLI
## 1469-1527

For most of us, Renaissance statecraft is typified by a single man, Niccolò Machiavelli—or rather, by a single name, a reputation, an epithet. After all, not many people have any clear recollection of the life and character of the man Machiavelli (not many, even, of the relatively few who have ever bothered to read anything about him). But everyone knows what the name stands for: all the complicated deviltry, hypocrisy, intrigue, secret murders, and public treacheries which for four hundred years the Western world has held typical of the Italian Renaissance. Seventy-five years ago a learned Frenchman identified the whole High Renaissance—the last decades of the fifteenth century and the first ones of the sixteenth—as the Age of Machiavelli. Certainly he realized the incongruity of labeling that bustling time after the drab little servant of a third-rate state, a man whose name even those princes and prelates to whom he had bowed probably never knew or, unless they were Florentines themselves, promptly forgot. But Maulde la Clavière was writing about Renaissance politics, and the name imposed itself. It came as naturally as saying the Age of Augustus, or of Louis le Grand, or of Napoleon, and it carried, like those labels, its own connotations, its own peculiar and, in this case, definitely sinister aura.

In a way it was appropriate that Niccolò Machiavelli should have become the interpreter of Renaissance politics to subsequent ages. He was a Florentine of the Florentines, and the citizens of his city were the quintessence of the new spirit that was then stirring in Italy. Not at first, of course: in the years after the great Guelph victory, after the

*Santi di Tito painted Machiavelli as the secretary to the government of Florence.*

By GARRETT MATTINGLY

popes had broken the power of the Empire in Italy forever, Florence was only one of the vigorous, turbulent city republics with which northern and central Italy swarmed. Some of these paid a token allegiance to the papacy, although the popes knew how little that really meant, and some professed a loyalty to the Holy Roman Emperor, since no emperor could endanger their liberties any more, but in fact they had all torn clean away from the hierarchical system in which the rest of Christendom was enmeshed, and were engaged in an external struggle against all their neighbors and an internal one of faction against faction, in which the only reality was the naked fact of power.

At first most of these new states were republics. Then, as the bigger fish devoured the smaller, not only were there fewer independent cities, but fewer of the survivors were republics. Presently came the anxious moment when on the Italian mainland only one republic was left, or only one that mattered. By force or guile the great Duke of Milan, Giangaleazzo Visconti, was building himself a kingdom. All Lombardy yielded to him from Piedmont to the Adriatic, and then Genoa and Pisa, Perugia and Siena, and finally proud Bologna. Guarded by its lagoons, the Republic of Saint Mark turned its aristocratic back on Italy. Only Florence still held out.

Florence had had as checkered a political history as any of her neighbors. In the century since she had exiled her greatest poet, the factional strife which Dante lamented so pathetically and joined in so energetically had never ceased and only occasionally diminished. In the moment of crisis there was, of course, a clique to say that it would be madness for Florence to pit her unaided strength against the wave of the future, that it would be better for Florentines to live as the subjects of a tyrant than to die as his victims. But the Florentines chose to resist. Apparently they preferred the uneasy vigilance which is the price of freedom to the smug lethargy of the Milanese, and were willing to risk death as free men rather than embrace life as slaves. They did not have to make so hard a choice. As he advanced against Florence, the plague struck down the tyrant, and his jerry-built kingdom fell into ruins. By resisting, the Florentines saved not just their own liberty but the liberties of Italy.

In a series of masterly studies Hans Baron has clearly shown how the outcome of this crisis altered the whole tone of Florentine and so of Italian thought. Florence became the center from which spread a new humanism, a new appreciation of political liberty and civic virtue, a new attitude toward the place of man in society. It was this attitude which ensured the independence of the major Italian states, and consequently, that vigor and diversity of Italian artistic and cultural development which characterized the Renaissance. Although he was himself no humanist, if we make that term include a polished mastery of Greek and Latin letters, Niccolò Machiavelli was soaked in the spirit of Florentine humanism.

He was soaked, too, in the Florentine obsession with politics. He came of a family which had played a great role in the political life of his city for more than two centuries. Ancestors of his had been honored, time and again, with the republic's highest offices, and if his father was too stiff-necked a republican to hold a place in a government which was becoming a more and more transparent mask for the boss rule of the Medici, we may be sure that papa Bernardo saw to it that son Niccolò was thoroughly imbued not only with the history of ancient republican Rome but also with the great traditions of his own city. When he was forty-four, Niccolò wrote that politics was the passion of his life, that he could think and talk of nothing else, and we may guess that this began to be true when he was still young.

For fourteen years he had a chance to indulge his bent in action. When the French invaded Italy in 1494, the Florentines, who had begun to be restive under the scarcely disguised rule of Lorenzo the Magnificent and had become more so under Lorenzo's incompetent son, rose up to reclaim their ancient liberties and drove the Medici out of Florence. In 1498 Niccolò Machiavelli, just turned twenty-nine, was appointed second chancellor of the republic. Shortly afterward he was given the additional charge of secretary to the influential committee known as the *Dieci di Balia*, the Ten of Liberty and Peace, or, more realistically, the Ten of War.

War was the chief preoccupation of the restored republic. Foreign armies were tramping back and forth across Italy. Spaniards slowly tightened their grip on Naples; Frenchmen periodically invaded the kingdom and were periodically chased out of Milan; Switzers and Germans were in the field, fighting sometimes for foreign paymasters, sometimes for their own hands; around Rome, first the bastard son of the Borgia pope and then that warlike old man who succeeded to the papacy as Julius II were trying to unify the anarchic Papal States; and once all the warring powers put aside their quarrels in order to combine against the one powerful, independent Italian state, the Venetian republic. In the midst of these big wars Florence was busy with an interminable little war, trying to reconquer Pisa, which, in the confusion of the first French invasion, had slipped from under the Florentine yoke. Since his nominal chief, the first chancellor, was more interested in Greek poetry than Italian politics, Machiavelli took a large part in these affairs. He was deep in the business of war and the diplomatic bickerings and hagglings which were the normal Renaissance accompaniments of war. Most of the correspondence of the republic passed through his hands. He wrote memoranda to inform and

*The archetype for Machiavelli's Prince was Cesare Borgia, who used cunning, good looks, and intrigue to control Italy for a pope who was also his father.*

advise his masters on a variety of subjects, and the signory sent him on numerous diplomatic missions in Italy, Germany, and France.

Early in his diplomatic career his path crossed that of the man who for most of us typifies the prince of the Age of Machiavelli, the typical prince of the Italian Renaissance—largely because he is the leading figure, the ostensible hero, of Machiavelli's famous little book. Actually, Cesare Borgia was not much more typical of the princes of Italy in his time than Caligula was a typical Roman emperor, or than Al Capone was a typical tax dodger of the Age of Herbert Hoover, but there is no denying that for a few years Cesare cut a wide swath and attracted a lot of attention, even eclipsing his notorious father.

Throughout his papacy, the whole family of Rodrigo Borgia, who ascended the papal throne as Alexander VI, was surrounded by a buzz of scandal. Other popes had kept mistresses in the Vatican, and simony and immorality were no more rife in Rome under the Borgia pope than they had been under his predecessors and would be under his successors. But there was a sort of childlike shamelessness about Alexander VI which invited comment. Other popes had auctioned off high ecclesiastical offices, doubled-crossed their associates and allies, and used their exalted position for the advancement of their families and for base personal ends, but usually they had pretended that they were doing something else. Rodrigo Borgia had either an honest scorn for hypocrisy or a naive ignorance of the force of public opinion. Other popes had thrown wild parties at the Vatican, but no other pope had made the parties so flamboyant or so public. And no other pope had had a portrait of his official mistress, robed as the Virgin Mary, painted over the door of his bedchamber or, at the same time, given his official mistress so many transient but reasonably well publicized rivals. Temperate, even ascetic in most respects (in spite, or perhaps because of, his gross body, he drank little wine and ate sparingly of coarse food), Rodrigo Borgia was a great lover of women, and this alone was the source of innumerable stories which grew more outrageous with each retelling.

*This view of Florence in 1500 shows the new cathedral dome that dominated the battlemented towers of Machiavelli's city-state.*

But neither his private conduct nor his carelessness of concealment can account for all the stories about the Borgia pope. The trouble was that although far from a saint, he was a first-rate administrator, with enormous energy and a driving will. He tried to police not only the streets of Rome but even the Roman Campagna, he tried to control the disorderly Roman nobility, he tried to make sure that the papal treasury received its proper cut of all the sums which the swollen papal bureaucracy and its hangers-on extorted from suitors at his court. He tried, and in part he succeeded, and this made him very unpopular with the Romans. Besides, he tried to assert the rights of the papacy and his jurisdiction over the Papal States wherever it was challenged, whether by the Duke of Milan or the republics of Venice or Florence, by the king of Naples or the anarchic Neapolitan barons, or by the petty tyrants of Umbria and Romagna. This made him unpopular with the ruling classes throughout Italy. Worst of all, he was a foreigner, a Spaniard, and Italians have always resented a non-Italian pope. Hence another whole cluster of stories, different and more sinister.

Two of Rodrigo Borgia's children, his eldest son, the Duke of Gandia, and his daughter Lucrezia, were poor targets for malicious gossip. Gandia, although he inherited somewhat his father's disposition to run after women, was otherwise a conventional and colorless type. Lucrezia, although she had a checkered and somewhat smirched history of successive marriages before she was out of her teens—a foundation on which Roman scandalmongers readily erected a towering superstructure—was really a bland, vapid creature with nothing remarkable about her except a cowlike disposition and long blonde hair. But the pope's younger son Cesare was something else again. Even as a mere stripling, just turned seventeen and newly made a cardinal, he was already a spectacular figure, taller by a head than most tall men, with massive shoulders, a wasp waist, classically regular features, a leonine mane, and blazing blue eyes. It was said that he could leap into the saddle without touching pommel or stirrups, bend a silver scudo double between his fingers, or straighten the iron of a horseshoe with a twist of his wrist. And he was a show-off. He dressed himself and his household with insolent magnificence, and he used to organize corridas in the Piazza Navona so that the Romans could watch him behead a bull with a single stroke of a broadsword. Before long he was trailing a legend gaudier and more lurid than that attached to his father.

It was said that he was his father's rival for his sister's incestuous bed. (Almost certainly false.) It was said that after the horrible sack of Capua he seized forty beautiful highborn maidens and added them to his personal harem. (Highly unlikely. Cesare does not seem to have shared his father's excessive appetite. The maidens were probably commandeered by Cesare's captains, though perhaps in his name.) It was said that he seduced that gallant youth Astorre Manfredi, and when he tired of him had him murdered. (Possible, but the motive for the murder was more probably purely political.) It was said that he had murdered his brother, the Duke of Gandia. (Probable. At least his father seems to have believed it.) And that he had his brother-in-law, Lucrezia's second husband, murdered. (Pretty certainly true.) But it was a dull week when one, at least, of the embassies in Rome did not chalk up another murder to Cesare's credit, sometimes by poison,

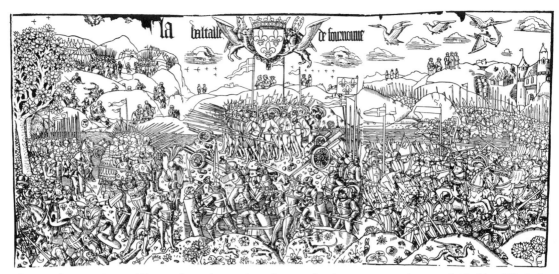

*Contests between foot soldiers and cavalry, such as the 1495 battle at Fornovo, devastated Machiavelli's Italy.*

sometimes by the hands of hired assassins, sometimes by his own dagger. Probably he really was responsible for a fair share of those bodies hauled out of the Tiber. Freed by his brother's death from his cardinalate, Cesare became Duke de Valentinois (Valentino, the Italians called him) and Gonfalonier of the Church, cousin and ally of the king of France, and commander in chief of the papal army. As he marched through the anarchic Papal States, seizing one town after another, by bribery or trickery or the sheer terror of his name, his legend hung over him like a thundercloud.

When Machiavelli first encountered the Duke, the spell of the legend must have been already at work on him, and it must have been heightened by the manner in which Valentino received him and his chief, at night, by the light of a single flickering candle which showed only dimly the tall figure clad in black from head to foot without jewel or ornament, the still white features as regular as a Greek statue and as immobile. Perhaps the cold beauty of those marble features was already beginning to be marred by the pustules which led Valentino later on usually to wear a mask. Perhaps the eyes, lost in shadow, already held that glare which another ambassador noted in them shortly afterward, the look of a savage beast at bay. And perhaps a shrewder observer might have reflected that there was the smell of comedy about these negotiations, the Duke endlessly repeating the same banalities about his eternal friendship for Florence and how wise the republic would be to employ the services of so good a friend, while his captains warned the Florentine envoys that the Duke's patience was growing short, that France would support him against Florence and the Venetians would not stir, that the army was poised to spring and could be at the city's gates before the news of its coming. It was really one of the cruder forms of blackmail, but something about the Duke's personality put the act over, and the Florentine envoys carried away the image of a great prince, subtle, inscrutable, dangerous.

Not long afterward Machiavelli had an opportunity to observe Cesare Borgia in action at the time of his greatest triumph. Cesare was not much of a general: he never learned the rudiments of tactics or strategy, logistics or supply. He was not even a good combat leader, and though he has been praised as a disciplinarian, the only available instance seems to be that once he quelled an incipient riot among some of his brawling soldiers by the terror of his presence. Similarly, if he ever gave any proof of ability as a statesman or ruler, no evidence survives. But he was a ruthless gangster and an expert confidence man, and the revolt of some of the smaller gangsters, his captains, gave him an opportunity to display his talents. Machiavelli watched, fascinated, while Cesare, all mildness and good will, lured his mutinous subordinates into a peace conference, lulled their fears, invited them to a banquet to celebrate their renewed friendship, and when they arrived unarmed and unescorted at a rendezvous where Cesare had hidden his bodyguards, had them seized and murdered. Machiavelli was delighted at the virtuosity of the performance and set it all down in detail for the edification of his countrymen and of posterity.

Machiavelli had a third opportunity to observe the Duke. He arrived in Rome on the business of the republic some months after the death of Alexander VI and just at the moment when Cesare, with incredible stupidity, had helped swing the election of his most implacable enemy. It was plain to see that Cesare was finished. Everything really had depended on his father's being pope, and as soon as his father died, his allies deserted him, his people rose against him, and his army fell apart as his captains scrambled for the service of some luckier master. Machiavelli assessed the emptiness of the man at a glance, avoided him when he could, wrote of him and no doubt looked at him with cold contempt. But later Machiavelli seems to have preferred to forget the cringing, whimpering, blustering, dithering creature his hero had become. The picture is spread out in detail in his dispatches, but Machiavelli never openly alluded to this aspect again.

One thing Machiavelli admired about Cesare was that he raised his soldiers in his own domain instead of hiring foreign mercenaries. Cesare's action was like a project very close to Machiavelli's heart, one which after years of urging he finally got the Florentine government to adopt. They not only adopted it, they put him in charge of it, so that for the last six years of the republic, he had added to his other duties most of those of minister of defense. Instead of the cut-rate mercenaries who had prolonged the Pisan war for twelve years (being a republic in which the taxpayers held the purse strings, Florence hired only the cheapest mercenaries), Machiavelli persuaded the government to raise a militia in its own territory. Since the militia were not Florentine citizens, but conscripts from the wretched peasants of the *contado,* a folk without political rights or any material stake in the success of their bourgeois masters, the scheme had an obvious weakness, but it did not work badly at first. In 1509 Pisa fell, and Machiavelli's militia could claim a share in the long-delayed triumph. Three years later the militia failed a harder test. When the veteran Spanish infantry moved in to attack Prato, the militia ran like rabbits, and the Medici epigoni came back behind a column of Spanish pikes to rule once more in Florence. Machiavelli's active career in politics was over. But not his interest in politics. The next year he wrote that he could think about, talk about, nothing else, and from then on until he died in 1527, only a few weeks after the Florentines had again expelled the Medici, most of the writings with which he sought to allay the boredom of his exclusion from office were concerned, one way and another, with statecraft. He also wrote some verses—pretty wretched verses— and a not unamusing version of an old, smutty joke, and comedies, one of which is a masterpiece. But mostly he wrote about politics. Had he been asked to name his political writings in an ascending order of importance, surely the top three would have been his *History of Florence,* his *Art of War,* and his *Discourses on the First Ten Books of Livy.* Into these writings, and particularly into the last, Machiavelli had poured, or so he thought, all his practical experience of government and diplomacy and all his wide reading of ancient and modern history. However surprised some of the successful statesmen of his day might have been to find the little Florentine secretary the political spokesman of their age, Machiavelli himself would not have been too surprised. He would have regarded the reputation accrued as a poor compensation for the fame as a statesman which fate had denied him, but he had often said that he was the first modern man to look at politics with a clear and open eye, and he would certainly have taken the recognition of posterity as no more than due to the merit of his books.

Only, of course, the recognition of posterity has nothing to do with the books Machiavelli would have named. When people speak of the Age of Machiavelli, they are not thinking of any of them, but of one little pamphlet apparently dashed off at white heat in 1513 just after the fall of the Florentine republic. It is called *The Prince,* and it bears only an ambiguous, tangential relationship to Machiavelli's big, serious works or, some people think, to the actual history of the time and place over which its fame casts such a lurid and sinister light. The discrepancy between the impression of Renaissance Italy to be gathered from *The Prince* and that given by the rest of Machiavelli's writings, to say nothing of the writings of his contemporaries, who often turn out to be more reliable about matters of fact, is sufficient to raise some doubts about the appropriateness of letting *The Prince* describe the political atmosphere of its time.

Perhaps our doubts about letting Machiavelli speak for the age which bears his name ought not to be increased by our knowledge of his private life. But among his contemporaries, surely Niccolò Machiavelli was one of the least Machiavellian. It is true that he often professed a preference for drastic methods and for sweeping all-or-nothing solutions, along with a contempt for delay and improvisation and compromise, a set of attitudes usually more characteristic of academic theorists than of practical men of affairs. But though this quirk of temperament sometimes misled him into a temporary enthusiasm for a mountebank like Cesare Borgia, it does not seem otherwise to have affected his own behavior. If the discipline of the Florentine militia had been harsher, they might not have run so soon at Prato. Machiavelli not seldom praised the efficacy of hypocrisy and smooth deceit, but in his dealings both with his own government and with foreign potentates he was usually inept at concealing his feelings, likely to show his hand, and, in negotiation, blunt to the point of tactlessness. He often spoke of the value of clear-eyed, dispassionate observation and seems rather to have prided himself on the possession of this faculty, but, in fact, his views were usually clouded by wish and prejudice, he was easily deceived, and he was not, in the things that really mattered, those affecting the daily course of politics, a very acute, discriminating, or even very accurate observer. This judgment, suggested by comparing his dispatches with those of his contemporaries, is reinforced by the fact that his employers, the Florentine signory, never gave him the chief responsibility for any important mission.

Niccolò not only lacked the virtues he praised but possessed others even more incompatible with a picture of Old Nick. He was as anticlerical as most Italians of the last six centuries have always been, and, in spite of his pious mother's teaching, no more zealously practicing a Catholic than one would expect. But as he had been baptized, confirmed, and married, so he died in the arms of the Church, having seen to it that his children followed the same conventional course. Nor—and this is farther from the popular picture of his age—is there any evidence that he indulged in any fantastic crimes or vices. He was probably no more faithful to his wife than most middle-class husbands in any age or clime, but he seems to have been a kind, affectionate, considerate husband and father, as he was a warm and true friend, a man of his word in money matters, and an admired and respected citizen.

One inappropriate virtue is particularly surprising It even surprised Machiavelli himself. The man who wrote that men are moved so predominantly by self-interest that princes need take account of no other motives, that "a man will resent the loss of his patrimony more than the murder of his father," was himself the devoted, unselfish servant of his ungrateful state. He lived in an age when the use of public office for private gain was perfectly customary. He had during most of his fourteen years as a servant of the Florentine republic unrivaled opportunities to enrich himself at the expense of the *condottieri* and other contractors with whom as secretary to the Ten of War he had to deal. Yet he quitted the Florentine service as poor as the day he had entered it. His whole public career was a testimony to the inaccuracy of his own cynical maxims. It is hard to reconcile it with the trend of his major serious books. It is impossible to square it with the lurid picture which we have drawn from his one famous little book, *The Prince.*

Drawn, in part, quite unjustifiably. Most people, whether they have read *The Prince* or not, retain the conviction that somewhere, they cannot say quite where, Machiavelli commends the famous (quite mythical) poison of the Borgia and justifies the pagan debauchery which ever since the Reformation Protestant countries have associated with the Italian Renaissance.

*Decaying corpses, like the ones painted by Pisanello, showed Florentines the result of wrongdoing—or a change in political power.*

Most of these false imputations are quite old and go back to a book called *Anti-Machiavel* which a Huguenot pamphleteer wrote against Catherine de' Medici and her Italian entourage just after the Massacre of St. Bartholomew's. But even after these old vulgar errors have been cleared out of the way, *The Prince* remains a shocking book, shocking both for what it says and for the deliberately provocative way it says it, and for the discord between a part of its contents and the life and other writings of its author.

As for its contents: *The Prince* lays it down as a major premise that men in general are selfish, treacherous, cowardly, greedy, and, above all, gullible and stupid. It therefore advises a prince, and particularly a new prince who hopes to destroy the liberties of those he rules, to employ hypocrisy, cruelty, and deceit, to make himself feared even at the risk of making himself hated, to divide the people and destroy their natural leaders, and to keep faith with no one, since no one will keep faith with him. It views the world of politics as a jungle in which moral laws and standards of ethical conduct are merely snares for fools, a jungle in which there is no reality but power, and power is the reward of ruthlessness, ferocity, and cunning. In such a jungle, not the actual Cesare Borgia, but the picture of himself which Cesare succeeded in conveying at the height of his fame, a savage beast—half lion and half fox—would be the natural king. To a society which regarded the relations between its parts as ruled by justice and equity and santified by religion, all this was more shocking than we can quite imagine.

It was shocking, too, to find a man of staunch republican principles and flawless republican antecedents, a man who had served the Florentine republic with selfless devotion and suffered for that devotion more than most, turning, within months of his country's fall, to writing a handbook for tyrants, a book meant to teach the Medici, the enemies of his country's liberties, how to hold his fellow countrymen in thrall, and writing it all for the mean object of helping himself to wriggle back into some minor government post. If Machiavelli behaved so, he earned, for the only time in his life, the epithet Machiavellian. That his behavior seems to have been a momentary aberration, that when it was over Machiavelli returned to the defense of republican principles and the society of republican friends, makes his defection not less shocking but only more puzzling.

From the first there were at least two explanations of the puzzle. One was that Machiavelli had been inspired by the Evil One to write a book of advice for princes, meant to damn the souls and ruin the fortunes of princes who followed it and to destroy the prosperity of their subjects. This was the official view, shared by the cardinals and popes who placed and kept *The Prince* on the Index and by the Protestant pamphleteers who pointed to it as the manual of the Jesuits and the political inspiration of the Counter Reformation. Meanwhile, a second view was expressed openly by some of Machiavelli's fellow countrymen (those in exile) and hinted at by some who remained in Italy, where the banned book continued clandestinely to circulate. This was that *The Prince,* under the guise of giving advice to princes, was meant to warn all free men of the dangers of tyranny. One wonders whether the originators of this explanation of the puzzle may not have been the ardent Florentine republicans who always remained Machiavelli's friends. From this second view sprang the judgment, popular in the eighteenth century, that *The Prince* was, in fact, a satire on absolute monarchy, and that all its epigrams were deliberately double-edged. The nineteenth century offered other solutions to the puzzle. The one which gained ascendancy as the cause of national self-determination triumphed in western Europe was that, ardent republican though he was, Machiavelli made up his mind that only a strong prince could liberate Italy from the barbarians, and so chose to sacrifice the freedom of his city to the unity of Italy. Just before World War I this solution began to be questioned by those who said that Machiavelli was not a chauvinistic patriot but a detached, dispassionate political scientist who described political behavior as it actually was. After about 1920 this view took a powerful lead over all its competitors, and among orthodox Machiavelli scholars it still dominates the field.

Obviously, none of these answers is entirely satisfactory. It is possible that Machiavelli was mean enough to sell his birthright of republican ideals for the chance of some third-rate civil service post under a petty tyrant; but that he was at the same time stupid enough to believe that a book like *The Prince* was the best way into Medici favor, and to let advice which, if it was seriously meant, should have been highly secret escape into general circulation, seems much less credible. Both the notion that *The Prince* was inspired by the devil and the counternotion that it was the subtle weapon of republican idealism seem equally oversimplified. And, of course, the proposal that *The Prince* was conceived as a satire is the kind of anachronism which only the eighteenth century could have perpetrated. Machiavelli knew perfectly well that satires were compositions in verse after the manner of Horace and Juvenal, such as his friend Luigi Alamanni wrote. He would have failed completely to understand the proposition that *The Prince* was a satire. As for the theory that Machiavelli was willing to accept a tyrant prince in order to effect the unification of Italy, there is not the faintest indication anywhere in his writings that he would have grasped the idea if anybody had put it to him. There is nothing about unifying Italy anywhere in *The Prince,* only about driving out the barbarians, a commonplace of Italian rhetoric from Petrarch to Paul IV. But Machiavelli the Italian patriot is a little easier to swallow than Machiavelli the dispassionate scientist, unless someone can explain how the scientific temper can accord with facts distorted by emotion and prejudice.

Trying to explain the puzzle of *The Prince* is probably hopeless. How do you reconstruct the motives at a given moment of a man over four hundred years dead who has left only the scantiest and most ambiguous clues to what they might be? How do you tell, in the case of a man like Machiavelli, how much of the demonstrable distortion in *The Prince* was due to faulty observation (he was a passionate man), and how much to the deliberate irony which he certainly sometimes practiced? How do you probe the bitterness and agony of spirit which must certainly have been his on the collapse of all his hopes, and decide which wild statements come from anger, which from despair, and which from a calculated will to undermine his enemies by indirection?

Probably, like most insoluble problems about men of genius, this one has taken up more time and energy than it deserves. The real importance of Machiavelli, his claim to give his name to a whole period of history, lies elsewhere, not in the points in which *The Prince* differs from his other writings, but in those in which it agrees. Here the transformation of his legendary figure from a diabolist or a rebel, a spirit who says "No," to a major culture hero, offers the clue. What had happened, in almost three centuries between the time when Machiavelli was either praised as a daring rebel or denounced as an emissary of Satan and the time when he began to be acclaimed as a prophet, was that all Europe had become what Italy in Machiavelli's lifetime already was, a congeries of autonomous, purely temporal sovereign states, without any common end to bind them into a single society or any interest higher than their own egotistical drives for survival and expansion.

To pretend that the relations between such states were governed by Christian ethics seemed to Machiavelli a contemptible hypocrisy. Many Italians since Dante had lamented that the nearer one came to Rome the wider the gap between Christian teaching and Christian practice, and charged that the papacy had corrupted the morals of Italy. Indeed, the major assumption of the stern reformers of what we call the Counter Reformation was not much different. But Machiavelli went further. He compared his own embittered picture of the degeneracy of his countrymen with Livy's of the virtues of republican Rome, and without asking how much exaggeration there might be in either, he leaped to one of his drastic all-or-nothing conclusions. Christianity, whatever its value as a guide in private life, was not a viable fountain for the good society. So for the religion of Christ he proposed to substitute the religion of patriotism. In politics the Christian ethic was worse than valueless, it was positively harmful. It might serve to keep the masses more law-abiding in their private lives, but when it came to public actions the only test of good or bad was what best served the safety and aggrandizement of the state. Since every state was an autonomous entity, recognizing no superior and no interest higher than its own, no rules of ethics whatever applied to relations between states. The only test was success. This was Machiavelli's consistent position. It appears in his earliest state papers and is as firmly held in his writings in praise of republics as it is in *The Prince*. In 1513 it was a desperate paradox. By 1813 it was an axiom of statecraft. By 1914 it was the tritest of platitudes. Machiavelli did not invent it. It was apparent in the behavior of the Italian states of his time and more or less openly acknowledged in the memoranda of statesmen and diplomats. But Niccolò Machiavelli first gave the fresh attitude of his age toward statecraft a permanent literary form, and the progress of history compelled general recognition of his insight. For that reason, perhaps he does deserve to be accepted as the voice of the Renaissance state. Perhaps his age should be called "The Age of Machiavelli."

*A stern-faced* condottiere, *a professional soldier in the Italian wars, was portrayed by Machiavelli's contemporary Leonardo in an ornate, fanciful helmet.*

37

# DESIDERIUS
# ERASMUS
## 1466?-1536

**D**esiderius Erasmus is more than any other man the symbol of humanism. This powerful movement, which had begun in the Renaissance, culminated in Erasmus: his personality was formed by it, and for a lifetime he expressed humanism for all men. He was born about 1466 in Holland, but his mind was cosmopolitan, and it dominated intellectual Europe in his age as the mind of Voltaire was to dominate a later age. One of his friends confessed: "I am pointed out in public as the man who has received a letter from Erasmus."

The movement of humanism which Erasmus personified was (if one must find a single phrase for it) a liberal movement. Its history and its defeat, therefore, have a special interest for our time. The life of Erasmus has a modern moral and, indeed, a very modern ring. He had the respect of thoughtful men and, like his friend Sir Thomas More, for a time he had the ear of princes. Then, in 1517, the Reformation divided Europe into two religious camps, and soon each side outdid the other in dogmatic bitterness. Erasmus was helpless between two forms of intolerance, and the last years of his life (he died at the age of seventy in 1536) are marked with his own sense of failure.

Thomas More had lived the tragedy of an individual martyr. Erasmus lived the tragedy of a whole generation of intellectuals—and of later generations too. His rise showed that a movement of tolerance, such as humanism was, can inspire men only so long as it confronts a single intolerance. And his decline showed that tolerance as an ideal no longer moves men when two opposing intolerances clamor for their

*Erasmus, sedately at work in his study, was painted by Hans Holbein during 1523.*

By J. BRONOWSKI *and* BRUCE MAZLISH

loyalties. This has been the dilemma of the liberal spirit in every age since Erasmus.

Humanism was a movement in which many strands were woven together: the strand which leads directly to Erasmus was the new interest in the classical writers of Greece and Rome. This interest, which was strong throughout the Renaissance, goes back in its beginnings at least to the fourteenth century in Italy. It was first clearly expressed at that time in the works of Petrarch, whose poems already showed the characteristic coupling of ideas in humanism: classical literature was thought of, not as an end in itself, but as the expression of a wider love for man and nature.

In one sense, humanism was a pagan movement. It was impatient of the narrow asceticism which the Church laid down; it was not willing to abhor nature as a beautiful snare, to think the flesh evil, and to find virtue only in a monastic renunciation of life. The doctrine of the medieval Church was original sin—the belief that the soul and the body are sharply divided and that, because man cannot express his soul except through his body, he carries an unavoidable sin. The doctrine of humanism was original goodness—the Greek belief that the soul and body are one, and that the actions of the body naturally and fittingly express the humanity of the soul.

*This title page from Erasmus's* Complete Works, *published at Basel in 1540, was mutilated by the Spanish Inquisition in 1635.*

Just as the Churchmen leaned on the Bible and the Church Fathers, so humanists turned for support to the pagan classics. The literature of Greece and Rome, therefore, came to be regarded as a golden ideal in all things. Aeneas Silvius Piccolomini, an early humanist who later became pope, wrote: "Literature is our guide to the true meaning of the past, to a right estimate of the present, to a sound forecast of the future. Where letters cease, darkness covers the land: and a Prince who cannot read the lessons of history is a hopeless prey of flattery and intrigue." In the same spirit Machiavelli found it natural to support his realistic advice on the conduct of politics by references to Livy's *History of Rome.* But the appeal to classical literature was, at its best, an appeal to its spirit. Humanism was not a literary but an intellectual movement, a shifting of values and an awakening to a new self-consciousness of the human spirit.

In the setting of those times it was, of course, impossible for humanists to think of themselves as antireligious. Like all reformers, they felt their protest to be a protest only against abuses of religion. They criticized Churchmen and Scholastic philosophers; but in this, they felt they were not opposing Christianity, they were merely correcting the errors which the medieval Church had put on it. When Lorenzo Valla, a papal secretary, wrote a book which he called *Pleasure as the True Good,* he insisted that its moral was to show that elegant living was an expression of Christian virtue.

There were, indeed, elements of Greek Stoicism in the model of Christian virtue which the medieval Church had set up. But, at bottom, the link which the humanists tried to find between the medieval Christian vision and the vision of the Greeks was false. The Church idealized the ascetic and monastic virtues and allowed man the pleasures of the flesh only because man was by nature weak. By contrast, the pagan vision glorified the flesh, and for a time the humanists converted at least some leaders of the Church to accepting this vision. For a time, humanism persuaded the Church to take as its ideal the complete, the universal man.

In doing so, humanism had to attack the monastic virtues, and therefore had to represent these as false doctrines imposed on the true structure of Christianity. The work which made the reputation of Erasmus was a bitter satire on this theme, *The Praise of Folly*, in which he mocked both the monastic life (he had spent six unhappy years in a monastery) and the indulgences and abuses of the Church.

An attack on abuses is always an attractive refuge for those who do not want to be deeply involved in principle. By making fun of superstition, by showing the bigot at his most absurd, the critic can keep aloof from the deeper issues which drive men to commit themselves. But the critic deceives himself if he thinks that an attack on an established way of life can stop at what seem to be its accidental faults. What Erasmus said about the corruptions of the Church in fun, Luther soon said in earnest. And for Luther these corruptions became not accidents but essentials—evils that grew out of the structure of the Catholic Church itself. Humanism undermined the belief in medieval tradition and practices, and inevitably Luther turned its attack into a new theology.

Even the scholarship of the humanists had the effect of destroying respect for the medieval Church. When Lorenzo Valla studied the *Donation of Constantine*, he proved it to be a papal forgery; other critics uncovered the spurious history of other Christian texts. Research in history and in languages, which followed naturally from interest in classical literature, unexpectedly turned out to throw doubt on the authenticiy of much that was revered in the Church. As a result, the authority of the Church came to be doubted in other fields, and Aristotle and the Christian Fathers were no longer accepted as infallible. Luther took advantage of these infectious doubts, although, ironically, the new dogmatism that he created soon sustained itself by means no more scrupulous than the old.

Erasmus was an illegitimate child, as Leonardo da Vinci had been; and like Leonardo, he seems to have felt the slur. As a young monk, he believed that because of his birth he could hope for no great career in the Church. And when he was at the apex of his fame, in 1516, he

*These marginal drawings for a 1515 copy of* The Praise of Folly *were done by Hans Holbein. At top, the soul of the medieval philosopher Duns Scotus enters the body of Folly, Erasmus's mouthpiece for mocking man's foibles. At bottom is a traditional figure of fun, the fat monk.*

wrote to the pope in some embarrassment to ask him to lift the bar by which he, as an illegitimate child, could not legally hold Church office.

Erasmus's childhood, however, was not unhappy or isolated. His parents lived together and had another son, and Erasmus went to a school run by the lay society of the Brethren of the Common Life. Here the stress was on the spiritual teachings of Christ, the Bible, and the good life. These years of simple piety ended when Erasmus was fourteen; his mother died of the plague and his father died soon after. His guardian was anxious to be rid of responsibility for the two boys and had them prepared for the monastery. There was no escape; reluctantly, Erasmus became an Augustinian monk at the age of twenty-one.

In 1492 Erasmus became a priest and was able to move from the monastery to the court of the Bishop of Cambrai; and at last, in 1495, he was able to go to the University of Paris, the most famous school in Europe. But here, where he had hoped for a new spirit, he found that the theology again shocked and disappointed him: the Scholastic arguments were empty. As Erasmus wrote privately: "Those studies can make a man opinionated and contentious; can they make him wise? . . . By their stammering and by the stains of their impure style they disfigure theology, which had been enriched and adorned by the eloquence of the ancients. They involve everything while trying to solve everything."

The Schoolmen, who repeated the traditional philosophies either of Plato or of Aristotle, were bitter opponents of the new learning. Erasmus describes their bigotry in his *Letters:*

It may happen, it often does happen, that an abbot is a fool or a drunkard. He issues an order to the brotherhood in the name of holy obedience. And what will such an order be? An order to observe chastity? An order to be sober? An order to tell no lies? Not one of these things. It will be that a brother is not to learn Greek; he is not to seek to instruct himself. He may be a sot. He may go with prostitutes. He may be full of hatred and malice. He may never look inside the Scriptures. No matter. He has not broken any oath. He is an excellent member of the community. While if he disobeys such a command as this from an insolent superior, there is stake or dungeon for him instantly.

And Erasmus saw that the formalism which withered the minds of these men also withered their lives. If thinking was merely an arrangement of traditional arguments, then living was merely an arrangement of traditional observances. In 1501 he wrote *Handbook of a Christian Warrior,* in which he contrasted this mechanical worship with true piety:

Thou believest perchance all thy sins and offenses to be washed away at once with a little paper or parchment sealed with wax, with a little money or images of wax offered, with a little pilgrimage-going. Thou art utterly deceived . . . !

It was the abuse of indulgences which tipped over Luther's patience in 1517; and the sentences of Erasmus are, therefore, the prophetic rumblings, sixteen years before the thunderclap, of the storm which was drawing together over Rome.

When the *Handbook of a Christian Warrior* was written, Erasmus had already made, in 1499, a visit to England which deeply changed his life. There he had met Thomas More and other English humanists, among them Grocyn, Linacre, and Colet. They were devout and even ascetic men, but their virtues seemed to grow naturally out of their personalities, and their lives and their minds were of a piece. Among these English idealists, Erasmus felt, Christianity was truly an expression of the spirit, and of the classical spirit. Argument and worship were not brittle forms here; the search for truth was generous and faith was not, as he had felt it to be in Paris, a dead superstition.

E rasmus had always longed for the liberal and humane vision of the classics, believing that it expressed the best in Christianity. Now, having seen the best in action, he felt Christianity could be an expression of broad and tolerant virtues, of the whole man. In the houses of Sir Thomas More and his friends, Erasmus could feel that his longing was realistic and that he in his own person could bring this vision to Europe. This, he saw, should be his life's work: the reconciliation of the classics with Christianity. To a later age the noble savage became the model for a natural morality; to Erasmus the simplicity of the classics spoke with the same inspiration. The classics were a natural gospel; reading Cicero and other moralists, he was carried away: "A heathen wrote this to a heathen, and yet his moral principles have justice, sanctity, truth, fidelity to nature, nothing false or careless in them. . . . When I read certain passages of these great men I can hardly refrain from saying, Saint Socrates, pray for me."

All this Erasmus believed, but believed in part on hearsay, from his English friends. For in fact Erasmus, like others trained in the monastery, did not at this time read Greek. Yet his belief was so strong that he at once began to learn Greek when he went back to Paris, though he was already thirty-four, in need of money, and often ailing. He wrote: "I am determined, that it is better to learn late than to be without that knowledge which it is of the utmost importance to possess. . . . We see, what we have often read in the most weighty authors, that Latin erudition, however ample, is crippled and imperfect without Greek." And he mastered Greek in three years.

He now began to translate, to edit, and to popularize the works of antiquity. He had already published, in 1500, a collection of about eight hundred *Adages,* or tags, from the Latin classics, which, like the collection of wise saws which Benjamin Franklin made later, went through countless popular editions. He enlarged this to more than three thousand sayings, many now drawn from Greek authors. He translated Aristotle, Euripides, Plutarch, Lucian, and Seneca.

At the same time, it was part of Erasmus's sense of his own mission that he should also translate and edit Christian documents. His work here has been called "the foundation of modern critical study of the Bible and the Fathers." He published editions of a number of Church Fathers, among them Saint Jerome and Saint Augustine.

Saint Jerome had translated the Greek Bible into Latin, and this translation was the accepted Vulgate. This was the center of Erasmus's interest in Saint Jerome, and in the same year, 1516, he printed his own translation of the Bible, in Greek and Latin together. On one page stood the Greek text as Erasmus had revised and edited it, and on the opposite page his translation into Latin, which differed markedly from the Vulgate of Saint Jerome. Erasmus felt that he was giving the Bible freshly to common men, as the Brethren of the Common Life had given it to him. He wrote in his preface: "I wish that all women might read the Gospel and the Epistles of Paul. I wish that they might be translated into all tongues of all people, so that not only the Scots and the Irish, but also the Turk and the Saracen might read and understand. I wish the countryman might sing them at his plow, the weaver chant them at his loom, the traveler beguile with them the weariness of his journey." In a few years Luther broke tradition still more abruptly by translating the Bible into the everyday language of his country, German.

For some years from 1504 on, Erasmus had traveled through Europe and in particular had spent time in Italy. When Henry VII died in 1509, Erasmus's English friends urged him to come there in the hope that he might find advancement under the new king, Henry VIII. He left Italy at once; and it was while he was crossing the Alps on his way to England that he conceived the idea of writing his famous satire on monkish life. He wrote the satire in a week in the house of Sir Thomas More, with whom he again stayed in England; and by way of acknowledging his friend's hospitality, he gave it a title which was meant as a pun on the name of More: *Moriae Encomium,* or in English, *The Praise of Folly.*

*The Praise of Folly* was published in 1511 and was at once read with delight everywhere. It was printed in many languages and editions, and in 1515 Hans Holbein the younger, who was then eighteen, added a set of marginal drawings to it. It inspired many other satiric books, among them those of Rabelais.

The satire in *The Praise of Folly* seems oddly lacking in humor to us now. The attack on the formalism of Churchmen and the greed and stupidity of monks is not noticeably gayer than it had been in Eras-

*Holbein drew Erasmus's friend the humanist Sir Thomas More (seated at center) with his family in 1526. Erasmus wrote* The Praise of Folly *while visiting More.*

mus's serious books. Yet, to his own generation, Erasmus in *The Praise of Folly* seemed somehow nimbler and more carefree; it was possible to side with him in laughter without being committed to a more profound criticism. The fool was a familiar device in the tales of the times; and by speaking in the universal person of the fool, Erasmus made himself one with all his readers.

Erasmus was speaking the discontent of his age, in his satire as much as in his serious translations. The monks and the Schoolmen had ceased to be a vital intellectual force; they no longer reached the minds of their hearers, nor did their own minds give anything fresh to their doctrines. Thus the Churchmen no longer commanded intellectual respect. But since they claimed that their doctrine spoke to men's minds, there was no other form of respect that could be given to them. They were, therefore, seen simply as figures of pomp, offering empty words of superstition.

The age had had enough of clerical pomp and of obedience without respect. In fun and in earnest Erasmus voiced the discontent of the powerful minds of the age; and princes and popes heard him with pleasure and were his friends. The simple minds of the age felt the same discontent; but for them it was voiced more dramatically by Martin Luther.

Luther had studied the works of Erasmus and had been guided by them—by the *Adages,* by *The Praise of Folly,* and above all by Erasmus's edition of the Greek New Testament, which Luther used as the basis of his own lectures. In 1516 he had prompted a friend to write to

Erasmus to criticize his interpretation of Saint Paul's Epistle to the Romans—characteristically a text on which the liberal and the zealot would fall out. Luther sensed from the outset that Erasmus was not, either in temperament or in opinion, radical enough for him. Six months before he nailed the theses to the door of the church at Wittenberg, Luther already wrote about Erasmus that "human considerations prevail with him much more than divine."

Erasmus was a supporter of the Ninety-five Theses, in principle; he sent copies of them to Thomas More and to Colet in England, with a letter of approval. But Erasmus was not—and this again both by temperament and by opinion—a man to push the criticism of the Church so far that both sides would find themselves committed to positions which allowed no movement. A year after the theses, in October, 1518, Erasmus wrote to a supporter of Luther, John Lang, approving them but pointing out that their result was likely to be just this: that those who were allied to the Church would be forced to take up an inflexible position. "I see that the monarchy of the Pope at Rome, as it is now, is a pestilence to Christendom, but I do not know if it is expedient to touch that sore openly. That would be a matter for princes, but I fear that these will act in concert with the Pope to secure part of the spoils."

Luther had now been commanded by the Church to recant, and had refused. In general, the humanists supported him. Erasmus's Swiss publisher, Froben, printed a book of Luther's pamphlets. Their violence alarmed Erasmus; he was both more timid and more far-sighted than others; above all he saw that humanism itself, the revival of learning, the cause of "good letters" which he had nursed so long, would be threatened. He wrote privately to Froben to advise him not to publish Luther's writings, "that they may not fan the hatred of the *bonae literae* still more."

Meanwhile, Luther in his first struggles needed what support he could get, and he particularly needed the open support of Erasmus. He therefore wrote to him in March, 1519:

Greeting. Often as I converse with you and you with me, Erasmus, our glory and our hope, we do not yet know one another. Is that not extraordinary? . . . For who is there whose innermost parts Erasmus has not penetrated, whom Erasmus does not teach, in whom Erasmus does not reign? . . . Wherefore, dear Erasmus, learn, if it please you, to know this little brother in Christ also; he is assuredly your very zealous friend though he otherwise deserves, on account of his ignorance, only to be buried in a corner, unknown even to your sun and climate.

But Erasmus was not to be drawn. In his reply he carefully dissociated himself from Luther's writings:

Dearest brother in Christ, your epistle showing the keenness of your mind and breathing a Christian spirit, was most pleasant to me. I cannot tell you what a com-

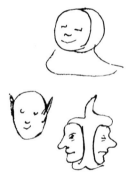

*These doodles by Erasmus are from the margin of one of his manuscripts.*

motion your books are raising here [at Louvain]. These men cannot be by any means disabused of the suspicion that your works are written by my aid and that I am, as they call it, the standard-bearer of your party. . . . I have testified to them that you are entirely unknown to me, that I have not read your books and neither approve nor disapprove anything. . . . I try to keep neutral, so as to help the revival of learning as much as I can. And it seems to me that more is accomplished by civil modesty than by impetuosity.

What Erasmus wanted was moderation. He did not want Luther to be wronged: rather, he tried to guard him from persecution, and even wrote to the Archbishop of Mainz to plead for Luther's safety—and this though the indulgences which Luther had attacked in his theses had been preached precisely for the coffers of this Hohenzollern archbishop.

At the same time Erasmus wanted Luther to be moderate. In encouraging John Lang, he wrote in a tone which is wishful to the point of being absurd: "All good men love the freedom of Luther who, I doubt not, will have sufficient prudence to take care not to allow the affair to arouse faction and discord." It was, in fact, absurd to believe that in such a quarrel either side could be reasonable. And Erasmus knew that Luther was a less moderate man, indeed less a humanist, than many Church dignitaries. What made Erasmus helpless was that he believed Luther's criticisms of the Church to be just, but that he also knew they would merely entrench in the Church the uncompromising men, the monkish bigots whom the humanists had worked so hard to displace. If Luther was defeated, then the reactionaries would also sweep away all that the humanists had gained. "I am deeply disturbed about the wretched Luther. If they pull this off, no one will be able to bear their intolerance. They will not be quiet until they have utterly ruined the study of languages and 'good letters.' "

In the summer of 1520 a papal bull declared Luther a heretic, giving him sixty days to recant or be excommunicated. Luther's answer was to burn the papal bull, and the canon law with it, in public. After this, in spite of further searches for a compromise, there was in effect no going back. Erasmus was already under attack from the University of Louvain, where he had lived since 1517, and where the Churchmen now accused him of double-dealing. The Church was making it clear that those who were not openly against Luther must be counted to be for him. Albrecht Dürer made a last appeal to Erasmus to take the side of Luther, at a time when Luther was thought to be dead or in hiding: "O Erasmus of Rotterdam, where will you be? Hear, you Knight of Christ, ride forth beside the Lord Christ, protect the truth, obtain the martyr's crown. . . . I have heard you say that you have allowed yourself two more years, in which you are still fit to do some work; spend them well, in behalf of the Gospel and the true Christian

*The Latin inscription on this engraving by Holbein declares that it shows Erasmus "as painted from life."*

faith. . . . O Erasmus, be on this side, that God may be proud of you."

Erasmus knew that he was not the man for such heroics, and in his view the heroics had already done harm to his cause. With that unposturing simplicity which gives all his writings their modest personal air, he wrote sadly: "All men have not strength for martyrdom. I fear lest, if any tumult should arise, I should imitate Peter. I follow the just decrees of popes and emperors because it is right; I endure their evil laws because it is safe."

It was not only his temperament that made Erasmus retreat from the side of Luther. He found Luther's opinions more and more distasteful. He did not care for Luther's German nationalism, for his fanaticism, his intolerance, and above all for his belief in the essential helplessness of man under the divine will. For Luther was now outspoken in beliefs which we should call Calvinist, and which left no room for the humanist belief in the goodness of man. To Erasmus, Luther's belief in predestination was no better than the medieval belief in original sin.

Therefore, when the Church pressed Erasmus to speak out against Luther, he chose an issue, free will, on which he was indeed intellectually opposed to Luther and to the rising shadow of Calvinism. Luther replied by writing *The Bondage of the Will,* and left no doubt that there was no longer common ground between them. He sent a copy of *The Bondage of the Will* to Erasmus, with a letter which at last stung Erasmus to speak his mind:

Your letter was delivered to me late and had it come on time it would not have moved me. . . . The whole world knows your nature, according to which you have guided your pen against no one more bitterly and, what is more detestable, more maliciously than against me. . . . The same admirable ferocity which you formerly used against Cochlaeus and against Fisher, who provoked you to it by reviling, you now use against my book in spite of its courtesy. How do your scurrilous charges that I am an atheist, an Epicurean, and a skeptic help the argument? . . . It terribly pains me, as it must all good men, that your arrogant, insolent, rebellious nature has set the world in arms. . . . You treat the Evangelic cause so as to confound together all things sacred and profane as if it were your chief aim to prevent the tempest from ever becoming calm, while it is my greatest desire that it should die down. . . . I should wish you a better disposition were you not so marvelously satisfied with the one you have. Wish me any curse you will except your temper, unless the Lord change it for you.

Alas, Erasmus had not succeeded in mollifying the Church either. He left the Catholic University of Louvain and went to Switzerland. Catholic hotheads insisted that he was the man who "laid the eggs which Luther and Zwingli hatched." Although Erasmus protested that "I laid a hen's egg; Luther hatched a bird of a different breed," the eggs were all broken together. *The Praise of Folly* was placed on the Index of forbidden books; his work on the New Testament was expurgated; and Erasmus himself was condemned by the Council of Trent as "an impious heretic." His cause had failed; he was at home in neither of the two camps now at war; and he had lived beyond his time.

What had failed when Erasmus failed was not a man but an outlook: the liberal view. He gave his life to the belief that virtue can be based on humanity, and that tolerance can be as positive an impulse as fanaticism. Above all he believed in the life of the mind. He believed that thoughtful men would become good men, and that those who knew and loved the great writings of all ages must live more justly and more happily in their own age.

When Erasmus was appointed to the court of the young emperor Charles V in 1516, he wrote for him *The Education of a Christian Prince*. The word "Christian" in the title points the contrast to *The Prince*, which Machiavelli had written three years before, and so do the opening words of Erasmus's dedication, ". . . no form of wisdom is greater than that which teaches a Prince how to rule *beneficently*." But the sense in which Erasmus used the word "Christian," his longing for universal good, could not survive the violence of both sides in the coming struggle.

Part of that struggle was national: Luther was very German, and the Reformation of Henry VIII was very English. In this also Erasmus was out of place; he had hoped to make humanism a movement of universal peace from one end of Europe to another. And in his great years he had traveled Europe as if this empire of the mind, his free Christian community, had already been created. For a time the courts of Italy and England, the universities of France and Spain, the houses of cardinals and reformers, were open to him. But the time was short, and it has not returned.

*Erasmus dictates to a clerk in his Rotterdam study.*

# NICOLAUS
# COPERNICUS
## 1473-1543

H e was the only begetter of the Copernican Revolution, we
say. He was the restorer of astronomy, a second Ptolemy,
they said in the sixteenth century. Both statements are
true, and between them they tell us as much about the difference between the scientific outlook of our day and that
of his day as they do about the man they honor. And in the making of
this difference, Copernicus, or rather, his ideas, played a vital role.

Not that this was his intention. The only revolution he visualized
was that incorporated into the title of his last great work, of which,
tradition says, a copy was placed in his hands on his deathbed. *On the
Revolutions of the Celestial Spheres* it was called—*De revolutionibus*
it has ever since been called for convenience. Like most truly important scientific works, its greatest impact on men's minds was delayed
until lesser men had worked on it; like any seminal work on physical
science, it was difficult, highly technical in exposition, and had an
influence far beyond those who could read and understand it.

The basic idea was simple, and in an age when astronomy was the
science whose rudiments were most widely understood by the lay public, readily comprehensible—as was the implication for astronomy if
the idea was accepted. "The fool will turn the whole science of astronomy upside down," said another intellectual revolutionary, Martin
Luther, not realizing that this was what astronomy required.

Copernicus did indeed turn accepted astronomy upside down by
reversing the age-old theory that what we observe is what actually
happens; for anyone who looks and thinks unblinded by prejudice

*This portrait of Koppernigk, or Copernicus, was painted by an anonymous artist.*

*By* MARIE BOAS HALL

will agree that we see the sun moving and feel the earth to be at rest, not, as Copernicus insisted, the other way around. And while Virgil's acute poetic summary of the relativity of motion—"We sail forth from the harbor, and lands and cities retire"—could be used by Copernicus to support the moving earth, it could equally be used by traditionalists to oppose it. And the latter long had the greater following.

Not that the world in which Copernicus grew up was intellectually stable; far from it. When he was born, in February, 1473, the first agitation of humanism was past, but its excitements lingered and were just beginning to be felt among astronomers. This was especially true of the central European culture of which Copernicus was to be a part. He was born in Toruń (Thorn) on the Vistula, in the plains of northern Poland, a town in territory claimed both by the Teutonic Knights, who had Christianized Prussia two centuries earlier, and by the Polish crown. The diplomatic niceties required to keep this area afloat were to exercise the mind of Copernicus in later life, since thanks to his maternal uncle Lucas Watzelrode, bishop of Ermland, he was to pursue an active career as an ecclesiastical administrator.

Copernicus came from solid Germanic merchant stock, but his uncle's influence—Bishop Watzelrode undertook the education of his sister's family when his brother-in-law died in 1483—ensured that he and his brother should go to the University of Cracow, founded in 1364, where the new ideas of the Renaissance were flourishing. Mathematics and astronomy, as well as classical languages and literature, were thriving, and it is tempting to assume that it was here that the young Copernicus was taught the fascination of mathematical astronomy, man's rational organization of the tangled facts of planetary motion, first systematically attempted twenty centuries earlier, in the time of Plato.

Certainly he was deeply concerned with astronomy by 1496, when he migrated to the University of Bologna. There he took the degree of M.A., prepared for his future career by attending lectures in canon, or church, law, and made his first recorded astronomical observation, to be incorporated in the future into his investigations of the motion of the moon. At Bologna Copernicus met Domenico Maria da Novara, who lectured on astronomy and taught his pupils that all was not well with that science. He was an ardent Platonist, as was fashionable in advanced Italian circles at the time, and this inclined him to the belief that purely mathematical considerations might restore the order and harmony conspicuously lacking in contemporary astronomy.

Late fifteenth-century astronomy was a confused collection of systems inherited from a diverse past, with no certainty of fact or theory. Medieval astronomical theory was based on Aristotelian cosmology,

*Poland and Prussia fought over Toruń, Copernicus's birthplace, for centuries.*

Ptolemaic mathematical astronomy, and Islamic modifications of both. To the layman, like Dante, it was easy, for Aristotle sufficed, and the universe was a tidy nest of spherical boxes, with the earth at the center and the planets arranged on solid crystalline spheres ranging ever outward until one reached the sphere of the fixed stars and the *primum mobile,* the "first mover," or cause of motion. For the astronomer, who knew that simple motion on a sphere, or even a system of spheres, could not "save the appearances" or account for the observed motions of moon, sun, and planets, the intellectual position was full of distress.

The philosophical position was equally difficult. Both Platonic and Aristotelian metaphysics taught that the heavens and the region around the earth obeyed different physical laws; the heavens being perfect and unchanging, heavenly bodies possessed perfect motion— that is, uniform motion in the circle. But since shortly after the time of Aristotle, astronomers had known that the motion of the planets was too complex to be represented by a system of either circles or spheres centered on the earth.

The first suggestion was to make some circles or spheres eccentric to the earth, which solves some problems. The next was to employ the method of epicycles, the epicycle being a small circle on whose circumference lies the planet, the center of the epicycle itself lying on the circumference of a larger circle, the deferent, either centered on the earth, or eccentric to it. When epicycle and deferent rotate, a series of complex curves is obtained. (Nowadays we would express these curves algebraically, but Greek mathematics was geometric.) As if this were not enough, there was also the device of the equant point—a point that is not the earth or the center of the deferent, with respect to which the velocity of the deferent is uniform. (In fact, as Kepler was to show, the velocity of a planet is not uniform, but faster when the planet is near the sun.) All this was nominally pure circular motion, but it was not easily seen as such.

There was a literary problem for sixteenth-century astronomy as well, very important in that age of flourishing humanism. Humanistic tradition dictated the need for pure texts; the first step toward understanding was to go to the original text and make a critical edition. But Greek texts of Ptolemy were few and far between, to be found only in Rome, and the available Latin versions were suspect because translated from Arabic. The Viennese astronomer Georg Pürbach had been distressed by this fifty years earlier; his pupil Regiomontanus had gone to Rome about 1470 to find a Greek manuscript—but he never printed it, only his own commentary on it. Finally, there was the very practical problem of the calendar, clearly inaccurate by 1500, but requiring more knowledge of lunar motion and of the length of the year for rectification.

There was plenty here to exercise the mind of the young Copernicus, and it is clear that he thought long and deeply upon it. Certainly he made a number of astronomical observations. But other things occupied him as well. In 1497 his uncle had succeeded in obtaining his election as canon of Frauenburg Cathedral, one of the chapter of ecclesiastics who, independently of the bishop, ran the secular and religious affairs of the cathedral. But Copernicus was in no hurry to settle down, and preferred to stay in the intellectually exciting world of Italy. He went to Rome for the jubilee year of 1500, partly as a tourist, partly to enjoy the riches of its great libraries. He stayed in Rome for a year, supporting himself by teaching mathematics; his lectures, presumably on astronomy (often called simply mathematics at this time), were later reported to have drawn "a throng of great men and experts." In Rome, too, he recorded his observation of an eclipse of the moon.

After this obviously exciting year he went back home to be installed as canon—and promptly secured leave of absence to study for another five years. This time he went to Padua, famous for law and medicine and with a distinguished tradition in astronomy as well. Here he completed his legal studies (though he actually took the degree of Doctor of Canon Law at Ferrara in 1503), here he obtained the knowledge that later permitted him to practice medicine, and here he acquired a sufficient knowledge of Greek, all in the best tradition of the humanists.

In 1506, his leave of absence up, Copernicus returned to Frauenburg, only to have his uncle call him away to the episcopal palace at Heilsberg in the center of Ermland. Until the bishop's death in 1512 Copernicus acted as his uncle's physician and administrative assistant, helping to keep Ermland independent of the Teutonic Knights and the king of Poland and gaining valuable diplomatic experience. Evidently his uncle also encouraged his intellectual pursuits, for in 1509 he published a Latin translation of an obscure seventh-century Byzantine poet, dedicating the work to his uncle. This scholarly contribution also contains a laudatory poem by a friend, which speaks admiringly of the translator's classical learning and, as well, of his study of the motions of the moon and the planets.

*This 1559 English engraving shows Atlas holding up the Ptolemaic universe, with the earth at its center surrounded by the orbits of the sun, moon, and planets. The Copernican system, with the sun at the center surrounded by the orbits of the earth and the planets, is shown below as it appeared in the first edition of Copernicus's work.*

It is thus clear that his friends knew of his astronomical preoccupations, and probably it was during these years that he planned a new approach to the problem of the structure of the heavens. Certainly it was no later than this (and may have been many years earlier) that he wrote a first and tentative summary in what he called his *Commentariolus* (little commentary), a work that circulated in manuscript in a manner still common in the century after the invention of printing. Through its hand-written pages his ideas became known to a wider circle than that of his immediate friends—who, however, scattered ecclesiastics and scholars as they were, had access to a wide audience.

In the *Commentariolus* the Copernican system was not yet full-grown, and it omitted, as the author explained, "for the sake of brevity" any "mathematical demonstrations which are reserved for my larger work." But it clearly stated the defects that Copernicus felt to obtain in existing astronomical theories and proposed to remedy these by assuming (the word is that used by Copernicus) that the center of motion of the universe is the sun, not the earth. He went on to suggest that the earth rotates on its axis, thereby accounting for the rising and setting of the stars, sun, and planets, and also revolves about the sun, "like any other planet," thereby accounting for many of the observed irregularities of the motion of the other planets. Here, then, is a hypothesis that, according to its author, is "pleasing to the mind," simpler, and more uniform than any complete astronomical system proposed before.

Whatever the reaction later, those who first saw the sketch of the Copernican system evidently regarded its author appreciatively. In 1514 the Lateran Council under Pope Leo X, debating the problem of the calendar (of peculiar concern because of the difficulty and importance of fixing the date of Easter), called on astronomers to give advice; a personal plea was conveyed to Copernicus by an old acquaintance of Roman days, now the pope's chaplain. But Copernicus replied "that the lengths of the years and months and the motions of the Sun and Moon . . . have not yet been determined with sufficient exactness," although he promised to continue to investigate the matter, as indeed he did in continuing to develop his great theory.

Meanwhile he was busy with mundane affairs. His uncle's death sent him back to Frauenburg, where he was much in demand both as a medical consultant and as an administrator. From 1516 to 1521 he managed certain estates belonging to the cathedral, living at Allenstein Castle, south of Heilsberg. Here he experienced the turmoils of war between 1519 and 1521, striving successfully to fend off both sides. He attended the meeting of the Prussian Diet in 1522, with other ecclesiastical rulers, and there presented a notable report on coinage reform, still remembered as containing a statement of what English-speaking economists know as Gresham's Law: that debased money drives out good money.

Back in Frauenburg, in the early summer of 1524, he was led into astronomical controversy by a friend, thereby fully displaying his mastery of the techniques of mathematical and computational astronomy. The friend was a canon of the Church of Cracow and secretary to the king of Poland—like many of Copernicus's friends, a successful ecclesiastical administrator—and he had sent to Copernicus for comment a work on "The Motion of the Eighth Sphere" (the sphere of fixed stars) by a minor German mathematician named John Werner. The *Letter against Werner* criticizes Werner's calculations, in substance and method, and is scathing about his competence. It was an age of controversy; his mathematical friends enjoyed Copernicus's easy mastery of the subject and saw to it that the piece circulated in manuscript, as did the *Commentariolus*.

The *Letter against Werner* undoubtedly added to his reputation as an able and original astronomer, although it contains no hint of his revolutionary astronomical system. But this itself was far from unknown, and in 1533 Pope Clement VII and various cardinals listened to an exposition of the new theory. One of these cardinals, a friend, was so impressed that three years later he wrote to Copernicus to urge him to communicate the details of his system to the world.

Meanwhile, although Copernicus seems to have been very little affected by it, another revolution in thought was taking place—the Protestant revolt. It may have been Andreas Osiander, returning in 1525 from converting the Grand Master of the Teutonic Knights to Lutheranism, who spread the word in Protestant circles of the strange new theory on which the canon of Frauenburg was working. Although Osiander settled in Nuremburg in southern Germany, he may well have passed through Wittenberg, where Luther was living and where the new Protestant university was intellectually active. It is tempting to suppose that it was he who informed Luther of "the new astronomer who wants to prove that the Earth goes round, and not the heavens, the Sun and the Moon; just as if someone sitting in a moving wagon or ship were to suppose that he was at rest, and that the Earth and the trees were moving past him," as Luther described it in his "Table Talk" in 1539. Clearly, the canon of Frauenburg's plan for the reformation of astronomy was by no means the guarded secret one might imagine, and clearly, too, there was as yet no intellectual barrier between Protestant and Catholic circles.

This tolerant view was to become increasingly alien in the growing violence of Reformation and Counter-Reformation Europe, but its

*Cracow was a European center of culture when Copernicus attended its university.*

existence among at least some of the clergy of Frauenburg perhaps explains why the ultimate publication of the entire Copernican system came to be ineluctably linked with Protestant mathematicians. In the spring of 1539, the same year in which Luther showed his surprising knowledge of the new system, a young Protestant professor of mathematics from the University of Wittenberg, Georg Joachim Rheticus, arrived unannounced at Frauenburg, seeking Copernicus and desperately eager to learn the details of his system. Copernicus received him into his household, gave him the run of his manuscripts, explained any difficulties Rheticus encountered, and granted him permission to write a short summary, which under the title *A First Account of the Books on Revolution (Narratio Prima)* was published at Danzig in 1540.

It is a breathless but fairly thorough account, nearly three times as long as Copernicus's own *Commentariolus,* and it describes not the earlier theory but Copernicus's final and considered system. Rheticus is full of respect and praise for his "teacher," as he always calls him, comparing him favorably with the greatest astronomers of past ages. He was utterly captivated by the widespread interest in astronomy he found in Prussia, where it was pursued, he says, not only by Copernicus and by his friend Bishop Giese of Kulm but by the mayor of Danzig and by many others. Rheticus returned to Wittenberg after two years, his head filled with Copernican astronomy and in his luggage a manuscript of the trigonometric sections of Copernicus's work, which he published as a separate tract in 1542.

The departure of Rheticus, though his name was never mentioned by his teacher, seems to have decided Copernicus, now an old man by the standards of the age, that the time had come to cease his labors and let his manuscript be made available for all to read. He gave it to Bishop Giese, who promptly sent it to Rheticus for publication under the title *De revolutionibus orbium coelestium.* Rheticus gave it for printing to a friend in Nuremburg interested in astronomy, and asked Osiander to see it through the press. Eminent churchman and devout

Lutheran that he was, Osiander introduced an extra unsigned preface in which he warned those who may have heard of the author's work not to be alarmed, since the motions of the earth there described were hypothetical only. Copernicus never knew of this preface; for at least six months before his death on May 24, 1543, he was partially paralyzed and bedridden, and although he saw a copy of the finished book, it is unlikely that he was fully aware of it.

If he had been, he almost certainly would not have agreed with Osiander. He may have been cautious, and slow to venture into print because of "the scorn which I had to fear on account of the novelty and incongruity of my theory"—scorn that might come from the unlearned, and indeed had come from Luther and others as a result of his letting the *Commentariolus* circulate widely; yet his friends, far from hissing him off the stage, had encouraged him on every hand. Finally, reflecting that "mathematics are for mathematicians," who would understand, and that the work would be useful for the Church's calendar reform, he had decided to let the long-matured book appear. All this he confided in his own preface to *De revolutionibus*, addressed to Pope Paul III and therefore written after 1534.

In this preface, which appeared along with Osiander's, Copernicus gave his reasons for having tried to reform astronomy by thinking about the motion of the earth. "I should like your Holiness to know," he declares, "that I was induced to think of a method of computing the motions of the spheres by nothing else than the knowledge that mathematicians are inconsistent in these investigations." Their computations are inexact and inconsistent with their hypotheses; their mathematical devices are clumsy, and they cannot make the universe a coherent whole. Long reflection convinced Copernicus, he said, that it was not right to abandon the attempt to find a true system, and, good humanist that he was, he read the ancients "to seek out whether any of them had ever supposed that the motions of the spheres were other than those demanded by the mathematical schools." Finding that there had indeed been Greek astronomers who had taught the mobility of the earth (he does not seem to have known of late medieval speculators like Nicole Oresme and Nicholas of Cusa), he ventured, he says, to try its effect upon astronomy. And he found it offered a "sound explanation," for if the earth were taken to be in motion, then the whole universe seemed to fall into a harmonious whole, even though it was necessary to assume that this universe was far larger than had previously been thought.

How did this come about? First, by assuming the daily rotation of the earth upon its axis, he found that one motion explained many: the rising and setting of the fixed stars, of the sun, moon, and planets, were all accounted for. There was no need to assume that the sphere of fixed stars whirled around every day at immense speed, nor to postulate some extra mathematical device to account for the diurnal motions of the sun, moon, and planets. Next, by assuming that the earth was not the center of the universe but itself a moving planet, and by making all the planets revolve about the sun, the motions of the planets became simpler. For example, Mars and Jupiter have the awkward habit of appearing at some points in their orbits to move backward, contrary to their normal motion. This "retrograde motion" Copernicus correctly explained as being the result of the earth's motion. The terrestrial year is shorter than the Martian or Jovian year, and so the earth sometimes appears to overtake the so-called outer planets, those that are located beyond the sun, making it appear that these planets are moving backward.

Two points must be noted here. The first is that Copernicus differed from his predecessors in his postulation of the motion of the earth by the fact that he genuinely believed it represented physical reality. Indeed, his very belief that a knowledge of physical reality was attainable is in itself in marked contrast to the beliefs of Scholastic thinkers, who held that only Revelation, which came direct from God, gave certainty and that man could by reason attain only to possible, probable, or contingent truths.

*The quadrant, above, and astrolabe, below, were the medieval astronomer's basic tools. The quadrant had sighting devices and a plumb line; the astrolabe was used to determine the movement of the stars. The instruments shown were made in Italy about 1500.*

Copernicus was aware that the observations available to him, whether his own or those of others, were necessarily insufficient and probably not as accurate as they might be, and this might mean the necessity of correcting his tables and figures, but he never doubted that the aim of astronomy was to achieve a description of physical reality, of nature as it really was. Osiander's preface is therefore the absolute denial of one of Copernicus's greatest contributions to astronomy—the conviction, which his successors readily adopted, that it was the business of the astronomer to describe the motions of the planets as they really are.

The second important aspect of Copernicus's work in which he differed from his predecessors is that, far from offering a hint or a suggestion or a sketch of an astronomical system, he offered the complete system itself, in thorough and efficient detail. Only one man had done this—or even tried to do this—before, namely Ptolemy in his "great synthesis," which we know by the Latinized Arabic title *Almagest*. Here Ptolemy had set out the arguments for a geostatic universe, and then had gone on to give a mathematical exposition of the motions of the moon, the sun, and the planets, with tables showing what the positions of these heavenly bodies ought to be in the future.

Copernicus produced in *De revolutionibus* a mirror image of the *Almagest:* in the first book is what he called "the general system of the

*The Danish astronomer Tycho Brahe, top, developed a system incorporating elements of both the Ptolemaic and Copernican theories. His associate Johannes Kepler, middle, accepted the Copernican theory and corresponded with Galileo, whose observations further expanded the science of astronomy.*

universe," that is, the arguments in favor of the earth's mobility (Ptolemy's arguments for its being at rest all carefully refuted), followed, as in the *Almagest,* by a short trigonometric treatise intended to provide the more advanced mathematics to be used in later books. Then, again like the *Almagest,* Book II applies his trigonometry to various problems concerned with the apparent motions of the planets, improving on Ptolemy, and ends with a star catalogue, that of Ptolemy corrected for the passage of time. There follows in Book III an exposition of the motions of the earth, in Book IV of the moon, and in Books V and VI of the inner and outer planets, each exposition ending with a theoretical discussion of the particular body's motion and with tables intended to show future positions.

Much of the immediate importance of Copernicus's work lies in these later books, for the methods of calculation and the tables themselves were, although imperfect, a great improvement upon earlier ones. It is clear why Erasmus Reinhold (like Rheticus, a Protestant professor of mathematics at Wittenberg) called Copernicus "a second Ptolemy." In fact, Reinhold was not a believer in the Copernican system, but he recognized the merits of the calculations and tables, and in 1551 he published the *Prutenic* (Prussian) *Tables,* based on those of Copernicus. Reinhold's printing costs were paid by Duke Albert of Prussia, whom Osiander had long before converted to Protestantism. So, curiously, the work of the Catholic Copernicus continued to be linked with Protestantism.

It is difficult to tell what the immediate effect of *De revolutionibus* was on the world. For on the one hand, the chief novelties—the motions of the earth and their effects—had been known by those who had read either the *Commentariolus* or the *Narratio Prima* of Rheticus, or had even heard these spoken of. And on the other hand, the *De revolutionibus* was an extremely difficult work to master. Nevertheless, it was reprinted with the *Narratio Prima* in 1566 at Basel, and it is clear that many astronomers who shrank from the implications of the Copernican system still found it useful for reference. Rather oddly to the modern mind, it was the fresh observations that struck astronomers most forcibly; these are not very numerous—Copernicus mentions only twenty-seven—nor very accurate, but they very much impressed astronomers in the decades before Tycho Brahe revolutionized observational astronomy.

Too much can be made of the reactions of poets and literary men, often speaking from hearsay. These frequently reacted like Luther, or like Du Bartas, who expressed the view in his didactic poem of 1578, *La Semaine,* that Copernicus represented the "brainsick" generation overblown with novelty—"how absurd a jest" to suppose the earth moves, as if a passenger on a ship should think he was at rest while the shore moved away. On the other hand, the more intellectual Pléiade (the French court poets, the best known of whom was Ronsard) discussed, if they did not entirely accept, the Copernican system, and their astronomical member, Pontus du Tyard, in 1557 published an accurate summary of it.

In England Robert Recorde in his *Castle of Knowledge* of 1556 expressed a view that must have been common among teachers of astronomy—that the Copernican system was an important one but not suitable for beginning students. For the rest of the century even Copernicans taught the old system to elementary students and the Copernican system only to advanced students. Yet one of the few vernacular translations of Book I of *De revolutionibus* was presented to the layman—by Thomas Digges, a competent mathematician and astronomer, who in revising his father's *Prognostication Everlasting* (a perpetual almanac) in 1576, added an appendix entitled *A Perfect Description of the Coelestiall Orbes*. This differs from Copernicus only in extending the sphere of fixed stars to "the palace of felicity ... the very court of celestial angels," the theological heaven, so that the stars are no longer hung on a crystalline sphere but are scattered through an immensity of space. It is, perhaps, not entirely fortuitous that it was in England that the heretical runaway monk and pantheistic philosopher Giordano Bruno expanded his dithyramb of oneness to include the infinity of the universe and espoused Copernicanism because it was easier to adapt to infinity than the Ptolemaic universe was.

Bruno was burned at the stake in 1600, though not for accepting Copernicanism. But his death reflects the growing and bitter religious tensions of the sixteenth century, which made it more difficult for Protestants and Catholics alike to dissent from the literal truth of the Bible. Copernicus had rightly pointed out that in his time no one seriously followed Lactantius in denying the sphericity of the earth on Biblical authority, and hence, he argued, one need not reject the mobility of the earth on Biblical authority. But others were less sure, especially when they reflected upon the physical arguments that could be advanced against a moving earth: its heavy, sluggish nature, the enormous size of the Copernican universe, the belief that a stone dropped from a tower could not land at its foot if the earth were rotating.

These were the arguments that moved the Danish Lutheran Tycho Brahe, the first great observational astronomer of modern times. Tycho was no Copernican, but his own system, geocentric and geostatic, was really more revolutionary than that of Copernicus. For Tycho did more than anyone to destroy the Aristotelian heaven-earth dualism. His observations of the nova of 1572 convinced him that its appearance meant that the heavens were not perfect and unchanging; and his observations of the comet of 1577 convinced him that, since it traversed the regions where the planets lay, there were no solid, crystalline spheres to hold the planets in their orbits. Many Copernicans accepted his reasoning, and the Copernican system was expanded thereby.

But if there were no crystalline spheres, what kept the planets in position, and how did they move? Answers to these questions were attempted at the very end of the sixteenth century by brilliant, original scientists. William Gilbert, born three years before the publication of *De revolutionibus,* saw no difficulty in accepting at least the daily rotation of the earth, for had he not discovered that the earth was a magnet, and therefore capable of rotating on its axis? And he further postulated that magnetism was responsible for keeping the moon in its orbit—a view that was to be extended to all the planets by Kepler.

Kepler, born in 1571, was the first since Copernicus himself to attempt a mathematical assessment of the Copernican system. Unlike Copernicus, he was driven on by a spirit of mysticism, curiously tempered by an equally profound belief in observation, especially when the observations were the supremely accurate ones made by Tycho Brahe. Tycho had obliterated crystalline spheres; now Kepler threw away all the computational devices of circle, epicycle, and deferent, representing the planets as moving in elliptical orbits according to certain simple mathematical laws, under a quasimagnetic force emanating from the sun. This theory was too remote from conventional astronomy to find an immediate audience, and Kepler's work was assimilated only in the mid-seventeenth century.

The nearest approach to a proof that the Copernican system ever received before the nineteenth century came from the telescopic discoveries of Galileo, published in 1610. He observed that Venus had phases, like the moon, as it should if the Copernican system was true; that the earth was not unique in having a moon, for Jupiter had four; that the stars really were enormously far away, for they could not be resolved in a telescope, but that they were not so huge as people had thought, for they were only points of light. Galileo crowned all these wonders by announcing a firm belief in Copernicanism, to which he even tried to convert a Catholic Church increasingly alarmed by intellectual novelties. In 1631 he published his *Dialogue on the Two Chief Systems of the World,* in which he clearly, although not professedly, espoused Copernicanism. The result was a clash with the Inquisition, and Galileo was forced to abjure his astronomical beliefs. Although this made Catholic scientists cautious, it attracted much sympathy to Galileo, and many readers. These were converted by Galileo's clever arguments, and above all, by the fact that his new physics fitted in with the Copernican system as well as the old Aristotelian physics had with the Ptolemaic.

A hundred years after the publication of *De revolutionibus* Galileo died, Newton was born, and the best scientists everywhere were inclining toward Copernicanism. Even Catholics were Copernicans—for example, Pierre Gassendi, like Copernicus a cathedral canon. Only priests in orthodox orders like the Jesuits held out, to be won over quietly in the eighteenth century. By the time that observational proof of the Copernican system was forthcoming—in the late 1830's—even the Catholic Church had capitulated. But the effects on science and thought had been incalculable ever since Copernicus had first let those outside his immediate circle know of his truly revolutionary theory of the celestial orbs.

*This engraving depicts Copernicus and Tycho Brahe as new pillars in the temple of science.*

# MARTIN
# LUTHER
## 1483-1546

Born in 1483 at Eisleben, Saxony, Germany, he became a law student at Erfurt University in 1501, turned monk in 1505, and was appointed professor of Biblical studies at the University of Wittenberg in 1512. In 1515–16 he arrived at his theology of justification, which prompted him to formulate the Ninety-five Theses the following year. In 1520 he publicly burned the codex of the canon law representing the established Roman Church and was duly excommunicated. In 1521 at the Diet of Worms (an assembly of the supreme legislative body of the German Empire), he refused to recant his teachings and writings, was abducted while in protective custody, and remained in hiding until 1522, when he returned to Wittenberg. There, in 1525, during the turmoils of the Peasants' War, he cast off his priestly vows of celibacy and married an ex-nun. He died in 1546, the year after the convocation of the Council of Trent, which in its eighteen-year course was to initiate the responsive Catholic Counter Reformation. The Western Church remained divided, in a pattern that finally emerged at the end of the Thirty Years' War of 1618–48.

Such are the bare outlines of the life and influence of that extraordinary man who may be said to have brought to birth the literally epoch-making movement known as the Reformation.

The Reformation got its name when, unlike previous similar attempts, it succeeded. In the act of survival, what had started as a religious-institutional overhaul turned into a comprehensive revolution. A change of climate was effected to which, like it or not, for

*Holbein painted a Martin Luther whose peasant face was "black like my parents."*

better or worse, we are still the heirs. It created a new historical concept, that of a medieval, *middle* period set between antiquity and modern times, as clearly differentiated in point of outlook from the one as from the other.

Until then, in Western reckoning, B.C. and A.D. were the only valid subdivisions in the story of man, with its fixed plot of the Fall and Redemption. Adam had sinned and forfeited Eden, Jesus had lived and died to regain Paradise for him. The break was indicated by the birth unto human ken of the incarnate Saviour. Otherwise, pending the Second Coming, the Last Judgment, and Finis, history was seen entirely in terms of variations on the two basic themes, perpetually re-enacted in allegoric form.

Religion suffused all existence, on every plane and ranging from the most rudimentary intellectual apprehension to the subtlest. The accent everywhere was on the supernatural. Matter represented evil. Partly this was a side effect of the inversion of success and failure under the Christian doctrine, which equated poverty and lowliness on earth with spiritual riches, worldly defeat with victory in salvation —as exemplified by the crucified carpenter. The primeval identification of success and failure respectively with good and bad being ultimately unalterable, their terms of reference had been turned inside out: a circumstance that was at the bottom of the whole elaborate code of the pervasive medieval symbology. But as paradox was thus meat and drink to the medieval mind, and as the spiritual object had to be made intelligible by analogy to a material one, it became possible to reinvert the system, until mundane wealth and power might claim to be, in fact, symbolic of privation and humility. So long as the initial premise was not questioned, you could have it both ways.

Axiomatically, the yardstick of status evaluation was not wealth, not power, not birth, not even usefulness, but rather, the quality of holiness. Under God there were degrees of holiness in heaven, even as on earth there stood at the top of the social scale not the king but the saint. Yet, holiness being a compound of sacrament and merit rather than a matter of simple virtue, it happened that the gradings of class and sanctity were mostly congruent. The king, having to be consecrated by a high-ranking member of an entire consecrated class, the priesthood, that intervened between the hierarchies of heaven and earth, naturally received a greater share of holiness than what he dispensed to his vassals, and they in turn to theirs, in ever-diminishing portions, down to a level of traceless dissipation among the mass of the people whose functions carried no sacerdotal diploma whatsoever.

Still, something remained of the primal principle of the equal brotherhood of all souls in Christ. For one thing, holiness could be acquired and it could also be lost, irrespectively of human categories.

*These are bookplates from Martin Luther's Old Testament, displaying (above) his initials and (below) the Lamb of God giving up His blood into a Communion cup.*

For another, Christendom formed a truly international body, under the aegis of the universal Church. And the Church, styled catholic, or all-embracing, and *semper reformanda,* or ever-reforming, that spiritual entity, had taken on material shape. Though having no intrinsic terrestrial substance and recognizing no frontiers, it had become a state, with all the territorial, fiscal, judicial, and military attributes of such a thing, under a monarch, the pope, who claimed all Western Christendom for his subjects and maintained landed enclaves, immune from local dues and legislation, in the countries of Europe. Moreover, he had all islands in his gift, among which were numbered the newly discovered transatlantic areas.

Such, in most of Europe, was the overall situation until about the middle of the sixteenth century. Even before the close of that century, the world and the human condition had got a new look.

The world, which God had not just dreamed up but created, was as real while it lasted as the realm of the spirit. Everything was itself and not something else; events were actual and not mere paraphrases, life no mere, incurable charade. Perfectibility was not confined to the hereafter, nor inevitably backward-looking in design. Counting the sojourn in Eden and the years of Jesus' ministry on earth as the first two golden ages, the millennium would be a third one, not necessarily a reversion. One had to do something about it. The end of time was no longer just around the corner, no longer rendering technological advances, industry, education, welfare, and so forth at best incidental or irrelevant.

The nature of time had altered, along with the approach to it. The religious controversy had made chronology a vital aspect of the study of Church history, and the flat panorama of the past had revealed unguessed perspectives and dynamism, like the universe itself. The new age developed a craze for clocks, and if the modern respect for research was still this side of latter-day idolatry by a long way, factual-critical investigation had come into honor.

To work was to be honorable, not underprivileged; all human occupations had alike become blessed. Where once neglect of hygiene had been a mark of saintliness, cleanliness was now an important adjunct of the godly life. Holiness was by the grace of God, indivisible yet equally accessible to all men; it no more adhered to station than it could be acquired by set actions. Charity, previously an oblation, became philanthropy, a humane duty; medicine became consciously divorced from both magic and alchemy. Skill, discovery, invention, had come into their own. Any extraordinary accomplishment ceased to be automatically attributable either to assistance from the devil or the immediate agency of God. Man had begun to feel that there was nothing beyond him. Nothing was impossible, one only had to learn how it was to be done. Learning might specialize, no longer wholly geared to and tied up with devotional purposes. The vernaculars of different countries were promoted to the rank of languages, formerly monopolized by Latin, Greek, and Hebrew as the vehicles of Scripture. Nationhood and nationalism, unknown not long before, were phenomena now taken for granted.

There was no universal Western Church. An undesired split had taken place, whereby the one side upheld the canon of papal supremacy while the other side acknowledged no doctrinal authority save the actual Word of God, the Bible, and accepted overriding civil authority in matters temporal. On the evangelical side there were many heterodox mansions, often mutually hostile but sparing of the outright charge of heresy. The ideas of freedom of conscience, human rights, and progress, without antecedent parallels in Christian civilization, had made their appearance.

On the Roman Catholic side ecclesiastical reforms had been carried through, of such proportions that a small part of them, if conceded earlier, would have sufficed to keep Martin Luther quiet and obscure in his provincial backwater where the cataclysm had originated.

In what ways did Luther determine those developments? To what extent was he responsible? What part was played by the character of the man as distinct from the historical forces operating through him?

Much of the time Luther had no inkling of what his actions would be leading to. Often propelled, now victimized, now benefited by the confluence of circumstances, chance, or mistiming and miscalculations on the part of his adversaries, he followed his own imperious conscience. Personal ambition and vanity had no part in his make-up, and by temperament he was conservative. He hated change. He abhorred rebellion. He condemned heresy and "enthusiasm" (a word that in his book comprehended everything from political radicalism to sectarian mysticism). He had a passion for truth, and in the end acquired the arrogance of total conviction; he never wittingly started a fight but only defended himself, the faith, mankind, and even Jesus Christ against oppression, with fitting vigor. That was how he saw the matter. To him it was the religious Establishment that had defected from orthodoxy.

Sensitive, affectionate, unsure of himself, thoroughly intimated by his upbringing—all he had wanted was to stand well with God and man, longing to lean on authority for paternal support, security, and warmth. However, he also possessed a ready intellect, shrewdness, imagination, a sense of humor, boundless energy, the gift of words and music, and the capacity to win friends and influence people. He

*Cranach depicted Luther's preaching as powerful enough to make the dying Christ real to a rapt congregation.*

was good company. He was loyal and never more courageous than when most afraid. As he said, Stubbornissimus was his middle name.

Indeed, arbitrariness, insult, and menaces were to him irresistible stimuli against knuckling under. If his own treacherous metabolism joined forces with the enemy—for Luther fell ill at every serious crisis in his career—he would not give in to psychosomatic pressures either. Time and again at the eleventh hour he would rise to the occasion that had threatened to prostrate him.

A lively interest in the wonders of nature mitigated the standard medieval loathing of the flesh, which smacked too much of self-pity where Luther was concerned, as he was of a practical turn of mind, instinctively realizing that problems to be tackled must be faced before they are bemoaned. His understandable preoccupation with intestinal processes—Luther was a lifelong martyr to constipation and dysentery—informed a coarse imagery that hit the mark with larger numbers of his contemporaries than it scandalized. There was a striking correlation between the state of his bowels and that of his head: periods of toilsome blockage alternated with a creative diarrhea. So far from agreeing with that dominant strain of theological thinking that had contrived to narrow down the evil of matter particularly to its procreative manifestation, further concentrated in its unsavory hatching place, the womb, the mature Luther looked upon the miracle of birth as second to none in goodness and beauty.

The contradictions that dwell in every person, and that on closer scrutiny most often resolve themselves into complementary rather than conflicting traits, worked in him, too, with all the lusty force characterizing every aspect of his being. He was fair-minded, he was cantankerous; he overflowed with loving kindness, he could erupt with venomous hate; he was modest yet overbearing; down to earth yet hardly what one would call a realist—it is not the realist who will attempt, much less achieve, the impossible. Ever uncompromising in his faith and stance, his worst errors sprang from compromise. That

*Luther's pen furnishes quills for other reformers in this contemporary allegory, while a figure symbolizing the Church lies dying in the upper right-hand corner.*

is the trouble: men, especially revolutionary leaders, have to perish young to be adjudged consistent and to die with wholly clean hands.

To the end of his life Luther never ceased to be amazed at his own survival and, for that matter, at the avalanche resulting from the pebble he had first set rolling. It could only be proof of the hand of God: a belief hardly calculated to induce diffidence and caution. Intelligent and sane enough to appreciate some of the factors that had contributed to the spectacular chain reaction (for instance, the invention of printing: "God's latest and best work!" according to Luther; and an initial, acute public concern about indulgences: "Nobody else had come forward and opened his mouth"), Luther lacked the equipment to discern many more.

Much of Luther's biographical data testifies to the currents of his times. He came of Thuringian peasant stock, sturdy and swarthy ("black like my parents"), and later liked to flirt with a lowly origin from which, however, his father had already risen to the position of part owner of a few small copper mines and foundries—illustrating the arrival of capitalism and of a social mobility incompatible with the feudal order until the latter had begun to lose its grip.

The age of chivalry, of social organization centered on the horse as the sovereign means of military power, was past, though many features of it lingered in mostly vestigial, unfunctional form. Especially was this the case in the German Empire, which, not so much a federation as a conglomerate of some three hundred autonomous states, was in every political sense behind the times. Nevertheless, even in Germany manufacture and trade were supplanting private war as the key to the pattern of society. Status was no longer inseparable from land. There were now broad sections of the nobility without territorial possessions and broad sections of the lower orders freed from territorial bondage, a situation favoring violence and disaffection on the one hand and the steady increase in growth and power of an urban middle class on the other.

Aspiring recruits to that class, the Luther family were subjects of the Count of Mansfeld, who was vassal to the Elector of Saxony, one of the seven sovereign, hereditary rulers of a country that was at once the largest physical unit in Europe and the most disunited and disorganized. These seven Electors pledged allegiance to the German emperor, whom they voted into office and whose title needed no German territorial suzerainty. (Thus Henry VIII of England and Francis I of France were among the candidates for the imperial crown at the election of 1519, which was won by Charles V of Spain and which, as it happened, furnished one of the turning points in the Romano-Lutheran controversy.) Owing to the absence of an effective central authority, the encroachments of the Italian-based Church on German secular affairs had not become reduced as in most other countries, so that Germany was dubbed, with small injustice, the "private milch cow" of the papacy; while the revival of imperial Roman law for a uniform civil code placed some restraint on the living anachronism of feudal anarchy. This supreme law code had brought into being a species of professional administrators who were neither lords nor clerics as theretofore and who could expect to do well in the world. Martin, the second son of Hans and Margarethe Luther, was set to study for the law.

The parents, plain, hard-working, thrifty folk, were anything but pleased at his abrupt decision to become a monk. Yet they had not a little to do with it. The fear of God and of themselves his domestic deputies, in which they had raised their children, had so permeated this son that it secretly blighted his youth, until in a moment of superstitious dread he, as it were, made a peace offering of himself to the deity.

The cure, however, proved worse than the disease, since the introspection prescribed as a part of the monastic curriculum only enhanced Martin's existing tendencies in that direction, and with them, that agonizing consciousness of guilt, sin, and ineluctable damnation under which he labored. ("Love God? I hated Him!") It was partly in an attempt by sympathetic superiors to get him out of his recurrent depressions that he was appointed lecturer in Biblical studies to the young University of Wittenberg. The university, near and dear to the heart of its founder, the Elector Frederick of Saxony, was largely staffed by the Augustinian priory to which Brother, now Doctor, Martinus belonged.

The internal fragmentation of the German Empire had one fruitful effect in that there was considerable cultural rivalry between many of its diverse units. A university was a status symbol as well as an attraction to visitors and revenue. But meanwhile, education, and higher education most of all, was dominated by theology, the Queen of Sciences, as it was styled: a discipline that had become well and truly academic. Scholasticism, pursuing the knowledge of God by rational means through a system of analytic debate, had turned divinity into an arid dialectical wilderness and a byword of dissatisfaction, a butt of satire everywhere, not just in Germany.

Since the Scriptures, held to be of divine authorship, were being used principally as a mine of abstruse symbolism, and since humanistic scholarship had recently uncovered serious mistranslations in the Latin Vulgate, a return to the straightforward contents of the Bible, by way of the original Greek and Hebrew, was being advocated in enlightened circles. Even so, the Word of God would remain in truth a book with seven seals to the laity at large, who had only their own native tongues and for whom the all-Latin liturgy was a rigmarole of magic gibberish—nicely demonstrated, some say, in the popular rendering "hocus-pocus" of the phrase *hoc est corpus* at the climax of the mass, the central act of Christian worship.

This matter was one of many on the agenda of a reformation such as thoughtful men in every walk of life had mooted for close on two centuries, and which included manifold abuses and malpractices recognized as such within the Church itself. But, "Never refuse [to convoke] a Council [to deal with reform]," as a certain papal legate artlessly defined the prevailing papal policy in that respect, "and never grant one. Thus you will continually stave it off." It was not that, even on the summit, reforms were deemed redundant, merely that it was always inconvenient to get down to the business, chiefly for reasons of finance and power politics.

None of this touched Luther to begin with. His lectures were conventional, and he took no interest in current affairs. But his duties at Wittenberg also embraced that of parish priest in the town, causing the chronic concern with his own salvation to become overlaid by a concern for others. He was no less perturbed by the low level of piety and morals in his parishioners than by the fatal imperfections of his soul.

Somewhere there must be a key to these related problems. He immersed himself in the Scriptures, taking up text after text and worrying it like a dog, always still in the despairing hope of overcoming his enduring difficulty—how to reconcile the love of God with the concept of divine justice—which hinged on the word *iustitia*. "That word used to give me seasickness . . . ay, even to this day I feel a pang when I hear God called 'the just'!" Then, as he "raged with a wounded and confused spirit . . . laboring day and night," the solution came suddenly when least expected, in a flash of revelation from one phrase in Saint Paul's Epistles to the Romans: "The just shall live by faith."

"All at once I began to understand the justice of God as that by which the just live by the gift of God, which is faith: that passive righteousness with which the merciful God endues us in form of faith, thus justifying, rendering us just . . . At this I experienced such relief and easement, as if I were reborn and had entered through open gates into paradise itself. The whole Bible all at once looked different . . . And then, what a game began! The words [texts] came up to me on every side jostling one another and smiling in agreement . . ."

Rather than equating *iustitia* with justice, which metes out deserved punishment, it had been given him to interpret it as righteousness in the sense of purest good, dispensing mercy. Imperfect man, he found, does not need to attain a perfection that is forever beyond him to be saved: let him but have perfect faith, and he shall find grace. Salvation is contingent on forgiveness, which is contingent on repentance: that is all there is to it. Repentance is of the heart; it can be neither feigned nor commuted into outward "works" whether sacrificial or ritual. There is no buying and selling in heaven: mercy can only come as a transcendent gift.

That was the foundation of Martin Luther's "Practical Theology," theology applied to the interests of man and treating Scripture as a manual of instruction and guidance rather than philosophical word-play—"our" theology, as it was soon spoken of at Wittenberg with some pride. Its development boosted Luther's reputation and sent up university enrollments. Luther's preaching also grew more direct and ranged farther afield in human interest. One thing led him to another. From elucidating justification by faith to castigating mercenary piety in the form of worship of saints and relics was but a logical step.

*This anti-Luther cartoon gives the reformer seven heads for the various areas of society in which he was thought to be treacherous.*

His strictures were not so well received. The Elector Frederick had built up a famous and lucrative collection of relics, no less dear to him than his academic project, and the laity on the whole preferred what seemed to be the easier road to salvation, via *quid pro quo:* you paid your oblation, and it was charged to your credit on high. To bring home to the people that this was a most dangerous fallacy became Luther's foremost concern. It was shared by many; neither was it altogether new. But he did not know that. He busied himself trying to find out what other qualified professionals thought and what rulings might be culled from the great teachers of the past. Communications in the sixteenth century were primitive, and although that recent godsend, the printing press, was working overtime to replace rare and costly manuscript books with duplicated ones, the bulk of a huge body of source and exegetical material was still hard to come by.

Then came the great indulgence campaign, launched to finance the rebuilding of St. Peter's basilica in Rome and promoted in Germany by a noted fund raiser, the Dominican friar Tetzel. Tetzel, whose methods were notorious for overstepping every bound of dogma and decorum (since he explicitly promised wholesale release from purgatory against receipted money contributions, with an amount of showmanship to put the gaudiest circus to shame), was an abomination to the serious-minded of every degree, not least the Elector Frederick, against whose relics the indulgence competed with utmost success.

"All the world was complaining about the indulgence," said Luther, exaggerating slightly in an attempt to explain what happened, "and since all the bishops and doctors kept silent, for the Dominican Inquisition had frightened everybody with the terror of the stake . . . to this Luther was praised for daring to take a stand in the matter." He himself, he added, did not know precisely what indulgences were.

*A letter from the emperor summoned Luther to Worms.*

That was the point. The celebrated ninety-five point disputation program that Luther fastened to the door of the castle church, or acting university notice board, on All Saints' Eve, 1517, was a probe to clarify the position. "Those who cannot be present and discuss the subject orally are asked to do so by letter." Copies went to Luther's diocesan bishop, to the Archbishop of Mainz, under whose license Tetzel operated and who was himself deeply involved on the financial side, and to some colleagues at other universities. (The Elector Frederick did not get a copy because, as Luther let it be known, politics were to be kept strictly out of a purely scientific conference.)

There was no conference. The debate did not take place, as no one came to it and nobody wrote in. Luther's placard appeared to have fallen flat; the probe had elicited nothing. But then, as everybody knows, the contrary was seen to have occurred. All at once Luther was inundated with letters of acclaim, many from people he did not know in towns where normally he had no correspondents. Specialists conveyed their delighted support, laymen their thanks for the illumination he had brought them. Without reference to him, the theses had been variously copied, passed from hand to hand and town to town, reprinted in sizable editions, including a translation into German—for of course they had been written in Latin, the official instrument of all academic proceedings. Even so, the document was highly technical for the most part: the question of indulgences really must have been a very sore point in the collective conscience.

"Within a fortnight," Luther marveled, "the Ninety-five Theses ran throughout all Germany"—more, they were being read in England, Holland, and Switzerland. Again remembering the slowness of communications at the time, and the fact that they would be at their worst in late autumn, the wildfire publicity that was attained strikes one today as scarcely less miraculous than it did him.

Luther was alarmed. Intended only as a challenge, the theses had been taken as a positive critique—and who was he to lay down the law? So jeered the personalized Devil—the only outright supernatural manifestation in his day and age that Luther credited and with whom he was in almost constant skirmish. The jeer was echoed in the appropriate quarter: Tetzel exulted that within the month he would have "the heretic" burning at the stake. No more was needed to firm Luther's assurance, unless it was that his brother friars at the priory now took fright and importuned him to retract.

What was there to retract? To show that the heresy was on the other foot and explain himself beyond misunderstanding, Luther elaborated the theses into a proper treatise as well as publishing a simplified version in German for the people. The treatise was forwarded to Rome, besides being widely circulated among all those whom it concerned in Germany; it and the vernacular abstract became runaway best sellers. Rome took no notice, in spite of the growing clamor of the Dominicans in high places to liquidate the author. It was thought at the Holy See that a small, localized "monkish squabble" of this kind did not warrant attention; just as Luther, too, was under the misapprehension that he took issue in a case of local and particular aberration.

*Above is the room in Wartburg Castle where Luther was hidden after the Diet of Worms and where he threw an inkpot at Satan.*

Within a month or two, Tetzel's prediction was disproved to the extent that the fame of Dr. Luther, that "mangy" small-town teaching friar, had been bruited far beyond his familiar stamping ground. Within the year, every educated person in Europe knew whom the various epithets referred to, from Holy Doctor to Pestilent Boil, from Saint Paul (or alternatively Saint John the Divine) Reborn to Infamous Blasphemer. Within two years, the common people were as well informed and as embattled as an ever-escalating war of publications could ensure, while monarchs, bankers, Princes of the Church, had to name Luther as a factor in their calculations. Within three years almost to the day, Luther by the unprecedented step of publicly burning the codex of the canon law captured the imagination of the world, both pro and con: he had taken it upon himself to excommunicate the papacy before it finally excommunicated him. And only a few months after that, the "drunken mini-monk," or "German Hercules," alone and quailing, stood up in person before the full array of empire, complete with Roman plenipotentiaries, at the Diet of Worms, refusing to recant a single thing that he had said or done.

That was the moment of Luther's apotheosis, in which his image was enshrined for transmission to posterity. Inasmuch as he lived to head and help consolidate the movement he had inspired for another twenty-five years, the subsequent developments, though not without their high spots and setbacks, were less starkly dramatic by comparison, lending themselves less to heraldic representation, as it were, less stirring at a remove in time. Human beings have never quite lost their taste for symbols and allegorical postures.

What, then, was the nature of the things Luther had said and done in those few, short, formative years that they should have led to such a climax?

The man who is often called a "healthy philistine" had much of the Bohemian in his make-up. The bourgeois virtues he commended —prudence, patience, conformity, subservience to routine—were not his. He was incapable of standing still and of repeating himself. Each time he was moved to justify or further clarify his thoughts, he was pushed deeper into researches and conclusions that neither he nor his opponents had anticipated. Every treatise, sermon, or epistle that he wrote, every argument produced in oral confrontation, broke a little piece of fresh ground, though he had merely meant to see to his defenses. Once he had been brought to question certain modal effects, he was led step by step to the doctrinal causes. Propositions he had sincerely believed unassailable crumbled before his searching gaze—infinitely to his own distress. To

*Reformation leaders gathered at Marburg Castle in 1529 in an abortive attempt at unification.*

the last he strove to avert a schism. But just as the Ninety-five Theses turned into "Resolutions" as soon as he set about expanding them, so, gradually but inexorably, Luther, from wishing to disabuse the minds of his compatriots as regards indulgences, traveled all the way to identifying the papacy with the Antichrist, no less.

The interpretation of the indulgence principle, which he had attacked, *was* untenable; the Holy See in due course confirmed this and threw Tetzel to the wolves, but too late to halt a conflict that by then had passed far beyond the point of departure. At every juncture it was the Holy See's automatic reaction against the merest breath of criticism that delayed concessions until they were out of date. At every juncture, too, the political elements that Luther fondly declined to have anything to do with intervened—until political events hinged as much upon him as his fate hinged upon them, until even he had to realize that there is no ideological upheaval without commensurate political corollaries.

Added to this, a general hunger for spiritual refreshment, regeneration, and yes, recreation came to his assistance, together with a not unrelated longing for some new folk hero having superhuman stature, yet flesh and blood. Emperors like Maximilian I and Charles V, champions of strong-arm individualism like Sickingen, ingenious humanists like Erasmus, had been tentatively cast for the vacancy, which somehow they had never entirely measured up to. Luther emerged with all the right qualifications.

He was a David pitched against Goliath; at once pious and robust, learned and earthy. He was saint and soldier, holy and romantic— for, abducted in the interests of his own safety directly he was outlawed after Worms, Luther spent some time disguised as a knight with bushy beard and sword: a time, incidentally, that he used to translate the New Testament into the language of the people.

Even had he not already become the German people's favorite author—printers and booksellers made fortunes out of everything he wrote—Luther's version of the Bible secured for him a lasting, seminal position in the literature and the idiom of his country. Since, during the period of his quasi-exile, he was widely believed murdered, some of the martyr's aura accrued to him as well, notwithstanding his punctual resurrection.

*Katherine von Bora, Luther's wife, was a former nun who bore him six children and provided him with a happy household.*

During that same period Luther's aides and disciples took over from him at Wittenberg. Already his young colleague Melanchthon had shouldered the task of systematizing Luther's surging insights into an ordered theology, and now one of the seniors, Karlstadt, sped a drive to put Luther's preaching into practice—long before the leader would have considered doing so. But the leader was absent, and after the event could not well veto a logical implementation of his teachings concerning the equal priesthood of all believers, the validity of only two out of seven sacraments (baptism and the Lord's Supper), the sinfulness of vows and all other outward hieratic forms, the urgency of intensive propagation of the Gospel, and the right of civil authority to take a hand in rectifying ecclesiastical wrongs if the ecclesiastical authorities would not. In secret correspondence with his followers, Luther could only applaud, a little wistfully ("How happy I am to see you don't need me!"), practical reforms that included celebration of the mass in German with Communion in both species (wine as well as bread), voluntary dissolution of monasteries, municipal supervision of church administration, and priests relinquishing celibacy, which set them apart from their fellow men, to marry. All these were epoch-making, even terrifying, innovations, of much civic as well as religious consequence.

But they went too far for Luther. Under Karlstadt the left wing of the movement gained ascendancy, and a lunatic fringe sprang up for good measure. Iconoclastic vandalism joined hands with civil lawlessness, brutality with a spate of dissident perversions. Luther made a precipitate return, disregarding the ban of Church and state and against the stated orders of his temporal overlord: "I will protect you more than you could ever protect me!" he declared, repudiating the Elector's warning. Nothing should stop him, who now would sometimes sign himself "God's notary," from putting down disobedience and revolt in other people.

In spite of his consistently disclaiming personal honors and credit, Luther undeniably had acquired authoritarian aplomb while he lived as a knight and listened to the echoes of his fame as a popular hero and prophet. If he had previously believed himself to be working to the limits of his capacity, after his return he found that he grew busier still. Although the shaping of policy and definitions devolved more and more upon Melanchthon and others, Luther's literary output never had a chance to decrease; meanwhile, there were ceaseless demands on his advice, rulings, and active ministry. The only real crime that he committed arose from a mixture of imperiousness, haste, and white-hot emotional response to the German peasant rebellion of 1524–25, which claimed Luther among its fathers. That got Luther on the raw. The tract *Against the Murderous and Thieving Hordes of Peasants* with which he obliged the cause of law and order was nothing less than an incitement to mass slaughter, a license of which the victorious nobles availed themselves horribly. Neither his repute nor his peace of mind was ever fully to recover from this.

To bear out his precepts by example, he married. Fittingly, the former monk took to wife a former nun, a woman of intelligence, resource, and evident fertility. Although for some time beforehand Luther had protested a rooted disinclination to the married state, he honestly enjoyed it on the whole and reveled in parenthood. Without the full patriarchal trappings and, of course, a greater understanding at first hand of the more intimate, humdrum human problems, the father-figure of the Reformation might have lacked that serviceable, durable solidity with which he came to be invested.

The Reformation itself did not attain to that state until a century after Luther's death. For many years its very viability hung in the balance; for decades the movement advanced at the rate of two steps forward and one step back and one step sideways, so to speak. But advance it did.

The founder died not knowing that it would succeed, in fact, believing the opposite—not that Luther would have accounted it a success so long as Christendom was left divided. His own endeavors to save it by steering a pragmatic middle course were doomed to impair its purity and helped to brake its impetus: and gradualness means compromise. But then, living is all compromise. Only the beginning and the end, birth and death, will be uncompromising; in between, everything is change and adaptation. Opinion as to whether such a process went in the right or in the wrong direction can never be unanimous. Luther tried.

Had he been crucified in his early thirties there would have been no wear and tear to deface him or modify his stand. To die unbeautiful, respectable, and eroded by a typical syndrome of executive's ailments, including spleen and disillusionment, may be the price of survival in such cases.

It was Luther's tragedy, perhaps, that once the evangelical movement had got under way the creator became its creature. He was forced into the positions of planner, administrator, public-relations officer, party organizer, oracle and judge, scribe and bottle washer, when—as he himself well knew—"theologizing" and communicating the result was his true métier.

"I have no head for politics." He could say that again. "They try to make me into a fixed star. I am an irregular planet." No more than the truth. Well, he loved the truth; and what, as mankind will have to go on asking to the end of time, is that? Luther believed he knew; but in the upshot he made it legitimate and proper that man shall go on asking, never accepting any answer as absolutely final. Neither is the spectacle of an individual defying and surviving the concerted pressure of the major powers of his age one that we could have done without. Without Luther, we might have thought that the wages of integrity is, always, defeat.

*In Cranach's painting of an imaginary congress of reformers, Luther appears in the foreground left of center, with Melanchthon at far right.*

# JOHN
# CALVIN
## 1509-1564

"When the honor and service of God are at stake, there can be no excuse for timidity." The words are more than a simple statement of priorities; they embody the faith that unexpectedly transformed a shy, introspective, and pathologically sensitive French academic into a religious activist who was the intellectual architect of international Protestantism and the living model of militant Puritanism. The willful recasting of John Calvin, the son of a provincial ecclesiastical lawyer and petty city magistrate, into a spiritual soldier dedicated to the service of God is not merely a homily on the triumph of will over mortality; it is the drama of the Reformation in capsule as it moved from simple dissatisfaction with the medieval established order of things into a massive effort to remodel Christendom according to a dynamic vision in which all men were expected to "act so that God may be the more strong."

The spiritual drive and religious energy that Calvin marshaled represented a greater break with the past than had the New Learning of Erasmus or the new religion of Martin Luther. Luther was essentially a medieval man, closer to Wycliffe and Huss than to John Calvin or John Knox. The German monk's words brought fear to his enemies, his voice struck down the walls of Satan, and his faith moved mountains, but his appeal was to the heart, not the mind. He began as an academic reformer of abuses, and even when he was driven into open revolution, he was unhappy about the logical consequences of his protest, the abandonment of ancient ceremonies simply because they had

*A stern Calvin appears to be lecturing his flock in this portrait by an unknown artist.*

*By* LACEY BALDWIN SMITH

been misused by evil men. Always, if foolishly, the hope of religious reconciliation remained, the expectation that Christian men of good faith could settle their differences and live in brotherhood and peace.

It remained for the second generation, for John Calvin, to dress the Reformation in modern garb, to fit out Lutheranism in the armor of military discipline, and to carry God's truth throughout the Western world. Calvinism spread under many labels and to many lands—Dutch Reformers. French Huguenots, Scottish Presbyterians, English Congregationalists, even South African Boers—but it found its most receptive and aggressive audience in the Anglo-Saxon world, especially in the wooded wilderness of New England where God-fearing Pilgrims sought to establish a Puritan paradise in "the place that God will show us to possess in peace and plenty."

John Calvin, or Cauvin, was born on July 10, 1509, in the episcopal city of Noyon, fifty-eight miles northeast of Paris in Picardy. His father, Gérard Cauvin, was caught up in a world in which religion was more a matter of livelihood and the maintenance of privilege than of inner devotion, and he used the Church as a ladder to social and financial prominence. His influence won for his son John a chaplaincy at the cathedral at the age of eleven and a curacy at eighteen. Gérard's misappropriation of chapter funds in 1528, however, earned him an excommunication, and three years later he died, still excommunicate, a matter that did not seem to have concerned him any more than the furious quarrel between the canons of the cathedral and the monks of the abbey of Noyon as to who possessed the authentic remains of Saint Eloi. As Calvin said in later life, it was quite impossible to be sure who was "reverencing the bones of some thief or robber, or of an ass, a dog or a horse."

It was into this Church, tolerant, cynical, and secular, that the elder Cauvin destined his son and sent him at the age of fourteen to the University of Paris to be educated in medieval scholarship. The Collège de Montaigu, where John took up residence and where four years later Ignatius Loyola would begin his studies, was the center of theological conservatism, its master one of the leading enemies of humanism. For four years the young Picardy student was drilled in the great medieval Schoolmen—Aquinas, Bonaventura, Duns Scotus. and Gerson—and became so proficient in Scholastic logic that legend records he was nicknamed "the accusative case" for his didactic and argumentative spirit.

In 1528 Gérard Cauvin changed his mind about his son's career. He now demanded that John leave Paris for the University of Orléans and study law as the "surest road to wealth and honors"; he would not dedicate a son to an organization that held him excommunicate, even if the Church was the traditional path to social position and material well-being. Calvin approached jurisprudence with the same compulsive energy he had shown while studying theology, laboring daily until midnight and awakening early to lie abed mulling over what he had absorbed the day before. Four years were given to the law, first at Orléans and then under the more liberal atmosphere at Bourges, until the theologian had become an accomplished and eloquent jurist. Jurisprudence and theology, however, were not the sum total of John Calvin's intellectual diet; humanism was on the move and the young scholar was soon swept up in the new learning. After his father's death Calvin dropped his legal studies, and once again returned to Paris to immerse himself in the classics, producing in 1532 his *Commentary on Seneca's Treatise on Clemency,* a precocious study bristling with classical quotations and high ethical principles and written in impeccable Latin prose.

At twenty-four the ark of Calvin's education was complete. The rather priggish Picardy registrar's son by grinding industry and the aid of an extraordinary memory had transformed himself into a jurist, theologian, dialectician, and consummate Latinist. The price, however, was high; his health was shattered and his soul was as empty as the Church in which he had been reared. For all of his marvelous talents and learning John Calvin could not find "true peace of conscience"; there was no solace left save that of deluding himself by "obliviousness." Oblivion, the deliberate closing of the mind to the spiritual woes of Christendom, had been the accepted solution for his father's generation. It was not to be Calvin's, for at some time between November, 1532, and May, 1533, the Lord spoke, and despite his timidity and love of tranquillity, despite his family training and medieval education, John Calvin was obliged to listen.

God called, of that there was no doubt. Calvin's conversion cannot be questioned, but the suddenness, the speed with which God's will and Calvin's were forged into a single entity is a matter of intense debate. Who, if anyone, were the human instruments involved? Was the entire spiritual man transformed in a twinkling of the eye or did the process involve the galvanizing of a will to act upon convictions long held as intellectual verities but not as living realities? Certainly Calvin had been exposed to Protestant notions, humanistic piety, and family anticlericalism, and many of his closest friends and associates stood on the brink of heresy. At first he was offended by the novelty of Lutheran ideas and lent them only "an unwilling ear," desperately and passionately denying any suggestion that the Church of his birth could have been in the wrong for fifteen hundred years. Suddenly, miraculously, he was converted, and the recluse became God's trooper, the medieval scholar shed his Scholastic training, the boy from Noyon

*Calvin, Luther, and the pope engage in a hair- and beard-pulling match, while symbols of the established Church fall all around them, in this sixteenth century French cartoon.*

became an international leader, and the terror of spiritual uncertainty gave way to the knowledge that "when God calls us to Himself, He dedicates us so that our whole life may set forth His honor."

Inexplicably, Calvin was filled with the will to act. He was consumed with a bottomless fury that God's Word should be "hidden, perverted, corrupted and depraved." It was impossible to condone that "gentleness which allows the wicked to go on with impunity, which confuses good and evil, and which does not differentiate between black and white . . . As for me, I would rather be transported with rage than never be angry at all." It was no longer sufficient to ignore the world or escape from it, for "we live in a time of war, and there is no better lot for us than to gather round the standard where we can gain courage to go on fighting until death." Whatever the cause—the slow formation of associations and the growth of intellectual conviction or divine intervention—the result was fateful: the humanist and jurist became the Biblical theologian who knew that God spoke simply and directly in the Scriptures. Calvin had no choice, he was committed to speak the truth even if it meant going into exile.

In May of 1534 he resigned his chaplaincy and curacy and almost at once was charged with heresy and imprisoned at Noyon. He escaped the stake, but it was too dangerous to remain in France, and early in 1535 Calvin wisely left his native land for Basel, already a citadel of the Protestant faith and a retreat for reformers the continent over. There he wrote the first draft of that true, perfect, and final pronouncement of God's Word—*The Institutes of the Christian Religion.*

First published in abbreviated form in 1536, *The Institutes* was brief by theological standards, only 519 pages, and within nine months every copy had been sold to men desperate to be told the truth in terms they could understand and defend. Calvin did for Protestant knowledge what Thomas Aquinas had done for medieval, and he did for his church what the Council of Trent would shortly do for sixteenth-century Catholicism. He summarized and systematized the creed and disciplined and ordered the ranks of the true believers, so that the truth could be protected against the spawn of new heresies from within the Protestant faith as well as against the papal Antichrist and the Romanist court of darkness. *The Institutes* was the quintessence of Protestant thought as formulated by Luther, Zwingli, Erasmus, and Melanchthon. It was a faultlessly rational and convincing statement of the ultimate logic of the Protestant Reformation, which Jonathan Edwards called "a delightful doctrine, exceeding bright, pleasant and sweet."

The central tenet around which all others revolved was the existence of an inscrutable God who was bound neither by compassion nor the laws of science but was "the Arbiter and Governor of all things," a sovereign and capricious force who "by His own power, executes what He has decreed." Every event is a manifestation of His divine plan. The inescapable corollaries to such a thesis were the doctrines of providence, predestination, and election. For Calvin it was impossible for a leaf to fall or a decision to be formed without the express command of the deity, and the gates of the kingdom of heaven were open only to those chosen few who were the elect of God. Man, according to the Calvinistic creed, was the product of sin and disobedience, and in justice God found it unworthy of His omnipotence to save any man, yet He selected for salvation certain men, irrespective of their deserts, in order to reveal to the world the full capriciousness and total freedom of His authority. Calvin's God could not even be bound by His own sense of justice. That Adam disobeyed God and brought upon posterity the wrath of heaven by divine command, and that the mouth that tasted of the apple was moved by God's will, were historic facts that might seem unjust to man's faulty reason, but in the divine scheme of things they were in no way illogical, for God was "above logic; indeed, God made logic just as He made the apple."

*Idelette de Bure, a "grave and honorable" widow, married John Calvin in 1540, not long before his return to the city of Geneva.*

In this divine scheme of things, man, by definition, took a secondary position, for man did not belong to himself: "God's glory, and everything which belongs to His kingdom must always come first." Calvin made it clear that even to a king there was something far more precious and important than man's fate: "namely the glory of God and the spread of the kingdom of Jesus Christ, wherein lies the salvation" not only of royalty but also "of the world." To have spoken of man's salvation would have detracted from God's glory; it would have placed humanity at the center of existence and made God a means to a personal end. Instead, it was cruelly evident that the faithful lived and died for God, and in doing so they worked for no personal end. They did not even glorify God by their puny efforts, for Calvin's deity glorified Himself in the faithfulness of His followers. "Our Lord has desired to glorify His Name in you" was the crucial message.

It might have produced the fatalism of the Orient, but instead the knowledge was a spur to action, for "God uses the service of men . . . to do His work through them, just as a craftsman uses his tools." There was profound psychological insight in the assertion that the faith that did not witness God quickly and completely was deformed and must die, for Calvin sensed that "faith cannot stay asleep for long without being extinguished." It was fatal to the truth and therefore to action to sit on the fence or seek to "serve God and the devil" at the same time. The man who understood God's Word was compelled to act, for only in action was there proof of true understanding. To Calvin the whole world was "the theatre of God's glory," and the divine doctrine could never be victorious without commotion and suffering, for only the Devil's creed was ever accepted by all without contention.

Calvinism appealed to the most dangerous and restless element of any society—the hyperactive personality, be it religiously or economically oriented. The link between the Protestant ethic of laboring in the Lord's vineyard and the spirit of capitalism with its emphasis on frugality and hard work has often been noted, and without a doubt, the capitalist seeking economic prosperity on earth and spiritual security in heaven found the parable of the talents peculiarly satisfying. But to load John Calvin with the sins of capitalism is to do him an injustice; his vision was theological not commercial, and his appeal was to souls in need of grace not merchants in quest of profits.

The author of *The Institutes* and the creed of action was himself the tireless tool of God, for as William James noted, the gods we worship are "the gods whose demands on us are reinforcements of our demands on ourselves and on one another." Heavy as the demands were that Calvin made on his followers, they cannot be compared to those he made on himself. Throughout his life, despite stomach trouble, chronic headaches, bouts of malaria, ulcerated hemorrhoids, gout and gallstones, and in the end tuberculosis, coughing blood and gasping for breath, he labored in the Lord's vineyard. By sheer strength of will, he found the energy to produce sixty-two massive octavo volumes and forty thousand pages, which flowed from a mind that refused to accept physical suffering or constant interruption as an excuse worthy of God. He confessed that he found it difficult to recall "two consecutive hours without interruption." The cry is that of a frustrated scholar, but the fault was in fact his own. In God's service nothing was too insignificant, and when he took up his pastoral burdens in Geneva his ordinary day involved the writing of four letters, a lecture, and a sermon, the settlement of a dispute, and "more than ten visitors, all of whom required attention." His will was prodigious, and his strength of mind branded every facet of his creed, for it was but a pale reflection of God's sovereign omnipotence. Toward the end, when he could not walk, he demanded that he be carried to the pulpit to preach; when he could no longer write, he dictated.

The iron tenet by which the Christian of unbending will lived was stark and uncompromising: "Even if the whole world hisses, my soul will not weaken." Clearly, "if God will not open a door, we must creep in through a window, slide in through the narrowest crack, rather than lose the opportunity of doing good." In July, 1536, that opportunity came—the city of Geneva was in need of a pastor who had the will and imagination to convert riot, insurrection, and senseless commotion into a vision—the founding of that "most perfect school of Christ that ever was on earth since the days of the apostles."

For more than a decade Geneva had been in the throes of religious and political revolt. In May of 1536 the city elders, gathered together in the Council of Two Hundred, voted without dissent their "desire to live in this holy evangelical law and Word of God, as it has been announced to us, desiring to abandon all masses, images, idols and all that which may pertain thereto."

God's Word had been trumpeted from every city pulpit and square in stentorian tones by Guillaume Farel, one of the more impetuous, if irritating of the elect. Farel was as inflammatory as his brilliant red hair. Earlier in his tempestuous career, he had stood up while mass was being celebrated, walked up to the surprised priest, knocked the consecrated bread from his hand, and calmly announced to the incredulous audience that God was above in heaven and not in a piece of ritualistic trickery on earth. Such an ardent Protestant could spearhead revolution but he could discipline neither himself nor his followers; he needed the iron will and organizational talents of Calvin to complete the transformation of the city of Geneva into the kingdom of God. When Calvin chanced to pass through the city, Farel prevailed upon the young author of *The Institutes* to remain and make his home and lifework in Geneva. There was no doubt in Calvin's mind that Farel was the vehicle of the Lord's will, and he claimed that the passionate reformer "kept me at Geneva not so much by advice and entreaty as by a dreadful adjuration, as if God had stretched forth His hand upon me from on high to arrest me."

In January of 1537 the "perfect school of Christ" was outlined in a series of articles establishing a system of church-state government that, from the start, smacked more of the schoolhouse than of the house of God. Church and state were fused into a theocracy in which the two swords of Christ—the civil and the ecclesiastical—lived together in perfect harmony: the Council of Two Hundred ruling the city and the "Venerable Company" of clergymen inspecting civil morality and governing the church. The state remained politically separate from the church, and conversely, the ecclesia was free from civil interference to initiate its members in right doctrine and right living. The council retained the power to legislate and punish, but the Venerable Company was expected to scrutinize the life of every citizen, report any moral lapses, and inspire the secular government to acts of devotion and godly legislation. Discipline and her handmaiden, inspection, were the hallmarks of the new Geneva, for if the church consisted of all the believers and not merely the clergy, then it was essential that every member be wholesome of heart and pure in mind. "To accomplish this," Calvin wrote, "we have decided . . . to appoint and choose certain persons of upright life and good reputation among all the faithful" who shall have "an eye to the life and conduct of each one." For the good citizens of Geneva there were not only to be windows into their souls but also great doors into their domestic, social, and business affairs. The grand experiment in applied theology had begun, and henceforth the life of every man was to be held up to the standards of Scriptural purity.

Attendance at church and morning prayers was strictly enforced. Popery was exterminated root and branch, and even the celebration of Christmas was prohibited, under pain of imprisonment, as a devil's mass and bacchanalian brawl. The theatre was denounced, especially the introduction of the new and degenerate Italian custom of allowing women on the stage instead of the older and safer use of boys to play female roles. The women who appeared in theatrical productions, according to Calvinistic argument, had no purpose in mind other than "to expose their bodies, clothes, and ornaments to excite the impure desires of the spectators," all of which was utterly "contrary to the modesty of women who ought to be shamefaced and shy."

It is far too easy to caricature Calvin's Geneva as a dreadful combination of a reformatory for juvenile delinquents, a Christian revival meeting, and a school for saints, a veritable "dictatorship of the praying classes," in which neither common sense nor common happiness prevailed. The concept of an organic commonwealth imbued with the spirit of God was not unique to the Reformation; it was as much a medieval belief as a sixteenth-century ideal. Long before the Reformation, Catholic episcopal authority had sought to eliminate gaming, dancing, and bawdy singing, and a full year before Calvin's arrival in the city, the Council of Two Hundred had prohibited blasphemy, oaths, and card playing and had issued precise orders regulating the sale of liquor and the reception of travelers in the city's taverns. Nor was Calvin himself without his belly wisdom. There was always a heavy dose of administrative common sense about his vision of Christ's kingdom on earth, and he understood that even godliness palled when presented in excess. "I am given to understand," he wrote one over-zealous preacher, "that your very full sermons are giving some ground for complaint. I beg you most earnestly to restrict yourself, even forcibly if necessary, rather than offer Satan any handle which he will be quick to seize. . . . We must remember proportion in teaching, so that boredom does not give rise to disrespect." Indeed, Calvin, the pastor and pedagogue, knew the secret of his academic trade!

Calvinism, moreover, was never "the haunting fear that someone somewhere may be happy," for Calvinistic Genevans, Puritan English, and Huguenot French were not devoid of laughter and fun. Puritans danced, wined, and made merry in the privacy of their homes,

*A sketch of Calvin, made shortly before his death in 1564, was done by one of his academy students.*

and *The Institutes* themselves stated that it was not "anywhere forbidden to laugh, or to enjoy food or to add new possessions to old and ancestral property, or to be delighted with musical harmonies, or to drink wine." The problem was one of purpose: gaiety for man's sake was to be avoided, good fellowship that was the fruit of godliness was to be welcomed.

The trouble with God's elect in the eyes of more politic men was their determination to thunder against the evils of this world and their conviction that it was the minister's duty to God to speak as "a dying man to dying men." Calvinist preachers were rarely known for their tact and moderation, for John Calvin never regarded the clerical office as so limited that "when the sermon is delivered we may rest as if our task were done." The preacher had to take care that souls were not lost as a consequence of slothfulness and lack of vigilance. The need to bring the Lord's way to all men made the elect of God a busybody, and nothing was too obscure, nothing too inconsequential, to be considered by the church elders. The consistory, a body of the clergy sitting in company with twelve lay elders who were elected by the city council, decided cases involving fortunetelling, the singing of obscene songs, overindulgence, blasphemy, adultery, witchcraft, and heresy. Matters of apparel, women's hair styles, the propriety of a woman of seventy marrying a man of twenty-five, and two cases of adultery involving Calvin's own sister-in-law and his stepdaughter were brought to the consistory's attention. The names given to children at baptism by too eager and too old-fashioned parents were carefully culled, and if found objectionable, were prohibited. Such Catholic names as Claude and Martin were barred as indicating a secret and idolatrous reverence for saints, while such questionable designations as Sepulcher, Sunday, and Jesus were outlined as being in poor taste. In 1546 the inns of the city were reorganized as "abbeys" and placed under strict government supervision, and a precise code for guests and hosts was laid down that included among other items the following:

If any one blasphemes the name of God or says: "By the body, 'sblood, zounds," or anything like, or gives himself to the devil or uses similar execrable imprecations, he shall be punished . . .

*Item:* the host shall not allow any person, of whatever quality he be, to drink or eat anything in his house without first having asked a blessing and afterwards said grace.

*Item:* the host shall not allow any dissoluteness like dancing, dice or cards, nor shall he receive any one suspected of being a debauche or ruffian.

*Item:* he shall only allow people to play honest games without swearing or blasphemy, and without wasting more time than that allowed for a meal . . .

*Item:* nobody shall be allowed to sit up after nine o'clock at night except spies.

Calvin demanded that the city of Geneva should become the armed citadel of God and that absolute discipline of behavior and orthodoxy of thought should be maintained as an example to all Europe. The self-appointed pope of the Protestant world was more than a pastor, he was a general; his followers were soldiers in the Lord's service, and it was essential to success that God's army should be built on obedience to the divine Word as revealed in the Scriptures and interpreted by Calvin. It was not always easy doing the Lord's bidding, and in April of 1538 the forces of evil temporarily triumphed. There were those who detested the moral rigor of the new regime; there were those who on principle believed in the supremacy of the state over the church and argued that man's faith should be subject to civil control; and, of course, there were those who disliked Calvin and his French friends. For a time God's enemies succeeded in evicting Calvin from the city, but within two years the Lord had wrought such changes that His shepherd was asked to return to his flock.

Master Calvin recommenced where he had left off thirty months before, but with one difference—he was married. The decision suited his character, for he entered matrimony as an act of intellect, not of love. He was harshly frank on the subject: "I am not of that insane class of lovers who, once captivated by beauty, kiss even its faults. The only comeliness that attracts me is this—that she be modest, complaisant, unostentatious, thrifty, patient, and likely to be careful of my health." This feminine paragon was discovered in the person of Idelette de Bure, a "grave and honorable" widow and a lady of extraordinary Christian devotion who survived nine years of married bliss with her new husband and was content to remain in the shadow of his intense personality. It was a highly satisfactory union though it produced no living children, and after it was all over, Calvin was content to say that "she was the faithful helper of my ministry. From her I never experienced the slightest hindrance," a statement that could not have been said about others in Geneva who were only too willing to interfere with God's work.

One of the first to clash with Geneva's warden of morality was Pierre Ameaux, whose ancestral livelihood—the manufacture of playing cards—had been endangered by the new discipline. In 1546, at a supper party given in his own house, Ameaux indulged in the ill-advised luxury of calling Calvin a preacher of false doctrines and prophesied that the government would soon be in the hands of fanatic French religious exiles who were flocking by the hundreds to the city. Ameaux's confidences were reported to the consistory by one of his guests. His attack was viewed not as a mere personal affront to one of God's ministers but as an insult to "the honor of Christ" whose servant Calvin knew himself to be. The Council of Two Hundred ordered Ameaux to appear before it and on bended knee to seek humble pardon of Calvin. That outraged defender of the Lord would have no such mildness shown to a man who had insulted the "name of God," and he prevailed upon the council to reconsider its verdict and change the punishment to a more suitable one: Ameaux, clad only in a shirt, was forced to walk the streets of the city and on his knees beg the mercy of God and the city magistrates for his ill-advised words.

Ameaux's defiance was largely the result of economic spite; the case of Jérôme Hermès Bolsec was far more dangerous. Bolsec was an admirer of Calvin on every point save the doctrine of predestination, which he said was ridiculous, for it made God into a tyrant, and, moreover, was contrary to the Scriptures. From public disputation he moved in October of 1551 to an open avowal that the Master was not a true interpreter of the Bible. Clearly, Bolsec was the devil's instrument and had to be destroyed. At Calvin's instigation, the council exiled Bolsec forever, for "false opinions, contrary to the holy Scriptures, and pure Evangelical religion."

Serious as Bolsec's defiance had been, it struck only at Calvin the man; the heresy of Michael Servetus, who denied the Trinity and the doctrine of original sin, went to the very core of God's authority and omnipotence. Michael Servetus was a Spanish physician whom history has treated as a hero, but whom contemporaries, both Protestant and Catholic, viewed as a vicious criminal. He was seen as a murderer of the soul, and his death by slow fire in 1553 was greeted with applause by the entire Christian world. Calvin had known of Servetus in their university days in Paris, and he had been horrified even then by the Spaniard's pseudo-Unitarian arguments. Servetus represented a pernicious threat from within the Protestant ranks, for he embodied the tendency of the Protestant faith to explode into a warring spectrum of religious sects ranging in alphabetical frenzy from Adventists and Boehmenists to Salmonists and Tyronists.

Servetus lived in France for a decade, but finally fled to Vienna and in 1553 published the *Restitution of Christianity*, a work that brought him to the immediate attention of the Catholic authorities. He escaped from prison a month before being condemned to the fire, and for reasons bordering on lunacy he sought safety in the city of the man who had denounced him in his university days, who had been expounding against his views, and who, in fact, may have betrayed his identity to the Catholic Inquisition in Vienna. The moment Servetus set foot in Geneva, he was recognized, arrested, tried and found guilty of heresy, and sentenced to death by burning. Still possessed of Satan, he died on October 26, 1553, at the hands of those who accounted the agony of the stake as slight compared to hell's fire. To Calvin the ranks had to be preserved and heresy stamped out, for Geneva was more than a Protestant stronghold and *The Institutes* more than a state-

MICHAEL SERVETVS DE ARAGONIA

*Michael Servetus, a Spanish physician, was the Devil incarnate to Calvin for his anti-Trinitarian views. Servetus was burned as a heretic in Geneva in 1553.*

ment of righteousness. His city was the tabernacle of the Lord and a model for all believers, and his book was the tablet of God's Word.

Calvin's reputation rests not simply on his record as Master of that "perfect school of Christ" but even more on his achievement in building a rival to Catholicism, a tightly organized, self-sufficient, and international church dedicated to bringing the standards of heaven to earth. To Roman Catholics, Calvin's Geneva had become the cesspool of an international and diabolic conspiracy to overthrow all established order and to subvert the true faith; to Protestants, the city was a source of inspired preachers and organizers who went forth in God's name to every country in Europe. Calvin was in touch with kings of England, Poland, Denmark, and Navarre. He advised Thomas Cranmer in England, John Knox in Scotland, John Lasco in Poland, and Admiral Coligny in France; and in each case his militant message was the same: "If He pleases to make use of you even to death in His battle, He will uphold you by His mighty hand to fight firmly, and will not suffer a single drop of your blood to remain useless." Always his priorities were the same, and he wrote Edward VI of England that "It is a great matter to be a king, but I am sure that you count it a far greater privilege to be a Christian."

By definition, Calvinists were poor security risks because no earthly authority could claim their obedience. They were the soldiers of the Lord, and true believers, said John Knox, could never be expected to "frame their religion according to the appetite of their princes." In Calvinism Protestant minorities found the strength to resist and the justification to disobey established authority. Puritans in England, Presbyterians in Scotland, and Huguenots in France were the chosen instruments of sublime grace, and in abandoning themselves to the majesty of God's will, they felt themselves to be the equals of any earthly king. The structured and hallowed hierarchy of established social and political authority was meaningless to men who harkened to the voice of inner conscience. The Word of God spoke in their hearts and it was of greater import than the most weighty instructions of pope, magistrate, or king. Calvin never argued the right of revolution, but the spirit of disobedience was implicit in his statement that "where the glory of God is not made the end of government, it is not a legitimate sovereignty, but a usurpation." Peter Wentworth summed up the Puritan position in England and elsewhere in Europe when, during a debate in Parliament, he presumptuously but positively told Archbishop Parker: "We will pass nothing before we understand what it is; for that were but to make you popes."

John Calvin died on May 27, 1564, in his fifty-fifth year. For months his suffering had been almost unendurable, and he confessed to Melanchthon that "illness presses me from this world as much as

*The Calvinist tradition was extended to France by the Huguenot Gaspard de Coligny (top) and to Scotland by the Presbyterian John Knox (bottom). In his zeal, Coligny, aided by Charles IX and Catherine de Médicis, precipitated the horrific St. Bartholomew's Day Massacre. Knox failed to convert the "Jezebel," Mary, Queen of Scots, to Calvinism, but he did succeed in establishing Presbyterianism as Scotland's state religion.*

old age does you." He was eager even in death to do God's bidding, asking only "Lord, how long," and characteristically, he found the energy to give explicit instructions that no stone should mark his grave—it was too inconsequential. For all the portraits of the man and the intimate details recorded by his flock, Calvin remains strangely inhuman. Eventually, the slender scholar of university days slowly burned away, leaving an emaciated body and a face dominated by an uncompromising nose, tight and unsmiling lips, and eyes that looked with sorrow upon a world filled with ignorance and evil. Calvin the man was replaced by Calvin the elect of God. His anger was monumental, his will uncompromising, his logic irrefutable, and his task herculean. He was never beset by doubt, only by ill-health and exhaustion, both of which he willed away. He was not merely neat and orderly in his habits, but fastidious to the point of frenzy, for he could not endure even a speck of dust to mar the blackness of his gown. No detail was too trifling, no task done in the Lord's name too inconsequential. John Calvin must be numbered among the saints, if only because the intensity of his emotions, the strength of his convictions, and even the adjectives required to describe him are all beyond human scale. Like the saints, he is of interest to humanity, but he lies outside its power of compassion or comprehension, for, as he said himself, his strength was not his own but belonged to the Lord.

> I'm here a pillar in thy temple
> > Strong as a rock.
> A guide, a buckler, an example,
> > To a' thy flock.

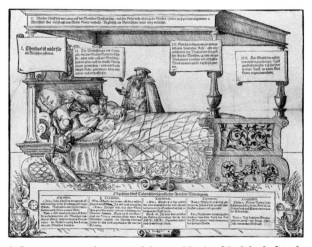

*A German engraving of Calvin on his deathbed includes the numbered articles of faith to which Calvinists subscribed.*

# FRANCIS
# BACON
## 1561-1626

I n January of 1561 a son was born to Nicholas Bacon, Lord Keeper to Elizabeth I. In twelve years this bright, grave child, Francis, would be called by Elizabeth her little Lord Keeper, but all his life she would deny him great office (as one denies, yet counsels with, a wizard), and all his life poverty and ill fortune would dog him in the midst of luxury. Yet it is this man who first fully visualized in all its splendor the "invention of inventions"—the experimental method which would unlock the riches of the modern world.

The most curious aspect of the technological environment which surrounds us today is one we rarely think about—namely, that it exists. How did it arise and why? We define ourselves vaguely as *Homo sapiens*, the wise, and we assume, if we think about our surroundings at all, that man's innate wisdom has, in the course of time, automatically produced the scientific world we know. Yet the archaeologist would be forced to tell us that several great civilizations have arisen and vanished without the benefit of a scientific philosophy. Similarly, Western society, down to the last three centuries or so, betrays but feeble traces of that type of thinking known today as "scientific," with its emphasis upon experiment and dispassionate observation of the natural world.

There is only one great exception in Western thought—Greek philosophy and Greek science before that tiny but enlightened world was destroyed by internecine conflict and the expanding power of the Roman Empire. In other words, we are faced with the problem that this wise creature, man, has rarely shown any penchant for science

*This portrait by James I's court painter shows Francis Bacon as Lord Chancellor.*

**By LOREN EISELEY**

and would much rather be left to his uninhibited dreams and fantasies.

Scientific thought demands some kind of unique soil in which to flourish. It has about it the rarity of a fungus springing up in a forest glade only to perish before nightfall. Perhaps, indeed, its own dynamism contains its doom. Perhaps the tendency of science to fragment and crumble also partakes of the qualities of the mushroom. This much at least we know: science among us is an *invented* cultural institution, an institution not present in all societies, and not one that may be counted upon to arise from human instinct.

Science is as capable of decay and death as any other human activity, such as a religion or a system of government. It cannot be equated with individual thought or the unique observations of genius, even though it partakes of these things. As a way of life it has rules which have to be learned, and practices and techniques which have to be transmitted from generation to generation by the formal process of education. Neither is it technology, although technology may contribute to science, or science to technology. Many lost civilizations—Roman, Mayan, Egyptian—had great builders, whether of roads, aqueducts, temples, or pyramids. Their remains show enormous experience of transmitted and improved techniques, but still we are not precisely within the true domain of science.

*A terra-cotta bust of the ten-year-old Francis Bacon still stands in his father's house at Gorhambury.*

Science exists only within a tradition of constant experimental investigation of the natural world. It demands that every hypothesis we formulate be subject to proof, whether in nature or in the laboratory, before we can accept its validity. Men, even scientists, find this type of thinking extremely difficult to sustain. In this sense science is not natural to man at all. It has to be learned, consciously practiced, stripped out of the sea of emotions, prejudices, and wishes in which our daily lives are steeped. No man can long endure such rarefied heights without descending to common earth. Even the professional scientist frequently confines such activity to a specific discipline, and outside of it indulges his illogical prejudices.

Since the dawn of the scientific world is a strangely unique, almost unnatural one, the life and times of the great statesman who played a major part in the half-light of that spectral morning will be of perennial interest so long as science and its world endure. Of all those who dreamed in secret, experimented but confined their endeavors, Francis Bacon alone walked to the doorway of the future, flung it wide, and said to his trembling and laggard audience, "Look. There is tomorrow. Take it with charity lest it destroy you."

Time dulls the horrors of the past. A traditional monarchy like that of Britain has much in its history which both subjects and later monarchs desire to forget. We remember Elizabeth as an adept ruler of men; we remember her sea rovers and the destruction of the Spanish Armada. As the centuries recede the screams of tortured men sound faraway; the fall of the headsman's axe is no longer heard upon the block. But to understand the Elizabethan world in which Francis Bacon rose to a Lord Chancellorship we must know the realities of that world.

Its bloody legacy came straight from Henry VIII. It was a world in which the English language was still being shaped into the vehicle of great literature. It was also a world of terror, corrupted by absolute power. A world where the throne defined treason and where to rise was also to invite one's fall, a world where rulers expected to be struck in the dark and where the logical paranoid act was to strike first. "Every public man in the England of the Tudors and the Stuarts," writes one historian, "entered on his career with the familiar expectation of possibly closing it on the scaffold."

Spies and informers swarmed everywhere. *Agents provocateurs* promoted treason for pay. Bestial crowds swarmed to torturings and hangings in public. The heads of executed men withered on the city gates as object lessons. Withal, this was Shakespeare's world and Francis Bacon's. It was the latter who was to write of himself and his generation as wearing out days few and evil. It was he who was to say, in weariness, that his soul had been a stranger to his pilgrimage. It was he, the last great Elizabethan, who was to murmur when they came to summon him back to the court of Charles I, "I have had enough of that vanity."

All along the way he had done the will of princes, had been a true servant of the state. Why was disgrace his reward? The world forgives his treasonous, intemperate patron, Essex, who died under the axe. The world remembers with favor the great freebooter, Raleigh, who ate his heart out in the Tower and could not believe his age was dead until he had tried the seas once more. These men were truly Elizabethans. They died bloodily as their age demanded, and were understood.

Francis Bacon, by contrast, walks masked and cool through this age of violence. Traps snap on either side, associates perish, he remains. Even when he is caught between parliament and king, and a powerful enemy demands his imprisonment in the Tower—even then, he goes free, though robbed by a strange combination of events of his personal honor, his fortune, and his place at court.

Yet among all these plots and subplots a curious mythology lives on: that Francis Bacon "took a bribe"—a not very respectable thing for a judge to do, a thing to moralize upon in the safe seclusion of a modern study. The men of violence have been forgiven. A romantic halo envelops them. But the man who outlived the violence and who

*Bacon's parents were molded in terra cotta about 1571. Sir Nicholas was Lord Keeper of the Seal for Queen Elizabeth, the highest judicial position in the land. Lady Bacon, his second wife, translated ecclesiastical tracts and knew Greek, French, and Italian.*

*Gorhambury House, built by Bacon's father in 1568, was a gracious Tudor manor.*

husbanded his power of survival in order to communicate a great secret, our age finds it oddly difficult to forgive. Perhaps it is because he was truly a stranger in his own age—a civilized man out of his time and place, dealing with barbarians and barely evading the rack and gallows in the process. It affronts our sense of dignity to see him bowing painfully to titled fools and rapacious upstarts, while presenting his books hopefully to learned men who scornfully fling them aside. He walks hesitantly toward us through history as though he could see our century but not reach it; he is out of place.

In a grim moment he whispers in *The Advancement of Learning* that one must consider how one's nature suits the state of the times. If one is out of place then one must walk "close and reserved." This is all we ever learn of the man except that he had one burning passion: to change the world through thought, through an "engine" he had devised. Otherwise there is nothing of himself; nothing, that is, save the cry of the painter Nicholas Hilliard, who wished he could have painted Bacon's mind, and the words of Ben Jonson, who spoke of his eloquence, and of another who remarked upon his generosity.

Bacon died, appropriately enough, in the midst of an experiment. He had gone out in a carriage on a winter day and decided suddenly to investigate the effects of cold in delaying putrefaction. He stopped his carriage, bought a hen from a cottage woman, and stuffed it full of snow. Immediately aware of having taken a chill himself, he sought the hospitality of a friend who lived nearby, and in that house he died.

It is symbolic that Bacon died in a borrowed bed. The century in which he found himself was equally borrowed, and he had no genuine place within it. One might say, if one were a student of literature, that here was Everyman engaged in that great pilgrimage which runs through the centuries. Perhaps this is why he repulses us. He is Faust and something more. In some fashion he is ourselves, and we project upon Bacon the fear we have of what he has brought to us. His work is not a gift that can be recalled, and the more we fear the gift, the more hatred we extend to the giver of it. Before we can understand and forgive the giver, we must understand the intention of his gift.

Rumor has it that Francis Bacon, his father's favorite child, the boy whose courtesy had caught the eye of the queen, played alone a great deal. Once he was found investigating the nature of echoes in some rocky spot, the story goes, and a likely enough incident it is, for what boy has not shouted into a well or bounced experimental sounds in reverberating places? But it is also likely that his intent, listening ear caught sounds not heard by ordinary, boisterous children. In the fey mind of this solitary, gifted youth it might have seemed as though fate whispered, or an echo sounded from some yet distant century. For Bacon, at least in his adult years, was to show an uncanny sensitivity to time.

In 1573 Francis, along with his brother Anthony, went to Cambridge. He was just twelve, unusually young even for that day of early university training. Cambridge, at the time, had sunk to a low intellectual level, and Bacon did not linger long. The school was given over to bitter theological disputes. "Men of sharp wits," Bacon was later to describe his tutors, "shut up in the cells of a few authors, chiefly Aristotle, their Dictator." A strong admiration for the lost classic literature could not conceal the fact that at Cambridge learning was largely pretense, that all was of the past. Men endlessly wove and rewove a spider web of ideas derived from Greek and Roman sources.

At the age of fifteen the youth returned home, indifferent to his abandoned degree. In 1575 he turned, as was natural in a legal family, to Gray's Inn and began to study for the law. The next year, however, he was sent abroad by his father in the company of the English ambassador to France.

For nearly three years Bacon experienced not only events at the foreign court of Henry III but the enormous stimulus of a society in which letters were honored. It was the time of the French Renaissance. Montaigne was being read, the great poet Pierre de Ronsard was writing his autumnal verses. It is likely that in this morally corrupt but brilliant society Francis Bacon received much of the literary stimulus that was to haunt his strangely divided career in the less literate circle of the English court.

In the winter of 1579 Francis had a strange dream. He saw his father's house "plastered all over with black mortar." The dream was prophetic: three days later Lord Keeper Nicholas Bacon was dead.

Francis, the youngest of the several children of two marriages, received only a pittance from the divided estate. His father's unexpected death had left him unprovided for. The student, the man of dreams, was never again to be totally free of financial insecurity. By birth and training he had been fitted for a life far beyond his financial station. And now, where others could be independent, he must humble himself to petition. He was doomed to strive impatiently after what others, securely entrenched, might confidently expect the stream of time to bring to them.

Yet, seen in the afterlight of history, perhaps his misfortune contained a secret blessing. Until the near close of his career he possessed no estates worth confiscating, nothing likely to strike the covetous eyes of kings or their favorites. His chief danger—in spite of his recognition of the necessity of going masked, so to speak—would be a certain stiff-necked, aristocratic pride showing through in unexplainable odd moments, in books, in Parliament.

"I have taken all knowledge to be my province," he once wrote in importuning aid from his uncle, Lord Burghley, the Secretary of State. Burghley, that sturdy, imperturbable minister, must have shuddered. His nephew talked as though from a place beyond the century, while at the same time he revealed a vaulting ambition likely to cause an experienced courtier to frown. Bacon was eager, and like all bright youths, occasionally uncertain and gauche in his impetuous demand for place. Burghley would give the young man little aid. He was intent on furthering the career of his own son, Robert Cecil, and held the Bacons—Francis and his brother Anthony—at arm's length.

All through Elizabeth's reign—and even though his cause had been promoted by the Earl of Essex, who had become his patron—Bacon was given only crumbs. There was an exception: Elizabeth's lease-gift of the pleasant country residence of Twickenham Lodge in 1595. It was evident that the Cecil faction would never tolerate Bacon's accession to any post of power. Essex's brief rise to royal favor, and his sudden fall, brought Bacon nothing but danger and the animus of powerful foes.

All of the more able biographers of Bacon repudiate the canard that he aided in the fall of Essex and ungratefully abandoned him. In vain Francis had given Essex sound advice and had pleaded with the frustrated man to abandon the course which led to his downfall. But the hotheaded, impetuous courtier, full of the proud violence of a sea dog's age, had run headlong into revolt and his own death by the axe. Surveying his career today, one might suspect that Essex was not totally sound, mentally. Yet he was a brave man and a generous one, and the way his life ended tore many hearts.

Elizabeth herself was never the same afterward; for days at a time, it is said, she would brood motionless, or else suddenly drive a sword into tapestries and hangings, as if in fear of lurking assassins. Bacon was ordered to draw up a state paper explaining the treason of the Earl and his accomplices to the restless populace, who had adored Essex. Painfully he did so. His affection for his old patron made the document too lenient for the queen's taste. Those who accuse Bacon of ingratitude might well examine Elizabeth's sharp reaction to Bacon's document: "It is my Lord of Essex, my Lord of Essex on every page; you can't forget your old respect for the traitor; strike it out; make it Essex. . . ."

Until the death of Elizabeth, Bacon's life was lived in the shadows where he wrote state political tracts and advised the queen as a "Counsel Extraordinary." He once remarked, not unfondly, to her successor, James I, "My good old Mistress was wont to call me her watch-candle, because it pleased her to say I did continually burn and yet she suffered me to waste almost to nothing." At another time he had spoken bitterly of the way in which he was forced to trudge after small favors like a child pursuing a pretty bird that hops away. Elizabeth could be parsimonious and fickle. As long as Robert Cecil, Bacon's secret enemy, lived, the shadow of that cunning little hunchback would fall across Bacon's path. And when that shadow lifted, Bacon's last great elevation spelled his doom even as he walked into the full sunlight of eminence. He learned what it was to hold power without personal wealth under a king without greatness.

Elizabeth died in 1603 leaving no heirs, or at least none acknowledged. In her final illness, men—swept like sea birds before a rising storm—had posted hard up the great north way to the court of James in Edinburgh: by remote lines of descent he was now heir to the English throne; courtiers had to look to their fortunes. James was not Elizabeth. Essex had favored him. The wheel was turning. "By the mutability of fortune and favor," as the old Elizabethan documents would put it, Bacon's hour would seem to have struck. The Scottish king was reputed to be a learned man. Bacon sought his favor.

*Elizabeth I, whom Bacon's father served for twenty years, kept Bacon dangling for political favors throughout her long reign.*

The first results were inauspicious: the king had not recognized Bacon, and his former office was not renewed; Robert Cecil, by contrast, remained Secretary of State. The new king intended to knight several hundred people, and Francis—after some correspondence with his cousin Cecil—was one of those selected. But the honor, done hastily to a large body of people, was a small one. A little pension was given him in remembrance of his late brother Anthony's services as an intelligence messenger between Essex and James. He was made a "King's Counsel." The term meant little: there was a plethora of counselors. There is evidence that Bacon was in despair and contemplated withdrawing from court life to become a recluse and scholar.

It is here, while Bacon's star seems waning, that we may seize the opportunity to examine the intellectual life of this man who was so long entangled with the affairs of state. One thing seems clear: Bacon, so far as we are allowed to penetrate that aloof mask, preferred the cloister. He had, however, one trait which would never have suited the life of a recluse: he was a man of action. By family and tradition he had been bred to serve the state. Moreover, he was a reformer more than he was a philosopher. Reserved and shy though he appeared, he was eloquent. In Parliament he could sway men. He was honored there. Curiously, it was this, and neither his vast learning nor his dreams, that finally caused James's eye to fall upon him.

In the meantime, however, in the period between Elizabeth's death and the aroused interest of James, Bacon had little to do. He turned vigorously to the completion of a book—a book destined to be one of the great books of all time, even though it was finished in haste in the hope of interesting the learned James. By no means Bacon's first venture into scholarship (his equally well-known volume of *Essays* having appeared in 1597), *The Advancement of Learning* contains the essence of his inner life and his long-frustrated hopes for man.

It is incredible, now, to realize that this great statesman of science was sneered at as a fool by many of his literate fellows in law, government, and the universities. In despair, he had all his works put into Latin because, in that barbaric time, he feared that the rapidly altering English tongue would not survive. Time-conscious as no other man of his era, he viewed books as boats with precious cargoes launched on the great sea of time. One can catch the quality of this time sense, as deep and brooding as that of a modern archaeologist, when he writes:

But howsoever the works of wisdom are among human things the most excellent, yet they too have their periods and closes. For so it is that after kingdoms and commonwealths have flourished for a time, there arise perturbations and seditions and wars; amid the disturbances of which, first the laws are put to silence, and then men return to the depraved conditions of their nature, and desolation is seen in the fields and cities. And if such troubles last, it is not long before letters also and philosophy are so torn in pieces that no traces of them can be found but a few fragments, scattered here and there like planks from a shipwreck; and then a season of barbarism sets in, the water of Helicon being sunk under the ground, until, according to the appointed vicissitude of things, they break out and issue forth again, perhaps among other nations and not in the places where they were before.

Through all his trials Bacon's faith in his books, even as lost and bobbing "planks" in the wreckage of time, never faltered. "I have lost much time with this age," he wrote a friend, as if, from some high place, his eye spanned centuries.

We of today have difficulty in realizing that the world of Bacon and Shakespeare was only semiliterate, steeped in religious contention, with its gaze turned backward in wonder upon the Greco-Roman past. Oswald Spengler justly remarks that human choice is only possible within the limitations and idea-forms of a given age. More than three hundred years ago, Francis Bacon would have understood him.

Bacon's world horribly constricted his ability to exert his will upon it. At the same time, he would have had a slight reservation. "Send out your little book upon the waters," he would have countered, "and hope. Your will may be worked beyond you in another and more favorable age."

For a man whose personal life had been disappointing, Bacon was singularly sure of his destiny. All that he wrote of it has come to pass. The men who destroyed him are remembered, if at all, only because of their perfidious roles in the life of a man whose name now stands with Shakespeare's as the light of the Elizabethan Age.

Other men of Bacon's period were beginning to grope with the tools of science. Only he, however, would clearly perceive its role and the changes and dangers it would introduce into the life of man. In the years left to him, and particularly after his fall from office in 1621, a flood of works poured from his pen. It was almost as if he foresaw that this would be his last chance to speak "to the next ages."

There is no doubt that his concentration on philosophy contributed to his downfall. It closed his ears to signs of danger; it closed his eyes to the machinations of his enemies. His single-minded devotion to duty, his curious ebullience of temperament, would make him the easy victim of a political ambush. Nevertheless, the forces that brought about Bacon's fall might well have achieved their purpose even against a more unscrupulous and cunning man.

The times were running against the king, and Bacon was expendable. In a weird way he would be trapped in a portion of his own political philosophy. But of that, more later. Here let us examine the essence of that remarkable book, *The Advancement of Learning*, along with those works which bear upon his significance as a harbinger of the modern age.

"This is the foundation of all," wrote Bacon in his masterpiece, "for we are not to imagine or suppose, but to *discover*, what nature does or may be made to do." Bacon's gift for condensation is so remarkable that it is easy, three hundred years later, in a different intellectual climate, to overlook the significance of his words.

The remark just quoted lies at the root of the modern scientific method. Distilled into one brief phrase, it is the very essence of science as we know it today. We would search unavailingly among the practical experimenters of Bacon's time—even the greatest of them—for any comparable analysis of science throughout the whole range of its activity. In a breath he had chained the imagination to reality, but at the same time had left it free to explore "the dark crooks and crannies" of nature.

We must enter into the intellectual life of Bacon's period if we are fully to grasp the enormity of the task that confronted him, or his challenge to his epoch. I have said that science does not come easily to men; they must be made to envision its possibilities. This was Bacon's role, and it is sheer folly to dismiss him, as some have sought to do, because he personally made no inventions. He did far more; by eloquence and an unparalleled glimpse of the possibilities contained in the new learning, he forced a backward-oriented culture to contemplate its own future.

The magnitude of his educational vision can be perceived only when we realize that well into the nineteenth century the greatest universities in England were still primarily devoted to the classical education of gentlemen. This fact is both a measure of Bacon's perception and a revelation of the glacial slowness with which ancient institutions are modified. Most of Britain's great scientific contributions in the post-Baconian years had come from members of the Royal Society (an association of scholars which was largely the result of his posthumous stimulus) or from other enlightened amateurs working alone.

"I say without any imposture," wrote Bacon, "that I . . . frail in health, involved in civil studies, coming to the obscurest of all subjects without guide or light, have done enough, if I have constructed the machine itself and the fabric, though I may not have employed or moved it." Before examining the forces that shaped Bacon's thought, let us now consider his mysterious "engine" and see wherein his originality can be said to lie. This is always more difficult to do in the case of a great philosophical thinker than in the relatively simple case of a man who produces a new mechanical invention.

We have to face the fact that the world of scholarship is sometimes a contentious and prickly one. By and large, as the mass of knowledge grows, men devote little attention to the dead. Yet it is the dead who are frequently our pathfinders, and we walk all unconsciously along the roads they have chosen for us. We find what they warned us to look for, and sometimes, also, we are unknowingly entrapped in some half-enchanted circle of ideas woven by a vanished mind. It is a credit to Bacon's perception that, at the very dawn of science, he warned the scholar against this kind of bewitchment, of which the later history of science can provide many instructive examples.

Bacon has long been known as an advocate of inductive reasoning. Indeed, this is a substantial part of his engine for the discovery of the truths of the natural world, the secondary causes which he believed to control all the phenomena of nature. Bacon's emphasis upon induction—that type of logical thinking by which one ascends from specific, observed facts to the establishment of general laws or principles—need not be regarded as original with him, since the classical world was not unaware of the distinctions between inductive and deductive logic.

Bacon, in fact, never claimed such originality. What he did seek to do with his new *use* of induction was to avoid the sterile logic of the Aristotelian Schoolmen. Since this type of thought has practically vanished from the modern world, we forget that education, in Bacon's day, was largely confined to metaphysical argument along with the reading of Greek and Roman classics. The techniques of logic, in other words, were being expended upon abstract controversy, while nature itself passed largely unexamined.

Men, to paraphrase Bacon, were spinning webs out of their own substance. To recapture reality it would be necessary to bring speculation into conformity with reality, to ascend from genuine facts to deductions, and to avoid hasty and unsubstantiated theory. As one student of the time has remarked, people "decided all questions not by investigating the observable facts, but by appealing to the infallible authority of Aristotle." Around the scholars of Elizabeth's century lay a natural universe scarcely investigated except for the exploration feats of the often unlettered voyagers.

Bacon was convinced that once man came to understand this unexplored nature about him, he could attain power over it, but that this potential power could be achieved only by the right methods of investigation exerted on a very large scale. "Looking back," says the philosopher C. D. Broad, "we can see that he was right, and we may be tempted to think that it was obvious. But it was not in the least obvious at the time; it was, on the contrary, a most remarkable feat of insight and an act of rational faith in the face of present appearances and past experience."

*Bacon's uncle, Lord Burghley, above, and his cousin, Sir Robert Cecil, had illustrious careers paralleling his own, but they thwarted the young man at every opportunity, and he did not achieve the office of Lord Chancellor until 1618, after they both were dead.*

Bacon's associates in government, such as Elizabeth and James, had been brought up in the traditional learning. James, in particular, prided himself on an antique, pretentious classicism. Neither was impressed by so unconventional an idea as Bacon's and one which, if adopted, would upset the prevailing school system. Both rulers were dancing bewitched in a ring out of which he was powerless to lead them. The more he wrote in the vein of his own convictions, the more warily he was regarded by his political contemporaries.

Experimenters—such as William Harvey, the discoverer of the circulation of the blood—were beginning to appear, but none seems to have had Bacon's total vision of what science and the experimental method could achieve over the centuries. Harvey, in fact, referred amusedly to Bacon as writing of science "like a lord chancellor." His remark is true, but imperceptive. Bacon was the first great statesman of science. He saw its potentiality in the schools; he saw the necessity of multiplying researchers, establishing the continuity of the scientific tradition, and promoting government-supported research for those studies which lay beyond private means and which could not be accomplished "in the hourglass of one man's life."

This vast vision could only have emerged from a mind trained to state affairs, to the management of kingdoms, and withal, a mind equally devoted to discovery. It is ridiculous to bemoan Bacon's practical experience of statecraft; it contributed enormously to his insight. The pity lies in the fact that he came so close to the seats of power without the opportunity to realize his dreams. It is an apt illustration of the degree to which even a great genius can be restricted and made helpless by his time. Yet in justice we must add, not totally so. The prestige of Bacon's final offices gave greater weight to his literary pronouncements, financed his publications, and in other indirect ways, lent wings to his words beyond what would have been possible for an obscure scholar opposed by many of his compatriots.

Another aspect which deserves attention is Bacon's conception of the *mundus alter*—"the other world" produced by human culture, a world drawn out of the void and made possible by the arts of man. It is, in a sense, a latent world filled with novelties which man, by his own ingenuity, can bring out of nature. Until the time of Bacon, man had more or less "drifted" in the natural world. His culture, with all its rational and irrational elements, had grown up largely without conscious self-examination or attention to the fact that man might possess the power successfully to mold and improve his own society through science.

"If we must select some one philosopher as the hero of the revolution in scientific method," said William Whewell, a learned nineteenth-century historian of science, "beyond all doubt Francis Bacon occupies the place of honor." He based his estimate upon Bacon's conception of the dawn of a new era and the shifting of logic from contention to its use in the analysis of experiments. "In catching sight of this principle, and in ascribing to it its due importance," continues Whewell, "Bacon's sagacity wrought unassisted and unequalled." Ungrounded argument must be replaced by a logic applied to reality. Only then could the second world come into being.

Considering the time at which he wrote, Bacon's numerous insights are phenomenal. For example, although he himself was not a mathematician, he foresaw the necessity for using mathematics in some of the more subtle examinations of nature. Similarly, Bacon reveals perceptive insights into biology and anthropology. He raised, in a quite objective way, the question of whether the transmutation of species could occur, and commented that the problem required deep research. He refused the arbitrary abandonment of the idea. He observed that the lower organisms might reveal secrets of life which in the higher organisms "lye more hidden."

His analysis of the "cave of custom" and the necessity for understanding the "Idols" that distort the thinking of the average man are the product of long observation of men under emotional stress. Jonathan Wright, a number of years ago, commented that it is to Bacon that we owe the idea of utilization of controls in scientific experiment.

One could point to many other evidences of Bacon's wide-ranging mind—his early recognition of the value of the history of science, his contention that biography should not be confined to rulers, and last, but not least, his recognition of the value of the division of labor in science. Above all else he dwelt upon science "for the uses of life." He warned that knowledge without charity could be as dangerous as the modern world has finally discovered it to be. In contrast to today's warring nationalisms, Bacon spoke in *The Great Instauration* of bearing a strong love for "the *human republic,* our common country."

If one now asks why science arose when it did, and why at its dawn so great a spokesman should have appeared to spread its doctrines, one would have to pursue innumerable beams of light into that globe of crystal which Bacon termed the human understanding. His own mind serves as a kind of condensing lens in this respect. Analogies in language drawn from the great voyagers dot his pages. It is evident that the geographic discoveries of his time, and the circumnavigation of the earth, had set wise men's statements at nought and promoted the independent examination of the natural world. The historian Merle Curti, commenting upon his influence in pioneer America, remarks, "It was no accident that Francis Bacon's ideas were rediscovered and put to work in an era characterized by the rise of the common man."

Formal theology had been shaken by observations in continents unmentioned in the Bible. A second Book of Revelation, the book regarded as unclouded by human error and confusion—the book of Nature—was becoming increasingly respectable to devout minds. Bacon's mother was under strong Puritan influence. The Puritan desire to rebuild an earthly Paradise, even in the wilds of the New World, was growing. It is no secret that later, in New England, the Puritan clergy promoted the new astronomical discoveries. This is not to equate science with Puritanism alone, but it does suggest that something about the Reformation played a part in the emergence of a full-bodied scientific movement which, a generation or so after Bacon, recognized his significance as the great spokesman for the scientific method itself and all that was to follow in its train.

We left Bacon's political career at a time of crisis, but with a hint of what was to come. He had desperately hurried forward the completion of *The Advancement of Learning,* in order to impress the new king James. That monarch, whose backward-directed classical learning would find little it could comprehend in the *Advancement,* was eyeing quite another aspect of Bacon's diversified career: his role in Parliament. Bacon was highly respected there.

Bacon had sat in the Commons since the days of Elizabeth; in fact, he had once aroused her fury by opposing a tax requisition which he felt to be inordinate, and which would cause suffering among the poor. For those who conceive of Bacon as an unscrupulous manipulator for favor, his letter to Lord Keeper Puckering on that occasion is worth quoting: "It mought please her sacred Majesty to think what my end should be in those speeches, if it were not duty and duty alone. I am not so simple but I know the common beaten way to please."

*Under England's King James I, shown here holding the royal arms, Bacon was recognized for his abilities, and also impeached.*

In 1603 the problems of Parliament versus the king were to emerge once more in another guise. There were church problems, there was the problem of the political union between England and Scotland. James was a newcomer from a more absolutistic and barbaric land. He needed advice and a trusted statesman who could mediate between the Lords and Commons. Bacon's moderation, his ability to sway audiences, the respect accorded him in the lower house, all fitted the needs of the new regime. It was a time when, in the words of Fulton Anderson, one of the most careful students of Bacon's career: "A wise king would decrease the area of his prerogative and gradually increase the range of his subjects' privileges. For some sixteen years," Anderson records, "Bacon would be trying to make James aware of these things; but the King would prove neither wise nor teachable."

Bacon assumed his first important administrative post under James as Solicitor General in 1607. It was an exacting office, made more so by Bacon's diverse abilities as a statesman. Frequently he was engaged in carrying out duties that ordinarily would have been assigned to others. For a man of frail health his energies seem almost superhuman. In the midst of difficult affairs of statecraft he still yearns over his "rebirth" of the sciences, and studies ways that Cambridge or Oxford might be encouraged toward the new learning—toward laboratories, "engines, vaults, and furnaces."

All this time the king's treasury, in the hands of Robert Cecil, was sinking into debt. Taxes and impositions levied upon the public were growing more onerous. Opposition to James and the high-handedness of his favorites was growing in the House of Commons. These events were the first weather signs that were to lead to the Puritan revolution. Bacon could read them, but those around him could not. Blind though he might sometimes be to his personal interests, he was never blind to the interests of the state. A long list of state papers and unheeded advice testifies to his efforts.

He would have been an able replacement as Secretary of State for Robert Cecil, who died in 1612 leaving James's treasury empty. Bacon sought the post, but James, wary of Bacon's association with the now-feared Parliament, turned aside from the one logical candidate. He named instead an inexperienced man with no obligations to the House; Bacon was appointed Attorney General. He would yet be made Lord Keeper in 1617 and rise to the high office of Lord Chancellor of England in 1618.

Meanwhile his new office of Attorney General, as events were to prove, was a far more vulnerable post than his previous one. Ironically, the suspicious James, in spite of not trusting Bacon sufficiently to allow him to succeed Cecil, continued to seek his advice on the financial affairs of the kingdom. Once more, in the words of Professor Anderson: "The courts and the constitution were to be preserved in a continuity through great trials and hazards by one man and one man alone, Francis Bacon. In this regard he became for a period the chief axial officer of the kingdom. He managed, without ill-deserving, to keep the constitution intact . . . to maintain the law and liberty of subjects, and to preserve 'the King's honor,' through wise, skillful, and just resorts."

Only in the reign of James's son Charles I would the great storm of the Puritan revolution finally strike. To Bacon is owed no small credit for delaying that storm by a generation. If James had earlier given heed to Bacon's counsels, if Buckingham and Cecil had been less venal, the interruption of the British monarchy and the sorry death of Charles need never have occurred at all. A people's great tragedy was winding to its conclusion—a tragedy which would not end with Bacon's death but only when James's son would lay his head upon the block in payment for his own and his father's obstinacy.

As part of his monarchial creed, Bacon had once written: "It is well, when nobles are not too great for sovereignty nor for justice, and yet maintained in that height, *as the insolency of inferiors may be broken upon them before it come too fast upon the majesty of kings.*" This maxim is practiced even in modern democracies, though generally under less severe conditions. Francis Bacon, the moderate monarchist, Parliament's man, the sensible compromiser, was now to act out in life his own observation.

He had risen to high office. The Lord Chancellorship of England, given to him in 1618, had brought along with it the title of Baron Verulam. In the very year of his tragic fall—1621—he was to receive yet another honor: the investiture as Viscount St. Alban. On January 27, five days after the event of his sixtieth birthday, his new dignity was conferred upon him in full ceremony. In a letter to the king, thanking him for this new advancement as well as the previous ones, Bacon added: "And so I may without superstition be buried in St. Alban's habit or vestment."

He was not to die for five years. But he was to be broken by the mob pressing more and more angrily upon the "majesty" of James. High office could not save him. In Parliament a majority of the members, manipulated by such enemies of Bacon's as the sadistic Sir Edward Coke, would turn against him. In frustration at their inability to vent their rage on the king, or upon his favorite, George Villiers, they would destroy the one man who had sought to temper the royal excesses and preserve the state.

It was not all ingenuous. Old enemies would scurry on black errands, traditional homage would be deliberately redescribed as bribery in order to fit the scene, the lapses of servants would be laid upon the overworked master. Southampton, former conspirator with Essex, would charge Bacon with corruption in office. One has only to consider the way the majority of these men were to end, amidst their own violence and rapacity, to realize the nature of Bacon's judges. James wept; Villiers vacillated. "My lord," said Bacon when confronted with the charges, "if this is to be a Chancellor, I think if the Great Seal lay upon Hounslow Heath, nobody would take it up."

James did not dare dismiss Parliament; the unscrupulous George Villiers, though obligated to Bacon for advice in earlier years, was not a man of sentiment. We need not linger over the intricacies of things said and done, nor over Bacon's personal agony. He intended his defense, but there came before it a fatal interview with James. James advised him—and to a man in Bacon's position this was a command—to avow his guilt and trust his protection to the crown.

It was the royal will. When Bacon left the king's presence, he is reputed to have remarked: "I am the first sacrifice; I wish I may be the last." He was face to face with his own dictum that in times of crisis the king's circle was expendable for the protection of the monarch. Without land or title of his own, he had been raised high by James. He owed him much. Bacon bowed to the king's wishes.

For more than three centuries the intellectual world has contended, censured, moralized, and probed into a world that is gone. The man behind the mask gives back no answer, the man who took care with his documents, those frail vessels in which he put his final trust, utters to posterity no word of vituperation or defense. He was a man who lived by his code, a servant to his monarch and the state.

The world was changing. Even that monarch, in spite of his avowals and a few protective gestures, did little to alleviate Bacon's lot or clear his name. Neither did Charles after him. A terrible loneliness descended on the dying man, the last and least publicized of the Elizabethan explorers—the stay-at-home discoverer of the New Atlantis, the opener of the great door into the future.

About him the storms of a new era were gathering. In a generation men would begin to talk of Bacon again, scientific societies would arise on the plans he and other dreamers had modeled. Men would grow curious about him, but the stain would be there, the ineradicable, terrible stain, unexamined in its time or place or condition, spreading endlessly as his name spread, as it still spreads today.

Strangely, the mask dropped just for a moment after his death. Long ago he had courted the Lady Hatton, who had cast him aside for his old rival, Sir Edward Coke, one of the undoubted contrivers of his downfall. She had grown to hate her overbearing, quarrelsome husband; Bacon had been equally unfortunate in his own marriage. When the sharp winter airs struck him down at last, there was found in his will an intended gift to Lady Coke. The episode is unexplained to this day. Perhaps Bacon's legacy was dedicated to some lost spring by a man who, rumor says, was cold to the ways of love.

The harsh accusers of his own time have long been silent, but Bacon's ordeal has not ended. What we find in him now may essentially be a measure of the nature of ourselves as individuals. "Bacon's wisdom," said the archbishop Richard Whately, "is like the seven-league boots which would fit the giant or the dwarf, except only that the dwarf cannot take the same stride in them."

*The title page from Bacon's* Great Instauration *shows the ship of philosophy sailing rough, uncharted seas.*

# THOMAS
# HOBBES
## 1588-1679

**T**homas Hobbes, like Machiavelli, has always had something of a bad name. He was a great philosopher, that has been universally admitted. But was he not also an atheist, an apologist of despotism, a materialist, a cynic? Did he not depict God's supreme creation, man, as a mere machine, and what is worse, a machine that was moved by fear and pride? How could Hobbes expect to be popular? He certainly hoped to be; and indeed, his whole life as a theorist was inspired not only by an abstract curiosity about truth but by a concrete desire to serve his contemporaries and deliver them from the evil consequences of false opinion. His was intended to be an essentially useful philosophy.

Hobbes often described himself as a timid man. He was born in the west of England on Good Friday, 1588, born, as he told his friends, prematurely because his mother was frightened by the approach of the Spanish Armada. "Fear and I," Hobbes said, "were born together." As a man he was undoubtedly prudent; he took care of himself and avoided danger. Death possessed for him none of the sweetness it was said to have had for Socrates and the Stoic philosophers. Hobbes was afraid even of the dark, and as he did not believe in the kind of God who could answer prayers, he used to sing to keep his spirits up. As an author Hobbes was far from timid; he was bold, even reckless, and toward the end of his life he was forbidden by Charles II to publish his writings, only because that king was fond of him and wanted to protect him. He lived to the extraordinary age of ninety-one.

Hobbes grew up in a century, like our own, of ideological confronta-

*Thomas Hobbes, somber in his black robe, was painted by J. M. Wright about 1669.*

*By* MAURICE CRANSTON

tion and war. Peace became for him an overwhelming preoccupation. He tried to teach men both to appreciate the value of peace and to understand how peace can be maintained. Traditional attitudes and arguments, he felt, were no longer of any use. The nation was falling apart. The new world that had come into being after the Renaissance needed a new political philosophy to restore its cohesion: a political philosophy constructed in the method of the new age, in a word, a scientific one. Francis Bacon had already proclaimed the idea that science could save us, that the systematic mastery of nature could immeasurably better the life of man on earth. Hobbes developed the idea that political science could save us politically, by halting the relapse of civil societies into war and anarchy.

Hobbes was born poor, the son of a dissolute clergyman, but he was fortunate in having a rich childless uncle who paid for his schooling and sent him to Oxford. He did not greatly relish the Aristotelian philosophy taught at the university or the Puritan type of religion already coming into fashion there, but he acquired the education that enabled him to become a professional scholar and tutor. It was a post as a private tutor in the family of the Earl of Devonshire that enabled him to travel and to meet the men who stimulated his thought.

Hobbes became a friend of Francis Bacon himself at a time when that great man had fallen from office as Lord Chancellor and was devoting himself to his scientific interests. Hobbes was undoubtedly infected by Bacon's hostility to traditional Aristotelian philosophy and to medievalism generally, and he was perhaps also influenced by Bacon's authoritarian politics; but if Bacon gave him his zeal for science, Hobbes did not accept Bacon's conception of what science was. Bacon, the founder of Anglo-Saxon empiricism, understood science as substantially a matter of collecting data, conducting experiments, recording the observable regularities in nature, and formulating the laws that those regularities suggest. Hobbes thought differently. He learned about the work of science from the great savants of Continental Europe, who were rationalists rather than empiricists; that is to say, they regarded the crucial part of science as the exercise of reason, the deployment of a mathematical method, something that could be done, as Hobbes put it, "sitting in one's closet in the dark." Hobbes's rejection of empiricism led him into a series of quarrels, throughout his long life, with the Baconian school of English scientists. He did not always get the better of these encounters. But this hardly matters, because Hobbes was never himself a practicing natural scientist: he was a philosopher who applied what he conceived to be the method of science to metaphysics, psychology, and politics.

Among the illustrious men whom Hobbes came to know on his travels in Europe were René Descartes, the French philosopher and geometer; Galileo Galilei, the astronomer who revealed the existence of the principles of motion that governed the solar system; and William Harvey, the Italian-trained Englishman who discovered the circulation of the blood. Each of these men contributed to the evolution of Hobbes's thought. Descartes prompted him to think that geometry constituted an ideal model of systematic knowledge. Galileo, who had combined theoretical and practical science in his study of the workings of the heavens with such remarkable success, gave Hobbes the idea of using the same approach to the study of man and society. Galileo also provided Hobbes with what he felt to be the key to the understanding of the universe: the principle that motion is the natural state of bodies. This was a direct inversion of the traditional Aristotelian doctrine that the natural state of bodies is rest. Since Hobbes was already convinced that Aristotelian philosophy was false, he was delighted to see it thus contradicted.

It seemed to follow from what Galileo had discovered about the workings of the solar system that the whole universe was a vast machine. William Harvey's discovery of the circulation of the blood suggested to Hobbes a parallel conclusion: that man was a small machine. Before Harvey published his book *De Motu Cordis* in 1628, people believed in Aristotle's theory that the blood flowed and ebbed through the same vessels in the body, giving rise to "animal spirits" that differed in different organs. Harvey demonstrated that the blood literally circulated; that the heart was a pump that pressed the blood through a series of tubes, the arteries and veins, some of which were equipped with valves. It was this that led Hobbes to think of the human body as a mechanical device.

But Hobbesian man was a thinking machine. Unlike animals, men (Hobbes argued) possessed the faculty of reason, which meant that they could reflect, calculate, and be instructed by arguments. Men's instincts alone tended to make them harm and even destroy themselves. Reason served to guide them in the pursuit of their natural satisfactions. Nature gave men one overriding objective, to prolong their lives as long as possible. The universal principle of motion took the form in men of life.

When Hobbes looked around him and saw that his contemporaries were hastening toward violent death in civil war and anarchy, he concluded that their reason was not instructed as it should be. Hence the importance of the task that Hobbes set himself: that of calling men back to a true understanding of themselves and their situation in the world. Events conspired to make political philosophy the most pressing of his concerns.

It was a commonplace belief in Hobbes's time that the new age could not be governed by the methods of the old. In England the

*Changes in an engraving reflect changes in the political scene. Pierre Lombart first depicted Charles I in an equestrian pose (top). But with the coming of the Commonwealth, the head was expunged and later replaced by that of Oliver Cromwell (bottom).*

Stuart kings, James I and Charles I, tried to modernize at the expense of some traditional rights of Parliament, and Parliament tried to modernize at the expense of the traditional prerogatives of the king. The result was the civil war that Hobbes foresaw.

Hobbes's sympathies were on the side of the king. But he criticized Charles I for making too many concessions to the demands of Parliament. He blamed him especially for assenting to the Non-Dissolution Bill, which enabled Parliament to grow into an independent power in the realm beside the king. Sovereignty by its nature, Hobbes believed, should be undivided, for it was the unity of the sovereign that enabled the sovereign to preserve the unity of the state. When there were two sovereigns in the realm, there was bound to be war. So far as England was concerned, Parliament had been allowed to build itself up to the point where it possessed one half of the sovereignty, and the king the other half. And this, said Hobbes, was a formula for war. In England in the 1640's, it assuredly proved to be one.

By the time the Civil War started, Hobbes was well out of the country. As he afterward confessed, or boasted, "I was the first that fled." In Paris he already had many friends, and when the defeated Royalists followed him into exile, Hobbes became tutor for a while to the Prince of Wales, who was later to be Charles II. Hobbes occupied his time during the years of exile in Paris completing his masterpiece, *Leviathan*. This book set forth a case for absolute sovereignty based on what the author conceived to be sound philosophical principles.

Most Royalists believed more or less in the idea of absolute sovereignty. But they had their own reasons for doing so, reasons that had been ably expounded by King James I himself in a book called *The Trew Law of Free Monarchies*. Briefly, they believed in the divine right of kings, based on the authority of the Scriptures. They believed that God's word compelled them to give their allegiance to the anointed king, and that after the death on the scaffold in 1649 of Charles I, his son and heir had become their true and lawful sovereign. Hobbes had no sympathy for religious arguments such as these, thinking that the principle of absolute sovereignty could and should be derived from purely rational foundations. This very enterprise made the Royalists suspicious; but what really disturbed them was the conception of sovereignty that came out at the end of Hobbe's argument. For what emerged was not that the rightful sovereign was the head of the lawful royal house but that the rightful sovereign of any realm was the person who exercised actual or effective sovereignty. And since the head of the royal house of Stuart was no longer effectively exercising sovereignty in England, Hobbes's *Leviathan* plainly implied that allegiance should go to another, namely to the victor of the Civil War.

It was a curious irony that this book, which had been prompted by the desire to give a better intellectual basis for the Stuart claim to absolutism, should prove in the event to serve the interests of the Stuarts' enemies. For when Hobbes sent one copy of *Leviathan* to Charles II, he sent another to a bookseller in London, to have it published. The book came out in 1651, by which time Oliver Cromwell, having already conquered England, was fast on the way to subduing Ireland, Scotland, and the Channel Islands. It was plainly Cromwell and not Charles who was enacting the role of sovereign in the British Isles.

Cromwell and his fellow Puritans could no more relish Hobbes's style of argument than could the Royalists in Paris. They had conquered England in the name of liberty, and Hobbes was scornful of "the specious name of liberty"; they appealed to the rights of Parliament, which he denied, and to the inner light of the individual conscience, which be believed to be mischievous nonsense. Nevertheless, his book could hardly fail to make pleasing reading for those who had won the Civil War, since it told them that their very success had justified their claim to rule. *Leviathan* offered Cromwell and his friends the philosopher's title to their office. And since they were sadly wanting any other forms of legitimacy, they were not prompted to take any action against either the book or its author.

All this Hobbes must have foreseen when he sent the book to be published, for the Royalist cause was already lost in 1650. But he was impetuous in his urge as an author to be printed, and once *Leviathan* was published and read, there was no alternative for Hobbes but to quit Paris and make his submission to the new rulers of England. Most of the Royalist exiles regarded him as a turncoat, and even his French friends were set against him by his manifest antipathy to the Catholic religion. Hobbes was squarely opposed not only to Catholic theology but equally to the existence of the Catholic Church as an institution that sought to rival the authority of the state, and thus to divide sovereignty in two. So Hobbes was virtually expelled from Paris; although the future king, who shared, perhaps, his preference for science to religion, remained his friend.

The starting point of Hobbes's political theory is, characteristically, a denial of Aristotle's central belief that man is by nature a political animal. Men's basic natural instincts, Hobbes says, are competitive, not co-operative. They are instincts that tend to war, not to peace. Ants and bees are naturally social, Hobbes agrees; but he refutes the Aristotelian suggestion that men have anything in common with such creatures. Men, he reminds us, vie continually for honor and privilege, which ants and bees do not; men's private advantage differs from the common good, which is not the case in insect communities; and while ants and bees have no use of reason with which to criticize the administration of their societies, men have such a faculty and use it either well or ill.

It is, in fact, this faculty of reason, as opposed to natural impulse, which leads men, Hobbes suggests, to form societies. The state of nature for man is a state of war, and it is reason that prompts men to escape the perils of this condition by instituting civil government. In an eloquent passage near the beginning of *Leviathan*, Hobbes writes:

> During that time men live without a common power to keep them all in awe, they are in that condition which is called war, and such a war is of every man against every man . . . In such a condition there is no place for industry, because the fruit thereof is uncertain, and consequently no culture of the earth, no navigation nor use of the commodities that may be imported by sea, no commodious building, no instruments of moving and removing such things as require much force, no knowledge of the face of the earth: no account of time, no arts, no letters, no society, and, which is worst of all, continual fear and danger of violent death, and the life of man solitary, poor, nasty, brutish and short.

*The Prince of Wales, later Charles II, was Hobbes's pupil during the Paris exile.*

Fear of violent death in a condition of natural anarchy, Hobbes argues, gives men the motive to quit that condition: reason suggests to each man that if everyone surrendered his right to kill others on condition that others surrendered their right to kill him, all could be safe; reason further suggests that such a bargain would require a supreme authority to ensure that it was upheld; in short, reason teaches men that it is better to live safely under a system of law than to live dangerously in total freedom. Hobbes believed that all men were equal; that is to say, they were all equally vulnerable. Even the strongest man had to sleep, and while he slept anyone could kill him. Brute strength was no protection against cunning, and no one could rely on his own power to protect himself. No one could be safe in a condition of anarchy. Hence, everyone possessing reason could understand the folly of remaining in the state of nature and the desirability of living under a sovereign. The Hobbesian man naturally loves liberty and dominion over others, but he realizes that he cannot prosper when each is at war with all, and therefore gives up his natural liberty for the sake of his own preservation and a more congenial life. Once he is in society, man's second natural impulse, pride, or the desire for honor and glory, keeps him active.

The basis of political society is thus a contract, or what Hobbes called a "covenant," by which each man yields his natural rights to a civil ruler or sovereign on condition that all other men do the same. The covenant is a kind of nonaggression pact between naturally rapacious men to live under a law. Hobbes defined law with his usual briskness as the "command of the sovereign." The sovereign, as Hobbes depicts it, is almost by definition absolute. It does not have to be a single man, or a monarch; it may equally well be a republican council, or a democratic assembly. The crucial feature about the sovereign is that it makes the law and enforces it, for it is the enforcement of law that preserves the peace. The law gives me my security by punishing you if you injure or threaten me. Hobbes preferred monarchy to other types of sovereignty because it was more unified, less prone to that ruinous division within itself by which sovereignty was destroyed. But there is only one real test of sovereignty—namely, what person or institution actually enacts and enforces the law.

Hobbes noted that sovereigns permitted different sorts of civil liberties in different countries, but he was impatient with people who tried to differentiate between "free" and "despotic" forms of government. There was no such thing as a completely free commonwealth, because all states had laws, and laws were "artificial chains" by which men agreed to be bound. It followed that for Hobbes there was not much point in trying to change or replace any existing government by another. Indeed, Hobbes deplored reformist or revolutionary movements because they brought the danger of a relapse into natural anarchy. However, if a revolution took place and another party seized power in the state and ruled successfully, or if there was a war and an enemy power invaded the state and set up its own rule—then the rebels or the invaders became the legitimate government as soon as they exercised the function of that office. Might makes right; or more precisely, *de facto* rule is *de jure* rule.

Hobbes is often spoken of as a bourgeois philosopher, or as a mere spokesman of his age, which witnessed the rise of the Renaissance prince and nation-state on the ruins of medieval Christendom. Neither judgment does him justice. His conception of man is certainly unmedieval: it reflects the experience of an age in which the traditional social hierarchy had given way to a competitive struggle between ambitious and adventurous individuals, the Christian faith had become more a source of conflict than a bond of peace, and all the old principles of feudalism were being challenged both by kings and by the rising middle classes. But Hobbes was not a bourgeois theorist. He had no belief, as had Locke, in the sanctity of property. Hobbes did not think of the desire for gain as a basic force in human life. Hobbes stressed rather the desire for honor, or pride, which he believed to be the one sentiment in man that could sometimes be stronger than fear. And what is bourgeois about the notion of honor?

It is an error, also, to think of Hobbes as some kind of ideologue of his time. His contemporaries did not understand him any more than they liked him; and it has been left to much later generations to develop his insights in the fields of psychology, philosophy, and sociology. Twentieth-century theories of human aggression, of the conflict between culture and nature, of the origin of human society, stem from Hobbes and not from Aristotle. Such fashionable theorists as Freud, Sartre, and Konrad Lorenz are deeply indebted to Hobbes; and our common twentieth-century experience, not only of the horrors of war, but of a peace based on nuclear terror, has helped make the pessimistic Hobbes the most "contemporary" of political philosophers.

Hobbes can, of course, be criticized, both for his account of the origin of societies and for his deductions from that theoretical construction. He may have been correct in thinking that men's desire to live under a sovereign is absolute, but that is not to say that they desire to live under an absolute sovereign. Bad government may indeed be worse than no government at all, but it does not follow that the only choice that confronts men who live under a bad government is a choice between that evil and the worse one of anarchy. Hobbes did not believe that the anarchic state of nature had ever been a historical reality; it was something he conceived as he reflected "in his closet in the dark" by stripping man in imagination of everything man owed to civil society. Thus, if the state of nature had not been a condition of man's past history, why should there be a danger of man's *relapsing* into it if he engaged in hazardous political adventures? The difference between free governments and despotisms, which Hobbes treated as trivial distinctions, have seemed to other men to be supremely important ones; and although most governments known to history have been despotic, many people have felt the evils of despotism to be worse than the evils of war. They have not necessarily been deceived by the illusory promise of enjoying (what Hobbes thought to be impossible) perfect freedom under law: they have seen the alternative of partial freedom or bondage and risked their lives in a struggle for partial freedom against bondage. More often than not, perhaps, they have lost their lives or succeeded merely in exchanging one type of bondage for another, but they have not always been disappointed; they have sometimes improved their lot. Hobbes may condemn all risks as foolish risks, but in a phrase of the much-maligned Aristotle, it is only the wearer who knows where the shoe pinches, or how far present pain is more intolerable than the risk of a different kind of pain in future. Although Hobbes's politics can be derived from his philosophy, it is not the only politics his philosophy entails.

No one has yet written a full biography of Hobbes, but we have a marvelous sketch of him by the incomparable John Aubrey, who was one of his closest friends:

He walked much and contemplated, and he had in the head of his staff a pen and inkhorn; he always carried a notebook in his pocket, and as soon as a thought darted he entered it in his book, for otherwise he might have lost it ... He had few books; I never saw above half a dozen in his chamber. He was wont to say that if he had read as much as other men, he would know no more than other men. He seldom used any physic. In his youth he was unhealthy, but from forty or better, he grew healthy, and then he had a fresh, ruddy complexion. In old age he was very bald ... He was not a woman-hater neither had he an abhorrence of good wine. In the last thirty years and more his diet was moderate and regular. He rose about seven, had his breakfast of bread and butter, took his walk meditating till ten. His dinner was provided for him exactly by eleven. In the afternoon he penned his morning thoughts. He was never idle. Besides his daily walking, he played tennis—still at seventy-five. He lived to the age of ninety-one. He died worth a thousand pounds, which considering his charity, was more than I expected.

The people who knew Hobbes best liked him most. The restoration of Charles II to the throne of England in 1660 was a happy moment for his former tutor, and a fortunate one as well, for the Anglicans who came to power in Parliament during the reign of Charles II detested Hobbes, and when there were national disasters in 1666—the Fire of London and the Great Plague—Parliament ascribed it to the wrath of God, and ascribed that wrath in turn to Atheism and Profaneness. A committee of the House of Commons was instructed to report on books tending to atheism, including "the book of Mr. Hobbes called *Leviathan*." For the rest of his life Hobbes was forbidden to publish anything. By 1668 he had completed his history of the English Civil War called *Behemoth* and submitted the text to Charles II. The king saw that the argument would give offense to both parties and commanded Hobbes, in his own interest, to refrain from publishing. *Behemoth* was not published until 1682, three years after the author's death. But even then *Leviathan* was not reissued. In Pepys's diary for September 3, 1668, we read: "To my booksellers for Hobbes's 'Leviathan,' which is now mightily called for ... and is sold for 30s., it being a book the Bishops will not let be printed again."

As the scandal of Hobbes's atheism waned, prices fell. When the original manuscript of *Leviathan* was auctioned in London in the 1850's, it fetched only nineteen shillings. In the comfortable years of English history between 1688 and 1914 it was doubtless rather easy to assume that Hobbes was wrong and that peace was man's natural state. Today we read his account of the human condition with a more uneasy feeling. In the Hobbesian *homme machine* for whom "there is no good but being foremost," driven by fear and the desire for glory, rapacious and belligerent, respecting only the law he is compelled to respect, mistrustful, vulnerable, and anxious, depending for his tranquillity on submission to force, and saved from slavishness only by his insatiable pride—in such a portrait we can, if only in certain disagreeable moments, recognize ourselves.

*The monarch, surveying his realm, presides over symbols of church (right) and state on the title page of Hobbes's* Leviathan.

# RENÉ
# DESCARTES
## 1596-1650

C lose to four score and seven years ago, Henry Adams was making a summer trip to France when he reached Chartres cathedral. Overwhelmed by the polychrome radiance of its windows, he wrote to his niece that "In my sublimated fancy, the combination of the glass and the Gothic is the highest ideal ever reached by men"—higher than the mosaics of Ravenna, higher than the temples of the Greeks and the Egyptians. Sublimated though his Bostonian fancy may have been, Henry Adams was troubled by something that may well have puzzled many another visitor to Chartres: why it is that the choir, the very heart of the cathedral, should be dominated by clerestory windows composed of gray panes that offer a bleak contrast to the watery blue, the rich ruby glow, the golden effulgence of the rest? Unable to explain this paradox, Adams concluded that the art of the grisaille "is a separate branch of color-decoration which . . . will have to remain a closed book because the feeling and experience which explained it once are lost."

Though he taught medieval history at Harvard, Adams's knowledge of French Church history was, here at least, defective. For the dreadful truth—which would have brought his Brahmin blood to a fiery boil had he known it—was that the choir of Chartres was originally lighted by the same glorious windows that ornament the rest of the cathedral; windows that were later dismantled, not by the Phrygian-bonneted regicides of 1792 who multilated the statues on Notre Dame's great Gallery of Kings. No, those grisaille windows were put there in the

*René Descartes gazes haughtily at the world from a portrait attributed to Hals.*

*By* CURTIS CATE

early eighteenth century by members of the chapter of Chartres cathedral so that they might more easily peruse their missals!

Nothing could more graphically illustrate the colossal change that swept over Europe in the age of Descartes and Newton than this "capitulation" of the clergy to their contemporaries' new and more "rational" attitude toward life. Whereas, six centuries before, Abbé Suger could declare that *"Mens hebes ad verum per materialia surgit"* —man's feeble mind can only attain truth through (the beauty of) material objects—these eighteenth-century clerics were closing their eyes to beauty in the name of a loftier, less primitive, more "sophisticated" ideal. No less than to Johann Gutenberg and his printed word, they were paying homage to Saint John, whose Logos, after centuries of internecine warfare, had at last got the better of the mystic faith of Saint Paul. For in dispelling the medieval mystery and "gloom" with which their cathedral was once uniformly filled, the canons of Chartres were exalting the new spiritual fashion that had made Hardouin–Mansart's Invalides in Paris, like Christopher Wren's Saint Paul's in London, domed temples of light. Stout Catholics though they remained, the canons of Chartres were yielding to a new faith that was to move more mountains than ever had the faith of Thomas Aquinas—a faith that, like all faiths, was to prove as destructive as it was constructive, as cramped and blinding as it was enlightened. This was the new faith in man's *lumen naturale,* in the "natural light" of truth and the "sweet" powers of reason, the faith of which, as much as any man since Socrates, René Descartes was the epoch-making prophet.

Because he was both mathematician and philosopher, Descartes has never been easy to pigeonhole. There have been greater mathematicians and great philosophers, yet none since ancient times has exercised a comparable influence. More specifically than Kepler and Galileo, he universalized the deductive, mathematical approach they had so brilliantly applied to astronomy and physics. His critical attitude toward the past and inherited tradition helped to deal a deathblow to the medieval faith in God. This made him Europe's first great revolutionary, the spiritual ancestor of Robespierre and Danton, of Marx and Lenin. From this time on, what was new and "modern" came to be regarded as *ipso facto* better than what was old, antiquated, and "out-of-date." It is off the substratum of this conviction—that the new *qua* new is better than the old—that the West has lived for the past three hundred years. No one, not even Christopher Columbus, did more to promote this explosive idea than the eloquent, soft-spoken, secretive René des Cartes (as he always spelled his name).

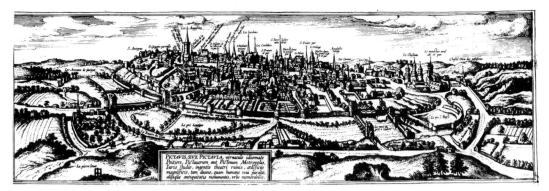

*Descartes studied law (which bored him) and medicine (which didn't) in Poitiers, shown above in the 1500's.*

Of Descartes's infancy we know practically nothing, beyond the fact that he was born in 1596 in the hamlet of La Haye, on the river Creuse. His father, Joachim Descartes, had helped the town of Poitiers repulse a Huguenot siege, and the young René's early education was stoutly Catholic. Descartes's mother, from whom he inherited a "dry cough," died when he was a year old, so that he was brought up with an elder brother and sister by his maternal grandmother, while their father, a councilor in the Breton parliament, spent half each year in Rennes.

At ten René was sent to La Flèche, near Le Mans, and entered in the Jesuit school that Henry IV had founded a couple of years before. The nine-year curriculum included six years of study in the "literary humanities" (grammar, history, poetry, and rhetoric) followed by three more in "philosophy," including mathematics, ethics, theology, Aristotelian logic, metaphysics, and physics. Though the Jesuit teachers at La Flèche were the best in France, they could not disguise the fissures that had begun to appear in the elaborate structure of traditional Scholasticism. The attempt to wed Aristotelian logic to Augustinian faith was like trying to mix fire and water, and the one conclusion to be drawn from the "ceaseless disputations of the schools" was that since no Church Father had been able to produce an argument that hadn't been ground to pieces by another, the truth had to be looked for elsewhere.

In April, 1610, when Henry IV was assassinated by a Catholic fanatic, his heart was cut out and brought to La Flèche, to be buried, with great ceremony, by the candle-bearing fathers while the fourteen-year-old René walked behind, in the procession, with other "gentlemen boarders." Dramatic though it was, this event was rapidly eclipsed by astonishing news from Padua, where an Italian mathematician named Galileo, using the recently invented "spy-glass," claimed to have spotted four moons circling the planet Jupiter—an epoch-making discovery that hastened the collapse of the Aristotelian conception of the universe.

His studies at La Flèche completed, Descartes was sent to Poitiers to study law and medicine. He cared little for the first, but was so fascinated by the second that he seems to have indulged in anatomical dissections, a risky occupation still associated in the public mind with witchcraft and superstition.

In July, 1618, he obtained his father's permission to sell a piece of family property, which brought him an income sufficient to sustain him comfortably thereafter without his having to take up a trade or a profession. Instead, he chose a military career, probably feeling that this was as good a way as any of sowing a few wild oats. Trained to be a gentleman as well as a scholar, he learned the use of the rapier, which he invariably wore next to his green doublet, along with a cloak and feathered hat. He was, in fact, something of a swordsman, and so interested in the subject that one of his earliest works was a treatise on fencing, a "science" that through precise analysis of the "long position" and the "short" (i.e., thrust and parry) could lead its practitioner to "infallible victory."

The same scientific temper prompted Descartes in 1618 to leave Paris and journey north to Holland, to study siegecraft and ballistics. At Breda he met Isaac Beeckman, a thirty-year-old student of medicine turned teacher, who awoke him to the realization that what had hitherto been a dilettantish interest in mathematics could be transformed into a lifetime vocation. Beeckman seems to have been astounded by the range of Descartes's scientific curiosity—and well he might have been, for over the next few weeks the young Frenchman showed him how mathematics could be applied to a more precise spacing and tuning of lute strings, proposed an algebraic formula for determining the rise in the water level when a heavy object is lowered into a tank, drew a geometric graph to demonstrate how the accelerating speed of a falling pencil in a vacuum could be precisely calculated for any moment of a two-hour period, proposed an explanation for why a spinning top remains upright and how this could be used to help man become airborne, and composed a treatise on music.

Beeckman's invaluable journal (which first came to light in 1905) makes it clear that by the end of 1618 Descartes was already applying algebra to the solution of geometric problems and that it was during these fruitful months at Breda, and not later, as has so often been written, that he invented analytic geometry. What the young Frenchman had perceived was that a geometric, or spatial, proposition can be transposed into algebraic terms. This can be done by the use of two axes—a vertical one measured in terms of $a$, and a horizontal one measured in terms of $b$. Any position to the right or left of the vertical axis can then be expressed as an algebraic function of $a$ and $b$—a function that can be manipulated algebraically in a way quite impossible with a mass of geometric tangents juxtaposed to follow the slope of a curve.

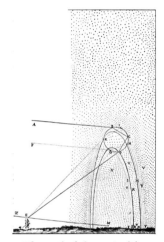

*The optical decomposition of the rainbow is pictured in a diagram from Descartes's work on dioptrics.*

Just five days before his twenty-third birthday Descartes wrote Beeckman a rhapsodic letter in which he boldly declared his conviction that there was no problem in geometry that could not be solved through the use of axes, lines, and curves, even though, he conceded, the task confronting him was too "infinite to be the work of one person, and incredible as it is ambitious."

Soon after this, he set off on a tour of central Europe. The outbreak of the Thirty Years' War and the election of a new Holy Roman Emperor forced an abrupt change of plans; and after attending the imperial coronation in Frankfurt, he joined the staff of Maximilian of Bavaria, head of the Catholic League formed to combat the dissident Protestant of Bohemia. Descartes's motives are far from clear. Though he always considered himself a devout Catholic, he was anything but a religious fanatic, as his friendships with Beeckman and other Protestants prove. Nor was he, like d'Artagnan, a Gascon hothead burning to fling himself into the fray. Indeed, his brief involvement in the Thirty Years' War was so discreet that there is no record of his having ever actually fired a musket or even bloodied a sword.

Travel in those parlous times was a risky business, and a good way to see something of the world without having one's purse snatched or throat cut was in armed company. But a more revealing motive is hinted at in the first of a series of "private cogitations" which Descartes began recording in Latin while still at Breda: "Just as players, fearful lest the blush show upon their brow, assume a role, so I who am about to step out onto the stage of a world of which I have been a spectator heretofore, do go forth masked."

Who, peering beneath the brim of his cavalier's hat, could have guessed that the innocent-looking young man with the dark meditative eyes under whimsically arched brows might be planning to stand the world of learning on its head, in a revolution as earth-shaking as the one Copernicus had launched a hundred years before? The "incredible" and "ambitious" undertaking that Descartes had begun to conceive as his life mission demanded a discretion bordering on secrecy. This was still a rough age in which an errant philosopher could expect no more mercy at the hands of the Church than an unorthodox medic or a heretical divine. He would need years of patient, plodding cogitation, he realized, before he could hope to tear off the disfiguring Scholastic mask and reveal the sciences in their quintessential beauty. So, rather than risk premature exposure, why not masquerade as a God-fearing soldier in the service of the arch-Catholic Duke of Bavaria?

Maximilian's forces had taken up their winter quarters in the vicinity of Augsburg. It was here that Descartes experienced three dreams that struck him with the force of "visions." They came to him on the eve of the Feast of Saint Martin, traditionally celebrated in Germany with wild wassailing and debauchery, though not by the abstemious René, whose intoxication was purely mental.

Descartes had spent the whole of November 10, 1619, indoors, enjoying the warmth of a porcelain stove, when he lay down, overcome by elation at the idea that he had discovered the basis for the "wondrous science" he had dimly conceived in Holland. Falling asleep, he dreamed that he was met in the street by several ghosts, who so frightened him that he had to lean heavily to the left to keep from keeling over. Next, he found himself being pushed by a furious wind toward a college chapel. But before he could enter it to pray, he was hailed by a stranger, who told him that a Monsieur N. had brought a melon from a foreign land to give him. Amazed to see the stranger standing straight while he was still bowed over by the wind, he woke up.

Feeling a pain, which he attributed to some "evil genius" that might have sought to seduce him, Descartes turned onto his right side and dropped off to sleep again. He was awakened by an ear-splitting noise, like a thunderclap, and was horrified to see sparks of fire dancing before his eyes.

In his third and final dream he was pleasantly surprised to find a dictionary on his table, mysteriously joined a moment later by an anthology of poetry. Opening the latter, he came on the verse *"Quod vitae sectabor iter?"* (What path of life should I follow?) At that moment a stranger appeared and handed him a copy of a verse play beginning with the words *"Est et Non."*

On awakening, Descartes began interpreting the dreams. "He judged that the Dictionary meant nothing aught than all the Sciences together joined, and that the Collection of Poems, entitled *Corpus Poetarum* . . . denoted the union of Philosophy and Wisdom," wrote his biographer Adrien Baillet, copying Descartes's account in 1690, a few years before this priceless manuscript vanished, never to be seen again. Descartes interpreted this to mean that poets gifted with imagination could give expression to truths as fundamental as those conceived by philosophers. The thunderclap which had so frightened him had been "the Spirit of Truth descending to possess him," and the melon he had been offered signified "the charms of solitude, but presented by purely human solicitations"—a phrase that has mystified more than one Descartes scholar.

It is curious, to put it mildly, that the crucial "illumination" in Descartes's life, which was to orient the rest of his career and through him transform the scientific thinking of the West, should have taken the form of a triple dream, followed by a session of analysis. These dreams have fascinated more than one psychiatrist. But their real significance is not to be found in Freud's suggestion that Descartes's guilt complex (symbolized by his leaning to the left, the "sinister" side) stemmed from sexual desire, represented by the melon. His sense of guilt, as Henri Lefebvre pointed out long ago, was linked to the sin of pride—one of the seven deadly sins of the Middle Ages—and more specifically, to the pride that comes from excessive knowledge. Hence the mysterious sparks flashing about his eyes in warning.

In terms of Christian theology and symbolism, the melon can be considered an enlarged version of the fatal apple Eve presented to Adam. It was here associated, however, not with carnal lust but with an all-embracing, *global* knowledge. Much as Christ had once been tempted by the devil, so Descartes was being invited to accept the forbidden fruit of limitless knowledge—not for his own satisfaction, like Faust, but for the common good. For if the melon was associated with the "charms of solitude," it was because he was haunted by a guilty feeling that he was reserving for his private enjoyment the global, universal science he had just stumbled on.

But what was the nature of this blinding truth which could arouse in him such a schizophrenic nexus of temptations and taboos? The key is to be found in the words *"Est et Non,"* which, though derived from Pythagoras, really sum up the fundamental weakness of Aristotelian logic.

Unlike Plato, who was more interested in the universal than the particular, Aristotle was a pragmatic naturalist with a passion for biology. The logic he created, the first to deserve the name, was designed to classify the world's myriad things and beings into genera and species. Syllogisms, such as the classic "All men are mortal; Socrates was a man; therefore Socrates was mortal," were logical exemplifications of a system of classification which, since no important truths could be derived from it, turned into a science of verbal definitions—that particular form of philosophizing known as Scholasticism.

What had begun as an admirable endeavor to classify and organize the myriad phenomena of the universe thus ended up a totally ossified system. As time passed, it came to be regarded as axiomatic that, just as each genus is a whole that admits of no partial or intermediary category (the genus "animal" as totally distinct from the genus "plant" or the genus "mineral," for example), so the four sciences recognized by the Greeks—arithmetic, geometry, astronomy, and physics—each formed an essentially distinct, self-ordering, and independent whole. Thus the rules governing astronomy, the "science of celestial phenomena," were declared to be radically different from those governing physics, the "science of sublunary phenomena." Arithmetic was defined as the "science of numbers," and considered radically distinct from geometry, the "science of magnitudes."

While developing his logic, Aristotle realized that the validity of genera and species ultimately depends on an even more overriding principle—that of negation (echoed in the *"Est et Non,"* "Yes and No," formula of Descartes's third dream). An affirmation can be false, just as a negative statement can be true. For example, "A horse is an animal" is true, but the no less affirmative statement "A horse is a bird" is false. Given a negative twist, "A horse is not a bird," it is true again.

Had Aristotle grasped the full import of this realization, he would have applied his omnivorous curiosity to a systematic search for the overriding categories of human thinking to which even genera and species must pay homage. Instead, he proceeded on his way without giving further thought to the question. His successors did likewise, with the result that though no astronomer could function without recourse to geometric figures, any more than a geometer could work without arithmetical notations, the axiom of "the incompatibility of (different) genera" remained the official dogma for close to two thousand years.

Increasingly critical though they were of the sterility of the Aristotelian system, no prominent thinker of the late Renaissance—not even Bacon, Galileo, or Hobbes—seems to have been able to put his finger on what was fundamentally wrong. But this is what the twenty-three-year-old Descartes did during that momentous November of 1619. He had already seen that if arithmetic is defined as a "science of discontinuous quantities" and geometry as a "science of continuous quantities," the artificial barriers separating them simply collapse (the result being analytic geometry). He had also realized that arithmetic, and by the same token, algebra, are not so much sciences of numbers as of proportions—a realization that justifies the use of "irrational" numbers and opens up vast mathematical possibilities. It only remained for him to universalize the principle, as he did in the first of his "Rules for the Guidance of the Mind"—the *Regulae ad directionem ingenii:* "For, inasmuch as all the sciences are naught else but human wisdom, which remains one and the same, however different may be the objects to which it is applied, and which is no more changed by these objects than is the light of the sun by the variety of the things which it illuminates . . . one must therefore convince oneself that all the sciences are so linked together that it is easier to learn them all at once than to isolate them from each other."

For an Aristotelian, brought up to regard the "incommunicability of genera" as in "the nature of things," this was heresy pure and simple. No one knew it better than Descartes, who preferred to keep these rules unpublished during his lifetime rather than risk a head-on clash with the Schoolmen, like the one that was to cause Galileo such trouble and embarrassment.

*An illustration from* De Homine *shows Descartes's theory of perception: the nervous impulse, he thought, was transmitted to the eye, then to the pineal gland in the brain, and finally to the muscles.*

He made this even clearer in his Fourth Rule, where he noted that mathematics could be applied to all measurable things "without its mattering that this measure be sought for in numbers, figures, stars, sounds, or any other object; and thus one observes that there must be some general science explaining everything that one can look for regarding order and measurement without application to a particular matter, and that this science is called . . . universal mathematics."

When Isaac Newton, some sixty-five years later, published his *Philosophiae Naturalis Principia Mathematica* (The Mathematical Principles of Natural Philosophy), he was simply following Descartes's prescription and deliberately violating the old Aristotelian frontiers between physics, mathematics, and astronomy. Einstein was proceeding in exactly the same spirit, more than two centuries after that, when he set out to develop a universal field theory capable of reducing electromagnetics and gravitation to the dominion of a single all-embracing set of formulas. A good half of the great scientific breakthroughs that have been made since Newton's time have followed this same pattern—with the result that the "universal mathematics" Descartes first surmised in 1619 has since been applied to optics, astronomy, meteorology, acoustics, chemistry, architecture, physics, engineering, accounting, and warfare (all of which he clearly foresaw), as well as electronics, cybernetics, microbiology, genetics, economics, and even politics—public-opinion polls, budget estimates, and all forms of statistical planning.

The Damascene revelation Descartes experienced on the 10th of November, 1619, is thus a landmark in the evolution of modern thought. His conviction that "scientific" thinking is, in essence, mathematical thinking led him to reject the Aristotelian–Scholastic emphasis on the classification of *things,* in favor of a new mode of thought focused on the *ideas* we have about these things. Just as the number 4 is a compound number made up of 2 and 2, or 3 and 1, so every composite idea can be analyzed down to its simpler components. This was the start of what deserves to be called "microscopic analysis"—the mode of thought that has effectively dominated the Western mind ever since. Before examining the universe, with its myriad forms and objects, man must begin by examining his way of looking at it; he must become what even the most brilliant of the ancient Greeks was never really able to be—intellectually critical and introspective.

All of the great European philosophies that followed—Locke's *Essay Concerning Human Understanding,* Leibnitz's *Nouveaux Essais sur l'entendement humain,* Hume's *Treatise of Human Nature* (in large part written at Descartes's old school, La Flèche), Kant's *Critique of Pure Reason,* Hegel's *Phenomenology of the Spirit*—all proceeded from this fundamental Cartesian insight: that the essential task of philosophy is to analyze and regulate the concepts and operations of the human mind.

Descartes's original intention was to write an account of his "revelation" under the title *Studium bonae mentis*—"A Study of Sound Thinking." But he soon thought better of it. The Counter Reformation was now in full swing, Europe was in the throes of a witch-hunting frenzy, and there was no telling on whose neck the axe of the Inquisition might next fall. Keeping his heretical ruminations to himself, he dutifully followed the Duke of Bavaria's troops into Bohemia, where he is said to have taken part in the Battle of the White Mountain, fought near Prague on November 8, 1620. Eight months later, he decided he had seen enough of the Thirty Years' War and bade good-bye to the career of arms forever.

The one-time soldier now became a traveler. On his way back to France, via Poland and northern Germany, he almost lost his life. During a North Sea crossing near Emden, the sailors of the skiff he had hired decided to steal his purse and toss him and his faithful valet overboard. Whipping out his rapier, Descartes told them to sail on or be prepared to die.

After a few months in France, he rode off to Italy, where he spent two years. On his return to Paris in 1625, he renewed old acquaintances with various religious fathers and savants who had succumbed, like himself, to the new passion for catoptrics and dioptrics, or as we would say today, mirrors and lenses. This was a period of intense intellectual ferment, ready-made for the reception of his new "method of philosophizing." Indeed, almost too ready-made; for one of those whom it mightily impressed was the influential Cardinal de Bérulle, who thought to enlist Descartes's talents in the cause of the Counter Reformation. Descartes thought differently, and in the autumn of 1628 he hastened back to Holland.

Convinced that *bene vixit, bene qui latuit* (he lives well who hides well), our philosopher-mathematician first sought refuge in a small Frisian township north of the Zuider Zee, and then moved to Amsterdam, where he found lodgings in the house of a cloth merchant. Happy to be able to live a life of total anonymity in the great port city, he slept ten hours a day, enjoyed wonderful dreams, and spent most of each morning in bed, occasionally rising to jot down a new argument or thought sequence he had worked out in his head. Fascinated by the problems of reflection and refraction, to which he applied his discoveries in analytic geometry, he now plunged into a study of the rainbow. But the deeper he delved into this subject, the more it dawned on him that it could only be treated as a particular aspect of a universal theory of light—embracing "the heavens, since they transmit it; the planets, comets, and the earth since they reflect it; and particularly all those bodies which are upon the earth since they are either colored, or transparent, or luminous; and finally, man, since he is their spectator." From an inquiry into atmosphere and meteorology, his treatise thus came to include geology, mineralogy, fermentation, combustion, smoke, plant and animal life, embryology, anatomy, physiology, and oneirology (the science of dreams).

There is something both admirable and pathetic in this endeavor to fashion a new and all-embracing philosophy of nature from the scientific bric-a-brac at his disposal. But nothing could be more mistaken than the notion that this prophet and propagator of the deductive method had no use for experimentation. In Amsterdam Descartes made almost daily visits to the nearby butcher, watching him carve up animals and often having a special piece delivered to his lodgings. He made painstaking dissections of brains, eyes, and nerves in a grim effort to determine what memory and imagination consist of. Intrigued by the fact that the pineal gland in the brain of an ox is relatively large, whereas it is almost invisible in the human brain, he concluded that this was the "seat of the soul and the place wherein all our thoughts are made." He had long since developed a kind of plumber's theory of physiology, according to which human muscles work with pumps and valves, but what worried him more was how the "animal spirits" that proceed from the heart to the brain communicate their vitality to the muscles and how the material body is connected to the immaterial soul. The conclusion he came to—that they are linked by a "highly subtle fluid"—can be dismissed today as moonshine, but Descartes was working with extraordinarily primitive instruments (vacuum pumps, thermometers, and microscopes did not yet exist), and the serious study of anatomy was barely in its infancy.

In 1633 he was putting the finishing touches on his "universal" treatise on *Light, The World, and Man* when his friend Mersenne wrote to him from Paris that Galileo's *Dialogues on the Two Systems of the World* had been ordered seized and burned by the Sacred Congregation in Rome, and Galileo himself forced to "make amends." Unwilling to run the same risks, Descartes immediately put his work into cold storage. Since his own system of "physics" was based on a heliocentric planetary system, he knew he could never get it approved by the Church's censors.

To combat his discouragement, he visited his friend Beeckman in Dordrecht, then returned to Amsterdam, where he took up new lodgings with a bookseller. In the house worked a tempting young damsel named Helen. One Sunday, while the bookseller was out, the former musketeer briefly surrendered to passion and soon found himself, like Dumas's Athos, the prospective father of a child. The embarrassingly

*These entries in Galileo's notebook record his observations of the four moons of Jupiter, an epoch-making discovery that led to Descartes's subsequent rejection of the Aristotelian conception of the universe.*

pregnant Helen was bundled off to friends of his in Deventer, there to give discreet birth to a daughter, who was to be called Francine.

Descartes himself headed for Utrecht, where he composed a substitute, stopgap opus to replace his no longer publishable treatise *The World*. From this work he selected three fragments—the first devoted to dioptrics (the making of telescopes and lenses), the second to meteors (essentially a geometric analysis of rainbows), and the third to his analytic geometry. To these he added a philosophical preface entitled *Discours de la Methode,* or *Discourse on Method*.

It is not easy for today's casual reader to appreciate the colossal impact that this relatively brief work was to have on later generations. Though it was more an expression of philosophical intent than a systematic elaboration, it became the New Testament of scientific and "rational" thinking. At a time when philosophical debates were still carried on in Latin, it was written in a simple, unpedantic French, still regarded a *langue vulgaire* among scholars. It was thus made accessible to all, including women. *The Discourse on Method* did for French what Cervantes's *Don Quixote* did for Spanish: it established a classic style of graceful, easy-flowing limpidity that was to be a model for French prose writing for the next century and a half, and it thus contributed to making French *the* language of intelligent conversation in eighteenth-century Europe. Its admirable brevity marked another break with traditional philosophizing, as did the personal tone, something no one had seriously thought of attempting since Saint Augustine.

The *Discourse*'s opening words—*"Le bon sens est la chose du monde la mieux partagée"*—were in themselves epoch-making, stating a credo that has the ring of a rationalist manifesto:

> Good sense is, of all things in this world, the most equitably distributed; for so well provided thereof does each man think himself, that even those who are the hardest to please in all else, do not usually desire more of it than they already have. Wherein it is unlikely that all be mistaken; rather does it attest that the faculty of judging aright, and of distinguishing the true from the false, which is properly what is called good sense or reason, is naturally equal in all men.

The audacity of this opening assertion is so staggering that even recent scholars have wondered if the author's intention was not ironic. But the rest of the *Discourse* makes it clear that he was being quite straightforward. That many human beings are stupid, as Descartes was privately willing to concede, does not mean that they have been denied the gift of "good sense" or reason; it merely means that they have not been properly employing this God-granted faculty.

No longer was Descartes willing to accept the traditional notion that the gap between sovereign and serf or between sage and imbecile was as great as that separating man from beast. In decreeing that man

DISCOURS
**DE LA METHODE**
Pour bien conduire sa raison,& chercher
la verité dans les sciences.
PLUS
LA DIOPTRIQVE.
LES METEORES.
ET
LA GEOMETRIE.
*Qui sont des essais de cete* METHODE.

A LEYDE
De l'Imprimerie de IAN MAIRE.
CIƆ IƆC XXXVII.
*Avec Privilege.*

*The title page of Descartes's masterpiece,* The Discourse on Method, *also gives the titles of the three fragments that he included from his unpublishable treatise* The World.

is not accidentally but *substantially* a reasoning being, Descartes was placing all men, and for that matter, women, on a new philosophical pedestal. Wittingly or unwittingly, he was aiming a trenchant blow at the intricate, hierarchical structure of medieval and Renaissance society and laying the groundwork for modern democracy.

If for the influence it subsequently exerted it can only be compared to Rousseau's *Social Contract* or to Marx's *Communist Manifesto,* in its scope and implications *The Discourse on Method* is the most far-ranging of the three. So stuffed with seminal ideas is this rich fruit-cake of a book that there is hardly a major theme or tendency in the evolution of the modern mind that was not either hinted at or here foreseen.

A summary thematic listing includes the following: the idea that the conduct of one's life should be not haphazard but methodical and systematic, which makes Descartes the philosophical father not only of bourgeois capitalism but of all forms of economic (and even city) planning; the glorification of human "reason" as opposed to animal "instinct," a trend so deep-rooted in the modern psyche that ethologists like Konrad Lorenz and Robert Ardrey are still actively combating it; a systematic distrust of the senses combined with the belief that genuinely important "subjects" can be given mathematical expression, a concept that underlies the technocratic numeromania of our times, according to which everything from human welfare to questions of aesthetics can be reduced to essential quantitative terms; the rejection of theology as too "lofty" for man's rational powers, which makes Descartes the grandfather of nineteenth- and twentieth-century positivism; the rejection of "myths" and superstition, which makes Descartes the father of modern criticism and the inspirer of Pierre Bayle and Voltaire no less than of Jean Paul Sartre and Simone de Beauvoir; the repudiation of bookish erudition and traditional authority in the name of clear, simple, distinct, and "evident" ideas, combined with the *tabula rasa* principle, that is, since the past has accumulated so much error and confusion, it is better to wipe the slate clean and start again from scratch, which makes Descartes the spiritual ancestor of all revolutionary movements, from the French Revolution of 1789 to the cultural and other revolutions that have recently shaken China and so many Western universities; the notion that we have a more immediate and intimate awareness of our thoughts than of external reality, combined with an advocacy of self-analysis and introspection, which makes Descartes the founder of German idealism and the distant ancestor of Stendhal, Proust, and Sigmund Freud; the belief that the worth of a proposition is not derived from the innate beauty of its definitions but from the usefulness of the conclusions that can be derived from it, which makes Descartes the anticipator of the utilitarians no less than of William James's robust Yankee conviction that what counts is the "cash value" of an idea; the specific affirmation of a mechanistic credo, according to which man's intellectual efforts should be devoted to making life more comfortable and human labor less burdensome; the idea that physics (a better knowledge of fire, water, air, heavenly bodies, etc.) can be transmitted to artisans, thus helping make men "the lords and possessors of nature," which makes Descartes the prophet of the Industrial Revolution; and an optimistic view of his century, "as fertile in good minds as has been any of the preceding ones," and destined, furthermore, to improve, which makes Descartes, along with Francis Bacon, one of the great promoters of the idea of human progress.

"Descartes, in the history of thought, will always remain that French horseman who set out at so sure a pace," the poet Charles Péguy once wrote. He added that the four prescriptions for sound thinking outlined in the second section of the *Discourse*—never to accept anything as true that one does not clearly know to be such, to divide all difficulties into parts adequate to their solution, to conduct one's thoughts in order, proceeding from the simplest to the most complex, and to keep reviewing one's enumerations to make sure that nothing has been overlooked—had "revolutionized the world and thought." Though this is the kind of lyricism which the name of Descartes is still apt to inspire in France, it was a pardonable exaggeration.

The first precept—never to accept anything on trust—was packed with enough dynamite to rock Europe to its foundations. Curiously, this was the opposite of the author's intention. Descartes wanted to make it the first principle of a new rationalistic philosophy in order to show up the purely "arbitrary" character of dogma, and precisely of those narrow religious dogmas which had kept Europe in a state of war and turmoil for more than a century. (Thomas Aquinas, he once wrote in a private letter, was ultimately responsible for producing Calvin; and if anything of Christian faith was to survive, Scholastic theology would have to be exterminated!) Making systematic doubt the foundation of a new philosophy would have been a self-defeating enterprise had Descartes not been fortified by a Platonic faith in the universal science he was bent on unfolding. For what he was asking man to doubt was not mathematics or deductive reasoning but "treacherous" sense experience, the fountainhead of the illusions and hallucinations that mortal man is heir to.

The central argument he propounded—that since thought cannot exist unless someone is doing the thinking, a thinker cannot doubt his own existence—was not as original as it might seem. More than a thousand years before he produced the celebrated formula "I think, therefore I am" (*Cognito, ergo sum*, in its later Latin formulation), Saint Augustine had written *"Si enim fallor, sum"* (Even if I err, I am). Saint Augustine, however, was only making the point in passing, whereas for Descartes it was fundamental and designed, as Pascal rightly pointed out, to establish the primacy of thought over matter-of-fact "existence." What Luther did for religion, Descartes thus accomplished for philosophy. The first made the individual "conscience" the ultimate depository of faith and ethics; the second made the individual "consciousness" the touchstone of existence.

That the once docile pupil of the Jesuits was a curious "defender of the faith" the Scholastics, and not least the Jesuits, soon perceived. Even Mersenne felt obliged to point out that the proof of the existence of God and of the immateriality of the soul in the *Discourse* had received less than half the attention accorded to the functions of the human body. Descartes, who had sent copies of his work to Richelieu and other prominent ecclesiastics in the hope that it might win favor with the hierarchy, assured his friend that he would develop his arguments on the subject more fully in an accompanying work. Thus were born the *Meditations,* which he completed in the little pine- and dune-surrounded village of Santpoort, close to the Haarlem of Frans Hals (who painted his portrait during his stay). Reunited with Helen and their daughter, he spent three happy years there until, in September, 1640, his happiness was abruptly darkened by the death of five-year-old Francine.

From this misfortune Descartes never fully recovered—though he hastened to get rid of Helen. Increasingly, he was concerned to defend himself against his enemies, who derided his "libertine" life and "heretical" opinions. Catholics vied with Protestants in damning him and his "method." Fearful of the criticism his new *Meditations* might incur, Descartes had Mersenne print up a score of copies of the Latin text, which were sent to a number of Dutch and French theologians, as well as to Pierre Gassendi and Thomas Hobbes. Thanks to this ingenious artifice, several editions of the *Meditations* were published, together with a fascinating series of objections and answers.

Fame now caught up with the one-time Frisian recluse with a vengeance. Accused of atheism and sued for libel by a fanatic Calvinist who headed the theological faculty at Leyden, Descartes moved up the coast to a small fisherman's village called Egmond-an-den-Hoef. Here he wrote *The Principles of Philosophy* and *The Passions of the Soul* for his most illustrious disciple, Elizabeth of Bohemia, the granddaughter of Mary Stuart, niece of Charles I of England, and sister of the future mother of England's first Georgian king.

His interest in medicine remained as keen as ever. Experimenting with his diet, he came to the conclusion that meat was a harmful food and that by eating plenty of vegetables a person could live to the age of a hundred. Here, too, his expectations were doomed to disappointment. Letting vanity get the better of his doubts, he finally agreed to go to Sweden, to "tutor" its young queen, Christina.

Accompanied by his Dutch valet, he reached Stockholm in October of 1649 and soon realized how right he had been to distrust "this land of bears, between the rocks and the ice." At his first meeting with the headstrong daughter of Gustavus Adolphus, he was shaken to discover that her extraordinary appetite for languages was matched only by her ignorance of philosophy. With a caprice which struck Descartes as sadistic, this energetic Amazon insisted on having him turn up at the palace for "lessons" at 5 o'clock in the morning, in the bitter cold of the long Nordic night. In December she commissioned him to write a "pastoral play" to celebrate her twenty-third birthday, after which she had him draft a project for a Swedish Academy of Sciences.

It was Descartes's last undertaking. Returning to the French Embassy from a 5 A.M. session with the queen, he began to shiver and drank down half a bottle of aquavit to combat the cold. Feeling feverish, he took to his bed, and for two days ate nothing, while his cold developed into pneumonia. For another week he fought off the queen's physician (an avowed adversary of his philosophy), steadfastly repeating, *"Messieurs, épargnez le sang francais!"* (Gentlemen, spare French blood!); but finally he gave in and let himself be bled. This weakened him without lowering his fever, to the disgust of the physician, who left him to his fate. Two days later, on February 11, 1650, Descartes died, after making a last pathetic attempt to climb out of bed and warm himself by the fire.

There being no Catholic churches in Lutheran Sweden, his friend the French ambassador had him buried without the elaborate state funeral which a chagrined Queen Christina would have liked to stage for "her philosopher." Sixteen years later, Descartes's body was brought back to France, by which time his published works had gone the way of Galileo's and been placed on the Index. After eight more years of heroic struggle, a fanatic Cartesian member of the oratory, Nicolas Malebranche, persuaded Rome to revoke the decision. "First denounced and pilloried, persecuted and condemned, the disciples of Descartes, a mere half century later, occupy the university chairs, dictate the courses, write the books, and enjoy all honors and authority," as the French historian Paul Hazard was later to put it.

More papist than the pope, as disciples so often are, the mystically inclined Malebranche soon showed to what pathological absurdities Descartes's antitraditionalism could lead. One day, on seeing a copy of Thucydides on the table of a friend, he walked out in a huff.

Though he never actually said, like Henry Ford, that "History is bunk!" the fanatic oratorian was proclaiming his conviction that, Descartes having supplanted Aristotle, there was henceforth nothing of importance to be learned from the ancients.

The revolutionary worm was now in the European apple, and the resulting ferment was to work on to its logical, if not preordained, conclusion. Leibnitz, at the start of the eighteenth century, could not help but note the creeping rise of opinions which, "insinuating themselves in the minds of those men of the world who rule others and on whom business depends, and slipping into fashionable books, dispose all things to that general revolution with which Europe is threatened." D'Alembert, fifty years later, was echoing the same premonition when he wrote that his century "believes itself destined to change the laws in everything." And even Gibbon could write, in a strangely Cartesian phrase, that "History is little more than the register of the crimes, follies, and misfortunes of mankind."

Such being the case, the logical thing to do was to make a clean break with the past and try and start all over—which is just what the French revolutionaries of the Year 1 (A.D. 1792) did when they abolished the *ancien régime,* discarded the old calendar, and voted enthusiastically that the body of Descartes, the man "who has smashed the chains of superstition," should repose, alongside those of Voltaire and Rousseau, in Paris's Panthéon. A new age had dawned, one determined to uproot the past in order to improve the future, with convulsive repercussions we are still experiencing today.

*An imaginary gathering, painted after Christina's visit to Paris in 1656–58, shows the queen attended by scholars, including Descartes (third from right). Descartes actually met the queen in Stockholm in 1649, and died there in 1650.*

Mon pere sest servi de
le droit pour son ou
de Mr pascal fait par mon pere

# BLAISE
# PASCAL
## 1623-1662

E very now and then humanity produces an intellectual sport, a genius, a mental monster. We expect the great mind to serve us, and so, usually, it does. But with its higher order of values it is likely to dismiss our own and to perceive and pursue aims that astonish our earthliness. Thus Isaac Newton abandoned science to spend his incomparable mind on unriddling the prophecies of Daniel. Thus Joseph Priestley, the discoverer of oxygen, came to America and settled in Pennsylvania, to write twenty-five volumes of unreadable, or at least unread, theology. Thus also Blaise Pascal.

What made the great mind? The genes, of course, or if you prefer, God. But notice Pascal's background and development. He was born in Clermont-Ferrand, in the center of France, in 1623. His mother died when he was three. His father, a civil servant and amateur scientist, recognized that he had fathered a prodigy and resigned his post to devote himself entirely to the education of Blaise and his two remarkable sisters. The father's views were unorthodox. He believed that the need of knowledge must precede knowledge, that reason and judgment must precede formal study. He taught the experimental method: observe, classify, generalize. Thus Blaise, at eleven, noticed that a china dish struck with a knife hums until silenced by a touch of the hand. "Why?" he said, like any child. Unlike any child, he found the answers unsatisfactory and made a series of experiments on sound and wrote a treatise much applauded by his elders. Having been kept in ignorance of geometry, he invented, at twelve, his own, and was discovered doing his version of Euclid's thirty-second proposition on the

*This notebook sketch is the only portrait of Blaise Pascal made during his lifetime.*

*By* MORRIS BISHOP

kitchen floor. At sixteen he printed some remarks on conic sections that herald our projective geometry.

Thus he was trained to originality, to genius. He never knew the orthodoxies and subjections of a school, nor the group spirit and rivalries of a school; he was destined for lonely apartness. Nor did he ever play, or build his body in sports and games. Nature shook her head and sighed.

When Blaise was sixteen his father was appointed collector of internal revenue in Rouen. The post was an exacting one; Blaise was drafted to aid in the endless calculations. Promptly bored by drudgery, he wondered if the mechanical work could not be done by a machine. Characteristically, he proceeded from the problem to its practical solution. He created the first calculating machine.

His momentous idea was to conceive the digits of a number as arranged in wheels; each wheel, after making a revolution, should turn its left-hand neighbor a fraction of a revolution. It was an extraordinary mechanical achievement. "Pascal knew how to animate copper and give wit to brass," said an admiring friend. Pascal made at least fifty machines and built on them great hopes of gain. But the *pascaline* did not sell. Since accurate gear-cutting was impossible, the mechanism was forever getting out of order, and only Pascal or one of his workmen could fix it. And it was too expensive. Though it could do the work of half a dozen men, the men were still cheaper than the machine. Technology had to wait for economics to catch up.

In mathematics Pascal's work is known to every professional. He created the theory of probability, gave Leibnitz the hint that became his infinitesimal calculus, and—as a diversion from a toothache—solved the problem of the cycloid. Most of his mathematical work is too technical for exposition here. But physics, or the world we live in, is everybody's business. We are all physicists, or we would be dead.

In Pascal's time there was much learned talk of the vacuum, or the void, which was identified by verbal habit with *nihil*, nothing. Philosophers argued that nature abhors a vacuum, that a Nothing cannot be a Something. But Pascal was impressed by reports of Torricelli's famous experiment, today a high-school commonplace. A forty-inch glass tube is filled with mercury, then turned smartly upside down, with the open end in a bowl of mercury. The mercury in the tube sinks to a height of about thirty inches, leaving a ten-inch gap at the sealed top of the tube. What is in the gap and how does it get there? Pascal concluded that it is a real vacuum, that the weight of mercury in the tube balances the weight of air on the mercury in the bowl. He developed his thesis with a sensational series of experiments. He had, for instance, forty-six-foot glass tubes made. He bound them to ships' masts, pivoted in the middle. He filled the tubes with water, wine, or oil, reversed them so the open ends sat in tubs of liquid, removed the stoppers, and saw the fluids fall and create measurable vacuums.

If air has weight, he argued, there should be less at the top of a mountain than at its foot; hence the measure of mercury in a Torricellian tube should vary with the altitude. The Puy de Dôme stands conveniently four thousand feet above his native city of Clermont. He commissioned his brother-in-law, Florin Périer, to make the great experiment. Two Torricellian tubes were borne by a party of enthusiastic amateurs to the summit. The mercury dropped about three inches, and rose again on the return journey. Meanwhile control tubes set up in the city had remained unchanged. Thus the weight of air was not only demonstrated but measured. And thus Pascal propounded the principle of the aneroid barometer.

Pascal continued with important work on hydrostatics, or the equilibrium and pressure of liquids. He enunciated the general rule of the transmission of pressure in fluids, known as Pascal's law. He proposed the hydraulic press. He stated, apparently for the first time, the principle of the elasticity of gases. He tried to relate the behavior of fluids and gases in corresponding formulas. And he wrote some precious analyses of scientific method and of the scientific mind.

*Pascal built the first workable calculating machine in 1642.*

But science palled for him. He wrote: "I had passed a long time in the study of the abstract sciences; and the limited number with whom one can treat thereof had disgusted me with them. When I began the study of man I saw that these abstract sciences are not proper to man and that I was straying farther from my natural state in penetrating them than others were in their ignorance of them, but I thought at least to find many companions in the study of man, and that this was the true study proper to him. I was mistaken; there are still fewer who study man than geometry."

He plunged into the study of man in society, or social psychology, with a scientist's thoroughness. He had his entrée at court, in literary salons, in the high bourgeoisie of Paris. He attended the theatre, and gambled like a gentleman. Did he know love? Very likely; but if so, most of the evidence was carefully suppressed after his death.

His father died; his beloved sister Jacqueline became a nun; his married sister Gilberte was far away in Clermont. He was alone, sick, wretched. Science and man had failed him. He turned to God.

His God was the God of Jansenism. This was a movement within the Catholic Church, proposing a rigorous, fundamentalist interpretation of sacred texts and of the early Fathers. Its doctrine was grim, dwelling all on man's guilt, from which he can be redeemed only by God's rare predestined grace. The chief enemies of the Jansenists were the Jesuits, who had developed a more modernist theology, more kindly toward errant man. The headquarters of Jansenism were the convents of Port-Royal de Paris and Port-Royal des Champs. About the two Port-Royals clustered a group of adherents, the *solitaires,* mostly men of distinction fleeing the void of their world, seeking to fill the vacuum in their hearts. They devoted themselves to the meanest of labors in the service of the nuns, their Ladies.

To this center Pascal turned, in disgust with the world. And on the evening of November 23, 1654, from half past ten to half past twelve, God came in fire to give him a mystic revelation. This was the capital experience of Pascal's life. His record of that fiery vision, of the coming of certitude, joy, peace, and grace, he wrote on a sheet of paper, which is now one of the treasures of the Bibliothèque Nationale. We call it his Memorial, for during the rest of his life he carried it always with him, sewed in the lining of his coat. It was discovered only when his body was laid out for burial.

Was it God who spoke to him? Or was he victim of a hallucination? Abnormal psychology can give of his experience a description that has no need of God. But abnormal psychology can never prove anything to a mystic. He smiles, and says: "I was there. I know."

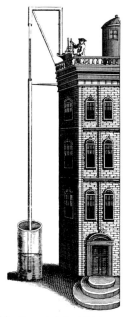

*This 1744 print depicts an experiment Pascal had performed a century before to prove that air had weight.*

After his night of fire Pascal abandoned the world and science to devote himself to the care of his soul. "What would you say of a leper who, indifferent to his gnawing disease, would talk of botany or astronomy to his doctor?" He made long retreats, doing his own housework, delighting in the earthen dish and wooden spoon which, his sister in religion told him, are the gold and precious stones of Christianity. He is said to have designed, during one of his visits, the well-windlass, still in operation. The ascription of the device to Pascal rests only on an old tradition first recorded in 1723, but there is nothing unlikely about it. His habit was always to pass from the recognition of a need to its satisfaction. Visiting Port-Royal's Little Schools, he was annoyed by the illogicality of the traditional system of teaching reading. He devised a new method, which became standard throughout the Western world. And even in little things: Irritated by waiting for sedan-chair bearers, the taxis of the time, he established in Paris the first omnibus company. Annoyed at fishing for his watch, he strapped it to his wrist.

Jansenism was under attack in those days, and Pascal was summoned to aid its defense. He did so in his *Provincial Letters,* a series of polemics addressed to the general public. These turned from defense to offense, to a savage attack on Jesuit theology and practice, particularly on casuistry and on the relaxation of moral principle by comforting concessions to man's weakness. To reach the large public Pascal found an easy, colloquial style, based on speech, which determined the form of French prose even to our own time. The effect of the *Provincial Letters* on Western man's common fund of ideas has been immense. They seem to render theology so clear and easy that every man felt himself competent to argue with the doctors. They broadcast the legend of Jesuit duplicity for all the world to read. The weapon forged against the Jesuits fell into the hands of Catholicism's enemies, and soon into those of Christianity's enemies.

The *Provincial Letters* angered rather than convinced the high Churchmen. The pope condemned Jansenist theology and forbade the order to propagandize or to recruit new members. Pascal then turned to a new and greater task—the defense of the Christian doctrine by purely rational means, an Apology for Christianity.

As his health steadily grew worse he could no longer trust his clouding memory. "Escaped thought, I wished to write it; I write instead that it escaped me." He jotted down his thoughts as they came to him, now in an illegible invalid's scribble, now in a clear, confident hand. When too weak to write he would dictate the scheme of an idea or a few happy phrases. He would return from church with a suggestion scratched on his fingernails with a pin.

These notes are the *Pensées* of Pascal, as we possess them today. Some are incomprehensible; some are commonplace memoranda; some are fragments of dialogue, imaginary conversations with objectors; some are careful developments, pages long; some are lyric outbursts, forever memorable and unforgotten. The *Pensées* make one of the great books of French literature, of all literature. They are admitted to every Five-foot Shelf, to every collection of Great Books. They are the comfort of soldiers, the companions of exiles, night voices to fevered men, songs in solitary hearts.

One can construct from the *Pensées* the general scheme of his unwritten *Apology for Christianity*. Let me string together some of his thoughts on a connecting thread:

Look first at the natural state of man. What is man in nature? A nullity in relation to infinity, an all in relation to nullity, a mid-point between nothing and everything. . . . Forever uncertain and drifting, we sail on a vast middle sea, impelled from one shore to another. To whatever fixed point we think to tie and cling, it quakes and fails us; and if we follow it, it escapes our clutch, slips away and flees us in eternal flight. Nothing stops for us. This is the state which is natural to us, and yet the most unwelcome to us; we burn with the desire to find a firm footing, a last constant base whereon to build a tower rising to infinity; but all our foundation cracks, and the earth opens, down to the abyss. . . . "The eternal silence of infinite space terrifies me."

Man is worse than weak, ignorant, and vain; he is evil. His actions are determined by self-interest, a marvelous instrument for putting out our own eyes agreeably. We would do anything for the applause we love. We even lose our life joyfully, if only people will talk about it. We hate the truth and those who tell it to us; we are only disguise, falsehood, and hypocrisy. All men naturally hate each other. What a sink is the heart of man, how full of ordure!

But look closely; something noble peers from the eyes of that ogreish face. The creature thinks; he is not utterly a stone or a brute. Visibly he is made to think; that is his dignity and merit. Man is only a reed, the weakest in nature; but he is a thinking reed. There is no need that the whole universe arm itself to crush him; a vapor, a drop of water, is enough to kill him. But even if the universe should crush him, man would still be nobler than that which kills him, because he knows he dies; and of the advantage the universe has over him the universe knows not at all. By thought man has learned the truth; by it he conceives a possible nobility. He knows himself to be wretched; a tree, a ruined house, does not know itself to be wretched. Man's very wretchedness proves his grandeur, for his are the woes of a great lord, a king unthroned.

This is man—part misery, part grandeur—two opposites which cannot be resolved. What a monster is man, judge of all things, witless worm; casket of truth, sewer of incertitude and error; glory and refuse of the universe!

Of man's duality God has given us a lucid and convincing explanation. Man was once perfect and has become corrupt through sin. His misery is natural to his present condition; his grandeur indicates his lost perfection.

Christianity offers a means of rescue from this parlous state. A sensible man will test the proposition that the Christian God exists. You could bet on that proposition. If you bet that God exists, and win, you win everything; if you lose, you lose nothing.

You will examine the overwhelming proofs of Christianity's truth, the miracles, the fulfillment of prophecies, the persistence of the faith. But in the end you will have no need of proofs based on fallible human reason. The heart has its reasons that reason does not know. It is by the heart that we know the first principles, and reason must rest on the perceptions of the heart and of instinct. There is nothing so conformant to reason as the disavowal of reason. Christianity, so rich in proofs, miracles, witnesses, signs, and wisdom, dismisses them all and declares to you that none of these can change us and make us capable of knowing and loving God, but only the virtue of the folly of the cross, without wisdom and signs.

Thus in the end Pascal surrenders all his proofs, to rest on man's need to love his God.

As Pascal meditated and wrote, his health continued to fail. He was tortured by frightful headaches, but he blessed God for his sufferings, regarding them as a fire burning away his sins little by little by a daily sacrifice. Sickness, he said, is the natural state of Christians.

He hurried the end of his sufferings by austerities. He refused any concession to appetite. He made secretly a wire belt, with sharp points turning inward against the flesh, and when he felt any stirring of pleasure or vanity he would rub his elbows against it, to wound his spirit through the body. He tortured also his sisters, forbidding any show of affection toward him, forbidding even Gilberte's children to embrace their mother: "Jesus shakes off his disciples to enter his agony. We must shake off our nearest and dearest to imitate him."

He died in 1662, aged thirty-nine. The direct cause was a hemorrhage of the brain. The great mind was poisoned by the corruption of the blood, the corruption of life.

He was as authentic a genius as our world has produced. But the logic of genius would not permit him to rest satisfied with the reasonable work of genius, the service of human knowledge. He was trying, by force of will, to pass from what he called the order of minds to the higher order of charity. He was attempting sainthood, attempting to take the heavenly city by storm. He tried to surpass and abandon humanity; he succeeded only, in pain and misery, in abandoning himself. We commonplace men and women, content with our humanity, must regard him with wonder and pity, recognizing in him a victim of the curse of genius.

*In 1710 Louis XIV drove the Jansenist nuns from Port-Royal, where, half a century before, Pascal had spent the last years of his life.*

# LOCKE

John Locke was a versatile man: an economist, diplomat, theologian, pedagogue, political scientist, and physician, as well as a philosopher. He was also an enigmatic, even a romantic figure—handsome, elusive, more than once involved in revolutionary intrigue. He guarded with elaborate care his anonymity as a political writer; he invented all kinds of little ciphers, he modified a shorthand system for the purposes of concealment, he sometimes used invisible ink. And yet it was this same John Locke who taught the world its least romantic philosophy: the theory that the only things worth saying are those that can be said clearly, that the only things worth having are those that are useful, and that the only things worth knowing are those that can be learned by methods of science.

He was one of the founders of the Age of Reason, and the one whose influence has been the most enduring. For Locke's liberal empiricism did not perish with the eighteenth century but lives on in our own day as one of the most substantial elements of the Western intellectual tradition. What is not Lockian in our culture is in a certain sense anti-Lockian. The great modern thinkers who have thought differently from him—Rousseau, for example, and Hegel and Marx—have all acknowledged Locke as the supreme exponent of ideas they wished to reject. And those who have in one way or another followed him—Benjamin Franklin and Jefferson and the pragmatists of America, or Montesquieu and Voltaire and the innumerable positivists of Europe—have invoked the name of Locke almost as a talisman.

Our modern world has been made by practical men—scientists,

*This painting of the versatile John Locke was based on a portrait by Kneller.*

By MAURICE CRANSTON

technologists, industrialists, merchants, reformers, and pioneers. Locke was the first philosopher to articulate their view of life, to encourage their aspirations and justify their deeds. No philosopher has spoken for a wider public. A Jesuit wit once said that this was because Locke was not a philosopher at all. And assuredly Locke was not a metaphysician. Unlike his great seventeenth-century contemporaries Descartes, Leibnitz, and Spinoza, Locke devised no all-embracing system to explain the nature of the universe. On the contrary, he tried systematically to show that human understanding is so limited that such knowledge is beyond men's powers to achieve. Hence the importance, for Locke, of concentrating on learning what could be learned in a piecemeal, workmanlike way, rather than elaborating intellectual structures of perfect logical coherence independent of the realm of experience.

How "Anglo-Saxon" Locke seems to the modern reader, how conspicuously different his approach from the "Continental" style of Descartes and the others. But this impression is really the measure of the effect Locke has had in shaping the modern Anglo-Saxon mind. The English philosophers who preceded Locke were every bit as rationalistic as Descartes. Thomas Hobbes was a thoroughgoing system builder, and so, in his more amateurish way, was Francis Bacon. It was Locke who made the break from the common heritage of European metaphysics, Locke who separated philosophy from speculation and confined the empire of knowledge within the boundaries of men's five senses. "Our portion," Locke wrote, "lies only here in this little spot of earth, where we and all our concernments are shut up."

*A drawing made in 1829, almost two hundred years after Locke's birth, shows the small house in Wrington in which he was born.*

But if Locke was in this sense a materialist, he was no skeptic. He detested atheism, which he regarded as the product both of a defective moral character and of rationalistic speculation about the unknowable realm of metaphysics. Locke approved of religion for one good reason: that religion was useful. Where religious doctrines had proved injurious to men's welfare, those effects were to him proof of the error of the doctrines. The basis of religion was not knowledge but faith. And Christianity he thought the most reasonable of religions because it required assent to only one essential proposition: that Christ is the Messiah. Needless to say, many of Locke's contemporaries, and many Christians of other generations, believed that the Christian religion required assent to more than this one, almost tautological article of faith. But Locke's restatement of Christianity was far removed from Hobbesian or Voltairian cynicism; Locke had a pious faith in the divine ordering of the universe and the prospect of happiness in the life after death. He had no belief in miracles, and no patience with people who had mystical experiences or visions, but in his own quiet and decorous way he was a deeply religious man.

He was born in August, 1632, in Somersetshire in the west of England. His grandfather on the paternal side had been a prosperous clothier, his father was a rather less prosperous lawyer. The years of his childhood were years of political crisis, and he was ten when the Civil War broke out between the Puritans and King Charles I. Locke's father fought on the Puritan side, as a captain in a troop raised by a local landowner named Alexander Popham. Locke afterward complained he had been "born in a storm," but it was a storm that brought him one immeasurable advantage. After the defeat of Charles I, Westminster School came under the control of Parliament, and Alexander Popham was named one of the new governors; he used the position to secure a place for the son of Captain Locke.

At Westminster Locke was taught by men whose political views were Royalist rather than Puritan. The execution of Charles I nearby in Whitehall readily stirred the sympathies of the boys for the royal victim. When Locke left in 1652 to go to Oxford, he was well prepared to react against the rule of the Puritan saints that then prevailed in the university. He had been born and bred in a Calvinist family, and his temperament remained in some ways a recognizably Puritan one; but a Royalist school opened his eyes to the virtues of the other side. The long-term effect was to make him averse to extremism of all kinds, whether in religion or politics. The short-term effect was to make him a conservative.

Locke was twenty—rather older than was usual—when he entered Oxford, and as soon as he had taken his degree he was offered a post as college tutor. His college, Christ Church, was then the most important in the university, and its senior members included men of various political persuasions. One of Locke's colleagues was a man named Edward Bagshawe, who published pamphlets advocating religious toleration, political liberty, and natural rights: ideas we now associate with the name of Locke. But Locke was far from being one of Bagshawe's supporters. In 1661, shortly after the restoration of Charles II, Locke wrote a pamphlet attacking Bagshawe's liberalism and asserting that the civil ruler had the right to enforce conformity to the established religious order. Locke never published the pamphlet; and indeed, he may have felt that there was no occasion to, since Anglican conservatism was dominant in the Restoration Parliament. The unfortunate Edward Bagshawe suffered wretchedly for his premature advocacy of liberalism: he was expelled from his place at Christ Church and died soon afterward while out on bail from Newgate Prison.

By that time Locke himself had come to agree with Bagshawe. The excitement of the restoration of Charles II stirred an authori-

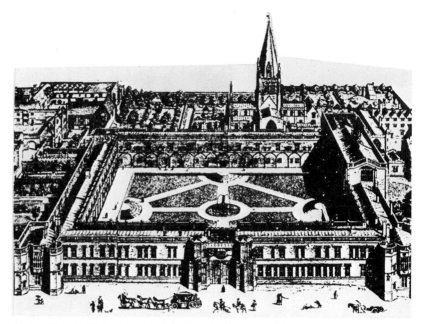

*Christ Church, Oxford, included in Locke's time such thinkers as Edward Bagshawe, whose views on toleration, liberty, and rights are now associated with Locke.*

tarian zeal in many Englishmen besides Locke, but with him it was short-lived. Then, in the summer of 1666, Locke met and made friends with a man who was to play a decisive role in the development of his political thinking, and indeed, in his thinking generally, Anthony Ashley Cooper, later the first Earl of Shaftesbury. Shaftesbury was not yet the leader of a party, but he was already the outstanding liberal politician of the time and the most forceful champion of religious toleration. Shaftesbury had spoken in Parliament against the Corporation Bill, the Bill of Uniformity, the Five–Mile Bill, and every other measure designed to curb the freedom of Nonconformists. He had thus been a spokesman for liberty while Locke still wanted to see obedience enforced, but if at the time of their first meeting Locke had not already come over to Shaftesbury's way of thinking, Shaftesbury must soon have pulled him across the last few hurdles.

Shaftesbury has a bad name in the history books. He was small, ugly, and vain; he had the reputation of a turncoat and a brothel-creeper; he was pilloried by satirical dramatists, such as John Dryden, who wrote so well that the caricature is better remembered than the truth. But Shaftesbury was certainly no fool. He was what would nowadays be called an intellectual, with a real interest in philosophy and science. And there can be no denying that he did much in his career in Parliament to defend and enlarge the liberties of all men subject to English law. Admittedly, his concern for religious toleration was prompted less by Christian forbearance and compassion than by the calculated belief that religious persecution divided and weakened a nation that would be stronger and richer if it were united. Although Shaftesbury was a nobleman and a landowner, he had all the sentiments Marx afterward ascribed to the bourgeois capitalist class. He saw more clearly than most of his contemporaries that colonial expansion and international trade might bring at the same time great fortunes to men like himself and great power to the country as a whole.

Friendship between Shaftesbury and Locke ripened quickly, and within a year of their first meeting Locke went to live at Shaftesbury's house in London, a stately *palazzo* between the Strand and the river Thames. Locke's Oxford career had been to some extent a frustrating one. As a college tutor of Christ Church he had had to teach the traditional kind of Aristotelian philosophy, which, like Thomas Hobbes before him, he regarded as a waste of time. He had been introduced by Robert Boyle to the new style of natural science, but had had no opportunity to do much laboratory work. He had taken up medicine, partly because as a doctor he would not be required by his college to take holy orders, but he had not succeeded in obtaining the Doctor of Medicine degree. Even so, it was as a domestic physician that Locke entered Shaftesbury's household, and he soon proved himself an able one. He saved his patron's life, as Shaftesbury believed, when it was threatened by a suppurating cyst of the liver. Locke had a silver tube inserted by a barber-surgeon, and this served to drain the cyst; Shaftesbury wore a tube for the rest of his life, but being a stylish man, he had the silver one replaced with another made of gold.

After the successful operation Shaftesbury decided that Locke was far too great a genius to be spending his time on medicine alone, and work of other kinds was found for him. It was under Shaftesbury's patronage that Locke discovered his true gifts. Instead of teaching Aristotle, he began reading Descartes, and the Cartesian method of systematic doubt suggested to Locke for the first time the possibility of a type of philosophy entirely different from the arid disputations of the schools. In Shaftesbury's London house Locke met regularly with a group of friends for philosophical discussions, and these conversations prompted him to write, in his fourth year under Shaftesbury's roof, the first draft of his masterpiece, the *Essay Concerning Human Understanding*. In London Locke also met Thomas Sydenham, the eminent physician, who introduced him to the new clinical medicine he had learned at Montpellier in France. Shaftesbury himself introduced Locke to the study of economics and gave him his first experience of political administration. He also urged Locke to turn his mind to political theory.

When Shaftesbury pleaded in the English Parliament for religious toleration, he wished to have it mainly for Protestant dissenters. Charles II, who favored religious toleration primarily for the sake of Catholic recusants, was for a time in agreement with him against the intolerant Anglican majority in Parliament. This was the situation in the earliest years of Locke's connection with Shaftesbury. Shaftesbury was then anti-Dutch. He had studied Holland closely, and his commercial imperialism was largely inspired by the Dutch model. He saw Holland as England's greatest rival in trade, and hence as her greatest potential enemy. Later Shaftesbury came to see France, not Holland, in this light, and he altered his policy accordingly. Since Charles II was pro-French, this change put Shaftesbury into opposition against the king, but it also gave him a principle besides trade and toleration on which to take his public stand. That principle was the Protestant religion. France was Catholic, and everything Catholic served the interests of France. France was England's natural enemy, therefore everything Catholic was inimical to England's interests. The case was easily argued, though it hardly needed to be: the very name of "popery" was enough to agitate the public.

Shaftesbury, however, as an intellectual, liked to argue and to argue well; he wanted to express his ideas in theoretical terms, and since his domestic physician was also a philosopher, he invited Locke to reflect on the general principles involved in these matters of political expediency. Was it illogical to stand both for religious toleration and for the suppression of Catholics? Locke provided Shaftesbury with a chain of reasoning that concluded it was not illogical. Catholics, Locke suggested, were not simply religious dissenters, they were a body of men who acknowledged allegiance to a foreign potentate, the pope, and who were therefore allied through Rome with the pope's true friends, the French. No country, Locke maintained, could tolerate within it people who adhered to a subversive doctrine even though it could, and should, tolerate all manner and varieties of religious worship. Catholics, he argued, were potentially disloyal; and the toleration of them was a question not of religious liberty but of national security.

Locke lived in Shaftesbury's house, on and off, until Shaftesbury's death in 1683. In those fifteen years Shaftesbury's Protestant zeal carried him to the point of organizing a rebellion. This was part of what was known as the Exclusion Crisis. Charles II refused to deny his Catholic brother, James, his legitimate right to succeed him as king. Shaftesbury persuaded Parliament to pass a measure designed to exclude James, as a Catholic, from the throne. When Charles II thwarted this maneuver, Shaftesbury replied by calling on his friends to enforce a Protestant succession by an appeal to arms. The Protestant successor Shaftesbury unwisely named was Charles's bastard son the Duke of Monmouth. Shaftesbury's supporters hesitated to back the illegitimate against the legitimate; the plot was nipped; and Shaftesbury himself escaped to Holland, there, soon afterward, to die.

These are the events that stand behind Locke's chief work of political theory, his *Two Treatises of Government*. The book was not pub-

*Locke's patron and friend, Anthony Ashley Cooper, the Earl of Shaftesbury, was depicted by an artist in the studio of John Greenhill.*

lished until six years after Shaftesbury's death, by which time Englishmen generally had come to feel sufficiently in agreement with Shaftesbury to take up arms to expel the Catholic prince—enthroned as James II—and to give his crown to his Protestant nephew William of Orange. In the preface to the published version of his book Locke said that he hoped it would "help to justify the title of King William to rule us." But Locke had conceived the book, and written most of it, while Charles II was still alive, and while the question of whether a people had the right to rebel against their king was not a backward-looking moral problem but a forward-looking moral challenge.

Much of what Locke has to say in his *Treatises of Government* is a veiled reply to the theories of Thomas Hobbes, by whom Locke had been influenced in his youth and to whom he still owed a conspicuous debt. However, the immediate purpose of Locke's argument was to attack not Hobbes but Sir Robert Filmer, author of *Patriarcha*. Filmer was not, like Hobbes, a man of genius; his name is now almost forgotten, but he was important at the time because he expounded what was substantially the official Tory ideology. Whereas Hobbes recommended obedience to any sovereign on prudential, or as we might say, scientific grounds, Filmer justified obedience to the anointed monarch by reference to the divine right of kings. The authority of lawful monarchs, including the Stuart kings, derived from God, and Filmer set out to prove this on the authority of Holy Writ. People of the time understood and responded to this kind of language, and it was because Filmer was so influential that Locke chose to answer him.

*Locke's sovereign and enemy (because of the king's Catholicism), Charles II, is portrayed above in a portrait by an unknown artist.*

Locke met Filmer on Filmer's ground. He championed the rights of men against the rights of kings, and appealed, as Filmer did, to the Scriptures. But Locke produced a more philosophical argument by combining his appeal to Biblical authority with an attempt to analyze the nature of civil society and the basis of political obligation at the highest level of abstraction. In these sections of his *Treatises* Locke comes closest to Hobbes. Like Hobbes, Locke suggests that civil society is based on a covenant, or agreement, among men to exchange the anarchic state of nature for a commonwealth ruled by law. Both are social-contract theories; but Locke has a different conception of the social contract. Locke writes as if the social contract is something that actually happened. He treats it as a fact of history that men once lived in a state of natural anarchy and then banded together to form political societies. For Hobbes the social contract is only an analytic device, a model conjured up to explain the existence of systems of law among men who are by nature selfish, rapacious, and haters of constraint.

Locke does not depict human nature in anything like these unflattering colors. He took a more Christian view of man, albeit a Christian view purged of the notion of original sin. Man, according to Locke, is a reasonable being who is subject even in the anarchic state of nature to the rule of natural law, which is the law of God made known to man by the light of reason. Locke also believed that men were endowed in the state of nature with certain natural rights, notably the rights to life, liberty, and property. And whereas Hobbes said that these rights were necessarily surrendered when men entered civil society, Locke argued that men formed civil societies precisely to defend these rights and that political sovereignty was a kind of trust given to princes by the men they ruled. It followed from Locke's analysis that if a prince's title to rule derived from a contract with the people, the people had the right to revoke the title if the prince betrayed the trust.

In this sense Locke gave men the right to revolution, the right, as he put it, to "appeal to heaven" in certain circumstances, namely in a situation in which the prince had clearly ceased to respect the rights of the people and in which a resort to force had a fair chance of instituting a just regime in place of the unjust one. But Locke was mindful of the dangers of abortive rebellions and chronic unrest, and he clearly did not intend the right to revolution to be invoked in anything except the most exceptional and critical conditions.

Locke published his *Two Treatises of Government* anonymously, and even after the Revolution of 1688 had made his opinions permissible, and fashionable, he kept his authorship a secret. He never forgot that his friend Algernon Sydney had been executed for expressing rather similar opinions during the reign of Charles II. After Shaftesbury's exile in 1682, Locke returned for a time to Oxford, but he soon became aware that several of his colleagues at Christ Church were spying on him, and when the search for Shaftesbury's political supporters reached fever pitch, Locke fled, as his patron had done, to Amsterdam.

In 1684 Locke was expelled in absence from his studentship of Christ Church by the king's express command. The following summer, after James II's accession to the throne, came the unsuccessful rebellion led by the Duke of Monmouth in the west of England. Locke was named by the English government as one of Monmouth's agents in Holland and went into hiding as Dr. van der Linden. He had certainly been in touch with Monmouth's circle in Holland, but he is unlikely to have encouraged their endeavors, for the prospects of success, which Locke considered an essential part of the justification of any revolutionary action, did not exist. In 1688, when the Prince of Orange was invited by leading English Protestants to invade the country and save them from James II's popish rule, the situation was altogether different, and Locke approved of the enterprise. He did not actually sail with William's invading fleet. He complained of ill-health and stayed in Rotterdam. At the age of fifty-six he could reasonably feel that he had had his share of danger. He returned to London quietly in 1689 in the company of the Princess of Orange, who was to become Queen Mary II of England.

Locke had spent a great deal of time during his exile in Holland in conversation with scholars and in writing. Among other things, he completed his masterpiece, the *Essay Concerning Human Understanding*. This was published under his own name in 1689, and it won him renown throughout the civilized world. He might well then have decided to spend the rest of his days in intellectual work of this same kind. But Locke had strong views about the vocation of a scholar. He had the liveliest contempt for the kind of academics "who converse with but one sort of men and read but one sort of books." He thought the philosopher should live in the world of action, and move among men of affairs. He himself, but for his poor health (he suffered from asthma), would have been willing to accept the post of an ambassador or some other administrative job. In fact, he gave a good deal of his time to the Board of Trade, which in the time of William and Mary he helped to establish. It was only the need to breathe a cleaner air than that of London that finally drove Locke into what he thought of as retirement in the country, where he did little besides reading and writing and talking with his visitors, who included the great astronomer Isaac Newton.

In the preface to his *Essay Concerning Human Understanding* Locke says that in an age of such "master builders" as "the incomparable Mr. Newton," it is for him "ambition enough to be employed as an underlabourer in clearing the ground a little and removing some of the rubbish that lies in the way of knowledge." Despite this modest explanation of his purpose, Locke is generally, and rightly, believed to have done more. He provides among other things the first modern philosophy of science.

A recurrent word—perhaps the most important word—in Locke's *Essay* is "idea." He uses this word in a distinctive manner. He does not say merely that we have ideas in our minds when we think; he says that we have ideas in our minds when we see, hear, smell, taste, or feel. The core of his epistemology is the suggestion that the objects of perception are not *things* but ideas that are derived in part from objects in the external world and that also depend to a large extent on what is contributed by the observing mind. Locke defines an "idea" as the "object of the understanding," whether that object is a concept, an entity, or an illusion.

It follows from this account of perception that men have no knowledge of things in themselves but only of those ideas in the mind that things help to generate. The human predicament, according to Locke, is that of a man permanently imprisoned in a sort of diving bell, receiving some signals from inside and some from outside the apparatus, but having no direct knowledge of the external world. However, with the range of knowledge thus diminished, Locke does not deny us the possibility of an assurance that falls short of perfect certainty. We can have probable knowledge, which is the kind of knowledge obtained by scientists. And unlike some of his more extreme successors in the empiricist tradition, Locke believed in the existence of substance. He says that substance is what stands under and props up qualities the mind perceives. Beyond that, there is only mystery. "It seems probable to me," Locke writes, "that the simple ideas we receive from sensation and reflection are the boundaries of our thoughts, beyond which the mind, whatever efforts it would make, is not able to advance one jot, nor can it make any discoveries, when it would pry in the nature and hidden causes of those ideas."

This is the reason Locke called on his readers to turn their minds from speculation to the practical activities of living. Since knowledge of the nature of things is impossible, men should "direct their thoughts," as he put it, "to the improvement of such arts and inventions, engines and utensils as might best contribute to our conveniency and delight." Locke was a utilitarian. He did not respond to the beauty of buildings and fine art, and in his writings on education he demanded, "What is the *use* of poetry?" He did not even rate scholarship very highly: "Learning," he said, "is the least part of good breeding." The proper end of education, for Locke, was the cultivation of a good character, gentlemanly manners, and an aptitude for business or some other vocation.

But if Locke was to some extent a philistine, his philistinism was in no sense an aberration. He wanted to get away from the imagination, from the vague glamour of medieval things, from unthinking adherence to tradition, from enthusiasms, mysticism, and *gloire;* away from all private, visionary insights and down to the publicly verifiable, plain, measurable facts. This desire was central to his whole mission as a philosopher and reformer.

His influence over all manner of men has been so pervasive and far-reaching as to be strictly incalculable. It is a commonplace that his political writings inspired the makers of both the American and the French revolutions. Locke's type of religion—cool, tolerant, and stripped down to a minimum creed—became fashionable among Protestants in the eighteenth century, and after an interlude of religious enthusiasm in the nineteenth century, has returned to favor in the twentieth. Locke's empiricist philosophy has never ceased to be of central importance to a civilization in which science and technology have occupied an increasingly dominant position. Even literature, for which Locke himself had so limited a taste, has been shaped by his teaching. Defoe and Sterne and Smollett are among those who were conscious of their debt to Locke; to read Samuel Richardson and Jane Austen is to be instructed in the Lockian view of life, to enter a world in which virtue is rewarded and calm self-love prevails and no one but a fool seeks to penetrate the mysteries lying beyond appearances. It could almost be said that the novel as such, at any rate the realistic, naturalistic novel, is a Lockian literary genre.

Locke is often spoken of as a prophet of democracy, and indeed, it is possible to elaborate his principle that legitimate government is based on consent into the doctrine that the people's consent should be expressed in continuous participation. But Locke himself did not care for "numerous democracy," on the grounds that practical politics is a form of estate management that only the owners of property are likely to understand. He would have detested socialism. When William Penn told him about the social services he wished to introduce in Pennsylvania, Locke protested that such innovations would be inimical to the liberty of individuals. To sacrifice liberty for the sake of philanthropy seemed to him mistaken; and if anyone had suggested sacrificing liberty for the sake of equality, he would have thought that person mad.

*Thomas Jefferson freely acknowledged his indebtedness to Locke for many of the ideas that shaped the American Republic.*

But Locke did not make a fetish of liberty. In the preface to the English translation of Locke's first *Letter for Toleration* is a sentence that reads, "Absolute liberty . . . is the thing we stand in need of." Locke did not write these words; they were contributed by the Unitarian translator. Locke did *not* believe in absolute liberty, any more than he believed in absolute knowledge. He wanted as much knowledge as possible, and he thought that the way to achieve it was to recognize how limited our information is. Hence the seeming paradox of Locke's enterprise in his *Essay* of showing how much men can know by showing how little they can know.

In Locke's political writings the technique is much the same. By demonstrating the liberty that men cannot have, Locke shows the liberty they can have. The limits of freedom are set not by the nature of political societies as such but by the necessity of protecting the life, property, and freedom of each from invasion by any other, and the safety of all from common enemies. Once these limitations are understood, no other limitations need be borne, indeed, no other limitations *should* be borne. Locke set men on the road to the greatest possible liberty by the method he used to set them on the road to the greatest possible knowledge—by teaching the impossibility of the absolute.

# ISAAC
# NEWTON
## 1642-1727

He voyaged, wrote Wordsworth, "through strange seas of Thought, alone." Such, to the poet, was "Newton with his prism and silent face." In life the eyes of that silent face were protuberant, and often they appeared glazed, which made Newton look somewhat less than intelligent. He had the dim expression of a man whose thoughts turn inward, incessantly. This was not from love of solitude or contempt for the world, for Newton looked upon the world of men and affairs with admiration, and expressed, in moments of irritation, a corresponding dislike of "mathematical trifles." He was often irritable and almost invariably somber. It was said of him by an intimate that he only laughed "but once." The event was occasioned by someone asking him what use in life geometry was. At that, Newton laughed.

The incident illustrates a profound characteristic of Newton's: he always gave the briefest possible answers to questions—even at the risk of being misunderstood. In doing so he was faithful to an austere ideal: that of mathematical elegance, the aesthetic quality that mathematicians find in the most concise of demonstrations. This formal austerity Newton elevated into a personal style and the mode of his thought. In the prime of his scientific career he compressed all of mechanics into three concise laws of motion. At the end of a long life he labored to reduce all Christian doctrine to what he took to be its minimal number of essential propositions. At all times he spoke laconically, as if an excess number of words was as inelegant as an excess number of steps in a proof. Once someone asked Newton how he had

*This portrait of Newton was done in 1710 by the court painter of King George I.*

*By* WALTER KARP

made all his discoveries, and Newton replied with perfect Newtonian concision: "By always thinking unto the problem." The answer is indisputable. He would concentrate his awesome mental powers on a problem for days, until, as he said, "gradually the light would dawn." The light that dawned was the most monumental achievement in the entire history of science, and Newton is, beyond dispute, the greatest scientist who ever lived, the only one of whom it can be said: had he not lived, the course of science might have been radically altered.

The nature of Isaac Newton's vast achievement is easier to state than to grasp, but a singular lexical fact may suggest its magnitude. During Newton's lifetime, what we know as modern science was known to many simply as "the Newtonian Philosophy." It seemed to be his own personal doctrine, and to a remarkable extent it was. He did not himself "discover" science. No one man could have done that. Science was not some compact instrument simply waiting to be used. It was rather a complex invention that men had painstakingly to put together out of quite disparate elements. Physical science is an abstruse meld. It unites, for one thing, the abstractions of mathematics, which have no physical meaning, with concrete physical phenomena, which have no inherent mathematical form. It employs a skeptical and exacting experimental method but combines that method with the most sweeping assumptions about the mechanical nature of reality. Being empirical, it assumes that truth will emerge from the investigation of things as they are; being mathematical and mechanical, it also assumes that things as they are, are never what they seem to be. How these elements might be combined is not readily apparent, but their combination and synthesis was Newton's. If modern science and its methods can be likened to a machine, then it was Newton who assembled its parts and demonstrated its power.

Newton was a great genius, and he was born, as Einstein once wistfully remarked, at exactly the right time. Around 1642, the year in which he was born, science was most markedly in pieces, although four of the greatest figures in the scientific revolution had already completed their work. The monk Nicolaus Copernicus, who began the vast enterprise by reconstructing the heavens with the sun at the center, had been dead for a century. Francis Bacon had died in 1626, Johannes Kepler in 1630, Galileo in the very year of Newton's birth. A fifth great figure, René Descartes, had already published his *Discourse on Method* and was within two years to publish his monumental treatise on the mechanical principles of philosophy. Still, it can be said that science did not yet exist; its methods and its goals had not yet been agreed upon. What the great pioneers shared (the long-dead Copernicus excepted) was not science but a deep disdain for the Aristotelian philosophy and an overriding desire to replace it with something better. In the parlance of the day, they were "new philosophers," united against the "old philosophy" of Aristotle.

Within this broad unity, however, the disunity among these pioneers was sharp and deep. For example, Galileo, Kepler's peer and acquaintance, looked with utter scorn upon Kepler's most fundamental conceptions. With characteristic audacity Kepler had supposed that an invisible "moving force," emanating like spokes from the sun, drags the planets around in their orbits and that a "mutual gravitation" between the earth and its companion the moon—like moving toward like—causes the tides. This radical conception, that even the unchanging heavens require some natural force to keep them in motion, was the foundation of all of Kepler's work in astronomy, yet Galileo professed to be "astonished" that so acute a man as Kepler "has nevertheless lent his ear and given his assent to the moon's dominion over the waters, to occult properties and to such puerilities." This was not mere backbiting; Galileo's disdain flowed directly from his deepest conception of what the new philosophy must be. That philosophy, first and foremost to Galileo, had to bid a good riddance to solar emanations, occult forces, and all such quasi-magical explanations of why things are as they are. It was not, in Galileo's view, the task of philosophers to fabricate fanciful hidden causes of things. It was their object to demonstrate *how* phenomena occur and to express this "how" in the simple, precise terms of mathematics. So Galileo himself had studied falling bodies and demonstrated that, in falling, a body will cover a distance proportional to the square of the time it spends falling that distance. But *why* bodies gravitate toward the earth's center in the first place he did not choose to say.

Descartes, arriving later, disagreed with both thinkers. That invisible forces and similar occult causes must be eliminated from philosophy was indeed one of Descartes's fundamental beliefs, as it was Galileo's. Apart from "mind," the world consists only of corporeal substance, and this matter has but one real property: extension—its size, shape, and volume. No body, for example, possesses color. It merely arouses in us, due to its particular physical structure, a certain subjective sensation that we deem its color to be. The only real differences between any two things are the differences in size, shape, arrangement, and motions of the tiny corporeal particles comprising them. Bald matter and its motion must—and will—explain everything. In this stark mechanical world of Descartes's no forces, powers, spirits, or attractions exist. If a body begins to move, that motion can have but one cause: the impact upon that body of another moving body. So, according to Descartes, bodies fall to the earth because they are pushed downward by extremely fine particles that swirl around our

*Newton's family were yeoman farmers who had bought Woolsthorpe Manor. It was here that an apple's fall suggested to Newton his gravitation theory.*

planet, while other vast whirlpools of these same fine particles keep the planets moving in circles.

Descartes also found Galileo's new science inadequate. Galileo had hoped to derive certain truths through a mathematical analysis of how particular phenomena occur. In Descartes's view, however, no certainty could come of such a piecemeal enterprise. There was, he believed, but one means to certainty. The philosopher must begin with a few indisputable axioms, which he discovers by introspection. From these axioms, he then proceeds, as far as possible, to deduce by strict logic all the other basic laws and rules of nature. Galileo had supplied no such first principles. Therefore, in Descartes's eyes, he had attempted to build a house from the roof down.

The Cartesian philosophy was lucid, comprehensive, and enormously persuasive; yet not even Descartes was taken to represent all that was valued in the new philosophy. Contemporary students of nature had also to reckon with Francis Bacon, whose new program for "the advancement of learning" was diametrically opposed in spirit to the philosophy of Descartes.

Between these two new philosophers the disparities were glaring. Descartes bade men to start with first principles and then, by deduction, to explain the phenomena of the world. Bacon bade men to begin by examining phenomena and then, by induction, to work up gradually to the most general principles. Bacon called upon men to open their eyes wide to the subtle powers of nature, and he recommended experimentation as the prime means to force nature to reveal yet more of her hidden powers. Descartes, on the other hand, asked men to shut their eyes and meditate on the "clear and distinct ideas" they found within themselves.

Thus there existed, in no clear interrelationships, the mathematical approach of Galileo, the mechanical philosophy of Descartes, the experimentalism of Bacon, and, more obscurely, the abstruse astronomy of Kepler. Such were the leading elements of the "new philosophy" when Newton was growing up in Lincolnshire.

The Newtons were yeoman farmers who lived for some time in a meager hamlet known as Woolsthorpe. They had only one known distinction: whereas their neighbors resided in small farmhouses and thatched cottages, the Newtons had scraped up enough money to purchase the hamlet's only stone manor house. They looked on themselves as distant kinsmen of a certain Sir John Newton, Bart., and this keen sense of rank stayed with Newton all his life. As a child, however, he was virtually an orphan and a somewhat neglected one. His father had died some months before he was born, and his mother, upon remarrying a neighboring rector, left him for several years with his grandmother. In and around Woolsthorpe he was remembered

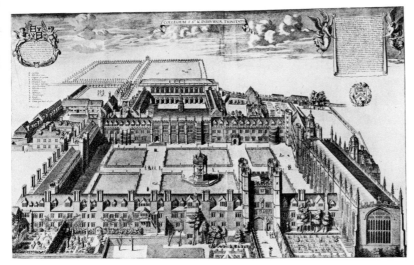

*Trinity College, Cambridge, was Newton's home as an undergraduate and a fellow.*

as "always a sober, silent, thinking lad, and was never known scarce to play with the boys abroad." He amused his elders by devising ingenious instruments such as sundials and water clocks. He also collected magic tricks and formulas for compounding colored inks, which he duly recorded in a notebook.

Altogether he was the kind of solitary, self-sufficient youth we would instantly describe today as "mechanically inclined." Newton was also, even as a boy, much given to laying down magisterial rules of method. "Of Drawing with ye Pen," he solemnly entitled one section of entries in his notebook, and offered the following basic rule for drawing "landskips": "If you express ye sunn make it riseing or setting behind some hill; but never express ye moon or starrs but up on necessity." Thus Isaac Newton on art, aged about sixteen. The human subjects of this kingly impulse to legislate would not materialize for a long time; outwardly Newton was humble, mild, and anxious to please.

A slight scholarly superiority to the other local farm boys saved him from his preordained fate of plowing furrows in Lincolnshire. At eighteen, thanks to his uncle's intercession with his mother, he was sent off to Trinity College, Cambridge, which was to be his home for the next thirty-five years. Humbleness followed Newton to the university. At Trinity he was a subsizar, a scholar who paid his way by doing menial chores for his fellow Trinity men.

As an undergraduate Newton was particularly interested in mathematics, astronomy, and optics, but he was mainly learning what there was to learn, and he won no special honors beyond being accepted for graduate studies. Awarded his bachelor's degree in January, 1665, he probably seemed merely another future don destined to teach mathematics to an endless line of indifferent Trinity students.

This lack of distinction, however, was not due to the fact that Newton's genius was ripening slowly. His genius did not ripen. It simply burst forth. Two years after Newton completed his undergraduate studies, it could be said that of all the achievements of seventeenth-century science the better half were located, then and there, inside Newton's head—and there they stayed for some time, unknown to anybody. By the end of 1666 he had invented calculus, one of the supreme accomplishments in mathematics. He had discovered a profound truth about the nature of light and color, one of the foremost achievements of experimental investigation. He had, while espying an apple fall at Woolsthorpe, conceived the moon as a body "falling" perpetually toward the earth, like the apple, and had devised a mathematical way to express the power producing these falls. He was on the way, that is, to arriving at his theory of universal gravitation, the greatest single discovery in physical science.

The gifts of mind Newton brought to bear on these topics were, of course, extraordinary, but the most extraordinary thing about them was their presence in the same person. The gifts were such that the possession of any one of them seems to preclude possession of the others. In the history of science the most brilliant experimental investigators have rarely been notable theoreticians; the finest theoreticians—Einstein, for example—have rarely been superior, or even adequate, experimental scientists. Yet Newton was a supreme experimental scientist and a supreme theoretical scientist as well. What is more, he alone among the very great scientists was one of the supreme figures in the realm of pure mathematics. He was to achieve in three distinct modes of thought what only a few scientists have been able to achieve in one. Such were the gifts that Newton, in his twenty-fourth year, was applying to certain comprehensive topics that took his silent fancy.

Newton's optical work—his favorite study and his first published effort—took its departure from the phenomenon of color and from the new mechanical philosophy of Descartes. There was nothing unusual in this. By the 1660's there was scarcely a new philosopher who was not, in some degree, a "mechanical" philosopher as well. Even professed Baconians resorted to invisible particles and the motions of these particles to explain their experimental findings. With such principles they could explain virtually anything. Given a set of facts, say those concerning air pressure, the philosopher would construct a hypothetical mechanism of invisible aerial particles endowed with hypothetical shapes and motions that seemed capable of producing the observed phenomena. Devising such mechanisms was becoming the chief business of natural philosophy; experimentation, as a result, tended to be merely illustrative. If a thinker likened air particles to little balls of wool, he could experiment with little balls of wool to show that they will expand after they are compressed—like the air.

Light, according to the leading men of science, consisted of wave-like motions in Descartes's whirling subtle matter, or ether. These waves radiated evenly from a light source, like ripples in a pond when a pebble is dropped into it. Light from the sun was pure, homogeneous, and, of course, colorless. Color, then, was the effect produced when this uniform sunlight became disturbed or modified in some mechanical way or other. Light modified in one way produced one sort of color sensation. The same colorless light striking a body with a different sort of surface structure would be modified in a different way and so produce a different sort of color sensation. Since light when it passes through a prism will appear as a spectrum of colors on a wall, it was held that the prism, in refracting (i.e., bending) the light passing through it, also disturbed white light and so produced the spectrum. Such was the prevailing view when young Newton bought some prisms and pushed the experimental method farther than it had probably ever been pushed.

What Newton did was grasp a certain discrepant fact that he refused to explain away until it yielded the basis of an extraordinary discovery. This discrepancy arose in a precise experiment he made with a prism after many months of trial. He cut a circular hole, one-quarter inch in diameter, in the closed shutter of his room at Trinity College. Through this hole a narrow beam of sunlight entered his darkened chamber. Placing a prism near the hole, he cast the well-known spectrum of colors against the opposite wall. What he now saw, with the eye of a mathematician, others had seen but overlooked: the spectrum of colors, instead of being circular—because the hole in the shutter was circular—was an oblong. This curious elongation of the circle seized his attention.

As Newton well knew, there existed a mathematical law, discovered by Descartes, for determining how much a ray of light will be bent when it passes through a prism at any given angle. According to that law the beam, in passing through Newton's prism, ought to have cast upon the opposite wall a circle of colors $2\frac{5}{8}$ inches in diameter. The oblong image, he found, was indeed $2\frac{5}{8}$ inches *wide,* but it was $13\frac{1}{4}$ inches *high*—five times longer than it should have been. The top part of the beam had been bent more than it ought to have been according to the law of refraction; the bottom part of the beam less, which was why the beam's height was elongated. Something was radically wrong with the beautifully precise law of refraction.

Here Newton might have stopped. There was a ready means to explain away the odd elongation. Such an explanation followed, moreover, from the very nature of color itself. Newton could have said (as his adversaries eventually *did* say) that the prism, in modifying the light waves to produce colors, also spread them out somewhat to produce this elongation. It was that simple, and quite in line with mechanical principles. The explanation by "spreading," however, had one drawback; it would mean setting aside the law of refraction, and this Newton found disagreeable. Great scientists, it has been said, are perfect mixtures of credulity and skepticism. Newton, for reasons that go straight to the heart of his scientific method, chose to believe the law of refraction and to doubt the doctrine of colors.

He set aside for the moment the whole question of colors and focused his attention solely on this apparent flaw in the regularity of refraction. Taking a second prism, he placed it between the first prism and the wall and intercepted different parts of the refracted beam. This was the "crucial experiment." In making it Newton discovered that the part of the beam that was bent too much the first time was also bent too much when refracted a second time—exactly the same amount too much. The part of the beam that was bent too little was, when refracted again, again bent too little—exactly the same amount too little. Any time a given part of the beam was refracted by the prism, it always exhibited the same fixed degree of bending, or refrangibility. Refraction, in other words, was lawful and regular for the several parts of the light beam, though not for the beam as a whole. "And so," Newton concluded, "the true cause of the length of that Image was detected to be no other, than that *Light* consists of Rays *differently refrangible,* which . . . were, according to their degrees of refrangibility, transmitted towards divers parts of the wall."

Now it was not lost upon Newton that rays "differently refrangible" were also differently colored. When his second prism intercepted the blue part of the refracted beam, not only did that part bend to the same degree, it also remained blue. No amount of further refraction could change the color, just as no amount of further refraction could change that ray's degree of refrangibility. "To the same degree of Refrangibility," he then concluded, "ever belongs the same color, and to the same color ever belongs the same degree of Refrangibility."

As Newton now saw, something was wrong with the prevailing theory of colors. The doctrine that colors are produced when pure colorless light is disturbed could not be sustained. According to that theory, the prism causes a change in homogeneous light that results in the production of a color. A second refraction of this changed light ought, therefore, to change it more, producing yet another color. This was not the case. Blue remained blue, red stayed red. These and five other "primary colors" could not be changed no matter how many times they were refracted. The prism, therefore, did not modify

*A page from Newton's early account books lists a gift of thirty pounds from his mother for his college fees.*

pure white light, it merely *separated* different parts of white light according to their fixed and distinctive degrees of bending. So Newton concluded: "Colors are not *Qualifications* [i.e., modifications] *of Light,* derived from Refractions, or Reflections of natural Bodies (as tis generally believed), but *Original* and *connate properties,* which in divers Rays are divers. Some Rays are disposed to exhibit a red color and no other; some a yellow and no other . . ." White light, pure homogeneous light from the sun, was not, as everyone believed, pure and homogeneous at all. It was, said Newton, "a confused aggregate of Rays" endowed with different degrees of refrangibility and different dispositions to cause a color sensation within us. Against all reason, so it seemed, colors were inherent in ordinary colorless light.

In an essay of thirteen mercilessly concise pages Newton set forth his discovery. Then in 1672, six years after making it, he presented it to the world of science, or rather to its illustrious new epitome, the Royal Society of London. With no false modesty whatever he described it to the membership as "the oddest if not the most considerable detection wch hath hitherto beene made in the operations of Nature." With that, Newton sat back to await acclaim. Instead, to his dismay, he found himself in the most exasperating of disputes.

The two great students of light, Robert Hooke at the Royal Society and Christian Huygens of the French Académie des Sciences, had their own theory of colors—the prevailing one. More decisively, they had their own ingrained conception of what the new mechanical philosophy was supposed to be. To them it meant devising mechanical hypotheses to explain given sets of facts. Newton had, as they saw it, explained colors by *supposing* that seven primary colors somehow pre-existed in white light, a hypothesis hard to believe. Then, to explain how a prism produces the colored spectrum, Newton, in their view, had further supposed that these differently colored rays were differently refrangible. It was, they conceded, an "ingenious" hypothesis, though distinctly inferior to their own.

With increasing vexation Newton tried to explain to his critics that they had turned his discovery upside down. He had not invented a hypothesis about color and then fitted it to the facts. The very reverse was true. He had found directly from experiment "certain properties of light . . . which if I did not know to be true, I should prefer to reject as vain and empty speculation, than acknowledge even as hypothesis." He had not supposed that white light was a confused bundle of rays differently refrangible; he was driven to that conclusion by his experimental findings. These findings could not be explained by the prevailing theory, as he pointed out to Hooke with biting scorn. His critics remained unconvinced.

For Newton it was a bitter experience. He felt cheated and victimized. He had offered the world a great new discovery, but the grandees of science had robbed him of his credit because his discovery did not square with their own mechanical preconceptions. To Newton, who had not the smallest doubt about his own immense superiority, there was only one recourse: the grandees must be taught like children what the true method of philosophy is. He told them: "First, to inquire directly into the properties of things, and establish them by experiment; and then to proceed more slowly to hypotheses for explaining them. For hypotheses should be subservient only in explaining the properties of things, but not assumed in determining them." To call an experimentally discovered property false because it contradicts a plausible hypothesis is to reverse the order of inquiry. Such was Newton's advice to his elders, but he was only a young and obscure mathematics professor, and it would take more than a few irate letters to imprint his conception of science on the minds of men.

After this, his first public encounter with other men, Newton was bitter in the way that a haughty and capricious child is bitter. He fumed and sulked and withdrew into the thick shell of his temperament. From Cambridge he was heard to mutter peevishly that natural philosophy was "litigious" and filled with "no end of fancying." When men approached him with scientific questions, he could reply loftily that he had "laid aside philosophical speculations"; and in fact he often did. For long periods of time he preferred investigating the doctrine of the Trinity (which he secretly doubted), the legal authority of the Nicene Council (which he wished to undermine), and the prophecies in the Book of Daniel (which he hoped to decipher). For Robert Hooke, who dared to criticize him before the Royal Society, he burned with barely concealed hatred. It was to Hooke, actually, that Newton addressed his famous "modest" remark that if he had seen farther, it was by standing on the shoulders of giants. He meant the remark as a pointed reminder that he did in fact see farther.

Rule or sulk was the principle of Newton's life, until the day would come when he would rule like a monarch. In the meantime he led a monkish life at Cambridge as a fellow of Trinity College and Lucasian Professor of Mathematics who gave abstruse public lectures that few students attended and nobody understood. He did not have many friends at the university, which he looked on as a backwater not quite fit for a gentleman. There was little warmth in his character, and what there was seemed reserved for his widowed mother, whom he duly visited each year at Woolsthorpe.

For a man who hated to be wrong—who dreaded even appearing to be wrong—the theory of universal gravitation presented a vexatious quandary, and one that Newton lived with for a long time. Unless that theory could be proved true beyond a doubt, it would be rejected by every rational thinker as false, pernicious, and even laughable. This is the most important historical fact about the theory of gravitation.

As its prime challenge to credibility the gravity doctrine proposes that the center of a material body can, in some utterly mysterious fashion, draw, or "attract," another body across millions of miles of space without being in any way in contact with it. This inexplicable "action-at-a-distance" is further held to act instantaneously, regardless of how far apart the two bodies are. It is, moreover, a power that is miraculously inexhaustible, for it never seems to weaken. It is a power, too, that nothing whatever can balk or diminish, since it penetrates every known substance. It is everywhere and nowhere, a parodoxical principle that cannot, on the face of it, be accepted.

At the time that Newton conceived it, this principle of attraction was never less likely to be accepted, for it ran counter to everything that the new philosophy so confidently represented. By most people who thought about the matter at all, action-at-a-distance was held to be impossible. To mechanical philosophers the only conceivable cause that could operate in nature was the impact of one body upon another. Attractive powers were simply part of that vast arsenal of nonsense that the "moderns" had relegated to the ash heap: something not to be proposed, as one new philosopher remarked, "if you do not wish to be laughed at." A philosopher who was merely rational would not have entertained the idea of a universal attraction even in the privacy of his thoughts. This is not a rhetorical assertion. The fundamental discovery that points the way to universal gravitation was made independently by both Newton and Huygens. With this discovery—great in itself—Huygens did nothing, Newton everything.

This discovery is known as the law of centrifugal force. As a problem to be solved it arose from Descartes's inertia principle: a material body, unless impeded by another body, will naturally move in a straight-line course at constant speed forever. When a body travels in a circle, therefore, it must be constantly "endeavoring" to move in its natural rectilinear course along a tangent to the circle. A body twirling on a string is pulled back by the string, but the endeavor, as Huygens observed, is felt as a "tension" on the taut string. Both Newton and Huygens found a means to express mathematically this endeavor to fly from the center of rotation. Gifted with hindsight, we see its immediate application to the heavens, where the planets, too, move in orbits. Plainly they must be endeavoring to fly from their centers of rotation. Some power, therefore, equal to this centrifugal tendency must be exerted in the opposite direction, because the planets do not, obviously, fly away. Great scientist though Huygens was, it never occurred to him to conceive of this counterpower as a pull, or attraction. Indeed, why should it have? Planets are not attached to the sun by strings, and imagining invisible strings or immaterial pulls would be puerile. Huygens supposed, as Descartes had, that ethereal whirlpools continuously *push* each planet back into its orbit, just as a whirlpool surrounding the earth causes a piece of fruit to be pushed toward the earth's center. Apples could have fallen at Huygens's feet through eternity, and he would never have supposed otherwise. Being a rational philosopher, he was a prisoner of the "true and sane philosophy" all his life. Newton was not, for he was never merely a rational philosopher.

Once again, a perfect mixture of credulity and skepticism lay behind the intuitions of genius. A conviction more powerful than the "true and sane philosophy" colored Newton's thoughts, and in doing so, liberated them. The conviction was a religious one. Consistent with his doubts about Christ's divinity, Newton believed as fervently as any Lincolnshire Puritan in the fierce, absolute God of the Old Testament, the Hebraic God of arbitrary power and mysterious ways. Newton believed, and longed to find reason for his belief, that the providential God had not only created the world but ruled it and sustained it every moment by his will. A Supreme Being who merely created a world that then ran by itself was, to Newton, the god of disguised infidels like René Descartes, whom he detested as vehemently as any rustic clergyman.

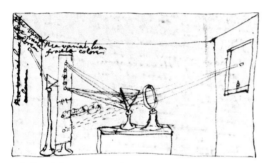

*A sketch by Newton shows the result of a crucial experiment—the diffraction of light by a prism.*

To prove that God truly governed and sustained his creation was the deepest purpose of Newton's life. This purpose and conviction gave Newton the liberty to doubt that the impact of bodies was the ultimate cause of all natural phenomena. He was willing, indeed eager, to imagine that the ultimate principle was not matter at all but immaterial powers: "active principles," he called them, directly propagated by the lawful will of God. If such immaterial powers demonstrably existed, then the world could not survive without the Creator, and the providence of God would be upheld against the infidelity of the mechanical philosophy.

So it was not inconceivable to Newton, for example, that bodies should fall toward the earth's center by means of an immaterial attractive power exerted toward the earth's center. Thus, when the famed apple fell, he was free to conceive that the very same power extended far beyond the earth's surface and caused the moon, too, to "fall" toward the earth. Never mind that such a power would make no sense to the new philosophers; it could be investigated nonetheless. Clearly this "fall," which was directed toward the earth's center, was equal to the moon's tendency to fly from that center, since the moon remained in its path. Because he now knew how to measure the centrifugal force, Newton could also calculate this balancing tendency. Specifically, he could calculate how far in any one second the moon was being pulled toward the earth. Also he knew how far gravity would draw a falling apple in one second's time: 16.1 feet. Were the force pulling the moon and the force pulling the apple the same force? By comparing the two one-second falls Newton reached an interesting result. The power, if indeed it was the same power, grew weaker the farther away from the earth it had to act. What was more tantalizing, it grew weaker almost but not quite according to a simple mathematical rule: the gravitational force diminished in proportion to the square of the distance; at three times the distance, it was one-ninth its strength, and so forth. Almost but not quite, since Newton's first calculations were somewhat crude. This was the point he had reached as far back as 1666 at Woolsthorpe, before anybody but his professors knew his name. For thirteen more years Newton kept his gravitational work at the back of his mind.

The next great move came in 1679, when Newton discovered to his dismay that there was one other man entertaining the idea of a gravitational attraction varying inversely with the square of the distance. He was none other than the man Newton hated most: Robert Hooke. Gravitation was, in Hooke's hands, only a daring idea, and beyond a few close friends, including the mathematician-turned-architect Christopher Wren, nobody paid the least attention to Hooke's grandiose "hypothesis." Nobody, that is, until he flaunted it before Newton in the course of a frigidly polite exchange of letters. That a "mere smatterer in mathematics," as Newton referred to Hooke, should discourse boldly to *him* about an inverse-square law of gravity was more than Newton could bear. He sat down to prove to himself that he knew more about the matter than Hooke would ever know. Using calculus, the mighty mathematical tool that he himself had invented (and so far kept to himself), Newton brought the gravity law one giant step closer to reality. He demonstrated mathematically that such a force, varying inversely with the square of the distance, would "bend" a moving body into an exactly elliptical orbit. This was a fundamental confirmation of the theory, for by Kepler's law the ellipse is the actual path of the planets. Since such a proof was beyond the powers of anybody, including Hooke, Newton was satisfied to drop the subject again without reporting his results.

Such secretiveness is more bizarre even than it might seem. Had Newton turned his back, hermit-fashion, on the world, it would have been odd but understandable. But Newton had not turned his back on the world. In 1679 he hungered as much as ever for honors and acclaim and the friendship of celebrated men. He longed to be praised, but he feared being criticized. This was the fine torture Newton's character had contrived for him: to be wretchedly suspended between fear of the world and a hunger for worldly success. So, in the dim privacy of his chambers, he often wrote long, polished essays, drafting them not once but several times, as if the very act of writing them out allayed his hunger to be read and recognized.

The forces pushing and pulling at him must have been nearly in balance, because four years after triumphing over Hooke the coaxing of a tactful stranger convinced Newton to declare all that he knew about universal gravitation. The stranger, a brilliant young astronomer named Edmund Halley, simply approached Newton as he liked to be approached: as a supplicant begging help from the master. Halley now informed Newton that Hooke and Wren had been toying with the idea of a universal attraction but could explain nothing with it. If such a force existed, he asked Newton, what path would it move the planets in? "An ellipse," said Newton, remarking casually that he had proved the proposition but had mislaid the papers. The record of that famous meeting is lost, but we can image a thunderstruck Halley begging the strange man before him to set it all down. This Newton promptly did. In twenty months of incredibly concentrated effort Newton completed the greatest single work in the history of science: the *Philosophiae Naturalis Principia Mathematica,* or the *Mathematical Principles of Natural Philosophy.* Published at Halley's expense, it appeared in the summer of 1687 and sold for seven shillings.

Simply to look at, the *Principia* is dazzling. It appears to be some kind of awesome geometry book, packed with propositions and theorems that are rigidly demonstrated by geometric proofs accompanied by intricate diagrams. It looks, moreover, like a geometry raised to some higher power, for its subject is not static lines and areas, but "forces" that vary and "bodies" that move and accelerate; a geometry that is to the old geometry of Euclid as a motion picture is to a still photograph. Like a geometry book, too, the *Principia* is set forth in the grand deductive manner of ancient Greek mathematics. Beginning with a brief set of definitions and axioms—the three laws of motion—Newton proceeds step by step to deduce a vast array of propositions of ever-increasing complexity; some of them, indeed, deduced solely for the sake of deducing them. Having at last unburdened his mind, Newton, it seems, was determined to empty it. The relentless march of the proofs reaches its grand climax in Book III with Newton's demonstration of the truly astounding proposition that between *any* two bodies in the universe there exists a mutual attraction that varies inversely with the square of the distance between them and directly with the product of their masses. This is the law of "universal gravitation." *Quod erat demonstrandum* Newton could justly write. Nonetheless it is certainly action-at-a-distance with a vengeance, for gravity, according to Newton, acts not only between the vast heavenly bodies but between any two particles of matter whatever. How two flecks of dust can attract each other according to Newton's law is something no mechanism of hypothetical pushes could ever explain.

Nor does the *Principia* end here. With his law firmly established, Newton now "returns to the phenomena," as he says, in order to unravel mysteries that had baffled thinkers for millenniums. With his law he will explain mathematically why the twice-daily tides occur and why there are spring tides and neap tides. He will even calculate how high the tide reaches in mid-ocean. He will explain, at last, the mysterious path of the comets, demonstrate that the globular earth is flattened at the poles and calculate by how much. He will estimate the mass of the sun and planets and explain why the axis of the earth makes its own revolution once every twenty-five thousand years. He will explain the general motions of the moon and account mathematically for a variety of subtle perturbations in the moon's motions that had long puzzled other astronomers. By his law of gravitation he will not only explain a vast array of phenomena, he will explain them in terms more precise than anyone

*William Blake saw Newton as a demonic calculator.*

had dreamed possible. From only a few laws of motion, themselves derived from phenomena, he has locked the universe into one lawful system, as comprehensive as the most daring speculations of ancient Greek philosophy and as precise in its operation as a railway timetable.

Yet the fundamental problem remained: what, after all, is this impalpable attractive force that acts at a distance, against all reason, all philosophy, and all sound sense? The question haunts the pages of the *Principia*, as it must have haunted Newton himself. Time and again he anxiously warns his readers not to misunderstand him. He does *not* believe that a material body can literally "attract" another body from a distance. The attractive force of which he speaks is not a physical pull at all. He is, he explains, "considering those forces not physically, but mathematically: wherefore the reader is not to imagine that by those words I anywhere take upon me to define the kind, or the manner of any action, the causes or the physical reason thereof, or that I attribute forces, in a true and physical sense, to certain centres (which are only mathematical points); when at any time I happen to speak of centres as attracting, or as endued with attractive powers." And again, "I here design only to give a mathematical notion of those forces, without considering their physical causes and seats."

What, then, is "force" if it is not a physical cause? To this question Newton's revolutionary answer is this: force is the "efficacy" of a cause unspecified and unknown. It is the mathematical measure of the strength of whatever unknown cause it is "that propagates it." The gravitational force does not cause a planet to move toward the sun. It is the *measure* of the strength of whatever it is that causes this motion. Though the cause of this force (and other forces) is unknown, forces themselves can be determined exactly, and this is all that philosophy requires. The force of a cause can be determined, in fact, by the three laws of motion. As the first law states, a body moves naturally in a straight line at uniform speed. Therefore, by this law, when the uniform motion is changed in any way, we know that some cause is operating on that body. The strength, or force, of that cause is measured by the *amount* of change the cause induces, or more strictly, by the amount of acceleration the cause induces in a body of a given mass. As to the explanation of the gravitational force, says Newton, he has not been able to discover it empirically "and I frame no hypotheses. . . . To us it is enough that gravity does really exist, and act according to the laws which we have explained, and abundantly serves to account for all the motions of the celestial bodies, and of our sea."

*In 1679 Newton wrote Robert Hooke, including the erroneous solution of a gravity problem shown above. Hooke's blunt correction led Newton to perfect his theory of gravity.*

"To us it is enough." With that regal pronouncement Newton summed up the meaning of his revolution in natural philosophy. Just as he had expected, philosophers like Huygens declared that the *Principia* was incomplete. For all the book's grandeur, they said, its author had failed to give a mechanical explanation of his gravitational force. It may be true, they argued, that planets move toward the sun in accordance with Newton's law, but surely natural philosophy must explain why they do so in terms of the material push that must propel them. Newton had said that forces measure causes unknown, but why should philosophers leave these causes unknown? Such a question is not really answerable, and Newton's reply—it cannot be called an argument—was simply: "To us it is enough." He, Newton, was satisfied. Beyond such concepts as he had laid down— beyond force, mass, and acceleration—philosophy could not go without dribbling away into vain speculation.

"The whole burden of philosophy seems to consist in this—from the phenomena of motions to investigate the forces of nature, and then from these forces to demonstrate the other phenomena." Indeed, he suggested with truly prophetic intuition, there are probably other forces like gravity that operate in nature. "Have not small particles of Bodies certain Powers, Virtues, or Forces by which they act at a distance . . . for producing a great part of the Phenomena of Nature?" If so, philosophers must investigate them and find the laws governing their operation.

There was no way for Newton to prove that the "whole burden of philosophy" was one thing and not another. In brief time, however, men came to agree with him. He conquered, not by force of argument, but by the overwhelming power of his peerless example: the *Principia Mathematica* itself. If, as Newton said, the law of gravitation is but a sample of his "mathematical way," then men agreed that science need go no farther than Newton had already gone. Forces may measure causes unknown, but Newton's new mathematical science of forces was more comprehensive, more precise, and more rigorous than anything natural philosophy had ever seen before. It was also freer; for Newton's belief was not a shackle but a liberation, and that liberation is what distinguishes modern science from all previous philosophies.

The modern scientist, disciple of Newton, does not ask what causes a force, or what energy is, or how charged particles can attract each other. It is enough for scientists that concepts like force or energy be mathematically precise, derivable from experiment, and capable of explanation according to Newtonian standards of precision. What metaphysicians might say—what "reason" might demand—is of little concern to scientists; they have been freed by Newton's *Principia* to comprehend nature without deciding what nature ultimately is.

This was exactly how Newton wanted it to turn out, though his reasons were only partly scientific and only partly revealed. The truth was that he had no doubt about the mysterious cause that propagated the force of his system. It was God himself, "incorporeal, living, intelligent, omnipresent," though Newton never dared say so outright. He could only hope that men might follow his example and cease to arrogate to matter what properly belonged to God. Ironically, the mathematical method, through which science won its freedom, was the means by which Newton hoped to preserve God's place as ruler and sustainer of his creation. Like Janus, he faced two ways—toward the science of the future and the faith of the past.

Newton was forty-four when the *Principia* appeared. He had forty more years to live and to enjoy his fame, which grew more immense with each passing year until in time he found himself being looked upon as a kind of semideity. Honors and emoluments came one by one, but too slowly in the first few years to prevent Newton from suffering a nervous breakdown, during which he wildly accused John Locke of "embroiling" him with women. Shortly afterward he begged

Locke, like a child, to forgive him. Then his iron pose of aloofness cloaked him once more and did so until the end of his life.

In 1696 Newton's admirers obtained for him the very crown of his ambition: an honorable post in His Majesty's government. He was named first Warden, and later Master, of the Mint. With that appointment Newton packed up and left Cambridge and never looked back. The institution that had housed and sustained him for thirty-five years he now left behind as if it were a wretched village and he a young man burning to try the metropolis. He bought a handsome house in London, rode in a coach, and entertained splendidly. In 1703, when Hooke died, he condescended to become president of the Royal Society. In 1705 he was knighted by Queen Anne, and in an official pedigree he feigned the hypothesis that he was a gentleman by birth as well as merit. He became a favorite of the court and an acquaintance of the celebrated, who hung on his words—which were as few and as final as ever. Except for revising the *Principia* and publishing his early work in optics, he all but abandoned science. Once, when Continental mathematicians sent him a problem to be solved, Newton exploded in rage. "I do not love to be printed upon every occasion much less to be dunned and teezed by foreigners about Mathematical things or to be thought by our own people to be *trifling* away my time about them when I should be about ye King's business." No doubt it irked him to be taken for a mere mathematician.

To amuse himself, Newton delved deeply into the kind of crabbed erudition that was already growing old-fashioned. As his avocation for thirty years, he worked on a chronology that would co-ordinate the events in ancient pagan history with the events in basic history, namely the historical narrative of the Bible. He worked, too, to decipher such prophetic symbols as the seven vials and the seven trumpets and hoped that by translating the Biblical term "magi" into its proper meaning of "cheats and liars" he might infer post-Biblical history from prophetic Biblical texts. A skeptical Frenchman explained such scholarly aberrations in the great man by supposing that he had never recovered from his nervous breakdown. This was not true, yet it must be said there *was* something amiss with Newton in spite of his fame and his prosperity. Men noticed the glazed look in his eye and his curious inattention even in the midst of the bright society that he had longed for during his years at Cambridge. By now, his days of "thinking unto the problem" were over; perhaps he realized they were better days than he had ever thought. He seemed, at any rate, estranged and homeless. Once, late in his life, there was a gathering of Lincolnshire men at a London tavern, and upstairs, where the gentry mingled, a guest was told that a certain odd figure was sitting downstairs among the commoners. The man came down and found the aged Sir Isaac sitting among the sons of Lincolnshire plowmen, quite silent, but apparently content; Woolsthorpe's "sober, silent, thinking lad" momentarily at peace.

Doubtless Newton's heart was not in the age in which he now lived and which looked upon him as its special hero. Infidelity and skepticism seemed to be rising. There were signs that his own grand vindication of God's providence might prove futile in the end. Eager Newtonians were coming to conceive of gravity as an inherent property of matter and so were resuscitating materialism in a new, Newtonian form. He was an old man by now, and he felt urgently the need to set his faith upon lasting foundations. He sat down to write what he called "A Short Scheme of the True Religion," a set of propositions that would both contain the essence of religion and yet withstand skeptical assault. He wrote it once, then a second time; then again, and then twice more. He could not get it right. The true religion evaded him.

In the year 1727, at the age of eighty-four, Newton died, and six peers of the realm carried his coffin to Westminster Abbey. With his quaint Biblical prophecies and his Hebraic God he was by then something of a relic; for a skeptical, experimental generation was rising, and it was out of spirit with his deepest concerns. Ironically, historians sometimes call this dawning era the Newtonian Age.

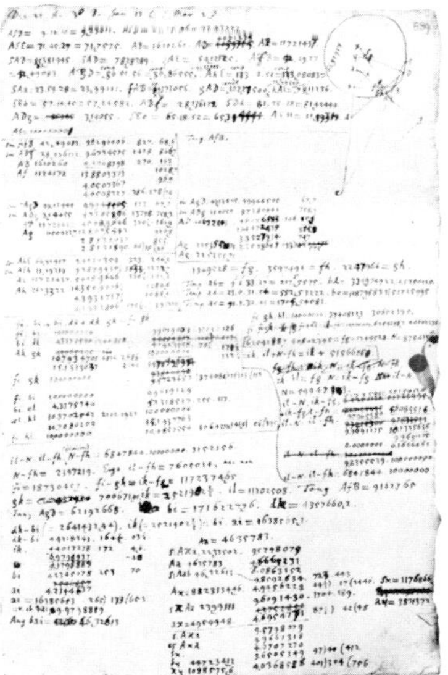

*A determination of the orbit of Halley's comet is shown above in a page of intricate calculations by Newton.*

# VOLTAIRE
## 1694-1778

Voltaire continues to surprise us. One might think his image had been fixed forever: by his twenty thousand letters; by the innumerable anecdotes illustrating his wit, his malice, his fervent humanitarianism; by his disenchanted stories, pioneering histories, and amusing poems; above all, by the famous Houdon bust, which seems to capture him for all time—emaciated, intelligent, fierce, cruelly quick-witted: the grinning philosopher of the Enlightenment.

But once we come to know him, the grin turns out to be a mask for a mystery rather than a revelation of character. The real Voltaire, it seems, continues to preserve his privacy. New discoveries only deepen his secret. A few years ago some letters were found revealing that early in the 1750's Voltaire had carried on a prolonged and intense affair with his niece. Like most prominent eighteenth-century figures, Voltaire lived in a goldfish bowl; his correspondence was treated like official bulletins, and his love affairs—his *other* love affairs—were conducted in the glare of gossip. But here was an affair that the sly Voltaire had kept private from his most intimate friends, his most prying enemies, and, for two hundred years, from his most diligent biographers. The testimony of these letters is incontrovertible: Voltaire was seriously, deeply in love with Mme Denis, his dead sister's daughter. He was in his late fifties when the affair began, an accomplished man of the world, the most famous literary man in Europe, a writer to whom all doors, including royal ones, were open. Mme Denis was about forty, a woman of real intelligence but with fading looks, greedy

*Despite the traditional toga, Houdon's Voltaire has an iconoclast's shrewd look.*

*By* PETER GAY

and self-centered beyond the normal. And yet, Voltaire wrote to her like a mooning schoolboy, appealing to her sympathy, longing for her body, and revealing (usually in Italian) a thorough and lascivious knowledge of her topography. It is a sobering experience to read these letters, for they are a reminder that Voltaire eludes cliché and resists easy classification. Whatever else this peculiar and untimely passion was, it was a paradox.

It was not the only paradox in his life. Voltaire was a Parisian who spent little time in his native city, a poet and philosopher who preached the life of action and preferred the turmoil of political agitation to contemplation and solitude, a crusader at once bold and timorous. Doubtless the real Voltaire, the man behind the mask, had a certain consistency, a character, but it is with the paradoxes that we must begin.

Mme Denis, above with Voltaire, was the philosophe's niece and mistress and the moving spirit behind a salon at which noted Parisian wits gathered. Mme de Pompadour, below, managed to obtain a position for Voltaire at the court of King Louis XV.

Voltaire, to start with, was a Parisian—he is unthinkable without Paris. He was born there on November 21, 1694, when the long and no longer glorious reign of Louis XIV was on the wane, and he died there, eighty-four years later, on May 30, 1778, early in the disastrous reign of Louis XVI. Paris was a frame for his life, physically and emotionally, even though he was rarely there. "I don't think," he wrote early in 1778, when he returned to Paris for the last time, "that I've lived in this city for more than three years at a time. I know it only the way a German does on his grand tour of Europe."

He knew Paris better than that. He grew up there as François Marie Arouet, the son of respectable bourgeois parents with some remote claims to aristocracy on his mother's side. He was educated there, at the Jesuit collège Louis-le-Grand, a brilliant and, as it turned out, ungrateful pupil. The Jesuits ran the best, and the most exclusive, schools in France, and his parents sent their precocious son to the famous Paris collège at least in part so that he might make some useful social connections. He did that, but he also did more: at Louis-le-Grand he acquired his love for the classics, exercised his gift for making rhymes and epigrams, and found some lifelong friends who remained his link with Paris.

After he completed his education in 1710, he began his wandering existence. At first, he was much in the city, a welcome guest in an elegant and rather decadent society, though he also traveled a good deal, making inimitable conversation in hospitable châteaux. But it was in Paris that he first discovered the limits of impudence: in the years 1716 to 1717 he spent eleven rather comfortable months in the Bastille, for some scurrilous verses against the regent that he might well have written but probably did not write. He emerged from prison with a new name—de Voltaire—symbol of his social ambitions and thirst for independence. And it was again in Paris, almost ten years later, in 1725—

*This contemporary view of a group of philosophes at supper was engraved by Jean Huber. In it, Voltaire appears in a cranky mood, with his head bound and his arm raised (1). The Encyclopedists Diderot (6) and d'Alembert (4) are also included.*

26, that he learned to his cost the perils of a hierarchic society. As the aftermath of an absurd quarrel with a decayed aristocrat (in which the aristocrat, not Voltaire, had been the aggressor), Voltaire was briefly put into the Bastille again. It was a lesson he never forgot: he went to London, full of rage, and discovered there a Paris in exile—Huguenot refugees from French persecution who had found a friendly welcome in an open society.

His long English sojourn confirmed Voltaire's radical views on religion and politics, but it did not estrange him from his native city—nothing could do that. In the 1730's and 1740's he lived mainly in the French countryside: he had acquired a wealthy, independent, and intelligent mistress, Mme du Châtelet, and he spent much time at her country seat at Cirey, in Champagne. But he refreshed himself by periodic visits to Paris, and then, in 1749, he lost his mistress through a fatality that was Parisian in its piquancy: Mme du Châtelet died in childbed, shortly after having given birth to a baby engendered not by Voltaire, her official lover, nor by M. du Châtelet, her husband, but by Saint-Lambert, a dashing, minor young poet.

After her death, Voltaire's long exile began. Rootless and miserable, he went back to Paris in 1749, meddled in politics on the king's behalf, and was asked, in 1750, to mind his own business. Louis XV found Voltaire an embarrassing political ally. This meant the end of Paris as his physical home. He moved to Prussia, on his famous, disastrous visit to Frederick the Great, which ended, as it had to end, in a quarrel. Finally, in the mid-1750's, Voltaire found a satisfactory substitute for his native city, near Geneva. There, on his properties, mainly at his

*All the world came to honor Voltaire in his old age at Ferney, his Swiss château.*

estate of Ferney, he lived out his life, active to the last. He returned to Paris only in 1778, to die, after an absence of almost thirty years.

All this hardly sounds like a Parisian existence, but it was. Wherever he was—in London, at Cirey, in Potsdam, or at Geneva—he kept steadily in touch with Paris. After all, Paris was the center of dramatic, political, and intellectual activity, and in spirit at least, Voltaire was never far from the center of that center. His Parisian friends informed him of literary and theatrical gossip, sent him the latest books and important political news, watched over the performance of his plays, and distributed his writings. Wherever he lived, Voltaire took Paris with him; at Ferney, with his stream of visitors and unending stream of letters, he ran a literary government in exile. Even Mme Denis was, in her rather special way, a reminder of Paris.

It was in Paris, too, that he became a writer, and he always needed the good opinion of Paris. Today, most of his literary productions lie forgotten; academic specialists read his plays, his poems, and his polemics, but they are not in general circulation. *Candide* alone, and perhaps selections from his letters and excerpts from the histories, have survived. But to understand Voltaire and his age, we must set aside the harsh and, I think, unjust verdict of modern taste.

In his own day Voltaire was chiefly known as a writer—a great writer. He had a vast and appreciative public: his first tragedy, *Oedipe,* was hailed as a worthy successor to Racine's best efforts; discriminating readers such as Lord Chesterfield devoured his historical works; polemics like the *Dictionnaire philosophique* went into edition after edition to satisfy an enormous demand.

Voltaire was happy to accept the high opinion of his contemporaries, and strove to deserve it. His sense of style was almost instinctive, but he rewrote constantly. He was always clear, never dull; always varied, yet always himself. He was the best of explainers, the most memorable of wits. No one wrote quite like him, and even the productions he most vehemently disavowed were manifestly his own.

His consciousness of himself as a professional writer was of central importance to him. It gave him a vocation, a self-respect that permitted him to take a stand in the world and to consider his views as significant as those of the best-placed aristocrats. Until the end of the seventeenth century writers had been hired hands, docile courtiers, dependent, as their effusive dedications to noblemen testify, on the goodwill of the aristocracy. In the eighteenth century all this changed: Pope dedicated one of his translations to Congreve, a mere commoner, and Samuel Johnson, in a famous letter, refused the help of Lord Chesterfield. These were signs that merit was beginning to count in the world and that literary men were becoming respectable. Voltaire admired the English situation, witnessed it at firsthand during his stay there, and sought to duplicate it on the Continent. It has often been said that Voltaire egregiously flattered the great, and that his letters to monarchs like Catherine of Russia make embarrassing reading. So they do, even if we take eighteenth-century conventions of politeness into account. But Voltaire's flattery was part of his struggle for independence. The eighteenth century was a century of censorship and suppression; even English writers restrained themselves in religious and political matters. If a writer had subversive opinions—and Voltaire did—he needed a variety of tactics to enable him to bring these opinions before the public, and survive. Voltaire was an expert tactician: he flattered kings that he might publish in their realm, he denied that he had written what he had obviously written that he might be free to write more. Goethe said, a little severely, that few writers had made themselves so dependent in order to be independent, but that paradox is more apparent than real: Voltaire judged that the social and political situation demanded these tactics of him. He was a writer, not a courtier, and a writer needs freedom. We may disagree with his appraisal of the situation—there were others, like Rousseau, who refused to lie and flatter, and who paid the price of being hunted through Europe—but we can hardly dispute his aim.

Voltaire was not only a poet but a poet who had something to write about. Diderot, who had mixed feelings about Voltaire, preferring to admire him from afar than meet him at Ferney, recognized the value of his intellectual equipment. "What is it that particularly distinguishes Voltaire from all our young writers?" he wrote to Catherine the Great. "Instruction. Voltaire knows a great deal, and our young poets are ignorant. The work of Voltaire is full of matter, their works are empty." This is a perceptive remark. Ever since Alfred North Whitehead observed in an unfortunate epigram that the philosophes were not philosophers, it has been widely assumed that Voltaire and his associates were merely loose talkers, coffeehouse wits with irresponsible opinions and unrealistic programs.

To be sure, if one restricts the word "philosopher" to the lonely theoretician, the maker of grand metaphysical systems, then Voltaire was not a philosopher. He was opposed to contemplation for its own sake, and to metaphysics, though his opposition sprang not from incapacity but from principle. For Voltaire, as for the other philosophes, philosophy was the supreme discipline; it was intelligent critical thinking for the sake of appropriate action. To deny Voltaire the title of philosopher, therefore, is to prevent us from understanding the character of his philosophy, and hence his character.

His philosophy did not come to him easily; it was the fruit of hard and patient labor. Even before he went to England, he had studied the philosophical writings of Locke and made Locke's empiricism his own. In England, and after, he studied Newton, and in 1738 he published an intelligent and influential popular account of Newtonianism. And with Mme du Châtelet, he studied the higher criticism of the Bible. He was as well informed in science and theology as any eighteenth-century amateur could be.

The elegant silhouette above shows Voltaire impatiently dangling one slipper. Benjamin Franklin, at the center of the contemporary sketch below, presents his grandson to Voltaire for a blessing.

His philosophy pervades all his work, even his poetry. Voltaire was a deist: he was confident that the world had been created by a Divine Intelligence, a Supreme Watchmaker, who had set the universe going by means of admirable, universal, unchanging laws. One could worship this divinity only by admiring its accomplishments, without articles of faith, without priests, without miracles, without prayers. Voltaire's notorious slogan, *écrasez l'infâme,* was not directed merely against superstition, or persecution, or Roman Catholicism. It was directed against all revealed religions.

As a deist, Voltaire was also confident that the world subsisted on universal moral laws, which profound teachers like Socrates and Confucius had preached to the world but which any reasonable man could discover for himself. At the same time, Voltaire's confidence in this life was severely limited: despite his reputation, he was not much of an optimist. He appreciated the caprice of fate, he sympathized with suffering, and he urged that men make themselves at home in this hard world by accepting their lot, understanding their place, and tolerating their neighbor. One of his lesser known stories, *"Le monde comme il va, Vision de Babouc,"* sums up his disenchanted, wryly tolerant philosophy best. A high-ranking angel commands Babouc to go to Persepolis and observe men in their activities. If he finds them all bad, the city will be destroyed. Babouc learns the ways of Persepolis and discovers that its citizens are a mixed lot: some are honest, others are crooked; some kindly, others cruel; some beautiful, others ugly. Then he goes to a goldsmith in the city and has him make a small statue, composed of materials both base and precious, and with this statue he reports back: "Would you break this pretty little statue, just because it isn't all made of gold and diamonds?" The lesson is plain; the angel understands. Let the city live: if all is not good, it is at least passable.

But while things might be passable, they could be much better. I have said that Voltaire was a poet, a philosopher, and a crusader, but to Voltaire himself—especially in old age, when he understood himself and his place in the world very well—these three words would have designated the same thing. "Man is born for action," he had written early in the 1730's in his famous book on England, the *Lettres philosophiques,* and indeed, from the beginning, he had written with a moral and political purpose in mind. He was a reformer all his life.

Yet it was not until the end of the 1750's and the early 1760's, when he was rich, famous, and old, that he became a full-time crusader. It was in these years, while settled at Ferney, that he raised his battle cry, *écrasez l'infâme.* He signed his letters with it, urging his fellow writers to propagandize for the good cause of anticlericalism and secularism and toleration, to lie if necessary, and never to give up. It was at this time, in early 1762, that he launched his campaign to reform the French legal system—a campaign to have certain forms of behavior, like blasphemy and homosexuality, removed from the catalogue of crimes; to have punishments reduced, trials made public, lawyers secured for defendants, torture abolished. These are the years in which Voltaire the humanitarian emerges in full armor.

In one sense, of course, this crusading spirit was anything but paradoxical, for it followed quite logically from his definition of philosophy. As a good pagan and an admirer of such Roman thinkers as Cicero, he considered social ethics the heart of philosophy, despised what he called "mere disputes about words," and thought it a philosopher's main task to make the world a better place in which to live. In another sense, his activity was deeply paradoxical, and his contemporaries sensed, and appreciated, this. Here he was, the best-known writer in Europe, with friends and admirers in all civilized countries, of uncertain health and at an age at which most men sit quietly by the fire, a man subject to seizures of panic, yet taking great risks, working full time for the obscure, the unhappy, the persecuted. That is why Diderot wrote in astonishment to his mistress and beloved friend Sophie Volland in the midst of Voltaire's intervention in the Calas case: "Oh! *mon amie,* what beautiful use of genius! . . . Eh! What are the Calas to him? What can interest him in them? Why should he suspend work that he loves in order to occupy himself in their defense? If there were a Christ, I assure you that Voltaire would be saved."

In fact, Voltaire's participation in the Calas affair is extremely revealing. Voltaire was passionately interested in politics, but he had no patience with political theory. He needed a specific case, an outrageous incident, to awaken his concern. He had a poet's love of the concrete. The Calas case was ideal for a man of Voltaire's temperament: it was odd, even mysterious, it lent itself to propaganda, and it was dramatic.

In October, 1761, one Marc Antoine Calas, son of a Huguenot cloth merchant at Toulouse, had been found hanged in his father's shop. He had been a morose young man, prevented as a Protestant from entering the legal career he craved. But while suicide seemed extremely probable, the authorities thought it was murder. It was asserted that Marc Antoine had been about to convert to Catholicism and that his father had murdered him to prevent that conversion. The family was arrested, interrogated, and finally Jean Calas, Marc Antoine's father, was found guilty, tortured, and executed in March, 1762. When Voltaire heard of the case, he did not know whether Jean Calas was guilty, but guilty or innocent, the case was fodder for his antireligious campaign. Guilty, the elder Calas was a splendid example of a Protestant bigot committing a ritual murder; innocent, the Toulouse authorities were perfect examples of cruel and credulous Roman Catholics. Voltaire studied the case with care, and the sympathetic humanitarian won out over the cold-blooded propagandist, as it usually did. Voltaire became convinced that the Calas family was innocent, and he mounted a great campaign to rehabilitate Jean Calas's name. After three years, he was successful, and the verdict was overturned.

From this case, and other, less well known cases, Voltaire moved into a large-scale, principled program for legal reform, and when he returned to Paris in triumph, early in 1778, the crowds in the streets hailed him, not as the author of *Candide* or *Oedipe,* but as the savior of the Calas family. Thus, public opinion mirrored the growth of Voltaire.

As we look back from the aged Voltaire, *l'homme aux Calas,* to his earlier incarnations—including Voltaire, lover of Mme Denis—much becomes clear. Voltaire was human, like the rest of us, but with his literary talent, his pure ear, his immense intelligence, he translated his needs into hilarious comedy or poignant drama. He needed sympathy and approval and confirmation; he needed the intimate sense of being loved. He could not bear cruelty: his God was a kindly father, not a harsh one. From the beginning of his religious ruminations he had been appalled by the God of the Old Testament, the implacable, remorseless judge, and had searched for a father whom he could love, but in whom he, the disenchanted student of modern science, could believe: He, his God, must be lovable, but He must be plausible too.

And as he tried to remake God into just such a father, so he tried to remake the world into a place closer to his heart's desire. To say this is not to charge him with a flabby universal benevolence: he was not a Christian; he did not love his enemies. On the contrary, much of his crusading fervor came from his secure conviction that men must destroy before they can build. He once wrote to a friend, "I know how to love, because I know how to hate," and this is one of the most revealing things he ever said about himself. He knew how to love, but he could not love everyone, abstractly, indiscriminately. Some things were hateful, some people were hateful, but others, like Mme Denis, could be loved.

His need to be loved, then, was one spring of action. But there was another, related spring, one that came out in the open most clearly in his later years. He needed to be justified in this world; he needed, that is, not merely to be loved but to deserve that love. As the great and terrible Seven Years' War raged all about him, he sat at Ferney, hating his enemies, passionately wanting to improve the world—and happy. And this happiness bothered him. In letter after letter he told friends that while he was happy, he was also ashamed of being happy in a world that was so stupid and so miserable. Hence he worked to become worthy of his happiness.

Behind the grin, then, behind the biting wit and the cool classical style, there stood a passionate man, controlling his passions without destroying them. Voltaire used to say that he would run a fever on the anniversary of the St. Bartholomew's Day Massacre, that great, treacherous slaughter of Huguenots in Paris in the year 1572. It sounds improbable, but we have independent corroborating evidence that he spoke the truth. Such a man, celebrating a far-off event in such a manner, knew how to hate because he knew how to love. It is eternally to his credit that he loved the right things and that he thought it worth his while to fight for them.

*Voltaire (at upper left) was apotheosized in 1778 when his bust was crowned with laurel on the stage of the Comédie Française.*

# JEAN JACQUES
# ROUSSEAU
## 1712-1778

When, in 1778, Rousseau died at the age of sixty-six, one of the most tortured existences ever recorded came to an end. He had spent the better part of his life as a tramp. Suddenly shot to fame, he had been at the same time hunted like a criminal over the face of Europe and consulted like an oracle. He had made enemies of all his friends and had spent his final years in a state close to insanity. He had suffered from a variety of bizarre physiological complaints and from almost every conceivable form of neurosis. He had never owned a house or founded a family (he abandoned his five illegitimate children to an orphan asylum). He had been ostracized in his native land. He had published, in his lifetime, a body of works that contained the most radical and comprehensive social criticism ever formulated up to his time, a criticism whose impact on modern society was and remains incalculably great. Misunderstood and misrepresented by his contemporaries, he had written his *Confessions*—a unique act of self-exposure designed to prove to his detractors that even with all his weaknesses he was, like all men, fundamentally good. The posthumous publication of the *Confessions* only added to the misunderstanding and misrepresentation. Always his own worst enemy, and endowed with a sure instinct for making enemies of others, he saw to it that he would have a large number of them as long as people read books: the *Confessions* alone have supplied his detractors with virtually the entire arsenal of weapons they needed to attack him.

Rousseau was the victim not only of his enemies and of his mania

*Rousseau, in his furry Armenian costume, was painted by Allan Ramsay in 1766.*

*By* J. CHRISTOPHER HEROLD

for self-exposure but also of his most enthusiastic followers. Indeed, like his critics, the majority of his admirers have obstinately persisted, down to our own times, in distorting his thought. They took from his writings only what they pleased, either to propagate or to attack what they chose to regard as his doctrine. He has been both claimed and damned by Marxists and conservatives, by atheists and mystics, by anarchists and totalitarians. He has been blamed with some plausibility for such disparate developments as the Reign of Terror, Hitlerism, progressive education, romantic love, liberalism, communism, nudism, momism, and the revival of square dancing. Everybody has read something about him, everybody thinks he knows what Rousseau said and preached; yet hardly anybody, whether admirer or enemy, seems to have taken the trouble to read him as attentively as he deserves. As a result, he has been almost universally credited with ideas that he either did not hold or that he held in common with most of his contemporaries, whereas the gist of his thought remains misunderstood. Before attempting to formulate what Rousseau did think, it is essential to dispose of at least five stereotyped falsehoods about him.

Falsehood 1: Rousseau preached a "return to nature." It is true that Rousseau assumed that man had lived in a state of nature before living in the state of society. Yet he insisted in his *Discourse on the Origin of Inequality* that this hypothetical state of nature may never have existed and probably will never exist; he merely used it as a critical tool, a yardstick. He did not ask man to *return* to nature but simply to *turn* to her, and he expressly defended himself against the imputation that he wished man to turn back on the road he had already traveled. "Human nature does not retrogress," he wrote toward the end of his life; and, referring to himself in the third person, he continued: "He has been obstinately accused of wishing to destroy the sciences and the arts . . . and to plunge humanity back into its original barbarism. Quite the contrary: he always insisted on the preservation of existing institutions, maintaining that their destruction would leave the vices in existence and remove only the means to their cure."

*Falsehood 2: Rousseau extolled primitive man, the "noble savage."* The idea of the savage's moral superiority over the civilized European can be traced at least as far back as Montaigne, who wrote two centuries before Rousseau. The phrase "noble savage" occurs in Dryden; Rousseau never used it. American Indians and South Sea Islanders were extolled by Diderot, but not by Rousseau, who looked to Sparta, republican Rome, and his own native Geneva rather than to primitive societies. There is not a single exotic note in all his writings.

*Falsehood 3: Rousseau began the cult of sensibility.* He did not begin it; it was in full swing when he appeared on the scene, and though he contributed to its spread, so did the novelists Richardson and Sterne and the philosophers Shaftesbury and Diderot. The morbid sentimentality of the late eighteenth century—the fashionable fainting fits, floods of tears, suicides, romantic landscaping, and artificial rusticity —cannot be imputed to Rousseau, even though those who indulged themselves in these fads claimed him as their patron saint. Artificiality was precisely what he wished to eliminate from men's lives, and the antics of his misguided followers filled him with misgivings and scorn.

*Falsehood 4: Rousseau reacted against the rationalism of his time and substituted feeling for reason as man's guide.* This cliché contains two falsehoods. Far from being rationalist, the entire Enlightenment was a rebellion against Cartesian rationalism, metaphysics, and system making. It was an age of experimental science and empiricism, with Bacon, Locke, and Newton its guiding spirits. Voltaire, Diderot, and Hume no more rejected feeling than Rousseau rejected reason; what Rousseau did reject was intellectualism and the arrogance that goes with it. In assigning a primary place to feeling, conscience, or instinct, Rousseau was in complete harmony with his times.

*Falsehood 5: Rousseau was the spiritual ancestor of the French Revolution.* The early leaders of the Revolution looked more to Thomas Jefferson and the American Declaration of Independence than to Rousseau. Leaders of the later stages, such as Marat, Hébert, and Danton, were indifferent or hostile to Rousseau. Mme Roland and Robespierre, it is true, were fanatic Rousseauans—and two more opposed political thinkers it is difficult to imagine. All that can be said is that many revolutionists invoked Rousseau's name, and that Robespierre made the mad attempt to put his own version of Rousseau's political theory into practice; he emphasized the totalitarian features of Rousseau's *Social Contract* at the expense of its very spirit. *The Social Contract* is a theoretical blueprint for a society of equals; how such a society should come into existence Rousseau did not say, but it is quite plain that he never advocated the violent overthrow of existing institutions. Such was his respect for the customs and traditions of nations, such his aversion to forcing social change by mere legislation, that when he was asked by Polish liberals to propose a new constitution for Poland, his suggestions did not even provide for the immediate abolition of serfdom.

Every idea, every book, every act, has two sets of consequences— those intended and those not intended. It has just been shown that in at least five instances Rousseau is credited with an influence that he did not intend or that can be just as readily credited to others. Indeed, it may perhaps be said that no man since Christ has had more follies committed in his name. But it cannot be said that his *real* thought, the thought that was original with him, was of less consequence than were the ideas falsely imputed to him. Contemplating him from the vantage point of our own time, we see the gigantic and tortured figure of the prophet of modern man's predicament. Weak, sick in body and mind, perverted, unfit for society, he knew all the distress of the human condition, and he said, in essence: all man's sufferings are brought on him by man, not by God, who has given man the means to save himself.

"Everything is good as it leaves the hands of the Creator; everything degenerates in the hands of man"—the celebrated opening sentence of *Emile* contains all of Rousseau's thought in germ. The conclusions he reached, no matter how mutually incompatible they may seem, can each be traced to the same point of departure. And yet, for all the inner consistency of Rousseau's thought, it does not form a system; rather, it represents the application of the same emotional conviction to various fields. It is the intensely personal, subjective tone of his writings that lends them their force and that sparked the enthusiastic response they received. Regarding himself as both unique and universally human, Rousseau drew all his ideas from subjective experience. To understand what he thought, we must feel what he felt—hence the continuing emotional character of our reactions for or against him. It was the misery of his neuroses as much as the brilliance of his genius that made him the prophet of man's discontent with modern civilization. If we share his malaise (and who does not?), we should at least listen to him, though we do not have to agree with him.

Rousseau's birth, which took place in Geneva in 1712, cost his mother's life. His father, a watchmaker with a taste for travel, gave him an odd early education: he kept the boy up nights reading novels while he wept over the loss of his wife. Rousseau's elder brother ran away to Germany as a boy and was never heard of again. When Jean Jacques was ten, his father had to leave Geneva as the result of some fracas. All in all, not a very settled family. Shortly after his father's flight, the boy experienced his first sexual pleasure while being spanked by the sister of the pastor with whom he was boarding. The perverse desire to repeat that experience remained with him all his life—although, as he asserts, he was too shy ever to ask from a woman the thing he desired most. Apprenticed to a watch engraver, he ran away at sixteen; became a Catholic convert (in return for a cash bonus) in Turin, where he served for a while as a lackey in a noble household; wandered off to Savoy, and there, in Chambéry or its environs, spent several years as the protégé, helpmate, adoptive son, and bedmate of a strange and remarkable woman, Mme de Warens, whom he called *Maman*.

Promiscuous in a motherly and dispassionate way, Mme de Warens

was at the same time a devout Catholic in her own fashion, unbelievably kindhearted, and unbelievably irresponsible. She did not succeed
in making Rousseau into a great lover, but she profoundly influenced
his religious thought. Also, in the rustic idyll that he shared with her,
Jean Jacques experienced—as he was to recall a few weeks before his
death—the only period in his life when he felt entirely himself, the
only time of which he could say that he had truly lived. *Maman*'s
growing financial difficulties eventually forced him back into the
world. We find him in Geneva, returning to the Protestant faith in
order to regain his citizenship; we find him at Lausanne, giving piano
lessons to young girls without himself being able to read a note of
music (he was later to become a thoroughly competent musician); we
find him wandering about Switzerland with a bogus archimandrite
from Jerusalem, making speeches to raise funds; we find him in Paris,
trying to make a fortune with a new system of musical notation he had
invented. Everywhere his attractive looks, his obvious gifts, and the
impression he conveyed of being made for better things, earned him
the personal interest and patronage of those he met. It was largely
with their help that he educated himself in the course of his wanderings. None of his writings betrays a lack of formal schooling.

His musical notation scheme was a fiasco, but he eventually obtained the post of private secretary to the French ambassador in Venice, where he gained an insight into the seamier sides of practical
politics, had several bizarre and inconclusive love affairs, and, above
all, gorged himself with music. The ambassador was an eccentric if
not a maniac; after a while a resounding quarrel between the two men
ended Rousseau's diplomatic career.

Back in Paris and now in his thirties, Rousseau still had accomplished nothing, yet the happier half of his life was behind him. He
fell in with the circle that soon was to acquire universal fame as the
philosophes and Encyclopedists—Diderot and d'Alembert at their
head, the publicist Friedrich Melchior Grimm, and Grimm's mistress
Mme d'Epinay. He also acquired a companion, Thérèse Levasseur,
who worked as a servant girl at his lodgings and who was to remain
by his side throughout the rest of his stormy and tragic career. In the
winter of 1746–47, Thérèse bore him the first of five children, all of
whom, according to his own testimony, he deposited at a foundling
home, never to see them again. "In letting them become working people and peasants rather than adventurers and fortune hunters, I believed that I was acting as a good citizen and father," he explained
later, without much conviction—though he may well have been right
in his own case. Some have questioned whether Thérèse's children
were really his; but even though Rousseau's sexual passion, extraordinarily intense as it was, remained largely confined to his imagination

DU
CONTRACT SOCIAL;
OU,
PRINCIPES
DU
DROIT POLITIQUE.
PAR J. J. ROUSSEAU,
CITOYEN DE GENEVE.
— fœderis æquas
Dicamus leges. Æneid. xi

A AMSTERDAM,
Chez MARC MICHEL REY.
MDCCLXII.

The Social Contract, *published in 1762, opens with
the words, "Man is born
free, and everywhere he is
in chains," a thought
echoed nearly a hundred
years later by Karl Marx.*

and to daydreams, there is no indication that he was impotent; or rather, he was impotent only with women whom he desired and loved passionately—and Thérèse was not one of them. It is certain that with his meager savings and his sporadic earnings as a literary hack and a music copyist he was scarcely in a position to support a family.

It was on a summer day in 1749, when he was entering his thirty-eighth year, that chance drove him into the career which was to make him both famous and wretched. He was walking to Vincennes to visit his friend Diderot, who was briefly and very comfortably imprisoned there. As he walked, he glanced at an announcement in a literary journal he was carrying, and read that the Academy of Dijon had proposed the following subject for its annual prize competition: Whether the restoration of the arts and the sciences has contributed to the purification of morals.

"If anything ever resembled a sudden inspiration," Rousseau wrote

*The idyllic view of the "noble savage" was a distortion of Rousseau's thought: he never used the term, nor did he extol Indians and Pacific islanders.*

several years later in a letter, "it was the emotion that worked in me as I read that. I felt my spirit dazzled by a thousand lights; swarms of lively ideas presented themselves to me at once, with a force and confusion that threw me into an inexplicable turmoil; I felt my head seized with a dizziness like that of inebriation. A violent palpitation oppressed me and made my chest heave. Since I could no longer breathe while walking, I let myself drop under one of the trees by the wayside, and there I spent half an hour in such excitement that as I rose I noticed that the whole front of my jacket was wet with my own tears which I had shed without noticing it. Oh, Sir, If I could ever have written one fourth of what I had seen and felt under that tree, with what clarity I should have revealed all the contradictions of the social system! With what force I should have exposed all the abuses of our institutions! With what ease I should have shown that man is naturally good, and that it is through these institutions alone that men become bad. All I have been able to retain of these swarms of great truths that enlightened me in a quarter of an hour under that tree has been scattered quite feebly in my three main works."

Diderot afterward claimed that it was he who advised Rousseau to answer the academy's question in the negative and thus launched him on his career. Perhaps so; Rousseau later blamed Diderot for having made him insert extreme views in his *Discourse of the Sciences and the Arts* as well as in his *Discourse on Inequality*—views that indeed do not reappear in his later writings. It seems strange that the man who was just then editing the epoch-making *Encyclopedia, or Dictionary of the Sciences and the Arts,* should give such advice; but then Diderot probably felt that his friend had a better chance of winning the prize if he took the more original view, and besides he must have known that a negative answer would be more congenial to Rousseau's *farouche* temperament. At any rate, Rousseau's own account of his epiphany under the tree sounds completely convincing, and to imagine him answering the question as easily in the affirmative as in the negative is rather difficult.

Though overrhetorical, intemperate, and slightly confused, Rousseau's *Discourse* is so passionate and incandescent an indictment of civilization and material progress that even after two centuries it cannot leave the reader indifferent. In some respects the indictment was nothing novel: it echoes Thucydides, Cicero, Tacitus, and Plutarch, all of whom denounced the debilitating effects that luxury and ease produced on the moral fiber of society; yet, at the time when Rousseau's *Discourse* appeared, the more commonly held view was that the civilizing effect of higher living standards, industrial progress, luxury, and art would also produce a beneficent influence on man's moral conduct. To Rousseau, things looked different. Paris, that apex of civilization, appeared to him like a vast and nightmarish agglomeration of some five hundred thousand people who had come there to sell or prostitute their minds or bodies, to exploit others if they could, to impress each other with their wealth, their rank, their power, or their wits; half a million people busily scurrying about either to produce superfluous goods and services for their exploiters or doing nothing with an air of busy importance; polite to each other when expedient, but ready for treachery and caring only for themselves; alienated from the sources of true happiness; wretched in their hunt for success; stripped of the proud dignity of active citizens; thinking, acting, and striving not according to their own conscience and nature but according to the artificial standards of society. "No one," he wrote toward the end of his life, "cares for reality; everyone stakes his essence on illusion. Slaves and dupes of their self-love, men live not in order to live but to make others believe that they have lived."

Rousseau's *Discourse on the Sciences and the Arts* won the first prize it deserved. Though launched on a literary career and famous virtually overnight, he never renounced what he thought was his real vocation: he continued to write about music and even composed it. His opera *Le Devin du village,* a slight but charming work, was successfully performed before the king in 1752. Yet, half against his will, his newly gained reputation drew him into philosophy. He was accused of attacking the arts and sciences and of wanting men to go back to walking on all fours. The accusation, though unfair, forced him to explain himself and to clarify his position. If the arts and the sciences had failed to make men happier or more virtuous, the fault was not theirs but must be sought in the social institutions which perverted their ends. In his discourses *On the Origin of Inequality* and *On Political Economy* Rousseau's thought takes on a sharper focus: social institutions, almost everywhere and at all times, rest not on true law but on power; laws and conventions aim to consolidate the wealth and power of the "haves" and to reduce the "have-nots" to increasing dependency. Under the existing social institutions men had renounced the freedom of the state of nature without gaining the advantages of associating as equals for the common good. The law of the jungle still prevailed, but the innocence of animals was lost: "Thinking man is a depraved animal."

How man could raise himself above this wretched state is the theme of the two great works of Rousseau's maturity—*The Social Contract* and *Emile.* Perhaps Rousseau found the key to his quest in his epistolary exchange with Voltaire concerning the latter's poem on the Lisbon earthquake of 1755. Shocked by that terrible disaster, Voltaire questioned the existence of a benevolent God or Providence: God is said to be free, just, and clement. Then why, asks Voltaire, do we suffer so much under so mild a master? In reply, Rousseau pointed out that if people did not insist on gathering in large cities and on dwelling in six-story stone buildings, disasters on the scale of the Lisbon earthquake would be statistically less likely to occur. He went further: disbelief in God, or the possibility of a cruel or unjust God, was utterly unacceptable to him. "All the subtleties of metaphysics would not lead me to doubt for a moment the immortality of my soul or a spiritual Providence. I feel it, I believe it, I desire it, and I will defend it to my last breath." And again: "In this strange contrast between what you prove and what I feel, I beg you to relieve my anxiety and to tell me where the deception lies—whether on the side of feeling or of reason."

In the words just quoted lies the key to Rousseau's religious and moral philosophy as he developed it in *Emile* and in his novel *Julie, or the New Héloïse,* and to which he gave expression most movingly and succinctly in the section of *Emile* entitled "The Profession of Faith of the Savoyard Vicar." Philosophy and theology, he contends, in all the thousands of years of their existence, have led us nowhere. We cannot be certain of anything except what we feel. Judgment and reasoning can enter only into our correlation of what we perceive through our senses. Yet while we can never be wrong in feeling what we feel, we certainly can reason erroneously in relating our sense perceptions to one another. Reason and feeling must never be in conflict, but since reason is subject to error, it must always be controlled by feeling. The paradox disappears if one realizes that by "feeling," in this context, Rousseau always means "conscience."

To Rousseau, the purposes of God were unfathomable, as they are to most of us, and he derided as empty metaphysics any attempt to explain them. The hypothesis that the universe was the purposeful creation of a Supreme Being seemed to him incontrovertible simply because he *felt* it to be true, and who could convince him that he did not feel what he felt? Why there were seeming imperfections in the Creation he did not presume to say; like Alexander Pope, he felt that "in erring reason's spite/One truth is clear, Whatever is, is right." And yet —this is the second great paradox in Rousseau's thought—it was plain that everything was wrong. "Everything is good as it leaves the hands of the Creator; everything degenerates in the hands of man" and the opening sentence of *The Social Contract,* "Man is born free, and everywhere he is in chains," are but two formulations of the same thought. What had gone wrong? Rousseau did not share the conviction of Voltaire's Dr. Pangloss that all was for the best in the best of all possible worlds; nor did his feeling allow him to accept the fashionable despair of later romantics and existentialists; nor did he find it possible to ascribe the sad state of our affairs to the fall of Adam and Eve. To suppose that God would be so unreasonable and, one might say, inhuman as to create man simply in order to punish him for acting human went counter to reason and feeling. By endowing man with reason and with conscience, God had equipped him, in Rousseau's view, with everything he needed to pull himself up by his own bootstraps. Then why did everything degenerate in the hands of man? In answering the question, Rousseau substitutes for the devil and original sin a new hypothesis: man is born good, but society corrupts him.

When we say that society is responsible for the crimes and sufferings in the world, we usually are unconscious of being Rousseauans; yet this idea did originate with Rousseau, and it is the weakest part of his philosophy. Rousseau's apparent inconsistency is twofold: (1) If man is good, then why does he become evil through association with other men, who are also good? (2) If society is the villain, then why does Rousseau prescribe the social contract as man's sole salvation? The questions would be well taken if it could be shown that Rousseau said society must necessarily corrupt man. But he never says such a thing. On the contrary, his entire social-contract theory is based on the assumption that the social state is a step forward from the state of nature. What is more, Rousseau maintained not only that just and beneficent societies were theoretically possible but that they had actually existed in the past—as in Sparta and republican Rome—and even in his own times, as in Geneva.

It is true nevertheless that, in Rousseau's opinion, society tends to corrupt man because it generally rests on power and exploitation rather than on law and co-operation. In a society not governed by law the individual moral will is stunted, social conventions take the place of inner conscience, men scramble after false values, self-love and vanity drown all benevolent instincts, and the gifts of life and nature pass unnoticed. All these evils are man-made and result from society, yet they are inherent neither in man nor in society. For man, it was Rousseau's conviction, is born not only with a conscience and with reason but also with a free will. He is the author of his fate, collectively speaking. Social redemption can be found in a collective exertion of the will by which men surrender all their individual rights to the body of society. Under such a "social contract," the state would be governed solely by the law, and the citizen could function at the same time as a free individual and as a member of a society whose exclusive goal is the common good. Indeed, "each man, by giving himself to all, gives himself to nobody"; and as long as no individuals or interest groups gain ascendancy over the rest, there will be a free and responsible citizenry.

Such are the basic features of *The Social Contract*. That this theory should have been proposed by one of the most notorious social misfits in history must seem ironic, but it is not particularly surprising, nor does it invalidate its importance in modern political thought. But Rousseau was not content with abstract theory. A perfect society, he realized, would have to be a society of gods, and all human institutions carried the germs of their own decay within them. A good society could neither come into existence nor maintain itself for long unless its members had the necessary moral will. In *Emile*, which he wrote concurrently with *The Social Contract*, Rousseau attempted to show how man's inborn good instincts could be fostered and developed through education and how citizens worthy of the good society could be formed. Since existing society is corrupting, the pupil Emile is brought up far away from urban civilization by a tutor who serves as guide rather than teacher. No ready-made knowledge or moral code is imparted to him: all his learning is derived from direct experience, all his judgments spring from his own intellect and heart. While Rousseau failed in *Emile* to prove the innate goodness of man, he undoubtedly succeeded in laying the basis for modern pedagogy. All education since his day, whether progressive or traditional, rests to a large degree on Rousseau's psychological insights and moral goals.

*The Social Contract* deals with the good society, that is, a collective body; *Emile* deals with the good citizen, that is, the individual. Unlike some of his critics, Rousseau could see no contradiction between the two works. Within the collective state, the individual potentialities of its members could and should be developed in all their diversity, since free and rational men willing the common good could not help but agree on all essentials. While the two books complement rather than contradict each other, they nevertheless reveal the tension between two poles in Rousseau's temperament. Rousseau the champion of civic virtue and activity was also Rousseau the contemplative, solitary dreamer; a forerunner of Marxist collectivism, he was also one of the ancestors of romantic individualism and of Thoreau's civil disobedience. In both roles—the dour patriot and the eternal adolescent who plays hooky from class—Rousseau reacted against his social environment. This soon became apparent to his friends the philosophes, who tried to enlist him in their cause only to discover that he was not one of them. Although, like him, they criticized society, society was the very air they breathed, whereas he revealed himself increasingly as a crank who shunned society and took offense at everything. The parting of the ways was gradual, but thanks to Rousseau's hypersensitive and morbidly suspicious nature, and to his radical alienation from society, it eventually became complete. "[He] makes me uneasy," Diderot wrote of their final meeting, "and I feel as if a damned soul stood beside me. . . . I never want to see that man again. He could make me believe in devils and in Hell."

The years Rousseau spent at the *Ermitage* and at Montmorency as the guest of Mme d'Epinay and, after breaking with her, as the guest of the Maréchal de Luxembourg were a period of growing isolation. To his friends, Rousseau was guilty of misanthropy, the worst crime in their eyes. To him, their devious methods to regain him for their fold appeared as persecution. At the same time he fell passionately in love with a much younger woman, the beautiful Mme d'Houdetot; since she was in love with another man, she did not reciprocate the middle-aged philosopher's ardor, and even if she had, she would have been disappointed, for, as Rousseau confesses, his passion was invariably spent in anticipation of their trysts. The ludicrous affair further envenomed Rousseau's relations with his meddling friends and undoubtedly helped to unhinge his mind. Yet it also produced a positive result. Jean Jacques, who was addicted to daydreaming and to populating (as he put it) the world with imaginary creatures, dreamed not only of ideal societies and ideal citizens but also of the ideal woman. He incorporated many of Mme d'Houdetot's features in her, called her Julie, and made her the heroine of his epistolary novel *Julie, or the New Héloïse*. With its sensuous descriptions of nature, its vibrant evocation of passion at its paroxysm, and its almost hysterical sensibility the book began a new era in literature, for better or for worse. At the same time its purpose is moral and its tone often quite preachy. Here the theme is the same as in *Emile* and *The Social Contract*: passions, pure in themselves, may overwhelm people whom society has not spoiled, but they can be transcended by the moral will.

*A memorial temple to philosophy, located at Ermenonville, includes the stone shown in detail above, inscribed with Rousseau's words.*

By May of 1762 Rousseau had produced, within the space of two years, three of the most influential works of modern times. His later writings added nothing new and were intended only to justify himself before his fellow men. Indeed, the publication of *Emile* brought catastrophe upon him. It was, in particular, his merciless attack on revealed religion and on the authority of the Church (in "The Profession of Faith of the Savoyard Vicar") that drew him the simultaneous anathema of the Catholic Sorbonne in Paris and the Calvinist Consistory in Geneva. In both places warrants of arrest were issued against the author; in Paris, *Emile* was burned by order of Parliament, and as far away as the Netherlands and Switzerland it was officially condemned.

With the connivance of some very high-placed protectors, Rousseau escaped to Switzerland, finally settling at Motiers in what was then the Prussian principality of Neuchâtel. Though the works that had been condemned were reprinted in innumerable pirated editions, Rousseau saw in his fame only a new cause for persecution. The authorities denounced him as a godless rebel and a destroyer of society; his former friends, the philosophes, while ostensibly deploring the attacks on him, privately denounced him as a monster of ingratitude, a hater of men, a savage. His eccentric ways and clothes and his reputation for godlessness drew upon him the hatred of the local population; when he was stoned by a mob, he left Motiers and took refuge on the island of St. Pierre, in the Lake of Bienne, in Bernese territory. Two months later the government of Berne expelled him, although he had engaged in no more subversive activities than botanizing and boating. He accepted David Hume's invitation to join him in England. But his stay at Hume's country seat, at Wootton, ended with another resounding quarrel. In the eyes of the philosophes his blackness was demonstrated; they called him a tiger, and open war was declared.

Thus far, it would seem unfair to accuse Rousseau of persecution mania. His persecution had been very real. It is true that his isolation was due more to shyness and his exaggerated sensibility than to any initial hostility on the part of his friends, who at worst did not understand his neurotic personality. Even his persecution by the authorities can be largely ascribed to himself; the authorities had bent over backward to help him escape the consequences of measures they themselves had been forced to take because Rousseau insisted (unlike most of his contemporaries) on signing his most subversive writings with his real name. But that he was persecuted, that his friends had turned hostile and occasionally even vindictive, there can be no doubt. After his quarrel with Hume, however, his self-isolation and suspiciousness took on all the symptoms of paranoia.

Returning to France, where he was tolerated on condition that he refrain from publishing his writings, he wandered from place to place

*An eighteenth-century water color depicts the elderly Rousseau as a herbalist, "cultivating his garden" at Ermenonville.*

with his inseparable Thérèse, and finally fixed himself in Paris, living in poverty on his wages as music copyist, refusing to see anybody for long periods, brooding over his persecution. Everything that had happened to him in the past twenty-five years now appeared to him quite clearly as a universal plot for his destruction. His friends had secretly laid their traps years ago, while he was still unsuspecting; even those who had remained loyal were now suddenly revealing themselves as diabolical accomplices of the archplotter, Grimm. Occasionally he would try to defend himself against their slander by posting public notices, or would denounce their machinations in readings of parts of his *Confessions*. The second part of the *Confessions* reveals these paranoiac traits only too painfully; the dialogues entitled *Rousseau As Judge of Jean Jacques*, despite some brilliant flashes of reason, are even more tragic testimony to the growing darkness in his mind. Yet it would be bold to assert that Rousseau was demented. His last works, soliloquies really—the *Reveries of a Solitary Wanderer*—show by their serenity what a heroic victory he had gained over himself. He still believed in a universal plot against him, but reminding himself of the guiding principles of his own philosophy and of his capacity to find happiness in mere existence, he transcended his mania and found long periods of inner peace. "I laugh at the plots hatched by men," he declared, "and I enjoy my own being in spite of them." He died soon after writing these lines, at Ermenonville, north of Paris, where he was staying as the guest of one of his protectors.

Rousseau's *Confessions* probably remain his most widely read work. They are a unique, amazing, fascinating, shocking, moving, exasperating document. They have done more harm to the appreciation of Rousseau's thought than all the weaknesses that may be found in his other works put together. To psychiatrists, the document is perhaps as interesting for what its author reveals as for what—despite his genuine effort to say everything—remains concealed. It is only natural and fitting that students of the human soul should look at the *Confessions* with a clinical eye and regard the rest of his writings as the outpourings of a psychological cripple. It would be futile to deny that his attack on society was the result of resentment and social inadequacy, or that his compulsion to re-create the world in his imagination was induced by his inability to function "normally," by his sexual inhibitions and his autoerotic tendencies. Rousseau's personality was what psychologists would call immature; moreover, he suffered from a number of psychosomatic problems in addition to his psychological ones. Thus, while he was the reluctant lover of the motherly Mme de Warens, who regarded the act of love as a matter of male hygiene, Jean Jacques suddenly contracted some unusual and alarming symptoms, which, according to him, lasted with undiminished intensity throughout the rest of his life; they involved a constant throbbing of his arteries accompanied by a loud noise in his ears in four different pitches. He also suffered from a malformation of the urethra, which caused urine retention. It was this condition that once made him refuse Louis XV's invitation to the court and thus miss a chance of obtaining a royal pension. He was afraid of wetting himself in His Most Christian Majesty's presence, but he made his refusal appear the proud gesture of a citizen of a republic. The same weakness made him adopt, later on, what he called an Armenian costume—a caftanlike garment that was more comfortable than breeches but that seemed un-Christian to the inhabitants of Motiers.

Undoubtedly his physiological and psychological handicaps go a long way toward explaining his reaction to society, yet such clinical discussions fail to explain his influence or to invalidate his diagnosis of our social ills. It will never do to brush aside *The Social Contract* because its author lost his mother at birth or suffered from enuresis as a grown man. Such criticism is standard; but not only is it irrelevant, it also misrepresents Rousseau's personality.

Far from being the antisocial recluse that he became after his contact with the world of fashion, finance, and intellect, Jean Jacques as a young man had been an exceptionally amiable and good-natured tramp. His penchant for vagrancy never left him. He loved to travel on foot, and he did not always end up at his intended destination. Though he did not shun work, he disliked working more than was necessary for his subsistence, and he treasured idleness above all things. The son of a watchmaker, he looked upon the day he threw away his watch as the beginning of his wisdom. He was fundamentally companionable, at least for the first five decades of his life. He was by no means prudish and, while no Casanova himself, was never a puritan censor of other people's sexual mores. Lacking the drives and ambitions of more settled and responsible men, he found his chief pleasure in the enjoyment of existence for its own sake, in daydreaming, in strolling through the countryside with his dog, in lying down under a tree. Until he experienced his famous illumination on the road to Vincennes, he was the most harmless fellow in the world. Surely his sudden change from amiable vagabond to social and moral prophet must have had more immediate causes than a urethral obstruction.

The most obvious explanation is that the social evils which Rousseau diagnosed after his clash with Paris do in fact exist. While more robust temperaments could adjust to them, partly submitting to the inevitable, partly seeking a remedy in practical action ("Let us cultivate our garden," says Candide), Rousseau was by his nature compelled to challenge the entire system. Whether this was practical or wise is a matter for argument; it was inevitable and necessary, and it enabled him to penetrate to the very roots of modern man's dilemma. Science and material progress had not made men happy. On the contrary, in their pursuit of false values, men had forgotten to learn from nature. Rather than be themselves, they strove for the creation of a desirable image of themselves in the eyes of their fellow men. Governed by the opinions of others, they had ceased to be individuals without becoming members of a community. Sacrificing their birthright as citizens and self-determined beings for the sake of security, pleasure, and comfort, they invited the destruction of all freedom. Born free and with the gift of reason, they lived as slaves and dupes. These causes of unhappiness could be blamed neither on God nor on human nature: far from commanding man to submit to fate, God or nature had endowed him with the means to shape his fate. Nature, to Rousseau, did not appear cruel—only natural. But man had become perverse since he used his natural gifts to impress and oppress other men instead of living with them in a free and brotherly community.

Whether one agrees or disagrees with Rousseau's prescriptions, it is impossible not to recognize that his persistent theme, that man's alienation from nature is the price of modern civilization, continues to vex us. His insistence that only man can save himself, that the tools are not lacking but only the will, is truer in our technological age than it was in his own. It is because of this that Rousseau was a prophet. How to simplify man's existence in an increasingly complicated culture remains the great problem. If man is not born good, as Rousseau thought he was, at least he is born with the potentiality for good; and he has reached the point where, if he does not realize that potentiality by a collective effort of the will, he must perish.

*Rousseau died in 1778 and was buried, as he wished, on an island at Ermenonville. Sixteen years later his body was placed, with Voltaire's, in the Paris Panthéon.*

ADAM SMITH
N.B. 64TH YEAR
1787

# ADAM
# SMITH
## 1723-1790

As late as the 1790's, the view of the economic life of the nation taken by government in England (and England was far advanced over the Continent in this respect) was essentially the mercantilist view. In the mercantilist system the wealth of the community was thought to be produced only by favorable trade. We ought not to despise this view of economics; it is the view still held to some degree by the man in the street, who assumes that a nation cannot rise unless another nation falls, and that a nation cannot grow rich unless another grows poor.

It is, of course, natural for the individual to think that money in his pocket must come out of somebody else's pocket. This view is especially tempting in a stationary society, in which the sum total of goods is for practical purposes constant. In such a society the individual could maximize his power by making a corner in that part of the fixed market which represented the most widely salable good, for example, spices. And such attempts were made. This was the individual's approach to mercantile economics.

At the level of government, the approach was the same, but the commodity was different. The government, assuming a constant total sum of goods, believed it should concentrate on those goods which were always sure to find a market; and the commodity in demand was the means of exchange itself: gold. Therefore, what the country did was to hoard gold. If the ruler, or even the individual, lived as frugally and as miserly as possible with gold, he would eventually have a great accumulation and thus a great power over everybody else.

*The economist Adam Smith was sculptured in a medallion by James Tassie in 1787.*

By J. BRONOWSKI *and* BRUCE MAZLISH

In reality there was no unified economic system or philosophy of mercantilism but only a loose set of beliefs. The core of mercantilism, however, was the developing territorial, or national, state, and the main purpose of mercantilist theory was to make economic activity subservient to the requirements of the state. The primary requirement was external power in relation to other states. Thus it was not consumption on the part of the subjects but production serving the authority and power of the state which was the aim of mercantilist economic activity.

As to the means of achieving this end, different writers differed. In general, however, mercantilism resolved itself into a "monetary system" and a "protectionist system." It was under both aspects that Adam Smith attacked it, devoting almost a quarter of the *Wealth of Nations* to the task.

As a monetary system mercantilism was concerned with the balance of trade. It was considered desirable to have a favorable balance of trade—more is exported than is imported and, therefore, a net gain in bullion is made—not only in general, but with every particular nation. To achieve this, the state fostered production (by subsidies, bounties, etc.) and commerce, hoping thereby to exchange manufactured goods for the precious metals. To prevent the outgo of bullion, the state passed sumptuary laws and prohibited foreign luxuries. The furthest step in this direction was the total prohibition of the export of bullion.

As a protectionist system the mercantilist doctrine favored the use of tariffs and direct prohibitions to prevent the country from being flooded with foreign goods (for which gold would have to be paid). The desideratum of this aspect of mercantilism was self-sufficiency; the fortunate country, one that was blessed with everything it needed.

In sum, the aim of mercantilism was neither to raise the standards of living of its own people nor to contribute to the well-being of other countries; its only aim was to regulate commerce and industry and to manipulate financial policy so that the power of the state might be promoted relative to other nations.

The mercantilist view first began to be undermined about the middle of the eighteenth century. It was attacked primarily by a sect of men in France who called themselves Economists, or Physiocrats, and whose motto was *"laissez faire."* The leader of this new group was François Quesnay, who strongly influenced Adam Smith. He was the physician to Mme de Pompadour (mistress of Louis XV) and used her salon to spread his new ideas.

Impetus to the movement had come during the reign of Louis XIV. Outwardly glorious, France under the Sun King was described by

*Edinburgh, seen here from Calton Hill, was Smith's home for most of his adult life.*

one of its critics as a "rotting white sepulchre." In fact, Louis's wars and financial policies left France in 1715 with a debt of 3,460 million francs, of which over 3,300 million had been contracted since the death in 1683 of Colbert, Louis's mercantilist finance minister—a vivid proof that wealth was used in forwarding the power of the state and not the prosperity of the people.

It was characteristic of the Physiocrats that they attacked the mercantilist position by stressing the primacy of land and with it the notion that rent was the center of wealth in the community. They singled out the soil (from which rent was derived) and, accordingly, contended that agriculture was productive and industry sterile. Such a view was typical of French landed society: no important doctrine of this kind arose in England or elsewhere.

A further sign of the originality of the Physiocrats was that they started with a kind of flow sheet of society. Even though in their flow sheet the total of goods was still kept constant, or nearly constant, they did begin to take a view of society which was quite different from the static mercantilist view. Their attention to the distribution of wealth and its "circulation" meant that, in this sense, their economics was dynamic.

Under the influence of the Physiocrats, Adam Smith pushed this view further. He concentrated, too, on the origin and circulation of wealth. What he changed was the central good that was being pushed around—the central source of wealth—hitherto regarded by the Physiocrats as rent. Smith, in the growing manufacturing and trading community of England, realized that although land was fundamental to the creation of wealth, so, too, was labor. And on this basis he went beyond the Physiocrats and formulated his famous "labor theory of value."

Adam Smith was born in the little Scottish town of Kirkcaldy a few months after his father's death, in 1723. After schooling in his home town, he went at fourteen to the University of Glasgow, where he studied mainly mathematics and Greek and where he attended the lectures of Dr. Francis Hutcheson, to whose chair in moral philosophy he was later to succeed. At seventeen he went to Oxford University, and there, instead of taking religious orders as his mother had wished, he spent six years studying literature (Greek, Latin, Italian, French, and English). Upon his return to Scotland, after two years of virtual unemployment, he eventually became professor of logic in 1750 and then, in 1752, professor of moral philosophy at Glasgow.

Gradually, however, Smith's mind seems to have turned from philosophical subjects per se to economics treated philosophically. It is true that from the very beginning Smith followed Dr. Hutcheson's division of moral philosophy into four parts—Natural Theology, Ethics, Jurisprudence, and Political Economy—and gave his lectures accordingly. And we know that in 1763 he was already lecturing on material that was later published (although not until 1896) under the title *Lectures on Justice, Police, Revenue and Arms*. We have further proof of Smith's interests: the draft of another treatise, *On Public Opulence*, was made by him just before his trip to Europe in 1764.

There is evidence to show that Adam Smith had formed for himself liberal and large views of trade early in life. We know that by 1752 he had become friendly with the philosopher David Hume, also a Scotsman. Hume, although he never wrote a major work directly on economics, wrote some essays on the subject and included a good many remarks about commerce in his general works—all of them in support of free trade. It seems clear that Smith was strongly influenced by Hume.

*François Quesnay, the founder of the Physiocrats, or Economists, is shown in an engraving based on a portrait by Vigneron.*

What stimulated Smith to go further and write his great work on economics was the offer made to him to go to the Continent as a private tutor for the Duke of Buccleuch. Smith resigned his professorship at Glasgow and traveled, for about two and a half years, on the Continent, spending most of the time in France. During that period he began writing his book on economics, the *Wealth of Nations,* or, in full, *An Inquiry into the Nature and Causes of the Wealth of Nations.*

The impulse to begin the book came, at first, from boredom. As he wrote to Hume from Toulouse (where he and his pupil were staying for eighteen months), "The life which I led at Glasgow was a pleasurable dissipated life in comparison of that which I lead here at present. I have begun to write a book in order to pass away the time." Thus came into existence the modern science of economics.

Hume later relieved Smith's boredom in another way, by introducing him to the prominent literary figures of the Paris salons. In this manner, Smith met such men as d'Alembert, Holbach, Helvétius, and the Abbé Morellet, as well as Turgot and the founder of the Physiocrats, Quesnay. The influence upon Smith of the last two men was important; that of Quesnay, as we have indicated, was fundamental.

Upon his return from France, Smith retired to his home in Kirkcaldy, near Edinburgh. Here, almost in seclusion, he spent the next ten years writing his work on economics. The book, from the moment of its appearance, was hailed as a monumental work, and Hume wrote to Smith in great relief:

EUGE! BELLE! DEAR MR. SMITH,—I am much pleased with your performance, and the perusal of it has taken me from a state of great anxiety. It was a work of so much expectation, by yourself, by your friends, and by the public, that I trembled for its appearance, but am now much relieved.

Relieved of his anxiety, Hume then added: "If you were here at my fireside, I should dispute some of your principles."

The *Wealth of Nations* was published in 1776, a date easily remembered because the American Revolution broke out in that year. One of the things that made the *Wealth of Nations* nicely topical was that it contained a sentence saying that he, Adam Smith, expected the American nation beyond the sea to become one of the foremost nations in the economy of the world.

Smith, by writing the *Wealth of Nations,* had become the father of modern economics. Businessmen before him had elaborated a "political arithmetic," dealing with problems, as they arose, of credit, banking, or balance of trade; in the course of these treatments a mass of statistical information had been collected. On the other hand, enlightened thinkers in France had built up a speculative system, based on the notion that natural laws were in as much control of society's economic movements as of the movements of physical nature. What Smith did, like Newton before him, was to combine the rational and empirical into one scientific method. Smith joined French "physiocracy" with English "political arithmetic" to form a science of economics.

What were Adam Smith's own and specific contributions to economics and to thought in general? He made essentially two contributions. First of all, he introduced the historical method into economic discussion, and secondly, he gave a central place in his economics to the value and the division of labor.

First, the historical method. In the hundred years that preceded Smith, the deductive method of trying to set up physics or the laws of society or anything else was dominant. A glance backward to Hobbes or Locke shows us their methods. They started with certain propositions about what human beings are like in a simple state of nature. These propositions, with almost no factual background at all, are in effect a set of axioms. They are not wild inventions, but they are essentially the axiomatic background from which everything is deduced.

*David Hume, who not only influenced Smith's thought but also introduced him into the French salons, was painted by Allan Ramsay.*

Adam Smith did not believe in an axiomatic background; and his book is not presented so that it looks like a book of propositions. Instead, the *Wealth of Nations* was written in an amiable, chatty way, and for this reason, it is difficult to find one's way about in it. True, the book was ordered by a strong intelligence with a very clear idea of what he was talking about, but with a willingness to be repetitious and long-winded, if necessary, to be understood. Thus, the style reflects the fact that Smith had little belief that an economic system consists of a set of fundamental axioms from which further propositions are deduced. As early as the *Theory of Moral Sentiments,* he had poked gentle fun at "A propensity which is natural to all men, but which philosophers in particular are apt to cultivate with a peculiar fondness, as the great means of displaying their ingenuity—the propensity to account for all appearances from as few principles as possible."

There were many reasons why Adam Smith did not think that economics was a pure, axiomatic science; we would like to point to one which is of especial interest. The great discovery that Hume made, and he made this as a very young man, was that ever since the time of Hobbes people had incorrectly supposed that the laws of cause and effect had the same kind of finality and rational certainty as the laws of logic. For attacking this notion, he was once called an atheist and generally blackballed by all decent members of society, who had spent a hundred years struggling with the idea that the universe really worked by cause and effect and were not going to have some Scottish whippersnapper upset the notion that had been so difficult to learn.

Richard Arkwright, founder of the factory system, was a prototype of Smith's new laissez-faire capitalist.

Smith did not go as far as Hume in freeing himself from the bondage of cause and effect, but he achieved a healthy skepticism. Smith employed cause-and-effect relations when he said "The constancy and steadiness of the effect supposes a proportionable constancy and steadiness in the cause" or "The suddenness of the effect can be accounted for only by a cause which can operate suddenly." But he also handled these relations in a more sophisticated way. He was aware that the same cause can have different effects: "The rise and fall in the profits of stock depend upon the same causes with the rise and fall in the wages of labour, the increasing or declining state of the wealth of the society; but those causes affect the one and the other very differently"; that effects may be mistaken for causes: "The carrying trade is the natural effect and symptom of great national wealth; but it does not seem to be the natural cause of it. Those statesmen who have been disposed to favour it with particular encouragements seem to have mistaken the effect and symptom for the cause"; that the mere fact of being posterior in time does not make a thing an effect: "Though the period of the greatest prosperity and improvement of Great Britain has been posterior to that system of laws which is connected with the bounty, we must not upon that account impute it to those laws."

In general, Adam Smith was wary of simple causal explanations and preferred to treat economics as a historical rather than as a logical or even as an empirical science. Hume had written a fine *History of England* and thereby given a strong impetus to the historical method. Smith followed his friend and filled the *Wealth of Nations* with historical interludes. It will be well to give some idea of the subjects Smith covered. He traced the historical origin of freedom; the history of Rome; the origin of city independence; the rise of the third estate; and the changes in war and militias. He investigated the origin of money and gave an extensive disquisition on the history of price movements. He also devoted a large chapter to the history of colonies, in the process of which he formulated a refined theory of imperialism.

In part, Smith anticipated Marx in the theory of economic determination of history. Marx's formulation is more dogmatic, but was influenced by this idea of Smith (as well as by the idea of the labor theory of value, which we shall discuss in a moment). Smith, who had little respect for feudal society, contended that the great lords lost their power when they chose to sell their surplus produce to the towns in exchange for luxuries. In Smith's words: "But what all the violence of the feudal institutions could never have effected, the silent and insensible operation of foreign commerce and manufactures gradually brought about. These gradually furnished the great proprietors with something for which they could exchange the whole surplus produce of their lands, and which they could consume themselves without sharing it either with tenants or retainers." Thus the merchants unintentionally supplied the nobles with the instrument of the latter's own destruction: luxuries. Instead of using their surplus produce to maintain tenants and military followers, the real source of their power, the nobles sold the surplus to the towns for "trinkets and baubles." It was in this manner that, to borrow Hegelian terms, the "dialectic of history" played itself out. As Smith phrased it:

*William Pitt the Younger used Smith's teachings to help push his free-trade bill through Parliament.*

A revolution of the greatest importance to the public happiness was in this manner brought about by two different orders of people who had not the least intention to serve the public. To gratify the most childish vanity was the sole motive of the great propietors. The merchants and artificers, much less ridiculous, acted merely from a view to their own interest, and in pursuit of their own pedlar principles of turning a penny wherever a penny was to be got. Neither of them had either knowledge or foresight of that great revolution which the folly of the one, and the industry of the other, was gradually bringing about.

Adam Smith's second major contribution to economics was his theory that the source of all wealth is the labor of the people who produce it. The mercantilists had no real theory about the origin of wealth because they believed that wealth was more or less constant.

The Physiocrats held, generally, that wealth resided in land; they believed that new wealth, i.e., agricultural products, was created as a gift of nature and that man's industry merely transformed but did not add to this wealth. Adam Smith, however, held that wealth is created by man, and he believed that man creates it by work.

Thus, in the *Wealth of Nations* Smith stated that the wealth of a community increases by the amount of work which it puts out. But he did not leave this as a superficial statement. He traced everything back to the original labor. He did not say merely that wealth was added to a bale of wool when you made it into cloth; he traced the labor back to the shepherd, and then to the man who sowed the grass on which the sheep fed, and so on in an exhaustive and complex fashion.

Adam Smith was aware that improved productivity comes most readily from the division of labor. In his analysis he pointed out that division of labor fosters increased dexterity on the part of the worker, saves valuable time, previously wasted in passing from one phase of work to another, and through the use of machinery facilitates and abridges labor. The famous example Smith used to illustrate these advantages was the pin-making trade.

Unfortunately, Adam Smith often treated labor as a commodity rather than an activity; very much like the things one buys and sells. For example, he writes: "It is in this manner that the demand for men, *like that for any other commodity* [our italics], necessarily regulates the production of men; quickens it when it goes on too slowly, and stops it when it advances too fast." In this respect, what he said had quite a disastrous effect during the next thirty or forty years. When one propounds a labor theory of wealth in which labor is treated mainly in terms of supply and demand, a very inhuman kind of civilization is implied; and the implication became reality in the years after Smith's death.

Smith did the worker one other disservice. By concentrating on the division of labor as being, along with greater capital investment, the source of increased productivity, he was drawn into thinking of man as a mere "machine of production." He knew the price to be paid for this view, and he was keenly aware that "gross ignorance" characterized the inferior ranks of people when they were cut off from a full and rich work life. It is worth quoting at some length Smith's indictment of the division of labor:

In the progress of the division of labour, the employment of the far greater part of those who live by labour, that is, of the great body of the people, comes to be confined to a few very simple operations, frequently to one or two. But the understandings of the greater part of men are necessarily formed by their ordinary employments. The man whose whole life is spent in performing a few simple operations, of which the effects are perhaps always the same, or very nearly the same, has no occasion to exert his understanding or to exercise his invention in finding out expedients for removing difficulties which never occur. He naturally loses, therefore, the habit of such exertion, and generally becomes as stupid and ignorant as it is possible for a human creature to become.

Though he knew the degrading effects which could result from almost all specialized employment, Smith eulogized the division of labor as one of the two prime sources of the wealth of nations. He left too little room in his commercial society for the Renaissance "whole man" or "universal genius"; opulence might exist in modern society, but society would not be rich in many-sided men. This implied resignation in Smith's thought is especially strange because of his frequent laudation of the farmer as an independent and intelligent personality.

Was Smith simply accepting the inevitable direction of history? In extenuation he might have pleaded, as he did, that "It is the great multiplication of the production of all the arts, in consequence of the division of labor, which occasions, in a well-governed society, that universal opulence which extends itself to the lowest ranks of the people." It was Smith's contention that as a result of the division of labor, the average English worker was richer than an African king who was "absolute master of the lives and liberties of ten thousand naked savages." The brutalization of the masses was compensated for by their relative opulence.

Eighteenth-century debates over foreign trade are reflected in this playing card of 1720, one of a set called "Bubble Schemes."

Smith was really feeling his way to a problem whose solution most of us today glibly take for granted. He asked the frank question: "Is this improvement in the circumstances of the lower ranks of the people to be regarded as an advantage or as an inconveniency to the society?" Smith's answer was to go forward with the division of human labor and to compensate for the resultant brutalization by having the government intervene and educate the laboring poor—strange doctrine for a supposed free enterpriser.

The possible solution of substituting actual machines for the worker as a "machine of production" was not yet apparent to Smith. Machines were, of course, one way of expanding the productivity of labor, but they were less important in his mind than increased capital and increased division of human labor. He claimed, for example, when talking of the textile industry, that machines had contributed little in the way of increased production and—an astoundingly bad prediction—were not likely so to contribute in the future.

Adam Smith did, however, realize that the well-being of the worker depended not on the absolute wealth of the nation but on the fact that the wealth was expanding. The *real* wages of labor depended, he declared, on the "advancing, stationary, or declining condition" of the society, and only in an advancing society was the worker's lot tolerable. It was at this point that Smith came to the heart of his theory:

a continuously advancing and expanding economy could only exist in an atmosphere of *laissez faire*. The worker, as well as the manufacturer, had to be free to pursue his own advantage, without let or hindrance.

This leads us directly to what is called Smith's theory of "self-interest." One difficulty in following his account of self-interest is that he had discussed the matter thoroughly in the *Theory of Moral Sentiments;* and he assumed that the reader of the *Wealth of Nations* would not think that he, Smith, considered self-interest the only or even the main motive, or virtue, of humanity. His teacher, Hutcheson, indeed, had taught that the only virtue was benevolence; but Smith, while agreeing that this was the major virtue and the one which aimed "at the greatest possible good," felt strongly that the system of benevolent ethics was too simple and left no room for the "inferior virtues." Therefore he devoted himself to a more naturalistic theory of morals, in which man's nature was accepted as it was. He felt that it was not beneath the dignity of man to admit that "Regard to our own private happiness and interest, too, appear upon many occasions very laudable principles of action. The habits of economy, industry, discretion, attention, and application of thought, are generally supposed to be cultivated from self-interested motives, and at the same time are apprehended to be very praiseworthy qualities which deserve the esteem and approbation of everybody."

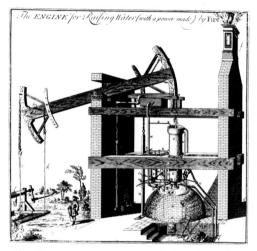

The Newcomen engine, an "Engine for raising water (with a power made) by Fire," was one of the Industrial Revolution's key inventions.

Benevolence was undoubtedly the highest morality, but the workaday world ran on the motives of self-interest. It was the latter motive which drove men to the division of labor, the basis of society's affluence. In a famous passage, Smith declared: "It is not from the benevolence of the butcher, the brewer, or the baker that we expect our dinner, but from their regard of their own interest. We address ourselves not to their humanity, but to their self-love, and never talk to them of our own necessities, but of their advantage."

Smith's task in the *Wealth of Nations* was to analyze the butcher's, brewer's, and baker's world. From his work on morality, however, he brought one other very important notion to this task—a belief in Providence. According to Smith, "Human society, when we contemplate it in a certain abstract and philosophical light, appears like a great, an immense machine whose regular and harmonious movements produce a thousand agreeable effects." Even his belief in cosmopolitanism is grounded in his belief in Providence. Thus, the wise man realizes that the subordination of himself and of his country to the interests of mankind is for the "good of the whole"; that he must trust himself in this matter to the "great Conductor of the universe."

In the *Wealth of Nations* Smith combined the two doctrines: God's providential benevolence and man's earthly self-interest. The result is his famous "invisible hand" theory in which the individual, intending only his own gain, is led "to promote an end which was no part of his intention," the well-being of society. From then on, the inevitable benefits of self-interest became a doctrine to which rising manufacturers and owners of newly enclosed land constantly appealed.

A close inspection of Smith shows how ridiculous it is to say that he favored the uncontrolled pursuit of self-interest. He was constantly inveighing against the farmers, the workers, the manufacturers, and the banks on exactly this point and complaining that they did not understand their own particular interests. For example, on the question of paper money, after an exhaustive analysis of the real factors involved, Smith said: "Had every particular banking company always understood and attended to its own particular interest, the circulation never could have been overstocked with paper money." He chided the mercantilists that their very cupidity, by imposing a heavy duty on certain goods, called into being a smuggling of the goods which ruined their business. Country gentlemen were told that in their demand for a bounty on corn "they did not act with that complete comprehension of their own interest" which should have directed their efforts.

We could extend this list almost indefinitely. One of the very practical purposes of the *Wealth of Nations* was to enlighten self-interest by pointing out its *real* interest. Smith was sophisticated enough to realize that it is the long-range effect of an action, and not the immediate and obvious one, which is to be attended to, and that this requires an understanding of principles. It was for this reason that Smith entitled his book an *Inquiry into the Nature and Causes of the Wealth of Nations.*

Smith was quite adamant that experience without explanatory principles was insufficient. For example, as he said: "That foreign trade enriched the country, experience demonstrated to the nobles and country gentlemen as well as to the merchants; but how, or in what manner, none of them well knew." None of "them" might know, but Smith did. His method was to form out of experience an abstract principle, to state this as a general rule, and to give evidence and examples to support it. Thus, he and his science of economics could show "how" and "in what manner."

In order to discover such a science of economics, however, Smith had to posit a faith in the orderly structure of nature, underlying appearances and accessible to man's reason. It was essentially the same faith which long before had inspired the researches of Copernicus, Kepler, and Galileo—the faith that nature moves in a regular and harmonious fashion in spite of the bewildering variety of appearances. This, in our judgment, is what Smith really meant by the "invisible hand"; that, so to speak, an "order of nature" or a "structure of things" existed which permitted self-interest, if enlightened, to work for mankind's good.

Man's task, therefore, was to understand the nature or structure of things and to adjust himself harmoniously to the necessary results of this structure. On one level, this might mean the acceptance of a "natural" price of things (reached when the supply, whether of goods or of labor, exactly equaled the demand).

On another level, Smith applied his faith in a structure of things when he said: "A nation of hunters can never be formidable to the civilized nations in their neighbourhood. A nation of shepherds may." This is true, he thought, because the nature of hunting is such that large numbers cannot indulge in it; the game would be exterminated. On the other hand, shepherds can grow in number as their flocks grow; and can carry war into the hearts of civilized nations because they carry with them their food supply.

On the highest level, there existed a "natural course of things," or, as Smith more frequently phrased it, "the natural progress of things toward improvement." The principle behind this "natural course" was "the uniform, constant, and uninterrupted effort of every man to better his condition." Thus, self-interest drives civilized society; the duty of the scientist and the legislator is not to castigate it but to accept and enlighten it. In so doing, they will act in harmony with the order or structure of things.

Smith was fully aware that a totally free-trade or "natural" society was a utopia. The main obstacles to the realization of such a "natural" society were prejudices (i.e., unenlightened ideas) and partial interests (i.e., the desire for gain at the expense of the general good; ultimately, therefore, at the expense of one's own eventual good). He had no illusions that either of these barriers could ever be fully overcome. But he did believe that *gradual* change in the right direction was possible and that his book, by truly exposing the nature and causes of the wealth of nations, would indicate to the legislator, scientifically, what that right direction was.

What effect did Smith's work actually have? First, it gave the rising manufacturers and merchants a rationale for their desire to change existing government policy. Thus, for example, it helped Pitt to pass a free-trade agreement, the Eden Treaty of 1786 with France, through

Parliament. And Pitt openly acknowledged his debt to Smith. The story is told that at a dinner party Smith was late and apologized. The whole company (men like Pitt, Grenville, Addington, and other British leaders) rose, and Pitt exclaimed: "We will stand till you are seated, for we are all your scholars."

The second effect of Smith's work was in the shaping of thought. His influence in introducing historical method into political economy was far-reaching. He made the foundation of all subsequent economics the notion that wealth was created by labor. But more than any of these things, he introduced science into the study of economics. Although he talked much about the "invisible hand" and the "natural course of things," Smith really freed man from the tyranny of chance by forming for him the analytic tools with which he might learn to control his economic activities. This he did in spite of the fact that selfish men later twisted his ideas to make it seem that Smith was subjecting man to cold, harsh economic forces beyond his power to control.

Smith provided the stalking-horse behind which the new manufacturers of England could peacefully accomplish the "revolution" of freeing Britain from outworn and outmoded regulations and hindrances to economic progress. He was able to do this because his free-trade doctrines were fortunate in fitting the necessities of the time—a time when British industries were ahead of their neighbors' and were therefore sure to benefit by free rivalry.

This in itself was a momentous reason for Smith's importance. It pales, however, in comparison with his second service to mankind. He provided a lasting contribution to man's ordering of his material life. Thus, Smith ranks high in the history of ideas as the philosopher who, exemplifying his own belief in the division of labor, founded the specialized science of economics and gave to the mind of man another means of controlling the world of matter.

*This portrait medal of Adam Smith, engraved in 1797 by Boog, has symbols of the* Wealth of Nations *on its obverse.*

# IMMANUEL
# KANT
## 1724-1804

I n understanding any great philosopher of the past, it is necessary to distinguish that which made him the philosophical
spokesman and leader of his age and that which is of permanent, and therefore also contemporary, relevance and importance. Kant's philosophy was a penetrating examination of the
foundations of Aristotelian logic, Euclidean geometry, Newtonian
physics, and the optimistic utilitarian ethics of the eighteenth century. All of these were superseded in the century after his death,
leaving the impression that however great Kant may have been in
his time, the progress of knowledge since his day has left his teachings behind as a mere historical curiosity. Yet one cannot be dogmatic about this; it may well be that the same *kinds* of problems
that concerned him are still with us, and that his questions and
some of the patterns of his answers may still produce fruitful insights into the foundations and methods of reasoning employed in
modern life. Recently many leading philosophers have begun a re-
examination of Kant's works in an effort to see how his teachings
can be adapted to present-day problems, or how present-day problems can be illuminated by his work. It is not too much to say that
there is a Kantian renaissance in Anglo-American philosophy comparable to that in Germany eighty years ago; but it is still too soon to
know the outcome of the re-examination that has been undertaken.

Immanuel Kant was born in Königsberg, Prussia (now Kalinin-
grad, Russia), on April 22, 1724. His father was a saddle maker; his
family were Pietists, members of a church somewhat like the Quak-

*A bachelor, Immanuel Kant was throughout his life a dapper, sociable gentleman.*

By LEWIS W. BECK

ers in England in their quietist faith in the inner light of conscience, their moral strictness tempered with active benevolence, and their stubborn indifference to the subtleties of sectarian theological speculation. These religious teachings had a profound influence on Kant that continued even after he had outgrown the anti-intellectual restraints often characteristic of members of this community. His family was too poor to give him an education; but he was aided by their pastor to attend school and then the University of Königsberg, where, it is said, he helped support himself by his winnings at billiards and by writing sermons for his classmates studying for the ministry. He seems to have matriculated at the university as a student for the ministry; but his main interest was physics, and his dissertation upon leaving the university was on the subject of the proper formula for measuring kinetic energy.

When he left the university, in 1746, Kant took employment as a tutor for a noble family near Königsberg. He says he was a poor teacher, but he was loved and respected by his patrons. Perhaps he learned as much from them as he taught their children; for when he returned to Königsberg, he was a "gentleman," spruce in his dress and courtly in his manners. Unfortunately, he was still dreadfully poor. For fifteen years he worked as a *Privatdocent* in the university, supplementing the students' lecture fees with a small salary he earned as a librarian. During these years he was busy lecturing his students eighteen hours a week and writing papers and books that got him a modest reputation as a promising young man but would be forgotten now had he not later done the work that brought him lasting fame.

In 1770, after several disappointments, Kant was finally awarded a professorship, and for the first time in his life he was economically comfortable. Eleven years later he published his most important book, *Critique of Pure Reason*. During the next ten years of incredible intellectual labor he produced work after work: *Prolegomena to any Future Metaphysics, Foundations of the Metaphysics of Morals, Metaphysical Foundations of Natural Science, Critique of Practical Reason,* and *Critique of Judgment*.

Kant was a frail man, "never sick but never well," he said. He was barely five feet tall, had a shrunken chest and a hump on one shoulder. His character was strictly puritan. He was sternly self-disciplined and jealously guarded his independence. He made a fetish of punctuality; it was said that the housewives of Königsberg set their clocks by his daily walk. His life, like his ethical philosophy, was rigorously governed by rule and precept. Yet, paradoxically, he was a convivial man and popular teacher. One of his greatest students, Johann Gottfried Herder, recalled after many years: "Play-

*Kant never traveled more than a dozen miles from his birthplace, Königsberg, above.*

fulness, wit, and humor were at his command. His lectures were the most entertaining talks. . . . The history of men and peoples, natural history and science, mathematics and observation were the sources from which he enlivened his lectures and conversation. He was indifferent to nothing worth knowing. No cabal, no sect, no prejudice, no desire for fame, could ever tempt him in the slightest from broadening and illuminating the truth. He incited and gently forced others to think for themselves; despotism was foreign to his mind.'' In his younger days he was called "the gallant doctor" and much enjoyed the company of the Prussian (and during the Russian occupation of Königsberg, the Russian) officers who were garrisoned there. When older he was noted as an excellent host whose dinners brought out the best conversation in Königsberg. Most of his writings are of great difficulty, but as a man he was simple, humane, and polished. One of his biographers who knew him well spoke of "childlikeness" as his most distinctive character trait.

It has been said that it is impossible to write a life of Kant because he had no life; Heinrich Heine said his life was like the most regular of regular verbs. Yet the 1790's, when Kant was already an old man, were a period of disturbances in his life. In 1792 he was forbidden by the king of Prussia to lecture or write on religious subjects because of his unorthodox views. He came to be known as "the old Jacobin," i.e., an adherent of the French Revolution, at a time when this was politically hazardous. It was even rumored and believed that this old man, who had never ventured farther than twelve miles from Königsberg, was going to Paris as adviser to the Revolutionary government! In 1795 he published his *Perpetual Peace* in favor of nonintervention in the Revolutionary government in Paris; it is one of the principal defenses of representative government in the eighteenth century and one of the first proposals for the establishment of a league of nations for securing lasting peace.

In 1798 he retired from lecturing at the university. He spent the remaining six years of his life trying to perfect his system of philosophy, but feebleness and increasing senility thwarted his efforts. He died on February 12, 1804. By that time his philosophy was taught in most German universities and was beginning to be known in France and England. The next great movement in Germany philosophy, known as German idealism, was on the upswing, being led by his former pupil Johann Gottlieb Fichte. Though German idealism was far different from Kant's philosophy, it grew out of his teachings and cannot be understood without them.

Heine, with characteristic wit, called Kant "the Robespierre of philosophy." To see what Kant destroyed in philosophy, and what new structure he erected on the ruins of the old, we must consider the *ancien régime* in philosophy that Kant pulled down.

Modern philosophy begins with Bacon and Descartes. These men differed on many details, but they were one in demanding a fresh beginning in our efforts to understand man and nature and to use our knowledge of the latter for the benefit of the former. For both men, knowledge was power; for both men, most of what was then regarded as knowledge was mere "idols of the mind." When we say that modern philosophy, as instituted by Bacon and Descartes, is based on the faith in the infinite extendability of the scope of human reason, we are using the word "reason" ambiguously, simply as an opposite of faith, superstition, and ignorance. When we try to define what is distinctive of human reason that gives it power, we come upon a contrast between the Baconian and the Cartesian conceptions of the nature and proper use of reason. One emphasizes experience, the other intellection.

For Bacon, the careful observation of nature, without prepossessions drawn from Aristotelian philosophy, was the fundamental act of reason. For Descartes, it was the rational apprehension of self-evident propositions and deductions from them. For Bacon, natural history and experimental science were the highest form of knowledge; for Descartes, mathematics. From the first of these inspirations there grew, in the next century and a half, the philosophy known as empiricism, which taught that all our knowledge comes from sense experience and extends no farther than we can experience. From the latter there came the philosophy known as rationalism, which denigrated sensory knowledge as uncertain and held that true knowledge is like mathematics, dependent on reason alone.

Much of the history of philosophy from about 1600 to 1781, the year of the publication of Kant's *Critique of Pure Reason,* is the history of the conflict between these two interpretations of how man can best obtain knowledge. Empiricism and rationalism were alternative interpretations of the sciences of nature, mathematics, psychology, religion, and even ethics and political theory. Empiricists and rationalists differed in their estimation of the possibility of metaphysics, that part of philosophy claiming to give knowledge of ultimate reality. The rationalists held that reason can give such knowledge once it is freed from contamination by sense experience; the empiricists usually denied that there can be such knowledge since it cannot be based on sense experience. Newton, the empiricist who did more to explain the phenomena of nature than any other scientist, said, "I frame no hypotheses," i.e., conjectures about the ultimate forces underlying observable nature.

Kant's philosophical education was that of a rationalist. Early in his career, however, he came under the influence of Newton's science. In fact, he pushed Newtonian astronomy farther than anyone else of his time, using Newtonian principles to explain the origin and evolution of the solar system and not merely, as Newton did, its present structure. (He did this in his "nebula hypothesis," theorizing that the solar system originated by the gradual stratification of a whirling mass of gas, which he thought a nebula to be. This theory was further developed by the French astronomer Pierre Laplace and is now known as the "Kant–Laplace theory.")

Only gradually did Kant become aware of how little his Newtonian science fitted in with his rationalistic theory of knowledge and metaphysics. He was awakened, he says, from his "dogmatic slumber" (his unquestioning assumption of the power of reason, unaided by experience, to give us knowledge) by David Hume, the last of the great British empiricists.

Hume had taken quite literally the basic axiom of empiricism: "There is nothing in the intellect which was not first in the senses." By a careful examination of our common sense and scientific knowledge, he concluded that experience is necessary for us to say that one event, for example, lightning, is the cause of another event, thunder. But sense experience teaches us merely that one is usually or almost always followed by the other; it does not teach us that it is necessarily so, that the first *makes* the second happen, or that they will be joined together in the future. The concept of causality, i.e., the thought that two different events are necessarily connected, cannot be got from sense experience. Nor can it be got from reason, for it is not a logical law that it would be self-contradictory to deny. If, therefore, we are to remain faithful to the doctrines of empiricism, we have to declare the principle of causation to be based on neither reason nor sense experience. It is rather a subjective product of the custom or habit of seeing two events together and merely expecting the second to follow whenever the first occurs. This subjective principle of the association of ideas cannot be known to be objectively true. It is essential to us to act as if it were true; we could not, Hume says, live an hour without believing it. But believing is not knowing, and beyond the sphere of our practical needs there is no warrant for the principle at all. Thus Hume showed that empiricism, strictly interpreted, leads to skepticism.

The rationalists and empiricists had disputed also about the nature of space and the validity of geometric knowledge. Newton had argued that there is an absolute space accurately described by Euclidean geometry, and not just described as it is but as it must be. But our sense experience teaches us merely what is or what appears to be the case; it does not instruct us that something must be so. Hence, the empiricists had the problem of explaining the necessary truths of geometry, which they could not derive from sense experience. Hume undertook such an explanation by saying that the "truths" of geometry are merely logical consequences of definitions and are not necessarily true of things; they are like rules of a language we human beings speak, not laws necessarily applying to the things we talk about. Empiricism thus failed to explain the great accomplishments of Newton; it showed, rather, that a strict interpretation of empiricism conflicted with the mathematical principles of natural science presumably erected on the foundations of experience. Empiricism once again issued in skepticism.

But what was the alternative? Hume had shown that pure reason, without benefit of sense experience, was not able to give us knowledge of even the simplest facts; how much less is pure reason to be trusted when, renouncing sense experience as delusory, it pretends to pronounce confidently on metaphysical problems such as the existence of God and the ultimate nature of reality!

This was the situation in philosophy around 1780, when Kant undertook his revolution in philosophy and, for the first time, succeeded in assigning the two components of knowledge, sense experience and intellection, to their proper roles. He did so by means of his so-called Copernican Revolution. Copernicus, he reminds us, had been puzzled by the motions of the planets, which were supposed in ancient astronomy to move on circles about imaginary points that themselves moved around the earth in circles. He found that he could explain the apparent motions of the planets by supposing that the earth as well as the planets moved in circles around the sun. The apparent motions of the planets were their changes in perspective from a moving earth, and by knowing the *real* motions of the earth, Copernicus could explain the *apparent* motions of the planets. Kant reasoned by analogy: things we call real are not realities but the way realities appear to the human mind. In order to understand things, we must take into account the operations of the mind that knows them.

Another analogy will make this thought of Kant's more lucid. Imagine that everything appears blue to my sight; I ask, "Will things always appear blue to me?" They will if I am wearing blue spectacles; the things themselves may not be blue, but they will necessarily appear blue to me. Kant would say, "They will be blue a priori," meaning that I can know that they necessarily will appear blue and not merely that they just happened up to now to appear blue and therefore probably will continue to do so. *What* I see will depend on what the objective facts are; *how they appear* will depend on the spectacles I am wearing. Once again, as in the Copernican Revolution, attention is directed to the knowing mind and away from things as they are.

It is now time to interpret these analogies. The structure and operations of the mind are always with us; the things we observe come and go. The former determine how things must appear, and they are the basis of our a priori knowledge that things must always appear in Euclidean space and will be related to each other by the law of necessary causation. The latter, which we learn from sense experience, tells us, for example, merely that the figure on the blackboard is a triangle and not a circle and that it is lightning and not something else that is related to thunder as cause to effect. Without the operations of the mind our experience would be a "blooming, buzzing confusion," which Kant calls a "rhapsody of sensations." Without sense experience reason would present us only with empty thought-forms, such as "————— is the cause of —————," but not tell us what specific events to put into these blanks. Therefore, neither reason alone, as the rationalists believed, nor sense experience alone, as the empiricists believed, is able to give us knowledge; the former is empty, the latter is blind. Knowledge is the rational interpretation of sense experience in the light of some concepts and principles that are not derived from experience but are furnished by the operations of the mind alone.

This has been one of Kant's most fruitful thoughts. The developments in science and mathematics since his day have shown that some of the laws he believed to be necessary and to be known a priori were not so. He believed in the necessary truth of the logic, Euclidean mathematics, and Newtonian science of his time. All of these have been modified in the progress of knowledge since then. Yet the fundamental doctrine of the Copernican Revolution appears and reappears in the history of modern philosophy. From

*Kant's departure on daily walks from his house was so punctual that Königsberg housewives were said to set their clocks by it.*

the anthropologists we learn how other peoples with the same sense apparatus as ours interpret what they see in different ways and say they are seeing different things. The sociology of knowledge has relativized the Kantian categories of interpretation, which he believed were absolute, and teaches that they are culturally determined; thus we find that there are categories of magic and mythology that function in other societies much in the way the categories of science function in ours, and no community sees reality uncolored by the intellectual spectacles it wears. Marxian philosophy has taught that the modes of production in a society are responsible for its class structure and that each social class has its own categories ("ideology") for interpreting and controlling its history. Modern work in linguistics has pointed out the ways in which language functions as a kind of a priori filter through which sense experience must be pressed to become communicable and intelligible; the laws of grammar and semantics play a role in experience that Kant ascribed to his categories and principles. Even geometry and natural sciences have alternative structures within our own scientific community; it is possible to organize our spatial experience under Euclidean and under non-Euclidean principles, and for some purposes the one is simply more appropriate than the other. But ever since Kant it has been commonly recognized by philosophers that we don't see reality naively, we don't take it neat; rather, we doctor it up to fit in with our unconscious intellectual and cultural expectations.

*During the French Revolution Frederick William II of Prussia forbade Kant to speak or write on religion, fearing that his ideas might prove revolutionary.*

Kant could not have anticipated the developments I have just mentioned. He was writing at a time of unchallenged triumphs of Euclidean geometry and Newtonian science; he thought that the scientists had at last, under the tutelage of Newton, answered, or at least found the key to answer, all questions about the physical world. He lived in the Age of Enlightenment, the confident and optimistic eighteenth century, when men felt that not only in science but also in ethics and politics they had found the broad highway that would lead them inevitably to repeated triumphs of reason in the subjugation of nature and control in the affairs of men. It was the nineteenth century that found out how historically limited this optimism was, and how weak a reed human reason is; it discovered new forms of art, new ethical and political alternatives, and new world-pictures Kant could not have dreamed of. Yet all of these attested to a fundamental truth discovered by Kant: experience must be interpreted in order to be intelligible, and all human endeavors—science, mathematics, art, morals, politics, history, religion—can be understood only if the human contribution is properly estimated.

It is this human contribution to knowledge that keeps our knowing from being a perfect mirror of reality. In Kant's language, we do not know the thing in itself but only phenomena. Just as a rainbow is an appearance of drops of water that are not colored, the drops of water are in turn appearances of a thing in itself that is not even spatial. The thing in itself is completely unknown. Yet Kant is not a skeptic in regard to our knowledge of nature, as Hume was. Nature is knowable because it is nothing but phenomena under laws of the mind. It is odd, no doubt, to speak of a chair or a table as an appearance, and when Kant calls them appearances, he does not mean something illusory or dreamlike or subjective in the individual's consciousness. Appearances or phenomena are what we ordinarily take to be independent realities; but since we know something about them independently of experience—viz., that they *must* be spatial, they *must* have causes and effects—they can be only appearances, the joint products of an unknown thing in itself and the necessary operations of the mind in organizing the sense data we have of them. Hence Kant argues that the physical world is as Newton said it must be; there is no place for Hume's skeptical doubts about the laws of nature.

Still, there is something paradoxical about this answer to skepticism. We *know*, we do not just *believe*, truths about the physical world. The physical world is not ultimately real but only organized appearances; if it were real, we could not know about it a priori, as we do. Within the physical world we experience, we can distinguish true facts from illusory appearances. The stick in the water is really straight, and only appears to be bent. But in a deeper sense of "appearance," even the straight stick is an appearance of something that is nonphysical and nonspatial and unknowable. About it, Kant is as profound a skeptic as Hume. This is the price Kant had to pay for his answer to Hume's skepticism of science. And his answer leads directly into metaphysics, the study of ultimate reality.

It was here that the rationalists were most at home. For if sense experience is the lowest form of knowledge, to reach the highest degree of knowledge one should carefully exclude sensory knowledge and avail himself exclusively of rational principles. By doing so the rationalists professed to prove, without any appeal to empirical facts, that God exists, the soul is immortal, the will free, and other metaphysical theses. Hume was skeptical of these claims; he held that beliefs about causes and effects were indispensible in the practical affairs of life but had no warrant when used in speculation beyond practical needs. If the rationalists *could* prove them, well and good; but metaphysics is a battleground in which no rationalistic proof is ever so strong as to rout a proof of the opposite.

Kant agreed with Hume in his skeptical attitude toward metaphysical knowledge, but he argued that belief, which Hume had shown was essential in the ordinary daily affairs of life, was also essential and sufficient in metaphysics. He did not agree with Hume that a thinker could simply wash his hands of metaphysical speculation, using them only for empirical scientific work.

Since the categories of the mind do not originate from experience, but rather are presuppositions for there being any organized experience, Kant confesses that it seems they need not be usable only within the realm of experience. For example, what could be simpler than saying that the category of causality, relating one experienced event in a series to the next, also explains the series of events as a whole, relating the series of events in time and space to an ultimate cause which is neither spatial nor temporal? (This is one of the classic arguments for the existence of God, used by metaphysicians from Aristotle and Saint Thomas Aquinas to the rationalists Descartes and Leibnitz.) Kant regards it as inevitable that the human mind should think like this in its pursuit of completeness of explanation, but as nevertheless wrong. We can find *what* is the cause of *what* only by experience, guided by the rational principle of causality; but the principle by itself cannot supply the information that would verify any statement about what the cause is. The systematic effort to make reason do what only a combination of reason and experience can do is called metaphysics. No wonder, then, that for every "proof" in metaphysics there is an equally good "counterproof" and that metaphysics is a "wide and boundless ocean" with no landmarks by which the philosophical mariner can orient himself.

Kant thus faced a dilemma. Metaphysics is inevitable to a mind constituted like the human mind, bent on getting the *full* explanation of everything. Metaphysics is impossible to a mind constituted like the human mind, limited to organizing knowledge out of the raw data of the senses. To see how Kant escaped this dilemma, we must go back in history.

There has been a long debate in the history of Christianity about the respective claims of faith and reason. Saint Thomas Aquinas divided truths into two kinds: the truths of reason and the truths of faith. They could not be in conflict with each other, but truths of faith lie beyond the competence of reason to prove or disprove them. Reason was held by Saint Thomas to be capable of proving, for example, the existence of God; but that God is Three-in-One is an article of faith, vouchsafed to man by revelation, beyond reason but not against reason. In this distinction most modern philosophers (including even Sir Isaac Newton) followed Saint Thomas. But not Kant. He held that what was *beyond* reason was *against* reason, but not that everything it is reasonable to believe can be known to be true. Thus he modified Saint Thomas's classic distinction and said, "I found it necessary to deny knowledge [in metaphysics] in order to make room for faith." Note that he denied knowledge, not reason. He held that there could be a rational faith. It would be rational, because it is based on the rational capacity of the mind, which, in the world of sense experience, gives us knowledge and permits us to distinguish from error. But it would be faith, because it does not give us knowledge of what lies beyond sense experience.

The categories of the mind not only are necessary for the constitution of what we know, they also govern our vain but unavoidable pursuit of complete knowledge. As a regulative principle the law of causality does not tell us merely that every event we experience has a cause within experience; it tells us also to look for ever higher and simpler causes for the uniformity and harmony of nature. "God" is the name metaphysicians give to the cause of the world as a whole; and the belief that there is one cause of all the myriad variety of specific empirical laws of nature ought to regulate or govern our efforts to find simple explanation for them. It would therefore be unreasonable, Kant believed, for a scientist to deny the existence of God and thus rob himself of this regulative ideal that can give him confidence of success in the empirical study of nature. On the other hand, it would be dogmatic of him to claim that he knows that God exists, because our knowledge is restricted to what we can experience and integrate using such categories as that of causality.

One modern school of philosophy, called variously "logical positivism," the philosophy of the "Vienna Circle," and "logical empiricism," has followed Kant part of the way in his renunciation of metaphysical knowledge. Proponents of this school say that a proposition is meaningful if it can be verified or falsified in experience. Only such a proposition has "cognitive meaning." "The cat is under the table" is cognitively meaningful because we know what experiences would verify it or disconfirm it (you look under the table and see). "Atoms exist though they cannot be seen" is cognitively meaningful, because we know what experimental results in physics and chemistry would count for or against it. "God exists," on the other hand, is cognitively meaningless because we cannot say what experience would either confirm or disconfirm it. Literally speaking, "God exists" is nonsense (non-sense), like the words "Snarks are boojums." But the sentence "God exists" may have another kind of meaning, an "emotive meaning." Stating it in a certain tone of voice may motivate men, who believe that it is meaningful, true, and important, to act in certain ways. The job of the philosopher, according to these recent doctrines, is to teach us to distinguish cognitive from emotive meanings, to assign

Critik
der
reinen Vernunft
von
Immanuel Kant
Professor in Königsberg.

Riga,
verlegts Johann Friedrich Hartknoch
1781.

*Above is the title page of Kant's greatest work, the* Critique of Pure Reason.

the former to scientists who can find out empirically whether they are true or false, and the latter to preachers and poets, who may speak edifying nonsense, and to propagandists, who control men's behavior by persuading them that emotive meanings are cognitive meanings. Kant's regulative principles of metaphysics, according to the logical positivists, are merely emotive, encouraging the scientist in ways that the logical positivists think are dangerously misleading.

Another school of modern philosophy, the pragmatism of William James, has developed Kant's idea in a slightly different way, putting more emphasis on the "faith" Kant had in his regulative principles than in his denial of knowledge as if that were the most important concern of man. According to James, there are propositions like "God exists" that cannot be known to be true, and yet if one doubts their truth, the practical and emotional consequences are the same as if one had denied their truth. On these metaphysical problems, James holds, one cannot sit on the fence. And if the evidence for and against them is in equal balance, one should consider the consequences of believing or disbelieving them, which will be almost the same as the consequences of their actual truth or falsity, which we cannot rationally decide. James calls this situation the "will to believe," but his philosophy is a defense of the "right to believe" beyond what the evidence shows when momentous issues in human life and morals depend on belief or disbelief. We have a right to do "wishful thinking" when no other kind of thinking gives answers to our inescapable questions. Only in this respect do James and Kant disagree: Kant holds that one can be rational even beyond the evidence that is required for knowledge, while James holds that the only alternative to knowing is to let "our passional nature" decide for us. Yet it is remarkable that most of what Kant thought it was rational to believe was held by James to be warranted by the need of satisfying our "passional nature." Thus both believed in the existence of God, the immortality of the soul, and the freedom of the will.

Let us consider the third of these beliefs. Man himself is a part of the spatiotemporal world in which all events are linked to each other by inexorable causal laws. Human behavior is as predictable, Kant says, as eclipses of the sun and the moon. Only because of this can there be a science of human nature; and the science of human nature has not made the progress that the exact physical sciences have only because the phenomenon of man is the most complicated one we can observe. But psychology is predicated on the category of causality, the principle that there is a cause of every human action and that these causes can be described in general laws. There is no more place in psychology for uncaused actions, chance, and freedom than there is in chemistry. All is necessity, fate.

*Kant used the Andromeda Galaxy, above, to explain his nebula theory of the origin of the solar system.*

Yet we must remember that the world of phenomena, including human actions, is not a world of things as they are, but only as they appear. They appear under these laws because we have imposed these laws on phenomena in order to render them intelligible, explicable, and predictable. Man, however, is a citizen of two worlds. There is the world of spatiotemporal events, including human actions as they appear to us, and there is the world of the realities, including human beings as they are in themselves but unknown to us. Maybe, Kant is saying, causal mechanism holds only for the world of appearances, while the true reality is made up of free agents. If that is the case, there is no contradiction between determinism and freedom. Men may be free and only appear to be determined.

That there is no contradiction between them does not, of course, prove that men really are free; it merely means that it is not unrea-reasonable (illogical) to believe it. But Kant thinks that he has a stronger argument to show that men are indeed free.

Not only may man be a citizen of two worlds; his role in the world of appearances is twofold. He is first an observer, trying to make sense of his experience and build up an edifice of laws of nature that will explain what he observes. This is the attitude of the scientist, the psychologist, and the historian. Second, he is an actor, trying to decide what he ought to do. As observer, I can predict; as actor, I have to decide. Kant holds that as actor I have to believe that I am free to do one thing instead of another. If I were not free, I could not decide anything but would simply react to the strongest stimulus; and if I did not believe I was free, I could not even have the experience of deciding. I might wonder what I am about to do, but I could not understand what it means to deliberate on alternatives and decide between them.

At the beginning I mentioned Kant's pietistic upbringing. It made him take the actor-role of man as seriously as his scientific training made him take the spectator-role. Kant was as intent upon answering the skeptic in morals (the man who is indifferent to moral distinctions because he thinks they are illusory) as he was in answering the skeptic of scientific knowledge. He wanted to understand the experience of conscience, which tells us what we necessarily ought to do, just as he wanted to understand the experience that tells us (in our observer-role) what must happen. He did not believe that the empiricist in morals, who bases his moral judgments on feelings or observations, can explain the inexorability of the moral law and its universal applicability to all men any better than the empiricist in knowledge can explain the inexorability and unexceptionability of the causal law.

Just as Copernicus had furnished a model for Kant's theory of knowledge, now Rousseau gave him the clue to his ethical theory. Rousseau was a man very different in character from Kant, yet Kant admired his work so much that legend tells us he missed his afternoon walk when Rousseau's *Emile* arrived. Rousseau was concerned with the following problem: how can a citizen be free if he must obey the law? Rousseau's answer is that a man is free if and only if the law he obeys is one he has participated in enacting. Otherwise, he obeys the law only out of fear of the consequences of disobedience, and this means that he has the heart of a slave and not of a free citizen, even if he is fortunate enough to live under a benign government. Rousseau's *Social Contract* is a political document; but Kant took this teaching from it and made it the basis for his ethics.

Thus there is in Kant not only a Copernican Revolution against the thought that the laws of nature can simply be read off from observations; there is also a Rousseauan Revolution, that the laws of morality are not given to men (by God, by society) but are dictated by man, as a rational being, to himself as a creature of sense and emotion. It is our moral obligation to act in the way that reason guides us, not just to act in a way that will perhaps secure us happiness and well-being in the world of sense. We are to ask of any precept on which we are inclined to act: would I be willing for all men to act on this precept? If I make an exception to a general rule that I want all men to follow, and do so for the sake of some possible benefit that might accrue to me by exempting myself from the general rule, then I am acting irrationally. I am like the slave in Rousseau's state, who is following a law he himself did not make but takes from his psychological make-up and social circumstances. But when I follow a law I (my reason) make, then, like Rousseau's citizen, I am free even though I (as a sensuous being) am under a law.

Kant's political theory is based on the same consideration. There are two ways in which representative government has been defended by philosophers. One is that a government is likely to be most responsive to the needs of the citizens if they are consulted; in other words, a representative form of government is justified by its contribution to the well-being of the citizenry. Kant believes that this is so; but it is not the reason he favored representative government. He was more devoted to the dignity of man than he was to man's happiness. He held that only a representative form of government is compatible with the dignity of man as a free, autonomous agent. Any form of government that does things for, or to, citizens that they cannot, or will not, do for themselves demeans them, either patronizing them like children (if it is a benign rule) or using them as tools in the interests of the ruler (if it is not benign). Kant wrote too late to have an influence on the French and American revolutions; but his political philosophy is an ex post facto justification of what they were fought for.

In Kant's theory of the absolute autonomy of each moral agent and citizen, one can see some of the contributions he made to contemporary existential philosophy. Existential philosophy takes man as actor and subordinates his role as spectator. It is the business of philosophy to understand man as an actor who transcends the exigencies of the momentary state of the world and thereby exercises his absolute freedom from being determined by circumstance. That existential choices cannot be governed, indeed, ought not be governed, by reason is one of the chief tenets of existential philosophy, for existentialists regard even rationality as an infringement of absolute individual freedom. But Kant thought a lawless freedom was no freedom at all, and held that in obeying reason man was truly free because he was only obeying his higher self.

Kant was troubled by attacks on reason in his own time from men who were the immediate forebears of the romantic reaction against his philosophy and the distant ancestors of philosophers like Kierkegaard and Sartre. He addressed them: "Men of intellectual power and broad minds, I honor your talents and love your feeling for humanity! But have you considered what you do, and where you will end, with your attacks on reason?" In these words the Age of Reason admonishes our troubled age, in which reason rules in science and unreason governs man.

*Kant was a convivial host who used a dinner party as he did his classes, to stimulate the guests' own ideas.*

# JEREMY
# BENTHAM
## 1748-1832

I n Gower Street in London, among the gray early-nineteenth-century squares of Bloomsbury and not far from the British Museum, is University College, the oldest college of the University of London. After crossing the courtyard, past the great Corinthian portico, and turning into the main entrance hall, one finds oneself confronted, at the far end on the right, by what appears to be a large and rather handsome clothes cupboard. Lettered in gilt across the top are the words JEREMY BENTHAM. It is, in fact, a bald and entirely accurate description of the contents. For when the doors are opened, one indeed finds, screened by a pane of glass, Jeremy Bentham—legal philosopher, reformer, oracle, and sage to many influential disciples in all parts of the world—who died a hundred and forty years ago. His garments drab with age, he sits, in the manner he himself directed, as though poised to write one of those characteristic sentences, original in content but grammatically a calculated assault upon the English language, that appear so frequently in the vast piles of Bentham manuscripts housed in another part of the college.

In only one respect is his "Auto-Icon," as Bentham called this bizarre legacy of himself, inauthentic: the head, with its aged broad-brimmed hat and mild, benign half-smile, is a wax replica. The actual head, after resting a trifle obscenely for a while at Bentham's feet, is now housed on a shelf above, in a box rather like a large tea caddy. Bentham, in the clause of his will that provided instructions for this disposal of himself, added the slightly macabre wish that if his friends should care to hold occasional gatherings to honor the memory of the

*Jeremy Bentham's mummy (with a new wax head) still sits in its London cabinet.*

By J. W. BURROW

founder of the "philosophy of utility," he might be physically present.

There is a literalness about all this—a desire always to evoke the concrete nub of the matter, leaving as little as possible to the imagination—that is typical of Bentham's thought. He once observed it was a pity the apple that had supposedly suggested to Newton the idea of gravitation had not been preserved in a glass case. He himself, who had written of his aspiration to be the Newton of legislation, was to miss no such opportunity: *si monumentum requiris*—if you are seeking a memorial . . . open the cupboard doors.

It would be false and ungenerous, however, to imply that Bentham's real legacy could be confined within a nicely polished wooden box. When he died in 1832, just two days before the passage of the great Reform Act enlarging the franchise for which he and his followers had worked, his name was already both revered and controversial. For the greater part of his long life he had worked with little recognition, covering endless sheets of paper with diverse and often uncompleted projects that were written, in his later years, in an increasingly obscure and uncouth jargon of his own perverse creation. It was a style that led the critic William Hazlitt to remark that, Bentham's works having been translated into French, they should now be translated into English.

Bentham must often have seemed merely a gifted crank, toiling over tasks doomed to remain unfinished and unappreciated. Apart from what was, in a sense, the central work of his life, a constitutional code, there were plans for a model prison, perpetual peace, and a new universal grammar; long essays and pamphlets on economics, education, the poor law, usury, and rules of evidence; and radical and anticlerical tracts. Much of this mass is still unpublished, but the doyen of Bentham scholarship, Charles W. Everett, has estimated the total quantity to be some twenty million words. Bentham was, in some ways, the archetype of the unrecognized inventor, though his practical inventions were only a side line. He slept in a sleeping bag of his own design, experimented with refrigeration, and drew up projects for a harpsichord, speaking tubes, and a canal in Central America. But it was his work on the reconstruction of law and institutions that remained his abiding passion.

He eventually achieved a partial reward. Bentham lived to the age of eighty-four, and in the last two decades of his life he acquired a measure of recognition and a devoted band of disciples who proclaimed his philosophy and made it a vital and highly influential element in the great movement of reform that culminated in the early 1830's. Abroad, he became famous from Russia to South America, a revered father-figure for liberals in all parts of the world. "His name,"

Hazlitt wrote, slightly exaggerating the contrast for rhetorical effect, "is little known in England, better in Europe, best of all in the plains of Chili and the mines of Mexico. He has offered constitutions for the New World, and legislated for future times." John Stuart Mill, the eldest son of Bentham's chief disciple, James Mill, bracketed Bentham and Samuel Taylor Coleridge as "the two great seminal minds of England in their age," and went on to say that "there is hardly to be found in England an individual of any importance in the world of mind, who . . . did not first learn to think from one of these two."

In his earlier years Bentham had been a friend of the Whig prime minister Lord Shelburne; he had corresponded with the French revolutionary statesman Mirabeau and with the Autocrat of all the Russias, Catherine the Great. But it was in his later years, through a superficially drab group of younger followers, middle-class journalists, and educated artisans, that the influence of Bentham's ideas made itself felt: men like the dour Scotsman James Mill, the intellectual mastermind of the radical party, and his brilliant son John Stuart Mill, one of the mentors of the Victorian age. Other disciples included the historian George Grote and the jurist John Austin, key figures in the new London University; radical politicians and agitators like John Arthur Roebuck, Joseph Hume, and Francis Place; and Edwin Chadwick, the great pioneer of public health and the poor law, who had been Bentham's secretary. Limited and philistine though some of them were, gray and forbidding though their creed often seemed to more impulsive and emotional natures (Thomas Carlyle called Benthamite utilitarianism "pig-philosophy"), these men were among the makers of Victorian England.

*A Cruikshank engraving depicts the divided society Bentham hoped his theories would heal.*

There were wide differences of temperament among them, but to outsiders they often seemed to be simply members of a new, aggressive, doctrinaire sect, whose points of similarity merged into a single caricature: the Utilitarian. Charles Dickens drew an unforgettable picture of one in the character of Mr. Gradgrind. The Benthamite utilitarian, seen in this light, was a bloodless calculator, intent on reducing the richness and complexity of human life and human feelings to "Mr. Bentham's oracles of utility," remorselessly processing such intangibles as pity, sentiment, beauty, and poetry through a kind of intellectual machine called "utilitarian philosophy" and coldly evaluating the results. He was a stony-faced philistine who turned men's moral and emotional life into a sort of double-entry bookkeeping of profit and loss, pleasure and pain. Some of the accusations were even contradictory. Thus, the Benthamite was both a doctrinaire man of theories and abstractions and a crass materialist who could appreciate nothing but hard facts and crude satisfactions. It would not be too difficult to find evidence to substantiate these charges, though they do not really apply to any single member of the group.

There was also, however, a natural tendency to identify this collective portrait with the founder himself and to identify the word "Benthamite" with the man Bentham. To Karl Marx, for example, Bentham was the epitome of the narrow-minded bourgeois intellectual, the English shopkeeper turned philosopher: "the arch-philistine Jeremy Bentham, the insipid pedantic leather tongued oracle of the commonplace bourgeois intelligence of the nineteenth century." To Hazlitt he was a benign freak, a comically impractical enthusiast with no experience of life.

Hazlitt was a dramatic critic, and he presented Bentham like some old character actor's stock notion of "the philosopher." "He has lived for the last forty years in a house in Westminster, overlooking the Park, like an anchoret in his cell, reducing law to a system, and the mind of man to a machine . . . He regards the people about him no more than the flies of a summer. He meditates the coming age. He hears and sees only what suits his purpose, or some 'foregone conclu-

Bentham sought to alleviate the pointless monotony of prison life shown in this Doré engraving.

sion,' and looks out for facts and passing occurrences in order to put them into his logical machinery and grind them into the dust and powder of some subtle theory."

The members of the Benthamite school contributed to this picture. Francis Place said he was as "simple as a child." The young John Stuart Mill, in revolt against the narrowness of his upbringing, wrote, rather recklessly, of him he had known personally only as an old man: "He had neither internal experience nor external; the quiet, even tenor of his life, and his healthiness of mind, conspired to exclude him from both. He never knew prosperity and adversity, passion nor satiety; he never had even the experiences which sickness gives; he lived from childhood to the age of eighty-five in boyish health. He never felt life a sore and weary burthen. He was a boy to the last."

How much truth is there in this portrait of an elderly bachelor by a brilliant but discontented younger man? Was Bentham a half-man, a stranger to all but a fragment of the full range of human passions and experience, a benevolent calculating machine? Was he really benevolent? (Even this has had doubts cast upon it.) We shall never get a final answer. But it is at least clear that Mill's portrait is overdrawn. For a fuller understanding of him, we must turn from the old Bentham to the young one, to the Jeremy Bentham whom John Stuart Mill did not personally know.

Jeremy Bentham was born in 1748, in Houndsditch, London, the son of a prosperous businessman. Undersized and weakly but intellectually precocious, he was sent by his father to Oxford at age twelve. There, set apart from his fellows by his youth, he found little that appealed to him except a portion of the instruction in logic. He also endured an experience he never forgot: like all members of the university at the time, he had to affirm his adherence to the Thirty-nine Articles of Religion required by the Church of England. Unbelieving, Bentham did so with a passionate shame and resentment that left him lastingly embittered against both the clergy and judicial formalities.

After Oxford he became a student of law at the Inns of Court and met another disillusionment, for the law, like the universities, was passing through a period of decadence. The English lawyer's love of precedent and judge-made law, and his dislike of rigid systematization and the constricting logic of a legal code, had been carried to extreme lengths. By the late eighteenth century this had produced a situation approaching total chaos, a tangle of unsystematically related branches of law, of precedent piled on precedent, often contradictory, of gross anomalies and absurd legal fictions. To be able to pick one's way through even a part of this unpruned jungle required an erudition as profound as it was pointless for any purpose except to make the law profitable to lawyers, slow in operation, inequitable in its results, and totally incomprehensible to the unfortunate layman who became enmeshed in it. In criminal law callous injustice was supplemented by brutal atrocity—men were hanged, and women still sometimes burned, for trivial offenses, while graver ones frequently carried lighter sentences.

Such was the system whose operation the young Bentham set out to study by attendance at the courts held in Westminster Hall, the great medieval hall outside the houses of Parliament, where Charles I had been tried and where England monarchs still lie in state before their funerals. In Bentham's mature philosophy he would attempt to reconstruct men's habits of moral judgment—taking nothing on trust, allowing no appeal to habit, however ingrained, or sentiment, however profound, devising a new set of rules, a new language virtually, for legislative and judicial procedure and for moral appraisal. If there seems at times to be something almost maniacal about the sheer comprehensiveness of this program, something blatantly unrealistic about the determination to undercut everything habitual and historically given, one has only to remember that Bentham as a young man had closely observed a system in which men's ordinary moral habits and sentiments had become warped or rendered powerless by tradition and blind respect for precedent.

Yet, it was in the heart of this chaos that Bentham found his vocation. The law was a snare of unco-ordinated precedents; he would be for system and codification. The law was incomprehensible; he would devise a legal language, and a legal system, that was comprehensible even to the layman. The law was riddled with fictions, whereby things were described as something they manifestly were not; he would be against all fictions—in law, in morals, and in politics. The law was full of arbitrary, burdensome, and useless procedural rules and rituals; he would bring everything, in law and in life, to the test of its usefulness. "And have I indeed a genius for legislation?" he wrote. "I gave myself the answer, fearfully and trembling—Yes!"

Bentham knew he would never practice the law as it then existed. Such impracticality had its price; when he fell in love with a girl more than ten years his junior and wished to marry her, his ambitious father was unsympathetic. Bentham's worldly prospects were not good, the girl became impatient, and the affair fizzled out. Bentham remained a bachelor, and became a critic, a reformer, a would-be legislator, and the founder of a truly scientific jurisprudence.

In contrast to the archaic muddle of English law, Bentham had three main resources. The first was his own sense of equity and a cast of mind both orderly and systematic, even to excess. At Oxford he had discovered an aptitude for logic; he always liked to order and arrange, to group into classes and subclasses, to define, and then to define the elements of the definition, in a kind of bureaucracy of the intellect. The second was a hobby in which he found an order and precision that his profession so significantly lacked. He had always had a bent for science and technology; now he performed physical and chemical experiments in his lawyer's chambers and corresponded with the eminent chemist Joseph Priestley. The third resource was the self-consciously enlightened philosophy of eighteenth-century Europe, which for Bentham combined intellectual system with philanthropic purpose. In the writings of philosophers and psychologists working within the theory of knowledge established during the seventeenth century by John Locke, he found the notion that all complex ideas arise from sense experiences; if our concepts are not simply meaningless words and rhetoric, they must be reducible to terms that refer to our sensations.

The complexity of human motives, Bentham came to think, could similarly be resolved into two basic drives: the desire for pleasure and the avoidance of pain. The French philosopher Helvétius and the Italian jurist Beccaria had suggested how these ideas might be applied to devising a science of legislation and punishment, with the pains imposed by legal penalties nicely judged to provide just the right amount of disincentive for the various forms of antisocial behavior. From the philosophical writings of the Englishman Priestley, Bentham took the formula that for him expressed the end to be sought in every action: the greatest happiness of the greatest number. It was a discovery that evoked from him Archimedes' cry of exaltation: "Eureka!"

Henceforth, everything must be brought to the judgment of this test. There was no law, no punishment, no action good or bad in its very nature; it was made so only by its consequences, measured by the standard of the "principle of utility." Legal codes, governmental institutions, prisons, schools, the moral judgments of mankind—all must be reorganized in accordance with this central idea. It would be pointless, he held, for the moralist to wish men to desire something other than pleasure, or to want "higher" pleasures than those they now want. There are no higher or lower pleasures, for this introduces an arbitrary and personal standard of judgment: "Pleasure for pleasure, push-pin is as good as poetry." Since pleasure is what all men want, no pleasure is bad in itself.

So far, this sounds like a recipe for universal permissiveness and anarchy. But there is *one* standard for judging between rival pleasures that is not arbitrary—that is a necessary consequence of deciding that pleasures or happiness is what is good and to be sought. This is *quantity* of pleasure. It would be irrational, if pleasure was the only good, for us not to esteem a greater quantity of pleasure more than a lesser one, and not to discourage or prohibit pleasures that, although good in themselves, ultimately caused an amount of pain that outweighed the pleasure.

Bentham, in what he called his "Felicific Calculus," tried to devise ways of measuring pleasure by such qualities as certainty, intensity, duration, and so forth. All pleasures, for Bentham, were innocent until proven guilty by their consequences, however unsavory their traditional reputation. He pointed out that we only use words like "lust" and "avarice" when we have already decided that the consequences of these motives are bad; the neutral terms are "sexual desire" and "desire for gain." But an action or institution that failed,

*James Mill, top, was the leading promulgator of Bentham's ideas. His son John Stuart, below, was raised on utilitarian principles but rebelled against them before expounding them later in his writings.*

when all the calculations had been made, to come out on the plus, or "pleasure," side of the ledger was useless or pernicious, and should be prohibited or abolished. He took into account, of course, the fact that legal prohibition, backed by punishment, was itself the infliction or threat of a pain, and hence, always an evil and justified only by the prevention of a greater evil.

Bentham published these ideas in 1789 in his chief theoretical work, *An Introduction to the Principles of Morals and Legislation*. But the path to practical reform proved a long and weary one. The outbreak of the French Revolution, and the Reign of Terror, made reforming ideas suspect among the English governing class. Bentham himself allowed his time and energies to be dispersed among a number of different projects. Among them was one that absorbed the personal fortune he had inherited from his father and gave him the severest disappointments of his life. This was a project that became for a number of years an overriding obsession: the panopticon. The name derives from the Greek, meaning "all-seeing," and it was a plan for a model prison, which was later also adapted to the purposes of a paupers' workhouse.

The original idea seems to have come from Bentham's brother Samuel, who was a naval engineer, and Bentham saw in it a remedy for the prison conditions that had already become a scandal in the late eighteenth century. In the jails of the period scenes of Hogarthian squalor were normal. Prisoners—men, women, and children—were herded together in stench and filth, without discipline or supervision. The jailers were corrupt, and the jails formed a concentrated, exaggerated image of the world beyond their walls: the poor starved and the rich lived high, if disease did not take them, for jail fever was a recognized and lethal condition, which struck down lawyers and judges as well as prisoners.

Bentham's panopticon was to be an antiseptic place of silence and order and industry and minute supervision. The world of Hogarth was to give way to the world of the laboratory mouse. The building was to be circular, with the cells around the periphery; at the center, like a spider in its web, stood the jailer. By a special arrangement of slats, he would be able to observe every cell while himself remaining invisible, communicating with the inmates by a system of speaking tubes. All the squalor and disorder and overcrowding, the rioting and vice of the existing system, were to be replaced by a healthy, centrally heated, silent penal utopia, from which human viciousness, human contact, and human warmth were alike eliminated.

Perhaps the most remarkable feature was that the system was to be run by private contract, and as the contractor Bentham proposed— himself. For years he pressed his scheme, against all criticism, on a

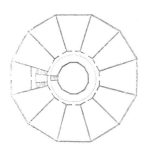

Bentham's circular panopticon plan for a prison enabled a single attendant to keep an eye on all inmates.

reluctant government. He sank his fortune into the purchase of land for the project. The great antislavery reformer William Wilberforce reported seeing Bentham with tears running down his cheeks in frustration and bitterness at the government's indifference. It is little wonder that in later years he did not care to bring up the memory of his panopticon: "it is like opening a drawer where devils are locked up."

Eventually, in 1813, Bentham's personal situation was restored by substantial government compensation. The ensuing years, as the admired head of a growing band of followers, seem to have been the happiest of his life. The disappointed man of Wilberforce's description gave way to the blithe old boy of John Stuart Mill's. In his bachelor comfort he became the benevolent eccentric of the legend, making little jokes, singing little songs (he was always devoted to music, especially Handel), fussing over his small domestic rituals, and endlessly writing. He was fond of animals, particularly "pusses and mouses," and gave pet names to his household possessions. The teapot was Dick, or Dicky. "Has my Dick begun his song?" he would ask. And when duly boiling: "Take down Dicky; he is in a passion."

Whether one finds this endearing, harmless, or repellent is, perhaps, a clue to one's attitude toward Bentham and Benthamism in general. There will never be a unanimous verdict on either. For to define one's reactions to Bentham involves reference to a set of dichotomies in human life that are as basic as the distinction between light and dark, or between hot and cold: logic versus sentiment; facts versus imagination; rationalization and system versus habit and tradition; calculation versus impulse. Most men would be willing to admit the necessity for both in some measure. But in the case of Bentham, who observed that "all poetry is misrepresentation," one seems forced to make a choice.

To his critics Bentham is a man who erected his limitations into a system, as John Stuart Mill implied. All his life Bentham was frightened—quite literally—of ghosts, and he connected this fear with his hatred of vague abstractions in moral and political philosophy. Knowing this, it is tempting to see something obsessive in his search for clarity and order.

But at what cost? Traditionalists and existentialists, Marxists and aesthetes, find it hard to say much good of Bentham. And he is hardly likely to become a cult figure for the young. Others find him more sympathetic. He was not strictly a behaviorist, but behaviorist psychologists find him a kindred spirit, as do logical positivists and social scientists interested in game-theory models. Logicians and philosophical jurists can admire his subtle and penetrating exploration of the logic of commands and the elegance of his principles of legal codifica-

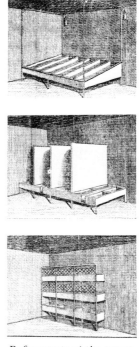

*Refinements of the panopticon included "bed-stages" for single people, top, and for married couples, center, with the couples separated by partitions and infants' cribs. Some babies would be put into caged cribs.*

tion. Criminologists now generally share his emphasis on deterrence and reformation rather than retribution for its own sake.

But as a moral and political philosopher Bentham continues to arouse not merely specific criticisms of his logical deficiencies but also a certain pervasive uneasiness. This uneasiness has been strikingly crystallized by Gertrude Himmelfarb in a recent essay on the panopticon. Bentham's model prison emerges as a nightmarish image of his own mind, of a desire to retreat into a perfectly ordered, insulated world, in which he would assume, at its center, the omnipotence and the omniscience—and the invisibility—of God. The totalitarian parallel is too close for comfort, and at the heart of the system there seems to be a kind of fear.

All pleasures, in themselves, are desirable. This principle could be a motto for a hippie commune. But it is not only Bentham's emphasis on calculation, his denigration of impulse and neglect of spontaneity, that set him apart from such a context. It is true that there is a strong libertarian and equalitarian strain in Bentham's thought; all pleasures are good and all are equal—except in quantity. But liberty is not a good in itself; it is only a means to good, which is pleasure, or the maximization of happiness. Bentham generally endorsed private judgment as a more efficient means than government action, just as he generally endorsed private property rather than large-scale expropriation. But these principles are not intrinsic to the utilitarian position. They are not conceded as rights but adopted as means.

The possibilities of conditioning human beings, stressed by Helvétius, is not ignored by Bentham, though generally, it is true, he displays an agreeably libertarian concern for getting people the maximum amount of what they actually like, rather than with getting them to like the maximum amount of what they are actually getting. Nevertheless, there is no defense in Benthamite principles against the benevolent despot who wants to make men happy by placing a drug in the water supply or electrodes in the brain, provided he takes the trouble to do it efficiently. The examples were unknown to Bentham, but the spirit was not altogether so. "Call them soldiers, call them monks, call them machines," he wrote, "so they were but happy ones, I should not care."

The vague terms that Bentham despised and tried to eliminate, terms like human rights and human dignity, are in some respects, it seems, a better defense of what most of us think of as our interests and our humanity than Benthamite utilitarianism is. To see other people and ourselves essentially as potential recipients of stimuli, pleasant or painful, has a kind of impartiality that can on occasion be a salutary dissolvent of prejudice, but if systematized into a view and a rule of life, can become impoverishing and even sinister. The limits of my language, Ludwig Wittgenstein said, are the limits of my world, and Bentham's language, in his search for concreteness and precision and system, became increasingly like the Newspeak of George Orwell's *1984.*

Our ordinary language, in its vagueness and imprecision, with its load of often unacknowledged prejudices, reflects and accommodates a diversity of values and ways of living. It is, therefore, richer in possibilities than a language tailored to the requirements of a theoretical consistency. The latter is useful in specific and limited contexts, where precision is required above all; generalized, it can become uncomfortably like a prison. It can be argued that it is with just such a specialized field—law—that Bentham was chiefly concerned. But his aspirations were wider. "We shall for we will," he wrote to his French translator Étienne Dumont, "be despots of the moral world." It was a figure of speech, but figures of speech are sometimes significant.

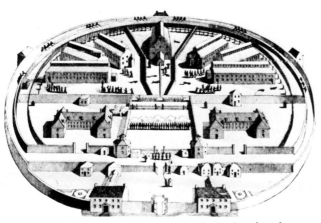

*Bentham's panopticon was never built, but its plan was adapted for institutions like England's Dartmoor.*

# MARY
# WOLLSTONECRAFT
## 1759-1797

<br>

T he first person—male or female—to speak at any length and to any effect about woman's rights was Mary Wollstonecraft. In 1792, when her *Vindication of the Rights of Woman* appeared, Mary was a beautiful spinster of thirty-three who had made a successful career for herself in the publishing world of London. This accomplishment was rare enough for a woman in that day. Her manifesto, at once impassioned and learned, was an achievement of real originality. The book electrified the reading public and made Mary famous. The *Vindication* has gone through almost a score of editions and is in print today, but, like many another revolutionary tract, it has probably been more talked about than read. The core of its argument is simple: "I wish to see women neither heroines nor brutes; but reasonable creatures," Mary wrote. Any of today's militants who look into the book may be disappointed to find that their ancestress did not demand day-care centers or an end to woman's traditional role as wife and mother, nor did she call anyone a chauvinist pig. The happiest period of Mary's own life was when she was married and awaiting the birth of her second child. And the greatest delight she ever knew was in her first child, an illegitimate daughter. Mary's feminism may not appear today to be the hard-core revolutionary variety, but she did live, for a time, a scandalous and unconventional life—"emancipated," it is called by those who have never tried it. The essence of her thought, however, is the gentle proposal that a woman's mind is as good as a man's and ought to be developed equally.

*This portrait of Mary Wollstonecraft was painted shortly before her death in 1797.*

*By* SHIRLEY TOMKIEVICZ

Not many intelligent men could be found to dispute this proposition today, at least not in mixed company. In Mary's time, to speak of *anybody's* rights, let alone woman's rights, was a radical act. In England, as in other nations, "rights" were an entity belonging to the government. The common run of mankind had little access to what we now call "human rights." As an example of British justice in the late eighteenth century, the law cited two hundred different capital crimes, among them shoplifting. An accused man was not entitled to counsel. A child could be tried and hanged as soon as an adult. The first law acknowledging the rights of children, as distinct from the rights of their employers, came forth only in 1802. The right to vote existed, certainly, but because of unjust apportionment, it had come to mean little. The ten or fifteen inhabitants of a "rotten" borough in the south could send their man to Parliament while the densely populated new factory towns in the north usually had no representation at all. In the United States, where much was being said about the rights of man, some of these abuses had been corrected—but the rights of man did not extend past the color bar and the masculine gender was intentional. In the land of Washington and Jefferson, as in the land of George III, human rights were a new idea and woman's rights were not even an issue.

In France, in 1792, a Revolution in the name of equality was in full course, and woman's rights had at least been alluded to. The Revolutionary government drew up plans for female education—to the age of eight. "The education of the women should always be relative to the men," Rousseau had written in *Emile*. "To please, to be useful to us, to make us love and esteem them, to educate us when young, and take care of us when grown up, to advise, to console us, to render our lives easy and agreeable: these are the duties of women at all times, and what they should be taught in their infancy." And, less prettily, "Women have, or ought to have, but little liberty."

If Rousseau had visited England in the late eighteenth century, he would have found little cause for complaint. An Englishwoman had almost the same civil status as an American slave. Thomas Hardy, a hundred years hence, was to base a novel on the idea of a man casually selling his wife and daughter at public auction. Obviously this was not a common occurrence, but neither is it wholly implausible. In 1792, and later, a woman could not own property, nor keep any earned wages. All that she possessed belonged to her husband. She could not divorce him, but he could divorce her and take her children. There was no law to say she could not grow up illiterate or be beaten every day.

Of course, a system so harsh tends partially to nullify itself by being unenforceable, but such was the legal and moral climate in which Mary Wollstonecraft lived. How she came to value education above all else is easily seen through an account of her early years. Mary was born in London in the spring of 1759, the second child and first daughter of Edward Wollstonecraft, a prosperous weaver. Two more daughters and two more sons were eventually born into the family, making six children in all. Before they had all arrived, Mr. Wollstonecraft came into an inheritance and decided to move his family to the country and become a gentleman farmer. But whatever agricultural efforts he may have made came to nothing. His money dwindled, and he began drinking heavily. His wife turned into a terrified wraith whose only interest was her eldest son, Edward. Only he escaped the beatings and abuse that his father dealt out regularly to every other household member, from Mrs. Wollstonecraft to the family dog. As often happens in large and disordered families, the eldest sister had to assume the role of mother and scullery maid. Mary was a bright, strong child, determined not to be broken, and she undertook her task energetically, defying her father when he was violent and keeping her younger brothers and sisters in hand. Clearly, Mary held the household together and in so doing forfeited her own childhood. This experience left her with an everlasting gloomy streak, and was a factor in making her a reformer.

Original Stories, *a book for children, was Mary's first literary success. William Blake did the illustrations, many of them depicting scenes from family life, like the pair shown here.*

At some point in Mary's childhood, another injustice was visited upon her, though so commonplace for the time that she can hardly have felt the sting. Her elder brother was sent away to be educated, and the younger children were left to learn their letters as best they could. The family now frequently changed lodgings, but from her ninth to her fifteenth year Mary went to a day school, where she had the only formal training of her life. Fortunately, this included French and composition, and somewhere Mary learned to read critically and widely. These skills, together with her curiosity and determination, were really all she needed. The *Vindication* is in some parts long-winded, ill-punctuated, and simply full of hot air, but it is the work of a well-informed mind.

Feminists—and Mary would gladly have claimed the title—inevitably, even deservedly, get bad notices. The term calls up an image of relentless battle-axes: "thin college ladies with eyeglasses, nononsense features, mouths thin as bologna slicers, a babe in one arm, a hatchet in the other, grey eyes bright with balefire," as Norman Mailer feelingly envisions his antagonists in the Women's Liberation Movement. He has conjured up all the horrid elements: the lips with a cutting edge, the baby immaculately conceived (one is forced to conclude), the lethal weapon tightly clutched, the desiccating college degree, the joylessness. Hanging miasmally over the tableau is the suspicion of a deformed sexuality. Are these girls man-haters, or worse? Or merely cryptonymphomaniacs? Mary Wollstonecraft, as the first of her line, has had each of these scarlet letters (except the B.A.) stitched upon her bosom. Yet she conformed very little to the hateful stereotype. As she began her adult life, however, she would have chilled Mailer's bones in at least one respect. Having spent her childhood as an adult, Mary reached the age of nineteen in a state of complete joylessness. She was later to quit the role, but for now she wore the garb of a self-sacrificing victim.

Her early twenties, grim as might be expected, were spent in this elderly frame of mind. First she went out as companion to an old lady living at Bath. "I am above the servants, yet considered by them as a spy," she wrote home miserably; the rest of the house looked down on her as a servant. After two years, Mary was called home to nurse her dying mother. Then the family broke up entirely, though the younger sisters continued off and on to be dependent on Mary. The family of Mary's dearest friend, Fanny Blood, invited her to come and live with them; the two girls made a small living doing sewing and handicrafts, and Mary dreamed of starting a primary school. Eventually, in a pleasant village called Newington Green, this plan materialized and prospered. But Fanny Blood in the meantime had married and moved to Lisbon. She wanted Mary to come and nurse her through the birth of her first child. Always ready to make a costly sacrifice, Mary borrowed money and made the journey. She reached Lisbon just in time to see her friend die of childbed fever, and returned home just in time to find that her sisters, in whose care the flourishing little school had been left, had lost all but two pupils.

Mary made up her mind to die. "My constitution is impaired, I hope I shan't live long," she wrote to a friend in February, 1786, shortly after returning from Lisbon, adding with the feeblest glimmer of hope, "Yet I may be a tedious time dying." Under this almost habitual grief, however, Mary was gaining some new sense of herself. Newington Green, apart from offering her a brief successs as a schoolmistress, had brought her some acquaintance in the world of letters, most important among them Joseph Johnson, an intelligent and successful London publisher in search of new writers. Debt-ridden and penniless, Mary now set aside her impaired constitution and wrote her first book, probably in the space of a week. Johnson bought it for ten guineas and published it. Called *Thoughts on the Education of Daughters,* it went unnoticed (without shaking Johnson's faith in Mary), and the ten guineas were soon spent. Mary had to find work. She accepted a position as governess in the house of Lord and Lady Kingsborough in the north of Ireland.

Mary's letters from Ireland to her sisters and to Joseph Johnson are so filled with Gothic gloom, so stained with tears, that one cannot

*William Godwin, the political philosopher, was Mary's husband and the father of her second child.*

keep from laughing at them. "I entered the great gates with the same kind of feeling I should have if I was going to the Bastille," she wrote upon entering Kingsborough Castle in the fall of 1786. Mary was now twenty-seven. Her most recent biographer, Margaret George, believes that Mary was not really suffering so much as she was having literary fantasies. In private she was furiously at work on a novel entitled, not very artfully, *Mary, A Fiction.* This is the story of a young lady of immense sensibilities who closely resembles Mary except that she has wealthy parents, a neglectful bridegroom, and an attractive lover. The title and fantasizing contents are precisely what a scribbler of thirteen might secretly concoct. Somehow Mary was embarking on her adolescence, fifteen years after the usual date. She was dreaming of herself with money and advantages and a lover whispering "dear creature!" in her ear. Mary's experience in Kingsborough Castle was a fruitful one, for all her complaints. In the summer of 1787 she lost her post as governess and set off for London with her novel. Not only did Johnson accept it for publication, he offered her a regular job as editor and translator and helped her find a place to live.

Thus, aged twenty-eight, Mary put aside her doleful persona as the martyred, set-upon elder sister. How different she is now, jauntily writing from London to her sisters: "Mr. Johnson . . . assures me that if I exert my talents in writing I may support myself in a comfortable way. I am then going to be the first of a new genus . . ." Mr. Johnson perhaps exaggerated Mary's uniqueness—London already had a few successful women journalists—but with pardonable delight in his protégé. As for Mary, she discovered the sweetness of financial independence earned by interesting work. She had her own apartment. She was often invited to Mr. Johnson's dinner parties, usually as the only female guest among all the most interesting men in London: Joseph Priestley, Thomas Paine, Henry Fuseli, William Blake, Thomas Christie, William Godwin—all of them up-and-coming scientists or poets or painters or philosophers, bound together by left-wing political views. Moreover, Mary was successful in her own writing as well as in editorial work. Her *Original Stories for Children* went into three editions and was illustrated by Blake. Johnson and his friend Thomas Christie had started a magazine called the *Analytical Review,* to which Mary became a regular contributor.

But—lest anyone imagine an elegantly dressed Mary presiding flirtatiously at Johnson's dinner table—her social accomplishments were rather behind her professional ones. Johnson's circle looked upon her as one of the boys. "Wollstonecraft" is what William Godwin calls her in his diary. One of her later detractors reported that she was at this time a "philosophic sloven," in a dreadful old dress and beaver hat, "with her hair hanging lank about her shoulders." Mary had yet to arrive at her final incarnation, but the new identity was imminent, if achieved by an odd route. Edmund Burke had recently published his *Reflections on the Revolution in France,* and the book had enraged Mary. The statesman who so readily supported the quest for liberty in the American colonies had his doubts about events in France. Mary's reply to Burke, *A Vindication of the Rights of Men,* astounded London, partly because she was hitherto unknown, partly because it was good. Mary proved to be an excellent polemicist, and she had written in anger. She accused Burke, the erstwhile champion of liberty, of being "the champion of property." "Man preys on man," said she, "and you mourn for the idle tapestry that decorated a gothic pile and the dronish bell that summoned the fat priest to prayer." The book sold well. Mary moved into a better apartment and bought some pretty dresses—no farthingales, of course, but some of the revolutionary new "classical" gowns. She put her auburn hair up in a loose knot. Her days as a philosophic sloven were over.

*Vindication of the Rights of Woman* was her next work. In its current edition it runs to 250-odd pages; Mary wrote it in six weeks. *Vindication* is no prose masterpiece, but it has never failed to arouse its audience, in one way or another. Horace Walpole unintentionally set the style for the book's foes. Writing to his friend Hannah More in August, 1792, he referred to Thomas Paine and to Mary as "philosophizing serpents" and was "glad to hear you have not read the tract of the last mentioned writer. I would not look at it." Neither would many another of Mary's assailants, the most virulent of whom, Ferdinand Lundberg, surfaced at the late date of 1947 with a tract of his own, *Modern Woman, the Lost Sex.* Savagely misogynistic as it is, this book was hailed in its times as "the best book yet to be written about women" and was widely used as a text for many "marriage and the family" courses in universities. Lundberg calls Mary the Karl Marx of the feminist movement, and the *Vindication* a "fateful book," to which "the tenets of feminism, which have undergone no change to our day, may be traced." Very well, but then, bewilderingly, he interprets the book as a sexual threat to men. Recounting Mary's life with the maximum possible number of errors per line, he warns us that she was "an extreme neurotic of a compulsive type" who "wanted to turn on men and injure them." But in one respect, at least, Mr. Lundberg hits the mark: he blames Mary for starting women in the pernicious habit of wanting an education. In the nineteenth century, he relates, English and American feminists were hard at work. "Following Mary Wollstonecraft's prescription, they made a considerable point about acquiring a higher education." This is precisely Mary's prescription, and the most dangerous idea in her fateful book.

"Men complain and with reason, of the follies and caprices of our

Sex," she writes in Chapter 1. "Behold, I should answer, the natural effect of ignorance." Women, she thinks, are usually so mindless as to be scarcely fit for their roles as wives and mothers. Nevertheless, she believes this state not to be part of the feminine nature, but the result of an equally mindless oppression. Subjection to absolute authority is degrading to anyone, and as demoralizing for the oppressor as for his victim. Mary would like to see a race of women fit to be their husbands' companions and to bring up their own children. She is willing to admit that woman is not the physical equal of man in matters of strength and endurance, though mercifully she avoids the whole irrelevant anatomical debate that adds bulk to so much feminist and antifeminist literature. Mary believes that a woman's basic mission is as a wife and mother. Need she be an illiterate slave for this?

The heart of the work is her attack on Rousseau. In *Emile,* his fictionalized, autobiographical, philosophical, pedagogical treatise, Rousseau set forth some refreshing ideas for the education of boys. But women, he decreed, are tools for pleasure, creatures too base for moral or political or educational privilege. Look at how stupid little girls are, he points out: always playing with dolls, never interested in anything worthwhile. Mary recognized that this view was destined to shut half the human race out of all hope for political freedom. *Vindication* is a plea that the "rights of men" ought to mean the "rights of humanity." The human right that she held highest was the right to have a mind and think with it. Virginia Woolf, who lived through a time of feminist activity, thought that the *Vindication* was a work so true "as to seem to contain nothing new." Its originality, she wrote, had become a commonplace. The Woman's Liberation Movement would obviously not agree; they might however join with Mary Wollstonecraft as she says, "Rousseau exerts himself to prove that all *was* right originally; a crowd of authors that all *is* now right; and I, that all *will* be right." The voice of the reformer speaks always in the future tense.

*Vindication* went quickly into a second edition. Mary's name was soon known all over Europe. But as she savored her fame—and she did savor it—she found that the edge was wearing off and that she was rather lonely. So far as anyone knows, Mary had reached this point in her life without ever having had a love affair. Johnson was the only man she was close to, and he was, as she wrote him, "A father, or a brother—you have been both to me." Mary was often now in the company of the Swiss painter Henry Fuseli, and suddenly she developed what she thought was a Platonic passion in his direction. She offered to move into his home as an intellectual companion, but Mrs. Fuseli ungratefully declined. Mary's partisans have devised various explanations for this gaffe of their heroine's, but the only possible inference is that she was extremely naive. In the winter of 1792 Mary went to Paris, partly to escape her embarrassment and also because she wanted to observe the workings of the Revolution firsthand.

Louis XVI was imprisoned at this time but living; the Terror had not yet begun. But soon after his arrival, as she collected notes for the history of the Revolution she hoped to write, Mary saw the king, "sitting in a hackney coach . . . going to meet death." Back in her room that evening, she wrote to Mr. Johnson of seeing "eyes glare through a glass door opposite my chair and bloody hands shook at me . . . death in so many frightful shapes has taken hold of my fancy. I am going to bed and for the first time in my life, I cannot put out the candle." As the weeks went on, Edmund Burke's implacable critic began to lose her faith in the brave new world. "The aristocracy of birth is levelled to the ground, only to make room for that of riches." she wrote, and worse, "Vice, or if you will, evil, is the grand mobile of action." By February France and England were at war.

Though many Englishmen were arrested, Mary and most of the colony stayed on. One day in spring, some friends presented her to an attractive American, newly arrived in Paris, Gilbert Imlay. Probably about four years Mary's senior, a former officer in the Continental Army, Imlay was an explorer and adventurer. He came to France seeking to finance a scheme for seizing Spanish lands in the Mississippi valley. This "natural and unaffected creature," as Mary was later to describe him, was probably the social lion of the moment, for in addition to having a fashionable nationality, he was also the author of a best-selling novel called *The Emigrants,* a farfetched account of life and love in the American wilderness. He and Mary soon became lovers. They were a seemingly perfect pair. Imlay must have been pleased with his famous catch, and—dear, liberated girl that she was—Mary did not insist upon marriage. Rather the contrary. But fearing that she was in danger as an Englishwoman, he registered her at the American embassy as his wife.

Blood was literally running in the Parisian streets now, so Mary settled down by herself in a cottage at Neuilly. Imlay spent his days in town, working out various plans. The Mississippi expedition came to nothing, and he decided to stay in France and go into the import-export business, part of his imports being gunpowder and other war goods run from Scandinavia through the English blockade. In the evenings he would ride out to the cottage. By now it was summer, and Mary would often stroll up the road to meet him, carrying a basket of freshly-gathered grapes. She spent her days working on her history of the Revolution.

This summer she seldom had any occasion to write letters to Imlay,

*Named for her mother, Mary Godwin (later Shelley's wife) is famous for her novel* Frankenstein.

but one of the notes she did write shows exactly what her feelings for him were: "You can scarcely imagine with what pleasure I anticipate the day when we are to begin almost to live together; and you would smile to hear how many plans of employment I have in my head, now that I am confident that my heart has found peace . . ." Soon she was pregnant. She and Imlay moved into Paris. He promised soon to take her to America, where they would settle down on a farm and raise six children. Mary thought of nothing else. But business called Imlay to Le Havre, and his stay lengthened ominously into weeks.

Imlay's letters to Mary have not survived, and without them it is hard to gauge what sort of man he was and what he really thought of his adoring mistress. Her biographers like to make him out a cad, a philistine, not half good enough for Mary. Perhaps; yet the two must have had something in common. His novel, unreadable though it is now, shows that he shared her political views, including her feminist ones, and set the same great store she did by "sensibility." He may never have been serious about the farm in America, but he was a miserably long time deciding to leave Mary alone. Though they were separated during the early months of her pregnancy, he finally did bring her to Le Havre, and continued to live with her there until the child was born and for some six months afterward. The baby arrived in May, 1794, a healthy little girl, whom Mary named Fanny after her old friend. Mary was proud that her delivery had been easy. "My nurse has been twenty years in this employment," she wrote to a friend, "and she tells me she never knew a woman [who did] so well—adding, Frenchwoman like, that I ought to make children for the Republic." And as for Fanny, Mary loved her instantly. "My little Girl," continues the same letter, "begins to suck so manfully that her father reckons saucily on her writing the second part of the Rights of Woman." Mary's joy in this child's sunny temperament, her intelligence, illuminates almost every letter she wrote henceforth.

*Born in the year the* Vindication *appeared, Percy Bysshe Shelley eventually read and revered the book*

Fanny's father was the chief recipient of these letters with all the details of the baby's life. Mary and Imlay hardly ever lived together again. Mary's mounting despair traces itself out painfully in her letters. A year went by; Imlay was now in London and Mary in France. She offered to break it off, but mysteriously, he could not let go. In the last bitter phase of their involvement, after she had joined him in London at his behest, he even sent her on a complicated business errand to the Scandinavian countries. She traveled as "Mrs. Imlay," and he wrote her occasionally, promising to join her somewhere along the way and take a holiday with her and the baby. He never came. Returning to London, Mary discovered that he was living with another woman. By now half crazy with humiliation, and forgetting Fanny and the rights of women into the bargain, Mary chose a dark night and threw herself in the Thames. She was nearly dead when two rivermen pulled her from the water.

Though this desperate incident was almost the end of Mary, at least it was the end of the Imlay episode. He sent a doctor to care for her, but they hardly ever met again. Since Mary had no money, she set about providing for herself and Fanny in the way she knew. The faithful Johnson had already brought out Volume I of her history of the French Revolution. Now she set to work editing and revising her *Letters Written during a Short Residence in Sweden, Norway, and Denmark,* a kind of thoughtful travelogue. The book was well received and eventually translated into Dutch, Portuguese, and German.

And it also revived the memory of Mary Wollstonecraft in the mind of an old acquaintance, William Godwin. As the author of the treatise *Political Justice,* he was now as famous a philosophizing serpent as Mary and was widely admired and hated as a "freethinker." He came to call on Mary. They became friends and then lovers. Early in 1797 Mary was again pregnant. William Godwin was an avowed atheist who had publicly denounced the very institution of marriage. On March 29, 1797, he nevertheless went peaceably to church with Mary and made her his wife.

The Godwins were happy together, however William's theories may have been outraged. He adored his small stepdaughter and took pride in his brilliant wife. Awaiting the birth of her child throughout the summer, Mary worked on a new novel and made plans for a book on "the management of infants"—it would have been the first "Dr. Spock." She expected to have another easy delivery and promised to come downstairs to dinner the day following. But when labor began, on August 30, it proved to be long and agonizing. A daughter, named Mary Wollstonecraft, was born; ten days later, the mother died.

Occasionally, when a gifted writer dies young, one can feel, as in the case of Shelley, that perhaps he had at least accomplished his best work. But so recently had Mary come into full intellectual and emotional growth that her death at the age of thirty-eight is bleak indeed. There is no knowing what Mary might have accomplished now that she enjoyed domestic stability. Perhaps, to be sure, she might have achieved little or nothing further as a writer. But she might have been able to protect her daughters from some part of the sadness that overtook them; for as things turned out, both Fanny and Mary were to sacrifice themselves.

Fanny grew up to be a shy young girl, required to feel grateful for the roof over her head, overshadowed by her prettier half sister, Mary. Godwin in due course married a formidable widow named Mrs. Clairmont, who brought her own daughter into the house—the Claire

Clairmont who grew up to become Byron's mistress and the mother of his daughter Allegra. Over the years Godwin turned into a hypocrite and a miser who nevertheless continued to pose as the great liberal of the day. Percy Bysshe Shelley, born the same year that the *Vindication of the Rights of Woman* was published, came to be a devoted admirer of Mary Wollstonecraft's writing. As a young man he therefore came with his wife to call upon Godwin. What he really sought, however, were Mary's daughters—because they were her daughters. First he approached Fanny, but later changed his mind. Mary Godwin was then sixteen, the perfect potential soul mate for a man whose needs for soul mates knew no bounds. They conducted their courtship in the most up-to-the-minute romantic style: beneath a tree near her mother's grave they read aloud to each other from the *Vindication*. Soon they eloped, having pledged their "troth" in the cemetery. Godwin, the celebrated freethinker, was enraged that a daughter of his could create such a scandal. To make matters worse, Claire Clairmont had run off to Switzerland with them.

Not long afterward, Fanny too ran away. She went to an inn in a distant town and drank a fatal dose of laudanum. It has traditionally been said that unrequited love for Shelley drove her to this pass, but there is no evidence one way or the other. One suicide that can more justly be laid at Shelley's door is that of his first wife, which occurred a month after Fanny's and which at any rate left him free to wed his mistress, Mary Godwin. Wife or mistress, she had to endure poverty, ostracism, and Percy's constant infidelities. But now at last her father could, and did, boast to his relations that he was father-in-law to a baronet's son. "Oh, philosophy!" as Mary Godwin Shelley remarked.

If in practice Shelley was merely a womanizer, on paper he was a convinced feminist. He had learned this creed from Mary Wollstonecraft. Through his verse Mary's ideas began to be disseminated. They were one part of that vast tidal wave of political, social, and artistic revolution that began in the late eighteenth century, the romantic movement. But because of Mary's unconventional way of life, her name fell into disrepute during the nineteenth century, and her book failed to exert its rightful influence on the development of feminism. Emma Willard and other pioneers of the early Victorian period indignantly refused to claim Mary as their forebear. Elizabeth Cady Stanton and Lucretia Mott were mercifully less strait-laced on the subject. In 1889, when Mrs. Stanton and Susan B. Anthony published their *History of Woman Suffrage,* they dedicated the book to Mary. Though Mary Wollstonecraft can in no sense be said to have founded the woman's rights movement, she was, by the late nineteenth century, recognized as its inspiration, and the *Vindication* was vindicated for what it was, a landmark in the history of society.

*Susan B. Anthony (left) and Elizabeth Cady Stanton helped revive Mary's reputation as the mentor of the feminist movement.*

# THOMAS ROBERT
# MALTHUS
## 1766-1834

P oor Tom Malthus has been persistently and almost wantonly
misunderstood for nearly a hundred and eighty years. To the
liberal optimists who see the future as a perpetual golden
dawn, Malthus is the kill-joy, the prophet of doom; he is the
warlock at the wedding that sanctifies sex, and the skeleton
at the feast that glorifies gorging. To the blessers of human fecundity—
Protestant and Catholic alike, though mostly Catholic—he is the chair-
man of a society that distributes free condoms. Even Aldous Huxley,
who should have known better, gave the name "Malthusian belt" to
the pessary bandoleers worn by the impregnable cuties of *Brave New
World*. Everybody pretends to know all about Malthus, but few seem
to have actually read *An Essay on the Principle of Population*. It is
time to set the record straight.

Malthus published the first version of his revolutionary essay in
1798—the year in which Coleridge and Wordsworth published their
equally revolutionary *Lyrical Ballads*. This latter volume was a kind
of romantic manifesto, in which the speech of ordinary men and
women was accorded a special reverence and the untrammeled imagination was given its head. The Age of Reason—an age of order and
hierarchy—was at its end, and the era foretold by Jean Jacques Rousseau seemed to be dawning. The brew of a new utopianism was making the intellectuals drunk all over Europe, not least in an England
that was permissive enough to allow free importation of that powerful libertarian liquor of France.

It was a liquor quaffed liberally by one English philosopher who,

*An engraving by John Linnell shows the amiable "gloomy parson," Thomas Malthus.*

**By** ANTHONY BURGESS

261

like Tom Malthus, had started a career in the Church of England but, unlike Tom Malthus, had resigned his ministry under the stress of the new French (and therefore most un-Anglican) ideas. This was William Godwin. He, in 1793 at the age of thirty-seven, published a book entitled *An Enquiry Concerning Political Justice, and its Influence on General Virtue and Happiness.* Godwin still had a good deal of the preacher in him, and he brought a pulpit eloquence to a radicalism that owed much to Rousseau and more to Condorcet. Rousseau had written about men being born free but still everywhere in chains; Condorcet had presented a program for actually hacking off the shackles. All existing institutions had to be destroyed: church and state were the joint oppressors of the spirit of man. The wealth of the community was to be divided up equally. Once established, the equalitarian society would maintain itself in perpetuity: men set free would be men enlightened.

Godwin's radicalism was total, but the technique he advocated for the achievement of utopia was more Fabian than Jacobin. He didn't call for the storming of Buckingham Palace and the guillotining of the House of Lords; he wanted calm discussion, slow debate, the gradual infusion of Truth through the social mass— a yeasty working, then the baking of the bread. His prophecies are heartbreakingly free of contamination by the doctrine of the Fall. "There will be no war," he says, "no crime, no administration of justice, as it is called, and no government." "Besides this," he promises, "there will be neither disease, anguish, melancholy nor resentment. Every man will seek with ineffable ardour the good of all." Bliss was it in that dawn, etc., etc.

Reading Godwin now, all we can do is smile sadly. The utopian experience is available only subjectively—in love-ins and LSD trips—and only in transitory bursts. The sad truth is that man is not perfectible. But intellectuals like Coleridge, Wordsworth, and Percy Bysshe Shelley, who had not yet seen the great butchering days of the French Revolution nor the start of the Napoleonic tyranny, were confirmed in their utopianism by the preacher's rhetoric of Godwin. "He blazed up as a sun in the firmament of reputation," wrote Hazlitt, who was also infected; "no one was more talked of, more looked up to, more sought after, and wherever liberty, truth, justice was the theme, his name was not far off."

Five years after the publication of Godwin's *Political Justice,* along came Malthus, death's-head and spoilsport. Strictly, Malthus should have been as ardent a Godwinian as any other young man (he was only thirty-two when he delivered his bombshell). After all, his father had been a friend of both David Hume and the great Jean Jacques himself. In March, 1766, a few weeks after the birth of Thomas Robert Malthus, Rousseau had come to visit the elegant Malthus mansion near Dorking, Surrey, and, presumably, had laid an archradical's blessing on the infant head. Again, when Tom was old enough to have a private tutor, it was Gilbert Wakefield—a heretical clergyman like Godwin—who took him in hand and nurtured him in the principles of the Rousseauan doctrines, using *Emile* as his textbook. But Wakefield didn't want proselytism; he wanted his pupil to argue, think for himself, generate, if he wished, his own heresies. It was as a man who had thought much, read much, but still retained an open mind that young Malthus passed through Cambridge and, a year before the storming of the Bastille, took holy orders. But it was no Christian ardor that countered the godless radicalism of Godwin; it was the cold skepticism of the scientific temper.

Malthus thought that Godwinian utopianism neglected the facts of life. Malthus was keen on data; Godwin thought facts an impertinent hindrance to free speculation. At Harvard a few years ago one young professor was heard to say to another: "Your theory won't hold; I've got data." The other replied: "Data, shmata—I *like* my theory." That was pretty much the Malthus–Godwin position, only more so. The data that Malthus presented was derived from history and economics, and he thought that Godwin had not just ignored these studies, he had deliberately distorted them, for he had been unwilling to accept that society was kept together only by the very restraints he inveighed against. Unrestrained by the horrors of the Godwinian thesis, society would collapse into the worst horror of all: that of a rapidly increasing population fighting for a rapidly diminishing food supply.

Malthus had discussed his own ideas with his father, who had encouraged him to order them into an essay. When the essay appeared, it was as an anonymously published book of fifty thousand words in nineteen brief chapters: Malthus's lifework was to consist of the expansion and corroboration of its thesis through the adduction of more and more data, making the *Essay on the Principle of Population* into the massive tome we know. But that comparatively brief pamphlet was the kind of thin, sharp weapon that was needed to puncture the adiposity of the Godwin optimists. Its author knew how unpopular it would be with liberal intellectuals; he knew that it would blot out their utopian sun with gloomy rain clouds.

"The view which he has given of human life," the author wrote in his preface, referring of course to himself, "has a melancholy hue, but he feels conscious that he has drawn these dark tints from a conviction that they are really in the picture; and not from a jaundiced eye, or an inherent spleen of disposition." And it was true that Malthus was not a melancholic, a dyspeptic hand-wringer rejoicing in the dark

AN

ESSAY

ON THE

PRINCIPLE OF POPULATION,

AS IT AFFECTS

THE FUTURE IMPROVEMENT OF SOCIETY.

WITH REMARKS

ON THE SPECULATIONS OF MR. GODWIN,

M. CONDORCET,

AND OTHER WRITERS.

LONDON:

PRINTED FOR J. JOHNSON, IN ST. PAUL'S CHURCH-YARD.

1798.

*Above is the frontispiece of Malthus's epochal work, the* Essay on the Principle of Population, *which was first published in 1798.*

shadow he was throwing across the sunny arena of optimism. He was a man who gave good parties, a smiling and kindly man whom, later in life, everyone was to call "Pop"—a nice, swinging name.

To look squarely and unflinchingly at the facts of life calls for a scientific temperament. Malthus undoubtedly had this. He said that theories were useless unless backed up by evidence. In his very first chapter he gave a grotesque but cogent example. "A writer may tell me that he thinks man will ultimately become an ostrich. I cannot properly contradict him. But before he can expect to bring any reasonable person over to his opinion, he ought to show that the necks of mankind have been gradually elongating; that the lips have grown harder, and more prominent; that the legs and feet are daily altering their shape; and that the hair is beginning to change into stubs of feathers." This is the Darwinian approach; or rather, the Darwinian approach owed a great deal to Malthusian objectivity.

The premises of Malthus's argument were not easily contradicted. His two main *postulata,* as he called them, were that food is necessary to man's existence and that the passion between the sexes is a constant force, unextinguishable and unmodifiable by either sermons or acts of Parliament. Godwin believed that sexual desire might, in a "pure" utopian society, be sublimated to a kind of fleshless angelic rapture, and Shelley, in his *Epipsychidion,* liked to think of love as a man and woman reading Plato in bed; but Malthus knew that sex was a self-perpetuating dynamo. And so: "Assuming then my postulata as granted, I say that the power of population is indefinitely greater than the power in the earth to produce subsistence for man. Population, when unchecked, increases in a geometrical ratio. Subsistence increases only in an arithmetical ratio."

*William Godwin, pacing in his study, was drawn by an English caricaturist.*

In plain figures, this means that the human race increases if unchecked in the ratio of 1, 2, 4, 8, 16, 32, 64, 128, 256, 512, and so on, while subsistence merely goes up a step at a time: 1, 2, 3, 4, 5, 6, 7, 8, etc. I don't think we have to take this disparity too literally, remembering that when Malthus came to write the "Population" article in the *Encyclopaedia Britannica* of 1824, he turned away from that sensational arithmetic and contented himself with the general law: "Life everywhere and always tends to exceed the warrant for it." Malthus was undoubtedly thinking not of the edible animal kingdom, which increases as man increases if it is allowed to, but of bean gardens and fields of cereal, which merely replace themselves. And there was another, more dynamic, factor: the pleasure principle, which found in sex the best and easiest gratification. The act of sex will always be preferred to the hard toil of keeping up the food supply. The husband's work at night is not to be compared with the husbandman's graft by day. This, again, is one of the facts of life.

What could be done about this wretched prospect—the death of the race through inability to feed itself? Well, there were certain "checks" to restrict population. Whatever tended to decrease the number of births was, in Malthus's terminology, a "preventive check"; whatever led to a greater number of deaths was a "positive check." The major positive checks were plagues, wars, famines—death-inducing catastrophes that, like earthquakes and floods, seemed beyond the control of the human will. Preventive checks included the postponement of marriage, the cultivation of continence, the vow of celibacy. Malthus added a third force he was rather vague about: "vicious customs with respect to women, great cities, unwholesome manufactures, luxury . . . All these checks may be fairly resolved into misery and vice." A Christian pastor, he was not prepared to be specific about nonreproductive modes of sex. Nor was he willing to condone the separation of sexual appetite from its biological consequences. He was a Malthusian, but not a neo-Malthusian.

That contraception was one of the facts of eighteenth-century life we know from the literature of the time, especially from the memoirs of randy young men like James Boswell. The condom was a regular item in the baggage of aristocrats making the grand tour—not cheap, but usually efficacious. Malthus would have nothing of such mechanical checks. He advocated late marriage and a sparing indulgence in marital comfort, and he practiced what he preached. He married at thirty-eight and fathered three children. (It is ironic that this optimum marrying age should have become the rule in a country that is fiercest in denouncing Malthusianism, meaning neo-Malthusianism. Ireland is not noticeably overspilling, and there is a lot of bogland to be reclaimed. Malthus could well be adopted as a northern Catholic saint.)

The dangers of Malthusianism—in respect to the tolerance of positive checks—were not slow to be indicated in his own time. Malthus was accused of defending wars, plagues, and famines, of denouncing soup kitchens for the poor, family allowances, parish relief. In other words, his doctrines were regarded as inhumane. Certainly, politicians who were influenced by him found a ready argument for retrenchment policies. The prime minister, William Pitt, dropped the Poor Bill of 1800, stating in the House of Commons that he did so in deference to the views of "those whose opinions he was bound to respect." The old shibboleths about the evils of a declining population were not now heard so much as formerly. Goldsmith had written a couplet in *The Deserted Village*:

> Ill fares the land, to hast'ning ills a prey,
> Where wealth accumulates, and men decay.

More than a century later, Hilaire Belloc suggested this follow-up:

> But how much more unfortunate are those
> Whose wealth declines and population grows.

Generally speaking, the poets—whose art has a basis of "paternity lust"—were not ready to write odes in praise of Malthus. His supporters were found in dubious quarters: among skinflints like Scrooge, who said that the poor ought to die and thus keep down the surplus population. Godwinianism preserved its attractions as late as H. G. Wells. Malthusianism was nasty. Data, shmata.

Perhaps if Malthus had not been a Christian and a clergyman, he would have boldly looked in the face one aspect of his primary *postulatum* and admitted that sin was often the only way of avoiding more sin. The sexual impulse does not easily hold itself in check until the times are propitious for the benefit of clergy. "Food breeds seed," said a seventeenth-century clergyman, and "seed will out." Despite the terrible human prospect, the sin of Onan remained a sin for Malthus: seed must be used for a biological end, otherwise it must not be used at all. This is, of course, still the doctrine of the Catholic Church.

It was left to the neo-Malthusians to dare the wrath of God and canonize Onan. Francis Place, a journeyman tailor, wrote a book in 1822, *Illustrations and Proofs of the Principle of Population,* in which he stressed the impossible idealism of Malthus's doctrines of moral restraint and late marriages. The only way to keep down the population, said Place, was to make contraceptive devices freely available and to cleanse them of the stigma of immorality or even blasphemy. He spread the word through handbills distributed among the poor. He knew the poor and the mores of the poor: he had been a struggling tailor, not a gentleman. He knew that deferred marriage could only encourage a greater immorality than already existed in the London slums; one had to face facts and at least ensure that a small harm would (almost literally) abort a greater one. If human nature would not be changed by sermons, let its worst excesses be harmlessly detonated through contraception.

Place was, inevitably, reviled, but neither he nor his followers were discouraged. The New World took over, and it was New York City that saw the publication of the first real best-seller of contraceptive advocacy, Robert Dale Owen's *Moral Physiology,* which sold seventy-five thousand copies in its author's lifetime. But New York was more permissive than Massachusetts. Charles Knowlton, a New England physician, produced a pamphlet called *Fruits of Philosophy, or The Private Companion of Young Married People*—an earnest and eloquent plea for the limitation of families—and was given three months' hard labor at Cambridge. But, back in England, Charles Bradlaugh and Annie Besant reissued Knowlton's pamphlet in 1876, forty-four years after its first publication, and fought repression even more uncompromising than that of puritanical Massachusetts. Sentenced to six months' imprisonment and a fine of two hundred pounds, Bradlaugh and Mrs. Besant appealed to a higher court. To their surprise, the indictment was quashed. The way was now open for a massive birth-control campaign, in which Knowlton's pamphlet—a British best seller—spread the primary gospel, soon to be followed by Mrs. Besant's own *Law of Population*. It was the beginning of a war that the white Anglo-Saxon Protestants made very much their own. Catholics, and other children of solar fertility creeds, have come closer to Malthus since those days, but they are slow to worship the juju of the condom.

The world picture since Malthus's time is both more frightening and more hopeful than ever he could have dreamed. In an article celebrating the Malthusian bicentenary in 1966, Lord Ritchie Calder pointed out that it took a million years to reach a world population of 3,250 millions and that it will take only thirty or so years to double it. But condoms, coils, and pessaries are spreading into the high-population areas, and the new food technicians are hard at work. The deserts can become fertile, the oceans can be probed for new items of diet, food can be synthesized in laboratories. For the privileged nations to help the starving ones means putting not only food into mouths but the family-planning philosophy into heads slow to accept it.

*William Pitt the Younger, aged thirty, was sketched in 1789 by James Gillray.*

The gloom of Malthus remains justified when we think solely in terms of "moral restraint"—a virtue difficult for our randy species to achieve. His spirit belongs, through a profound irony, to the Vatican. It is not he whom we invoke today so much as his successors, particularly Charles Bradlaugh and Annie Besant. But some of us are inclined to think that a society accustomed to their gifts—the means of copulation without population—must subtly change its culture patterns. Is the decline of Christian belief perhaps due to our rejection of the fertility cult that is at its heart? As a boy I was taught by my priests that the purpose of sex was to beget and to people heaven with new souls. Again, should not nonreproductive modes of sex—homosexuality and other inversions—be accepted not merely as tolerable but as positively virtuous? May we not end up with a hierarchy of pederasts and geldings? Are there not already signs that our sexual permissiveness is being countered by a new kind of animal—narcissistic, long-haired, of indeterminate gender? All this may be fancy, but if old "Pop" were still alive, there might be material there for a little appendix to the *Essay on Population*. And of course, in a sense, old "Pop" is still very much alive.

# GEORG WILHELM FRIEDRICH
# HEGEL
## 1770-1831

Until quite recently, Hegel's American reputation was that of a ponderous pan-Germanic philosopher, somewhat in Spengler's class but with an added halo of impenetrability. To be sure, there had been pockets of Hegelianism in American immigrant culture ever since the middle of the nineteenth century. And there had been a vagrant academic interest in Hegel's work, especially under the impulse of Josiah Royce. But after World War I this philosopher was little studied and certainly very poorly understood.

Today, much is changed. No longer can Hegel be paraded before common-sense Anglo-Saxons as a "mere peddler of metaphysical obscurity" or a "glorifier of war and carnage" or a "pompous defender of German power." Americans are not prepared to give lessons here, in any case. We begin to see this intellectual giant as one of the founders of our perplexed modernity. And this is a point of some paradox, because his own great achievement was to encapsulate the civilized past.

If there is no straw-man Hegel, there is equally no "Hegel without tears." Those who enter the Hegelian portal need not abandon all hope, but they should be warned that the way is tough and slippery. It is strewn not just with Hegel's uncommon uses of language but with elusive residues of a classical and Christian heritage that speaks to us less and less. Though not so brain-wrenching as, say, the philosophies of Kant or Spinoza, Hegel's thought is textured for the mind that circles to catch its prey, not for the intellect

*In G. W. F. Hegel's later years his ideas began to dominate German philosophy.*

*By* GEORGE ARMSTRONG KELLY

*Hegel studied theology from 1788 to 1793 at Tübingen, where he met the poet Hölderlin and the idealist philosopher Schelling, who both remained lifelong friends.*

that plunges ahead full-throttle from proposition to proposition.

Hegel is the last great founder of a philosophical system—complete, if not totally fleshed out, in all its specifics, from the bare bones of logic to the more concrete spheres of law, art, and religion. Yet Hegel's contemporary resurrection has not been for the sake of his total doctrine but for a variety of special insights that went into its building. Sixty years ago Benedetto Croce raised the question of "what is living and what is dead" in Hegel. For Croce's purposes, what was persistently relevant about this philosophy was not the system that it imposed on knowledge but the dynamism, or "historicity," that it conveyed, the sense of time as man's primary instrument of self-awareness. In an age where it has become banal to speak of "the permanency of change" many persons no doubt have reasons similar to Croce's for finding Hegelian thought congenial. For Hegel's method aimed to teach a complete speculative grasp of man's nature in time as conveyed by the unfolding of his highest works of spirit.

In Hegel's vision the world of men progressively reveals itself to itself as self-knowing thought. In this process, higher styles of consciousness are achieved that make collective human understanding more enriched and concrete. Nothing essential is shed in this movement of the human spirit, but what is kept is perpetually transformed at a higher level. The destiny of humanity is the liberation of the mind. This means the progressive appropriation by the mind of all that was previously alien or strange to it. Hegel's is a human philosophy of godlike proportions. Its imagery is typically Christian and its claims are bold. For Hegel, "the end of days is fully come" with the liberation of the spirit that accompanies his superior philosophical grasp of the root-meanings of Lutheran Christianity, a religion of which he affirmed in his later period: "I am a Lutheran and thus I will stay."

Still, latent within Hegel's translation of religion into philosophy were the critical elements for distintegrating his meta-Christian summary of the fullness of time. In closing his 1806 lectures at Jena, Hegel is quoted by his biographer Karl Rosenkranz as telling his students: "We find ourselves at an important epoch of time, a period of ferment, when the spirit has made a leap, gone beyond its previous form, and is busy taking on a new one. The whole mass of previous ideas and conceptions that tied the world together are dissolved and collapse as in the vision of a dream." This diagnosis, repeated in slightly altered form, in *The Phenomenology of Spirit* (1807), conveys a sense of restless surge and of the primacy of change, attesting the unwillingness of life to be bound within any system of thought, however spacious or ingenious. This mood also helps make Hegel our contemporary. Scarcely a decade after his death (1831), methodological disciples of Hegel—among them Marx and Engels—were busy destroying the synthesis he had thought to complete, often by the use of Hegelian critical techniques. Projected into a world a century and a half beyond Hegel's own, the diffuse set of problems these techniques created now constitute the better part of his living legacy. We return to Hegelian insights piecemeal, usually for their continuation or anticipation of burning social issues. This sovereign and completed philosophy has thus become a thesaurus for the development of fledgling ideologies. But to acknowledge that much of our interest lies here is not to deny that the real Hegel is also worth knowing.

Georg Wilhelm Friedrich Hegel ("Wilhelm" to his intimates) was born in Stuttgart in 1770 to a middle-class family. The man accused of being a "Prussian state philosopher" was not Prussian at all but Swabian, belonging to that Germanic tribe reputed to have both the most liberal and most intuitive talents. Of Hegel's parents and of his early childhood virtually nothing is known. We begin to pick up his traces in school and especially at the *Tübinger Stift* (advanced preparatory school), to which he was sent to study theology in 1788. Five years later, having become closely acquainted with the poet Hölderlin and the idealist philosopher Schelling at Tübingen, Hegel moved to Bern as a family tutor (*Hauslehrer*). In 1797 he went to Frankfurt, where Hölderlin was also employed, in the same capacity. Some remarkable essays and literary statements dealing with the cultural connections of Christianity, ancient Greek civilization, and Kantian philosophy date from this period. The usual title "Early Theological Writings" does little to convey the sense of these pieces. In some respects, they are profoundly antitheological, or at least, anti-Christian. They betray a distaste for established religion, a nostalgic wish for a unity of culture and worship, and a strident disaffection with reigning mores in Germany.

While Hegel was involved with these early essays, he and other young intellectuals, reared amid the tensions of Kant's critical philosophy and the titanic literary works of the *Sturm und Drang*, fell increasingly under the influence of the classicism of Goethe and Schiller. Their intellectual maturity was also marked by the experience of the French Revolution, to whose political ideals the young Hegel bestowed a temporary allegiance. Even in his later period, after he had condemned the French kind of liberty, Hegel could declare: ". . . not until now had man advanced to recognizing the principle that thought should govern spiritual reality. Thus [the Revolution] was a glorious spiritual dawning. All thinking men partook of its jubilation." Eventually he came to see that the Revolution had not renewed the free and substantial life of a political community. Accordingly, he denounced it as incomplete and one-sided. The Terror had dehumanized liberty by "cleaving off heads like cabbages."

*Johann Wolfgang von Goethe was the leading literary light of Saxe-Weimar when Hegel began teaching at Jena in 1801.*

In 1801 Hegel was appointed *Privatdocent* in philosophy (roughly comparable to our assistant professor) at the University of Jena, in the small but culturally important state of Saxe-Weimar. Here Goethe, Schiller, Wieland, and Herder had created a literary blossoming. Here, too, Fichte had taught—until forced out of his job on charges of atheism—and here Hegel's Tübingen friend Schelling was newly ensconced in a regular chair. But by now Weimar culture was on the skids. The shadow of Napoleon hung over Europe, and the Age of Romanticism was in the ascendant. While at Jena, Hegel labored at the architecture of a philosophical system designed to surpass the work of Kant and his immediate followers. In so doing, he drew further away from the ideas of his colleague Schelling. The result, obtained after many false starts and tribulations, was the work that many esteem as his highest achievement, *The Phenomenology of Spirit*. This book was distributed originally in only seven hundred copies, but it became the root-source of Hegel's impact on the world of modern thought. In the manner of a highly cerebral *Bildungsroman,* it traces the historical wanderings and accomplishments of the human spirit up to the point where, according to the author, philosophy is "able to relinquish the name of love of knowledge and become actual knowledge." The present favor of the *Phenomenology* is assured by Marx's critical reverence for the work (expressed in one of his 1844 manuscripts, not published until the third decade of our century). Taken as a whole, the *Phenomenology* betrays the atmosphere of one of its most famous phrases, "a bacchanale of reason where not a single member is sober," being altogether a tumultuous philosophical statement bridging the passage between rationalism and romanticism. It was written at a white-hot clip in the waning months of 1806 and finished, according to Hegel's own account, on the eve of the Battle of Jena, where Napoleon's Grand Army crushed the Prussian forces and their auxiliaries and changed the map of Europe.

After the fortunes of war closed the university, Hegel was driven to seek employment as a newspaper editor in Bamberg. In the autumn of 1808 he was appointed rector of the gymnasium (senior high school) in Nuremberg, where a modest financial security allowed him to marry in 1811 and to pursue his philosophical studies and writing. The outcome of the Nuremberg years was his second major work, the *Logic,* published in three installments between 1812 and 1816. Originally, the *Phenomenology* had been meant to encompass Hegel's philosophical system. But despite its forbidding length, it had proved to be only a preface to that system—a schooling for the adept who is about to acquire the philosophical viewpoint. Now the *Logic* was seen as the first part of the system, the dynamic method of thought, or, as Hegel put it so provocatively in his introduction, "the account of God, as he is in his eternal essence before the creation of nature and any finite spirit."

The challenge of the systematic task Hegel had set for himself in the *Logic* prefigured the addition of a "philosophy of nature" and a "philosophy of spirit" (metaphorically paralleling the two remaining persons of the Trinity). He never achieved the precise execution of these remaining parts of his system. But in 1816 he published the first edition of his *Encyclopedia of Philosophical Sciences,* which included these sections. Long as the work seems, it is composed of a cogent introduction and 477 austere paragraphs that carry the student through the entire realm of philosophical knowledge. Hegel did not intend the book to be his *summa;* he used the paragraphs as bases for lectures in his various courses. Yet the *Encyclopedia* contains the model and method of philosophy as Hegel conceived it.

Hegel did not remain long at Heidelberg. In 1818 he accepted a call to occupy the chair of philosophy at Berlin, vacant since the death of Fichte in 1814. In these times Berlin was the newest and most exciting German university, having been founded just prior to the War of Liberation under the genial auspices of Wilhelm von Humboldt and Karl August von Hardenberg. Moreover, it was

*The philosopher Friedrich von Schelling, above in an 1846 engraving, met Hegel during their school days.*

located in the capital of the most powerful German state. Hegel's inaugural address reflects both a confidence in the future of philosophy and a conviction that the state has the duty and task to protect speculative culture against its inner and outer enemies. This same speech has often been improperly interpreted as a glorification of the state per se. In Berlin Hegel lived out the remainder of his life, publishing only one more significant work, *The Philosophy of Right* (devoted to law, politics, and ethics), in 1822. It was in Berlin that he attracted students who were later to be influential in German academic life. Here his star rose. The acclaim he won in his lifetime (except from an inner circle of admirers, which included Goethe) came from his teaching activity in Prussia. He died prematurely of cholera in 1831, expiring, as his widow put it, "in the sleep of the blessed." Hegel reigned at the moment of his passing, and at certain intervals thereafter, as the loftiest figure in the German philosophical tradition.

His career had not been been exceptional, public, or adventurous. Aside from the misfortune of fathering an illegitimate child at the end of his Jena period (a transgression for which Hegel took full responsibility), there is nothing remarkable for a romantic biographer to get his teeth into. He appears to have been a winsome, pleasant youth whose early school reports do not destine him for philosophical immortality. At Tübingen he is described in a brief memoir left by his sister as a "gay but not dissolute" student who "loved to dance." The spiritual passion of his wrestling with antiquity and religion does not seem to be reduplicated in a proportionately passionate embrace of life.

*Johann Christoph Friedrich von Schiller, the poet and playwright, lived in Weimar while Hegel was teaching philosophy there.*

Though Hegel is no cardboard figure who lived in a private world of academic symbolism, he ordered his mature existence soberly amid its disappointments and triumphs. The portrait is very much that of a bourgeois professional in a somewhat prebourgeois culture. There are two existing love poems written to his fiancée Marie, competent and sincere but hardly sprightly. He appears to have been a loving brother, husband, and father. At Berlin he was a dedicated teacher (though a good deal less than spellbinding from the lecture platform) and a loyal professional colleague. For a space of time he was a good newspaper editor and the competent director of a high school. This grave philosopher admitted to loving the music of Rossini. And though a committed classicist, he marveled at the Gothic beauty of the Cologne cathedral when he visited it. His Bohemian friend Hölderlin, who eventually went over the brink into madness, described Hegel as "a calm person of the intellect." And, no doubt, he had both a catalyzing and calming influence on that disturbed poet.

Hegel had an appreciation of genius and passion, neither of which he lacked. In fact, he once wrote that "nothing great in the world is achieved without passion." But he was also able to declare that "an educated man is one who can act like others without show of personal idiosyncrasy." In both his teaching and conduct Hegel continually favored the value of public spiritedness against that of private rebellion. This temperamental preference (antiromantic to the core), which carries over consistently into Hegel's interpretation of ethics and politics, stamps him as a conservative, for whatever value the word has in this connection. In truth, all great philosophy is radical in its consequences. Hegel's is no exception to this rule. But he was not himself disposed toward the radical freedom of the individual or the supreme value of individual judgments.

Those things most important to men are what they achieve together. Genius itself cannot blossom unless the cultural substratum encourages it to emerge. This attitude underlies what some critics have taken to be a Hegelian complacency toward authority. But the fact is that Hegel's Germany was only a nation-in-embryo and that it seemed important to find ways of marshaling its cultural resources. Thus it is not surprising to find Hegel endorsing solutions that prize the cohesion of the body politic above the concerns of the individual, and favoring an implementation of this from above. His hope, like Goethe's, was that an impress of cohesion could stimulate the proper measure of genius and talent in an authentically national form. Subsequent abortions of this ideal are not to be blamed on Hegel, for they were carried out in a spirit of either positivism or fanaticism totally removed from the prescriptions found in *Philosophy of Right* and other texts.

H egel was a philosophical idealist—that is, a thinker who believed that the external world was animated, and in the final analysis, dominated, by a mental-spiritual power. Moreover, this force was collective and social. The spirit of culture was the generating force of human self-understanding. But Hegel was also very much of a realist regarding his own times. He was neither a brooding utopian aesthete nor an academic mummy. Though preoccupied by the problems of the culture in which he worked, he was not, needless to say, a Teutonic barbarian, either. He was a very brilliant flesh-and-blood man, quite sensitive to both the tragedy and comedy of existence and determined to push philosophy to the point where both could be contained in a reconciliation of history and destiny. History, in this sense, means the vital quest of man's freedom and self-understanding. But it is a destiny also because freedom and fate eventually lead to the same result. Man is most free when he learns, with his fellows, to will and achieve that which satisfies his goal of self-knowledge. To this end he discovers the essential human forms of consciousness, not just in the philosophical tradition, but in such works as *Antigone, Rameau's Nephew,* and *Wilhelm Meister.* And he sets out to create a philosophy that will rest not simply on a logic of formal argument but on a logic of being. The Hegelian dialectic is itself a mental mastery and containment of such forces as tragedy and comedy, lordship and bondage, struggle and contemplation. Each of the opposites mentioned here is irreducible at given moments of historical development; each is overcome only in the space of that development. For example, lordship and bondage is not simply, as some modern commentators appear to think, a millennial condition whereby the underdog is (rightly) transformed into the overdog. It represents a constant struggle in both society and the psyche in which estrangement is reduced and self-mastery (which means self-knowledge) is attained. There is no simple compromise of these opposing strains, nor is there any capitulation of the one to the other, but rather, a dynamic correlation of their modes of existence.

According to Hegel, "the truth is the whole," but the whole is to be understood as "the result together with its becoming." This notion makes Hegel's philosophy implicitly historical, a philosophy of change. In his system a category called "absolute knowledge," consisting of the trinity of art, religion, and philosophy, is set above the record of man's temporal strivings and above the realm of nature. Presumably, man's activity is to be judged by his accomplishments in creating "absolute knowledge." And yet these domains are seen to have a momentum of their own. Philosophy is set at a higher pinnacle of truth than what is formally contained in art or religion. Moreover, the apotheosis of art is connected with Greek classicism, that of religion with Protestant Christianity, and that of philosophy with the system of Hegel himself. In a sense, the movement of the spirit permits each of its absolute categories to be superseded by a higher form, the ultimate of which is philosophy.

This in itself would be a sovereign claim for any philosophy. If it supersedes all other forms of human activity as of 1806, it is worthy of the highest veneration. But philosophy seems not only to be cumulative of all other human forms and thus equivalent to the divine judgment of a culture; it is also the synthesis of all previous philosophical thought, expressed in terms not only of a specific culture but of what has been discovered in the entire tradition. If one follows the argument put forward by Hegel in his introduction to the *Lectures on the History of Philosophy* (published posthumously), one finds that philosophy is always the great summarizer

*In 1818 the University of Berlin was the most vital center of learning in Germany.*

of every age of culture, the wisdom that explains us to ourselves when our collective creativity has passed its prime. Thus Hegelian philosophy, as the totalizer of all human thought, is equivalent to truth, or at least to the method of knowing the truth; but this is in a peculiar way.

Theretofore, philosophers (among them, Kant) had claimed to replace previous philosophies categorically with their new systems. Hegel's claim is both more collaborative and bolder. For just as truth is "the result together with its becoming," philosophy is now visualized as the history of philosophy together with its Hegelian result. Previous philosophies were not wrong; they were merely partial. And they could not help being partial, for they were only competent to express the inner meaning of the cultures from which they derived, which were themselves incomplete or one-sided. Hegelianism, or, as it has sometimes been called, "absolute idealism," is not the brain child of Hegel, but the synthetic mastery of Hegel exerted first of all upon the culture of his time and secondly upon the entire tradition of philosophical discourse from Thales of Miletus to the present. It is one thing for a philosopher to assert that he has drawn a map of the truth, but it is quite another to say that this truth has been in dynamic evolution since the beginning of speculative thought and that philosophy has finally decoded the stages by which it appears. Yet this is the conclusion that Hegel encourages us to reach. And it has led quite naturally to the claim of some modern writers that Hegel "consummated" history by comprehending it, that he set his "immanent religion" in the place of God's transcendent one, and that he meant to propose his *Logic* as the Gospel for the new age.

Regarding such claims, Hegel himself was more circumspect. He did, in one instance, write to a correspondent: "I think [truth] dwells in every authentic consciousness, in all religions and philosophies, but our present point of view has been to understand its development." And, according to his major biographer, Hegel "grad-

*In 1808, when Napoleon routed a Prussian army at Jena, Hegel was teaching there. He claimed to have completed his greatest single work on the eve of the battle.*

ually became accustomed to the idea that his philsophy alone was the salvationary path to speculative education." But this was all. He was loath to set himself up as some sort of apostolic visionary because, at bottom, he was a rational problem-solver who regarded his work as a collaboration with the thought of all ages and an expression of the culture that had produced him. The spirit was a collective enterprise, "an I that is a we and a we that is an I." Its majesty carried none of the deceitful traits of one man's pretensions.

Hegel intends his philosophy to illuminate Christian truth as the account of a providentialism self-created from within man, rather than beyond man and his rational capacities. This mode of interpretation is not Christian orthodoxy, since it expressly asserts the primacy of reason over revelation. But neither is it disguised atheism, since it affirms the speculative truth of Christianity as reason and distinguishes the work of the spirit from the intentions and actions of particular men. Suspended between humanism and theism, it is largely indifferent to questions about the goal of history as a secularist would be apt to phrase them, just as it is jarring to the perspectives of an orthodox theologian. When Hegel declares in the *Philosophy of Right* that "world history is the judge of its own actions," he is not announcing a scandal but merely restating the truism that Providence can be justified through our understanding of its goal, but not challenged by the limited judgment one may make of it at some given point in time. Naturally, this view sits badly with anyone who posits enduring moral principles against the "slaughterbench" aspect of the historical record. Hegel did not intend his dictum to sedate human ethical responsibility; but that is, sadly, one of its obvious consequences. Moreover, as anxious philosophical agnostics, we find it difficult to accept that liberty and truth are bound to prevail in the sweep of world history portrayed by Hegel's brush strokes or in the forms he assigns to them.

Hegel's adoption of Christianity as the speculative matrix within which the spirit would advance to self-knowing fulfillment was not a conception that sprang easily to his soul. He did not begin his intellectual labors on the bosom of piety. Quite to the contrary, his earlier writings bristle with contempt for a religion that separates man from nature, robs him of the sacredness of his native community, and expresses itself in law rather than in love. In the culture of ancient Greece Hegel professed to find the cure of the ills that Christendom and modernity were heir to. Athens, according to Hegel—who was much in debt to the nostalgic Hellenism of his time —had been a cohesive popular community where, unreflectively, the stamp of beauty was placed on every action and production. There was no discrepancy between a man's life and the life of his city, no deviance between the works of nature and those of the spirit, no alienated wretchedness caused by the gap between self-esteem and the awesome worship of a transcendent deity. In anguishing over these themes, Hegel was much influenced by the analysis made in Schiller's *Letters on the Aesthetic Education of Man,* which appeared in 1795. Schiller, too, had been tortured by the seductions of Greek culture as distinguished from the style of life in gloomy Germany. He had also been influenced by Kant's austere morality. His solution to the problem had been to see Greek culture as a harmony that had to split between nature and spirit if the destiny of man was to make further progress. This bifurcation, according to Schiller, had promoted the most baleful psychic consequences during the next two millenniums. But contemporary man could not go back to the naive and natural art of the Greeks for his therapy. The intervening Christian centuries had disposed of that alternative. He could still be saved by artistic awareness and creativity, but he required a complex art that would marry his new subjectivity to the domain of wholeness and instinct.

Hegel took up this same challenge, deepening the perspective and charging it with philosophical insight. Whether or not—as scholars still debate—he ever accepted Schiller's notion of therapy through art, he quickly discarded this solution as archaic or inadequate. Modern men have ceased to be moved religiously by art; "we no longer bow our knees before it." He did, however, retain art (understood especially as Greek literature and sculpture) as a category of "absolute knowledge." Greece could not survive, except appreciatively. As Hegel puts it, somewhat crytically, in the *Phenomenology,* "reason must pass out of and leave this happy condition. For only implicitly and immediately is the life of a free nation the real objective ethical order." What Hegel means by this is that the Greeks had attained their civic excellence and religion of beauty unreflectively. Modern man must produce artificially and self-consciously the sort of harmony that for the Greeks was second nature. But in order to arrive at a point of knowledge and culture where this is possible, the spirit has had to pass through a bitter purgatory characterized by the alienations of Stoicism, skepticism, Roman private law, the Christian "unhappy consciousness," feudalism, absolutism, sentimentalism, dogmatic rationalism, and other forms of estranged knowledge. The new age will find healing power only when it can dialectically unite the Greek instinct for beauty and citizenship with the subjective power of modern self-awareness. Hegel calls such a condition *Sittlichkeit,* which means, literally, "ethicality," but for him bears the idea of an ethics that is not individualistic but rather the highest concrete expression of the laws, manners, and intellectual power of a collective culture.

This interpretation of the spirit's wandering retains a passionate admiration of Hellas, whose cultural artifacts Hegel once described as "golden apples in silver bowls." Hegel was more realistic than some of contemporaries, who either speculated on the remaking of Greece in Germany or were content to "internalize" Greece through their artistic withdrawal from public affairs. Hegel, on the contrary, was avid to explain and justify the mystery of Western civilization, and he was intensely interested in politics. Understanding meant a concession to the materials on hand, not their utopian refusal. "It is not what is that makes us irascible and resentful," he wrote in a characteristic passage, "but it is the fact that it is not as it ought to be. But if we recognize that it is as it must be, i.e. that it is not arbitrariness and chance that make it what it is, then we also recognize that it is as it ought to be." In other words, history has a plan in which dreams or complaints are idle unless we can marry them to that plan. Taking care to exclude the purely accidental from the historically real, Hegel imposed this doctrine impartially on both his view of political remedy and on his interpretation of culture. If philosophy means reason's clarity about the ultimate worth of man's works, and if these works can be grasped only in their historical evolution and "ideally," that is to say, as canceled in fact but preserved in the memory, then the task of the philosopher is both a submission to life as lived and a transfiguration of that life into its highest form of self-awareness.

Toward the turn of the nineteenth century Hegel recognized that the speculative schema of understanding that he sought for explaining culture was parallel to the Christian doctrines of the Passion, the Resurrection, Providence, and the Trinity. This insight enabled him to go beyond the secular rationalism of his predecessors. But Hegel entered the Christian fold more or less as a "conquered pagan." And it might be said that he took his revenge on the claims of this religion when he declared in an 1802 article entitled "Faith and Knowledge" that philosophy was the higher form of activity, even though both were adequate to the apprehension of truth. Indeed, his was a rather peculiar Lutheranism. "Our universities and schools are our churches," Hegel wrote. By exalting philosophy above religion and state above church in the way that he did, Hegel laid the groundwork for much of the radical theology and radical politics of later times.

It was precisely in his political claims that Hegel seemed weakest. Although only an egregious misreading of the *Philosophy of Right* can lead to the conclusion that Hegel was glorifying the Prussian state of his time as the consummation of political wisdom, it is fairly clear that he regarded conservative constitutional government as unsurpassable. If, as the Marxists claim, Hegel's philosophy as a whole is the highest form of "bourgeois truth," it is not obvious that the *Philosophy of Right* is a theoretical treatment of the highest form of bourgeois state. Indeed, that state included a fair number of prebourgeois residues. Hegelians have sometimes been embarrassed by the ethicopolitical system of the master and have been inclined to see weariness and old age as responsible for its construction. But Hegel was neither especially weary nor old in 1822, even if he no longer wrote with the flame of youth. Moreover, many of the themes of the *Philosophy of Right* can be traced back to lectures that Hegel gave at Jena as early as 1805.

*This etching depicts Hegel writing the* Phenomenology *at Jena in 1806.*

As mentioned earlier, the *Phenomenology,* the *Logic,* the *Encyclopedia,* and the *Philosophy of Right* are the only major works Hegel published in his lifetime. Yet his fame among the wider public rests chiefly on a book known as the *Philosophy of History.* Most thumbnail sketches of Hegel refer almost exclusively to this volume, which appears authoritative, readable, and unambiguous. The *Philosophy of History* (or the lectures that constitute it) are intended to show that history is justified in the operations of the whole and that its most brutal parts are necessary, that great men are not entirely the conscious agents of what they do, and that the course of history establishes the progress of freedom (as Hegel understood the word). But, in fact, the *Philosophy of History* is not just an easy version of Hegel's philosophical system, nor can it stand in its place. It is merely a portion of that system, or better, the system seen from a special angle. The *Philosophy of Art* (or "Aesthetics") is no doubt one of the least read and most rewarding of Hegel's lecture productions, while the introduction to the *Lectures on the History of Philosophy* is probably the clearest single guide to Hegel's thought system.

If Hegel is prized today, by our intellectuals, by our youth, by our new radicals, or by pathbreakers in general, it is not for the spirit of his system but for certain spirits that abound in the making of the system. Here there are three relevant bodies of work. First, the "early theological writings," which deal seminally with such fashionable themes as community, alienation, and discipleship and contribute new insight to the philosophical origins of the "God is dead" controversy. Second, some passages in the Jena lectures of 1803–1806, which were published only in the early 1930's in Germany. These reveal certain preoccupations about work and struggle that anticipate the early writings of Marx, though Marx had no knowledge of them. The first intellectual historian in English to refer extensively to the Jena material was Herbert Marcuse, whose classic *Reason and Revolution* (1941) has turned, deservedly, into a mild best-seller. Third, the *Phenomenology*, especially the early section called "self-consciousness," which presents the dialectic of master and slave and the complex portrait of the Christian "unhappy consciousness." Through the general revival of the radical Hegelian tradition in Continental Europe today, the antitheological and anti–status-quo aspects of the *Phenomenology* have once more become a living issue. They have joined with other strains of thought to accuse and challenge the politics of the Cold War and the claims of technology over human relationships. Unquestionably, advocates of these views have not rested their case on a pure understanding of Hegel. But they have been impelled by a genuine wish to update certain Hegelian methods for the criticism of our own times.

It is only in such a vicarious manner that Hegel is living, and not dead. The modern conclusions of our neo-Hegelian radicals would not have appealed to the master. He might, nevertheless, have been appeased to learn that many of his insights had helped shape a modernity beyond his vision. It would be interesting to go beyond the work of the radical Hegelians of the present to show that in a world where dozens of inchoate new nations have arisen in the past generation, the allegedly conservative dicta of Hegel might have much to teach them regarding the stabilization of their traditions and state systems—for the creation of civic pride and political breathing space.

In 1970 the bicentenary of Hegel's birth was celebrated by academic conferences and symposiums in Europe and North America. Hegel appeared to bind East and West in a way that no premeditated diplomacy could do. Hundreds of petty papers on Hegel and his philosophical accomplishments were given and politely applauded. But it was still clear to this observer that the radical Hegel and the conservative Hegel were at odds—not so much because of the Iron Curtain but because of the "generation gap." On historical evidence, it is extremely doubtful that Hegel would have wished to be the object of youth cultism or the inspirer of a radical acid thrown at a rational history of the spirit. But he has been gone these hundred and forty years, and is hardly in a position to object to what new ideologies will make of him. For it is through them, and despite Hegel, that Hegel lives.

*Hegel wore academic garb for this formal portrait.*

# ROBERT
# OWEN
## 1771-1858

erely to read some of the titles of Robert Owen's many books, pamphlets, journals, addresses, manifestoes, declarations, and open letters is to open a magic casement on fairy lands of benevolent optimism. Here is an early, relatively modest one dating from 1815: *Observations on the Effects of the Manufacturing System; with Hints for the Improvement of those Parts of It which are most injurious to Health and Morals.* But from simple hints toward simply improving the worst parts of the economic order, we pass to a *Report to the Committee of the Association for the Relief of the Manufacturing and Labouring Poor* in 1817, which has a more ambitious goal, namely, *to reduce the Poor's rate, and to gradually abolish Pauperism.* By 1830 the scope is ballooning outward. There are *Addresses . . . Preparatory to the Development of a Practical Plan for the Relief of All Classes, Without Injury to Any.* And there is *The New Religion; or, Religion founded on the Immutable Laws of the Universe, contrasted with all Religions founded on Human Testimony.* That new set of beliefs will be indispensable to understanding *An Outline of the Rational System of Society,* which, though first promulgated in 1830, too, promises in an edition of a few years later to furnish *the only effective Remedy for the Evils experienced by the World; the immediate Adoption of which would tranquilize the present agitated State of Society.*

In 1841 he hails *The Signs of the Times; or, the Approach of the Millennium* in a tract addressed impartially to "Tories, Whigs, radicals and chartists; churchmen, Catholics, dissenters and infidels; to all

*In this 1834 portrait, Robert Owen has a characteristically kind, abstracted gaze.*

By BERNARD A. WEISBERGER

producers of wealth and non-producers; in Great Britain and Ireland." In 1849 he is discussing nothing less than a *Revolution in the Mind and Practice of the Human Race,* and the next year commences the publication of *Robert Owen's Journal; Explanatory of the means to well-place and well-feed, well-clothe, well-lodge, well-employ, well-educate, well-govern, and cordially unite, the population of the world.* And in 1856, two years before his death, he is composing text for *Robert Owen's millennial gazette; explanatory of the principles and practices by which, in peace, with truth, honesty, and simplicity, the new existence of man upon the earth may be speedily and easily commenced.*

What a world Robert Owen carries under his hat: A "new moral world," he calls it in a journal begun in 1834, believing that it can and will be attained; that all classes can be blessed without injury to any one; that all nations can be cordially united; that rationality can banish, with a wave of a necromancer's wand, pauperism and all the evils of society. Pure cloud-cuckoo land, lit by the beams of a sunny mind seemingly out of place in an era of Malthusian gloom, Ricardian dismalness, Manchesterian blackness. Yet a mind that was able, until late in life, to stimulate the visions and energize the labors of thousands of devoted followers. A mind, too, that made its owner a successful and respected businessman by the age of thirty, in 1801.

Robert Owen was more than the Don Quixote of immediate pre-Victorian England. He is a reminder of two sides of the Industrial Revolution—the one, its relentless erosion of established institutions; the other, its power to instill in men a *hubris* that led them to believe they could really achieve heaven on earth. Owen, thanks both to his talents and the luck of an expanding market, surmounted modest beginnings as the son of a saddler and ironmonger to become a successful entrepreneur, a self-made man in a new society. But he likewise was a dreamer of utopias.

His benevolence was no surprise. Benevolence was in the model of Christian virtue taught everywhere in the nineteenth-century Anglo-Saxon world; for every few Gradgrinds there was at least one Cheeryble. What *was* unique was that his schemes went beyond benevolence, to an insistence, in the teeth of a reigning doctrine of economic individualism, that co-operation was better than competition. He believed that a special fortune had unbandaged his eyes at a tender age and revealed to him a mighty truth: man was the child of circumstance. He could not be blamed for the evil that he did, but on the contrary, in a mighty bootstrap tug, he could abandon his outworn institutions, based on a false morality of individual responsibility, create perfect social conditions, and therefore mold a perfect humanity. Cool minds would make pure hearts. From this simple faith Owen

*The mills of New Lanark brought Owen riches and a chance to play the patriarch.*

never wavered. Its reiteration through a lifetime made him a kindly bore, but it also made him, in the words of no less a critic than Friedrich Engels, "one of the few born leaders of men."

Owen's thinking was set in the eighteenth century. After reaching maturity, he never really added to his intellectual equipment. As Harriet Martineau noted, he might be induced to look at opposing arguments, but he was not the man to think differently of a book for having read it. But his intellectual dogmatism, normally a disqualification for winning men's hearts, was tempered by an extraordinarily attractive nature. Frances Trollope heard him debate religion with a minister in 1829, in Cincinnati, and was struck by the contrast between his uncompromising assertion that "the whole history of the Christian mission was a fraud" and the mild manner in which the charge was couched. "The gentle tone of his voice," she wrote, "the absence of every vehement or harsh expression; the affectionate interest expressed for 'the whole human family'; the air of candour with which he expressed his wish to be convinced he was wrong, if he indeed were so—his kind smile—the mild expression of his eyes . . . disarmed zeal" in a way that those who did not hear him could not have conceived.

He did regard the human family as if it were his own, and the best title for him is that bestowed upon him by one set of disciples, "the social father." His life went through several phases, but the first to bring him fame was as a paternalistic factory owner, housing his workers in a model town. From there he passed to a period in which he became a demiurge of co-operative villages, aimed at putting society on a rational footing. He actually inaugurated such a community in Posey County, Indiana, wishfully named New Harmony, while friends and disciples established three others—at Orbiston and Queenwood, in England, and at Ralahide in Ireland. They all failed but, somehow, left many Owenites no less devoted to the master, and Owen himself as confident as ever in the natural goodness of humankind.

Then, in the 1830's, he became something of a patron saint to producers' and consumers' co-operative associations and trade unions. Though he was neither a serious economic planner nor sensitive to the patterns of working-class life, and abandoned these movements as soon as they proved unlikely to become the nuclei of ideal communities, he nevertheless gave them the strength of his visions, on which they drew even after his own departure.

Finally, from 1838 to 1858, he was frankly, and somewhat dottily, a preacher and a seer. He patronized the dawning age of social science without in the least sharing its scrupulous concern with methodology. He offered unsolicited and untaken advice to monarchs and revolutionaries alike. And, turning to spiritualism, he conversed amiably with the shades of Jefferson, Franklin, and Shelley, among others, and found them all "very happy."

He was happiest, really, as an educator, and his most lasting contribution may well have been an almost unbelievably progressive school that he set up in 1815 for the children of his mill hands. He would have thought of it as simply one element in his "socialism"— a word that his followers more or less invented as the antonym to individualism. He was indeed, as Marxians labeled him, an unscientific romantic dreamer. But his dream glows for us across fifteen decades of the machine age: a dream of community persisting in the midst of alienation, of sharing and sensitivity surviving in a world in which men and societies are fragmented by their specialized skills. Owen saw that industrialism had produced a universe both inhuman and irrational. But the intelligence that created industrialism, he believed, could also improve its grimy world. And the sweetened humanity automatically generated in such an ameliorated environment would sit down to a perpetual feast of harmony.

If, somehow, he could peer through the curtain of death into a contemporary commune, one can guess that, as a rationalist and a diligent bourgeois, he would deplore the mind-bending drugs, the dirt, the flirtations with mysticism. But he might also, conceivably, enter a prideful claim to paternity.

Owen's career began in self-assurance, which rapidly peaked to the egotism of the early winner. He was born in 1771 in Newton, the youngest but one of seven children. In his sinewy *Life of Robert Owen, By Himself* (written in his eighties, when he was supposedly in his dotage) he assured the world that by the age of seven he had mastered the curriculum of the local day school and had been made an "usher," responsible for instructing others. He also read omnivorously—a book a day—everything from *Paradise Lost* and *Pilgrim's Progress* to works of travel and description and "all the lives I could meet with of the philosophers and great men." He also, he said, "excelled" in dancing and games. It was characteristic of Owen as an autobiographer to pin much of his early development on a single, simple, explanatory event. At a very young age he accidentally swallowed a spoonful of boiling-hot cereal and seriously injured his stomach. He was thereafter, he insisted, compelled to be cautious in his diet and to pay careful attention to it, and this gave him "the habit of close observation and of continual reflection" that "had a great influence in forming my character."

Shortly after his tenth birthday, Owen was apprenticed to a Northamptonshire draper. In the next four years he thoroughly learned business practices and fabrics. Then he was promoted to the post of assistant in a London haberdashery. That job proved too exhausting, and he snatched at an opportunity to take a similar, but less taxing position in Manchester. It was a key move. Manchester was a center of the rapidly growing textile industry. Owen heard progress in the clatter of those early machines. He went into partnership (on a borrowed hundred pounds) with a maker of crude cotton-spinning devices. The venture lasted only a short time before some better-endowed capitalist bought it out. Owen, the taste of quick profit fairly in his mouth, now rented a room and some more machines, and began to spin and sell yarn.

For the next ten years Owen rose in the Manchester business hierarchy. In 1795 he found partners with whom he formed an independent corporation, the Chorlton Twist Company. Then romance opened the door to a new career. One of the customers for Chorlton Twist's yarn was a Glasgow Scot, Mr. David Dale, proprietor of a successful cotton-textile factory at New Lanark, on the falls of the Clyde. On one of his numerous sales visits to Glasgow Owen met and fell in love with Caroline, Dale's youngest daughter. In due course, she accepted him, but he needed time and occasion to win her father's consent. However, as Owen put it himself, "Love is a wonderful suggestor of means to overcome difficulties." Hearing a rumor that Dale was ready to retire and sell his properties, he asked if it were true. It was. In a long series of ensuing negotiations Owen found the opportunity to sell himself as a son-in-law, and (with partners) to buy the Dale establishment for sixty thousand pounds. On September 30, 1799, he and Caroline were married. He was not yet twenty-nine—rich and well-married, and confirmed in the belief that the secret of his success lay in his intellectual penetration of the sources of human conduct.

As early as childhood, he said, he had begun his pilgrimage to enlightenment. Religious books given him by Methodist aunts had only awakened his doubts. There must be something wrong in all religions if they sowed "deadly hatred between the Jews, Christians, Mahome-

*Child mill laborers—much as Owen must have found them—were worthy subjects for social reform.*

*In Owen's factory school, tunic-clad pupils danced their way to free learning.*

dans, Hindoos, Chinese &c." Before he was fourteen, when he was still splashing with pubescent vigor in seas of print, he had been "compelled to abandon my first and deep rooted impressions in favor of Christianity." He promptly "examined" all other religions and found them rooted in the same error: that men were responsible for their own characters. His experience had already made it apparent to him that "I could not have made one of my own qualities—that they were forced upon me by Nature—that my language, religion and habits, were forced upon me by Society; and that I was entirely the child of Nature and Society;—that Nature gave the qualities, and Society directed them." Applying this discovery to all mankind made him an atheist (to the horror of the pious Dale), but also infused in him "a spirit of universal charity,—not for a sect or a party, or for a country or a colour,—but for the human race."

As senior partner in New Lanark, Owen had a singular opportunity to put his ideas into action. He was a philosopher-king, whose subjects were a labor force of about 1,300 families and 500 pauper children furnished by the workhouse—200 of them under ten. Dale was considered a model employer; he provided separate accommodations for single men and women, washing facilities, and a night schoolmaster for those of his moppets who could stay awake to learn reading after working a thirteen-hour day, exclusive of mealtimes. Most other factory masters treated their laborers like the brutalized population of an eighteenth-century jailhouse. The workers responded by becoming drunk, disease-ridden, and promiscuous beyond the redemptive hopes of all but the most dedicated ministers.

Owen changed all this, moving with initial circumspection to overcome the resistance of his Scottish hands to rule by a Welsh outsider. He suspended the drafting of children from the workhouse. He set up company stores to sell clothing of good quality, food, fuel, and whisky at cost (though there were fines for drunkenness). At company expense he added second stories to family cottages, sent carts to remove the dung heaps from before the doors, and paved the streets. He provided a doctor and a hospital, partly supported by small levies on wages. He even wooed his Scots with a local church and pastor. But his special pride was an instrument of social pressure that he called a "silent monitor." This was a little block of wood, colored differently on each side, hung on a peg at each workman's machine. The color turned to the front told how the operative had behaved the preceding day, in sobriety, cleanliness, punctuality, co-operativeness, and work quality. Black was bad, blue indifferent, yellow good, white excellent. Superintendents assigned the ratings and kept books, recording each worker's daily progress.

While, to a modern eye, this snoopervision sounds unpleasantly like *1984*, most of Owen's workers correctly took it as a sign that he cared for them as people and not as mere items on a wage bill. They responded by spectacular improvements, attested to by outsiders as well as by Owen. By 1815 they were an astonishing sight in industrial England—clean, healthy, model citizens of a model town. And Owen proudly noted that the predominant color of the "monitors" had turned from black to white.

Owen's deepest reforming wish, however, was to found a school for the town's children. His reason, a belief that early education was absolutely central to social improvements, was expressed in an essay in 1812, which became part of his book *A New View of Society.* "Any general character, from the best to the worst, from the most ignorant to the most enlightened, may be given to any community, even to the world at large, by the application of proper means; which means are to a great extent at the command . . . of those who have influence in the affairs of men." The time to begin applying means was virtually during infancy, when character was still plastic.

His partners, unsympathetic to most of his schemes, thwarted his educational hopes mercilessly. In 1810, with the works prospering grandly, he bought them out and found a new set. But in 1814 he quarreled with these, too, and finally had to agree to put the property up at public auction. This time he sought out partners whose ideas would better harmonize with his own. They included five wealthy would-be reformers—and Jeremy Bentham. All agreed that returns on their investment in excess of 5 per cent should go into education and other improvements in the workers' condition. After spirited bidding the new syndicate bought the mills for £114,000, and Owen at last could begin his school, or as he called it, the Institute for the Formation of Character.

It was an astonishing school for an England in which institutions like Dotheboys Hall and others rich in Dickensian horror and cruelty flourished. The children, who ranged in age from eighteen months to twelve years, dressed in identical cotton tunics, ankle-length for the girls, knee-length for the boys. Toddlers were only in class half the time, for the rest they were "allowed to amuse themselves at perfect freedom" in a playground. But even the older children were not subjected to anything "likely to prove unpleasant or irksome," according to the recollections of Owen's oldest son.

Lecture rooms were hung about with shells, mineral specimens, stuffed birds and fishes and reptiles, and preserved insects. All were designed to pique the curiosity of the young. Owen saw no need to stress reading and writing, which were "merely instruments, by which knowledge, either true or false might be imparted." In reading classes students were never given materials they could not understand and were encouraged to answer questions in their own words. Arithmetic was taught through practical examples. Natural history and geography stressed "whatever is useful, or pleasant, or interesting . . . to know," and were also the means of indoctrination in human kinship. The circumstances "which induce national peculiarities" were exhibited to the children, so that, in Robert Dale Owen's words, "they naturally asked themselves: 'Is it not highly probable that we ourselves, had we lived in such a country, should have escaped neither its peculiarities nor its vices? . . . in fact is it not evident that we might have been Cannibals or Hindoos, just as the circumstance of our birth should have placed us . . . ?'" By such training, the senior Owen hoped, he would lead the children to understand and accept "the inhabitants of every region of the earth, even including their enemies"—attaining, thereby, "the ultimate object of all former moral and religious instruction."

But there was still a practical streak to Owen. He taught his small philosophers military arts, "that they may be enabled to overrule the actions of irrational beings, and maintain peace." It was not particularly taxing; the drill was "never continued long at a time; and stiffness and unnecessary restraint [were] avoided as much as possible." The children seemed to enjoy it, as they also enjoyed a rather thorough program of music and group dancing, the latter performed "by some of the older pupils with a simple and unaffected ease and elegance" that enchanted observers.

As the youngsters marched and pirouetted in their tunics, under the glassy gaze of the stuffed birds and fish, they were supervised by a weaver named James Buchanan, who had "been previously trained by his wife to perfect submission to her will" and had "inexhaustible" patience with children, and a seventeen-year-old nurse named Molly Young. This sweet, henpecked man and adolescent girl, hand-picked by Owen, were given careful instructions. They were not to "annoy" their charges, particularly the youngest ones, with books. They were to teach lessons, drawn from familiar objects, only when asked. On no account were they to beat, threaten, or abuse the children; but were "always to speak to them with a pleasant countenance, and in a kind manner and tone of voice," only reminding them that "they must on all occasions do all they could to make their playfellows happy."

The factory and the school were unquestionable successes. Owen's already ample ego was expanded by the throngs of visitors—as many as two thousand a year—who came to New Lanark to marvel at how he took care of his "living machinery." Warmed by this attention, he easily persuaded himself that "he possessed the means, and was re-solved, to produce a great change in the manners and habits of the whole people" by a project "simple, easy of adoption, and so plainly efficacious that it must be embraced by every thinking man the moment he was made to understand it." Gradually, he lost interest in the routine operations of his school and factory. In the years between 1816 and 1824 he began to make the transition to the second major phase of his career—community planner.

There was a brief, unsatisfactory interlude as a reform lobbyist. During the hard times that followed the ending of the Napoleonic Wars, Owen proposed a law that would limit the workday in industrial establishments to twelve hours (including one and a half hours for meals), bar the use of children under twelve, and set up a state-financed primary-education system. Sir Robert Peel took up the sponsorship of such an act in 1815. Battered to death in three parliamentary sessions, it finally emerged (though vastly weakened) as the ground-breaking Factory Act of 1819. The experience confirmed Owen's distaste for the compromises of politics. Though he stood for Parliament in 1819, his chances of success were diminished notably by his public insistence that mankind would be ready for his schemes of salvation only when ready "to dismiss all its erroneous religious notions." In an England in which evangelicalism was a strong and growing force, one did not win influence by proclaiming from the housetops that religion was the poison of the masses.

A more sweeping Owenite proposal than factory reform was the one for a wholly new system of poor relief. In 1815 he began to develop a scheme to organize the unemployed into communes ("Villages of Co-operation" was his name for them), to become the nucleus of a new society altogether. For, as he was to say in 1817, the evils of modern life were deep-rooted, and *"while man remains individualized they must continue."* To an England officially enthralled with *laissez faire*, he issued proclamation after proclamation, in the fashion of a knight-errant declaiming challenges; each extolled the virtues of social planning and co-operation, the keys to a "rational, moral and intelligent" life for humanity.

As Owen first outlined his plan to a Committee for the Relief of the Manufacturing Poor, it was a strange mixture of forward-looking and regressive elements. The mechanical revolution in production, Owen's paper declared, could not be reversed, for to smash the machines would be "a sure sign of barbarism." But it would be equally barbarous to allow the workers displaced by machines to starve. His solution was to put them in agricultural villages, where the basic method of cultivating the soil would be—by turning it under with shovels! Under "spade husbandry," clearly the invention of a non-farmer, food production would forgo the benefits of modernization in order to employ the maximum of labor.

But that was only the beginning. Each village, of 1,000 to 1,500 unemployed workers and their families, would be built in the form of a hollow square of buildings, set amid the fields. The interiors of the squares would be subdivided into rectangles by still other buildings (which led William Cobbett, a fierce critic of Owen, to snort that the proposal envisaged "parallelograms of paupers"). The outer ring would contain family lodgings and dormitories for all children over three years old, or in excess of two in their family. In short, no couple would ever keep more than two infants at home. In this way, the young would escape their parents' bad habits and learn such "dispositions as may be most conducive to their happiness throughout life."

An additional motivation of this arrangement uncannily anticipated some of the radical attacks on the nuclear family launched by modern sociologists, educators, and feminists. In the words of J. F. C. Harrison, the most recent thorough student of Owenism, the family was responsible for "fragmentation and disharmony . . . Protected from the world at large by strong walls of legal and religious custom [it] seemed to him an autonomous and alien element in society. It served to isolate men from each other, and to breed loneliness and self-centredness. Moreover, it was an organ of tyranny, by which the wife was subjected to . . . her husband [and] condemned to a life of petty domestic drudgery and endless child-bearing."

Within the squares there would be communal kitchens and dining rooms, lecture halls, nursery and other schools, playgrounds, parks, and meeting rooms where the community would carry on the work of self-government through elected committees. While most of the men went forth to ply their spades, some—and some of the women—would tend to orchards, gardens, and stock pastures or work in such establishments as laundries, breweries, gristmills, and slaughterhouses.

It would be very Arcadian—the men and women marching to the

*New Harmony, on the quiet Wabash shore, was to be a model for a brave new world.*

shops, fields, and pastures between rows of gardens, the happy voices of children murmuring from the playgrounds and progressive classrooms—a society of men and women without selfishness, competitiveness, jealousy, or other vices. It would be so entrancing that all of England's population would rush to organize itself along these lines. Owen did not grapple with such questions as what would happen to the existing towns or how to secure credit, machinery, seed, or raw materials. As always, he saw no difficulties.

It *was* an enchanted vision. It even appealed to some hardheaded philanthropists as a cheap way to handle the poor. David Ricardo himself headed one group created to raise funds for such a village. Other men of affairs did likewise. But most of the sums collected fell far short of what Owen said was the absolute minimum required. The government magisterially did nothing to help. Owen was left to become a propagandist for his own views, through periodicals and visits abroad, where he called on highly-placed officials, was dutifully courted as the remarkable Mr. Owen of New Lanark, who knew how to meet a payroll, and received fresh nourishment for his self-esteem —but no money. By 1824, however, two developments had emerged that were to have future reverberations. One was the formation, throughout the country, of various Owenite societies: clubs of believers, ready to become the villagers of his blueprint should occasion offer. Many would become the nuclei of unions, co-operatives, and other progenitors of later English socialism. And, in 1824, Owen made a dramatic move. He sold his share in New Lanark and invested most of the proceeds in his own utopian community, far away in the wild interior of North America. Owenism transplanted proved to be an exotic, brief-flowering shrub. But it became a bridge between American and British reform.

The transatlantic adventure began when one Richard Flower appeared at the Owen home, acting as agent for "Father" George Rapp, the begetter of a religious community called "Harmonie" in southern Indiana. When Owen learned that Rapp had received a divine inspiration to move his flock elsewhere and sell the old location, he was interested enough to book passage to the United States. A look at the forty houses, the dormitories, the neatly laid out streets, the vineyards, orchards, granaries, distillery, brewery, and tannery that the Rappites had built, was enough to convince him that here was a "theatre," in his son's words, "on which to try his plans of social reform." On January 2, 1825, Owen paid approximately $125,000—a major share of his personal fortune—for twenty thousand acres of Wabash Valley soil, and then, characteristically, left at once for England to lay further plans.

On April 13, 1825, he returned to New Harmony to set up the machinery of the future Society of Equals. Several hundred brave souls had already assembled, with various quantities of household goods, tools, and capital to contribute. Owen stayed only a month, heartening the faithful ("I do not know how it is," wrote one, "he is not an orator, but here he appears to have the power of managing the feelings of all to his will") and then he was off to England again. In his absence, the community wrestled with the problems of maintaining high-mindedness amid the hardships of the frontier and the temptations of human nature. They frequented dances, concerts, and lectures in lieu of forbidden taverns and familiarized themselves with a credit arrangement whereby their services to the community were recorded in a little passbook and "exchanged" for bacon, chicken, coffee, and eggs at the official store. The limited supply of foodstuffs, however, was not expanded by this rational arrangement. Nor were skilled workers available to set up the pottery factory, the spinnery, the dye works, the bookbindery, the smithy, the glassmaking plant, and the other manufacturing establishments that would supply essential goods or earn the cash to buy them. So, while the co-operationists' motto, as given in the local newspaper, the *New Harmony Gazette*, remained, "If we cannot reconcile all opinions, let us endeavor to unite all hearts," complaints nonetheless increased in volume, and unity began to fissure.

Owen returned, in January of 1826, with inspiration and recruits—not the craftsmen and artisans who were needed, but so many scholars, artists, and assorted intellectuals who had fallen under the Owenite enchantment that the keelboat which brought them was dubbed "the boatload of knowledge." Its passengers included William Maclure, geologist, philanthropist, and educator; Mme Marie Duclos Fretageot, an early disciple of Pestalozzi, the educational pioneer; Thomas Say, zoologist and curator of the American Philosophical Society; Charles-Alexandre Lesueur, first curator of the Museum of Natural History of Le Havre; and an assortment of others. They blended into New Harmony's existing population of a thousand or so, and fell to botanizing,

*This title page of one of Owen's numerous publications is typical of his ebullient optimism, vanity, and dauntless wordiness.*

sketching, mounting fish, bugs, and birds, writing journals, and having a "wonderfully pleasant" time.

The social father stayed for eighteen months, devising names and constitutions, setting up and dismantling departments and governing committees, and issuing, on July 4, 1826, a Declaration of Mental Independence, declaring that the time had come to disenthrall men from the bonds of "a TRINITY of the most monstrous evils that could be combined to inflict mental and physical evil upon his whole race"—private property, absurd religious systems, and marriage founded on both of them. But it was all to no avail. The communitarians believed abstractly in all the co-operative virtues, but in practice they behaved like unregenerate individualists. Many moved out, taking their property with them. Other coalesced around strong individual leaders and seceded to form subcommunities. Arguments over the charges at the community store, the keeping of accounts, and the management of the schools threw meetings into turmoil. There were ugly accusations of profiteering and theft. By June of 1827 it was evident even to Owen that the experiment was breaking up, as it eventually did. He left in that month, and although he returned in 1828, he had no further interest in New Harmony. He eventually sold the property to his sons in return for an annuity upon which he lived for the duration of his life. He had staked almost everything he had accumulated in life, and lost it. Yet he did not give vent to recriminations of his own, nor cease to insist that his design was sound.

New Harmony's land gradually returned to private hands. Many of the members of the community moved onward to furnish energy for other reform movements. Owen's own children remained in the New World, and his three sons had distinguished careers, one becoming a congressman, another a college president, and the third an eminent geologist. The afterglow of New Harmony lit the way to humanitarian efforts for many Americans who knew of it only by report—for by report it offered sustenance to the continuing vision of a new heaven and a new earth that goaded men to struggle on behalf of society's victims long after Owen was dead and gone. The days of hope and harmony in Posey County did not add up to a long period, but they were enough to give Owen a place in the history of American, as well as British, reform.

In 1828 Owen, fifty-seven years old and still optimistic, entered upon a third phase of his life that would last for about six years. Temporarily downgrading communes in priority, he accepted the leadership of the many producers' co-operative associations springing up throughout England, and then of the young but growing trade-union movement. He was closer in spirit to the co-operationists because of their millennial hopes, well summed up in the title of one of their organizations: The Institution of the Intelligent and Well-Disposed of the Industrious Classes for the Removal of Ignorance and Poverty by Means of Education and Employment; and for Promoting Union and Kindly Feelings Among all Ranks, Sects and Parties.

In 1834 Owen became the head of a coalition of workingmen's associations called the Grand National Consolidated Trades Union. Its membership was gigantic for the day—in the hundred of thousands— and Owen thought that the members would raise a clamor for the new moral world too powerful for politicians to ignore. But his army was disunited, and he was an incongruous leader. Most of the unionists were interested in bread-and-butter issues and in girding for economic conflict. To Owen, strikes were anathema as the very obverse of cooperation and kindliness. His kind of advice to labor on building the New Jerusalem was expressed in a speech that counseled: "[You] will . . . effect this great and glorious revolution without, if possible, inflicting individual evil . . . without bloodshed, violence, or evil of any kind, merely by an overwhelming moral influence, which . . . individuals and nations will speedily perceive the uselessness and folly of attempting to resist."

Hard-pressed wage earners were, by and large, unready for such a pacific message. British conservatives, in turn, were appalled by the prospect of a powerful working-class movement. Employers and the government launched a strenuous antiunion campaign. Striking and nonstriking GNCTU members were harassed by firings, lockouts, arrests, and fines. By October of 1834 the infant organization collapsed under the pressure. It was reorganized, with Owen as Grand Master, simply as The British and Foreign Consolidated Association of Industry, Humanity and Knowledge, aiming only to "reconcile the masters and operatives throughout the Kingdom." Soon thereafter, Owen left unionism in effect, much as he had left New Harmony—in both cases with no rancor on his part and with a surprising residue of affection remaining among those he left behind.

In his remaining quarter of a century Owen was no longer an architect of live organizations. As head of the Association of All Classes and All Nations—later reincarnated, like so many of his periodicals and organizations, under another name, this time as the Universal Community Society of Rational Religionists—he lectured, traveled, and kept repeating his message to the world in an infinite variety of forms. He was presented at Victoria's court, to the scandalization of the pious. In 1848, when France underwent a brief socialist revolution, he rushed to Paris to hold interviews with leaders of the short-lived Second Republic, and to write a *Dialogue entre la France, le monde et Robert Owen*. Despite the widespread impression, created by his acceptance of spiritualism, that his mind had gone wholly soft, his *Life,* written in 1857, was lucid, condensed, and charming in its mixture of hard narration, egotism, and exhortation. In his last year, 1858, the author was still firm in the faith. Noting the highlights of the preceding century, he claimed the most outstanding among them to be the Industrial Revolution and "Robert Owen's discovery that *any* character, from the *worst* to the *best,* may be given to the human race; and that the *best* may be now be given to *all* from birth, *with the certainty of a law of nature.*"

Who could resist such a gospel? Who could not forgive his tautologies, his redundancies, his habit of "always thinking he had proved a thing" (in Harriet Martineau's recollection) "when he had only asserted it?" For in the end, it was easy to see that he was "always palpably right in his descriptions of human misery" and always matchlessly and truthfully eager to alleviate it.

His task was to inspire, not to fulfill. He was a child of his century—its high hopes and its often dismal performance in producing a livable world. If he was not free of its silliness, he escaped its cant and cruelty.

What he was seeking was a peaceful way for humanity to live with the forces it had unleashed. That he did not find the answer is not his failure alone. We have not yet found it. And if his schemes of instant perfection do not furnish us a practical guide, still, we could do much worse than to emulate his genial willingness to try new plans when old ones failed; to put up with a humanity that always seems to resist being reformed. He lectured, but never scolded mankind, like a boring but infinitely patient lover. In one who sets such a pattern, a touch of prolixity is, after all, something that may be easily forgiven.

Owen's utopias were tempting game to satirists and punsters, as in this cartoon entitled "New Harmony—All Owin'—No Payin'."

# KARL MARIA VON
# CLAUSEWITZ
## 1780-1831

S ince 1945, under the stimulus of the Cold War, an immense apparatus has been created in the United States to apply academic minds to the problems of war in international relations. Learned volumes and monographs, stuffed with impressive calculations and formulas, have poured forth. A new jargon has been invented to enhance the mystique of the authors and obscure their meaning. Mathematicians, lawyers, economists, sociologists—all have enthusiastically joined the Pentagon Irregulars.

However, the climax of more than twenty-five years of intense and nationwide intellectual study of war has unfortunately proved to be the American defeat in Vietnam. How much the academic think-merchants share in the responsibility for the mess cannot yet be known. Judging from the published literature, perhaps the United States would have found a better guide to action in the works of Karl von Clausewitz, a Prussian major general who died in 1831.

General Karl Maria von Clausewitz was the first man to make conceptual sense of war as a social and political activity and to deduce its governing principles. Clausewitz is the starting point of all later theorizing about war, and often the finishing point as well. He significantly influenced the German and French general staffs before 1914; he is the fountainhead of present-day Communist thinking about war; and he ought to be a part of every Western young man's education. His great work, *On War (Vom Kriege),* casts more light than any other single book on all the facets of collective human rivalry.

Clausewitz was an early example of that German phenomenon, the

*This lithograph of Karl Maria von Clausewitz was done by Franz Michelis in 1819.*

*By* CORRELLI BARNETT

intellectual soldier: a man whose professional worth lay not in powers of leadership but in powers of mind. Born in Magdeburg in 1780 (and therefore not Prussian by birth), he joined the Prussian army in 1792, at the outset of the French Revolutionary and Napoleonic wars. When thirteen and fourteen he served with the Prussian army in the campaigns on the Rhine. While he was studying at the Berlin Military Academy, between 1801 and 1803, he was noticed by the head of the school, Scharnhorst, who was later to carry out the sweeping reforms in the military system that followed the Prussian defeat at the hands of Napoleon in 1806. In that dismal campaign, in which the army bequeathed by Frederick the Great was smashed like an old clockwork toy, Clausewitz acted as aide-de-camp to Prince August of Prussia.

On his return, after the peace, he served on Scharnhorst's staff during the reorganization of the army. It was a mark of his intellectual reputation that he was also appointed military tutor to the crown prince of Prussia.

In 1812, when Prussia remained neutral under Napoleon's pressure, Clausewitz, with other Prussian officers, joined the Russian army and served through the campaigns of 1812, 1813, and 1814, first as an A.D.C. and then as chief of staff to an army, a post he filled with distinction. He took part in the negotiations that led to the Convention of Tauroggen in 1812, by which the Prussian army deserted Napoleon. During the Waterloo campaign Clausewitz was chief of staff to a Prussian corps and was present at the battle of Wavre on the same day as the Battle of Waterloo.

*David von Scharnhorst made sweeping reforms in the Prussian military system after the disastrous defeat by the French in 1806.*

Clausewitz had thus seen varied service in the first great conflict of modern times, in which the limited, formalized warfare of the eighteenth century was swept away by Napoleon, himself the embodiment of will power in violent action and backed by the mobilized moral and material resources of the largest nation in Europe. As a staff officer Clausewitz had had the opportunity to observe and reflect on war as well as to organize its conduct. He also knew by firsthand experience at Tauroggen the no man's land between strategy and policy. His experience helped him gain insight into both the nature of war and human behavior under the stress of conflict.

*On War* appeared in 1832, a year after Clausewitz's death as a result of cholera contracted while serving with an army of observation in Poland. He had nowhere near finished it. Of the eight books into which the massive work of more than a thousand pages is divided, only Book I was regarded by Clausewitz as being in its final form. Much takes the form of disconnected notes on particular topics, occasionally opaque and confused in language, and as a whole, the work is rambling and repetitious and even, at times, contradictory.

In treating warfare itself, strategy, and the conduct of war, Clausewitz was at pains to demolish the school of late eighteenth-century theoreticians who had reduced war to geometric formulas in which victory went automatically and bloodlessly to the commander with the correct angles between his base, his army, and the enemy, or to the one who occupied certain geographic points. Clausewitz has warnings for all armchair strategists:

War is the province of uncertainty: three-fourths of those things upon which action in War must be calculated, are hidden more or less . . . Here, then, above all a fine and penetrating mind is called for, to search out the truth . . .
War is the province of chance. . . .
. . . to get safely through this perpetual conflict with the unexpected, two qualities are indispensable: in the first place an intellect which, even in the midst of this intense obscurity, is not without some traces of the inner light . . . [that is, capability of] the rapid discovery of a truth which to the ordinary mind is either not visible at all or only becomes so after long reflection; and then the courage to follow this faint light. . . . *resolution*.

In a vivid metaphor Clausewitz explains the difference between flawless paper-planning and real war:

Activity in War is movement in a resistant medium. Just as a man immersed in water is unable to perform with ease and regularity the most natural and simplest movement, that of walking, so in War, with ordinary powers, one cannot keep even the line of mediocrity.

To such factors as exertion, uncertainty, error, and danger in real war, Clausewitz gives the general term "friction." It is one of his most illuminating concepts, explaining why even brilliant victories never go quite as hoped, why offensives lose their force, why "decisive" weapons or expedients (such as tanks, gas, or submarines in the First World War, or bombers in the Second) so rarely lead to decisive results, why wars always go on longer than most people believe they will. In Clausewitz's view, only two things serve to overcome friction: the will of the commander and the inurement of his army to war.

For Clausewitz the central points about war are that it is violent and that it is a contest of wills. Therefore, the basis of all strategy must be combat. The battle, even if it is for some reason unfought, remains the yardstick of war. In a simile that particularly tickled Engels (who passed it on to Marx), Clausewitz says that fighting is to war what cash payment is to trade: however rarely it actually occurs, everything must be directed toward it. After all, a battle avoided is often simply a battle that one side knows it will lose.

Clausewitz reckoned that in his own age the professional performance of armies was about equal, and that consequently, *"superiority in numbers becomes every day more decisive."* In Clausewitz's opinion, therefore, the essence of strategy lay in the calculations of space and time that enabled a general to give battle at the crucial point with all his available forces concentrated. Dispersion and diversion were

enticing traps to be avoided. Later critics, especially the modern proponents of small, elite mobile forces, have attacked Clausewitz for his
emphasis on the decisiveness of numbers. Yet it was numbers (and
industrial superiority) that determined the outcome of the two twentieth-century world wars.

Clausewitz believed that the critical point in strategy is the enemy's
"center of gravity." This is usually his principal field army, which,
once defeated, deprives the enemy of the means and will to resist.
However, in the case of a politically shaky opponent, the center of
gravity might well be the enemy's capital city. The center of gravity of
a coalition is the strongest member of it, the ally without whom the
others cannot sustain the war. (This almost self-evident point was lost
on those during the First World War who looked on Turkey, Bul-
garia, and Austria as the "props" of Germany, which, if knocked away,
would lead to a cheap victory.)

About the nature of battle itself Clausewitz says much that is penetrating. Far from being the dramatic clash of romance, it is a gradual
wearing away of physical and moral resources. The slowly tilting balance of defeat and victory is a moral one, manifested by loss of ground
and/or by the faster consumption of reserves and effort by the loser.

The insight of the general should tell him the moment when a battle is lost, and instead of committing more reserves to be consumed in
vain, he should husband fresh forces for another battle, which may
redress the balance. Casualties are usually about the same on both
sides in the battle itself; it is *after* the battle, in confusion and retreat,
that the defeated army suffers disproportionate losses. Even then, it
is the moral effect, rather than the casualties, that most upsets the
equilibrium of the campaign. Clausewitz points out, however, that the
equilibrium tends to right itself in time; the effects of victory are rarely
long-lasting.

In distinguishing between the defensive and the offensive, Clausewitz maintained that while the defensive is the stronger form of war
because it can be maintained with fewer forces, the offensive alone has
the positive object, and therefore the potentially decisive role. That
the defensive is inherently stronger is abundantly borne out by history: Napoleon's and Hitler's invasions of Russia, for example.

War for Clausewitz was no meaningless episode of violence, nor was
it absolutely distinct and separate from peace. War, on the contrary,

belongs . . . to the province of social life. It is a conflict of great interests which is
settled by bloodshed, and only in that is it different from others. It would be better
. . . to liken it to business competition, which is also a conflict of human interests
and activities; and it is still more like State policy, which again . . . may be looked
upon as a kind of business competition on a great scale.

This simple proposition is Clausewitz's greatest and most illuminating insight. In the words of his most quoted aphorism, "War is only a continuation of policy by other means." Clausewitz returns again and again to this theme of the continuity of international relations, from peace via war to peace again, speaking of a diplomacy that (in war) employs battles instead of notes. It follows that the conduct of war ought to be constantly governed by political considerations.

In Clausewitz's view, it is absurd to try to "win" wars by military means alone, because, as he says, no major plan of war can be made without political understanding and insight. The political setting not only determines the aims and decisions of war strategy but also colors the whole character of the war. The greater the issue at stake and the more ferocious the hostile emotions, the more ambitious will be the military objective (such as "unconditional surrender" in the Second World War) and the more violent the methods and immense the war effort (e.g., strategic bombing, nuclear weapons, total national mobilization). When political aims reach their ultimate, then war attains to what Clausewitz called "its absolute form." He himself was thinking of the Napoleonic wars. The two world wars of the twentieth century, however, were far nearer to the absolute.

Conversely, the belligerents may only be quarreling over an issue that neither feels to be vital or worth much effort and sacrifice. Such a war may be hardly more than a confrontation. Thus the scale and intensity of any war is determined by the importance of the issue at stake. Therefore, it is a mistake to speak of war itself as being "limited" or "unlimited"; rather, it is the policy behind the war that is limited or unlimited. It was not the nature of nineteenth-century warfare that made the American Civil War so long and bloody but the irreconcilable political and social issues of secession and union, slavery and emancipation. And it is political, not military, considerations that prevented the United States from using nuclear weapons in Vietnam—on the contrary, nothing would have so economically and efficiently blocked the Vietcong supply routes.

Unfortunately, the complete integration of war and policy requires Clausewitz's ideal of generals who are half statesmen and statesmen who are half generals—an ideal of which Cromwell and Frederick the Great are notably successful examples, and of which Napoleon was a crashingly unsuccessful one. As a rule, however, reality falls far short of this ideal—especially, perhaps, in the Western democracies, where we tend to find soldiers who think only in military terms, and especially of "military" victory, and statesmen who know little of strategy and believe that peace is something you fix up once the war is "won."

The classic example of this dichotomy is provided by the United States in 1944–45. Eisenhower and Marshall thought solely of com-

*Clausewitz's ideal of generals who are half statesmen and statesmen who are half generals was exemplified by Frederick the Great (top). Latter-day commanders who might have won Clausewitz's approval are Bismarck (center), and Mao Tse-tung (bottom).*

pleting the military victory over Nazi Germany; they were not concerned with the political aspects of the Allied Expeditionary Forces' deployment at the moment of cease-fire. Roosevelt, on the other hand, was thinking in terms of deals with Russia over the future of Europe, but it never seems to have occurred to him that the strength and location of Allied and Russian forces at the end of the war might have some bearing on such deals. Thus both American soldiers *and* American statesmen, although from different standpoints, saw the 1944–45 campaigns in Europe as merely the wrapping up of the war against Germany, instead of as the acquisition of positions of power for postwar international relations.

Even more disastrous is to reverse Clausewitz's principle and allow military considerations to dominate national policy. This "absurdity" (in Clausewitz's view) has been perpetrated more often by Clausewitz's own countrymen than by anyone else. In 1914 the Schlieffen Plan called for an immediate German attack on Belgium and France in the event of war between Russia and Austria. Once Russia had announced general mobilization, therefore, German diplomacy was completely shackled by military timetables. This not only made war inevitable but added Great Britain to Germany's enemies. And the Schlieffen Plan, with its awful political implications, had never been discussed or formally approved by any German government!

After 1916, when Ludendorff became virtual dictator of Germany, he made two momentous decisions that brought Germany down in catastrophic defeat. At the beginning of 1917 he persuaded the Kaiser to sanction unrestricted submarine warfare in the hope that it would "win" the war. The ruthlessness of such warfare made it certain that no kind of compromise peace—Germany's only real hope—would be acceptable to Allied public opinion, and it also brought the United States into the war. And at the beginning of 1918, the submarines having failed, Ludendorff launched a series of gigantic offensives on the western front. There was no attempt to put these in the context of reasonable peace offers; they therefore served no political purpose, and yet it was now beyond Germany's strength to "win" the war by military action. In the autumn, as Germany began to collapse, Ludendorff demanded instant peace to save his army, instead of backing peace negotiations by continued military resistance, and this final absurdity completed the German catastrophe.

It is not, however, Clausewitz's fundamental concept of the conduct of war that has made the most historical impact. This is partly Clausewitz's own fault, for instead of treating it in a set piece at the beginning of the work, he scatters references to it throughout, mainly dealing with it in the last book. His opening set piece is, in fact, a philosophical analysis of the nature of war. And apparently—although only apparently—it contradicts all he goes on to say about how, in real life, war is moderated by political considerations.

"War therefore," he writes, "is an act of violence intended to compel our opponent to fulfill our will." Violence leads to reciprocal violence, so that war tends ever to extremes—a concept now dressed up in fashionable jargon as "escalation." Therefore, it is absurd to introduce any principle of moderation into the philosophy of war.

It is this opening analysis, abounding as it does in memorably pungent phrases, that has come to epitomize Clausewitz for generations of careless or selective readers and to serve as the basis of all later demand for "total war," for outright victory, and for unconditional surrender. But, in fact, as Clausewitz tried to make clear, he was referring not to *real* war but to war in its ideal philosophical nature.

Even his statement that war is a continuation of policy has been twisted into meaning that war is the most effective of political instruments, or that war *is* policy. No wonder "liberals" have been so appalled by Clausewitz's apparent immorality and brutality that they have rarely bothered to read him through. The garbling of Clausewitz's thought by fire-eating military disciples has been compounded by similarly selective reading of his discussions of strategy and the conduct of war. His balancing qualifications and fundamental belief in the relationship of military means to political ends have been totally ignored.

In Germany the swift victories over Austria and France in 1866 and 1870 seemed to prove that the general staff's reading of Clausewitz was correct. However, those wars had been carefully prepared for by Bismarck's diplomacy, and Moltke subordinated military strategy to the Iron Chancellor's policies. It was Moltke's successors as chief of the general staff, Waldersee and Schlieffen, and military writers, like Bernhardi and Von der Goltz, who catastrophically misinterpreted Clausewitz and preached offensive war by a mobilized nation as the solution of all Germany's foreign problems.

Clausewitz exercised a hardly less disastrous influence on the French army. He was discovered by the French in the 1880's, in the guise of the theorist who had deduced an infallible doctrine from the great Napoleon's victories. Congenial extracts from Clausewitz married well with hero worship of the emperor and shaped French military thinking before 1914. The French, like the Germans, were mesmerized by the decisive victory, won with all forces united. Like other admirers of Napoleon, they failed to note that not one of the emperor's victories had been decisive, in the sense of leading to lasting peace on French terms, but instead had led ineluctably to the one decisive battle of the Napoleonic wars—Waterloo. Late-nineteenth-century French military thinkers, in evolving their own Clausewitzian caricature, garbled an-

*To illustrate the folly of the brilliant commander who wins all his battles except the last, Clausewitz drew frequent examples from Napoleon's campaigns. Others who might have profited from a reading of Clausewitz include Ludendorff (center), and F. D. Roosevelt (bottom).*

other of Clausewitz's insights, that of the importance of moral forces:

Moral forces . . . form the spirit which permeates the whole being of War. . . . And therefore most of the subjects . . . in this book are composed half of physical, half of moral causes and effects, and we might say the physical forces are almost no more than the wooden handle, whilst the moral are the noble metal, the real bright-polished weapon.

A succession of idealistic and rhetorical French soldiers, from Ardant du Picque to Foch, evolved from this the lunatic doctrine that an attack, if pressed bravely enough, could prevail over machine guns and quick-firing artillery by its sheer moral effect. In 1914 the French army attempted to win a decisive victory in Lorraine in obedience to such doctrines. The result was total failure, with such appalling losses that the French army—especially the officer corps—was weakened for the rest of the war.

If Clausewitz's influence has been so often catastrophic, there nevertheless *have* been those who have studied him with discernment and profit—the Communists. Engels, himself deeply versed in military history, carefully studied *On War,* and he and Marx corresponded about it. Lenin, too, was a devoted student. Of Clausewitz's concept that war is a continuation of state policy, Lenin wrote: "The Marxists have always considered this axiom as the theoretical foundation for the meaning of every war."

The most successful results of Communist study of Clausewitz have been in Asia. Mao Tse-tung read *On War* in translation as early as 1928, thus absorbing its ideas directly as well as through works by Engels, Marx, and Lenin. Revolutionary war as practiced by Mao and Vo Nguyen Giap presents the perfect manifestation of the Clausewitzian unity of war and policy, and a people's army is its perfect military-political instrument. Clausewitz's assertion of the continuity of policy through war and peace is superbly vindicated by the Communist method of "fighting while negotiating," that is, of winning a peace conference by a well-timed victory, as Dien Bien Phu decided the issue at Geneva in 1954. The Tet Offensive of 1968 in Vietnam, written off by the American command with incredible stupidity as a costly failure, achieved its political aim of shaking confidence in both the South Vietnamese regime and American military protection.

Mao's and Giap's whole theory of revolutionary war echoes Clausewitz. Thus Clausewitz lists the prerequisites for what he calls "people's war":

1. That the War is carried on in the heart of the country.
2. That it cannot be decided by a single catastrophe.
3. That the Theatre of War embraces a considerable extent of country.
4. That the national character is favourable . . .
5. That the country is of a broken and difficult nature . . .

Clausewitz's dictum that time works for the defender is the essence of Mao's "protracted war." Clausewitz describes the first stage of protracted war, the strategic defensive, in Mao-like language:

If the enemy follows us into the interior of the country . . . we have more time; we can wait until the enemy's weakness is extreme . . . The enemy is now, perhaps, in possession of the whole territory which was the object of his aggression, but it is only lent to him; the tension continues and the decision is yet pending . . . at the end of the aggressive career the enemy's forces by their own exertions, are half destroyed, by which our arms acquire a totally different value . . .

The very tactics of revolutionary war are laid down in *On War,* in metaphors that are once again reminiscent of Mao:

. . . a people's War . . . should, like a kind of nebulous vapoury essence, never condense into a solid body; otherwise the enemy sends an adequate force against this core, crushes it . . . and the arms fall from the hands of the people. Still, however, on the other hand, it is necessary that this mist should collect at some points into denser masses, and form threatening clouds from which now and again a formidable flash of lightning may burst forth. These points are chiefly on the flanks of the enemy's theatre of War . . . They serve to create a feeling of uneasiness and dread . . .

Stripped of its tactical detail, which was relevant only to the weapons of the early nineteenth century, Clausewitz's work still serves as a remarkable guide to the understanding of war and policy. Modern military technology, even the strategic nuclear weapon, does not invalidate Clausewitz's fundamental theses. And his emphasis on the study of history constitutes a needed corrective to the laboratory approach of some modern strategic thinkers and students of military institutions, with their dependence on sociological or mathematical "models" and their quest for tidy, finite, and verifiable certainties.

*Marshal Ney's charge at Waterloo was a last-ditch attempt to salvage the battle.*

GEORGE PERKINS
# MARSH
## 1801-1882

**W**hen urban Americans feel nostalgic for the simple life, they invoke Henry David Thoreau. There was, however, another American, born sixteen years before Thoreau, whose union with nature was equally mystic and whose impact on this century is likely to be more important. George Perkins Marsh, a Vermont lawyer, created the concept of modern ecology, or the study of the interrelationships between organisms and environment. He cut through the Victorian complacency of his own age to prove that men were no asset to the earth; they were wrecking it. Indeed, Marsh anticipated many of the crises in resources that plague our century.

Marsh once described himself as "forest-born," explaining that "the bubbling brook, the trees, the flowers, the wild animals were to me persons, not things." The intensity of his feeling for nature expanded, finally, to include *all* life; he became the complete watcher and the tireless collector of facts. (He calculated, for instance, that if all the domesticated four-footed animals of the United States were killed and piled together, they would, in one hundred years, form fifteen pyramids the size of Cheops's pyramid in Egypt.) He observed hummingbirds sipping nectar with the same attentiveness and appreciation he gave old John Quincy Adams dozing away during boring speeches in the House of Representatives.

It is fashionable today to sneer at the dilettante, yet each of Marsh's interests was strengthened by the variety of his life. He was a superb scholar who spoke twenty languages, an expert on architecture and an

*A rare photograph shows George Perkins Marsh with members of his family.*

By FRANKLIN RUSSELL

311

art collector, a congressman and a conservationist, a geographer and a historian, a lawyer, an ambassador, and a camel enthusiast. He was also one of the founders, and a director, of the Smithsonian Institution.

Marsh, like Darwin, had an immense breadth of vision, but, unlike Darwin, he was so far ahead of his time that even the most recent edition of the *Encyclopaedia Britannica* dismisses him in a paragraph as a "philologist" and a "diplomatist."

Yet soon after the American Civil War, Marsh expressed a devastating thesis: man, he said, was trapped in a crisis of environment. It involved him at every level of his existence, from his belly to his psyche. Moreover, the crisis was global and worsening rapidly. It could, and probably would, destroy civilization. This Marshian hypothesis was presented in 1864 in his chilling work *Man and Nature,* which was subtitled *Physical Geography as Modified by Human Action.* The destruction would involve forests, mammals, fish, and insects—life at all levels; and he foresaw the reduction of great areas of the earth to permanent deserts. Tied to this depreciation of environment was, he warned, the decay of man's moral being and the fall of empires. In an age of supreme optimism about the seemingly limitless possibilities of science Marsh wrote: ". . . we are, even now, breaking up the floor and wainscoting and doors and window frames of our dwelling, for fuel to warm our bodies and seethe our pottage, and the world cannot afford to wait till the slow and sure progress of exact science has taught it a better economy."

Marsh's genius, and his relevance to today, were that he saw the earth as a unit, a giant orchestra conducted by Homo sapiens—and making agonizingly bad music. He was obsessed by the chain of cause and effect. (The invention of the silk hat by a Parisian, he observed, caused the formation of many small lakes and bogs in the United States because it almost obliterated the demand for beaver fur, thus allowing the beavers to make their comeback). He saw the earth as a series of environmental systems, which in *Man and Nature* he broke down arbitrarily into "The Woods," "The Waters," and "The Sands." All were governed by geographic rules that, Marsh noted acidly, man did not understand. Today these environmental systems have a name—*ecosystems,* or a series of "living and nonliving units interacting in nature," as one definition puts it. An ecosystem can be almost anything—an ant colony, Chicago, Africa, or two people in love. It is the interaction and interdependence of the parts of the system that are important.

The concept of the ecosystem has demanded the creation of a new science—the study of ecosystems. Dr. S. Dillon Ripley, Secretary of the Smithsonian, recently indicated the significance of the new approach:

"The creation of this new science of ecosystem ecology is, without doubt, the most important single event that has occurred in the twentieth century. It may be the most important event in all history. It is our attempt to avoid the fate of the other great civilizations."

The genesis of Marsh's philosophy occurred, perhaps, in a Vermont forest fire. He was born in 1801 in Woodstock, then a village of some fifty frame houses. A year before his birth, fire burned off Mount Tom, a five-hundred-foot mountain that overlooks Woodstock. Until Marsh was three, the mountain remained bare of trees, and much of its soil probably eroded into the river at this time. Then new trees began springing up to cover it, as he, a precocious reader, was educating himself in his father's library. He saw the successive changes that followed the burn and noted them so carefully that years later he was able to write: "the depth of the mould and earth is too small to allow the trees to reach maturity. When they attain to the diameter of about six inches, they uniformly die, and this they will no doubt continue to do until the decay of leaves and wood on the surface, and the decomposition of the subjacent rock, shall have formed, perhaps hundreds of years hence, a stratum of soil thick enough to support a full-grown forest."

The Marshes of Vermont and their friends were gentleman landowners. Ethan Allen once described them as "A Petulant, Pettefoging, Scribling sort of Gentry, that will keep any Government in hot water till they are Thoroughly brought under by the Exertions of Authority."

Despite Allen's sour estimate, George Marsh was proud of his family heritage. In later years he would make a giant leap to link them to the Goths, whom he vastly admired: "The intellectual character of our Puritan forefathers is that derived by inheritance from our remote Gothic ancestry, restored by its own inherent elasticity to its primitive proportions, upon the removal of the shackles and burdens, which the spiritual and intellectual tyranny of Rome had for centuries imposed upon it. . . . The Goths . . . are the noblest branch of the Caucasian race. We are their children. It was the spirit of the Goth, that guided the May Flower across the trackless ocean; the blood of the Goth that flowed at Bunker's Hill."

The Goth whose name was George Perkins Marsh was an odd child with an oversized head, who liked to play with girls. His father, Charles, tyrannized the children, and George sweated over his studies to win paternal approval. As a country child, he began his thinking at the soil and worked upward. He wanted to know everything, in more than the usual childish sense, and he went about it through years of systematic study of an encyclopedia. In his usual fashion he overdid it; by the time he was eight, he was almost blind and for four years

*Idyllic pictures of Vermont concealed the ecological damage Marsh could already see.*

could read nothing. But his passion for knowledge was undiminished.

He went out into the fields and woods to study the natural world. His father often walked with him, identifying trees and explaining the workings of watersheds. Young George himself was at the center of the grand, interacting system of life that he observed. The fast-flowing river Quechee, which runs past Woodstock and which at that time was studded with mills, shrank to a trickle during the summer, and the mills shut down. George noticed that as the hills were cleared of spruce and white pine, the spring floods of the Quechee became higher. When he was ten, a July flood smashed his father's stone retaining-wall on the river and swamped his sawmill. The system in which he lived was close to nature, yes; but its philosophy was destructive, and he witnessed the despoliation of his environment. His childhood was spent within the span of pioneer days in Vermont, when entire forests were felled for fuel and lumber. The roar of the floodwaters and the crash of falling trees were somber lessons for an observant boy. Marsh never forgot that, as he watched, primeval Vermont was destroyed.

Erosion in New England may have carved the outlines of his philosophy, but to reach conclusions involving the world, Marsh was forced to make a lifelong journey through time and space. His boyhood experiences were forgotten while he followed in his father's footsteps and became a lawyer.

"Work is life," he once said, and he used work to get him through a life of sustained personal disaster. Calamities hit him about as frequently as the floods hit Vermont. His first wife, Harriet, whom he had married in 1828, died in 1833, and his four-year-old son, Charles, died of scarlet fever eleven days later. In 1843 he was elected to Congress as a Whig, but during his campaign his second wife, Caroline, suffered a stroke, and his surviving son, George, got typhoid.

*In the eroded hills of Lucania, Marsh saw the disastrous effects of deforestation.*

Politics, he found, dulled and degraded the mind. Besides, Marsh the politician needed a sinecure to support Marsh the scholar. In 1849 he wangled an appointment as U.S. Minister to Turkey. This, too, was a disaster. He had to spend thousands to supplement his meager government allowance.

On his return to the United States in 1854, pressed for money as usual, he tried the lecture circuit, but his fact-filled speeches stupefied his audiences. Marsh's biographer, David Lowenthal, explains that Marsh "never quite got rid of the notion that facts are virtues in themselves . . ." He had invested heavily in textiles a few years before the market collapsed, and now bought into a marble quarry that produced a type of marble nobody wanted. Eventually he went bankrupt from earlier investments in a railroad, losing valuable real estate in the process. "There have been Marshes," he wrote sadly to a friend, "who not only *had* money, but actually *kept* it till they died."

But none of this seemed to slow him down. He designed measuring and surveying instruments, wrote an Icelandic grammar, and launched a one-man lobby that was responsible for the Washington Monument's obelisk form.

In 1861 Abraham Lincoln came to Marsh's rescue, appointing him the first American minister to Italy. It was an odd choice, since Marsh was violently anti-Catholic; in the year of his appointment he expressed the hope that he would live to see Pope Pius IX hanged. Marsh set sail for Italy with his usual *mal de mer*. "I hate the sea," he once said, "and would be well content to pay my share of the cost of filling it up altogether."

When he finally sat down in a Genoa hotel room to work on *Man and Nature,* he was sixty-one. In addition to the Icelandic grammar and a work called *The Goths in New England,* he had published *Lec-*

*tures on the English Language* and a definitive book called *The Camel; His Organization, Habits and Uses, Considered with Reference to His Introduction into the United States.* No one could deny the dazzling variety of his work, but his life, though brilliant in parts, did not seem to add up to a significant whole.

However, Marsh's journey to Genoa and the beginning of the big book actually had nothing to do with his external life. This was the culmination of an *internal* journey—the summation of more than fifty years of watching and thinking. Added to Marsh's lifelong passion for collecting facts was an unmatched acuity of insight and an extraordinary capacity to observe, relate, interpret, and synthesize. He saw, for instance, that the great door of the cathedral at Ravenna was built of vine-wood planks, and calculated that the planks were thirteen feet long and fifteen inches wide. It was traditionally thought that the planks had been brought from the Black Sea, via Constantinople, in the eleventh or twelfth century. During his years in Europe he made a most careful search in Syria and Turkey, but he found no vine stocks more than six inches in diameter. From this he devised a commentary on what the state of Middle Eastern wine making had been a thousand years before his time.

It was, however, the ruins of civilization that really caught his attention. He analyzed ruins in North Africa, over much of the Arabian peninsula, and in Syria, Mesopotamia, Armenia, and other Roman provinces in Asia Minor, Greece, Sicily, Italy, and Spain. Dense populations of people had once occupied these areas, which in his time were little more than deserts. He recalled how the Persians, the Crusaders, and the Tartars had moved great armies, supporting themselves solely off the land, across areas that in the nineteenth century could scarcely support a few nomadic shepherds. What had happened?

The answer was clear to Marsh. A steady depreciation of environment had occurred, ending in the almost total exhaustion of its original fertility. On this exhaustion hinged not only the fall of civilizations but the corruption of the moral state of man.

The fall of the Roman Empire fascinated Marsh. He compared ancient descriptions of the empire with his personal experiences in the region. "Vast forests have disappeared from mountain spurs and ridges," he wrote in *Man and Nature.* Alpine soils were gone, cisterns and reservoirs dried up, and famous historical rivers were shrunk to "humble brooklets." He denounced the tyrannical, despotic, brutal Romans of the empire who had left a "dying curse to all her wide dominion, and which, in some form of violence or of fraud, still brood over almost every soil subdued by the Roman legions."

Marsh was intemperate about Latins, but he was right about the scope of environmental damage. Adria, situated between the Po and the Adige, was a famous Adriatic seaport in Augustus's time, but when Marsh got there, it was fourteen miles inland. Marsh calculated that the combined outflow of silt from the Italian Alps and Apennines amounted to 220,000,000 cubic yards annually, enough to cover 360 square miles with seven inches of silt. Marsh became so concerned about the silt outflow—most of it, he noted, being carried toward the equator—that eventually he came to believe the equatorial diameter of the globe would be increased, its center of gravity displaced, and its rotation affected. *Man and Nature* is full of such cosmic concepts. Locked in his hotel room, Marsh roared on around the earth, discussing the destruction of animal life, the transfer of plants, the damage done by fires, the effects of dams and dikes and floods, and the shifting of sand dunes.

In many ancient histories there are tantalizing clues to the range and period of man-made geographic change. Plato wandered in the Attic hills, chatting with his countrymen, and noted that the hills that in his time supported only thin grass and spring flowers had been covered just a few generations earlier with dense forests. Plato understood as well as Marsh that forested hills caused rain to be "received by the country . . . into her bosom" and prevented floods. Greek culture certainly did not flourish long after the loss of the upland soils.

Marsh witnessed the disastrous ecological consequences of the French Revolution. He climbed the Alps, wandered through the tributary valleys of the Rhone, and saw flood destruction that made Vermont (which he thought the worst-eroded region in America) look like a well-managed garden. The French catastrophe was caused by the elimination of the prerevolutionary forest-protection laws. The resentment of the masses for aristocratic landowners was enormous; chopping down the forests of the privileged became at once a social virtue and an ecological tragedy.

Although Marsh viewed coldly man's interference with the earth, he was a positivist. "The multiplying population, the impoverished resources of the globe," he wrote, "demand new triumphs of mind over matter." But he knew, too, that he was ahead of his time. "All I can hope," he said, "is to excite an interest in a topic of much economical importance."

In the ninety years since Marsh died man's relations with his world have excited more than "interest." Something nearing a hysteria of concern has infected almost everybody who has looked at the world through ecological, or Marshian, eyes. A minor flood of books and articles written by scientists and laymen predict catastrophe for the earth, citing its lack of food, its loss of soil, the pollution of its manifold parts. About one-third of all American topsoil has been blown or washed away, they say, and the soil is still disappearing at a grand rate. Lake Mead, formed by Hoover Dam, which was completed in 1936 to irrigate five hundred thousand acres in southern Nevada, Arizona, and California, may be filled with silt by the year 2000, according to some scientific prophets. Thousands of tons of topsoil are rapidly filling up other reservoirs through the United States.

Such statements—and more—have been cranked out so relentlessly by scientists that their shock value is pretty well gone. The most positive validation of Marsh's theories, however, is that the exhaust of man's engines is changing world climate. In the hundred-odd years since 1860, combustion of man-made fuels into the atmosphere has added nearly 14 per cent to the carbon dioxide content of the air. Carbon dioxide tends to pass ordinary light and to absorb infrared. It lets sunlight into the earth but prevents, or slows, the redistribution of heat back into space. Eventually this could melt the Antarctic ice cap, perhaps within four hundred years. By that time the rising oceans will have drowned most of the major cities of the world, unless Marsh's demand for "new triumphs of mind over matter" prevails.

Marsh worshiped technology, which he saw as the answer to man's problems of hunger and deprivation. It was, of course, technology—in the shape of axes, shovels, and plows—that had modified the geography he was discussing. However, in Marsh's view, that was the technology of ignorance. The technology of the future, he believed, would be in the hands of intelligent, informed, concerned men.

Unhappily, technology went right on being administered by the ignorant, the stupid, and the unconcerned. Farmers, equipped with the first steam plows, were breaking up the prairies in the west even as Marsh inveighed against erosion in the east. Ultimately, 280 million acres (or twice the area of France) of crop and range land were destroyed, and 100 million additional acres were so badly damaged that they cannot be restored. Former Premier Khrushchev, beset by food shortages, put plows into the Russian steppes and upset thousands of years of fragile ecological balance. Some scientists believe the land will never recover.

If Marsh's theories on man-made geography are to be meaningful to us, we must find ways to avoid the climax that his work so clearly implies. There *are* ways, or rather, there *is a* way, born out of the kind of holistic thinking that Marsh used and that ecosystemic thinkers today are trying to use.

"Ecosystemic thinking," says Dr. Frank Egler, an American ecologist, "co-ordinates the entire world—its plants, animals, soils, climate, man and other elements—as a single integrated whole which, though it must be 'managed' must also remain in relative balance if the human race is to persist in a healthy and culturally rich existence. It is a spider web where each strand is intimately connected with and dependent upon every other strand."

It is clear that a new type of man is needed in a future world where every man is dependent on every other man. Marsh, of course, would say that the new man should be a Goth, and because he understood the need so clearly, we can smile tolerantly at this small naiveté.

But was not Marsh himself the new man, or at least the *timeless* man who appears when he is needed? He was a combination of two Greek concepts: the Dionysian, or dynamic, ecstatic, and creative man, and the Apollonian, or reasonable, disciplined, and orderly man. Greek art synthesized these two concepts, and so did Marsh. He reconciled literature and science, reason and feeling, and this may well be the reason he tugs so hard on the scientific conscience today.

When Marsh died, in Italy in 1882, he was far from the "bubbling brooks" of his childhood, and he had become depressed because his optimistic hopes for man had coincided with the rise of the robber barons in America, the devastation and exploitation of the American South, and the "unification" of Italy—into apathy, poverty, and despair. Men learned nothing; they were stupid, dishonest, hopeless.

But if Marsh could hear the discussions about him today, he would not be so sure that man was hopeless. Men now listen to Marsh, and they understand him very well.

*Paul Davis painted Marsh as a living tree next to a chopped-off trunk, symbolizing the renewal of nature that Marsh taught us.*

# DARWIN

## 1809-1882

C harles Darwin's body lies in Westminster Abbey, close to the grave of Sir Isaac Newton. It is a proximity which few would challenge, nor is there any oddity in the presence there of Newton, devout Christian and Biblical scholar that he was. Yet the presence, in the Abbey Church of St. Peter, of Darwin, whom a clergyman had once pointed out in the British Museum to a friend as "the most dangerous man in England," arouses more contradictory reflections: a pleased sense, perhaps, of the appropriateness of the honor, and gratitude for the broadmindedness of Dean Bradley who, on Darwin's death in 1882, permitted it? Or wry admission of the anomalies created by combining in one building the functions of national pantheon and Christian worship? Satisfaction at a symbol of truce between science and theology? Or simply a sharper sense than usual of the ironies of death? Woe unto you when all men praise you; you are probably dead.

Yet though Darwin rests undisturbed in a Christian sepulcher, and his place in the history of science is now as assured as that of Newton or Galileo, his influence, the massive changes he wrought in the whole structure of men's ideas about themselves and the world they live in, is still immensely, even contentiously, alive—more alive today, perhaps, than half a century ago. The great nineteenth-century war between science and religion may have subsided into cheerful reconciliation, mutual indifference, or isolated border forays, but among the numerous books and articles about Darwin and his work which continue to appear, a fair sprinkling are critical and hostile, though

*A water color of Darwin, done in 1840 by George Richmond, shows him at thirty.*

*By* J. W. BURROW

perhaps for slightly different reasons from those which gave that Victorian clergyman such a *frisson* when he and his friend came across the archdestroyer pottering in the Bird Room of the British Museum.

The clergyman had probably been educated, as Darwin himself had been, in that school of Christian apologetics known as "Rational Christianity," of which the work of Darwin's neighbor in death and fame, Isaac Newton, had been the chief inspiration. Rational Christianity and its close but more radical partner, deism, represented a kind of compromise, a consciously created solution to the problems raised by an earlier conflict between religion and science; that earlier conflict was less overt but more insidious than the one of which the focal point was to be Darwin's *Origin of Species,* and it was profoundly disturbing to seventeeth-century Christian apologists like Pascal, who saw in the rise of experimental science a potential threat to belief. The crisis was overcome, at least in England, at a cost of some sacrifice of the miraculous and emotional elements of Christianity. A house of intellect was established in the eighteenth century in which men of widely differing views could conduct their arguments and all feel more or less at home, though of course there were always a few defiant atheists who refused to come in out of the cold. The England into which Charles Darwin was born in 1809 was in most respects a rougher and more dangerous society than the one in which he died, more vulnerable to organized and haphazard violence, to the social effects of callous indifference, and to the accidents of nature. Intellectually, however, the world was a far cozier and more reassuring place than it was later to become, and the chief, though not the only, agent of the change was to be that peaceable Victorian family man, Charles Darwin.

*Erasmus Darwin, Charles's paternal grandfather, was a poet, a physiologist, a temperance advocate, and the author of* Zoonomia, *a 1794 work on evolution.*

Much of this apparent coziness was due to a relative lack of historical sense, which, paradoxically, helped men to feel at home with the past. Educated men could speak familiarly of Moses, Abraham, and Solomon, and derive maxims from their words and deeds with no sense of estrangement; Dean Milman became very unpopular for calling Abraham a sheik. One reason for familiarity with the past was the relatively short time span it was thought to cover. Most men at the beginning of the nineteeth century thought that the world had been created only some six thousands years before, although perhaps few would have cared to be as specific as a seventeenth-century vice-chancellor of Cambridge University, according to whom "man was created by the Trinity on October 23, 4004 B.C., at nine o'clock in the morning." But when the Rev. John William Burgon apostrophized Petra as a "rose red city half as old as time," he meant it.

The world was not only imaginatively comprehensible, it was benevolently ordered. It is true that, ever since Copernicus and Galileo, the earth could no longer be regarded as the center of the universe; the music of the spheres was stilled. But God presided every instant, through the invisible filaments of gravitation, over the perfectly ordered harmony of the planetary motions. And if the earth was not the center of the universe, man was still emphatically the center—the end and purpose—of life on earth, a life which had issued, fully formed in all its variety of fish and flesh and fowl, directly from the hands of the Creator, to be subject to a man quickened into life, as in Michelangelo's famous fresco, by the outstretched finger of God: "fill the earth and subdue it; and have dominion over the fish of the sea and over the birds of the air and over every living thing that moves upon the earth." A characteristic treatise published in 1833 was entitled "On the Power, Wisdom, and Goodness of God as Manifested in the Adaptation of External Nature to the Moral and Intellectual Constitution of Man." It would be hard to think of a neater inversion of the Darwinian theory.

In harsher climates and in times when man's control over nature was more precarious, this doctrine often needed supplementation. The Fall was necessary to explain the tiger, and men wondered whether there were insects in Eden. By the eighteenth century, however, nature was sufficiently tamed to be idealized, at least by those who did not themselves labor on the land, and educated men were sufficiently leisured and urban to be sentimental about it. The eighteenth century was the heyday of the cult of a benevolent and edifying nature, while the Fall receded more and more into the theological background.

*Josiah Wedgwood, master potter, dear friend of Erasmus Darwin's, and maternal grandfather of Charles, appears above in a medallion by William Hackwood.*

Moreover, men were beginning to have some understanding of the complex interactions in nature, of the contribution to the animal and vegetable "balance" of even the noxious and disagreeable. To pursue in any detail the pleasing evidences of divine purpose and harmony in the Newtonian heavens required some rather abstruse mathematics; to trace the same evidences in each leaf, stamen, and insect was well within the scope of any country clergyman with a pair of good legs and a collecting basket. To follow the workings of nature was to explore the mind of its Creator and to receive renewed assurances of His benevolence. The proudly displayed "collection" was almost the equivalent of a Bible laid open on a table. God was sought, not in mystical exercises in one's chamber—that would have been "enthusiasm," which was both morbid and ungentlemanly—but at the bottoms of ponds and in the middle of hedges. "Natural Theology," as it was called, was the mainstay of Rational Christianity. Natural history became something of a craze in the first half of the nineteenth century and works on it outsold popular novels. When *The Origin of*

*Species* appeared in 1859, it went quickly through three editions and found a readership which, despite the many vulgar errors that grew up about what Darwin had said, was far better prepared, both by the trend of contemporary theology and by the taste for natural history, to appreciate arguments relating to the nature of species, plant life, and animal behavior, and also the effects of selective breeding, than the reading public would be today. Bug hunting was the Trojan Horse of Victorian agnosticism.

Darwin himself was a lover of nature, a collector and sportsman, before he was a man of science. He grew up with the tastes of an English provincial gentleman at a time when hunting, shooting, and the breeding of horses and dogs formed a staple amusement of upper-class Englishmen. In his father's unsympathetic words: "You care for nothing but shooting, dogs, and rat-catching, and you will be a disgrace to yourself and all your family." Darwin, in fact, belongs to the gallery of famous men whose school days were undistinguished and profitless. After he had shown no more aptitude for medicine, the family profession, than for the classical curriculum of Shrewsbury School, his father prepared wearily to follow the established English custom of bestowing the fool of the family on the Church, and so Darwin was sent up to Cambridge in 1827. He seemed destined to become yet another botanizing Victorian clergyman. From this he was rescued by an accident which seems almost to have been sent by Providence in a fit of self-destructiveness, for from it was to flow the work which so rudely shook men's belief in divine superintendence of human affairs. In 1831 H.M.S. *Beagle*, commissioned by the Admiralty to make a surveying voyage in the Southern Hemisphere, was in need of a naturalist. Darwin was recommended by his friend and mentor J. S. Henslow, Professor of Botany at Cambridge, and after some hesitation, he accepted. He was away for five years.

The voyage of the *Beagle* was, as he said himself, the formative experience of Darwin's life. He lived hard, working in the cramped conditions of a sailing ship, rounding Cape Horn and making expeditions hundreds of miles inland through dangerous and difficult country, collecting, observing, and interpreting the flora, fauna, and geologic formations of South America and the islands of the Pacific and the southern Atlantic, and visiting also Australia and South Africa. The forty-thousand-mile voyage of the *Beagle* gave Darwin, at first hand, a bird's-eye view of the natural world, from the tropical vegetation of the Brazilian jungle to the peaks of the Andes. It was an opportunity such as few scientists had had, though there were to be others later, including T. H. Huxley, who obtained a post similar to Darwin's on H.M.S. *Rattlesnake*.

Darwin took with him on his voyage, besides his own knowledge

*Darwin's schoolboy scribble, above, is preserved on the flyleaf of an atlas. Neater perhaps, though still rudimentary, is the sketch below, the first drawing of an evolutionary tree, taken from his notebooks on the transmutation of species. The original ancestor is labeled (1), and the letters show the branches that have produced surviving species.*

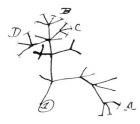

and aptitudes, one indispensable tool for interpreting what he saw. Before sailing, Henslow pressed upon him the recently published first volume of Charles Lyell's *Principles of Geology,* with instructions to read but on no account to believe it. Darwin obeyed the first injunction but not the second. Lyell was foremost among those geologists who refused to accept that the crust of the earth had been formed in a few thousand years by earthquakes, floods, and volcanic eruptions far more vast than anything now observable. He insisted that changes in the earth's formation must be accounted for only by geologic events similar to those with which men were familiar, which entailed an increase in the estimated age of the earth of many millions of years. There are few more dramatic episodes in the history of thought, not even the acceptance of Darwinism itself, than the change within a few decades from a prevailing view of geologic time that could be imaginatively grasped to one that, like astronomical distances, could be comprehended only scientifically and mathematically. The corresponding debate in biology, however, remained unsettled. Could biology, like geology, dispense with the sudden interventions of Providence, accountable for by no natural law, and explain the formation of species by the ordinary laws of nature? Noah's Flood was no longer a necessary scientific hypothesis. Could Adam be similarly dispensed with?

*Emma Wedgwood, Darwin's cousin and wife, is shown above in a water color by George Richmond, also done in 1840.*

The folklore of scientific invention and discovery has left no striking tale of the revelation to Darwin of the clue to the origin of species, like Newton's apple, Stephenson's kettle lid, or Galileo dropping weights from the leaning tower of Pisa. It was too gradual and subtle a process for that. Darwin had begun the voyage of the *Beagle* believing, like most people, in the fixity of species. During the voyage, and while writing up his notes on it, he underwent two conversions. He became converted to Lyell's interpretation of geology, and he began to doubt the fixity of species. The latter, however, was to remain for years a secret confided only to a chosen few, as Darwin wrestled with objections, accumulated evidence, and prepared his friends for the revelation that—as he wrote to Joseph Hooker in 1844—"I am almost convinced (quite contrary to the opinion I started with) that species are not (it is like confessing a murder) immutable. Heaven forfend me from Lamarck nonsense of a 'tendency to progression,' 'adaptations from the slow willing of animals,' etc! But the conclusions I am led to are not widely different from his, though the means of change are wholly so."

The theory of evolution in biology was already an old, even a discredited, one. Darwin, in his preface to *The Origin of Species,* listed more than thirty precursors—and was accused, in spite of this, of serious omissions. Greek thinkers had held the view that life had developed gradually out of a primeval slime. Diderot, Buffon, and Darwin's own grandfather, Erasmus Darwin, in the eighteenth century had held more or less fully worked out theories of the origin of species by evolution, or transformism, as it was called. The objections to pre-Darwinian theories of evolution were partly based on the assumption of a short geologic time span, which did not allow evolution time to operate, and partly on the speculative and puzzling explanations of how the process worked. In the most noteworthy pre-Darwinian evolutionist works—Erasmus Darwin's *Zoonomia* (1794) and J. B. Lamarck's *Philosophie zoologique* (1809)—it was supposed that the new needs of an organism somehow gave rise to new organs which were then transmitted to offspring, or even that some inner impulse toward perfection caused the new organs to develop. This was merely to explain one mystery by another. True, the same might at the time have been said of Darwin's own explanation, which assumed variations in offspring (though the explanation of these variations was still not understood), but if it was a mystery, it was at least one of everyday occurrence, which was not true of the development of new organs by mature organisms.

It was the unscientific character of earlier evolutionary theory that made scientists like Lyell and Huxley, and Darwin himself, skeptical. But their predecessors made some telling points. There were the improvements made in some domesticated animals and plant species by artificial selection—of which Darwin was to see the full significance. There were embryonic changes: the development of tadpole into frog and larva into butterfly. There were vestigial organs—noted by Erasmus Darwin—which seemed once to have served a purpose but now served none, suggesting that the modern species might be radically different from the ancestral one to which such an organ was useful. And there was the fossil record, unmistakable evidence of the *extinction* of species. The giant bones which lay embedded in the earth proved that the Creator could change his mind. Struggle and waste in nature were familiar to the nineteenth century long before *The Origin of Species;* Tennyson's "Nature, red in tooth and claw" is a pre-Darwinian quotation. But what naturalists did not see was that this could be used to explain the formation as well as the extinction of species.

Darwin had been struck during his voyage by a number of facts which seemed at odds with the special creation of each species. The organic life he studied so intensively and collected so assiduously seemed littered with clues, odd similarities, juxtapositions, and discontinuities, all surely significant, all part of some larger pattern if only one could discern it. Why did closely allied animals replace one

*The forty-thousand-mile surveying voyage of H.M.S.* Beagle, *seen above in the Straits of Magellan, gave Darwin a bird's-eye view of the entire natural world.*

another as one traveled southward? Why did extinct fossil species show such a close structural relation to existing animals? Above all, why, in the Galápagos Islands, did the birds and the famous Galápagos tortoises show slight variations from island to island, so that the local inhabitants could always tell from which island a tortoise had come? None of these things seemed to fit in with the special-creation theory. They began to tell an intelligible story once one doubted the fixity of species.

Ten months after his return to England, Darwin in 1837 opened his first notebook on "The Transmutation of Species"—the forge in which man's whole conception of the natural world was beaten into a new and enduring shape. The cause of change, Darwin was sure, must lie in reproduction, in heritable variations rather than in spontaneous changes in the living organism itself. By the end of 1838 the key was in his hand: natural selection of favorable variations in offspring. Because of these variations, and changes in the environment, nature was unstable, variable, not static, "those forms slightly favored getting the upper hand and forming species." Later, in the *Origin,* he was to describe in detail the "war between insect and insect—between insects, snails, and other animals with birds and beasts of prey—all striving to increase, all feeding on each other, or on the trees, their seeds and seedlings, or on the other plants which first clothed the ground and thus checked the growth of the trees!"

Darwin's own account suggests that in part he owed the inspiration for his theory to reading Thomas Malthus's *Essay on Population* (written in 1798), though the dates in Darwin's journal throw some doubt on this. Malthus's essay purports to show that population growth will always tend to outrun food supply unless checked by war, famine, or disease. Malthus's principle could obviously be extended in an evolutionary direction by concentrating on the struggle for existence and the question of why some survived rather than others. Seven years before the publication of *The Origin,* Herbert Spencer had already given Malthus such an interpretation in his brief essay on "The Theory of Population," but he applied it only to human beings, not to the problem of species as such.

Darwin was still planning a much longer work than *The Origin of Species* was in fact to be, when his hand was forced by the dramatic coincidence of the arrival of a paper from Alfred Russell Wallace in which the theory of natural selection was clearly set out. Darwin, in anguish, remarked, "I would far rather burn my whole book than that he or any other man should think I had behaved in a paltry spirit." But Darwin's priority was acknowledged, and the presentation of the Darwin–Wallace thesis as a joint paper before the members of the Linnaean Society on July 1, 1858, was one of the most unsordid episodes in the history of science. It was then more than twenty years since Darwin had begun his first notebook on "The Transmutation of Species." The Linnaean Society paper caused little stir; not so the publication in the following year of *The Origin of Species.* The "murder" Darwin had confessed to Hooker fifteen years earlier was finally out.

*Specimens collected on the* Beagle *voyage include large fossil bones, birds, beetles, a cat, and an armadillo (center).*

As a book, *The Origin of Species* gains enormously from the range of interests that a natural scientist could still, in the mid-nineteeth century, allow himself. It is a work of original research—as original as anything ever published—yet it is also a vast panorama of the natural world seen in the light of natural selection and in the almost endless perspective of geologic time as it was now understood. Its author was not merely another evolutionist, or even one who, like Wallace, had seen where the key to evolution lay. He was a geologist who had produced the modern theory of the formation of coral reefs, and explained, on geologic grounds, the gaps in the fossil record. He was a painstaking research worker, one of the world's leading authorities on barnacles, who devoted much of the latter part of his life to the fertilization of orchids and the activities of earthworms. His equipment as a student of nature was virtually complete. The former undergraduate beetle-collector was geologist, botanist, zoologist, and later, physical anthropologist. He was a paleontologist who had himself dug up a fossilized Megatherium (an extinct ground sloth), an ecologist who had observed the interrelations of organic life in tropical forests and in the grounds of Down House, his Kent home, and a former sportsman who was fully aware of the effects, in dog breeding, of selection by man. The first chapter of the *Origin* was called "Variation under Domestication."

The furor created by the publication of *The Origin of Species* was not due simply to the fact that it contradicted the literal word of the first chapter of Genesis. Many Christians had already reconciled themselves, for example, to interpreting the seven days allotted to the Creation in an allegoric sense. Religious doubt, that characteristic Victorian malaise, with its crop of social and spiritual catastrophes, of "dangerous" books and clerical resignations, had become almost a commonplace of the intellectual scene since the first impact of the new German Biblical criticism in the 1830's.

The *Origin* owed its notoriety mainly to two things. First, it destroyed the central tradition of rational Protestant religious apologetics—Natural Theology. All the beautiful and ingenious contrivances in nature, which Natural Theology had explained as the benevolent design of an Almighty Clockmaker, Darwin's theory explained by the operation of natural selection: the struggle for life, preserving random hereditary variations.

Second, the *Origin* became notorious for something it did *not* say, though anyone who read it intelligently could not fail to be aware of the implication: that man was first cousin to—*not descended from*, though this was an error often made—the ape and the orangutan. As Darwin had written in his notebook, "animals may partake from our common origin in one ancestor . . . we may be all netted together." Darwin only completed this aspect of his work in his later books—*The Descent of Man* (1871) and *The Expression of the Emotions in Man and Animals* (1872)—but the public seized on it at once. Darwinism was "the monkey theory," though monkeys are mentioned in the *Origin* no more frequently than other species. This was, however, the crux of the great Oxford debate in 1860 between T. H. Huxley and Bishop Wilberforce, at which Huxley made the famous retort, in response to the bishop's gibe, that he would prefer to have an ape for a grandfather than a man "possessed of great means and influence" who used his influence to bring scientific discussion into ridicule.

This episode was characteristic in many ways: of Wilberforce, whose nickname was "Soapy Sam"; of Huxley; of what was to the layman the central issue of Darwinism; and of the reasons why Darwin's supporters were victorious—not only because the weight of argument was on their side, but because they were always more righteous than the righteous. Infidelity had hitherto been equated with immorality and lower-class radicalism. Only a few years before, the geologist Hugh Miller had remarked, "it invariably happens that when persons in these walks [of life] become materialists, they become also turbulent subjects and bad men." It was an argument that died hard; Darwin was rebuked for publishing *The Descent of Man* "at a moment when the sky of Paris was red with the incendiary flames of the Commune." Hence it was of the utmost importance that the leading Victorian agnostics—Darwin, Huxley, Leslie Stephen (who resigned from holy orders as a result of reading the *Origin*)—were gentlemen and family men of unimpeachable sexual and financial respectability. They turned the tables on their opponents by taking a higher moral line. It was *immoral* to believe without proof, to refuse, as Huxley said, borrowing the language of religion, "to sit down before the facts as a little child. "

Of course, Darwin's theory was not immediately accepted by all scientists, either; in England its opponents were led by Sir Richard Owen, superintendent of the natural history department of the British Museum, while in America the chief protagonists for and against Darwin were Asa Gray and Louis Agassiz. Darwin himself played little part in the controversies that surrounded him, devoting his time to his orchids and earthworms and contenting himself with boyish shouts of applause from the sidelines. He was not interested in metaphysics and was not by nature combative. He was, moreover, by now an invalid.

There has been much speculation about Darwin's malady. Was it the aftermath of some tropical illness, caught during the voyage of the *Beagle,* which confined the mountaineer and explorer of the 1830's to his sofa at Down House for a large part of his later life? Or was it, as has been suggested, psychological in origin, due to a feeling that in removing God from his part in the Creation he had committed a kind of parricide? Much has been made, too, of Darwin's confession of the withering, in later life, of his feeling for beauty. He has been called "the fragmentary man," "the anesthetic man," and so on. It has been remarked, not altogether unfairly, that he debated whether to marry— he married his cousin, Emma Wedgwood, in 1839—rather as a man might decide whether to keep a dog, but it is difficult not to find something attractive in his reflection: "charms of music & female chit-chat, good for one's health; but forced to visit and receive relations, *terrible loss of time.*" There was always a childlike simplicity about Darwin, endearing him to some commentators and irritating others.

To some the implications of Darwin's theory were negative and desolating. The whole earth no longer proclaimed the glory of the

---

ON

THE ORIGIN OF SPECIES

BY MEANS OF NATURAL SELECTION,

OR THE

PRESERVATION OF FAVOURED RACES IN THE STRUGGLE FOR LIFE.

By CHARLES DARWIN, M.A.,
FELLOW OF THE ROYAL, GEOLOGICAL, LINNÆAN, ETC., SOCIETIES;
AUTHOR OF 'JOURNAL OF RESEARCHES DURING H. M. S. BEAGLE'S VOYAGE ROUND THE WORLD.'

LONDON:
JOHN MURRAY, ALBEMARLE STREET.
1859.

*The right of Translation is reserved.*

*Darwin's first title for his book was* An Abstract of an Essay on the Origin of Species and Varieties Through Natural Selection. *His publisher, John Murray, shortened it considerably before publication in November, 1859.*

Lord. Paradoxically, in revealing the closeness of man's links with the rest of creation, Darwin seemed to have cut the emotional ties between man and nature. The world was not, apparently, the rational creation of a Being whose purposes, though infinitely beyond man's full comprehension, were in some sense akin to the purposes and feelings of man himself (at least they *were* purposes). Nature, according to Darwin, was the product of blind chance and man a lonely, intelligent mutation, scrambling with the brutes for his daily bread. To some the sense of loss was irrevocable; an umbilical cord was snapped. Faced with "a cold, passionless universe," the only appropriate attitude seemed, at best, a dignified resignation "with close-lipped patience for our only friend." Unlike the beliefs of the Greeks and the Stoics, the eighteenth-century Enlightenment, and the rationalist Christian tradition, Darwinian nature held no clues for human conduct, no answers to human dilemmas. The modern ethics of the void—existentialism and all ethical creeds that make goodness not an innate property of things but a matter of human decision—have as an underlying assumption the purposelessness of the material world. So too, probably, did the rejection of "nature" as the prime subject for art by the aesthetes of the late nineteenth century. Man no longer characteristically expects to find nature suffused with divinity; he must create it out of his own visions.

But there were others for whom the ancient tradition of seeking prescriptions for human action in nature was hard to break. They found—and they were mostly the strong, the successful, or the embittered—the prescription they were looking for in "the survival of the fittest." They adopted natural selection as the key to "progress," though Darwin had not spoken of progress, only of adaptation. There were many fields, in the late nineteenth and early twentieth centuries, to which this formula seemed conveniently to apply. In Europe the nations watched each other, trained their young men, and waited for the day of reckoning. In America there were still great industrial and financial empires to be won by buccaneering methods. In Asia and Africa and the Pacific there were backward peoples to be brought within the orbit of the world's markets and taught their necessary subordination to the white man.

It is a strange paradox that Darwin, who gave up shooting because of the cruelty it entailed, should have been one of the begetters of the strident power philosophies of the later nineteenth century. The notion of the struggle for existence was not invented by Darwin, but the tendency to apply it to social relations was enormously reinforced by the apparent "scientific" backing given to it by Darwin's theory. Even Marx and Engels adopted Darwinism as the biological counterpart to

*Darwin, triumphant after his battles with scientists, churchmen, and laymen, posed for this photograph shortly before his death, at age seventy-three, in 1882.*

the class war, though Darwin respectfully declined the honor of having the English edition of *Das Kapital* dedicated to him. "The survival of the fittest" in a human context could be all things to all men. Everything depended on what you took as the competing units: individuals, classes, races, or nations. It even invaded academic sociology, in the work of Herbert Spencer and Walter Bagehot in England and Ludwig Gumplowicz in Austria, the Russian anarchist Prince Kropotkin, and William Graham Sumner in the United States. To Sumner "millionaires are a product of natural selection"—an argument which appealed to Andrew Carnegie. The doctrine of the survival of the fittest also recommended itself to Theodore Roosevelt and to the British imperialists of the late nineteenth century. The belief that war was "a biological necessity," as one of Germany's leading military thinkers put it, helped to shape that country's military and political thinking before the First World War; filtered through innumerable hack popularizations, it formed a vital ingredient in the pseudoscientific mess of racialism, nationalism, and anti-Semitism swallowed by the young Hitler in the public reading rooms of Munich and Vienna. Racial doctrines entered European thought before Darwin, as an offshoot of developments in anatomy and philology, and Darwin himself did not endorse the application of his theory in social contexts—Huxley, indeed, explicitly repudiated it—but inevitably it provided a kind of crucible into which the fears and hatreds of the age could be dipped and come out coated with an aura of scientific authority.

The bloodletting of two world wars, and the prospect that organized human aggression, far from improving the species, may actually eliminate it altogether, have dampened interest in this application, or rather misapplication, of Darwin's theory. Public attention now concentrates either on theological interpretations of evolution, in the manner of Teilhard de Chardin, or on the implications of the new factor which the development of human intelligence, with its powers of storing and communicating knowledge and hence of purposive control of the future, introduces into the evolutionary picture.

Seen in this way, evolution becomes a great adventure in which man, product of random mutations and of a suffering, blindly struggling creation, becomes, at least in part, the arbiter of his destiny. If this is to be so, a major contribution to control of the future will be the chief development in biology since Darwin: understanding the mechanism of heredity. Genetics places the thread of life in men's hands, the chemical ribbon linking past and future. In his notebook Darwin had written: "Given transmutation theory, instinct and structure become full of speculation and line of observation. My theory would lead to study of instincts, heredity and mind heredity."

When the *Origin* was written, the science of genetics did not exist.

Evolution was the result of natural selection acting on heritable variations in offspring, but, as Darwin admitted, "Our ignorance of the laws of variation is profound." The gap had begun to be filled by the experiments of the Moravian monk Gregor Mendel, but Mendel's work was rediscovered only at the beginning of this century. At first Darwinian natural selection appeared to have no application in the new science, and Darwin's reputation sank somewhat. Later, however, genetic theory began to explain variations as a consequence of environmental selection acting on the results of mutations of genes, and today selection is a controlling concept in the study of genetics, with its incalculable prospects, exhilarating and appalling, of insight into the nature of life and its possibilities for good and evil in the molding of man's physical and intellectual make-up.

Darwinism was a nineteeth-century *cause célèbre*, a fashionable formula, like Hegelianism, for applying scholarship or prejudice to the results of science. It was also, like the work of John Dalton or Michael Faraday, a permanent contribution to men's knowledge of the natural world. Yet even this comparison diminishes Darwin's real stature. As with Copernicus and Newton, before and after Darwin are different intellectual territories.

*Darwin's theories were a cartoonist's delight. "Man is but a worm," from* Punch, *purports to show his progress from crawler to monkey, ape man, dandy, and hoary evolutionist.*

# KARL
# MARX
## 1818-1883

One can imagine few greater shocks to our sense of the fitness of things than a revelation that Karl Marx without his beard had the face of a romantic poet, another Byron or Shelley. We are used to seeing him in the guise of an angry prophet, beard bristling with outrage at the iniquities of his opponents; or nobly marmoreal in profile, with a similar profile of Engels or Lenin apparently adhering to one of his ears, as one sees them on innumerable Communist posters. The beards of the saints of European communism seem a part of their roles: Marx's leonine and denunciatory; Engels's brisk and worldly; Lenin's a jutting icebreaker, forging forward toward the happy land over the always-receding horizon.

Yet the suggestion that the young Marx might have had a face of dreamy, romantic sensitivity—though literally speaking highly improbable, to judge from the clues among the bristles—is not altogether symbolically inappropriate. Marx was an idealistic young man, born into a romantic environment, whose early ardors bear unmistakably the marks of a youth of the generation of Hector Berlioz and Victor Hugo, a generation to which Byron and Napoleon, Prometheus and Faust, were the symbols of their own thwarted aspirations, pent up by the stuffy reaction that gripped Europe in the years after Waterloo. To many of that generation "revolution" was a holy word, and the spirit of freedom appeared, as in Delacroix's famous painting, as a beautiful bare-breasted woman leading the workers at the barricades. The years of Marx's youth and early manhood were the years before

*Karl Marx seems the kindly patriarch in this photograph taken in his later years.*

By J. W. BURROW

the European revolutions of 1848, when it seemed that with one final titanic effort humanity might throw off all its oppressors at one blow and create from the ashes of the old social order a new world of justice and freedom. Paris was revered by young men as the holy city of revolution. As the Russian socialist Alexander Herzen put it, "I entered the city with reverence, as men used to enter Jerusalem or Rome."

The fate of captive countries like Italy and Poland, ruled by oppressor nations whose domination had been reaffirmed at the Congress of Vienna, touched liberal consciences as Spain was to do in the 1930's and Hungary in the 1950's. Not only proletarians but artists and intellectuals of all kinds felt, during these years, the revolutionary itch; when revolution came to Europe's capitals in 1848–49, they went with the workers to the barricades.

This was the generation to which Karl Marx, born in 1818, belonged. There is no cause for surprise that he became a revolutionary; it would have been surprising if he had not. What distinguished him from most of his contemporaries was that in Marx youthful fervor soon became transmuted into scientific rigor, without abating its revolutionary character. Marx's revolutionary zeal thus acquired a staying power, while that of most of his contemporaries—vaguer, more hazily idealistic—faded with age and disillusionment. Nevertheless, Marx's "scientific" socialism never altogether lost a visionary, apocalyptic aureole that occasionally gives a lurid glow to the gray pages of *Capital* and recalls the ardent years before the false dawn of 1848. In his personal tastes, too, Marx remained a man of his generation; he shared that passionate love of Shakespeare that struck the intellectual youth of France and Germany in the early nineteenth century with the force of a revelation; for him, too, Prometheus, the archetypal rebel, the Titan who had defied Zeus, was a potent symbol, as he was for Shelley, Goethe, and Beethoven. Marx's taste in novels, again, was not chiefly for realistic novels of industrial England or Flaubert's brutal dissection of the French bourgeoisie, but for Sir Walter Scott and Alexandre Dumas the elder. Karl Marx, economist and visionary, German scholar and international revolutionary, contemptuous as he was of revolutionary phrasemakers and conspiratorial play-acting, was yet himself a powerful rhetorician and prophet of doom and regeneration, a romantic realist, a man of many faces.

The paradoxes begin with his birth. He was born of comfortably-off middle-class parents, not in one of the great centers of population and industry whose portentousness for the future he was so vehemently to proclaim, but in the ancient city of Trier. Marx was to experience poverty, but after, not before, he became a revolutionary. He never gained the firsthand experience of factory conditions possessed by his partner Friedrich Engels, the son of a Bremen manufacturer. Trier is a city of ancient monuments, set among the castle-dotted, vine-clustered terraces of the Moselle valley, only a few miles from the Luxembourg border and the forest of Ardennes. In one respect only was it an apt birthplace for Karl Marx. Trier, or Treves, which at the time of Marx's birth formed an outlying part of the dominions of the king of Prussia, had once been the gateway between the Latin and the Teutonic worlds; the great gate that marked the limits of the power of imperial Rome still stands, like a grandiose, abandoned Checkpoint Charlie, in the midst of Trier's traffic, a suitable reminder of a German who was also a cosmopolitan, to whom Paris and London were not only homes but the focus of his thoughts as the breeding grounds of revolution, a man who looked always to the West and has been honored in the East.

Marx's dreams were imperial in scale, ecumenical in scope, and grounded on a panoramic view of world history. Such cosmopolitanism, too, is characteristic of his generation. The French Revolution, the great beacon, extinguished yet still smoldering in the minds of men, especially of those too young to remember it, had been an ecumenical event; the fall of the Bastille, of little importance in itself, became a universal symbol, welcomed as eagerly in Britain and in Germany as in France itself. The nineteenth century is the classic age of the émigré intellectual, the cosmopolitan revolutionary, and the ideological *condottiere* fighting in a foreign land because liberty is every man's cause or because the proletariat has no fatherland.

*An unknown artist drew this romantic sketch of the young Karl Marx during the 1848 revolutions.*

In his secure niche in the placid, comely, preindustrial world of Trier and the German university towns, it was not personal oppression or the sight of proletarian misery and industrial squalor that first turned Marx into a revolutionary, but the enthusiasms of his generation and the theories of his elders, the intellectual diet he encountered as a student, on which young Germany was eagerly feeding. Marx the philosopher and the romantic humanist preceded Marx the politician and Marx the anatomist of industrial society. The philosophy Marx imbibed at the universities of Bonn and Berlin taught that man is truly himself, truly human, only when his activities are willed by himself, when he is not manipulated by others, by blind forces, or by brute *things* as a mere object, only when he chooses, rationally, to act as his own human essence dictates. The young Marx, applying this philosophy with his own uncompromising rigor, came to the conclusion that however free men might be in the abstract, legally speaking, as workers the majority were not free at all. Labor was, or should be, the highest expression of humanity, the activity by which men freely shaped and changed the world, subjecting *things* to the creative power of man. But labor, the essence of man's humanity, his godlike creative power, had itself been degraded into a thing and was bought and sold as a commodity. Instead of productive labor being used by humanity, human beings were used to produce products. The workers, the proletariat, were not free in practice, whatever the law said. The state was not their state, nor was it impartial, because it upheld the domination of the property owners. Man could only be free if labor was an assertion of men's own wills and creative power, rather than a commodity that they were forced to barter for wages, and this could only happen by the proletariat overthrowing the existing property relations and creating a state of real, as distinct from merely abstract, legal, freedom. As Marx wrote at this time: "Philosophy finds in the proletariat its material weapons." Marx the philosopher had become Marx the revolutionary politician.

He had also become a radical journalist, and it was this that led to his first self-enforced exile, to Paris and Brussels. In Paris Marx, now a committed socialist, saw for the first time the visible reality of the urban proletariat—which he had invoked as the savior of society—on a far larger scale than anything Germany could yet show. There, too, he found groups of other socialists. He learned from them, particularly from their critiques of capitalist economics; but chiefly it was in his intellectual struggles with them, his attempts to define his own position as a way of repudiating what he saw as the mistakes and eccentricities of theirs, that the "Marxism" of the *Communist Manifesto,* published in 1848, was born. The historian and social scientist was taking over from the idealistic philosopher of freedom.

A photograph of about 1860 shows Marx with his wife, Jenny, to whom he had been married in 1843.

The *Communist Manifesto* differs from most political pamphlets precisely in the breadth and grandeur of its historical perspective. The message is that history both promises victory and imposes conditions. From the ringing opening ("The history of all hitherto-existing society is the history of class struggles") to the final celebrated call to action ("The proletarians have nothing to lose but their chains. They have a world to win. Working men of all countries, unite!"), the idea is hammered home that capitalism is not the permanent state of mankind but simply the latest phase of historical development. The bourgeoisie is not respectable and law-abiding; it is dynamic and rapacious; it has won its way to power by smashing the ancient privileged regime of feudalism. Seldom has a political movement received such a gift as the *Manifesto:* at once an indictment, an analysis, and a promise of victory. Marx and his collaborator Engels, in the *Communist Manifesto,* join Jean Jacques Rousseau and Abraham Lincoln among the rare few who have given to a political attitude a classic rhetorical form. Like the Magna Carta and the Declaration of Independence, the *Manifesto,* especially in its concluding sentences, has the resonance and power of myth; like *The Social Contract* and the

Gettysburg Address, it gives definitive form to a hunger of the spirit.

In the short run the prophecy was false, nor has the ensuing century done much to make it valid. The specter of communism, which Marx and Engels had declared to be haunting Europe, proved in 1848, not for the last time, to be a wraith. The masses in France, enfranchised by the new Republican government, voted overwhelmingly for property and order; the resistance of the Parisian workers was trampled into the gutters of the capital by the government's cavalry, and Marx, doubly exiled now that he had made France too hot for himself, arrived penniless in London, the grimy citadel of capitalism itself, where he was to spend the rest of his life. For Marx the would-be man of action the best years of his life were already behind him; the years of patient research had begun. Here in London he was to work, mole-like, dogged by poverty, exasperated by the political moderation of the English working class, laboriously documenting his thesis of the inevitable downfall of capitalism, adding to the philosophy of human emancipation and to the incandescent rhetoric of the *Communist Manifesto* the technical apparatus of economic analysis, the patiently accumulated facts of a massive indictment of a whole social system, and detailed analyses of the failure of the recent revolutions on the Continent.

It is the last that, together with the economic sections of *Capital,* establishes Marx as a great historian—probably, in terms of sheer intellectual power and penetration, the greatest historian of the nineteenth century, an author to whom modern historians, no matter how hard they try, can scarcely avoid being indebted. His most masterly work of detailed history, a study of the rise to power of the new French emperor, Napoleon III, by a *coup d'état* over the ruins of the short-lived Republic established in 1848, is only an extended essay, yet it contains a revolution in the writing of history. Using the concept of a socio-economic class not merely as part of a political indictment but as a tool of historical explanation, Marx provides what is still the most penetrating and stimulating analysis of the character and the success of Napoleon III and also gives the classic account of the situation of the fascist dictator who claims to be "above" class and politics and to represent symbolically the unity of the nation.

Marx's essay is outstanding for the subtlety and minuteness with which he lays bare the ironies of history and the intricacies, the agitated twists and turns, of the various sections of French society, particularly the French bourgeoisie; parodying its cult of "order," Marx represents it as capitulating to Napoleon III by its bleating: "Only theft can still save property; only perjury, religion; bastardy [Louis Napoleon's legitimacy was doubtful], the family; disorder, order!" Marx's contempt is tellingly balanced by the glimpses he gives of the perspectives of world history; they are, in a sense, his justification for treating Napoleon's regime as a comic masquerade. The spectacle of the great Napoleon's nephew stepping into his uncle's boots offered opportunities that Marx was not the man to miss. The note is struck in the first sentence: "Hegel remarks somewhere that all facts and personages of great importance in world history occur, as it were, twice. He forgot to add: the first time as tragedy, the second as farce." This tone, sometimes of polished irony, sometimes sheer vaudeville, is maintained throughout. As an example of the first, take Marx's dismissal of French liberals' excuses for Napoleon III's success: "It is not enough to say, as the French do, that their nation was taken unawares. A nation and a woman are not forgiven the unguarded hour in which the first adventurer that came along could violate them."

Marx, his three daughters, and his friend Friedrich Engels were photographed during the 1860's.

The essay on Louis Napoleon is not only the work of a profound and original historical and sociological intelligence; it also has the verve and impact of first-class journalism. It was a talent Marx was to need in his exile, not merely as a political weapon but as a means of staying alive. One of the many ironies in Marx's career is that he quarried his indictment of capitalism from the British government's reports in the scholarly security of the British Museum Reading Room, but another is that in the 1850's he saved himself and his family from destitution partly by becoming the respected London correspondent of the New York *Tribune*. The managing editor, Charles Anderson Dana, had met Marx in Germany when the latter was winning notoriety as the crusading editor of the *Neue Rhenische Zeitung*. After Marx fled to London, Dana asked him for regular articles, at five dollars apiece. At first Engels wrote them for him, but when Marx's English improved he took heart from Engel's declaration that the *Tribune*'s own English was appalling and began to write them himself. Fortunately Marx's attitude toward British imperialism and the British governing class was pretty much the same as that of his American employers, and the relationship was a moderately harmonious one.

The meager pay of the New York *Tribune* and the subsidies of Engels enabled Marx and his family to survive the first bitter years of exile in London. Turned out of their first lodgings into the street because of a mix-up over the rent, the family settled in two small rooms at 28 Dean Street, Soho Square, in a poor exiles' quarter, where the house is now surrounded by restaurants and strip clubs. There they endured the hardships of genteel poverty. Marx wrote to Engels in 1852: "For a week past I have been in the pleasant position of being unable either to go out for want of my overcoats, which are at the pawnshop, or to eat meat because the butcher has stopped credit. The only good news we have here comes from my sister-in-law, the minister's wife, who announces that my wife's uncle is ill at last." In these circumstances, most witnesses agreed the Marx family created something very like a domestic idyll. Of the many faces of Karl Marx not the least surprising or remarkable is Marx the family man, a devoted husband, a jovial and indulgent father.

In 1843 Marx had married Jenny von Westphalen, the beautiful daughter of a neighbor in Trier, a Prussian government official. When they came to London, there were already three children, Jenny, Laura, and Edgar. Shortly after their arrival Guido was born and inevitably was nicknamed Fawkes, after the would-be dynamiter of the British Houses of Parliament; Marx's own nicknames were "the Moor"—a reference to his dark hair—and "Old Nick." Two more daughters, Franziska and Eleanor, were born later. The household was completed by "Lenchen," the Westphalens' family servant, who was said to be the only person who could subdue Marx. There may have been a reason for this. There were rumors at the time that Marx or Engels was the father of Lenchen's illegitimate son Frederick, and subsequent evidence points to Marx. Whether this was the result of an isolated lapse from fidelity to Jenny or of a protracted liaison, we do not know.

Details of the Marx's family life are preserved by another exile and a disciple, Wilhelm Liebknecht, in a series of descriptive scenes that have the slightly comic naiveté of the sentimental painting of domestic scenes of the period so beloved by the nineteenth-century bourgeoisie: pictures of a benign Marx patting urchins' heads like a Mr. Pickwick and giving them pennies and apples, or of the family picnics on Hampstead Heath. After lunch the adults would sleep on the grass, read the Sunday papers, or give piggyback rides to the children, Marx being, according to his daughter Eleanor, a splendid horse. On the walk home they would sing German folk songs, or Marx would recite Shakespeare or Dante from memory. To Eleanor he was the "cheeriest, gayest soul that ever breathed . . . a man brimming over with humor and good humor, whose hearty laugh was infectious and irresistible . . . His kindness and patience were really sublime."

Marx's political opponents would have been intensely surprised to hear it. They knew Marx in another of his incarnations, as a practical politician, a man of domineering temper, brutal speech, and implacable rancor. His opponents were, of course, not only the bourgeoisie, which was virtually unaware of his existence, but his fellow socialists.

Many of Marx's key works are polemics against the errors of some erstwhile comrade; again and again he showed himself ready to abandon or wreck a promising movement rather than allow it to fall into the hands of those he regarded as doctrinally in error. His deliberate destruction of the First Workers' International to save it from the Russian anarchist Bakunin and his followers was only the most notable of these fatal self-administered purges.

Marx's irritability was no doubt exasperated by ill health. When writing *Capital* he was troubled with hemorrhoids. As he wrote Engels plaintively, "to finish I must at least be able to *sit down*," adding grimly, "I hope the bourgeoisie will remember my carbuncles." Utterly dedicated to the idea of revolution, Marx spent his life as an exile, despite his attempt to organize the German exiles and to collaborate with English working-class leaders, essentially as a scholar. He would have nothing to do with merely conspiratorial politics; there was no substitute for the travail of history and the political education of the workers by the class struggle. Marx's rejection of conspiracy was not due to moral objections or to natural coolness of temperament, but to a massive intellectual self-restraint, a contempt for impractical revolutionary dreaming and frothy oratory. He was in fact a man in whose nature aggression and revolt ran deep. In a questionnaire composed by his daughter Laura he once gave the answers: "Your idea of happiness. *To fight;* The vice you detest most. *Servility;* Favorite hero. *Spartacus, Kepler.*"

The official name of Marx's circle was the German Workers' Educational Society, and the educational aspect was taken seriously even when it had nothing to do with politics. Marx in this context wears the face of the German *Gelehrter,* with all the strengths and weaknesses of the type. There was nothing narrow about his intellectual interests. He could read all the main European languages and taught himself Russian when he was in his fifties. He read Greek and regularly reread Aeschylus. He was interested in the natural sciences and, of course, technology; he acclaimed Darwin and became highly excited when he saw a model of an electric train engine in a shop window. For relaxation he would do mathematics; during his wife's last illness he could find solace only in working on calculus. In his dealings with his young followers one sees not only Marx the political doctrinaire but also, more surprisingly, Marx the pedagogue. On the whole the latter sounds a good deal more intimidating: "How he scolded me one day," Liebknecht lamented, "because I did not know—Spanish! . . . Every day I was questioned and had to translate a passage from *Don Quixote. . . .*" Educational bullying was obviously part of Marx's nature, even apart from politics, and one can see in these reminiscences the professor he at one time seemed destined to become.

But ultimately, of course, the politician and social scientist were uppermost. Marx had already, before he came to London, developed his characteristic theory of history: that a society's legal and political institutions are an expression of its economic substructure. But it was in England, in the British Museum, that Marx did his fundamental research as an economist and social scientist and prepared his most celebrated work, *Capital*. Marx's book is a strange amalgam: it is a highly abstract theoretical economic analysis designed to show that the capitalist annexed all the surplus value produced by the worker, leaving the latter nothing but his bare subsistence, and himself contributing nothing; there is a good deal of detailed economic history, of which Marx was a pioneer, analyzing the earlier stages of capital accumulation, the dispossession of the European peasantry, and the development of European industrial and mercantile civilization. And there is the statistical demonstration of the human cost of early industrialism, compiled chiefly from the evidence of the British government's own commissions and the reports of its factory inspectors. Marx here joins Dickens, Disraeli, Carlyle, and other Victorians appalled by the conditions of industrial and urban life. These pages of *Capital* are, for all Marx's attempts to refrain from mere denunciation, the work of an angry moralist who could see in the cold figures "the motley crowd of workers of all ages, and sexes, that press on us more insistently than did the souls of the slain on Ulysses."

*This is the title page of the 1872 edition of* Capital, *Marx's classic that was first published in 1848.*

Finally there is prophecy, deduced from a model of capitalist competition and production—intended to show the inevitability of increasingly frequent and disastrous economic crises and the ultimate revolt of the masses. In the *Communist Manifesto* Marx had called for this revolt and predicted its success. Now in *Capital* he thought he had demonstrated its inevitability, the result of the self-destructive character of capitalism, doomed to perish by its own inherent contradictions: "The centralization of the means of production and the socialization of labor reach a point where they prove incompatible with their capitalist husk. This bursts asunder. The knell of capitalist private property sounds. The expropriators are expropriated."

Marx thought that his conclusion was the verdict of social and economic science. More evident to us is the face and voice of the angry Hebrew prophet, denouncing the worship of the golden calf and the human sacrifices to a mechanical Moloch and trumpeting the wrath to come in the careless ears of the unrighteous. Capital is a "fetish," a false god. Marx's intellectual career comes full circle; the face of the economic theorist melts into that of the young idealist philosopher, to whom the ultimate evil is the subjection of mind and spirit to the domination of brute *things*.

# MICHAEL
# BAKUNIN
## 1814-1876

Michael Bakunin, a Russian aristocrat who became the great apostle of revolutionary anarchism, inspired, or at any rate foreshadowed, several valid trends in modern left-wing thought, along with others that appear manifestly pathological. Whether as a seer or as a symptom, however, he was a good hundred years ahead of his time, and has therefore sometimes been dismissed as a merely picturesque epiphenomenon of the nineteenth-century socialist movement. The error is understandable. Unless one recognizes the prophetic—or premonitory—elements in Bakunin's life and personality, it is hard to find anything truly impressive in his record. He seems too colorful to be taken seriously.

Bakunin was undoubtedly a charismatic leader and one of the first full-time professional revolutionaries of our epoch. He was a slipshod organizer, however, and an incorrigibly amateurish conspirator. He had a genius for mounting the wrong barricade at the wrong time in what from his point of view usually turned out to be the wrong revolution. His career was a succession of disasters and fiascoes, accompanied by still more tragic self-betrayals, but redeemed at moments by a heroic, almost saintly reverence for human dignity. The "scientific"—i.e., Marxist—socialists of his day denounced him as a romantic, a mountebank, a swindler, and a czarist undercover agent. They were at least partly right on all counts except the last one. "What a man!" exclaimed a French socialist. "The first day of a revolution he is simply wonderful; the second you had better shoot him."

*This photograph of Michael Bakunin, walking stick in hand, was taken by Nadar.*

*By* EDMOND TAYLOR

Bakunin was a huge, hairy giant and his mind was like his body, powerful but unkempt. Though in some ways he saw farther into the future, as a systematic thinker he was not in the same class with his famous antagonist, Karl Marx, whose historical materialism strongly influenced Bakunin's own world outlook. His thought was hardly less filled with contradictions than his life. Though passionately opposed to every form of authority, for many years he advocated the principle of revolutionary dictatorship that Lenin later adopted. The cult of the heroic, or simply violent, act that he introduced into anarchism has inspired fascist as well as libertarian ideologies. An evangelist of human brotherhood, he was vociferously anti-Semitic—and hardly less anti-German.

The basic anarchist blueprint for a free noncapitalist society organized from the bottom upward by spontaneous co-operation or association was taken by Bakunin from his friend and master, Pierre Joseph Proudhon, the first modern thinker to describe himself as an anarchist. Later the anarchist program was elaborated and rationalized by Prince Pierre Kropotkin, another Russian aristocrat. Bakunin himself contributed relatively little to anarchist theory. As his English biographer E. H. Carr says, he was essentially "a visionary and a prophet." His great achievement was to transform anarchism from a utopian social philosophy, attractive mainly to idealistic intellectuals, into a militant revolutionary force.

True, anarchism, especially of the Bakunin variety, has never entirely lost its nineteenth-century flavor, and has several times appeared to be on the point of fading away. For nearly twenty years after Bakunin's death certain of his spiritual heirs carried to psychopathic extremes his theory of "propaganda by the deed." Their reckless uprisings and spectacular bombings or assassinations terrorized bourgeois society so effectively that the movement was decimated by police repression. Its ideals became discredited even in the eyes of many workers. Kropotkin partially restored the intellectual prestige of anarchism, and as anarchosyndicalism, a form of revolutionary trade-unionism, it subsequently recovered some of its working-class appeal; it was only in Spain, however, that it put down solid roots. Anarchists played a significant part in the Russian Revolution (more significant than Soviet historians like to admit), but their refusal to accept the dictatorship of the proletariat—in practice that of the Bolsheviks—led to their suppression, generally by a Cheka or Red Army firing squad. Pro-Stalinist elements in the Spanish Republic liquidated with similar ruthlessness the interesting, if not wholly convincing, anarchist experiments in organizing free communes and collectivized production units during the Spanish Civil War.

"Clearly, as a movement, anarchism has failed," George Woodstock, one of its relatively sympathetic historians, wrote in 1962. "During the past forty years the influence it once established has dwindled . . . almost to nothing." James Joll, in a scholarly study published in 1964, offered an equally gloomy prognosis. "Anarchism," he concluded, "was a characteristic product of the 19th Century reflecting the impact of machinism and industry on a peasant or artisan society, and as such appeared to have little future in the modern world."

Abruptly, or so it seemed, the current of history reversed itself. Though what might be called the anarchist establishment showed few signs of rejuvenation, active new anarchist groups and study circles sprang up during the 1960's in a number of countries, notably in West Germany and Sweden. Their members, mostly young intellectuals or technicians, sometimes called themselves "pragmatic anarchists." Films like those on the Bonnot terrorist gang in France, or on the Sacco—Vanzetti case in the United States, further reflect the reawakening of interest in anarchism.

A diffuse anarchist influence is likewise discernible in the movement for "participatory" democracy that has developed in the United States and elsewhere. Certain schemes of neighborhood or community control have a particularly strong anarchist flavor. So, of course, do all the "communes," increasingly frequent in the United States and in the Scandinavian countries, which have a social aim more serious than group loafing, pot, or sex and are organized on a basis of freedom and equality. In fact, almost any type of collectivist organization, up to and including pure communism, that stresses voluntary participation approaches the classic anarchist model advocated by Proudhon, Bakunin, and Kropotkin. Consequently, many of the Israel kibbutzim, and to a certain extent the Yugoslavian system of local communes and workers' councils, can be considered as grass-roots experiments in anarchism. The results, while not especially brilliant to date, have encouraged the new generation of European anarchists to feel that viable alternatives to totalitarian socialism or cutthroat capitalism can be developed under twentieth-century conditions.

Western travelers in China during the Cultural Revolution reported the existence, particularly in Yunan province, of a youth movement with strong anarchist overtones. The program of the movement was officially condemned in 1968, but it seems doubtful that the impulse that produced it has been permanently suppressed. In western Europe underground groups describing themselves as anarchists—or labeled as such by the police—have renewed the tradition of propaganda by the deed with bombings, sabotage, and other terroristic acts in Italy, France, and the Federal Republic of Germany.

The most visible evidence of an anarchist revival is the reappearance of the black flag,* so often hoisted over the street barricades of nineteenth-century Europe, in cities where it has not been seen since the 1930's, if not the 1830's. Usually it is brandished—sometimes together with blown-up portraits of Bakunin—by hirsute students in blue jeans, taking part in general leftist demonstrations over such issues as the war in Vietnam, repression in the schools, police brutality, or the iniquities of the consumer society.

The anarchist revival is, in fact, essentially a youth phenomenon, as are the similar resurgences of revolutionary enthusiasm in other left-wing movements. Anarchists of the older generation sometimes view it with mixed feelings. The generation gap was particularly notable at the international congress of anarchist federations held in Carrara, Italy, a few weeks after the May Revolution in Paris. When Daniel Cohn-Bendit, one of the most publicized young activists of the Latin Quarter barricades, showed up to heckle the meeting as a gathering of "bureaucrats and war veterans," the forty-odd delegates, most of them veterans of far grimmer struggles, were indignant. "What's left of Proudhon, what's left of Bakunin?" one asked.

Apart from the explicitly anarchist organizations and mavericks like Cohn-Bendit, several left-wing youth movements in Europe can be classified as anarchist or para-anarchist. They include the Dutch "Provos," the international "Situationistes," and the "Spontaneous Maoists," particularly entrenched in the French high schools. (Jerry Rubin's Youth International Party in the United States might be described as anarchism with pimples.) A group of young French extremists who are seemingly superspontaneous ultra-Maoists publish in Paris a magazine formally sponsored by the philosopher Jean Paul Sartre and appropriately named *Tout* (everything). It promotes—or at least publicizes—such revolutionary causes as shoplifting, the sequestration of teachers and bosses, the abolition of incest taboos, the right of minors to be debauched by consenting adults, and the right of schizophrenics to be regarded as the only healthy members of a mad society.

To what extent can Bakunin's influence be credited with inspiring the serious young revolutionaries of today, or blamed for the more freakish symptoms of the current malaise in our civilization—and for the still more ominous rise in criminality or hard-drug addiction

---

*A traditional symbol of mourning or menace of death, the black flag was carried by unemployed French workers demonstrating for "Work or Death" as early as 1831. Its general use among anarchists, at least in France, dates from 1882. The Ukrainian anarchist leader Nestor Makhno adopted it during the 1917 revolution, and for a while it floated over much of the Ukraine. The emblem reappeared during the Spanish Civil War, especially in Catalonia, though the Spanish anarchosyndicalists usually preferred a red-and-black flag. Anarchists make a point of not reverencing their flag, which is generally a strip of coarse, black cloth nailed to a broomstick or something similar. During a commemorative ceremony for the martyrs of the Paris Commune held in 1970 at the Père Lachaise cemetery, several hundred young French anarchists fought savagely with the police, who had issued a ruling against flags inside the cemetery walls, and then, when they had finally succeeded in forcing their way through the gate, dropped their flag in the dust and ostentatiously trampled on it.

among adolescents professing vaguely anarchist opinions? The question is complex. As Luis Mercier-Vega points out, it is primarily the breakdown or malfunctioning of modern social institutions that turns the young into rebels; dimly remembered anecdotes of Bakunin's life or scraps from his writings, jumbled together with similar scraps from quite different revolutionary thinkers, then provide a vague rationale for their rebellion. Anarchism has never been a monolithic movement. In addition to the collectivist (or communist) anarchists stemming from Proudhon, Bakunin, and Kropotkin, there are individualist anarchists—including writers, avant-garde artists, and some more muscular types of terrorists—whose outlook has been shaped directly or indirectly by Bakunin's contemporary, the German philosopher Max Stirner. (Stirner, however, was also one of Nietzsche's masters, and exercised a considerable influence on twentieth-century fascist thought.) There are likewise pacifist anarchists ultimately inspired by Tolstoy. There are hippie anarchists. There are those who link revolutionary action with vegetarianism, sexual freedom, women's liberation, brigandage, homosexuality, or psychedelic drugs. To see how Bakunin figures—or does not figure— as an ideological ancestor of these different anarchist families, it is necessary to examine in more detail his life and thought.

*Pierre Joseph Proudhon and his children were depicted romantically by Gustave Courbet in 1865.*

Bakunin was born on May 8, 1814, roughly a year before the battle of Waterloo. His father, Alexander, was a country gentleman of good family but moderate means who waited to marry until he was past forty. Michael was the third of eleven children, and the oldest son. He spent an outwardly happy but in some respects emotionally crippling childhood on the family estate in Premukhino in central Russia. Looking back many years later, he attributed his "insensate hatred of every restriction on liberty" to his mother's "despotic" character. It appears more likely that she was simply lacking in warmth. Alexander was no despot; as Bakunin once wrote to him, he was a concerned and loving parent who inculcated in his children "the sacred spark of the love for truth." Part of the trouble may have been that Bakunin's childhood was too untrammeled, too idyllic. Brilliant, bold, imperious, he was constantly surrounded by adoring sisters and hero-worshiping younger brothers. Nostalgia for this lost paradise of childhood—the model for his later dreams of human freedom and solidarity, according to his biographer Max Nettlau—haunted Bakunin all his life. But the fact that the family group was composed of individuals with widely differing tastes and temperaments no doubt helped to instill in Bakunin a polyphonic sense of the richness of interpersonal relations conceivable in a freely ordered society. His vision of such a society is far more adult than the pot-scented global puppy-sprawl that some young revolutionaries of today mistake for the New Jerusalem.

The healthy elements in Bakunin's early background are reflected in his mature philosophy of anarchism. A lucid critic of the nascent nineteenth-century consumer society, he had no morbid hatred of life's amenities. The good society, as he foresaw it, would produce "less luxury, but unquestionably more wealth." Everyone would work, for "work is the highest law of life," and everyone would get an education. He advocated reforms in the patriarchal family system, but unlike some of the more fanatic present-day radicals, appears to have regarded the family itself as a valid social unit. Though he accepted Marx's theory of class warfare, in his mind it never had the almost racist overtones it would later acquire in Russia and China. Come the revolution, he reckoned, a few hundred of its most "odious" enemies would doubtless have to be abandoned to the just wrath of the people, but thereafter "Socialists will oppose with all their might hypocritical butchery perpetrated in cold blood."*

Among the less healthy aspects of life at Premukhino was Bakunin's emotional relationship with his sisters. As he grew up he became pathologically jealous of them, and he helped to spoil their lives by meddling in their already overabundant conjugal or sentimental problems. He once explicitly confessed to an incestuous passion for his younger sister Tatyana. She eventually died an old maid, and he struggled all, or most, of his life with a rare sexual aberration: chastity. Everywhere except in bed, Bakunin was a creature of strong, primitive appetites, bursting with animal energy. But his adult love affairs were ethereal, in all likelihood strictly Platonic. So was his marriage; the children that his wife bore were by someone else. Naturally, students of Bakunin have tended to see his repressed sexuality as seeking an outlet in his revolutionary activity. The fact is, however, that even his famous passion for destruction was largely Platonic, though he sometimes sounds as if he were mentally masturbating with dynamite, but by temperament he was not a desperado, merely a rebel.

Bakunin's vocation as a rebel probably crystallized during his adolescent years in St. Petersburg, where he was sent at the age of fourteen, first to a preparatory school, then to the army's artillery academy.

*Prince Pierre Kropotkin, geographer, philosopher, and revolutionary, was photographed by Nadar.*

---

*Traces of his concern for human life can often be found among even the most ruthless of Bakunin's latter-day disciples. According to a French friend who served as a volunteer with the anarchists in Catalonia during the Spanish Civil War, they generally treated with every courtesy the priests, landlords, and other "enemies of the people" they felt it necessary to shoot. In some cases the victims were driven miles to a beautiful promontory on the Catalan coast so they could meet their end in aesthetically agreeable surroundings.

After Premukhino, life in a cadet barracks was a traumatic experience. If there had been a war on and he could have started as a colonel, Bakunin might have become resigned to the army. He loved danger, drama, and battle—any kind of battle. In one of his later writings he exalts the tonicizing effects of civil war, almost irrespective of which side wins, because it "breaks up the brutalizing monotony of [the people's] daily existence." What he loathed for himself, or anyone, was mindless discipline, soulless bureaucratic routine, dehumanizing regimentation. It was in instinctive rebellion against these forces or manifestations of alienation, hardly less general in nineteenth- and twentieth-century industrial societies than in their armies, that Bakunin ultimately became a revolutionary. Social injustice he discovered much later.

Thanks to family influence, Bakunin managed to drop out of the army without having to face trial as a deserter, and soon afterward he left Russia to study at the University of Berlin. Hegel's philosophy made a profound impression on him, especially when stood on its head by the young left-wing neo-Hegelians he met in Germany. Bakunin's passionate faith that destroying something old automatically creates something new, and therefore better—the eventual foundation stone of revolutionary anarchism—stemmed from his highly personal interpretation of the Hegelian dialectic.

From being an expatriate intellectual, moving in politically advanced Western circles and supported by loans, as he euphemistically termed them, from wealthy émigré friends like Ivan Turgenev or Alexander Herzen, Bakunin gradually drifted into revolution as a career. Until the latter part of his life, he had no clear-cut revolutionary doctrine. He professed a vague socialism almost from the start, but in the 1840's it was the essentially nationalist liberation movements among the oppressed minorities of the Russian, Turkish, and Austrian empires that most engaged his sympathies.

The general European upheaval of 1848 furnished a release for his demonic energies. He missed the outbreak of the revolution in Paris, but made up for it by his exuberant activism when he got there. The government of the newly proclaimed French Republic gratefully—but promptly—packed him off with a modest slush fund to start things moving in Poland. En route he stopped in Prague, where he tried vainly to organize the Slavs of the Hapsburg empire into an effective revolutionary bloc, and took part in the bloody street battles against the imperial forces. He was in Dresden, still hoping to reach Poland somehow, when an insurrection against the royal Saxon government exploded there.

Accepted as a military adviser by the local insurrectionary committee, he soon became the key figure in organizing the defense of the city against the approaching royalist armies. The legend that he proposed taking the Sistine Madonna from the Dresden museum and hanging it on one of the barricades has no foundation. It is probably true, however, that when the enemy started closing in, he suggested blowing up the city hall, with the revolutionary committee—including its military adviser—inside. Bakunin stayed with the committee to the end, mainly because he had taken a liking to one of its leaders, a moderate German democrat whose fuzzy politics he disapproved of, but whose personal courage he admired. His chivalrous attitude cost him years in prison and Siberia.

Captured and condemned to death, first in Germany and then in Prague, he was reprieved in 1851 and turned over to the Russian police. After some two months of solitary confinement without trial in the notorious Peter Paul fortress in St. Petersburg, he was advised by

*Bakunin served as military adviser for the unsuccessful 1848–49 revolution in Dresden, above.*

an emissary of the czar Nicholas I to write out a full confession of his crimes and appeal for clemency. This confession, later released by the Soviet government, is deeply penitential in tone, but far less abject than many that have since been heard in Russian courts. It breathes scorn on the soulless Western bourgeoisie and its liberal leaders but exalts the unspoiled virtue of the common man. It names no confederates, and instead of abjuring the cause of Slavic liberation that Bakunin had championed, naively pleads with Nicholas—of all men—to become its supreme leader.

Naturally Bakunin stayed in prison. It was only six years later, after his forced return to Russia, that Nicholas's successor, Alexander II, commuted his incarceration to banishment for life. In 1861 he escaped from Siberia, aboard an American ship, by the unimaginative method of breaking his word of honor to the governer. He left behind his new wife, Antonia, the daughter of a deported Polish patriot. Pretty, vain, frivolous—perhaps the character-replica of Bakunin's mother—and twenty-five years his junior, she remained faithful to him in her fashion, and he cherished her until his death.

Back in western Europe, living mostly in Switzerland or Italy, Bakunin, now toothless and blubbery but hardened in his convictions, resumed his revolutionary career. Some of its details have only human interest: his farcical naval expedition to liberate Poland that fortunately never landed; his leadership of the revolutionary commune in Lyon in September, 1870, an abortive forerunner of the famous Paris Commune, that lasted nearly a whole day. Other details concern chiefly the specialist: the bewildering sequence of revolutionary factions or secret societies organized by Bakunin; his bitter struggle with Marx for the domination of the First International (founded in 1864); its breakup, because of the feud, in 1872; and the welding of the defunct International's Bakuninist wing into an anarchist international, for many years a powerful revolutionary force in the world.

What is important in terms of the influence Bakunin exercises today is the development of his thought in the last fifteen years of his life. It was only in that period that he explicitly formulated—in a series of articles, tracts, and books—the creed of revolutionary anarchism that had been germinating in him for years. Proudhon, Marx, Stirner, and other nineteenth-century thinkers fused in the passionate furnace of his mind into a millennialist religious faith, which, as Joll says, was at the same time a rational philosophy.

The Bakuninist version of anarchism is filled with insights and absurdities; it is at once hopelessly outdated and amazingly contemporary. Bakunin, like Proudhon, believed in material progress and in an integrated world society, with appropriate organs of planning and even of decision, but imagined it functioning literally without any agencies of enforcement at any level. In a planet haunted by hunger, overpopulation, and pollution, the dream seems more unrealistic than ever. But the decentralization and democratization of decision making, which was one of Bakunin's goals, is today more valid than ever.

Bakunin's suspicion of any socialism that stressed centralized control, and his analysis of the threat to freedom inherent in the Marxist formula of the dictatorship of the proletariat, were even more prescient. "Take the most radical revolutionist," he wrote, "and place him upon the all-Russian throne, or give him dictatorial powers . . . and within a year he will become worse than the Emperor himself." State ownership of the means of production, he foresaw, would inevitably lead to the loss of individual freedom; as an alternative to the exploitation that he believed implicit in the private ownership of property, he proposed collective ownership by local or professional bodies. (Kropotkin wanted to abolish property altogether.)

Bakunin was likewise far ahead of his age—perhaps still of ours—in recognizing that in the modern world the threat to freedom is not purely political. The worst kind of despotism, he wrote in *The Knouto-Germanic Empire,* perhaps the most philosophical of his major works, would be one of scientists, scholars, and what we today call technocrats. He believed that educators were particularly predisposed to tyranny by their calling. His proposal to keep society from falling under the yoke of the technocrats or from curdling into an elitist mandarinate were somewhat like those later put into effect by Mao Tse-tung; they involved spells of manual labor for the intellectuals and intensified education for the masses, the more mature students "exchanging experience" with their teachers. Though Bakunin preached the ultramodern doctrine of "the revolt of life against science, or against the rule of science," unlike some modern radicals, he never suggested solving the problem by systematically doing away with science, industry, education, and rational thought.

Bakunin's most valuable, and perhaps enduring, contribution to modern thought was his perception of the interdependence of individual freedom and collective solidarity. He condemned morbid individualism as sternly as he condemned totalitarian socialism. It was only in and through the social group that the individual could fulfill himself. Participation should be as complete as possible but free of compulsion: "To be free collectively means to live among free people and to be free by virtue of their freedom."

Unfortunately, Bakunin's stature as a moral philosopher, his true greatness, appears to be overshadowed today by his image as a kind of nineteenth-century Che Guevara or Trotsky, and by the mystical doctrine of revolution for the sake of revolution that is linked with it. Proudhon had already believed that an anarchist society could only arise by the spontaneous co-operation of the masses, after they were freed from the yoke of the state. Bakunin went a short but decisive step further. He argued that the total overthrow of the state, implying that of all the structures of authority or privilege attached to it, would automatically release the creative energies needed to build a perfect society. One hard push, and the millennium is literally here. This eschatology underlies the entire modern myth of revolution and, if only in a diluted form, tinctures every revolutionary ideology of our century, but Bakunin was its most extreme apostle.

Naturally, if revolution is virtually synonymous with humanity's definitive salvation, there is no need to worry about the future (though Bakunin was still old-fashioned enough to feel that perhaps it was useful to think about it a little). And the destructive act of revolution becomes, as Bakunin thought he had learned from Hegel, the most fully creative one. Pending the final triumph, any act that prepares or rehearses the ultimate assault, or simply keeps alive the sacred spark of rebellion, is likewise holy and creative.

Bakunin cannot be blamed for all the mindless violence perpetrated in the name of revolution that afflicts the world today, but his teaching often serves to rationalize and thus encourage it. It no more occurred to him than it does to many of his youthful acolytes now that such violence generally leads to dictatorship—whether revolutionary or counterrevolutionary in name—rather than liberation.

Perhaps Bakunin saw a glimmering of the truth at the end. That end was an absurd anticlimax, fraught with irony. One of his rich young disciples liquidated his inheritance to buy Bakunin a house, with considerable land, near Locarno. He also deposited a large sum to Bakunin's name in a Swiss bank. In the donor's mind the property was to serve as a headquarters for the anarchist movement, and the fund was to support the cause. Bakunin, however, squandered the money, partly on farfetched ventures in scientific farming, but mainly to make the house a sufficiently luxurious nest for his Antonia, summoned from Siberia.

When Bakunin's benefactor tried to recover what was left of his fortune, Bakunin firmly insisted that it was legally in his name and therefore his property. Proudhon's famous dictum, Property is Theft, apparently did not apply in this case—or applied too literally. The pricks of conscience finally drove him to a solemn decision. He would redeem himself in the eyes of his comrades by a heroic death on the barricades. Anarchist insurrection was brewing in Bologna, and Bakunin coaxed its local organizers into smuggling him into the town on the eve of the expected events. He was to remain disguised in his hotel room until the uprising started, then he would be led—he was sixty and walked with difficulty—to the scene of the action. There, he reasoned, he could find the heroic death he sought.

The insurrection proved a fiasco, however, and Bakunin eventually had to limp home to Switzerland, to die in bed, two years later—shamed, disillusioned, hardly believing any longer in the dream that had filled his life. "The time of revolution has passed," he wrote one of his old comrades. "Never were the forces of international reaction in Europe so formidably armed . . . There remains propaganda . . . and one other hope: general war. But what a prospect!"

*A spiritual descendant of Bakunin's anarchism throws a paving stone at the police during the 1968 Sorbonne riots.*

# WILLIAM
# JAMES
## 1842-1910

William James, the first American psychologist and philosopher to win world fame, was one of the major shapers of twentieth-century thought. His contribution was not, however, a great breakthrough, like Newton's law of gravitation, Freud's psychoanalysis, or Einstein's theory of relativity. He is probably best known for his book *Pragmatism* (1907), but he did not invent either the term or the basic concept, which he attributed to Charles Peirce, and John Dewey's pragmatism had a far greater impact on educational theory and practice.

James's *Principles of Psychology* (1890) was his most epoch-making book, but even in this work, his literary achievement outshone his contribution to science. An example is his chapter on "The Stream of Thought," better known as "The Stream of Consciousness" in the condensed version of the book. The concept, and even the metaphor, had been proposed by Franz Brentano in Germany nearly two decades earlier, but it was William James who developed, expanded, and expressed the theory in such vivid detail that no one who has read his exposition can ever forget it; and his chapters on "Habit," "The Consciousness of Self," and "Will" have been—and still are—only slightly less compelling.

It would be misleading, however, to reduce James's genius to a gift for literary style. He was a great thinker also, but on the order of an Emerson or a Goethe rather than a system maker like Kant or Spinoza. He was, in fact, one of the least systematic of philosophers, who de-

*William James was photographed during the 1890's, when he was in his fifties.*

*By* GAY WILSON ALLEN

clared that all philosophy is personal and subjective, "the expression of a man's intimate character, and all definitions of the universe are but deliberately adopted reactions of human characters upon it." This did not mean, however, that he reduced philosophy to impressionism or fantasy. On the contrary, his philosophy of man was so practical, so imaginatively understanding of the human condition, that it had remarkable therapeutic value both for himself and for the large audience that read and heard him.

To call James's teachings therapeutic suggests that he remained a psychologist even in his philosophy; and he was, indeed, more interested in healing the soul than in dissecting it. He wanted to take philosophy out of the academic sanctuary and make it available to all men and women. In *Pragmatism* he declared: "The world of concrete personal experiences . . . is multitudinous beyond imagination, tangled, muddy, painful and perplexed. The world to which your philosophy-professor introduces you is simple, clean and noble. The contradictions of real life are absent from it. The architecture is classic. Principles of reason trace its outlines, logical necessities cement its parts. Purity and dignity are what it most expresses. It is a kind of marble temple shining on a hill."

Time and again James insisted that the abstractions of systematic theology and the traditional problems of metaphysics had little meaning to real human dilemmas and were of no help in solving them. Even so, one of the oldest concepts in theology and metaphysics lay at the bottom of William James's psychologizing and philosophizing: the question of whether the will is free or determined. To understand why James had to answer this question to his own satisfaction, and why it is the key to his thinking, one needs to turn to his biography—as one should do, anyway, in deference to James's contention that all philosophies are personal.

The biographical influence began with James's grandfather, also named William, who came to America in 1789 as a poor Irish immigrant. The first William James brought nothing with him except his ability, but that was so extraordinary that at his death in Albany in 1832 his estate was worth more than three million dollars. His many business ventures left him little time for his large family, except to see that every son and daughter attended the Presbyterian Church and rigidly observed a "blue" Sunday. One of his sons, Henry, rebelled against his father's Calvinistic God and the suppression of "spontaneous affections" in the Albany home.

Having inherited an income that freed him from financial worries, Henry James, Sr. (to distinguish him from his son, who became the celebrated novelist), devoted his life to studying theology and giving his children the kind of home and education he had been denied. To

*Henry James, Sr., was a Swedenborgian mystic whose vague intellectualism was counterbalanced by the common sense of his wife (pictured below).*

his oldest son, William, born in New York City in 1842, and the four succeeding children, Henry James, Sr., was both a permissive and an overconscientious parent. Never satisfied with tutors and schools, he changed them frequently, as well as places of residence, and twice took his family and servants to Europe in search of ideal educational methods and stimulating influences. In these frequent uprootings William acquired a command of French and German, a restless disposition, and a nagging sense of frustration. At an early age he showed an aptitude for biology, though he really wanted to be a painter. His father objected to this ambition, but let him study under William Hunt for a year, long enough for him to discover that he preferred science.

It is paradoxical that William's father encouraged him to become a scientist, for Henry James, Sr., had a low opinion of scientists. They were materialistic, he said, and unappreciative of the spiritual nature of the universe that Swedenborg had revealed. His own theology was a mixture of Swedenborgian mysticism and unconscious vestiges of the Calvinist determinism that he thought he had rejected in his youth. None of his children could understand these doctrines, but they loved him as the most affectionate father imaginable. On the other hand, the intense spiritual and moral tone in the close-knit family was evidently not healthy for the children; as young men both William and Henry, Jr., suffered periods of serious emotional disturbances, and the one daughter, Alice, was a neurasthenic cripple after her twelfth year. Another son became an alcoholic.

William James's irregular education had not prepared him for admission to Harvard College, but he was permitted to enroll in Lawrence Scientific School. Later, he entered Harvard Medical School, and finally completed the requirements for his M.D. degree in 1869, after interruptions because of poor health and a specimen-collecting trip to the Amazon with Louis Agassiz, the famous comparative anatomist. He never practiced medicine, and for several years after his graduation from medical school he remained at home, nursing his hypochondria.

In the spring of 1870 James was so manic-depressive that he contemplated suicide, but the unexpected death of his beautiful young cousin Minny Temple shocked him into an awareness of the "nothingness" of his "egotistical fury." Then, on April 30, he recorded in his diary that reading the French philosopher Charles Renouvier had ended a crisis in his life, for he now saw no reason why Renouvier's "definition of free will—'the sustaining of a thought *because I choose to* when I might have other thoughts'—need be the definition of an illusion." He resolved that "my first act of free will shall be to believe in free will." For the present he would avoid metaphysical and skeptical speculation and try to strengthen confidence in his own will by

*William James drew his family as a "heavenly group" in this 1861 letter. His brother Henry, the novelist, is third from right.*

exercising it at every opportunity. Thus, when he later wrote the masterly essays on "Habit" and "Will," he drew upon his own intimate knowledge.

In 1873 President Charles William Eliot of Harvard rescued his former gifted student from brooding idleness by appointing him to an instructorship in comparative anatomy. From teaching anatomy and physiology, James advanced to physiological psychology, which he had studied during a health-seeking year in Germany and in exhaustive reading at home, and then to psychology and philosophy. This progression had the effect of relieving, to some degree, certain physical ailments—headaches, insomnia, indigestion, and back pains—that had been brought on by his agonizing difficulty in choosing a career and by his guilt over not sharing his father's passionate religious convictions. It also set him firmly, in his early thirties, on his true path.

By then brother Henry, a year younger, had made a brilliant start as a writer of fiction. Close since childhood days, the two brothers were to remain on terms of mutual affection and esteem and in almost constant contact. But the profound differences separating their respective personalities and outlooks—the source of much good-humored chaffing between them—were already manifest. The elder brother felt free to criticize the younger's stories and novels with impunity, and while Henry usually accepted William's blunt comments in good part, he avenged himself, at least once, by endowing a "morbid little clergyman" in his novel *The American* with some of William's characteristics. Meanwhile, the more the expatriate writer extolled the Old World's rich and many-layered social and cultural context, which he found necessary to his work, the more stubbornly did the scientist defend the virtues of the New World—stark and plain, no doubt, but alive and growing, the reverse of decadent. Yet William's attitude toward his homeland was never wholly free of ambivalence. In spite of his enthusiasm for the simple life in the wilds, he felt intellectually isolated in America and frequently traveled abroad to converse—in fluent French or German or passable Italian—with his peers in the great European centers of learning. A stabilizing element, and one that set him further apart from his confirmed-bachelor brother Henry, was added to James's existence in 1878, when, after a troubled two-year courtship during which each renounced the other "forever" at least once, he married a schoolteacher named Alice Gibbens.

Some of James's earliest publications were critiques of contemporary theories of the brain as an automatic mechanism, operating by reflex action. He did not question the reflex responses to external sensory stimuli, but insisted that the will could originate some impulses in the brain, and that these impulses then followed the usual neural paths of discharge. This was a defense of indeterminism on

*James did this pencil sketch of himself in 1866, after his return from a zoological expedition to Brazil organized by Louis Agassiz.*

psychological grounds. In 1881, in an address on "Reflex Action and Theism," he added a philosophical objection to determinism, though it was a negative argument. Determinism says that the world is one solid unit of interlocking causes and effects. This may indeed be true, James grants, but it is a world forever beyond finite intelligence. "The real world as it is given objectively at this moment is the sum total of all its beings and events now. But can we think of such a sum? Can we realize for an instant what a cross-section of all existence at a definite point of time would be? While I talk and the flies buzz, a sea-gull catches a fish at the mouth of the Amazon, a tree falls in the Adirondack wilderness, a man sneezes in Germany, a horse dies in Tartary, and twins are born in France. . . . Does the contemporaneity of these events with one another and with a million others as disjointed, form a rational bond between them, and unite them into anything that means for us a world?" James was sure that it did not. So far as human experience extends, the world is pluralistic, and James saw nothing of practical value to be gained by hypothetical rationalizing about an unverifiable absolute.

James's universe was unfinished, bristling with chance and possibility, a universe in which good and bad were real, and eternally in conflict. The outcome was so uncertain that at times even human effort might tip the scales. The uncertainty also added excitement and incentive for effort. "Regarded as a stable finality, every outward good becomes a mere weariness to the flesh. It must be menaced, be occasionally lost, for its goodness to be fully felt as such. . . . Not the absence of vice, but vice there, and virtue holding her by the throat, seems the ideal human state. And there seems no reason to suppose it is not a permanent human state."

*Alice Gibbens James, William's wife, was painted during the early 1900's.*

Some critics complained that this kind of reasoning was nothing more than moralizing, and it is true that James always felt a compelling need to believe in a moral universe. But the point is that he was a psychological pragmatist long before he began to talk about a pragmatic search for "truth." Countless religious teachers had insisted on the need for faith—faith in God, a church, a creed—but James was concerned not with "salvation" but with the health of the psyche. Perhaps his Puritan heritage prevented him from anticipating Freud, but he was as much a pioneer as Freud was in investigating the function of emotion in the human animal, first by introspection, then by scientific observation (in 1879 he started the first psychological laboratory outside Germany), and finally by philosophical speculation.

Since the time of Plato nearly all men had believed the human mind to be capable of impersonal, disinterested, coldly logical reasoning. Philosophy, in fact, had come almost to connote such thinking devoid of emotion. William James was, therefore, a philosophical iconoclast when he argued in "The Sentiment of Rationality" (1879–80) that impersonal reasoning is an illusion. How does a thinker recognize that he has attained a rational concept? He will recognize it, James contends, as he recognizes everything else, "by certain subjective marks . . . A strong feeling of ease, peace, rest . . . The transition from a state of puzzle and perplexity to rational comprehension is full of lively relief and pleasure."

In other studies, completed before he published his *Principles of Psychology*, James argued that there is no such thing as an emotion. The brain has no center for emotions as distinct from other aspects of consciousness. A so-called emotion is made up of a complex of sensations and motor responses. Emotion and thought are inseparable, an interrelated event in consciousness. The existence of consciousness itself James could not explain—nor has anyone else.

Still, as an empiricist, James could observe and describe the behavior of consciousness. The British school of epistemologists (Locke, Berkeley, Hume) had regarded consciousness as filled with separate objects or images because in introspection one becomes aware of this object and that, as if they were discrete. This atomic theory led to great logical difficulties in accounting for the experience of time, space, and cause—metaphysical puzzles like Zeno's arrow. The connections between the experienced atoms of time and space, said the "associationists," are supplied by the mind, so that one has the illusion of continuity and relation of cause and effect.

The associationists' logical difficulties did not bother James because he observed that consciousness flowed like a river. Even the objects in the stream seemed to come to the surface and merge into each other, like images in a dream. Moreover, he found on the outer limits of consciousness a fringe, containing objects that were vague, a little out of focus, which might either float into clear view or out of range of conscious attention. Later, James speculated on this fringe as the ambiguous edge of the subliminal world, but in his *Psychology* he was more concerned with clear applications. One was that a person's interests (his appetites, ambitions, and ego needs) determined what contents of his stream of consciousness he could keep in view and make use of. The stream flowed without ceasing; it might be slowed or speeded up by variations in stimulation, natural or artificial, but it could not be stopped or its direction changed. When objects of memory joined the stream, they were modified by other objects in the ever-flowing present, so that even in memory one continued to live—that is, have conscious awareness—only in the present.

James's stream of consciousness metaphor emphasized his predilec-

*Harvard College looked like this in 1861, when James went there as a student.*

tion for the primacy of experience over intellectual abstractions, but his concept of experience was not an automatic sensationalism. Man is not a clam waiting for whatever the wash of the sea may bring to his sensory organs. Instead, his interest causes him to bring some objects in the stream into focus and keep them there as long as they are needed. But this observation raised epistemological problems that James had hoped to avoid in writing a purely "scientific" description of psychological phenomena. He wanted to avoid positing a soul as knower, or mind stuff in which experience becomes conscious. He had to assume the awkward hypothesis that thoughts think themselves. He never, in fact, found a satisfactory theory of cognition; instead, he discovered a way to bypass it.

The solution was to eliminate the dualism of mind and body and make consciousness simply the flux of experience. To borrow a phrase from the European phenomenologists, "Mind cannot conceive independently of the world which appears to it." This was the basic thesis of the "radical empiricism" toward which James was striving through most of his career, though his book *Essays in Radical Empiricism* (1912) was not published until two years after his death. In a chapter on "A World of Pure Experience" he declared: "I give the name of 'radical empiricism' to my *Weltanschauung*. Empiricism is known as the opposite of rationalism. Rationalism tends to emphasize universals and to make wholes prior to parts in the order of logic as well as that of being. Empiricism, on the contrary, lays the explanatory stress upon the part, the element, the individual, and treats the whole as a collection and the universal as an abstraction. My description of things, accordingly, starts with the parts and makes of the whole a being of the second order."

In another chapter ("The Experience of Activity") James explains more concretely what he means by experience. In our consciousness, he says, there is no distinction between mental (or "spiritual") feeling and muscular activity. So far as experience is concerned they are the same, and any distinction must be imposed outside of experience. "The individualized self, which I believe to be the only thing properly called self, is a part of the content of the world experienced. The world experienced . . . comes at all times with our body as its centre, centre of vision, centre of action, centre of interest. Where the body is is 'here'; when the body acts is 'now'; what the body touches is 'this'; all other things are 'there' and 'then' and 'that.' These words of emphasized position imply a systematization of things with reference to a focus of action and interest which lies in the body; and the systematization is now so instinctive (was it ever not so?) that no developed or active experience exists for us at all except in that ordered form. So far as 'thoughts' and 'feelings' can be active, their activity terminates in the activity of the body, and only through first arousing its activities can they begin to change those of the rest of the world. The body is the storm centre, the origin of co-ordinates, the constant place of stress in all that experience-train. Everything circles round

it, and is felt from its point of view. The word 'I,' then, is primarily a noun of position, just like 'this' and 'here.' Activities attached to 'this' position have prerogative emphasis, and, if activities have feelings, must be felt in a peculiar way. The word 'my' designates the kind of emphasis. I see no inconsistency whatever in defending, on the one hand, 'my' activities as unique and opposed to those of outer nature, and, on the other hand, in affirming, after introspection, that they consist in movements in the head [brain]. The 'my' of them is the emphasis, the feeling of perspective-interest in which they are dyed."

*William James built this house in Cambridge in 1889, and lived there for the rest of his life.*

In writing his lectures on *Varieties of Religious Experience* (1902), James began by collecting hundreds of examples of experiences that he could classify as religious. He was interested not in theology, dogma, or institutions but in "the life of religion," which he said was characterized broadly as "the belief that there is an unseen order, and that our supreme good lies in harmoniously adjusting ourselves thereto." This definition emphasizes belief, and James's book is filled with experiences that had given individuals the empirical foundations for their faith. In all these experiences conviction grew out of emotions, a clear indication to James that feeling and not intellect or reason is the door to religious experience. Some of the biographies he collected were characterized by such violent and abnormal behavior that James felt it necessary to devote his first lecture to "Religion and Neurology." He freely admitted that some of his case histories seemed psychopathic and that there might well be some connection between mental illness and the religious life, but the investigation of this relationship was not the object of his study.

In all the religious confessions he had been able to collect, James found that each person had felt he had been in some sort of contact with a divine source of spiritual power, from which he had received a new charge of psychic energy—often transformed into physical energy and practical action. Reported "cures" of both mental and physical illnesses were frequent. He concluded that in all religions there were three basic techniques for attaining this psychic energy: (1) sacrifice (of objects, self, or pleasures); (2) confession (a "general system of purgation and cleansing"); and (3) prayer ("every kind of inward communication or conversation with the power recognized as divine"). Of course, these techniques often overlapped, as in self-sacrifice, or confession in prayer. But prayer, in whatever form, seemed most efficacious, and James called it "the very soul and essence of religion."

In prayer the worshiper finds purpose, guidance, and strength to meet the vicissitudes of life, says James, and "at all stages of the prayerful life we find the persuasion that in the process of communion energy from on high flows in to meet demand, and becomes operative within the phenomenal world." No matter how the effect is explained, whether as "miracle" by the devotee or "hypnotic suggestion" by the neurologist, the result is too real to be denied. The benefits may be of various kinds, but above all they are personal: "the religious individual tells you that the divine meets him on the basis of his personal concerns." As a psychologist, James suspected that the source of this psychic energy was the person's own subconscious, but no one really knows what the subconscious is; it may be the doorway to the supernatural, to a "World Soul," or Emerson's "Over Soul," which are but names for what men ordinarily call "God." Whatever the source or terminology, one must believe in its existence in order to derive benefits from it; then, says James, trust in its reality and reap the harvest—another application of his earlier "Will to Believe." He calls this a "thoroughly 'pragmatic' view" of religion, and adds, "I believe the pragmatic way of taking religion to be the deeper way. It gives it body as well as soul, it makes it claim, as everything real must claim, some characteristic realm of fact as its very own. What the more characteristically divine facts are, apart from the actual inflow of energy in the faith-state and the prayer-state, I know not." The resemblance of this view to phenomenology is also obvious.

So convinced was James that energy does flow into individual lives from a "faith-state" and a "prayer-state" that he was willing to confess his own "over-belief" that "our present consciousness is only one out of many worlds of consciousnesses that exist, and that those other worlds must contain experiences which have a meaning for our own life also; and that although in the main their experiences and those of this world keep discrete, yet the two become continuous at certain points, and higher energies filter in."

James had long been interested in the work of the Society for Psychical Research; in 1884 he helped organize the American branch, and in 1893 he served a term as president of the parent British society. He saw in psychic research a possible means of relieving people of delusions, personality disorders, and mysterious pains of the kind he himself had suffered in his early manhood. He took part in many investigations of reported phenomena, such as the claims of mediums, spiritualists, faith healers, experimenters in telepathy and communication with departed "souls," arguing that scientists had no right to dismiss these reports as hoaxes without first investigating them. As an investigator James was rigorously "scientific," though at the end of twenty-five years of "dabbling in 'Psychics,'" he ruefully admitted that "I am theoretically no 'further' than I was at the beginning; and I confess that at times I have been tempted to believe that the Creator has eternally intended this department of nature to remain *baffling*." However, James did not lose hope of future progress in this field; under his direction Gertrude Stein, then a student at Radcliffe, experimented with automatic writing, and he devised some of the basic experiments still used in the study of extrasensory perception. Altogether, he made notable contributions to parapsychology—for which he was denounced or laughed at by his more conventional colleagues.

Condemnation and even vilification came James's way as a consequence of his outspoken resistance to the "barbaric patriotism" that swept America into war with Spain. For years thereafter he expended much precious energy combating imperialism in public speeches and letters to newspapers. Then, in 1906, at the new Leland Stanford University in California, he delivered the most influential address of his career. Entitled "The Moral Equivalent of War," it was acclaimed by its hearers, later printed in *McClure's,* and finally published in pamphlet form in tens of thousands of copies. In his address, James admitted that human history was "a bath of blood," and that the instinct to kill, pillage, and overcome the enemy has survived in man. Although he looked forward to the time when civilized nations would outlaw war, he did not want to lose the martial virtues of "intrepidity, contempt of softness, surrender of private interest, obedience to command. . . ." This could be accomplished, he said, only by finding "moral equivalents," such as mobilizing men in the conquest of nature or in building a better society.

By now James was world-famous. In 1908 his leisurely trip to England, where he lectured at Oxford and received an honorary degree, was like a triumphal progression. But the attacks of angina pectoris that had plagued him in the past were becoming more frequent. The following year, at Clark University in Worcester, Massachusetts, he was crossing a green with Sigmund Freud when he experienced a seizure; the great Viennese psychoanalyst marveled at the courage his companion displayed in his moment of anguish.

In the summer of 1910 James and Alice again sailed to England to visit the ailing Henry; then William went on to Germany. By the time his wife and brother joined him there, his health had deteriorated badly. The three sailed home, and on August 26, a few days after reaching their New Hampshire retreat, James died. His death was important news on both sides of the Atlantic. In London Bertrand Russell hailed him as "the most eminent, and probably the most widely known, of contemporary philosophers"; in Paris *Le Figaro* called him *"un des plus grands esprit philosophiques de ce temps."* This last judgment was to prove prophetic: it remains no less true today after the intervening decades of dynamic effort, on the part of peoples everywhere, to achieve fuller social and political freedom. For James was pre-eminently the philosopher of freedom and human dignity, and in his psychology he anticipated the crises of humanity in this revolutionary century.

*William and Henry, eminent brothers, posed in the garden of Henry's house at Rye in Sussex in 1900.*

# FRIEDRICH WILHELM
# NIETZSCHE
## 1844-1900

The last decade of Nietzsche's relatively short life—he was born in 1844 and died in 1900—was spent first in a mental hospital, then for the last three years under the care of his sister, Elisabeth Förster-Nietzsche. In the end he was no more than a shadow of a human being. Yet his death mask shows no trace of madness or deterioration. Rather, it records an imperious face, with a fierce enigmatic mustache that completely covers the mouth and chin, and eyebrows that suggest Moses the Lawgiver. Above the hollowed temples and high forehead the hair curls back like Medusa's locks. There is an ominous quality to those features, inhuman, beyond humanity. Like much that has been concerned with Nietzsche, his death mask is an artifact, a contrivance. From an original flawed casting, his sister had the sculptor Rudolf Saudek reconstruct a portrait as she would have it. She, an obsessed fanatical woman of limited intelligence, lived on for a generation after her brother, long enough to greet Hitler in her old age as the personification of her brother's teaching and to present him with Nietzsche's walking stick. An "anti-Semitic goose," Nietzsche once called her. By her editing and often forging of her brother's letters and papers, particularly the posthumously concocted volume, *The Will to Power,* she aided in constructing the warped legend that has made Nietzsche seem the philosophical embodiment of German ruthlessness, intolerance, and world conquest. Just how much she had altered, toned down, rearranged, suppressed, and in some cases forged was not known until the evidence was unearthed after World War II.

*Friedrich Nietzsche glowers over his bushy mustache in this early photograph.*

*By* FRANCIS RUSSELL

Nietzsche wrote chiefly in aphorisms, in language that often burned to the touch. His masterpiece, *Thus Spoke Zarathustra,* is a dithyrambic prose poem, a many-faceted metaphor written with the passion of an Old Testament prophet, which he subtitled "a book for all and none." His electrifying phrases, when torn from their context, have been twisted to mean their opposite. He wrote of the Overman (unfortunately popularized by Shaw as the Superman). He used terms like "blond beast," "the will to power," "the master race," "Lords of the Earth." German nationalists, and later the National Socialists, claimed him as their own. He would have repudiated them with loathing. Christianity he detested, "the one great curse . . . the one immortal blemish of mankind." There is no mistaking his meaning. But when he wrote, possibly with deliberate provocativeness, that "it is the good war that hallows every cause," he was not thinking of the Schlieffen plan. And there are, in fact, times when he becomes intolerable. "You are going to women?" asked the little old woman of Zarathustra. "Do not forget the whip!"

*Nietzsche at sixteen, in 1861, appears in the traditional Napoleonic pose.*

Yet however willful or contradictory his aphorisms might make him appear, Nietzsche was a germinal force thrusting through the conventional surface of his age. Few men of the West since his death have remained unaffected by him, whether they were aware of him or not. He inspired or influenced such varied literary figures as Thomas Mann, Hermann Hesse, Rainer Maria Rilke, Stefan George—who once seemed a greater poet than Rilke—André Gide, André Malraux, Jean Paul Sartre, Albert Camus, George Bernard Shaw, W. B. Yeats, H. L. Mencken, and Eugene O'Neill. O'Neill acknowledged his debt and paid his tribute when he received the Nobel Prize. Oswald Spengler in his *Decline of the West* wrote that he owed "everything" to Goethe and Nietzsche. The circle around Stefan George derived their cold Caesarism—so far removed from the Hitler cult—from the Overman. One of the George circle, Count Stauffenberg, would later die in his attempt to kill Hitler. Freud admitted his indebtedness to Nietzsche, writing that the latter's "insights often agree in the most amazing manner with the laborious results of psychoanalysis."

For Nietzsche, the world he found himself in was purposeless, incomprehensible. He described himself as an atheist "by instinct." "God is dead," he wrote. "We have killed him." He meant that the God concept no longer had relevance for our age. Nothing existed for us but the world of phenomena as received by our senses. The thing-in-itself, whatever might or might not lie behind phenomena, was not only unknowable but meaningless. To Nietzsche the shadows moving across the wall of Plato's cave were not indications of a higher reality but themselves the only reality. "The reasons for which 'this world' has been characterized as 'apparent,'" he wrote in *The Twilight of the Idols,* "are the very reasons which indicate its reality; any other kind of reality is absolutely undemonstrable." What is left, what only is left, is for the individual to accept his given world, not with resignation, but with a fierce joy, disciplining himself to defy the empty glitter of the stars. The Overman is the perfected, the disciplined individual, who has overcome himself for the sake of himself, has ordered the chaos of his passions and impulses. He does not suppress but rather transforms his instincts—symbolized in *Zarathustra* by the wisdom of the serpent and the courage of the eagle. His is not the goal of humanity—for there is no goal—but he is the highest specimen. Freud's "sublimation" is the resounding echo of the Overman, but Nietzsche was the first to form this ringing concept. Through his self-mastery the Overman alone can face the tragedy of life with a glow of self-assertion that makes the tragedy a triumph. Nietzsche writes:

The individual shall be dedicated to something super-personal—that is what tragedy demands; he shall forget the frightful anguish which death and time cause the individual: for even in the smallest moment, in the shortest atom of his career something sacred can befall him which infinitely outweighs all struggle and all tribulation—that is what it means *to be tragically disposed.* Even though the whole of humanity must one day die—who could doubt it—the goal is given it, as the supreme task of all coming ages, so to grow together into oneness and community that it shall go to meet its impending extinction *as a whole* with a *tragic disposition.* In this highest task is comprised all ennoblement of men; from its final rejection would result the saddest picture a friend of humanity could put before his soul. That is how I feel it! There is only one hope and one guarantee for the future of what is human: it lies in this, *that the tragic disposition shall not perish.*

Nietzsche, the passionate seeker after truth, faced reality as if he were staring into a bottomless pool in which he could see nothing but the reflection of his own anguished face. It was a face he would have seen there an infinite number of times, for time itself, according to his doctrine of the eternal recurrence, was no more than a great wheel that turned and re-turned on itself. Everything that happened in this heartless, soulless universe had happened an infinite number of times before and would happen an infinite number of times again, in the exact same relentless sequence, down to the last fallen leaf, the last dust mote drifting in the sunshine, the last word written on the page or echoing in the mouth of Zarathustra: "And this slow spider creeping in the moonlight, and this moonlight itself, and you and I in the gateway whispering together, whispering of eternal things—must we not all have been here before? And return and walk in that other lane, straight ahead in this long fearful lane—must we not eternally return?"

The lives of most philosophers are independent of their philosophy, and it is not necessary to know the one to understand the other. It adds nothing to Kant's *Critique of Pure Reason* to be informed that Königsberg housewives could set their clocks to the given moment when the academic sage passed each morning on his way to the university. That Berkeley believed in the therapeutic value of tar water scarcely concerns his philosophy, nor does even the fact that he was an Anglican bishop. But with Nietzsche it is not possible to apprehend him as a philosopher without apprehending the details of his life. Man and thought cannot be separated, for Nietzsche wrote with his blood and his spirit as well as his mind. Among philosophers he is the defiant Prometheus figure.

Nietzsche's work [wrote the historian Golo Mann] is his life which pulsates in his writings. His work was a personal catastrophe which presaged and predicted Europe's general catastrophe. He himself was a catastrophe. Such a person must inevitably have made some irresponsible statements. He prophesied things which he claimed to welcome but at the thought of which he really shuddered. He prophesied a century of world wars, of revolution and universal turmoil. During it everything false, everything diseased would be stamped out, the weak would be crushed or disappear. Out of it would come a new force, the rule of the strong, of the merciless. Because life was the will to power and the struggle for it, all Christian virtue was merely the deceit of those who were too weak to fight.

Though Nietzsche's life was a tragic one, it began pleasantly enough in the Lutheran parsonage of the village of Röcken in Prussian Saxony. Pastor Nietzsche was carried away by the birth of his first son. "O blissful moment!" he wrote. "O exquisite festival! O unspeakable holy duty! . . . Bring me then this my beloved child that I may consecrate him to the Lord!" They called the boy Friedrich Wilhelm after the king of Prussia. Two years later, his mother bore a daughter, Elisabeth, and in 1848 a second son, Joseph. That same summer Pastor Nietzsche struck his head in a fall, injuring his brain. Before a year had passed he was dead. Six months later Joseph died, and young Fritz was left alone in a household of females: his mother, his sister, and his two managerial and dominating aunts. They were soon joined by the widowed Grandmother Nietzsche, who proceeded to take full charge of the household, moving the family to Naumburg an der Saale, where she had lived before her marriage.

Fritz was five and a half when he came to Naumberg, a solemn little boy who had absorbed the religiosity of the household and liked to recite Biblical texts and sing hymns. His grandmother wanted him to learn to mix with all social groups and sent him to the public Municipal Boys' School. Her democratic notion did not work out very well. The rougher boys of the town either ignored or made fun of the obedient, studious, neat newcomer. Soon his mother sent the unhappy little Fritz to a private school that prepared children for the Cathedral Grammar School. There he was happier than his relatives had expected. Although solitary by nature, he did make two friends, Wilhelm Pinder, the son of a judge, and Gustav Krug, whose father was a privy councilor. With these two and his sister he formed a little circle of which he was the leader. For this private world he invented toys, painted pictures, wrote verses and little plays, and made up fairy stories. At the age of ten he had written more than fifty poems and a motet for Christmas, and four years later he was writing his autobiography. Before he reached adolescence he began to develop the headaches that would dog him for the rest of his days.

In 1858 he was entered in the famous boarding school of Schulpforte, an institution as Spartan as an English public school but with more emphasis on the classics and less on sport. In the six rather isolated years he spent at Pforta he passed from boyhood through adolescence to young manhood. During his holidays he founded a small literary society, Germania, with his Naumburg friends. They discussed art, history, and literature, and in music made the, for them, astonishing discovery of Wagner. "I could not have endured my youth," Nietzsche wrote later, "without Wagner's music."

Just after his twentieth birthday he enrolled at the University of Bonn as a student of philology. In the free and easy academic atmosphere of that pleasant Rhineland town he found a freedom he had not before experienced. He expanded socially, sporting the colored cap and sash of Franconia, a student society to which Bismarck had once belonged. With his society brothers he danced and drank and sang and matched steins of beer in the Old Heidelberg tradition, and even managed to fight a duel. But after a semester of the roistering life he began to grow weary of his comrades' "beer materialism," and at the end of his second semester he left for Leipzig.

*This photograph of Richard Wagner was taken in 1867, about a year before the already-famous composer met the young Nietzsche, beginning a stormy friendship that was aggravated by the philosopher's deep devotion to the haughty, unconventional beauty below, Cosima Liszt von Bülow Wagner.*

Now he set out in undivided earnestness to acquire a mastery of classical languages and literature. His most overwhelming experience, however, was his encounter with the philosophy of Schopenhauer. In Schopenhauer's dark view, life itself was aimless, a mixture of suffering and pain. There was neither God nor immortality. All that a man could really know was that he existed. The force that gave him his sense of being was the will, blind and without purpose. Only through a private ascetic aestheticism could the will in its blindness be to some degree overcome. For the young Nietzsche this dark denial was a heady doctrine, making explicit much of what he had already come to feel about life.

Nietzsche spent five years at Leipzig, years in which he grew both in stature and reputation. In 1867 he began his required military service as a trooper in the horse artillery at Naumberg, though a riding injury prevented him from completing his year. His admiration for Wagner grew stronger than ever. It was about this time that he came to meet the composer himself on one of Wagner's visits to Leipzig, the beginning of a strange and tumultuous friendship.

In 1869 Nietzsche was offered an appointment as associate professor of classical philology at the University of Basel. He was welcomed to the social life of a patrician city often diffident to strangers. During those years he became an intimate of the Wagner family, then in Tribschen, near Lucerne, where Wagner was living with Cosima von Bülow, the illegitimate daughter of Liszt and estranged wife of the pianist and conductor Hans von Bülow. The unconventional couple—who were finally able to marry in 1870—treated the young Nietzsche as an equal. Two rooms in the Wagner family villa were set aside for his use, and he was free to come and go without invitation.

In 1872 Nietzsche published *The Birth of Tragedy from the Spirit of Music,* a book of unique apprehension of the Greek world. After Nietzsche, one could never accept the one-sided view of Greek art as the unrestrained and balanced classicism found in the serene sculpture of Phidias and Praxiteles, the aloof harmony of the Parthenon. This art of calm rationality Nietzsche called Apollonian, after Apollo, the deity of light. But beneath this serenity he saw the dark turbulence of the Dionysian, the worship of the dismembered but ever-reborn god who was the embodiment of the life-force, the irrational and instinctive, the primal energy that creates and destroys and in which creator and created become one. Apollo was the poised consciousness, Dionysus the erupting unconscious.

Nietzsche saw Greek tragedy as Apollonian form imposed on Dionysian frenzy. Ostensibly, his work was a discussion of how tragedy developed, but its importance was the tracing of the two strands of Greek life, the form-giving and the force-giving, reason and instinct. Nietzsche held up Socrates as the dessicating scientific spirit that destroyed Greek tragedy. While his book was being printed, he added an awkwardly inappropriate section on Wagner in which he tried to show that the tragic myth had been revived in Wagner's music as an antidote to the modern scientific world.

*The Birth of Tragedy* was received by the scholarly world with cold silence. Lacking the paraphernalia of scholarship, it was not what scholars had come to expect of professors. Before the negative impact of the book had made itself fully felt, Nietzsche gave five lectures on "The Future of Our Educational Institutions," not too successfully using the Platonic dialogue form to express his views on the vacuousness and overspecialization of contemporary scholarship and—in spite of his distaste for Bismarck's new Reich—holding up the German spirit as the gestater of a new tragic civilization. Increasingly, Nietzsche was moving away from the problems of language and literature to the problem of philosophy and to a criticism of his own times. Between 1873 and 1876 he wrote four *Untimely Meditations,* the last being on Wagner in Bayreuth, from whom Nietzsche had been growing apart ever since Wagner's removal from Tribschen. Nietzsche had become much more critical of the man whom he still called Master. "As early as summer of 1876," he later wrote, "I took leave of Wagner. . . . Ever since his return to Germany, he has lowered himself step by step to everything I despise—even anti-Semitism." Nietzsche found Wagner's tribal nationalism particularly offensive, but their final break did not come until the composer began work on *Parsifal,* a gesture toward Christianity that Nietzsche found intolerable.

As Nietzsche's health deteriorated—a combination of his childhood migraines and eye trouble and stomach ailments derived from the dysentery he had suffered as a medical orderly—his sister came to look after him, dividing her time between her brother and her ailing mother. On repeated leave from the university, he wandered through Germany, Switzerland, and Italy, searching for some environment he might find tolerable. At one time he even considered a marriage of convenience with, among others, a Dutch girl whose chief qualification seemed to be that she had found her life philosophy in Longfellow's "Excelsior."

So precarious was Nietzsche's health, so frequent his leaves of absence, so distasteful philology to him, that in 1879 he resigned his chair at Basel. Now his life became that of a wanderer, increasingly isolated, with only a few friends to break the loneliness. In spite of his racked body, he managed to fill copious notebooks with his evolving thoughts, even though he was unable to remain for extended periods at his desk. As Stefan Zweig observed, the ills of the flesh seemed to gather in on him:

*Nietzsche discovered the village of Sils-Maria in 1881. In a tiny back room of the house shown above, he lived and wrote, happier than ever before.*

headaches, deafening hammering headaches, that stretch the reeling sufferer senseless for days on his sofa or bed, stomach cramps with bloody vomiting, migraines, fever, loss of appetite, weariness, hemorrhoids, constipation, chills, night sweat— a cruel sequence. Added to that the "three-quarters blind eyes," that by the least exertion swell up and begin to water and allow the intellectual worker only "an hour and a half of light each day." But Nietzsche scorns this hygiene of the body and works ten hours at his desk, and for this excess the overheated brain takes its revenge with maddening headaches and a hyper-activity that does not cease when the body is long weary but continues to spin out visions and thoughts until it is subdued by narcotics. But larger doses are necessary—in two months Nietzsche uses 50 grams of chloral hydrate for a few hours' sleep—then the stomach refuses to pay so high a price and revolts. And now—a vicious circle—spasms of vomiting, new headaches that demand new medicines . . . never a pause in this conflict, never a span of contentment, a short stretch of well-being and forgetfulness of self.

In 1878 Nietzsche published *Human, All-Too-Human,* a book in which he abandoned his previous style and method to write in aphorisms derived from his notebooks. He was now chiefly concerned with human psychology. In lapidary phrases as polished as those of La Rochefoucauld, he set forth his views on immortality, the senselessness of Christianity, marriage, the world of dreams, war, Germanism, and European unity. Nietzsche looked forward to a Europe in which nations and nationality had been abolished. In the light of the crude perversions of Nietzsche's words by German nationalists and later National Socialists, his actual thoughts on race and nation have a singular significance. He wrote that

the whole problem of the *Jews* exists only in nation states, for here their energy and higher intelligence, their accumulated capital of spirit and will, gathered from generation to generation through a long schooling in suffering, must become so preponderant as to arouse mass hatred and envy. In almost all contemporary nations, therefore—in direct proportion to the degree to which they act up nationalistically—the literary obscenity is spreading of leading the Jews to slaughter as scapegoats of every conceivable public and internal misfortune. As soon as it is no longer a matter of preserving nations, but of producing the strongest possible European mixed race, the Jew is just as useful and desirable an ingredient as any other national remnant.

*In 1888 Nietzsche drafted the title page of a work he planned to call* The Will to Power. *The book was never published, but the title was later used by his sister, Elisabeth, when she published a distorted version of his notes in 1901.*

In 1881 Neitzsche finished his second aphoristic book, *Dawn*. That summer he discovered the village of Sils-Maria in the Inn Valley of the Engadine, one of the loveliest valleys in the world. Here he lived in a shady back room, happier than he had ever been before, and in better health than for years. In that clear mountain region he wrote his third aphoristic book, *The Gay Science*, in which at the end the enigmatic figure of Zarathustra first appears, Nietzsche's alter ego and his most inspired creation.

Nietzsche is remembered before all else by *Thus Spake Zarathustra*. In the guise of the Persian prophet of light and darkness, shielding himself with aristocratic disdain from the shallow and fickle rabble, he proclaimed the Overman, the death of God, the redemption of self, and the doctrine of eternal recurrence that is Zarathustra's underlying theme. The sonorous book with its echoing rhythms is Nietzsche's most personal work, into which he wove his deepest experiences, his ideals, his disappointments, his friendships, enthusiasms, and disillusionments, and the glimmer of his goals, all in a language unsurpassed in strength and brilliance, and which he rightly claimed bore comparison with Luther's Bible translation and with Goethe. "I am assuming," he wrote proudly in 1884, "that with this Zarathustra I have perfected the German language."

Zarathustra was a figure that had haunted him since his childhood when he first saw him in a dream. To this dream-born figure he gave various names at various times. The actual Zarathustra concept came to him in 1881—"600 feet beyond man and time"—as he was walking by Lake Silvaplana in the vicinity of Sils-Maria; but not until the following February, when he was staying near Rapallo (a region he loved equally with the Upper Engadine), did the whole Zarathustra legend seize him. He then wrote the first part under a spell of over-whelming emotional excitement, finishing it within a month and on the very same day that Wagner died in Venice. In this first segment, Zarathustra, after having spent ten years of solitude with his eagle and his serpent in the mountains, returns to the valley to bring his this-world wisdom to mankind:

Behold, I teach you the Overman. The Overman is the meaning of the earth. Let your will say: the Overman *shall be* the meaning of the earth! I beg you, my brothers, *remain faithful to the earth,* and do not believe those who speak to you of otherworldly hopes.

Nietzsche found in the mask of Zarathustra the sustained metaphor to express his most subtle thoughts, his most fulminating prophecies. Once he was able to articulate through Zarathustra, the phrases poured from him, sometimes in even too ample a flood. The second part he composed after his return to Sils-Maria in June, writing it in a period of ten days, seized again by the fierce joy of creation. Only at the end, however, does the awestruck Zarathustra dare hint at the eternal recurrence. In Part III he at last proclaims this doctrine of the recurring cycle that Nietzsche himself had first found so terrible. "Was *this* life?" asks Zarathustra. "Very well then! Once again!" In a gruesome vision Nietzsche sees the doctrine as a heavy black snake that has crawled into the mouth of a sleeping shepherd and fastened on his gullet. Zarathustra comes upon the shepherd writhing on the ground and cries: "Bite its head off!" And through accepting this loath-some heroic act, the shepherd is able to spew out the head and stand up "changed, radiant, *laughing.*"

Lou Andreas-Salomé, above in an 1897 photograph, was the only woman Nietzsche loved deeply, but their relationship was thwarted by Elisabeth's insane jealousy.

In January, 1884, Nietzsche had gone to Nice to spend the winter, and there in much improved health he wrote Part III of *Zarathustra* with the same incredible speed and eagerness that he had written the earlier parts. He had intended to end with Part III, closing with the Seven Amens in acceptance and praise of eternity that is the eternal recurrence. But then, when he was in Zurich in September, 1884, he felt that the three parts were incomplete and began working out a fourth part, which he reworked in Menton and finished in Nice the following February, concluding with the repetition of the *Drunken Song,* his ode to joy, from Part III and with the now-aged Zarathustra, "glowing and strong as a morning sun," knowing that his hour has come.

When Nietzsche was in Rome, the year before he began his *Zara-thustra,* he met and fell in love with Lou Andreas-Salomé, who came to him as a pupil and remained as an undisciplined disciple. Except for a buried attachment to Cosima Wagner, she was the only woman he ever loved deeply. Born in St. Petersburg, Lou, though only twenty-one, was remarkable both in spirit and intellect. Later she became Rilke's mistress and much later Freud's devoted friend and follower. Attracted to Nietzsche's enigmatic personality, she evidently expected him to propose marriage, but he never did. However, he did ask her to spend part of the summer with him and his sister at Tautenburg, near Weimar. Elisabeth was vindictively jealous, claimed Lou was Jewish, and did her best to poison the other woman's relationship with her brother. Caught between the two females, Nietzsche finally cut loose from his sister. He planned to meet Lou in Paris that winter. But, for all that they corresponded, Elisabeth had divided them, and the old relationship was gone. Instead of going to Paris, he went to Rapallo, and never saw Lou again. Nietzsche's anger with Elisabeth turned to fury and disgust when she married a vulgar anti-Semitic leader, Bernhard Förster. Not long after their marriage the Försters left for a German colony in Paraguay.

Nietzsche had had difficulty in getting the first three parts of *Zarathustra* published, and when they did appear, they entered a readerless void. He had Part IV printed privately in an edition of forty copies, which he planned to present to such friends "as deserved them." In the end he gave away only seven. His next two books, *Beyond Good and Evil* and *Toward a Genealogy of Morals,* are in a sense explanations of *Zarathustra,* an appeal to his readers, a clear and definite aphoristic setting forth of the ideas that he had expressed in veiled and symbolic form. But Nietzsche's time was running out. Only four years were left him before his mind gave way. His final year was his most productive one, though there were flickerings of madness in his work. He began with the brief, amusing *Wagner Case* and ended with *Nietzsche contra Wagner.* In between he wrote the *Twilight of the Idols* (a German pun on Wagner's Ring operas), a summary of his later philosophy and psychology, then planned to go on with a work to be called *The Will to Power.* Instead he wrote what he intended as the first part of a *Transvaluation of All Values,* an attack against what he considered the sickliness that was Christianity. In *The Antichrist* he defined Christianity as the cult of "every kind of man who was disinherited by life. . . . At the bottom of Christianity is the rancor of the sick, instinct directed *against* the healthy, against life itself." Christianity he saw as a perversion of Judaism, a religion of meek pity, a means by which the weak and the pariahs enslaved the strong. "All honor to the Old Testament," he writes in his *Genealogy of Morals,* "I find in it great human beings, a heroic landscape, and something of the very rarest quality in the world, the incomparable naiveté of the *strong heart.* . . . In the New one, on the other hand, I find nothing but petty sectarianism, mere rococo of the soul, mere involutions, nooks, queer things, the air of the conventicle . . . humility and self-importance cheek by jowl; a garrulousness of feeling that almost stupefies. . . ." He also completed his autobiographical *Ecce Homo,* a book of coruscant irony consisting of four chapters entitled "Why I Am So Wise," "Why I Am So Clever," "Why I Write Such Good Books," and "Why I Am a Destiny." This book was not published, however, until some years after his death.

Nietzsche's madness was the result of syphilis contracted as a student in a Leipzig brothel, if one can believe his own words after his mind gave way. By the end of 1888 his delusions were overwhelming him and he was even losing his sense of identity. On January 3, while staying in Turin, he saw a cabman flogging a horse, burst into tears, flung his arms round the horse's neck, and collapsed. Carried raving to his lodgings, he sent a postcard to a friend: "Sing me a new song: the world is transfigured and all the heavens rejoice. THE CRUCIFIED." He wrote a note to Strindberg, signing it "Nietzsche Caesar," and to Cosima Wagner he scrawled: "Ariadne, I love thee. DIONYSUS." "Have abolished Wilhelm, Bismarck and all Anti-Semites," he informed his old colleague, the art historian Jakob Burckhardt.

*This primitive typewriter was used by Nietzsche during his stay at Sils-Maria.*

Heavily dosed with chloral, Nietzsche was taken back to Germany and placed for a time in a mental hospital until his mother brought him home. The widowed Elisabeth returned from Paraguay and after her mother's death took over the care of her now thoroughly insane and partially paralyzed brother while assuming control of all his writings. Alert to his growing fame, she moved him to Weimar so that —even as a shell of a man—she could link his name to the classical city of German culture. Some years after his death she culled his notebooks, publishing selections from them as *The Will to Power,* a title he had once considered using but one she much abused in her own distorted promulgation of the Nietzsche myth. Nietzsche was buried in the churchyard at Röcken beside his father. More fittingly, on the mountain slope above Sils-Maria there is set in the rock a stone carved with the rhapsodic words of his *Drunken Song,* his ode to joy:

> O Man! Take care!
> What does deep midnight say?
> "I slept, I slept—
> Out of the deepest dream I woke:—
> The world is deep,
> And deeper than it seemed to the day.
> Deep is its woe—,
> Joy—deeper still than sorrow:
> Woe speaks: Go!
> But all joy wants eternity—
> Wants deep, deep eternity."

# IVAN PETROVICH
# PAVLOV
## 1849-1936

J oseph Cardinal Mindszenty of Hungary withstood his Communist interrogators for sixty-six hours before he broke. "End it," he gasped. "Kill me!" His body exhausted, his mind disoriented, the cardinal had become a mindless, helpless piece of meat, the victim of a scientific technique distorted and misapplied for political and antihuman ends. The technique is still alive, functioning, successful, and pervasive. It began with the discovery of the classic conditioned reflex by the great Russian physiologist Ivan Petrovich Pavlov. It is evolving into a more Orwellian conditioning, that of "operant behavior" manipulation, espoused today by B. F. Skinner.

There is no philosophical reasoning behind the classic conditioned reflex. It is a stimulus-response process in which the stimulus may have no connection with the response. Pavlov's dogs heard the sound of a bell and were conditioned to salivate as if for food.

It is B. F. Skinner's theory that the behavior of the living creature "operates upon the environment to generate consequences," though he believes in reward rather than in punishment during the training period. But in its more lurid forms, operant conditioning *does* use a punishment-reward system and may make men confess to nonexistent crimes—to "generate consequences"—in order to remove the unbearable psychological pressures being applied against them.

The techniques of conditioning, operant or Pavlovian, are having a profound influence today on education, medicine, psychology, and biochemistry. Some of these techniques are coercive, others voluntary, but all may be used to change or modify a man's individual behavior

*This photograph of Ivan Pavlov was taken sometime during his late middle ages.*

By FRANKLIN RUSSELL

and thus are capable of producing bizarre results in which otherwise intelligent men insist that Communism is democracy, that democracy is fascism, that peace is war, that good is evil, and so on through an Alice in Nightmareland.

Conditioning, no matter what adjective the practitioners care to use with it, classic or operant, has revealed the brain to be an organ of the body that may be regulated like a kidney or manipulated like a leg. The consequences of this knowledge are spreading through the civilized world in a series of ripples sinister to any humanist. B. F. Skinner's recent claim that man can no longer afford to be free and must submit himself, his behavior, and his culture to outside control for the greater good of the community is, in the opinion of many libertarians, the ripple turned into a tidal wave.

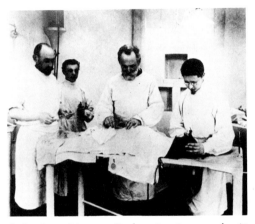

In Leningrad in 1927 Pavlov operates on a dog to prepare it by surgery for further experimentation.

And yet the technique of conditioning did not come from the inquisitional dungeon or from the laboratory of a mad scientist. It originated in the head of a visionary who had a dream of perfecting and dignifying the human race, and who would have been horrified to see any man degraded as Cardinal Mindszenty was in 1949.

Though he was born in the mid-nineteenth century under the reign of Czar Nicholas I, Ivan Petrovich Pavlov was a true twentieth-century man. He was a superb technician who ultimately came to see the human body, including the brain, as a perfectible machine. By studying the machine in motion, as if it were an automobile, he was convinced he could not only reach the central truth of human life but could also make the body and the man function more effectively. Thus, he differed from Freud, who recognized man's limits and understood the price the human psyche had paid for becoming civilized. Freud saw man as imperfectible; Pavlov saw the possibility of a perfect man.

Today, in a kind of sublime confrontation, these two giants, both seekers of the same truth, face one another across the turmoil of world civilization. Both have transcended their cultures, countries, and centuries. Both have penetrated the East and the West. The modern Freudian believes in the uniqueness of man and senses that his full potentialities and limitations are too deep to be easily plumbed. He insists that man's future is unpredictable in the face of the responsibilities placed on him by civilization. The Pavlovian believes in the computer, in the rebuilt man even, who can be governed by chemicals, electric shocks, scalpels, and conditioning.

In the no man's land between these two points of view there is a plastic explosion of rebellious youth and Establishment lawmen, of heart transplants and staggering increases in mental illness, of Chinese loudspeakers blaring slogans into a billion ears and television commercials pushing the hard sell, of the patterning of brain-damaged children and a pill for every psychic pain. Because the world cannot make up its mind whether man is perfectible (and who is to judge what is perfect?) Pavlov and Freud presumably must fight out their confrontation to the death.

Pavlov is now irrevocably connected in the world's mind with Communist science. Like Lysenko, he is a peculiarly Soviet scientific hero, with the politics of his life inextricably mixed with his work. And yet his background, and most of his legitimate international fame, were pre-1917. He was born into a time of profound intellectual activity, a contemporary more or less of Tolstoy, Dostoevsky, Rimsky-Korsakov, Moussorgsky, and droves of distinguished medical men, historians, economists, and chemists. Despite the repressions of czarism and its censorship, the age he grew up in was one of great liberal energy whose pressures, originating in the middle class, eventually wrenched Russia out of its feudal past.

Pavlov was twelve when the serfs won their freedom in 1861. The son of a poor parish priest in the old Russian city of Ryazan, he was indoctrinated—perhaps "conditioned" is a better word for it—to hard physical work in garden and orchard and to an intensive pursuit of scholarship. He always said later that the literature of the 1860's, with its emphasis on objective truth, had turned him to natural science at the university. The Nihilists Dobrolyubov, Chernyshevsky, and Pisarev were the modulators of Russian thought and influenced his thinking, particularly Pisarev, who believed strongly in Darwin's theory of natural selection. Science, it was clear, was to mold the new Russia.

The young Pavlov was slender, tall, athletic, his fashionably long beard setting off intense blue eyes and extraordinarily white teeth. His appearance caught the attention of a young woman named Seraphima Karchevskaya, who eventually became his wife. After the first physical attraction had passed, Seraphima remained transfixed by Pavlov's conversation, by his "hidden spiritual power," as she called it. He did indeed possess the unique quality of genius that would elevate him, regardless of the work he chose to do. This quality was matched by an incorruptible passion for pure truth.

After studying at the University of St. Petersburg, Pavlov was asked to work in the physiological laboratory connected with S. P. Botkin's famous clinics. His "lab" was a bathhouse with no equipment. He had no funds to buy the animals he needed. He had to extract and sell gastric juices (then used for treating human stomach ailments) from his few experimental dogs. In his farce of a laboratory Pavlov worked on the augmenter nerves of the heart, discovering that these nerves controlled not only the regularity of the beat but its force as well. He married Seraphima in 1881, but as he earned only twenty-five dollars a month in the Botkin laboratory, his family almost starved. His colleagues, worried about the pitiable state of his family, raised some money for him to lecture on the function of the heart. Pavlov gave the lectures, but he used the fees to buy more animals for research. His family got nothing.

While Pavlov might experiment with butterflies and measure heartbeats, he was always bound along an irresistible road toward the human brain. As a student, he had studied physiology under I. F. Tsyon, a dedicated experimenter. His mind was filled with the electrifying information he had mined out of *Reflexes of the Brain*, the classic work by I. M. Sechenov, the founder of modern physiology in Russia. Sechenov hurled a challenge at both church and state when he said he would attempt "to show the psychologists that it is possible to apply physiological knowledge to the phenomena of psychical life." Traditionalists, believers in the divine mystery of man, all closed ranks against Sechenov, yet for the young Pavlov the book was truth. But to reach the brain offered him by Sechenov, Pavlov had to make an incredibly circuitous journey.

It took him until 1890 to achieve some independence of research and a modicum of financial security for his family. In that year he was appointed professor of pharmacology at the Military Medical Academy in St. Petersburg. Five years later, he became professor of physiology at the same academy. It was a post he would hold for some thirty years.

Pavlov was an emotional man. But he became a mechanical monomaniac in his laboratory obsessions, as though, in this other way, he was presaging the century to come. He watched the ballet but his mind was on his work. He always walked fast and did not slow his pace even when walking with his pregnant wife. She miscarried and he overcompensated by carrying her, during her next pregnancy, up every stairway. If he could not win an argument, he shouted his rage, roaring his opponent into silence. But then he might just as readily apologize.

His impatience was legendary. He believed that every second of time was important. When assistants were doing class experiments for him, he would often leap to his feet and try to speed up the work, sometimes ruining the experiment. Then he would blame the luckless assistant. The students, delighting in these "circuses," would listen until Pavlov's shouts diminished down the corridors of the academy.

In the late nineteenth century the study of digestion was a neglected branch of physiology mainly because most experiments on the intricate workings of the digestive glands killed the animal subjects. Pavlov could not accept this drawback. He maintained aseptic conditions in the operating and recovery rooms so that his dogs would survive surgery. He insisted on dealing only with the functioning animal and was not concerned with classifying dead organs. He thus invented what came to be known as the "chronic" experiment, as opposed to the "acute," during which the animal died.

Pavlov quickly found that conventional methods of experimentation on anesthetized animals were unsatisfactory. Since anesthetics distorted the reflex action of the nervous system, he used a punishment-reward system to train conscious dogs to lie motionless in their restraint harness on the operating table. This achievement, not duplicated today, was partially helped by his incredible skill and speed as a surgeon. He often worked so quickly that he had finished operating while observers were still waiting for him to begin. He thus broke completely with tradition. Many of his dogs lived on for years, the subjects of countless experiments.

From his early work Pavlov concluded that all blood vessels and organs contained nerves sensitive to mechanical or chemical stimulation. The nervous system, he decided, was the grand regulator of the separate parts of the body, making of them a unified machine. He wanted very much to view his experimental animals as working organisms, and he figured out a way to do it. Early in the nineteenth century a Canadian trapper named Alexis St. Martin sustained an injury that left a permanent hole in his stomach and revealed its workings. Remembering this, Pavlov decided to create his own fistula, or hole, through which he could see the operation of the stomach during the digestive process. He lost nineteen dogs on the operating table before he finally succeeded. He enlarged the experiment by surgically separating one part of the stomach from the other so that he had, in effect, a "control" stomach and an "experimental" stomach with a viewing hole, which came to be known as a "Pavlov Pouch." The pouch had the same nerve and blood supply as the main stomach, and through the hole he was able to view the intricate workings of the stomach's digestive system.

*Pavlov's diagram of his basic technique: by cutting holes in dogs' stomachs and esophagi, he could observe gastric secretions.*

The work on the digestive glands led inexorably to the summit of the nervous system, the brain, and Pavlov understood this clearly. His dogs not only salivated when food entered their mouths, they salivated when he entered the room to work with them, or when they saw food in the distance. Gastric juices flowed in the same way. It was one thing for the body to respond to the taste and feel of food, but it was something else for it to react to what he called "psychic stimulation," where ears, eyes, and nose started physical changes. This put him at the crossroads where he either had to stick to his physiological methods or start thinking about the feelings and desires of his animals.

His resolution of this dilemma was preordained by the nature of his personality. Pure science so dominated his life that he was to dismiss the beauty of Paris, sneer at Switzerland's grandeur, and be bored in Vienna. He was always convinced that Italians washed their hands in their soup. Pavlov's immense scientific discipline made him a superb technician. But by so narrowing his view, he also limited himself. He would not consider anything that he could not see in his laboratory. A humanist or a Freudian might have predicted that research into the psyche, seductive and mysterious as it was, was not likely to appeal to a man who hated Italian soup and Paris.

His decision to follow only the hard and measurable physical facts wherever they were to lead him presaged the Russian Revolution itself. It hinted at the forthcoming transformation of the Russian theocracy into the materialistic society it was to become. "We endeavored," he said, "not to concern ourselves with the imaginary mental state of the animal."

Pavlov had come to his grand realization: if it was possible to examine the reactions of the body to a mental stimulus, then it was perfectly logical to assume he could study what happened in the mind by examining the body. He stood on the threshold of the conditioned-reflex breakthrough. He knew that the state of the external world produced some definite and predictable reactions on the animal. These were the unconditioned reflexes that had remained changeless for thousands, millions, of years. They were the adaptive responses that are built into an organism: flight from danger, migration in season, coughing, blinking. He felt that all animal behavior in an unchanging environment could be explained in physiological terms. Stimulation and response would be automatic.

But the natural environment was full of changes, and Pavlov knew how well he himself could manipulate an artificial environment. To cope with such changes as food scarcity or the onslaught of a hurricane, an animal needed to learn new reflex actions that would allow him to handle emergency situations. What Pavlov now proposed was to turn this learning mechanism into a nearly permanent reaction somewhat similar to the hereditary unconditioned reflex. He would make his dogs salivate when there was *no* food; in short, by using a system of reward and punishment, he would induce conditioned reflexes in his animals in situations where the stimulus had no recognizable affinity with the response, except through the conditioning.

That Pavlov's work on salivating dogs could lead to B. F. Skinner's pronouncement on the end of individual freedom little more than fifty years later is a measure of Pavlov's genius. But between Pavlov and

Skinner lies a veritable labyrinth—at least to the layman—of behavioral research. As Pavlov's work was developing in the first decades of the twentieth century, John B. Watson, a psychologist at Johns Hopkins, enthusiastically tried to absorb the principles of the conditioned reflex into his own concept of behavior. Watson, who believed that life responded to conditions set by the external environment, had decided as early as 1919 that a psychologist should be able, if he knew the stimulus, to predict the response. Conversely, if he knew the response, he should be able to specify the stimulus.

Watson was sure that thinking was only a stimulus response, like any other form of behavior. He is famous today, among scientists, as the father of behaviorism in America, and infamous, among humanists, as the man who wrote that if he were given a dozen or so healthy babies, "I'll guarantee to take any one at random and train him to become any kind of specialist I might select—doctor, lawyer, even beggarman and thief, regardless of his talents, penchants, tendencies, abilities."

The route from Pavlov to Watson to B. F. Skinner can be compressed into a paragraph, but it can say nothing of the many intervening years of argument, some of it ferociously bitter, as neobehaviorists grappled with Watson and their own theories of adaptive behavior. It became a morass of complexities as liberal psychologists struggled to handle perception, a subject previously *verboten* because it was presumed to stink of mentalism.

The roadway toward the mechanical man was wide open, but it was also studded with the wrecks of theories. Dr. Horsley Gantt, a lifelong Pavlovian, opened his laboratory at Johns Hopkins in 1932. There, he studied the effects of shock on the cardiovascular system and concluded that trauma, physical or emotional, might permanently damage the system. But even Gantt, who had met Pavlov, finally wrote that "the mind can never be equated with any physical measurement. It can be correlated, but whether it can always be correlated in every detail is open to question."

Meanwhile, for Pavlov, who had elected to travel the physiological road, no such doubts, no wrecks of theories, impeded his work on the conditioned reflex. He cut through the esophagi of his dogs and led both cut ends outside their bodies through the neck skin. This gave him total control over the gastric stimulation of the animal. When the dog ate, the food fell out of the cut esophagus, and Pavlov had a measurable gastric flow. When he actually wanted to feed his animals, he inserted food in the lower part of the cut esophagus. By checking through the hole in the stomach, he discovered that if the animal had not seen or smelled the food, no gastric flow followed. He devised scores of variations on this theme. He would not be hurried. More ebullient theorists, some of them psychologists, seemed at one time to be making faster progress along the path to the mysteries of nervous stimulation, but he limited himself to occasional icy criticism of psychology. All his work was incidental case-history material for the onslaught on the brain itself.

All during his digestive and conditioned-reflex experiments, there were dogs who seemed bitterly to resent their fate. They howled, suffered from insomnia, or became agitated in anticipation of the next experiment. Some grew unco-operative or panted as though running hard. The heartbeats of others quickened. These were experimental neuroses, accidentally created, but they pointed the way.

Pavlov worked on weak, inhibited dogs and on strong, lively types. He trained a dog to salivate at the sight of a circle, but not to salivate at an ellipse. Then, gradually, the ellipse was made more circular. The dog, which would be fed only after its correct identification of the circle, began to break down when the ellipse became nearly circular. It howled, bit through its tubes and restraining harness, and barked violently when the experiment was over. It had now, in technical language, decompensated. In this disturbed state, it was incapable of distinguishing between the circle and the ellipse.

*Cardinal Mindszenty of Hungary, above, is led from prison after police "conditioning." At a 1936 "purge" trial, below, innocent Russians willingly confessed.*

A weak type of dog was subjected, in forty-five seconds, to the impact of a gunpowder explosion, a crackle of gunfire, the explosive appearance of a figure in a horror mask, and a sharp movement of the swinging platform to which the dog was harnessed. The dog went berserk. He became rigid, limbs stiffly extended, head hurled back, eyes staring. His breathing was stertorous. All his conditioned- and unconditioned-reflex apparatus was paralyzed, and it took two weeks of rest before he could function normally again.

All his life Pavlov admired Anglo-Saxon motivation and deplored the Russian lack of it. In the 1920's the Communist rulers were faced with the gigantic barrier of a romantic, erratic, unreliable, feckless people. In the giant bureaucratic structure being built up during those years, Pavlov's work was immediately recognized as important to the state. It proffered, in Pavlov's own words, nothing less than the positive reconstruction of man himself, which from the beginning had been a basic tenet of Communist doctrine. Russia must not merely be united; its people must be remade into a new image. Pavlov and his family, on direct orders from Lenin, were given a luxury apartment and special rations. His laboratory was supplied by the state and in 1924, a new physiological institute bearing his name was built.

Pavlov relentlessly moved along his road, convinced he was very close to the mystery of the brain with his laboratory-induced disorders. He was totally obsessed by his discoveries. His experiments altered glandular functions, causing ulcers and other diseases. Some of his dogs howled on signal, became disoriented, and recovered. His desire throughout was to cure the diseases he created through what he called "scientifically sound psychotherapy." Eventually, he came to believe that neurotic behavior was caused by straining the nervous system so severely that one or another of its processes broke down, depending on the type of strain and the type of individual stressed. He did not realize that he had set the stage for a tragic drama in which his discoveries were to be relentlessly misapplied.

While disillusioned Marxists were documenting the horrendous mind-destroying techniques of the Soviet secret police, Pavlov moved steadily toward his analysis and understanding of higher and higher forms of nervous activity and operation. His dogs were fed and starved, castrated and loved, overstrained and terrorized, and hypnotized by weak and monotonous stimuli. They had their cortices removed, their thyroid, parathyroid, pituitary, and adrenal functions distorted. The dogs were poisoned to induce pathological changes in the cortex, drugged to intensify inhibitions or excitations, dosed with caffeine to exhaust cortical cells and Veronal to help them sleep it off. It would be unfair to suggest that Pavlov was some unique scientific monster; he did nothing in his laboratory that has not been done untold numbers of times in other experimental situations. His dogs were treated with kindness in excess of anything known in that age. But he lived by the principle that the end justifies the means, and since his aim always was to improve the condition of man, he considered his laboratory simply as a proving ground for theories that might further that goal. In the end he believed that all mental life came out of the fantastically complex physiological organization of the brain itself, although he never found the final proof he was looking for. Simply stated, Pavlov visualized the cerebral cortex as a reception center in which signals received by the body were broken down and analyzed before being synthesized into new connections and associations.

B. F. Skinner of Harvard, above, not only extended the theory of conditioning but raised an infant daughter in a glassed-in box.

His feelings about psychologists did not warm very much, but during the latter part of his life, he was steadily being drawn into Freudian territory. He became concerned with the mentally ill and experimented with sleep therapy in a clinic attached to his institute. He dosed his patients with narcotics, kept them in thickly-carpeted rooms with heavily-curtained windows where a dozen patients might be subjected to slow, blinking blue lights and metronomes beating. Therapists counseled the wakeful. Pavlov found that schizophrenics particularly responded to the rest cure.

By this time he was in his eighties and bore an astonishing resemblance to George Bernard Shaw (who considered Pavlov an imbecile). He was now a totally Soviet man. The cluttered bathhouse had become a gleaming, multimillion-dollar laboratory. A handful of assistants had become hundred of co-workers. He had been given all the honors of which the Soviet system was capable. A city was named after him, public squares and streets bore his name. He was, by any measurement, a giant thinker of the nineteenth and twentieth centuries. And he died in 1936, just as the astonishing confessions began coming out of the Moscow treason trials.

There is no final method of appraising Pavlov because each year that passes increases the ambiguity, brilliance, horror, and genius of what he began. Perhaps he was merely a vehicle of the times, but more likely he was its prophet. Among modern psychoanalysts, he is respected as the discoverer of the conditioned reflex. Among physiologists, he is recognized as perhaps their greatest pioneer. As one neurophysiologist in New York put it recently: "His techniques are still our crutches, but his ideas are not in our idiom any more."

His weakness, viewed in Freudian terms, is that he lacked subtlety. He was a mechanic, albeit a superb one, but he could not accept the ego since it could not be measured. He never recognized that the ego is capable of raising a series of defenses against conditioning of any kind. "It is," says the New York psychoanalyst, Dr. Bruce Ruddick, "a fantastic distortion to think you can change the core of a man's psyche by modifying his responses. Even psychoanalysis, in its concentration, frequency, and depth, is effective for a limited number of people."

A goat can be made to leap over a precipice if you beat him hard enough, but a man may stand there, enduring the pain, rather than make the fatal jump. Man *can* be conditioned, of course, either in the classic, salivating, Pavlovian manner, or in the operant, Skinnerian mold, but the process remains uncertain, faulty, and filled with imponderables. Some American prisoners in Korea confessed to war crimes, but others, with tougher egos and more cohesive social backgrounds, did not. Men in the process of being broken down in solitary confinement, in an atmosphere of threats, rewards, abrupt changes, terrifying events, have kept their equilibrium by counter-conditioning devices—building houses, plank by plank, in their minds, mentally solving abstruse mathematical problems, learning *Paradise Lost* by heart, or by confessing so voluminously to everything that their inquisitors became confused.

In some of today's communes where B. F. Skinner is revered by youngsters seeking cosmos in modern chaos, operant behavior techniques have not been able to do much with rebels or talented individualists. Many of them refuse to conform when their demands are denied, and move on. Conditioning techniques are used every second of the day by behavioral scientists and psychotherapists. A screaming maniac of a child, terrified of eggbeaters, may be quieted by brandishing an eggbeater in front of him. Homosexuals are given an electrical jolt when the picture of a good-looking boy is flashed on a screen, and a comforting massage at the sight of an undressed girl. Some people have learned to regulate their blood pressures and heartbeats.

The Chinese Cultural Revolution was a gigantic operant conditioning of a large and unwieldy mass of people. Such conditioning, a left-winger might say, is the difference between disciplined, industrious Peking and chaotic, corrupt Saigon. Such conditioning, a right-winger might say, destroys individuality. The political thinkers are in disarray about the conditioned society. Many scientists remain skeptics or are working at conditioning with personal reservations. But there are also many behavioral scientists who agree with B. F. Skinner that operant conditioning is mankind's only hope. "I have no doubt that society can be conditioned," a New York behavioral scientist said recently. "But do we want to? That is the crucial question."

The layman, bewildered by the complexities and contradictions of it all, may take note of the relentless repetition of television and radio commercials that promise him various "rewards" if he continues to buy and watch. He may be aware of the relentless sloganeering by almost everybody—government, the military, minorities—and suspect that this, too, is a form of conditioning. The repetition of certain words eventually creates an illusion of truth, even if it is a lie.

*A child of the czarist era, Pavlov, shown above with a pair of skittle clubs, was made a national Communist hero by the Soviets.*

Before Pavlov died, he understood that his road had lengthened as he traveled it. When Wilder Penfield, the great Canadian brain geographer, found that the brain's secrets proliferated faster than he revealed them, he sought refuge in his religion. When Pavlov's son Vsevolod lay dying of pancreatic cancer in 1935, Pavlov told him that perhaps the Communist state was making a mistake in trying to destroy the belief in an afterlife. "The common people need the churches yet for a while. I must write a letter to Stalin," he said.

Pavlov may, in the end, have had his tiny doubts, but our age is Pavlovian. We have found it much easier to put cool white men on the moon than to calm enraged black men on the earth. It is easier to rearrange brain molecules than it is to travel the contradictory road of the metaphysician. If we suppose that Pavlov is right and that man can be taken apart like an automobile, then reassembled for another 100,000 hours of useful life, then we have to renegotiate our own contract with being alive. If pleasure comes from the electrode and tears are dried with a drug, we must question the biological purpose of pain and pleasure, and wonder about the ethical usefulness of struggle. We have not heard the last of Ivan Petrovich Pavlov, and he himself, could he have seen the future, might well have had some unconditional comments to make about the quality of his immortality.

# FRAZER

## 1854-1941

T he scene is idyllic at first: a sunlit Italian landscape just outside Rome; a small lake nestling in a hollow of the Alban hills, and by its shore the grove that is the heart of the mystery. Once it was sacred to the goddess Diana, and its guardian in ancient times lived and died by a strange rule. It is here that the story begins. "In this sacred grove there grew a certain tree around which at any time of the day, and probably far into the night, a grim figure might be seen to prowl. In his hand he carried a drawn sword, and he kept peering warily about him as if at every instant he expected to be set upon by an enemy." He was a priest and a murderer: and the man for whom he looked was sooner or later to murder him and hold the priesthood in his stead. Such was the rule of the sanctuary."

These words from the opening of Sir James Frazer's *The Golden Bough* begin one of the longest, strangest, and most exotic detective stories in the history of scholarship. Why was the succession to the priesthood of Diana's grove at Nemi decided by mortal combat, and why was the victorious priest, while his precarious term lasted, also given the title of king? Why did the challenger, a runaway slave, have first to pluck a branch from a certain sacred tree before he could claim the right of combat? And what could such a rite, with its haunting evocation of many other practices sanctioned or required by prescientific ideas in every part of the world, reveal about the intellectual evolution of mankind? These questions set Frazer off on a scholarly quest that was to occupy him for more than a quarter of a century, and

*Sir James George Frazer was photographed in 1937, four years before his death.*

whose results, expanding from a mere two volumes in 1890 to an eventual thirteen in the years between 1907 and 1915, were to make him probably the most famous anthropologist of all time.

The solemn richness of Frazer's language, the drama and hushed suspense with which he invests the sinister scene by the peaceful wooded lake, and the feeling for the mystery and poetry inherent in uncovering the dark roots of primitive savagery and superstition are typical of the qualities that gave *The Golden Bough* an influence with the general educated public such as no other anthropological work has ever had. Readers were dazzled, too, by the sheer scope and erudition of a book that linked the ancient Greeks to the modern Eskimos and the rituals of Central African tribes to the seasonal festivals of English rustics. It was a book that truly seemed to take the whole world and human history for its subject, making it what Frazer himself called "an epic of humanity."

Everywhere, essentially, the human mind obeyed the same laws; everywhere reason and science were preceded by superstition in its successive forms of magic and religion, often manifested in bizarre, ludicrous, or appalling ways, but always, if approached in the right way—that is, scientifically and comparatively—ultimately intelligible. The apparently endless litany of names, examples, and comparisons was intoned by a master of vivid, opulent prose, which touched its weird subject matter with irony and pathos and a kind of magisterial, classical serenity. It is appropriate to introduce Frazer by his greatest work, for *The Golden Bough* grew in bulk, reputation, and influence until it must have seemed utterly to dwarf the tiny, tongue-tied Scotsman, with the shining blue eyes and pointed beard, whose molelike toil created it.

James George Frazer was born in 1854, and one feels it is typical of the somewhat obsessive regularity of his habits that the date should have been January 1. His parents, both of Glasgow merchant stock, were deeply religious, and strict observance of the Sabbath and daily reading of the Bible were part of the family way of life. Frazer's boyhood seems to have been a happy one, and in later life he wrote with deep affection of his home at Helensburgh, "the little white town by the sea," on the estuary of the Clyde. Even after Frazer turned away from the Christian certainties of his parents' creed, there seems to have been no family breach, and his mother died with her hand resting on one of her famous son's books. On Frazer, the family Bible reading left its mark. Belief disappeared but veneration of a sort remained, and one of his works was a selection of passages from the Bible "chosen for their literary beauty and interest."

At Glasgow University he encountered certainties of another kind,

*J. M. W. Turner's vision of Diana's ancient rites illustrated Frazer's* Golden Bough.

and these never left him: classical learning and physical science, nature's laws and the regimental precision of Latin syntax. Frazer never learned to carry his youthful learning lightly. There is a story that later on, when he was an internationally famous scholar, Frazer learned of a small grammatical error in a Latin sentence he had published and immediately offered his resignation to the head of his college. He rejected Freud, whose *Totem and Taboo* was heavily indebted to Frazer's work, perhaps partly from prudishness. Frazer was, after all, a Victorian, and his accounts of the fertility cults to which he devoted so much attention sometimes remind one forcibly of what might be called the "nameless abominations" school of nineteenth-century ethnographic description.

Frazer was rooted in the century of his birth, and his mind lost its elasticity fairly early. It is characteristic that when, in old age, he became blind, the books his secretaries read endlessly for his amusement were his own works, to which he would listen, as one said, "as if hearing for the first time the words of a promising colleague."

Virtually all Frazer's adult life was spent in Cambridge as a fellow of Trinity College, where he occupied rooms beside the great gate, on a staircase that in the past had housed Isaac Newton, the historian Macaulay, and William Makepeace Thackeray. Frazer wrote one of his word pictures of the scene: "the tranquil court of an ancient college, where the sundial marks the silent passage of the hours, and in the long summer days the fountain plashes drowsily amid flowers and grass; where, as the evening shadows deepen, the lights come out in the blazoned windows of the Elizabethan hall, and from the chapel the sweet voices of the choir, blent with the pealing music of the organ, float on the peaceful air, telling of man's eternal aspirations after truth and goodness and immortality."

Frazer began his scholarly career as a classicist and humanist, a student of ancient civilization, and never altogether ceased to be one. Anthropologists were sometimes puzzled as to whether they were dealing with one of themselves or with a classical scholar who had trespassed with outstanding success upon their discipline. Frazer himself spoke of *The Golden Bough* sometimes as science, sometimes as literature. Certainly he was always an intensely self-conscious stylist, a topographic and dramatic scene-painter, an artist in words. In many pages of Frazer's anthropological writings one can recognize the classical scholar who had tramped around Greece for his edition of the work of the ancient Greek traveler Pausanias, and who had supplied from his own observation, in the lush prose of his footnotes, the color and particularity of scene that Pausanias had unfortunately failed to provide. To Frazer places were never, if he could help it, bald geographic designations; they came in a package complete with vegetation and meteorology.

It is ironic, however, that the only fieldwork Frazer ever did was in order to edit a classical Greek text. For Frazer's life was unadventurous even by the standards of nineteenth-century anthropology. He was tongue-tied and self-effacing; he hated and avoided controversy and suffered badly from stage fright when he had to lecture. He took no part in university politics or administration, and when he accepted the chair of anthropology at Liverpool University, he quickly discovered his mistake and resigned after a year. Even to try to imagine the mannered classicist Frazer, who found all human contacts painfully difficult, as a possible field anthropologist in a primitive society seems almost an act of cruelty. When William James once asked him if he had ever met a savage, his reply was "Heaven forbid."

This repudiation was to him, however, not so much a rejection of danger and discomfort as an assertion of scientific objectivity. Frazer always stressed the danger to an anthropologist of too much immersion in one particular area. The anthropologist was to be a kind of clearinghouse, receiving, organizing, and putting into perspective the precious data about the primitive peoples of the world before it was too late, before native ways of life were adulterated or obliterated by the encroachments of Western civilization. The collectors of this information were to be missionaries, traders, explorers, and administrators, whose daily lives brought them into contact with primitive societies. Frazer's initiative lay only in maintaining a vast correspondence with them and drawing up a table of questions for their use. But they were to be eyes and ears only, and to keep as free as possible from theorizing, which might prejudice their vision. One of Frazer's chief informants was explicitly forbidden to read books so that he might keep his powers of observation untainted.

At the center of the web sat Frazer, the mastermind, in his quiet Cambridge room with the fountain plashing lazily outside the window, collating the odd, extraordinary, sometimes almost unbelievable facts they sent back, tinting their bare reports with artful adjectives and weaving them into a tapestry that he did not know whether to call science or literature. The division of labor that he justified as a requirement of scientific objectivity was, in fact, only another form of the old distinction between the practical man, the man of things, and the scholar, whom Frazer now sometimes called a scientist, the man of words and books. In that sense, Frazer remained the humanist classical scholar, who had won his fellowship with a dissertation on Plato's philosophy, to the end of his days.

But classical scholarship itself, the heart of a gentleman's education, was changing in the late nineteenth century under the impact of the science of anthropology, and Frazer put himself boldly at the head of that change, doing, in his own way, as much as any man to make anthropology academically respectable and to make some knowledge of primitive ways of thought and behavior part of the common cultural experience of Western man. He was able to do it partly because he had a gift for turning uncouth raw materials into a work of art and a vision of a strange world, alien and yet somehow close and almost familiar, which tugged at the imagination and provided poets and literary men with fresh and vital images, in a world where technology and urban civilization seemed to offer nothing but imaginative impoverishment and aridity. But it also mattered that Frazer, as an accomplished classicist and fellow of an ancient college, was at the center of the old gentlemanly culture that had often looked down on anthropology as a collection of nasty trivia.

Classical scholars of Frazer's generation, however, were beginning to think strange thoughts and to see the elegant mythology, the sublime Athenian tragedies, and even the sophisticated philosophical systems of classical antiquity in a new and startling perspective. Behind the Greek drama and festivals like the Olympian games there seemed to lurk other, more bloody and primitive rituals, performed by actors to whom their performance was a matter of life or death. Classical deities and heroes, Adonis, Hera, Persephone, Dionysus, whose ideal forms so many painters since the Renaissance had depicted, bore traces of cousinship not only, as had long been recognized, with the gods of other elaborate pantheons, Sanskrit, Babylonian, Egyptian, and Norse, but with the images of grass and wood, feathers and sun-baked mud, that were feared and revered by modern savages. Over Diana's chilly classical shoulder, like an uncouth relative insisting on an embarrassing kinship, leered a fat-bellied fertility goddess with pendulous breasts and interestingly unclassical proportions. The dark gods were claiming their place on Olympus.

There was, after all, nothing very surprising about it. According to the prevailing doctrines of social evolution, whose antecedents went back several centuries, all the elements of higher civilizations had sprung from savage roots and bore traces of their origin for those with eyes to see. If man, as Darwin had shown, was cousin to the apes, why should Zeus not submit to being cousin to a juju—different stages of the same mental process? It only remained to amass the evidence and mark the various stages. *The Golden Bough,* ostensibly an inquiry into a particular classical rite and legend, was actually an immense comparative study of primitive magic and superstition, culminating in a slightly oblique but unmistakable glance at Christianity.

Why, Frazer's argument begins, was the priest of the sacred grove of Nemi also a king? To answer this question, he plunges into what he takes to be the mental world of primitive magical ritual, with its guiding principles of sympathetic magic and taboo. Ignorant of the true relations of cause and effect, "the untutored savage" lives in a world in which any resemblance is enough to establish a relationship or even identity of one class of things with another. Men, beasts, vegetation, and weather are bound promiscuously together in a magical economy in ways for which science and reason offer no warrant, and the means of controlling nature is by ritual imitation of the desired events. But nature thus treated does not always respond, magic does not always work; so the momentous transition is made from magic to religion. Natural phenomena are thought of now as capricious deities, who must be made to work for their worshipers. But the heritage of sympathetic magic is not forgotten. The nature gods are personified in priests or divine kings who in a sense *are* the gods and natural forces they represent. The grove at Nemi was sacred to Diana, a goddess of fertility, and her priest was her divine consort, god of the wood and the rain.

*Frazer detected identical themes in diverse religions. Five centuries before the first Easter, a Greek vase painter depicted the springtime resurrection of Zeus's daughter Persephone (left).*

Frazer produces an immense number of alleged parallels, from other ancient mythologies, from the phallic gods and fertility goddesses of anthropology and the May kings and queens of European folklore. The function of the divine pair was to ensure continued fertility, and as Frazer rather primly puts it, speaking of the rites performed, "we may assume with a high degree of probability that the profligacy which notoriously attended these ceremonies was at one time not an accidental excess but an essential part of the rites, and that in the opinion of those who performed them the marriage of trees and plants could not be fertile without the real union of the sexes." For "profligacy," in other words, read sexual intercourse performed as sympathetic magic by nature divinities in human form.

But why, Frazer continues, was the divine king of the grove always killed by his successor? This leads Frazer on to the myths of the sacrifice and resurrection of a god, a ritual enactment of the natural miracle performed by the spring of every year. The god is killed in order that he may be renewed, and by his renewal guarantee that of the earth whose powers he embodies. So it was with the Greek Adonis, the Phrygian Attis, the Egyptian Osiris, and the Norse Balder the Beautiful, and so also, Frazer hints, with the founder of Christianity.

There is one last question: why did the challenger for the priesthood of Nemi have first to pluck a branch from a sacred tree, and why was this associated in classical tradition with the golden bough carried by Virgil's hero Aeneas to preserve him on his journey through the kingdom of the dead? Why *golden*? The answer Frazer finds in the myth of Balder. Balder, god of the oak, could be killed only by a piece of mistletoe. Frazer finds mistletoe regarded in the primitive world as the life or external soul of the tree to which it clings. Furthermore, Balder's body, to perform its work of renewal, had first to be consumed by fire; the legend of the phoenix is a variant of the same idea. Fire symbolized the rays of the reviving sun. The color and legendary significance of mistletoe, the golden light of fire and the sun, linked for Frazer the golden bough of Nemi with the fire festivals performed by the peasantry all over Europe at times of solstice and equinox. All elements of fertility and renewal fell into their places in the rite of the sacred grove; the riddle's solution was complete.

*Two millenniums after the fall of Athens, Matthias Grünewald portrayed the springtime resurrection of Christ, the Son of God.*

At one level, Frazer probably did not greatly care about the riddle. At times he seems almost to tease the reader with the pretense that all this erudition is deployed to provide a dubious interpretation of an obscure rite. For long periods he seems to forget about it altogether. His argument is often stretched to the breaking point by conjecture and remote analogy. "We may suppose that," "it is not impossible that," become more and more frequent introductions to a new line of argument. But far more important than the interpretation of the particular rite is the evolutionary drama of the transition from magic to religion and the theories of the mental processes underlying them.

Modern anthropologists have objected not merely to Frazer's particular interpretations, such as that magic always precedes religion or that primitives have no notion of cause and effect (when all the evidence indicates that they do), but to his whole strategy, to the way his examples are presented torn from their social context of habitual everyday behavior and strung together to form a speculative evolutionary sequence of primitive metaphysical ideas. Examples presented in this way are considerably more entertaining than the tables of kinship relations and the like that make such an effective deterrent to reading modern anthropology, but they are also seriously misleading. It is as though one were to portray the American mentality entirely from behavior at Thanksgiving, July 4, and New Year's Eve. A foreign people presented in this way is apt to sound more amiable, more childlike, and a good deal sillier than it is.

This, however, was the common anthropological practice of Frazer's time, and his readers could feel that they were being given the latest results of anthropological science in palatable form. Frazer's book is a product of four centuries of European superiority and domination, a map of the soul of the undeveloped world and of Europe's own savage past fossilized in the customs and superstitions of her peasantry. It is a kind of Victorian or Edwardian lantern lecture, on a vast scale and in gorgeous colors, with the voice of the lecturer, calm and ironic, coming reassuringly out of the darkness. Did one want to know of the absurd behavior of the Wawamba, the quaint superstitions of Breton peasants, the magical lore of the ancient Greeks, or the atrocious practices of the Mura-muras? Frazer could tell one. Readers could smile over stories of tribes who worshiped Queen Victoria or tried to copulate with trees. There were, it appeared, men on earth who would die if they spoke to their mothers-in-law; there were sorcerers who kept asylums for stray souls, and if you had lost yours, would supply you with a new one for a fixed fee. Savages, with Frazer as their impresario, provided an endlessly fascinating menagerie of exotic human behavior.

It was all splendid stuff for the cynical 1920's, when Frazer's reputation was at its height, just as the superior tone and faith in science and the pomp and circumstance of Frazer's prose appealed to the age of confidence and imperial grandeur that was passing away. Frazer's very inconsistencies and hesitations made his work acceptable to men of a wide variety of creeds and temperaments. The savage was absurd and one could look down on him, but he was also uncomfortably close, as well as rich food for the imagination. Science was destined everywhere to supersede and extinguish superstition—but was it? Frazer, like his contemporary Freud, another rationalist who devoted his life to studying the irrational, had a powerful and alarmed sense that beneath the civilized and rational surface of life there lay a dormant volcano of nonrational forces.

Beneath the confident evolutionist in Frazer there was a Manichaean who alternated between optimism and gloom. More persistent than any particular theory in his work, as Stanley Edgar Hyman has pointed out, were certain pervasive metaphors, especially light and the sun, and its opposite, darkness and gloom, so suitable to represent primeval forests and the confused thoughts of ignorant and frightened men. It is this as much as anything that gives *The Golden Bough* its literary zest; its pages abound in "gloomy recesses," "dark labyrinths," "phantasmagoria," and "subterranean forces." One is caught up in the drama of a dark and sleeping earth warmed into renewed life by the reviving sun, which also seems in the end to symbolize, for author and reader, the illumination of a dark world by knowledge and science.

Not the least of *The Golden Bough*'s excitements for its readers were its reference to a ritual and pagan origin of the central mysteries of Christianity. Eating the god—the title of one of Frazer's chapters—was a common ritual practice, rooted in magic. So was hanging divine scapegoats on a tree and even piercing their sides with a spear, that they might take upon themselves the sins of the people. The dying fall with which Frazer's immense book ends is obviously modeled on the famous conclusion of Gibbon's *Decline and Fall of the Roman Empire,* with the barefooted Christian friars chanting in the Roman temple of Vesta, representing the book's theme, "the triumph of barbarism and of religion." Frazer writes instead of a twilight of the gods, in a supremely effective elegiac passage, almost every word of which has been charged with meaning by what has gone before.

The great winding journey over, we return at last to Nemi. It is evening and "we look back and see the sky aflame with sunset, its golden glory resting like the aureole of a dying saint over Rome and touching with a crest of fire the dome of St. Peter's. The sight once seen can never be forgotten." The King of the Wood has gone, "But Nemi's woods are still green, and as the sunset fades above them in the west, there comes to us, borne on the swell of the wind, the sound of the church bells of Rome ringing the Angelus. *Ave Maria! . . . Le roi est mort, vive le roi! Ave Maria!"*

Frazer was not the first to be inspired by the image of the golden bough and its legendary association with the groves of Nemi. Apart from Virgil, the painter Turner had depicted the scene in a painting that Frazer used as the original frontispiece to *The Golden Bough.* Macaulay had written a verse:

> The still glassy lake that sleeps
> Beneath Aricia's trees—
> Those trees in whose dim shadow
> The ghastly priest doth reign
> The priest, who slew the slayer,
> And shall himself be slain.

But whatever the eventual verdict on Frazer's book as a work of anthropological science, one thing is certain. Frazer has taken possession of the grove of Nemi and its associated legends more tenaciously than any of its desperate priestly kings, and it belongs now, not to the Latin poet, the English painter, or the great historian, but to James Frazer. He, if anyone, is the King of the Wood.

The vast bulk and learning of *The Golden Bough* and the long list of Frazer's other works were the product of an astounding industry. There is something almost stupefying about the accounts of the sheer mechanical regularity of Frazer's working life, as though he were some half-naked drudge in a mine or factory of the early industrial revolution, instead of a distinguished scholar of worldwide reputation and fellow of a rich and ancient college. The story of Frazer's life is a story of unremitting labor. Day after day, year after year, the same story, the same working hours: 4–8 A.M., then breakfast; 9–12, then lunch and a nap; 3–6, then dinner; and finally, from 7 to midnight.

Bertrand Russell, another fellow of Trinity, mentions only one memory of Frazer. Fellows have free dinners in College Hall, and "as a Scot Frazer could not ignore this consideration." He grudged, however, "every moment taken from his studies for the gross work of self-nourishment." But fellows who arrived more than a quarter of an hour late were fined. Frazer therefore always arrived exactly a quarter of an hour late. In 1896 he married a Frenchwoman, Lilly Grove, a widow with two children, but it made no difference. They made a compact that his working hours should remain unchanged, and Frazer worked on his honeymoon. He never broke down and never revolted against this self-imposed slavery; the most he allowed himself was a sort of resigned self-pitying wistfulness in a verse he once wrote:

> Still, still I con old pages
> And through great volumes wade
> While life's brief summer passes
> And youth's brief roses fade.

From the moment of his marriage Frazer entered a new slavery, one accepted with the same unprotesting meekness. From that point all accounts of Frazer turn out, in fact, to be accounts of Lady Frazer, of her masterfulness, her ambition for her husband, her temper and meanness, and of how she would make lists of the governments, universities, and learned societies that had not yet given honors to her modest and already much decorated husband and scheme how to induce them to do their duty. When Frazer was aging, tired, and creatively spent, she made him rehash his earlier works until his publisher rebelled; there is perhaps an irony in Frazer's dedication of one book of snippets to her as its "only begetter." "James, go back to your work at once," she was heard to shout. Frazer's colleague and admirer the great anthropologist Bronislaw Malinowski described her guardedly as "unquestionably a puzzling element to most of Frazer's friends." A female colleague, uninhibited by chivalry, proposed the passing of "Game Laws for the Preservation of Eminent Husbands." Two of Frazer's secretaries, reading to the old man, over and over, his own works, were struck by his liking for the story of the Witch of

Endor and connected his preference with the jealous, grasping, devoted old woman, with the strong French accent, hook nose, beard, and untidy hair, who still dominated his life.

Few of us are likely to be edifying in our eighties, and the Frazers were harshly afflicted; he became blind and paralyzed, she stone-deaf. Their last years together were pathetic and dreadful, like some pitiless black comedy by August Strindberg. Seated side by side on seats like thrones, her hand possessively on his, they reminded observers of two images from the British Museum. She was as ruthless and strong-willed as ever, her suspiciousness aggravated to frenzy by deafness. All communication with him had to be through her. Frazer was polite, gentle, and fussed obsessively about his secretaries' comfort—was he or she too warm, too much in the light, and so on. Lady Frazer, seeing his lips moving, would jealously demand the reason. A note would be written: "HE ASKED IF I WAS TOO WARM." Frazer, unable to see but aware of trouble, would anxiously ask what was the matter, and the tragi-farcical cycle would begin again. One of Lady Frazer's last victories was to get Trinity College to send Frazer's dinner to their flat, a distance of more than a mile. The meal, covered with a green baize cloth and accompanied by a college servant, would travel through the Cambridge streets to the old man who did not want it, to be pushed into his protesting mouth by the indomitable woman whose will kept him alive and in doing so sustained her own life also.

In 1941, at the age of eighty-seven, Frazer rebelled and, as the saying is, went to his last rest. In less than twenty-four hours, "James, go back to your work at once," echoed in a heavy French accent through eternity. Lady Frazer had caught up with him.

*Sir James and Lady Frazer mirthlessly celebrate the scholar's eighty-third birthday in 1937.*

*And if something of the autocratic pose,*
*The paternal strictness he distrusted, still*
*Clung to his utterance and features,*
*It was a protective imitation*

*For one who lived among enemies so long;*
*If often he was wrong and at times absurd,*
*To us he is no more a person*
*Now but a whole climate of opinion.*

Of course, W. H. Auden is right. Freud, like Marx and Darwin, those other destroyers of nineteenth-century preconceptions with whom his name is so often linked, is no longer merely a person; he is a point of view, a way of thinking, an attitude to life, and above all, a continuing force to be reckoned with, who can be neither dismissed nor ignored by anyone who is concerned with the human predicament. His ideas have become so ubiquitous that it is difficult to imagine how men thought before he formulated them.

Before World War I our grandfathers would have considered themselves to be chiefly governed by reason, though subject to deplorable spells of irrationality. Freud reversed the picture, claiming that reason's voice, though persistent, had but a very small influence upon human conduct. Freud also made us regard both virtue and conventional morality with suspicion. In 1900 the man who displayed altruism and self-sacrifice would have been regarded as simply "good"; and,

*Sigmund Freud was sixty-six when this photograph was taken in Vienna in 1922.*

By ANTHONY STORR

if he was celibate, would have been congratulated upon his self-control and spirituality. It would not have occurred to the Victorians to suspect that unselfishness might be self-punishment; that kindness might conceal a patronizing superiority; that altruism could be a mask for self-centeredness, or celibacy an ignominious flight from woman.

Darwin shook man's self-esteem by demonstrating his humble origins and his kinship with other animals. Freud shattered it by showing that man's proudest spiritual achievements were rooted in primitive instinct. Not even children were allowed their "innocence"; and the cozy, comfortable love of the Victorian family was shown to be based upon violent sensuality.

Freud tore down many façades, leaving us naked and ashamed, but more realistic. Since his revelations Western man has become incapable of taking any form of human behavior at its face value. It is impossible to think of any other single individual who has so affected the way we look at the ordinary pursuits of our daily lives.

ꝋ   Freud was born on May 6, 1856, in Freiberg. His father, a Jewish wool-merchant, was over forty at the time, though his mother was only twenty-one. Jakob Freud was a kindly man, but a middle-aged father often appears somewhat formidable to a small boy; and it may be on this account that psychoanalysis, in its pristine form, is more concerned with the child's reaction to paternal authority than later developments would lead one to expect. C. G. Jung's psychology, for instance, is far more mother-based. Freud's mother, who lived to the age of ninety-five, seems to have been a warmhearted, gay person, who gave Sigmund, her eldest son, so much love, and regarded him with such pride, that he developed an inner confidence in himself which proved unshakable. When Sigmund was four the family moved to Vienna; and for seventy-eight years Freud continued to live and practice in this city, which he never ceased to talk of with distaste, but which he was extremely reluctant to leave. In 1938 he was forced to do so, and took refuge from the Nazis in England. In September, 1939, he died, having survived just long enough to witness England's declaration of war on Nazi Germany.

During his long years in Vienna, his outward way of life changed very little, although he progressed in the world's estimation from ignominious rejection to worldwide renown. He died as he had lived, patient, stoic, independent. Although his discoveries had an enormous influence on Western man's view of himself, Freud disdained the trappings of conventional success. The man who wrote that what men desired was "honor, power, and the love of women" was himself honored only late in his life after years of rejection, had little power, and enjoyed but a meager experience of sexual love.

As a boy Freud was mentally precocious, and notably successful at school. He became well-versed in the classics, learned French and English, and later taught himself Italian and Spanish. Already, in early youth, he showed an unusual application to work, and often took his meals apart from the family so that he could go on reading while eating. In his autobiography Freud writes: "At the 'Gymnasium' I was at the top of my class for seven years; I enjoyed special privileges there, and was required to pass scarcely any examinations." At school anti-Semitism seems not to have been a problem; but it was a different story when Freud entered the university. "Above all, I found that I was expected to feel myself inferior and an alien because I was a Jew. I refused absolutely to do the first of these things." But in old age he was able to see that his nonacceptance by society had had some positive results. "It was only to my Jewish nature, that I owed the two qualities that have become necessary to me throughout my difficult life. Because I was a Jew I found myself free of many prejudices which restrict others in the use of the intellect: as a Jew I was prepared to be in the opposition and to renounce agreement with the 'compact minority.' "

*Above, the eight-year-old Sigmund stands stiffly beside his middle-aged father, Jakob. Below, Sigmund's mother, Amelia, almost twenty years younger than her husband, sat for this portrait when her beloved son was sixteen years old.*

Freud's intellectual precocity was an important part of his character structure. He told Jung that if he had been neurotic, his neurosis would have taken an obsessional form. In a paper written in 1913 he says: "I do not know if it will seem too daring if I assume from the clues at our disposal that a premature advance of the ego-development ahead of the libido-development contributes to the obsessional disposition." Already one can discern hints that in the young Freud there was something of a split between reason and emotion, a split which led to his topographical conception of the mind as a divided structure. Originally, Freud thought chiefly in terms of "conscious" and "unconscious"; later, in 1923, he published *The Ego and the Id* and introduced the concept of the super-ego. His own super-ego must have been a powerful one, which denied him a good deal of pleasure.

It is still sometimes alleged that Freud discovered the unconscious mind. It is no disparagement of his achievement to point out that this, in fact, is not the case. As L. L. Whyte puts it in his book *The Unconscious before Freud*, "the idea of unconscious mental processes was, in many of its aspects, conceivable around 1700, topical around 1800, and became effective around 1900." Both philosophers and physicians had realized that man was less governed by reason and conscious deliberation than he liked to believe. What Freud did was not to invent the idea of the unconscious but to apply it and to make it operational. The manner in which this startling and original application came about is a fascinating story.

Freud started as a research worker who was chiefly interested in the anatomy and physiology of the brain. He published a number of papers on neurological subjects and had no wish to become a practicing physician. All his life he deplored and suspected "therapeutic enthusiasm"; and paradoxically, we owe his major insights to the fact that he was always more interested in understanding his patients' mental processes than in healing them direct. But his position in Brücke's physiological institute in Vienna was ill-paid and held little promise of advancement. Moreover, he wanted to get married and had not the money to do so. In 1882, with great reluctance, he decided to abandon his career as a research worker, and entered the General Hospital as a clinical assistant.

At that time the separation of psychiatry from neurology had not taken place; but, as Freud himself points out, no one could make a living from the treatment of the comparatively small number of patients with organic neurological diseases, especially as there was little that could be done for most of them. Like other neurologists, Freud made his living from the treatment of neurotics; and his principal therapeutic weapon was that of hypnosis, a subject of which Freud had more knowledge than most of his contemporaries, for he had studied its use in Paris at the clinic of the famous neurologist Charcot, who had demonstrated that hypnosis could produce and remove all kinds of physical symptoms at the will of the physician. Three years later, in 1889, Freud also studied for a brief period with Bernheim, founder of the Nancy school of suggestion. Of this period he writes: "I received the profoundest impression of the possibility that there could be powerful mental processes which nevertheless remained hidden from the consciousness of men." Hypnosis can still provide a spectacular demonstration of the reality of unconscious mental processes for those who need to be convinced of their existence, but, as other workers have repeatedly found, hypnosis, though producing some striking results, has many disadvantages. Not all patients can be hypnotized, and even those who can often relapse. Moreover, if hypnotism is used simply as a technique by which the physician issues suggestions to the patient, it reveals nothing of the origin of the symptoms nor throws any light on the causation of the neurosis. This latter fact alone must have been profoundly dissatisfying to Freud, who was deeply interested in causes and relentless in pursuing origins.

It was the observation made by another physician, Joseph Breuer, which first showed Freud that hypnosis could be used as a tool of investigation rather than simply as a technique for suggesting a cure. Breuer's case, now world-famous, was that of a young girl who had been taken ill while she was nursing her father. She had a number of paralyses, states of mental confusion, and other hysterical symptoms. What Breuer noticed was this: if, instead of merely suggesting to her

*The neurologist Jean Martin Charcot, at whose clinic Freud studied hypnosis, appears here in an embroidered, bemedaled jacket.*

under hypnosis that she would lose her symptoms, he made her tell him each time what was oppressing her mind, she would produce connections between her symptoms and her emotions which she was quite unable to do when in the unhypnotized, conscious state. Her symptoms all took origin in feelings and thoughts she had experienced while nursing her sick father. Many of these thoughts or feelings were unacceptable to her, and she had therefore tried to banish them from her mind; but no sooner did she do this than some hysterical symptom appeared. When Breuer put her into a state of deep hypnosis and made her recall the banished connections and thoughts, her symptoms disappeared. Breuer's observations gave Freud the key he was looking for. Instead of using hypnosis as a direct way of influencing neurotic symptoms, he started to use it as a tool for investigating them. Had Freud been born a therapeutic enthusiast, psychoanalysis might never have been born. As it was, the fact that he was a research worker by inclination rather than a physician bore rich fruit in the shape of the psychoanalytic understanding of the meaning and origin of neurotic symptoms.

Although hypnosis proved a useful tool for investigating symptoms, Freud finally abandoned it. There seem to have been two chief reasons. One, already mentioned, was that many patients, however hard one tries, cannot be hypnotized, or at least cannot be put into the deep trance then considered necessary to obtain a complete cure. Secondly, Freud began to realize that many of the cures brought about by hypnosis remained stable only so long as there was some positive emotional relationship between the patient and the physician. On one occasion a female patient suddenly threw her arms round his neck. It seems probable that it was at this time that he recognized something of the nature of the relationship between patient and physician. At all events, he said that he never hypnotized this lady again. Freud felt that if he was really to understand what he called "the mysterious element" at work behind hypnotism he would have to abandon its use. He then recollected that when he had been studying with Bernheim, Bernheim had maintained that even though a patient might seem to have forgotten everything that had transpired while in an hypnotic trance, the memory was none the less present. If the doctor strongly urged the patient to remember, it was often possible to recapture the missing memory even in the waking state. Bernheim used to do this by pressing his hand on the patient's forehead and assuring him that he would remember if he tried hard enough. Freud decided to follow this example. He soon found that even the pressure of his hand was not necessary. All that he had to do was to tell the patient to say exactly what came into his head without keeping anything back and without making any judgment upon what occurred to him. In

*This photograph of Freud and his fiancée, Martha Bernays, was taken in Hamburg in September, 1855, a year before their marriage.*

this way, the practice of free association was born and a new technique invented for the investigation of mental processes.

The importance of this discovery can hardly be overestimated. The term itself is actually a misnomer, being based on a mistranslation of the German *Freier Einfall*. *Einfall* does not mean "association" but "sudden idea," and the concept refers to ideas which occur spontaneously without straining. The use of free association depends upon several assumptions, one of which is that if a person says what comes into his mind without let or hindrance. he will inevitably be driven toward revealing what is really significant. Although no patient talks of what is significant all the time, the use of free association allows the analyst to detect and interpret underlying patterns and preoccupations. The patient is generally unconscious of these patterns, which thus cannot be altered or controlled. But when analysis reveals them, they become accessible to the patient's ego, and therefore modifiable.

In my view, however, this is not really the vital feature of the discovery of free association. What is revolutionary is that the use of this technique implies a change in status and relationship between the patient and the doctor. Hypnosis is essentially an active, authoritarian method, which depends greatly upon the prestige of the physician, upon the confidence with which he utters his suggestions, and upon the compliance or passive obedience of the patient. The use of free association transforms the physician's role from that of an authoritarian persuader to that of a passive listener who confines his activity to interpretation; that is, to helping the patient understand his own mental processes without attempting to persuade, cajole, or bully him into health. This is a most remarkable abrogation of the traditional role of the physician. Even today, in conventional medical practice, the good patient is the patient who believes implicitly in his physician, who does exactly what he is told to do, and who never queries his doctor's authority. Exactly the opposite is true of the successfully treated neurotic. Although friendly co-operation between analyst and patient is essential, and there are patients who are so rebellious, so aggressive, or so unco-operative that they cannot be treated, most neurotics have suffered in the past from accepting too readily the authoritarian ideas which have been impressed upon them in childhood. During their time on the couch they find out that it is safe to express resentment of authority and to question it, and thus learn to make progress toward freedom and autonomy. One of the main differences between psychoanalysis and other methods of helping people with neurotic problems is still the fact that the analyst confines himself to playing a largely passive role. There is a real difference between making interpretations and issuing instructions. Psychoanalysts are not particularly modest in their public utterances, but in the privacy of the consulting room they are notably less assertive than any other group of trained professionals. There has always been, and always will be, a plethora of people who are sufficiently sure of their own superior knowledge to tell people exactly how to behave in every conceivable circumstance. Indeed, the ordinary person finds it very difficult to imagine how it is that a psychoanalyst can listen so long and say so little. But Freud, who was both patient and persistent, realized that a person's emotional problems can never finally be solved by any external authority, and that the main task of the psychoanalyst is to help the patient to help himself, not by giving him advice, but by making him more conscious of what his problems really are.

Much of psychoanalytic theory is still the subject of controversy and debate. But even if none of Freud's original conclusions were to remain unmodified, the technique of investigation which he discovered, and its consequences, cannot be disregarded. It was Freud who taught psychotherapists how to listen.

[suicide rate of psychiatrists is highest of any other profession in this country]

Freud's passion for investigation into origins led to his exploration of the childhood of his patients. Breuer's case had convinced him that certain neurotic symptoms were concerned with the suppression of painful memories the patient could not face, and that the recovery of these memories was accompanied by the disappearance of the symptoms. Pursuing this idea, Freud soon discovered that many of the distasteful incidents which his patients recalled, and which seemed to have caused their illnesses, were sexual in nature. At the end of the nineteenth century the sexual factor in neurosis was not generally admitted. Both Breuer and Charcot had, in Freud's hearing, dropped hints that the secrets of the marriage bed were connected with neurotic symptoms. But Freud, who was easily shocked and puritanical in temperament, did not take these remarks seriously and dismissed them from his mind. However, when he came to investigate his own patients, he discovered that a great many of their anxieties and painful memories centered around the facts of sexuality. Moreover, he established that the sexuality which was causing the difficulty was not adult but childhood sexuality.

Today this is taken so much for granted that it is difficult to realize the shock and surprise with which Freud's announcements about infantile sexuality were originally received. Indeed, it was somewhat naive of him not to anticipate that people would be shocked, especially in view of his own primness. But Freud the conventional, bourgeois family man and Freud the relentless seeker after truth were two very different people. If neurosis in adult life was, as seemed probable, the result of trauma in early childhood, and if these traumata were chiefly sexual in nature, then it was Freud's duty as a doctor and a scientist to say so, however unpalatable these truths might be. Freud's original pronouncements on the nature of hysteria and upon infantile sexuality were indeed treated with such intemperate obloquy that a less determined man might have wilted and abandoned so unpopular a line of research. But Freud, like many another Jew, had little expectation of being generally popular, and abuse made him all the more obstinate. Instead of modifying his tone, he interpreted the attacks upon his opinions as further evidence supporting the psychoanalytic view that men are intensely reluctant to face the truth about themselves. For by this time, Freud's early belief that neurosis was due to traumatic incidents was gradually becoming modified. Although traumata could and did occur, what neurotics repressed was not simply the memory of such incidents, but whole aspects of the primitive and instinctive parts of themselves.

Among Freud's early cases of hysteria were a surprisingly large number of patients who reported to him incidents of seduction by one or the other parent. At first Freud took these stories literally (perhaps another instance of his naiveté), but later he came to realize that what his patients told him was largely phantasy and wish-fulfillment rather than an account of a real incident. This discovery was at first distressing to Freud, because he thought it represented a failure in his technique. However, his tenacity made him persist with his investigations, and what emerged from this was the importance of the patient's inner world of phantasy. Instead of concentrating on actual traumata in childhood, important though these sometimes are, it became more and more a part of psychoanalytic technique to investigate the patient's inner world: that world of hopes, daydreams, fears, loves, and hates, which originates in infancy, persists into adult life, and is only tenuously related to the hard facts of the real world.

Freud soon discovered that, as the long process of analysis went on, he himself became increasingly important in the patient's inner world. He wrote: "In every analytic treatment there arises without the physician's agency an intense emotional relationship between the patient and the analyst which is not to be accounted for by the actual situation. It can be of a positive or of a negative character and can vary between the extremes of a passionate, completely sensual love and the unbridled expression of an embittered defiance and hatred." It was about 1892 that Freud began to be aware of the importance of this phenomenon. The delineation of transference is the second important innovation for which every psychotherapist must acknowledge a debt to Freud. When Jung first visited Freud in 1907, Freud asked him, "What do you think of transference?" Jung replied, "It is the alpha and omega in treatment." "You have understood," said Freud.

Transference is, of course, a universal phenomenon. When we enter

*Vienna, above in a panorama of 1873, was Freud's home for seventy-eight years.*

a new situation in life, or are confronted by a new person, we bring with us the prejudices of the past and our previous experience of people. These prejudices we project upon the new person. Indeed, getting to know a person is largely a matter of withdrawing projections, of dispelling the smoke screen of what we imagine he is like and replacing it with the reality of what he is actually like. Moreover, we also bring to a new meeting the habitual attitude which our experience of life has taught us to adopt in relation to other people. In the same way, the analytical encounter becomes a microcosm of our previous encounters.

Thus, when a patient comes into an analyst's consulting room, he brings with him all his past anxieties, fears, prejudices, and hopes. If he is habitually dominant, he will tend to be dominant toward the analyst. If he is submissive elsewhere, he will also be so in analysis. The discovery which Freud made was that if these ingrained and generally unconscious attitudes and prejudices can be made conscious, they can be gradually modified. In this way, a person's relation with others can change.

At the time of writing, no psychotherapeutic treatment of any thoroughness can bypass a repeated discussion of the relationship of the patient to the analyst, and of the changes which take place in this relationship as treatment progresses. Once again, we owe the discovery of a powerful therapeutic weapon to Freud's reluctance to become too personally involved with his patients. I do not think that transference would have been so clearly delineated if Freud had been of a warmer, less controlled temperament. The fact that he developed a technique in which he said very little, sat behind the patient, and did not obtrude his personality made him much more of a blank screen than a more active doctor would have been. He therefore tended to receive his patient's projections in a way which a more conventional doctor would not have done. It is the unknown person upon whom we project our phantasies, just as it is the ink blot rather than the highly original painting which stimulates our imagination. Freud discovered that being an enigma to his patients produced material of psychological interest from them.

The opening of the inner phantasy world of patients led to the exploration and investigation of all kinds of psychological material which had hitherto been dismissed as meaningless. The delusions of the insane, the irrational fears with which many people are burdened, and the whole realm of dreams became open to analytical investigation. One of Freud's greatest claims to fame is that he showed a way of making sense out of things which had hitherto been considered nonsensical; and once again, although some of his theories have been superseded and others may yet not survive, his method of investigating such things as dreams and delusions, and the fact that he was able to take them seriously, remains a great achievement.

Freud himself regarded dreams as the royal road to the unconscious. His book on the interpretation of dreams was first published in 1900. To the end of his life he continued to regard it as his most important contribution to the understanding of the human mind. Ernest Jones reports Freud as saying that his two favorite books were *The Interpretation of Dreams* and *Three Essays on the Theory of Sexuality*. Of these two books he said to Ernest Jones: "It seems to be my fate to discover only the obvious, that children have sexual feelings, which every nursemaid knows, and that night dreams are just as much a wish fulfillment as day dreams." *The Interpretation of Dreams* is largely concerned with Freud's own dreams, partly because as a good doctor he was reluctant to reveal too much about his patients, and partly because, for a number of years in the 1890's, he was deeply involved with his own self-analysis. In October, 1897, he wrote a letter to Fliess in which he describes the basic elements of the Oedipus complex: love for the parent of the opposite sex and jealousy of the parent of the same sex. It was from a study of his own dreams that Freud made many of his discoveries. In his preface to the second edition of *The Interpretation of Dreams*, Freud writes: "For me, of course, this book has an additional subjective significance, which I did not understand until after its completion. It reveals itself to me as a piece of self-analysis, as my reaction to the death of my father, that is, to the most important event, the most poignant loss in a man's life."

This is by no means so for every man; and Freud's assumption underlines the point made above, that psychoanalysis was in its original form a father-oriented psychology. Freud, like most other people who became concerned with the treatment of neurotics, had his own share of neurotic symptoms. He suffered from anxiety attacks in which he had a fear of dying, and he was also overanxious about traveling.

*Carl Jung was a disciple and collaborator of Freud's during the years 1907 to 1913. But the two strong-willed men parted bitterly, each to go his own separate way in psychiatric theory.*

In addition, he suffered alternations of mood, being sometimes profoundly distressed, depressed, and unable to work, and, more rarely, full of excitement and self-confidence. During the time of his engagement he was tortured by doubts as to whether his fiancée really loved him. For a long time he could not tolerate any difference on her part between her own opinions and his and demanded that she should be completely identified with him. This may seem odd in a person so much opposed to current opinion and who appears always to have been extremely courageous in asserting his own view as opposed to the popular one; but it is surely endearing and a sign of Freud's basic humanity that in his private life he certainly did demand support, both from his wife and later from his pupils. The world owes a great deal to Freud's basic insecurity.

Like other men of genius, Freud possessed a personality compounded of many opposing strands. Perhaps its oddest and most interesting feature was his inclination to reduce everything to the lowest common factor. Freud's psychology has often been criticized by other people—notably Jung—on the grounds that it leaves little room for human aspiration, or indeed, for human goodness. On analytical investigation even the most self-sacrificing actions tend to be interpreted as distorted self-interest. Freud seemed to take an almost masochistic delight in reducing the whole of human endeavor to basic aggressive or sexual drives of a primitive kind. Psychoanalysis is a caustic discipline which allows little room for altruisim, for romance, or for spirituality. In this connection, it is significant that Freud was so fond of Jewish humor, which often depends upon the deflation of pretension and the reduction of sentiment to self-interest. *Wit and its Relation to the Unconscious,* Freud's study of humor, has many examples of the genre. Here are two he quotes: "Experience consists in experiencing what one does not care to experience." "Human life is divided into two halves. During the first one looks forward to the second, and during the second one looks backward to the first." There is little doubt that it was the deflationary aspect of wit which chiefly appealed to Freud, who had a sardonic edge to his temperament but seldom allowed himself the luxury of making an aggressive remark.

In his personal life Freud was exemplary; he was also inhibited. According to his own account, he had very little sexual experience before marriage, and at the age of forty-one he wrote, "sexual excitation is no more use to a person like me." All through his life, Freud was a fantastically hard worker. While he was in practice in Vienna he might be seeing as many as ten patients in a day, which, as any practicing analyst will aver, is exhausting. He would then have supper with the family and retire to his study to write until one or two in the morning. He had very little time off, and practically his only relaxation was playing cards or visiting museums. Freud had a long life, but even so, the amount of original work which he produced is astonishing, more especially when one remembers that by the time he had produced his most original work, *The Interpretation of Dreams,* he was already forty-four. In fact, he did not embark on his psychological discoveries until he was nearing middle age.

If ever a man was a living example of his own theories, it was Freud. His creative energy and his huge capacity for work were sublimations bought at the expense of inhibiting more primitive drives. The expression of both his sexuality and his aggression was severely inhibited. It is said that the most shattering discovery in his self-analysis was his deeply buried hatred of his father, whom he thought he had deeply admired and respected. Throughout his life Freud was particularly patient, tolerant, and kind. He always denied being a genius on the grounds that geniuses were intolerable in the home. His family, he said, could attest to the fact that he was unusually easy to live with. This was undoubtedly true, but it is probable that it was at the price of a certain lack of playfulness or vitality of a more ordinary kind.

Freud seems to have been a markedly controlled man, to the point where he revealed very little of himself, either to his patients or to his acquaintances. When his work was first beginning to reach a wider audience, he was asked, in 1909, to lecture at Clark University in Worcester, Massachusetts. He traveled across the Atlantic with two colleagues, Jung and Ferenczi; and the three men spent a good deal of their time analyzing each other's dreams. While in New York Freud apparently confided in Jung to the extent of telling him about some of his personal difficulties. An intimate dream came up for discussion and Jung asked for further associations. But Freud refused to give them, saying, so Jung reported, "I can't give you any further associations, for if I did I might lose my authority." Jung's retort was, "Analysis is excellent, except for the analyst." Even those who were his intimates, like Ernest Jones, felt that there were secrets about Freud which they would never know. Jones says of him: "He was beyond doubt someone whose instincts were far more powerful than those of the average man, but whose repressions were even more potent." He also says, "Everything points to a remarkable concealment in Freud's love life." In spite of the fact that aspects of Freud's self-analysis appear in *The Interpretation of Dreams,* there is a great deal about him which we should like to know but which we shall never know. It is very characteristic that his own autobiographical study contains practically nothing about his personal life and is concentrated entirely on the development of psychoanalysis. The man who spent his life investigating the secrets of other people more intimately than any man had done before was very reluctant to reveal his own.

Freud was dogged, persistent, and enormously courageous. For the last sixteen years of his life he was plagued by a painful cancer for which he had many operations. Yet he would allow himself no anodyne beyond an occasional aspirin. "I prefer to think in torment than not to be able to think clearly," he said to Stefan Zweig. In one of his letters he refers to the majority of the human race as trash; perhaps an unexpected sentiment for one who is generally considered a great humanitarian. He had the kindness bred of detachment, and the tolerance of one who has few illusions; but he did not love the human race. On the other hand he was not so entirely pessimistic as is sometimes supposed. Although he did not subscribe to the illusion that psychoanalysis could reform the world, he did believe that truth must ultimately prevail and that our present form of civilization could be replaced by something better. He was himself a man of great honesty and deep integrity. As a form of treatment, psychoanalysis may be superseded. But Freud's discoveries will remain, and his influence can never be eradicated. Thirty years after his death we salute him as the rationalist who taught us that it is the forces of unreason which chiefly govern us; as the pessimist who never gave up hope; as the doctor who never wanted to treat patients, but who was ultimately more help to them than physicians more intent on the direct relief of suffering.

*Freud walks arm in arm with his daughter after his return to England from the U.S. in 1938.*

# MOHANDAS KARAMCHAND
# GANDHI
## 1869-1948

I t is a bitter truism that politics and piety seldom go together. Zealots and messiahs may dictate the course of history, but good men by humanist reckoning, men of simple kindness, are rarely to be found on the hustings or in the seats of power. One legendary exception to this rule is Mohandas Karamchand Gandhi, called to his own distaste Mahatma, or "Great Soul," who founded a political career of almost unparalleled significance upon a personal creed of devout altruism, and who died a genuine martyr to his own ideals. Gandhi was a precursor of prophets, movements, ideologies even, and so compelling was his aura of godliness, so sweet his nature and so persuasive his presence, that the fakir in him has long been elevated above the polemicist and he is remembered everywhere in the world as a sort of saint.

Yet he was a man of ambiguities. His doctrines were not consistent, his methods were often devious, and he owed his political successes as much to the forbearance of his enemies as to the devotion of his friends. Often his conduct strikes a Western observer as amoral in precisely the kind of amorality that we allow only to professional politicians; often his concepts of pacifist protest led directly, as he knew they might, to tragedies of bloodshed. His political perceptions were limited. He was concerned all his life with the dignity of India, understood little of the wider world, and once advised the British to oppose the aggressions of Hitler with nonviolence. He was in many ways the epitome of the crank, dedicated to fads—dietary, economic, social, and sartorial. He could be simply maddening: "The saint has left our

*Mahatma Gandhi smiled for this photograph in 1948, the year of his assassination.*

shores," wrote General Smuts in exasperation, when Gandhi left South Africa for the last time, "I sincerely hope forever."

With it all, M. K. Gandhi, as the Indian historians call him, remains an epochal figure of the twentieth century. "One of the great men of the world," Smuts was later to say. He was great partly by virtue of his political impact: if the emergence of independent India marked the end of the imperial era of history, then Gandhi more than any other man is the creator of the modern world. But more expressly, he was great by virtue of his ideas, which were often muddled and sometimes specious, but which possessed to an astonishing degree the power of inspiration. He was a numinous figure—"like a good night's sleep," is how one contemporary described his presence—and he breathed paradox, puzzle, and surprise. "The cow," Gandhi once wrote in a famous phrase, "is a poem on pity"; and more precisely than any political manifesto perhaps, that single line, so complex, gentle, elegant, and haunting, expresses the elusive fascination of his genius.

*A photograph of Gandhi in about 1887 shows him as a serious young law student.*

He was first of all a rebel, in a plain political sense, and the times were made for him. He was born in 1869 in Porbandar, a small princely state on the seacoast of Gujarat, halfway between Bombay and Karachi: a British subject in the heyday of the British Empire, a Hindu at a time of Hindu humiliation. It was hardly more than a decade since the suppression of the Indian Mutiny, that last revulsion of traditional India against alien modernity; the raj was clamped implacably upon the subcontinent, and more than ever, the values of the Christian West were presented to educated Indians as the *sine qua non* of civilized behavior. Macaulay's celebrated sneer at Indian learning —"astronomy which would move laughter in girls at an English boarding-school, history abounding with kings thirty feet high"—was accepted as dogma not merely by Europeans in India but covertly by many Indians, too, so that the child of a worldly Hindu family was likely to find himself poised between cultures.

Into such a family Gandhi was born. His people were of middle caste—Gandhi means "grocer"—but were powerful in the little milieu of Porbandar. Gandhi's grandfather, uncle, and father were all at one time or another chief ministers of the state, which was one of the innumerable petty principalities allowed an ostensible sovereignty under the suzerain raj. His father was well aware of the advantages of European education: Gandhi learned English in childhood, and soon grasped the fact that in post-Mutiny India temporal success generally depended on Anglicized outlooks. At the same time, the family was devoutly Hindu, Gandhi's mother in particular governing her life by fasts, vows, and principles. Gandhi was married at thirteen, in the Hindu way, and grew up in the intimate knowledge of the Hindu sacred texts. The sectarians called Jains were strong in Gujarat: they combined a tolerance toward other faiths, including Moslems and Christians, with a belief in the sanctity of all forms of life, and their ideas were to influence Gandhi always.

So there was an early dichotomy to Gandhi's thought. When, aged nineteen, he sailed away to England to read law at the Inner Temple in London, the stresses of this duality came to the surface. His child-wife had to be left behind, and Gandhi was obliged to swear on oath never to touch women, wine, or meat. Even so, we are told, the elders of his community declared the sea voyage impious. Gandhi set off into the world a true figure of his own nation: in the one half of him, passionately dedicated to the oldest tenets of Hindu civilization; in the other, so dazzled by the confidence of the West that almost as soon as he landed in London he dressed himself in spats and wing collars and began a course of dancing lessons.

Then as now, London combined liberal urbanity with insular arrogance, but in those days it was also the central capital of the world. In a real but inner sense, Gandhi was always to remain a Londoner. There he acquired a wry affection for the British that was to survive all life's experiences, and that was bemusedly reciprocated, on and off. There he absorbed the classic theories of British parliamentary democracy, and so came to realize, perhaps instinctively, that the British Empire itself was an equivocation. Its global power was sustained by physical force—"India has been won by the sword," as the Governor General Lord Ellenborough had said, "and must be kept by the sword." Yet it was publicly dedicated to the idea of liberty, and possessed, buried away among the domes and pageantries of Whitehall, a humane and liberal heart. "Let it still be the boast of Britain," wrote Raffles of Singapore, "to write her name in characters of light."

*By 1897 Gandhi was a successful young lawyer in Durban, South Africa.*

If to its cruder practitioners the British Empire was merely a power system, or an economic device, to many other Britons it was a trusteeship, whose task it was to teach other peoples how to live, and eventually to hand over power to the subject races. For every imperialist bully in the field, there was a sensitive mind in London who was debating the rights and wrongs of imperial dominance. If capitalism was one strain of empire, and chauvinism another, a third was evangelicalism. Gandhi was quick to recognize all this, from his vantage point in the imperial capital; and in the end it was this very imperial conflict, this cross-bench ideology of empire, that alone enabled him to apply religious concepts to political ends, and so achieve a universal influence.

Gandhi first clashed with the British Empire in South Africa, and there, too, he discovered both his passionate nationalism (the politician in him) and his gifts of inspiration (the mark of the saint). Called to the bar in 1891, he went to Durban as legal adviser to an

Indian firm operating in Natal and the Transvaal. In South Africa the fundamental racialism of empire first revealed itself to him—"what *is* Empire," Lord Rosebery once asked, "but the predominance of race?" He experienced all the petty degradations of racial bigotry, from poll taxes to insults on railways trains, zoning restrictions to conveniently full hotels, and in angry reflex his legal career soon developed political purposes.

Most of the Indians in South Africa had first gone there as indentured laborers, and they were still treated with contempt. For twenty years Gandhi worked for them, without ever really succeeding. The Indians were never admitted to equality with the whites, and to this day they live in South Africa on sufferance, in a limbo between the races. But in Africa Gandhi forged his life's weapons. Even there, at the start of his revolutionary career, his objects were as much social as political. He was fighting not for the independence of a nation but for the dignity of a people. This was essentially a struggle of conscience, and Gandhi was not yet evoking nationalist passions. On the contrary, he repeatedly declared himself a loyal subject of the British Empire, and during the Boer War he raised an Indian ambulance unit to serve with the British Army: he spent six weeks in the field, and got a medal for it.

Nevertheless, during his years in Africa he began to discard the British veneer he had picked up in London. To be the spokesman of a minority required strength of mind, tenacity, endless self-discipline; and it was in the roots of his Hinduism, not in the practice of the stiff upper lip, that he found the power. He had always been a vegetarian and a teetotaler. Now he gave up milk, too, ate ever more austerely, experimented, like his mother, with fasts and vows. He made Monday a day of silence. He mended his own clothes. Finally, in 1906, he took a vow of complete sexual abstinence—thus stifling, he tells us in his autobiography, almost irrepressible instincts of lust. He read widely in the moralities. Tolstoy greatly influenced him, and Ruskin's call for a return to medieval simplicities struck a chord in his own nature. He had never been a large man; now, in his thirties, he began to look elegantly frail—rather elfin in appearance, in his high white collar and his tight trousers, and also distinctly urbane.

These personal philosophies he projected into a wider sphere, intending always to give the Indian minority more confidence, greater bargaining power, and a better sense of unity. Following Tolstoy's example, he established farm settlements, where followers lived a strict kibbutz life based on common self-discipline: manual labor was compulsory, smoking and drinking were forbidden, clothes were homemade, and celibacy was, if not a requirement of residence, at least a recommendation of zeal. He evolved the technique of passive resistance, as a means of political protest. Recognizing the impossible physical odds against the Indians, and perceiving that tolerance was the Achilles' heel of British imperial rule, he taught his people to defy iniquitous laws innocently: to break the rules openly, to court arrest, and so by simplicity of behavior and acceptance of consequences, at once to give publicity to wrongs and shame authority into reform.

Hundreds of Indians were imprisoned in the course of the campaigns, and Gandhi himself spent an aggregate of 249 days in jail. Starting sporadically with groups of zealous adherents, the movement became a mass protest. Gandhi, finding himself the unchallenged leader of the South African Indians, and a figure not to be ignored in the highest imperial councils, seems now to have realized his own power, and presently he gave it form. His system was a conglomeration of quirks, dogmas, foibles, contradictions—political aspirations, social theories, religious precepts, racial pride, personal intuition—but he rationalized it into a single metaphysic, and called it *Satyagraha*. This was the truth-force that was Gandhi's chief contribution to political practice. It was to remain the driving force of his activities, personal and public, for the rest of his life.

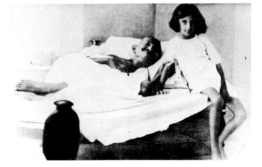

*Satyagraha* was active nonviolence, the spiritual energy that would prove in the end to be stronger than physical force, and it embraced not only the power of aspiration but also the power of suffering. Nothing could be more different

*Six-year-old Indira Gandhi, India's prime minister today, visited the Mahatma's bedside during his twenty-one-day fast in New Delhi in 1924.*

from the opposing ideology, the idea of imperialism—which was, however benevolent, essentially a glorification of strength. *"Satyagraha,"* Gandhi wrote, "postulates the conquest of an adversary by suffering in one's own person." Armed with this incalculable device, and experienced now in the ways of empire, Gandhi sailed from South Africa for the last time in 1914, and presently returned to Gujarat to apply his practices to more tremendous ends.

Gandhi's struggle against the raj in India, whose purpose was to broaden from the political particular to the humanist general, lasted more than thirty years. In the early years he was scarcely a nationalist in the modern sense. He believed in the Empire and supported the British cause in the 1914 war: he raised another ambulance unit, and though incapacitated himself by an attack of pleurisy, was awarded the Kaiser-i-Hind gold medal for his services. He did not want India to leave the Empire, only to take an honorable self-governing place within it, like Canada or Australia.

Indian protest then took two chief forms. On the one hand were groups of extreme Hindus and Moslems, generally antipathetic to each other, who worked for theocratic revivals and the expulsion of alien forms. On the other were the constitutionalists of the Indian National Congress, founded by a Scotsman in 1883 to work toward the parliamentary independence of India under the crown. Gandhi adopted a position that straddled the two. He believed, like the Congress, in constitutional progress, but he was ever more devoted to the ideal of an Indian India, honoring Indian customs, living in an Indian way, home-grown, home-educated, self-sustaining. And to these two impulses of rebellion he added a third of his own, the notion of *swaraj,* or independence—not only independence in a political sense but

*The last British viceroy of India, Lord Mountbatten, stands with his wife and Gandhi in the gardens of the viceregal palace in March, 1947.*

moral independence or self-sufficiency. In his view, national and individual dignity, political and personal morality, were indistinguishable, and his techniques embraced them all. *Satyagraha* itself, that potent new political weapon, was no more than moral restraint—nothing but a new name, said the Mahatma, for "the law of suffering."

More and more, too, Gandhi concerned himself with social reform—as a side issue of nationalist politics, as a cause in itself. Devout Hindu though he was, he pragmatically pursued his own convictions, distilled from such disparate sources as the New Testament, Shelley, Thoreau, the Book of Daniel, and the teaching of the Jains. He took up the cause of the Untouchables, to the horror of the orthodox. He made the practice of loom weaving and the wearing of homespun clothing (khadi) tokens of all his purposes. Pacifist Hindu though he was, he made common cause with the most virulent Moslem independence group, the Khilafat Movement. He argued passionately against the industrialization of India and established a celebrated ashrama, or communal hermitage, outside Ahmadabad, where his followers dedicated their lives to his ideals.

To the Indian masses he became semidivine. They believed him capable of miraculous feats, like flying or vanishing, and at the peak of his powers his hold over their emotions was absolute. His methods were often theatrical, or ostentatious in their humility. He adopted the fast, for instance, not merely as self-mortification but as a sort of political blackmail, so that the British authorities were repeatedly embarrassed by the prospect of this charismatic patriot dying on their hands. He gave up European clothes altogether and was seen only in homespun dhoti and sandals. He gave up all possessions, too, and lived in absolute poverty, even forswearing the hospitality of the rich.

If he looked frail in South Africa, by the 1930's in India he looked almost insubstantial: a little hunched spidery figure in white, walking with a stick taller than himself, his round steel-rimmed glasses perched upon a protuberant nose, his toothless smile sweeping with a self-deprecatory charm right and left. This queer image, projected partly by hearsay and legend, partly by skillful publicity, became familiar in every last village of India, and to most of his compatriots Gandhi stood alone. He was known everywhere affectionately as Gandhiji or reverently as Mahatma, and his word was law to half of India. Even the hardheaded politicians of the Congress, men as sophisticated as Nehru or Jinnah, acknowledged his ascendancy and regarded him as a kind of permanent *supremo*. Gandhi became, like Mother India herself, a myth figure—an Absolute, to whom millions of Indians of all ranks felt themselves personally in thrall.

As for the British, the rulers, they soon realized his significance. Puzzled as they were by Gandhi's eccentricities, baffled by his permutations of thought, attracted despite themselves by his fun and piquant charm, they knew him to be the most potent threat to their authority since 1857. For the thread upon which he hung all his activities, idealist or opportunist, social or patriotic, was opposition to the raj. If he wished Hindus and Moslems to live in friendship, it was partly for love's sake, but partly for political cohesion. If he encouraged khadi and cottage industries, it was partly because bucolic was best, but partly because a rural textile industry might release India from the hold of the Lancashire cotton magnates. *Satyagraha* might be moral restraint; it was also an effective system of political attrition.

*The wearing of homespun clothing became a token of all Gandhi's purposes in India. Above, he is at a spinning wheel in the Untouchables' colony in 1940.*

As the years passed, Gandhi's view of empire shifted, until he came to believe—or at least to declare—that the British presence in India was evil in itself and that India could only be regenerated by a complete break from London. It was only gradually, though, that he assumed this stance, and only by strikes, demonstrations, and lesser protests that he became the undisputed leader of a mass revolutionary movement—"the awakening of the masses," as he phrased it. His life was a long experiment. He was prepared to try almost anything, and to make a test case of almost any issue. Sometimes the gesture was obscure: he first achieved national fame as champion of the Bihar indigo tenants, a class of citizen nine out of ten Indians had never heard of. Sometimes it was inflammatory: his support for the Khalifat cause, for example, was steeped in violence, bigotry, and conspiracy. Sometimes it was flamboyant, like the Salt March of 1930, in which Gandhi, progressing triumphantly to the seashore in his native Gujarat, ceremoniously scooped some salt from the water's edge to symbolize the iniquity of the government's salt tax.

At other times, ironically, he was a formal participant in neodiplomatic exchanges. He negotiated directly with viceroys. He lunched with the king of England (asked if he had felt himself to be properly dressed, he replied that "King George wore enough for both of us"). He went to England as supreme Indian representative to the Round Table Conference of 1930—a meeting that, it was falsely hoped by the British, would finally chart India's constitutional progress toward self-government. He was recognized everywhere as the ex officio spokesman of India. Every important visitor to India wanted to meet Gandhi, and all over the world he acquired followers and imitators.

Yet all this he achieved through the cramped medium of nationalist agitation. His often squalid instruments were strikes, voluntary imprisonments, fasts "to the death," "civil disobedience," strokes of publicity, and propaganda. By 1939 his hostility to the British Empire was so absolute that he refused to support the war against Hitler, and at Britain's most difficult moment, in 1940, he sponsored a "Quit India" movement to embarrass her still further. After the war, when independence came at last, Gandhi never accepted the partition of India, played little part in the final negotiations, and boycotted the independence celebrations in Delhi.

Gandhi's few personal possessions, photographed after his assassination, include his spectacles, watch, and wooden sandals, bowls and spoons, a favorite book of songs, and a trio of monkeys: "See no evil, hear no evil, speak no evil."

His last months were spent in a final, dying attempt to reconcile a divided India, by then, as the British prepared to depart, caught in a maelstrom of sectarian jealousy and recrimination. He quelled a terrible riot in Calcutta by declaring a death fast; another fast he ended only when all the political leaders of Delhi—Hindu, Sikh, and Moslem—swore at his bedside to work for harmony. And so towering was his stature still, so fearful the passions he sought to calm, that on January 30, 1948, he was shot dead in a Delhi public garden on his way to lead the people in prayer. He was always a man of ironies, and it was a properly Gandhian paradox that his assassin should turn out to have been a man of his own faith, avenging not warfare or oppression but tolerance.

Gandhi was an enigma, especially to his opponents. From first to last the British were never quite sure what to make of him—and they are still in the same quandary, as a continuing flow of literature confirms. Sometimes they parleyed with him. Sometimes they imprisoned him. Sometimes they tried to ignore him. Sometimes they invited him to their palaces. Many recognized in him a true nobility. Others thought him a pure charlatan. When, in 1921, he received his first Indian jail sentence, the young British judge said in passing sentence: "Even those who differ from you in politics look upon you as a man of high ideals and of noble and even saintly life. . . . if the course of events in India should make it possible for the Government to reduce the period [of imprisonment] and release you, no one will be better pleased than I." On the other hand, when Gandhi entered formal negotiations with the viceroy Lord Irwin in 1931, Winston Churchill declared in a still more famous judgment: "It is alarming and also nauseating to see Mr. Gandhi, a seditious Middle Temple lawyer, now posing as a fakir of a type well-known in the East, striding half-naked up the steps of the vice-regal palace, while he is still organizing and conducting a defiant campaign of civil disobedience, to parley on equal terms with the representative of the King–Emperor."

He was from another world—as Nehru remarked of him, "through his eyes the unknown stared out at us." Simple people everywhere responded to him. "He spoke to them in their own language," Rabindranath Tagore wrote. "Here was living truth at last, and not quotations from books." In Lancashire the millworkers, though threatened with unemployment by his activities, welcomed him with familiar affection. Children loved him, as he loved them—"Hey, Gandhi," a Cockney urchin once amused him by yelling across a London pavement, "where's your trousers?" With his absolute disregard for rank or protocol, his contempt for wealth and trumped-up glory, he spoke for the dispossessed everywhere in cutting the mighty down to size.

Yet the ambiguities nagged. Repeatedly Gandhi was warned, by friends and enemies alike, that *Satyagraha* must lead to bloodshed. And so it did, most horribly in the 1919 Amritsar massacre, when mob violence resulted in the slaughter of 323 people by British Indian soldiers—probably the worst act of bloodshed in the whole history of the Empire. Gandhi well understood the dangers he was arousing in inflaming the masses, but he repeatedly took the risk. "I knew I was playing with fire," he wrote after the killing of twenty-two policemen by a mob in 1922. "I had either to submit to a system which I consider has done an irreparable harm to my country, or incur the risk of the mad fury of my people bursting forth when they understood the truth from my lips." Though Gandhi treated his adversaries on one level with unvarying fairness and courtesy, on another he was prepared to cheat them with cheap politician's tricks.

In many respects he was also a failure. He thought so himself, and he was right. Most of his mass campaigns ended in chaos or humiliation. As the Communist R. Palme Dutt has written of him, his name was "the best guarantee of the shipwreck of any mass movement that had the blessing of his association." His work for the Indians in South Africa made little lasting difference to their lot. His efforts to keep India united in independence ended only in partition, the most terrible of Hindu–Moslem riots, and a state of semiwar between India and Pakistan that has lasted ever since. He failed in his quixotic attempts to turn the Indian clock back, to demolish the factories and return the technicians to the fields. Even his campaigns to raise his people to a higher plane of national morality—*Satyagraha* in its loftiest sense—may raise a horselaugh today among observers of the Indian scene.

Yet in his prime political purpose he majestically succeeded. More than any other man, it was he who set India free, and so ended the era in which the peoples of western Europe imposed their views, their patterns, and their disciplines upon the colored peoples of the world.

More still, he succeeded symbolically. The fight for the liberation of India was, like the Spanish Civil War, the Algerian War, or Vietnam, one of those political struggles that epitomize the moral climate of the day. When we look back at Gandhi's life now, those distant diagrams of politics look blurred indeed; the constitutional issues of British India have lost their meaning, the gilded line of viceroys has faded into sepia. Only the Mahatma is left in brilliant relief against a shadowy background.

To Gandhi the field of nationalist revolution was essentially a proving ground, and patriotism was never an end in itself. That he succeeded as a nationalist was due largely to the sophistication of his opponents—a harsher empire would have shot him, a cruder one might have been less beguiled. He and the British were not really enemies. Gandhi always thought the best of Englishmen, and on the centenary of Gandhi's birth, in 1969, the British issued a postage stamp in his honor.

No, it is not as a nationalist that he will be longest remembered, but as a revolutionary, a liberator in a much more fundamental sense. He was concerned far more with the quality than with the pattern of life, and was one of those perennial mystics who, once or twice in a millennium, demonstrate to the world the power of immaterialism. Through all the contortions of his thinking, the sophisms and the casuistries, come messages that are clear, true, and timeless. Gandhi preached, above all, simplicity. "I do not believe that multiplication of wants, and machinery contrived to supply them, is taking the world a step nearer the goal. . . . India's salvation consists in unlearning what she has learnt in the last 50 years. The railways, telegraphs, hospitals, lawyers, doctors and such like have all got to go." This was the meaning of his crankier obsessions, and though it has not dissuaded India from proceeding headlong toward industrialization, nor persuaded the great Indian tycoons into khadi and communal asceticism, still we may recognize the legacies of the idea in the gentler philosophies of the young today, with their scorn, however transient, for material possessions, their backpacks, and their bearded poverty.

The nature of pacifism, too, has been transformed by Gandhi's practices. What was a religio-political dogma has become a life style, and nonviolence is no longer a curious Oriental device, but an instrument of persuasion throughout the Western world—wherever, in fact, authority is sufficiently humane to make it practicable. Its combination of sanctimony and infuriation is as telling now as it was in the hands of its great originator; now as then, it is vulnerable to manipulation, and tainted all too often by self-deception, for as Gandhi well knew, violence is a passion plucked from nowhere, by the best of causes and the kindliest of seers.

Civil rights, women's lib, conservation, the folk revival, the hippies, birth control, nuclear disarmament—in all these contemporary movements we may see reflected still the example of Gandhi, sometimes avowedly, sometimes without acknowledgment. Most paradoxically of all, Gandhism has helped to foster a strain of anarchy, even nihilism, that has played an important part in the genesis of today's New Left. Nothing, one supposes, would have surprised the Mahatma more. He was a man of order above all—not the order of authority, but order self-imposed: the order of religious restraint, the self-discipline of the silent Monday, the self-imposed tasks of spinning wheel and household chore, the fast, the celibacy, the hour of prayer.

Transmuted decades later by followers far away, fused with the very different reasoning of men like Kropotkin, Mao, and Marcuse, these ideals of individual responsibility have emerged in other forms. Gandhi's severely personal eccentricities have become a revulsion against conventions of any sort. His simple equalitarianism has become a distrust of all institutions. His austere paths of *swaraj* and *Satyagraha* are called "doing your own thing," and his pragmatic Hinduism, lifelong and heartfelt, has developed into a still vaguer altruism, without priesthood, prayer, or ritual.

At the heart of these hazed consequences, nevertheless, there stands a solid lesson. Gandhi proved once more the temporal power of spirituality. He achieved all by faith, only intermittently supplemented by guile, and faced with the greatest of worldly opponents, against all the stacked forces of power, wealth, prejudice, even logic, he emerged victorious. It is hard to write of Gandhi without emotion, or to read the story of his life's long pilgrimage without a tear in the eye. He behaved foolishly often, and sometimes perhaps dishonestly, but no public figure of our times has had more magnificent intentions. "What I want to achieve," he wrote in 1925, at the height of his struggles against the raj, when he had already been jailed and hero-worshiped, hailed as a saint and derided as a fake, sneered at by cartoonists, consulted by viceroys; when millions believed him capable of supernatural feats, and millions more thought him faintly comic—"what I want to achieve, what I have been striving and pining to achieve these thirty years, is . . . to see God face to face."

*During his lifetime Gandhi was considered semidivine by the Indian masses. The statue above stands in the pantheon of deities sculptured in a Hindu temple.*

# ALBERT
# EINSTEIN
## 1879-1955

"I have no particular talent, I am merely extremely inquisitive," Einstein remarked one day to a friend who asked him to speculate on the source of genius that had led him to be hailed as one of the immortal scientists of all time. Others included, of course, Sir Isaac Newton, who was extremely inquisitive about falling apples and planetary ellipses, and Charles Darwin, who was extremely inquisitive about the variant sculpture of finches' beaks on the Galápagos Islands. And what was Einstein extremely inquisitive about? "I want to know how God created this world."

Each member of that supreme triune of science pursued in his own way an identical goal, which was to discover the underlying order and architecture of the universe. Newton believed in an Old Testament deity who not only had created the cosmos but ran it by means of the mysterious, omnipresent force of gravitation. The third book of his *Principia* opens with the thunderous sentence: "I now demonstrate the frame of the system of the world." Darwin, a more modest man who omitted God from his masterwork, *The Origin of Species*, nonetheless sounds the same chord, pianissimo, in his classic coda, where he contemplates a "tangled bank, clothed with many plants of many kinds, with birds singing on the bushes, with various insects crawling through the damp earth," and reflects that "there is a grandeur in this view of life . . . that whilst this planet has gone cycling on according to the fixed law of gravity, from so simple a beginning endless forms have been and are being evolved." Einstein, who narrowly lost an academic post because he had proclaimed himself an "unbeliever,"

*Albert Einstein, already famous, was photographed near the end of World War I.*

By LINCOLN BARNETT

gazed out beyond Newton into the vast milky thickets of the galaxies and inward, deeper than Darwin, into the unseen, ineffable web of the atom.

"My religion," Einstein observed, "consists of a humble admiration of the illimitable superior spirit who reveals himself in the slight details we are able to perceive with our frail and feeble minds. That deeply emotional conviction of the superior reasoning power which is revealed in the incomprehensible universe forms my idea of God." It was this conviction that isolated Einstein in his later years from the amphitheatre of modern physics, which he had so brilliantly illuminated in the dawn light of the twentieth century. To his dying day Albert Einstein believed in causality, the mainspring of Newton's world, and rejected as a temporary compromise the statistical and indeterminate approach of modern quantum mechanics. "God is subtle," he declared, "but he is not malicious."

Einstein was only twenty-six when, as a bored, unhappily married, poorly paid clerk in the Swiss patent office at Berne, he produced in one year—1905, his *annus mirabilis*—three papers, any one of which would have assured him a place in the annals of science. The first analyzed Brownian (molecular) motion in stationary fluids. The second reinforced Newton's corpuscular theory of light and defined the interplay of matter and energy in the puzzling phenomenon known as the "photoelectric effect"—a study that not only added new concepts to Max Planck's quantum theory but also laid the groundwork for television and the laser and won Einstein the Nobel Prize in 1921.

*This photograph shows Einstein and his sister Maja. Only two years his junior, Maja was Albert's constant companion and confidant.*

Einstein's third paper, amplifying Newton's fundamental concepts of space, time, and mass, and stretching man's perceptions of his world into new domains beyond the horizon of the human sensorium—the realm of the infinite and infinitesimal, the macrocosm and the microcosm, of stupendous velocities approaching the speed of light, and apocalyptic temperatures like those in the interior of stars—became famous as the special theory of relativity.

Although this third and most revolutionary paper of the year 1905 was ignored by the Nobel Prize jury, and although it was bitterly attacked as illogical, incomprehensible, crazy, and perhaps an insidious Jewish assault on Christian dogma and common sense, it stands unshaken today beside Newton's and Darwin's insights.

Pragmatically, Einstein's paper on special relativity changed human history. Its crucial and climactic equation, $E = mc^2$, exploded the atomic bomb and remains the classic, precise, elegant, and compact expression of all transformations of matter and energy. Einstein's vision neither revokes nor repudiates Newton's laws, which laid the basis for the Industrial Revolution and stand valid for every ordinary mechanical operation from the flight of a Frisbee to that of a lunar module. What Einstein did was to generalize and extrapolate Newtonian precepts into a wider spectrum encompassing the extremes of both outer space and the atom.

Historians of science who chisel away at strata of heredity and environment for clues to the rock beds of dormant genius find little in Einstein's background to aid them. He was born in Ulm on March 14, 1879, the son of Hermann Einstein, whose hard-working, semi-prosperous forebears had lived in southwest Germany near the Swiss border since the 1750's, and of Pauline Koch of nearby Stuttgart. Einstein's father, a genial, rather happy-go-lucky man, ran a small electrical and engineering workshop, which failed a year after Albert's birth, forcing him to move his family and business from Ulm to Munich. Einstein's mother imparted to her son a love of music that was to endure as an important part of his life. When asked from which parent he inherited his enormous talents, Einstein more than once replied, "I think we can dispense with this question of heritage."

Only a few glimpses of Einstein's formative years survive. One incident that might be compared to the fall of Newton's apple occurred when Albert, at the age of five, had his first look at a pocket compass. The persistent pointing of the compass needle in the same direction convinced him that it was responding to unseen forces acting upon it from outer, supposedly empty space. What were those forces? What was space?

At ten Einstein entered the Luitpold Gymnasium in Munich. On being issued his first copy of Euclid's text on plane geometry he read it overnight, cover to cover, with breathless excitement and total recall. Yet Einstein hated the gymnasium. He performed indifferently in any subject that failed to absorb his deepest interest. When his father asked the headmaster what calling young Albert should pursue, the reply was, "It doesn't matter; he'll never make a success of anything." For the rest of his life Einstein remembered with deep distaste the ruthless discipline, physical force, fear, and insensitive authority that he associated with the gymnasium, German education, and the German mentality in general. However, on the credit side, the experience endowed him with a distrust of educational dogma and a skepticism that led him to question all the absolutes of science—and of any domain of thought.

In 1896, when he was sixteen, Einstein entered the Swiss Federal Polytechnic School in Zurich. It was a time of transition in science. Paradoxes had appeared—unexpected phenomena and inconsistencies that, though small, troubled physicists who had grown up believing in the immutability of Newtonian law. The work of the great Scottish physicist James Clerk Maxwell had disclosed the relationship of electricity and magnetism and shown that light is simply a narrow, visible band-width in a vast range of unseen radiation that pervades the universe. The German physicist Max Planck was puzzling over certain problems of radiant energy that led to publication of his revolutionary quantum theory in 1900, postulating that all forms of radiation, including light, must be conceived not as waves but as discrete, or discontinuous, pulses of energy. These shattering events in the world of science intoxicated Einstein's intense, inquiring mind.

"When young," Einstein later recalled, "I used to go away for weeks in a state of confusion, as one who at that time had yet to overcome the stage of stupefaction in his first encounter with such questions." And a longtime friend, Janos Plesch, recalled that Einstein hovered continually on the brink of a serious breakdown, partly nervous, partly digestive. "As his mind knows no limits, so his body allows no set rules. He sleeps until he is wakened; he stays awake until he is told to go to bed; he will go hungry until he is given something to eat; and then he eats until he is stopped."

Absorbed as he was in physical and metaphysical speculations, he did not distinguish himself in the required curriculum of the Zurich school. He often gave faculty members an impression of callow, supercilious, and somewhat overbearing conceit—quite in contrast to the gentle, kindly image of his declining years. Once on a geologic field trip his professor asked, "Now Einstein, how do the strata run from here? From below upward or vice versa?" Bored, Einstein replied, "It is pretty much the same to me whichever way they run." He also irritated his physics professor by addressing him as Herr Weber rather than Herr Professor. Although he graduated in August, 1900, with grades good enough to warrant the academic appointment he had expected, Professor Weber blackballed him, and Einstein found himself, as he wrote years later, "suddenly abandoned by everyone, standing at a loss on the threshold of life." In a way his rejection proved a boon, for he had detested academic discipline, and when he began work in the Swiss patent office at Berne in June, 1902, he found himself in a quiet atmosphere with regular hours, undemanding duties, and above all, "an opportunity to think about physics" and metaphysics.

Questions involving the relationship between the observer and "the outer world," between subject and object, had haunted philosophical thinkers since the dawn of human conjecture. Twenty-three centuries before Einstein the Greek philosopher Democritus wrote: "Sweet and bitter, cold and warm, as well as all the colors, all these things exist but in opinion and not in reality." And in the seventeenth century the great German mathematician Leibnitz wrote, "I am able to prove that not only light, color, heat, and the like, but motion, shape and extension too are mere apparent qualities." Just as our visual sense, for example, tells us that a golf ball is white, so vision abetted by our sense of touch tells us that it is also round, smooth, and small—qualities that have no more reality, independent of our senses, than the quality that we define by convention as white. Thus, gradually, philosophers and scientists together arrived at the startling conclusion that since every object is simply the sum of its qualities, and since qualities exist only in the mind, the whole objective universe from atoms to stars exists only as an edifice of conventional symbols shaped by the senses of man.

Speculations such as these played an important role in the train of logic that led eventually to the theory of relativity, wherein Einstein showed that even space and time are forms of intuition, which can no more be divorced from consciousness than our concepts of color, shape, or size can. Space has no objective reality except as an order or arrangement of the objects we perceive in it, and time has no independent existence apart from the order of events by which we measure it.

The philosophical basis of relativity was thus already in the air during the seminal period during which Einstein, who by now had taken out Swiss citizenship and had married a fellow student from the Polytechnic—a Serbian girl named Mileva Maric—was pursuing his leisurely duties at the patent office and reading physics nights and Sundays. Along with the contemplation of space and time, he found himself equally absorbed by new developments in the exploration of the microcosm: it was becoming apparent that the classic picture of the atom as the solid foundation stone of matter was inaccurate. The atom, it seemed, was a complex structure, composed of still smaller units endowed not only with mass but with an electric charge.

*Einstein was an indifferent student at the Swiss Federal Polytechnic School.*

But the event that inspired Einstein's first, great Nobel-Prize–winning treatise was the publication by Max Planck of the quantum theory in 1900. Laboratory physicists had long observed that when heated bodies became incandescent, they emitted a glow that turned successively from red to orange to yellow and then to white as the temperature increased. Many efforts were made to formulate a law defining how the amount of radiant energy given off by such heated bodies varied with wave length and temperature. All attempts failed until Planck found by mathematical means an equation that satisfied the results of experimentation. Planck's discovery—or assumption—was that radiant energy is emitted not in an unbroken stream but in discontinuous bits or portions, which he termed "quanta."

The far-reaching implications of Planck's conjecture did not become apparent until 1905 when Einstein, almost alone among contemporary physicists, saw its significance and carried the quantum theory into a new domain. Planck had believed he was simply evolving a correct mathematical formulation of the laws of radiation by his assumption of a discontinuous process of energy emission. But Einstein postulated that *all* forms of radiant energy—not only heat, but light, X rays, radio waves—actually travel through space in separate and discontinuous quanta.

He substantiated his idea by evolving a law accurately defining the puzzling phenomenon known as the photoelectric effect. Physicists had been at a loss to explain the fact that when a beam of pure violet light shines on a metal plate, the plate ejects a shower of electrons. If light of a lower frequency, like yellow or red, falls on the plate, electrons will again be ejected but at reduced velocities. The vehemence with which electrons are torn from the metal depends only on the color of the light and not on the intensity. If the light source is removed a certain distance and dimmed, the electrons that pop forth are fewer in number but their velocity is undiminished. The action is instantaneous even when the light fades to imperceptibility.

Einstein decided that these effects could be explained only by supposing that all light is composed of individual particles or grains of energy, which he called "photons," and that when one of them hits an electron the resulting action is comparable to the impact of two billiard balls. He reasoned further that photons of violet, ultraviolet, X rays, and other forms of high-frequency (i.e., short wave-length) radiation contain more energy than red and infrared (longer wave-length) photons, and that the velocity with which each electron flies from the metal plate is proportional to the energy content of the photon that strikes it. The expression of these principles profoundly influenced later work in quantum physics and spectroscopy, as well as leading to the development of television and all other applications of the photoelectric cell.

At the time he could not know what immense problems were to arise in the microcosm. So after submitting his first great paper, he turned his attention away from the infinitesimal and directed his gaze outward to the stars and beyond them to the vast drowned depths of empty space and time.

The problems of space and time are inextricably linked with the physical fact of motion, a subject that preoccupied Newton in the composition of his *Principia*. Newton had observed that on a calm day at sea a sailor, situated below decks, can perform manual tasks or drink soup as comfortably as when his ship is lying motionless in the harbor. The water in his basin, the soup in his bowl, will remain unruffled whether the ship is making 5 knots or 25 knots. Unless he peers out at the sea it will be impossible for him to know how fast his ship is moving, or indeed, if it is moving at all. If the sea should grow rough or the ship change course abruptly, he will then sense his state of motion. But granted the idealized condition of a glass-calm sea and a silent ship, nothing that happens below decks—no amount of mechanical experimentation performed *inside* the ship—will disclose its velocity through the sea. The physical principle involved was formulated by Newton into what is known today as the Newtonian relativity principle: "The motions of bodies included in a given space are the same among themselves, whether that space is at rest or moves uniformly forward in a straight line."

The ship Newton had in mind was the earth. For all ordinary purposes the earth may be regarded as a stationary system, upon which mountains, trees, and houses stand at rest and on which animals, automobiles, and airplanes move. But Einstein knew that to the astronomer the earth, far from being at rest, is whirling through space in a most complex fashion. In addition to its daily rotation on its axis at 1,000 miles an hour, and its annual revolution around the sun at 20 miles a second, the earth is involved in a number of less familiar gyrations. The entire solar system is moving within the local star system at the rate of 13 miles a second; the local star system is moving within the Milky Way at 200 miles a second; and the whole Milky Way is drifting with respect to remote eternal galaxies at 100 miles a second—all in different directions.

Although he could not know the full complexity of the earth's movements, Newton was nevertheless troubled by the problem of distinguishing relative motion from true, or "absolute," motion in a confusing universe. He suggested that "in the remote regions of the fixed stars or perhaps far beyond them, there may be some body absolutely at rest." While admitting there was no way of proving this by any celestial object within man's view, Newton thought that space itself might serve as a fixed frame of reference within which the wheeling of the earth and the visible rotation of the constellations around the polestar could be related in terms of absolute motion. He regarded space as a physical reality, stationary and immovable.

It was this fundamental assumption that Einstein challenged. With the development of the wave theory of light, physicists could only postulate that if light consisted of waves, there must be some medium to support these waves, just as water propagates the waves of the sea and air transmits sound. When experiments showed that light can travel in a vacuum, scientists invented a hypothetical substance, invisible and pervading all space, which they called the "luminiferous ether." Later, Faraday suggested that the ether must also be the carrier of electric and magnetic forces. When Maxwell finally identified light as an electromagnetic disturbance, the case for the ether seemed assured. The end product of classical physics was thus a universe permeated with an impalpable medium through which the stars wandered unimpeded and light and all forms of radiation traveled like vibrations in a bowl of jelly. The ether supplied the fixed frame of reference, the absolute space that Newton's cosmology required. Yet the existence of this hypothetical medium had never been proved.

To determine if the ether existed, two American physicists, Albert A. Michelson and Edward W. Morley, performed an epochal experiment in Cleveland in 1887. They reasoned that if all space is simply a tranquil sea of ether, then the earth's motion through that sea should be detectable and measurable and the velocity of light should be affected by the ether stream engendered by the earth's movement. Thus a light ray projected in the direction of the earth's movement should be slightly retarded by the ether flow, just as a boat going upstream is retarded by the current. Conversely, it should be slightly accelerated when projected aft in the wake of the earth's passage through the ether. The difference would be very small, for the velocity of light is 186,284 miles a second, while the velocity of the earth in its orbit around the sun is only 20 miles a second. Hence, a light ray sent forward, or against the ether stream, should travel at 186,264 miles a second, while one sent after, or with the ether stream, should be clocked at 186,304 miles a second.

To test this theory, Michelson and Morley constructed an instrument of such great delicacy that it could detect a variation of even a fraction of a mile per second in the enormous velocity of light. The experiment was carried out and the result was: absolutely no difference in the velocity of the light beams regardless of direction.

The discovery threw classical physics into a state of chaos, for science now had to choose between two embarrassing alternatives. It could scrap the ether, which had provided a medium for the propagation of light and all forms of electromagnetic radiation. Or if it retained the ether concept, it would have to conclude that the earth stands still. The dilemma was not resolved until 1905, when Einstein, who had pondered the problem for at least a decade, suddenly poured forth in the space of six weeks his special theory of relativity. He had never accepted the ether concept nor the idea of absolute space as a fixed system or framework within which it is possible to distinguish absolute from relative motion. The one indisputable fact established by the Michelson–Morley experiment was that the velocity of light is unaffected by the motion of the earth. Einstein seized on this as a revelation of universal law.

If the velocity of light is constant regardless of the earth's motion, he reasoned, it must be constant regardless of the motion of any planet, star, or other luminous system moving anywhere in the universe. From this he drew a broader generalization and asserted that the laws of

*Dr. Albert A. Michelson was one half of the team that conducted the epochal Michelson–Morley experiment in Cleveland in 1887.*

nature are the same for all uniformly moving systems. This simple statement is the essence of Einstein's special theory of relativity.

The inferences Einstein derived from this fundamental postulate revolutionized physics for all time. One is that within the restless universe—in which stars, galaxies, and supergalactic gravitational systems are constantly in motion—the movements of such systems can be described only with respect to each other, for in space there are no directions and no absolute, stationary frame of reference. It is futile for the scientist to try to discover the true velocity of any moving system by using light as a measure, for the velocity of light is constant throughout the universe and is unaffected by either the motion of the source or the motion of the receiver. Nature offers no absolute bases of measurement, and space is simply the order or relation of the objects it contains; without objects occupying it, space is nothing. Along with absolute space, Einstein discarded the concept of absolute time—of a steady, unvarying, universal time flow, streaming from the infinite past to the infinite future. Just as space is simply a possible order of material objects, so time is simply a possible order of events.

By referring our own experiences to a clock or a calendar, we think we make time an objective concept. Yet clocks and calendars offer man-made intervals geared to our local solar system. What we call an hour is actually a measurement in space—an arc of 15 degrees in the apparent daily rotation of the celestial sphere—and what we call a year is simply a measure of the earth's progress in its orbit around the sun. It is when science ranges beyond the neighborhood of the sun that all our terrestrial ideas of time become meaningless. Relativity states that there is no such thing as a fixed interval of time independent of a system of reference.

Max Planck published his quantum theory, one of the landmarks of modern physics, during the year 1900.

Suppose we try to ascertain what is happening on the star Arcturus "right now." Arcturus is 38 light-years away. If we should try to communicate with Arcturus by radio, it would take 38 years for our message to reach its destination. And when we look at Arcturus and say that we see it now in 1972, we are seeing a ghost—an image projected by light rays that left their source in 1934. Whether Arcturus even exists now, nature forbids us to know until 2010.

It is clear to any astronomer that as he looks outward in space he looks backward in time. Hence in the special theory of relativity Einstein took as a basic premise the fact that the cosmologist cannot employ concepts like "here" and "now" or think of physical events taking place simultaneously in unrelated systems. It is necessary in dealing with complex forms of motion to relate the magnitudes found in one system with those found in another. For the scientist, concepts of space and time take on significance only when the relations between events and systems are quantitatively defined.

The mathematical laws that define these relationships are known as laws of transformation. The simplest transformation, used as an example by Newton, depicts a sailor promenading the deck of a ship as it passes a jetty on shore. If the sailor walks forward along the deck at 3 miles an hour while the ship moves through the sea at a rate of 12 miles an hour, then the sailor's velocity with respect to the jetty is 15 miles an hour; if he walks aft, his velocity relative to the jetty is 9 miles an hour. Einstein used a different illustration. He imagined an alarm bell ringing at a railroad crossing. The sound waves produced by the bell spread away through the surrounding air at a rate of 400 yards a second. A train speeds toward the crossing at a rate of 20 yards a second. Hence the velocity of the sound relative to the train as it approaches the bell is 420 yards a second and 380 yards a second after the train has passed the bell. Serious difficulties arise, however, when this simple addition of velocities is used in connection with light.

Einstein emphasized these difficulties with another railway incident. Again there is a crossing, marked this time by a signal light that flashes its beam down the track at 186,284 miles a second—the constant velocity of light, denoted in physics by the symbol $c$. A train moves toward the signal light at a given velocity $v$. By the classic addition of velocities one concludes that the velocity of the light beam relative to the train is $c + v$ when the train moves toward the signal light and $c - v$ when the train has passed the light. But this result conflicts with the findings of the Michelson–Morley experiment, which demonstrated that the velocity of light is unaffected by either the motion of the source or the motion of the receiver. Since the velocity of light is a universal constant, it cannot, therefore, be affected by the velocity of the train in Einstein's railway problem.

Einstein saw that the dilemma presented by this situation lay in the irreconcilable conflict between the classical principle of the addition of velocities and his belief in the constancy of the velocity of light. Although the former appears to rest on the stern logic of mathematics—that two plus two equals four—Einstein recognized in the latter a fundamental law of nature. He concluded, therefore, that a new transformation formula must be found to enable the scientist to describe the relations between moving systems in a way that would satisfy the law of the constant velocity of light.

He found what he wanted in a series of equations developed by the great Dutch physicist Hendrik A. Lorentz. Like most physicists of the time, Lorentz had been deeply troubled by the Michelson–Morley experiment and subsequently intrigued by an imaginative explanation of the result adduced by George Fitzgerald of Trinity College, Dublin. Fitzgerald suggested that the constant velocity of light—affected by neither the motion of its source nor that of its receiver—might be explained if one presupposed that all moving objects are shortened along the axis of their motion. Thus a yardstick traveling at great velocity would be shorter than a stationary yardstick, and the faster it traveled the shorter it would get.

Although Fitzgerald confessed to Lorentz that "I have been rather laughed at for my view," Lorentz took the Fitzgerald contraction seriously and agreed that such an effect might well be produced when a body containing electric charges moved swiftly through the ether. Since Lorentz had been among the first to postulate the electron and had seen its existence proved, it seemed possible to him that electromagnetic forces could compress the distribution of electrons in a rapidly moving body and thus flatten it in the direction of its motion. But to agree that all measurements of length are foreshortened by motion is to shatter the classic Newtonian transformation.

Although the simple addition of velocities works in all situations involving compound motion within ordinary human experience, Lorentz thought it might not be valid when applied to bodies moving at velocities approaching the speed of light. He therefore evolved a new transformation formula that expressed the concept of the Fitzgerald contraction in mathematical language. Taking the velocity of light as a universal constant and regarding all measurements of distance or length as variables, the Lorentz transformation modifies measurements of distance or length on a moving system with respect to the velocity of the system and relates them to those observed on systems relatively at rest.

Einstein discerned in the Lorentz formula the revelation of a law of nature, and he incorporated it as a major pillar in the architecture of relativity. He reasoned that if spatial measurements varied with the relative velocity of moving bodies, then measurements of time should also vary. If a flying yardstick becomes shorter as its speed increases, then a clock attached to a moving system must slow down as the velocity of that moving system increases. If space contracts, time retracts. The chain of logic that led him to this conclusion began with a riddle he had invented for himself at the age of sixteen: if he could observe an oscillating electromagnetic wave flying into space, while flying along with that wave at its constant velocity of 186,284 miles a second, what would he see? His answer was "a spatially oscillatory electromagnetic field at rest."

But that answer presented a paradox that Maxwell's elegant equations did not encompass. For the inevitable inference must be that the laws of electromagnetism are different for stationary observers than they are for observers in motion. This inference offended Einstein's innate belief in the harmony of the universe and his conviction that the laws of nature must be the same for all observers, independent of their state of motion. Such considerations led Einstein to the conclusion that measurements of time, as well as measurements of space, cannot be absolute but must be regarded as relative to the combined motions of objects and observer.

Once again he envisaged a straight length of track, this time with an observer sitting on an embankment beside it. A thunderstorm breaks, and two bolts of lightning strike the track "simultaneously" at separate points, A and B. Now, asked Einstein, what do we mean by "simultaneously"? To define this term, he assumed that the observer is sitting precisely halfway between A and B and that he is equipped with an arrangement of mirrors enabling him to see A and B at the same time without moving his eyes. If the lightning flashes appear in the observer's mirrors at precisely the same instant, they may be regarded as simultaneous.

Now a train roars down the track, with a second observer perched on one of the cars with a mirror apparatus just like the one on the embankment. It happens that this moving observer finds himself directly opposite the stationary observer at the precise instant the lightning bolt hits A and B. The question still is: will the lightning flashes appear simultaneous to him? The answer is: they will not. For if his train is moving away from lightning bolt B and toward lightning bolt A, then B will be reflected in his mirrors a fraction of a second later than A. The velocity of light is not only constant, it is finite. And since he is moving away from B toward A at the instant the lightning strikes "simultaneously" so far as the stationary observer is concerned, he will always insist that—whatever the velocity of the train may be—the lightning flash ahead of him, flash A, struck the train first. Hence the lightning flashes that are simultaneous relative to the stationary observer are *not* simultaneous relative to the observer in motion.

This paradox dramatizes one of the subtlest and most difficult concepts in Einstein's philosophy: the relativity of simultaneity. Stated in Einstein's own words, it points out that "every reference body, or co-ordinate system, has its own particular time; unless we are told the reference body to which the statement of time refers, there is no meaning in the statement of the time of an event." Einstein's statement that time, like distance, is relative and that there is no such thing as a time interval independent of the state of motion of the system of reference, has become an established pillar of modern physics. The scientist who wishes to describe the phenomena of nature in terms that are consistent for all systems throughout the universe—the infinite and the infinitesimal—must regard units of time and distance as variable quantities. The equations of the Lorentz transformation do just that. So, although Lorentz had originally

*Einstein probably posed for this photograph with Hendrik A. Lorentz in Leyden shortly after World War I.*

developed his equations to meet a specific problem, Einstein made them the basis of a tremendous generalization, and to the edifice of relativity he added another axiom: the laws of nature preserve their uniformity in all systems when related by the Lorentz transformation. Translated into laymen's terms, the Einstein axiom asserts that a clock attached to a moving system runs at a different rate from a stationary clock, and a yardstick attached to any moving system changes its length according to the velocity of that system. The clock slows down as its velocity increases, and the measuring rod shrinks in the direction of its motion. The changes have nothing to do with the construction of the clock or the composition of the yardstick. They are not mechanical phenomena; an observer riding along with the clock and the yardstick would not notice these changes. But a stationary observer would find that the moving clock has slowed down with respect to his stationary clock and that the moving yardstick has contracted with respect to his stationary units of measurement.

It is, therefore, because of the relativity of time and distance that the velocity of light is a universal constant. Observers everywhere in the universe, regardless of their state of motion, will always find that light strikes their instruments at precisely the same velocity. As their own velocity approaches that of light, their clocks slow down and their yardsticks contract: the greater the speed, the greater the contraction. A yardstick moving at 90 per cent of the velocity of light shrinks to about half its length; thereafter, the rate becomes more rapid, and if the stick could attain the velocity of light, it would shrink away to nothing at all. Similarly, a clock traveling with the velocity of light would stop completely. It follows that nothing can ever move faster than light, no matter what forces are applied. Einstein thus found confirmation of his belief in another fundamental law: the velocity of light is the top limiting velocity in the universe.

*Einstein was introduced to the "scientific wizard" of General Electric, Charles P. Steinmetz, in Schenectady, New York, in 1921.*

Even today, more than half a century after the publication of the special theory of relativity, its concepts are difficult to digest. But that is because classical physics assumed without question that an object preserves the same dimensions whether it is in motion or at rest. In even the fastest vehicles of the space age, the slowing down of a watch is immeasurable. It is only when velocities approach the speed of light that relativistic effects can be detected. The equations of the Lorentz transformation show that at ordinary speeds the change of time and space intervals amounts practically to zero. Relativity does not contradict classical physics. It simply regards the old concepts as limiting cases that apply only to the familiar experiences of man.

Whenever Einstein's postulates have been put to the test, their validity has been confirmed. Laboratory work with charged particles moving in powerful magnetic fields has produced evidence of spatial contraction with accelerations approximating the speed of light. Remarkable proof of the relativistic retardation of time intervals came out of a famous experiment performed by Herbert E. Ives of the Bell Telephone Laboratories in 1936. A radiating atom may be regarded as a kind of clock in that it emits light of a definite frequency and wave length, which can be measured with great precision by means of a spectroscope. Ives compared the light emitted by hydrogen atoms moving at great velocities with that emitted by hydrogen atoms at rest and found that the frequency of vibration of the moving atoms was reduced in exact accordance with Einstein's predictions.

Some day, space travel may devise a more spectacular test of this principle. Since any periodic motion serves to measure time, the human heart, Einstein has pointed out, is also a kind of clock. According to relativity, the heartbeat of a person traveling with a velocity close to that of light would be relatively slowed, along with his respiration and all other physiological and metabolic processes. He would not notice the retardation because his watch would slow down in the same degree. But judged by a stationary—i.e., earthbound—timekeeper he would "grow old" less rapidly. In a science-fiction realm of the future, it is possible to imagine some cosmic explorer boarding a nuclear-powered spaceship, ranging the void at 167,000 miles a second, and returning to earth after ten terrestrial years to find himself physically only five years older.

A few weeks after publication of his paper on the relativity of space and time, Einstein added a kind of footnote, barely a page and a half long, which appeared in the *Annalen der Physik:* "The results of the previous investigation lead to a very interesting conclusion which is here to be deduced." Since any description of the mechanics of the universe requires three quantities—space, time, and mass—and since space and time are relative quantities, Einstein concluded that the mass of a body also varies with its state of motion. Indeed, the most stupendous results of Einstein's special theory have arisen from this third principle of relativity—the relativity of mass.

In its popular sense, "mass" is just another word for "weight." But in physics it denotes a rather different and more fundamental property of matter, namely, resistance to a change of motion. A greater force is necessary to move a freight car than to move a bicycle; the freight car resists motion more stubbornly than the bicycle because it has greater mass. In classical physics the mass of any body is a fixed and unchanging property. But relativity asserts that the mass of a moving body is not constant but increases with velocity. The old physics failed to discover this fact simply because man's senses and instruments are too crude to note the infinitesimal increases of mass produced by the feeble accelerations of ordinary existence. They become measurable only when bodies attain velocities approximating that of light.

Of all aspects of relativity, the principle of increase of mass has been most often verified and most fruitfully applied by laboratory experimenters. Electrons moving in powerful electric fields and beta particles ejected from the nuclei of radioactive substances attain velocities ranging up to 99 per cent that of light. For atomic physicists concerned with these great speeds, the increase of mass predicted by Einstein is not an arguable hypothesis but an empirical fact. Indeed, the mechanics of the proton synchrotron and other superenergy machines are designed to allow for the increasing mass of particles, which approaches infinity as their speed approaches that of light.

By further deduction from his principle of relativity of mass, Einstein arrived at a conclusion of incalculable importance. Since the mass of a moving body increases with its motion, and since motion is a form of energy (kinetic energy), then the increased mass of a moving body comes from its increased energy. In short, energy has mass. He expressed the relationship in the famous equation $E = mc^2$, which states that the energy contained in any particle of matter is equal to the mass of that body (in grams) multiplied by the square of the velocity of light (in centimeters per second: 300,000,000,000 cm/sec). One kilogram of coal (about two pounds), if converted *entirely* into energy, would yield 25 billion kilowatt hours of electricity, or as much as all the power plants in the United States could generate by running steadily for two months.

Apart from Hiroshima and Nagasaki, $E = mc^2$ has furthered knowledge in the still arcane realms of the atom and its elusive components. "We use it," said the late J. Robert Oppenheimer, "literally in almost every branch of nuclear physics . . . and in all branches of physics dealing with the fundamental particles. It has been checked and cross-checked and counter-checked in the most numerous ways and it is a very rich part of our heritage."

Finally, the great equation disclosed new truths about physical reality. Prior to Einstein, scientists had pictured the universe as a vessel containing two distinct elements, matter and energy—the former inert, tangible, and characterized by a property called mass, and the latter active, invisible, and without mass. But Einstein showed that mass and energy are equivalent; the property called mass is simply concentrated energy, and the distinction between them is one of temporary state. So from the epistemological standpoint, many puzzles of nature were resolved. The dual role of the electron as a unit of matter and a unit of electricity, the photon, the phenomena of radioactivity—all these seemed less paradoxical. Matter and energy are interchangeable. If matter sheds its mass and travels with the speed of light, it may be called radiation, or energy. Conversely, if energy congeals and becomes inert, it is called matter. Since July 16, 1945, on the sands of Alamogordo, New Mexico, man has been able to transform the one into the other.

Einstein's laws of motion, his basic principles of the relativity of space, time, and mass, and his deductions from those principles make up what is known today as the special theory of relativity. Summing up its impact in his own quiet words, Einstein wrote years later: "The most important result of a general character to which the special theory of relativity has led is concerned with the conception of mass. Before the advent of relativity, physics recognized two conservation laws of fundamental importance, namely the law of the conservation of energy and the law of the conservation of mass; these two fundamental laws appeared to be quite independent of each other. By means of the theory of relativity they have been united into one law."

In the decade following publication of this epic work, Einstein received no great acclaim. A few perceptive geniuses in the world of physics—Max Planck, Max von Laue—discerned its greatness. But as far as the world of the laity was concerned, Volume 17 of the *Annalen der Physik* might never have been published. For a while Einstein continued in his daily chores in the patent office at Berne. Then, in 1907, he accepted an appointment as *Privatdocent* at the University of Berne, where, like Newton, he sometimes lectured to a virtually empty hall. Later, at the urgent request of Max Planck, he moved to Berlin. From time to time his horizons were widened by meetings with Lorentz at Leyden and elsewhere with Rutherford, Mme Curie, Planck, and others. Gradually, an elite of the world's great physicists perceived that an incipient leader had arrived on the scene.

*Einstein was fifty when this photograph of him, his second wife, Elsa (seated), and his stepdaughter, Margot, was taken in Berlin in 1929.*

During this time, the second decade of the twentieth century, Einstein expanded his special theory of relativity into the general theory of relativity, through which he arrived at a new concept of gravitation and a new view of the architecture of the universe. The primary and crucial insight of the general theory is known to physicists as the principle of equivalence of gravitation and inertia. It states that there is no way to distinguish the motion produced by inertial forces—acceleration, deceleration, centrifugal forces, etc.—from motion produced by gravitational force.

Following publication of his special theory, Einstein had been deeply concerned that perhaps there might be one form of motion that could be described as absolute in that it could be detected without reference to any other moving system. He had conjectured that if all the objects in the universe except one were removed, then no one could say whether that one remaining object was at rest or hurtling through space at an immeasurable velocity. Hence it was meaningless to speak of the motion of a single body. Or was it? Suppose, Einstein reasoned, the earth, alone in the universe, suddenly began to gyrate wildly; its inhabitants would then become aware of their state of motion. Therefore, nonuniform motion, such as that produced by inertial forces and accelerations, might be absolute after all, which would mean that empty space provides a system of reference within which it is possible to distinguish absolute motion.

The sword with which Einstein slew the dragon of absolute motion was gravitation. He recognized a principle familiar to any aviator, that in blind flying it is impossible to separate the effects of inertia from those of gravitation. The physical sensation of pulling out of a dive is exactly the same as that of executing a steeply-banked turn at high speed; in both cases, the factor known as G-load draws blood away from the brain and pulls the body down heavily into the seat.

The gravitation of Einstein, however, is entirely different from the gravitation of Newton. It is not a "force." Newton's idea that bodies of matter can "attract" one another seemed to Einstein an illusion derived from erroneous mechanical concepts of nature. Rejecting the idea of the universe as a big machine, Einstein evolved a new concept of gravitation that contains nothing about force. Einstein's law of gravitation describes the behavior of objects in a gravitational field, not in terms of attraction but simply in terms of the paths they follow. The movements of the planets, galaxies, and all celestial systems stem from their inertia and are determined by the metric properties of space—or more properly speaking, the metric properties of the space-time continuum.

"The nonmathematician," Einstein wrote, "is seized by a mysterious shuddering when he hears of 'four-dimensional' things, by a feeling not unlike that awakened by thoughts of the occult. And yet there is no more commonplace statement than that the world in which we live is a four-dimensional space-time continuum."

When Einstein first published his general theory of relativity in 1919, the terms "four-dimensional" and "continuum" were by no means commonplace. Yet they swiftly became so, and Einstein's picture of the universe as a four-dimensional space-time continuum is the view upon which all modern conceptions of the universe are based. The ideas are perfectly clear. A continuum is something that is continuous; within it, the interval separating any two points may be divided into an infinite number of arbitrarily small steps. A railroad track is a one-dimensional space continuum, and on it the engineer of a train can describe his position at any time by citing a single co-ordinate—a milestone. A sea captain has to think in terms of two dimensions—latitude and longitude. An airplane pilot guides his plane through a three-dimensional continuum, consisting of latitude *x*, longitude *y*, and altitude *z*. But his traffic manager at the airport requires another co-ordinate—that of time. So time is the fourth dimension. If one wishes to envisage the flight of an airplane as a physical reality *in toto,* it must be thought of as a continuous curve in a four-dimensional space-time continuum.

What is necessary for an airplane traffic manager is even more necessary for the astronomer and the cosmologist who endeavor to discern and describe the stupendous reaches of the universe beyond the Milky Way. In his mind, man tends to separate the three dimensions of space from the dimension of time, but the separation is purely subjective. The world *is* a space-time continuum; all reality exists in both space and in time, and the two are indivisible. Measurements of time are really measurements in space, and conversely, measurements in space depend on measurements of time. Seconds, minutes, hours, days, weeks, months, seasons, years—all are measurements of the earth's position in space relative to the sun, moon, and stars. Similarly, latitude and longitude, spatial points, are measured in minutes and seconds, and to compute them accurately, one must know the time of day and day of the year. Such "landmarks" as the equator, the Tropic of Cancer, or the Arctic Circle are simply sundials that clock the changing seasons; the prime meridian is a co-ordinate of daily time; and noon is nothing more than an angle of the sun.

The astronomers' sensitive cameras can detect the glimmer of island universes 500 million light-years away—faint gleams that began their journey eons before the advent of man or his earliest forebears on the earth. His spectroscope, moreover, tells him that these huge outer systems are hurtling into limbo away from our own galaxy and away from each other at incredible velocities ranging up to 35,000 miles a second. Or, more precisely, they *were* receding from us 500 million years ago. Where they are now or whether they even exist now, no one can say. If man breaks down his picture of the universe into three subjective dimensions of space and one of local time, then these galaxies have no objective existence except as faint smudges of ancient enfeebled light on a photographic plate. They attain physical reality only in their proper frame of reference, which is the four-dimensional space-time continuum.

Einstein's next great leap in his development of general relativity was to postulate that within the space-time continuum that constitutes the universe every celestial object creates a physical condition around it, which may be described as a field. A simple analogy is the magnetic field surrounding a magnet, which can be rendered visible by sprinkling iron filings on a piece of paper held above the magnet. Magnetic and electric fields are physical realities. Their structures are described by the field equations of James Clerk Maxwell. A gravitational field is as much a physical reality as an electromagnetic field is, and its structure is defined by the field equations of Albert Einstein.

Just as Maxwell assumed that a magnet creates certain properties in surrounding space, so Einstein concluded that stars, galaxies, and all celestial bodies individually determine the properties of the space around them. And just as the movement of an iron filing in a magnetic field is guided by the structure of the field, so the path of a body in a gravitational field is determined by the geometry of that field. Einstein's gravitational laws merely describe the field properties of the space-time continuum. One group of these laws sets forth the relationship between the mass of a gravitating body and the structure of the field around it; they are called structure laws. A second group analyzes the paths described by moving bodies in gravitational fields; they are known as the laws of motion.

Einstein's theory of gravitation is more than a formal mathematical scheme. It rests on assumptions of deep cosmic significance. The most remarkable of these is that the universe is not a fixed, unchanging edifice wherein independent matter is housed in independent space and time; it is an amorphous continuum, plastic and variable, constantly subject to change and distortion. Wherever there is matter and motion, the continuum is disturbed. Just as a fish swimming in the sea agitates the water around it, so a star, a comet, or a galaxy distorts the geometry of the space-time continuum through which it moves. When applied to astronomical problems, Einstein's gravitational laws yield results that are close to Newton's. If the results paralleled each other in all cases, scientists might have retained the familiar concepts of Newtonian law. But a number of strange new phenomena were discovered, and at least one old puzzle solved, solely on the basis of general relativity.

*Einstein inspects the 150-foot solar tower telescope at the Mount Wilson Observatory in 1930.*

The old puzzle stemmed from the eccentric behavior of the planet Mercury. Instead of revolving in its elliptic orbit with the regularity of other planets, Mercury deviates from its course each year by a slight but baffling degree, which defied every attempt of astronomers to explain the perturbation within the framework of Newtonian mechanics. Of all the planets Mercury is the closest to the sun. It is small and travels at high speed. Under Newtonian law these factors should not account for the deviation; the dynamics of Mercury's movement should be the same as those of any other planet. But under Einstein's laws, the strength of the sun's gravitational field and Mercury's great velocity make a difference, causing the entire ellipse of Mercury's orbit to execute a slow, inexorable swing around the sun at the rate of one revolution every three million years. This calculation is in perfect agreement with observed measurements of the planet's course. Einstein's mathematics thus proved more accurate than Newton's in dealing with high velocities and intense gravitational fields.

Far more dramatic than this resolution of an old but minor problem was Einstein's prediction of a new cosmic phenomenon no scientist had ever imagined—namely, the effect of gravitation on light. Einstein concluded that light photons, like any material objects, travel in a curve when passing through the gravitational field of a massive body. He suggested that his theory could be tested by observing the path of starlight in the gravitational field of the sun. Since stars are invisible by day, there is only one occasion upon which sun and stars can be together in the sky, and that is during an eclipse. Einstein proposed that photographs be taken of the stars immediately bordering the darkened face of the sun during an eclipse and compared with photographs of those same stars made at another time. According to his theory, light from the stars surrounding the sun should be bent inward, toward the sun, in traversing the sun's gravitational field; hence, the optical *images* of those stars should appear to observers on earth to be shifted outward from their usual positions in the sky. Einstein calculated the degree of deflection that should be observed and predicted that for stars closest to the sun the deviation would be about 1.75 seconds of an arc.

Despite the Anglo–German hostilities of World War I, there were two men in England who became intensely interested in Einstein's hypotheses. One was Sir Arthur Eddington, Plumian Professor of Astronomy at Cambridge; the other was Sir Frank Dyson, the Astronomer Royal. Together they planned an expedition to photograph the eclipse of May 29, 1919, from equatorial regions. Since Einstein had staked his whole general theory of relativity on this test, men of science throughout the world anxiously awaited the result of the expedition. When the pictures were developed, calibrated, and painstakingly compared with previous pictures of the same star group, they revealed that defection of starlight in the gravitational field of the sun averaged 1.64 seconds—a figure as close to perfect agreement with Einstein's prediction as the accuracy of instruments would allow.

Public and general glory did not descend in full measure until November 6, 1919, when at a meeting of the Royal Society and the Royal Astronomical Society in London, in the presence of the greatest men of contemporary science, Eddington and Dyson read their reports, and Sir Joseph J. Thomson, president of the Royal Society, described Einstein's triumph as "not the discovery of an outlying island but of a whole continent of new scientific ideas. . . . one of the most momentous pronouncements of human thought the world has ever known." Alfred North Whitehead observed, "A great adventure in thought [has] at length come safe to shore."

Up to this point Einstein had been dealing with the phenomena of the individual gravitational field. But the universe is filled with incomputable masses of matter—stars, dust clouds, star clusters, galaxies, and supergalactic systems—grouped by the interlocking geometry of their gravitational fields. Einstein therefore asked: what then is the overall geometry of the space-time continuum in which they drift? In cruder language, what is the shape and size of the universe? All modern replies to this question have been derived directly or indirectly from the principles of general relativity.

Prior to Einstein, the universe was usually pictured as an island of matter in an infinite sea of space. The universe had to be infinite, most scientists agreed, because when they conceded that space might come to an end somewhere, the question arose: And what lies beyond that? Yet Newtonian law ruled out an infinite universe containing a uniform distribution of matter; for in such a universe the total gravitational forces of all the masses of matter stretching away to infinite would be infinite, and the heavens would be ablaze with infinite light. To man's eye, moreover, the lights of outer space beyond the rim of the Milky Way appeared to become ever sparser on the frontiers of the void. But the island universe presented problems, too. The amount of matter it held was so small by contrast with an infinity of space that the dynamic laws governing the movements of the galaxies would inevitably cause them to disperse like the droplets of a cloud, leaving the universe empty.

To Einstein this picture of dissolution and disappearance was eminently unsatisfactory. The basic difficulty, he decided, derived from man's assumption that the geometry of the universe must be the same as that revealed by his senses here on earth. Man assumes, as Euclid did, that two parallel beams of light will travel through space forever without meeting, and that in outer space a straight line is the shortest distance between two points. And yet Euclid never *proved* that a straight line is the shortest distance between two points; he simply *defined* it as such.

Is it not then possible, Einstein asked, that man is limiting his perceptions when he pictures the universe in terms of Euclidean geometry? Einstein had already shown that Euclidean geometry did not hold true in a gravitational field. Light rays do not travel in straight lines, for the metric properties of the field are such that within it there are no straight lines; the shortest course light can describe is a curve or great circle that is determined by the structure of the field.

*Einstein's letter to Roosevelt, written at the urging of his fellow scientists, warned the President that Germany had the knowledge to produce an atomic bomb.*

Since this structure is shaped by the mass and velocity of the gravitating body, it follows that the geometric structure of the universe as a whole must be shaped by the sum of its material content. For each concentration of matter in the universe there is a corresponding distortion of the space-time continuum. Each celestial body, each galaxy, creates local irregularities in space-time, like eddies around islands in the sea. The greater the concentration of matter, the greater the resulting curvature of space-time. And the total effect is an overall curvature of the whole space-time continuum; the combined distortions produced by all the masses of matter in the universe cause the continuum to bend back on itself in a great closed cosmic curve.

The Einstein universe is, therefore, non-Euclidean and finite. In it, there are no straight lines, only great circles. Space, though finite, is unbounded. A mathematician would describe its geometric character as the four-dimensional analogue of the surface of a sphere. In the less abstract words of the late Sir James Jeans: "A soap bubble with corrugations on its surface is perhaps the best representation, in terms of simple and familiar materials, of the new universe revealed to us by the Theory of Relativity. The universe is not the interior of the soap-bubble but its surface, and we must always remember that while the surface of the soap-bubble has only two dimensions, the universe bubble has four—three dimensions of space and one of time. And the substance out of which this bubble is blown, the soap-film, is empty space welded onto empty time."

Like most of the concepts of modern science, Einstein's finite, four-dimensional spherical universe cannot be visualized, any more than an electron or a photon can be visualized. But its properties can be described mathematically. And soon after publication of the general theory, cosmologists were applying the best available values of contemporary astronomy to Einstein's field equations, in an attempt to compute the *size* of the universe. Since, as Einstein showed, the geometry, or curvature, of space depends on its material content, the cosmological problem could be solved by obtaining a figure for the average density of matter in the universe. Fortunately, this figure became available through the painstaking work of Edwin P. Hubble of the Mount Wilson Observatory. By studying sample areas of the heavens over a period of years, he was able to compute the average amount of matter contained in them and concluded that in the universe as a whole there is .0000000000000000000000000000001 gram of matter per cubic centimeter of space. Hubble's figure yields a positive value to the curvature of the universe, which in turn reveals that the radius of the universe is 35 billion light-years. The Einstein universe, while not infinite, is nevertheless sufficiently capacious to encompass billions of galaxies. A sunbeam, setting out through space, would in Einstein's universe describe a great cosmic circle and return to its source after a little more than 200 billion terrestrial years.

At the time Einstein evolved his cosmology he was unaware of a strange astronomical phenomenon that was only interpreted several years later. He had assumed that the motions of the star systems were random, like the drifting of molecules in a gas. But astronomers were beginning to notice signs of a systematic movement among the outer galaxies at the extreme limits of telescopic vision; each distant galaxy appeared to be rushing away from our galaxy and from each other at a velocity proportional to its distance. The greater the distance, the greater the speed of recession. This concept of an expanding universe has presented cosmologists with problems of enormous subtlety. For the light by which the astronomer discerns the outermost galaxies has been swimming through space for millions of years—during which time the galaxies in question have traveled millions of light-years still farther away. It is for this consideration alone, if for no other, that Einstein's conception of the universe as a space-time continuum—with space and time inseparable—has become the basic overview today.

Although astronomy and cosmology continued, throughout Einstein's life, to adduce new and fascinating questions—such as the possibility that the curvature of the universe might be negative (i.e., saddle-shaped) rather than positive (i.e., spherical), as Einstein had conjectured—he left the field of cosmogony to others and turned to new and different things.

In the 1920's the rise of Hitler began to cast a shadow on Einstein's life. His family had never been active practitioners of the Jewish

*The first detonation of an atomic bomb, a product of Einstein's theories of relativity, took place on July 16, 1945, at Alamogordo in southern New Mexico.*

religion. He had always considered himself a freethinker, and it came as a shock to him to be told suddenly that he was a Jew. Rather plaintively, he remarked to a friend, *"Je ne suis pas très Juif."* But it became evident that for his own safety the world's greatest living physicist would have to leave his native land. In 1933 Einstein resigned as director of the Kaiser Wilhelm Institute and left Germany forever.

Any university in the free world would have cherished his services. He decided on the Institute for Advanced Study at Princeton because it offered him what he wanted—an intellectual sanctuary free of scheduled responsibilities. He settled there in 1934 with his second wife, Elsa (his first wife, Mileva, had divorced him a decade earlier). In 1940 he became an American citizen.

*The famous scientist relaxes, above playing the violin, below on a sailboat.*

During the final quarter century of his life Einstein labored in the quest of his personal grail—a unified field theory that would unite in one mutually consistent sequence of equations the physical laws governing both electromagnetic force and gravitation. To Einstein the importance of a unified field theory lay in the fact that virtually all the phenomena of nature arises from these two fundamental forces. There is only one other force in the universe that appears to operate outside their domain—nuclear force, the force that holds the nucleus of the atom together.

For many years scientists had wondered if gravitation might actually be a manifestation of electromagnetic force. There were grounds for this belief. The earth, the sun, and all stars have magnetic fields. And there is a physical analogy in the familiar concept of the atom as a miniature solar system, with its negatively charged electrons revolving around the positively charged nucleus like satellites around a central sun. Nevertheless, all past efforts to identify gravitation as a form of electromagnetic force met with failure. Newtonian law simply could not be harmonized with the laws of Maxwell's electromagnetic field. Yet Einstein felt that his own laws of the gravitational field could be reconciled with Maxwell's concepts; he thought that gravitation and electromagnetism were in a very real sense not "the same thing" but separate manifestations of a deeper underlying reality.

But over and above this minimum objective, Einstein strove toward a broader objective, which was to embrace in his unified field theory not only gravitational and electromagnetic phenomena but quantum phenomena as well—the phenomena of the world of atoms, protons, and electrons. The scope of this ambition can only be discerned when one realizes that the two great theoretical systems of modern science by which modern man has transcended his limited senses are relativity, which sets forth the physical laws of the macroscopic universe, and quantum theory, which sets forth the physical laws of the microcosm. Yet relativity and quantum theory rest on entirely different and independent basic concepts. They do not, as it were, speak the same language. It was Einstein's goal to bridge the gulf between the great and the small, and to show that all the multifarious phenomena of nature can be described in terms of a single harmonious edifice of cosmic law.

The unified field theory would thus carry to logical fulfillment the long drive of science toward unification of concepts. The progression began with the reduction of all material substances into elements, then of elements into certain basic particles. Ultimately, all features of the universe were reduced to a few basic quantities—space, time, matter, energy, and gravitation. In his special theory of relativity Einstein had shown that matter and energy differ from one another only as ice differs from water. And in his general theory he showed that time and space are inseparable and gravitation and inertia identical. Yet he could not fit electromagnetic field laws into general relativity.

The drive that fired his last years was a feeling that "the idea that there are two structures of space, independent of each other, the metric-gravitational and the electromagnetic is intolerable to the human spirit." For sixteen years Einstein worked on the problem. The mathematics were far more difficult than those of relativity, and Einstein, who often protested that his mathematical skills were limited, frequently sought assistance with the necessary computations. But finally, in 1949, he presented to the American Association for the Advancement of Science a paper, containing twenty-four pages of equations, that seemed to represent the attainment of his lifelong goal. The scientific world greeted it with respect but reservations.

It was not only the density of the mathematics that delayed expert acknowledgement of the unified field theory as Einstein's triumphant arrival, at the age of seventy, as the "grand aim of all science," which he once had defined as "to cover the greatest number of empirical facts by logical deduction from the smallest number of hypotheses or axioms." Even more forbidding was its abstractness, its remoteness from the physical world of experience. Einstein himself acknowledged this when he wrote to a friend, "The mathematical conclusiveness of the theory cannot be opposed. The question of its physical validity, however, is completely undecided." For, unlike the general theory of relativity, wherein he had specified three ways by which it could be empirically confirmed, Einstein's unified field theory contained no suggestions for experimental testing. When asked about the chances of obtaining experimental evidence to validate his theory, he replied, half jokingly, "come back in twenty years' time."

Today, more than two decades later, Einstein's unified field theory remains an abstraction, unsubstantiated by any experiment or physical observation. And in those decades the mainstream of physics flowed around and away from him. The advance of quantum theory, so enthusiastically adopted by the younger generation of physicists, propelled Einstein and field theory in general into a scientific backwater. He sadly recognized in his declining years that he had become, as he put it, "a genuine old museum-piece." Yet he was not about to surrender. The statistical approach and indeterminacy of quantum mechanics were abhorrent to him. He believed with all his heart in causality. The trouble with quantum theory, he felt, was not that it was wrong but that it was incomplete. Knowledge would advance.

Conversely, modern physicists felt that Einstein's pursuit of knowledge by deductive means was outmoded. He had long held that scientific discovery lay in formulating a theory and endeavoring to sustain it by experiment and observation. The whole thrust of modern physics lies with the inductive method—performing experiments and making observations first and then drawing conclusions from the results. It was his rejection of the "life-insurance methods" of quantum physics that led him to declare, "God did not play dice with the world."

Despite his awareness that in the eyes of his younger associates at Princeton, time and science had left him behind, he continued on his quiet way, resisting intrusions of the outside world. Because of his fame he was besieged by speaking invitations. "The only way to escape the personal corruption of praise is to go on working," he once observed. "One is tempted to stop and listen to it. The only thing is to turn away and go on working. Work. There is nothing else."

Only once during his residency at Princeton did Einstein become involved in the political world. That was in the summer of 1939, when, at the urgent request of physicists Leo Szilard and Eugene Wigner, Einstein wrote a historic letter to President Roosevelt, warning him that the Germans had discovered the possibility of setting up nuclear chain reactions in uranium: "This new phenomenon would lead to the production of bombs, and it is conceivable . . . that extremely powerful bombs of a new type might thus be constructed. A single bomb of this type . . . might very well destroy a whole port together with the surrounding territory." Einstein's letter led to the Manhattan Project, which six years later created the first atomic bomb and the holocaust of Hiroshima. Thus Einstein, a lifelong pacifist, became by virtue of his famous equation and his letter to Roosevelt the unwilling father of the atomic age.

He lived out his declining years tranquilly in Princeton, undisturbed except by one unexpected incident. In 1952, Chaim Weizmann, first president of Israel, died, and Einstein was entreated to succeed him. Slightly incredulous, Einstein refused, despite special pleadings by Zionists throughout the world. He declined the invitation in a gentle letter to Prime Minister Ben-Gurion: "I am deeply moved by the offer from our state of Israel, and at once saddened and ashamed that I cannot accept it. All my life I have dealt with objective matters, hence I lack both the natural aptitude and the experience to deal properly with people and to exercise official functions. For these reasons alone, I should be unsuited to fulfill the duties of that high office, even if advancing age was not increasing demands on my strength."

Einstein was not well at the time, and for the remaining two years of his life his illness advanced, although the clarity of his mind and his devotion to his world never waned. He died on April 18, 1955, mourned throughout the world and acclaimed universally as the greatest physicist since Sir Isaac Newton, and perhaps of all time.

"I sometimes ask myself," he once said, "how did it come that I was the one to develop the theory of relativity? The reason, I think, is that a normal adult never stops to think about problems of space and time. These are things that he has thought of as a child. But my intellectual development was retarded, as a result of which I began to wonder about space and time only when I had already grown up. Naturally, I could go deeper into the problem than a child with normal abilities."

*Einstein's chair and desk at the Princeton Institute for Advanced Study were photographed after his death in 1955.*

J. M. Keynes

LOW

# KEYNES

## 1883-1946

lmost everyone who knew Maynard Keynes—he disdained the banality of his first name, John—remembered him as just about the cleverest man in England. Lytton Strachey once remarked that "his common sense was enough to freeze a volcano." Leonard Woolf, Bloomsbury's judicious liberal conscience, said that Keynes had "absolutely the quickest brain of any man I've ever met, except perhaps Bertrand Russell's." But Russell himself admitted that he seldom emerged from an argument with Keynes without feeling something of a fool. Russell, the last of the Victorians, was demolished by Keynes as one successive age demolishes another: "Bertie . . . sustained simultaneously a pair of opinions ludicrously incompatible. He held that in fact human affairs were carried on after a most irrational fashion, but that the remedy was quite simple and easy, since all we had to do was to carry them on rationally." Let Keynes's loyal biographer, the economist Sir Roy Harrod, have the last of our opening words: "No one in our age was cleverer than Keynes, nor made less attempt to conceal it."

Inside this intellectual dandy was a genius crying to get out. When it finally did, in the depths of the depression, Keynes's brilliant intelligence devised a technique for steering capitalism off the rocks on which it was then stuck fast. He demonstrated beyond a doubt that the forces of the free market would not automatically bring prosperity if allowed to work themselves into balance in the long run; for, as Keynes said, "In the long run we are all dead." Adam Smith's "invisible hand" was simply not there to moderate self-interest.

*John Maynard Keynes was caricatured in his characteristic slouch by David Low.*

*By* LAWRENCE MALKIN

Keynes's classifications of aggregate income and expenditure, savings and investment, are as basic to modern thought as Freud's discovery of the emotional forces by which we are individually driven. The discovery of what was essentially a neutral fact—that there was no God in the economic machine—had an impact as forceful as the awesome discoveries of the atomic scientists. The scientists showed man that it was possible to harness the raw energy that runs the physical universe; Keynes showed him that it was possible to regulate and offset the greed that drives our capitalist world. He overturned Victorian economic morality at a stroke: "The engine which drives Enterprise is not Thrift, but Profit." These discoveries about ourselves and our environment, whether emotional, physical, or material, share one message: if man will be master of his fate, he must seize the power to control it. But Keynes, like the atomic scientists, was never quite at home with this brute fact of power. Politics, he said, is "a fairly adequate substitute for bridge." The clever Whig aristocrat, the gray eminence to two wartime governments, the patron of the arts, the prolific pamphleteer, the academic economist who outguessed the markets and made a fortune as a speculator, composed a life that was truly Mozartean in its grace, elegance, and success. But like Mozart and the Mysterious Stranger, Keynes at last came face to face with the irrational power of the self-perpetuating modern superstate, and his weak heart collapsed.

K eynes was born in 1883 and died in 1946. Fathered by an age of rational moralists (his parents were Cambridge dons), he grew up in an age of clever people—the fragile gadflies who led us out of Victorian certainty but not quite into the modern world; we know them as Bloomsbury. His life spans the period of change from individual enterprise to mass capitalism, and he was among the first to see the inevitability of this change in *The Economic Consequences of the Peace*. The book is seldom read nowadays because its conclusions are so obvious to us. Written in 1919, in the heat of resigning as Treasury representative to the British delegation at the Versailles Peace Conference, the book was a sensation and made Keynes internationally notorious at the age of thirty-six. Perhaps its most famous passage describes the capitalist system that gave birth to Keynes's class and sustained its self-confidence. It is worth quoting at length, to sample both his penetrating style and his view of a system that Marx wanted to destroy as passionately as Keynes wanted it rebuilt.

. . . this remarkable system depended for its growth on a double bluff or deception. On the one hand the laboring classes accepted from ignorance or powerlessness, or were compelled, persuaded, or cajoled by custom, convention, authority, and the well-established order of Society into accepting, a situation in which they could call their own very little of the cake, that they and Nature and the capitalists were co-operating to produce. And on the other hand the capitalist classes were allowed to call the best part of the cake theirs and were theoretically free to consume it, on the tacit underlying condition that they consumed very little of it in practice. The duty of "saving" became nine-tenths of virtue and the growth of the cake the object of true religion. . . . I seek only to point out that the principle of accumulation based on inequality was a vital part of the pre-war order of Society and of progress as we then understood it, and to emphasize that this principle depended on unstable psychological conditions, which it may be impossible to re-create. It was not natural for a population, of whom so few enjoyed the comforts of life, to accumulate so hugely. The war has disclosed the possibility of consumption to all and the vanity of abstinence to many. Thus the bluff is discovered; the laboring classes may be no longer willing to forgo so largely, and the capitalist classes, no longer confident of the future, may seek to enjoy more fully their liberties of consumption so long as they last, and thus precipitate the hour of their confiscation.

It took a depression and another world war for the capitalists and the workers to come to terms, with Keynes as their mediator. He was writing then under the shadow of the Bolshevik revolution, which he feared. When he visited Russia six years later, he came away horrified at this new and to him utterly drab religion: "Leninism is absolutely, defiantly non-supernatural, and its emotional and ethical essence centers about the individual's and the community's attitude towards the Love of Money." He asked himself: "How can I adopt a creed which, preferring the mud to the fish, exalts the boorish proletariat above the bourgeois and the intelligentsia who, with whatever faults, are the quality in life and surely carry the seeds of all human advancement?"

Now here is a curious type of economist, one who places personal development above material prosperity and assumes that others will, too. This is the key to Keynes; it was to be his triumph as an economist and at the same time his chief failing as a social thinker. He had grown up in an Edwardian late afternoon that cast deep and distinctive shadows on the personalities of those permitted to flourish in it. It is nice to be nostalgic about that age, but in fact it favored only the few. In 1910 poor-law relief in England reached a fifty-year high. Domestic servants in the middle-class London suburb of Hampstead outnumbered all other residents. Three-quarters of Britain's investment went overseas instead of building up home industry. The empire had not yet started running down, but its heart was; England made up its trade deficit with banking profits. British capitalism, once vigorously productive, had become essentially manipulative. Upper-class philistinism, with its shootin' and huntin' types, buried emotions and could be cruel to outsiders who seemed to violate the natural order of things. A Manchester industrialist might be a vulgar upstart, but he and his social betters shared a vast insensitivity for those trapped on the wrong side of the double bluff.

From their earliest days Keynes and his friends had gathered in secret sects to shut out this thick-skinned world. Perpetuating the individualism, even the eccentricity, of this life was one of his goals as an economist. His method was not mass organization but the intelligence of the precious few. Woolf and Strachey came to his rooms at King's College in 1903 to invite him into the Apostles, a society of Cambridge's intellectual elite that met secretly on Saturday nights. Their guiding philosophy was a kind of didactic aestheticism. The ideas were those of the Cambridge philosopher G. E. Moore, or at least their interpretation of him. They built on Moore's *Principia Ethica,* a work sweet and confident in its assumption of the existence of beauty and goodness and practical in its calculations of how to attain them. As Keynes later described their version of Moore, good was an attribute as morally neutral as, say, green. A little logical analysis—Keynes's father was a logician, the son's first theoretical work was a *Treatise on Probability*—leads quickly to a philosophy of finding the greatest good (as Keynes said he did) in the enjoyment of beautiful objects and the pleasures of human intercourse. The gravest sin seemed that of bad taste.

It certainly was in Bloomsbury—the group that took its name from the district of London where so many of its members lived. Much has been written about that ingathering of intellectual self-exiles that makes it seem a sort of conspiracy, at least to those who remember being withered by its conversation (unacceptable or insipid beliefs were quashed with a single word: "*Re*ally!"). But in fact it was a shepherd's reed hardly strong enough to be sinister. Years later, Keynes described its youthful genesis: "I can see us as water-spiders, gracefully skimming, as light and reasonable as air, the surface of the stream without any contact at all with the eddies and currents underneath." Bloomsbury was the original of the Beautiful People. The set gave famous parties, and one masquerade ball at which Keynes danced the cancan in 1923 has gone into the history books. The two Stephen sisters, who became Virginia Woolf and Vanessa Bell, were its queens, although their husbands were definitely not its kings. This honor was disputed, as was much else, between Keynes and Strachey. When Keynes defied Bloomsbury's positively Ptolemaic tradition of intermarriage and picked a bride from outside the set, the Russian ballerina Lydia Lopokova, Strachey dismissed her as "a half-witted canary."

To this day, the surviving members disagree on who belonged to this Upper Bohemia, where it met, even when it existed (roughly between 1910 and 1930, with time out for a detestable war in which Keynes was one of Bloomsbury's few participants, as a Treasury official managing external finance). The catfights of the memoir writers are

*In a photograph taken about 1917, Bertrand Russell (left) contemplates a verbal fencing match between the economist Keynes and the historian Lytton Strachey.*

of minor importance. What matters is Bloomsbury's essentially static sense. It was a kind of terminal moraine to the great Victorian glacier, the morality leached out; Stephen Spender described it as "the last kick of an enlightened aristocratic tradition." Bloomsbury was indeed the last of the Whig aristocracy, and except for Keynes, these intellectual oligarchs deliberately stripped themselves of public power. Keynes was Bloomsbury's man of action and adviser on the outside world, with a typical Whig zest that disdained all zeal. He would help arrange the finances for that Room of One's Own, which cost a neat £500 a year. He would advise Strachey where to go in the Mediterranean for the best value in "bed and boy." His homosexuality helped reinforce his sense of social separatism. Today we would call it alienation. But Keynes was never alienated from his society, except perhaps when he attacked it for sheer economic stupidity. He mastered society from above and quite naturally built his personal elitism into his economic techniques.

Reminiscences of Keynes's life make it a fine, sunlit, effortlessly spun web. His characteristic manner was sitting sunk deep in an armchair, each hand tucked into the opposite coat sleeve like a mandarin. His face was not handsome. He had a large spoonbill nose, which earned him the nickname "Snout" at Eton. But he allied his modulated, musical voice to his persuasive powers and delighted in argument for its own sake. "Like Dr. Johnson, he would talk for victory," recalled Noel Annan, a Cambridge colleague.

Keynes speculated on both money and commodity markets with the same languorous confidence. Operating from his bed every morning, equipped only with telephone, newspapers, and an uncanny knowledge of long-range trends—"my diversion," he wrote his mother—he built his personal fortune from an initial capital of £4,000 (most of it borrowed after losing his own savings in a first plunge on the markets).

"The dealers on Wall Street could make huge fortunes if only they had no inside information," he once said. He beat them at their own game in the 1930's by investing heavily in American utility stocks. Wall Street believed That Man in the White House would show his true socialist colors by nationalizing the public utilities. Keynes knew better. When the stocks eventually rose, he made a killing.

By 1937, when a heart attack curtailed his activities, his fortune was £506,450. His art collection was valued at £31,419 at his death. In the public interest he had also laid the foundations of the National Gallery's impressionist collection by attending a wartime Paris art auction armed with £20,000 of government money and Duncan Grant's advice; it was the spring of 1918 and Big Bertha was shelling the city, fortuitously depressing prices. "We have great hopes of you and consider that your existence at the Treasury is at last justified," Vanessa Bell wrote patronizingly, and indeed, ungratefully, for Keynes had risked his public position to testify for Bloomsbury's conscientious objectors. When his own call-up notice came, he replied on Treasury stationery that he was simply too busy to attend. For a man of such sheer practical genius life was a game, and the greater the intellectual or financial risk the better.

Keynes was a true Whig. This type of aristocracy is not found outside England. They did not accept the Victorian view of progress and the perfectibility of human nature, and they also rejected the Tory extreme of an Augustinian belief in the utter corruptibility of human nature. Keynes held to the skeptical Whig belief in tolerance and human intelligence as a way out of the thicket. But instead of democratically according these qualities to the citizenry at large, he transferred his faith in an intellectual elite to the government, to that supposedly sensible leadership beloved of the Whigs. He believed that an elite intelligence could manage things better than the citizens themselves, or more precisely, that it could define the arena for the play of individual interests. What he failed to recognize, until too late, was that in our time the government's own huge interests in that same arena would extend its role far beyond that of pure arbiter and that it would be equally subject to the deep irrationalities of the nation as a whole. The disinterested elite is ground to dust in the ring.

Every economist, like any social scientist, is a product of his times. Adam Smith observed and favored an agricultural society in which unemployment was impossible. Industry, cushioned by agriculture and fueled by thrift, operated from what Smith saw as a natural propensity to bargain. Of course this had its ups and downs; in the aggregate it was known as the trade cycle. When demand was slack, the farm families worked less at their cottage looms, sold less, ate less. But they survived, and national accumulations of capital slowly bettered their lot. (Bagehot said Smith believed there was a Scotsman inside each of us.) Malthus described an expanding urban society, and his predictions were consistently overturned by advancing technology. Ricardo and Mill described an early industrial economy of heavy saving and cutthroat competition. The dominant character was the Dickensian entrepreneur plowing his profits back into the firm; the subservient one was the worker robbed of his share of the reinvested profits and forced to sell his labor to the highest bidder.

All their speculations were turned into something close to science by Alfred Marshall, Keynes's teacher at Cambridge. This nineteenth-century mathematical economist devised calculations of supply and demand down to a hairsbreadth, and the more precise they became, the further they were from real life. These economists believed instinctively in the law of the eighteenth-century Frenchman Jean Baptiste Say: supply creates its own demand. Whatever could be produced —and this was natural in an economy of scarcity—would be bought. When the system got out of balance, it could be righted by cutting prices to increase demand, and that included a brutal cut in the price of the worker's labor. The system was beautiful in its self-regulating automaticity. Cheaper labor was supposed to encourage the capitalists to start up their idle factories and put people back to work.

Marx had already realized that workers wouldn't play and would one day refuse to cut their wages. Keynes looked around him and saw that the capitalists wouldn't play either. They refused to risk cutting their prices—and risk is the essence of capitalism. When it faced its crisis in the 1930's, it had lost the nerve to employ the tremendous resources lying idle in Europe and America. With populations declining and technology stuck fast, capitalism seemed to have lost its creative drive. There was a closing of economic frontiers. The Marxists thought the system was at last in its death throes, but Keynes restored its vigor by repealing Say's unworkable law of supply and demand and replacing it with a system that could make man a master of the economic machine instead of its slave.

But Keynes belonged nevertheless to the rationalist tradition of his predecessors, and out of this tradition came *The General Theory of Employment, Interest, and Money* (1936). This seminal work of the twentieth century is not in fact a general theory (Keynes never suffered from excessive modesty), but a system of short-run techniques for manipulating the economy, and in particular the level of employment, which was then capitalism's most serious threat. Their proof was in their practice: the techniques worked.

Keynes introduced the concept of a national balance sheet to regulate the level of employment and the level of consumption plus investment. The balance was not between the individual supply and demand, which never worked anywhere outside the daily cabbage market, but between the size of a nation's total resources and the demand for them. In short, what everyone produces and earns must equal what everyone saves and spends. If we earn less, we also spend and save less. We also produce and invest less. Then the machine begins to run more slowly, and resources are not used, human ones especially. Keynes demonstrated that nothing decreed the machine would ever start up again and call those resources back into use. It could idle along at half-speed for years, as it did during the depression. Nothing was built into the machine—no regulator, no invisible hand—to ensure that it would call on just the precise number of people who were available.

What to do? The answer seems absurdly simple now. The government must raise the level of what people spend, or lower it if there is not enough output to match. It can do this through taxation and through putting extra money into the economy by leaving the budget unbalanced. It must induce businessmen to invest more, by subsidies or lower interest rates. Or it must simply invest more itself, through public works. Naturally, the whole scheme can be thrown into reverse. It is a matter of shuffling the figures in the national equation to keep the machine running at optimum speed.

In the United States the New Deal acted more out of instinct than theory on Keynesian ideas that were already in the air. But without the underpinning of *The General Theory,* Roosevelt was eventually forced to bend to the classical economists and balance the budget. When he did this in 1937, unemployment rose at once. The economist and the President had met in the White House in 1934. Although Roosevelt wrote Felix Frankfurter that he had "had a grand talk with K and liked him immensely," he did not put Keynes's ideas systematically into effect, especially the vital technical ones on deficit finance and credit as a positive (rather than accidental) cure for slack demand. This did not happen until John Kennedy was reluctantly persuaded that it was necessary by his economic advisers.

Keynes admitted that he deliberately overstated his doctrine because he demanded action. "Words ought to be a little wild, for they are the assault of thoughts upon the unthinking." Paul Samuelson once described his master's chef-d'oeuvre thus: "It abounds in mares' nests or confusions . . . In it the Keynesian system stand out indistinctly, as if the author were hardly aware of its existence or cognizant of its proportions. An awkward definition suddenly gives way to an unforgettable cadenza. When finally mastered, its analysis is found to be obvious and at the same time new. In short, it is a work of genius." Keynes

*Keynes and his wife, the ballerina Lydia Lopokova, were photographed in 1945. He died a year later.*

knew it. On New Year's Day in 1935 he wrote Bernard Shaw: "I believe myself to be writing a book on economic theory which will largely revolutionize—not, I suppose, at once but in the course of the next ten years—the way the world thinks about economic problems."

So now the Keynesian revolution has been completed, and like any other, even one launched out of such a gentle and humane tradition, it has begun to devour itself. By demonstrating how to manipulate large forces in the economy, Keynes unwittingly drew the blueprint for an economic juggernaut that must eventually, if it has not done so already, kill the individual values and personal variety he passionately sought to preserve.

Like Freud's, Keynes's sensible ideas have been transported across the Atlantic and turned into a fake philosopher's stone of precise formulas for the supposed prediction of human behavior, a different kind of economic machine, but a machine nevertheless. It could hardly have been a benign intelligence that organized such unfettered production and shifted the control of investment, which is simply the control of economic creation, from the individual to the managerial elite, aptly described by Norman Mailer as "locked in common law marriage with the government for thirty-five years."

As a descriptive social scientist, Keynes saw this coming, but he encouraged it as the only way to keep capitalism going. It seemed self-evident to him that the creators of economic wealth would co-operate with their political rulers in its proper distribution. He explained how to use idle resources, but not misdirected ones; that was a task for simple intelligence. His system of short-term economic management is essentially static, like his very special society. Nothing in it allows for technological disruptions such as automation, nor for the huge concentrations of economic power that can fix the prices for goods or labor almost at will, nor for geometrical progression of ordinary human wants. Keynes provided the economic rationale for public investment in something as vague and rewarding as the pleasant English concept of public amenity—parks, schools, planned housing. He provided equally for public expenditure out of pure decency toward the forgotten, and significantly, nonconsuming parameters. But the will to do this is not necessarily comprehended in Keynes's system, only in his aristocratic soul. By invoking the state as a *deus ex machina* to extract the capitalists from their own contradictions, he assumed that the state would be beneficial, paternalistic, and sensible, if only it could shake off "a failure of intelligence."

But where in the world today can one find such a government of disinterested Whigs? Governments now are the major actors in the economic drama, seizing delightedly on the tools of taxation, investment, and credit that Keynes fashioned for them. Like the Renaissance princes who clipped the coinage, they now know how to manage the modern economy to suit their own purposes.

In the totally new type of economy created through Keynes—an economy neither of scarcity nor glut but of previously unimagined abundance—the master himself may be turning into a defunct economist. The size, complexity, and sheer force of modern productive power are proving less and less amenable to the fine-tuning of Keynesian levers. The economic managers have instead been forced to start swinging meat axes to chop off vigorous but unwanted growths in an economy of such heterogeneity as Keynes never imagined. Credit crunches work indiscriminately; businessmen damn the interest rate and invest even more fanatically. Across-the-board shifts in taxation only stimulate a new rush of money into goods, before they become even more expensive. A situation in which everyone expects rising prices promotes an irrational swirl that can destroy the necessary interplay of the market; for it to operate, buyers who believe prices will go up must balance against sellers who believe they will go down.

This is not to blame Keynes for the monster his followers have created. He had a secure faith in the forces of the market, but also a sensible awareness of their destructive potential. "For my part," he wrote in 1924, "I think that Capitalism, *wisely managed* [my italics], can probably be made more efficient for attaining economic ends than any alternative system yet in sight, but that in itself it is in many ways extremely objectionable. Our problem is to work out a social organization which shall be as efficient as possible without offending our notions of a satisfactory way of life." Later he came to realize that wise management was not as easily attained as good, or even green. In an essay on "My Early Beliefs," read to his old Bloomsbury friends in the Memoir Club, he wrote: "We were not aware that civilization was a thin and precarious crust erected by the personality and the will of a very few, and only maintained by rules and conventions skillfully put across and guilefully preserved. . . . I still suffer incurably from attributing an unreal rationality to other people's feelings and behavior (and doubtless to my own, too). . . . The attribution of rationality to human nature, instead of enriching it, now seems to me to have impoverished it. It ignored certain powerful and valuable springs of feeling." That was in 1938, just after the Mysterious Stranger had first knocked. But Keynes had already devised his system. It was too late to change mental habits to fit in with his new and perhaps darker beliefs.

During his final years Keynes was deeply involved in managing Britain's wartime economy and was given a peerage for it. He negotiated with the United States over the form of the postwar economic system and England's subsidiary role in it. He proposed the equivalent of a world-wide central bank to regulate the financing of world trade, and an international currency that would have downgraded gold ("a barbarous relic"). The idea, a product of sheer intelligence, would have provided the mechanism for solving the dangerous monetary problems we now face. The United States refused to accept anything but a watered-down version in the International Monetary Fund, lest this entail yielding too much of its newly won power to the embryo world authority that Keynes's central bank would have become. After surveying the faces of the American bankers, businessmen, and bureaucrats arrayed around the table at the Bretton Woods Conference in 1944, he remarked to a friend: "They look like knees." It was a look into a faceless future. In March, 1946, Keynes went to the founding meeting of the International Monetary Fund in Savannah and was reduced to quibbling over the location of the Fund's headquarters and its directors' salaries. "I went to Savannah expecting to meet the world, and all I met was a tyrant," he said. A month later he was dead.

Keynes had outlived his time, but surely not his usefulness. What he had missed about communism was that love of money would turn into love of power; and about capitalism, that the managerial elite, whether in business or government, would be suborned by the same thing. But capitalism could not have done without Keynes, and the question it now faces is what to do *with* him. His techniques may be subject to revision, but his essential idea of man controlling his economic destiny cannot be. The problem of capitalism is no longer economic, it is political. Success of this tremendously creative system now depends on whether we can bend the juggernaut to our social will. The key ideas now are not the elitist concept of management but democratic planning and personal participation. If Adam Smith's invisible hand was, in a way, actually created and made visible by Keynes, it now must be connected to those deeper springs of feeling he divined late in life. I do not know what the mechanism should be. But I do know that it demands new democratic institutions to deal with economic complexities. They probably must be drawn on a more intimate scale, but they must also reach far beyond the intellectual elite that Keynes believed was the repository of wisdom. If the ensuing dialogue entails a loss of economic efficiency, then so be it. Economists, Keynes was fond of saying, should be technicians "like dentists." He regarded members of his profession as "the trustees, not of civilization, but of the *possibility* of civilization." Today his intellectual heirs manipulate their slide rules and chortle, "We are all Keynesians now." Keynes would have shuddered at the expression, and if he were alive, I doubt he would be one.

*At the Bretton Woods Conference, Keynes discussed current economic policy with Henry Morgenthau, Jr., then U.S. Secretary of the Treasury.*

# LUDWIG
# WITTGENSTEIN
## 1889-1951

*In the elder days of art,*
*Builders wrought with greatest care*
*Each minute and unseen part,*
*For the Gods are everywhere.*

L udwig Wittgenstein copied this verse of Longfellow's into one of his notebooks with the comment: "Could serve me as a motto." His philosophical work was indeed "wrought with greatest care." The intensity of his striving for complete understanding, his uncompromising integrity and power of genius, make him a heroic figure in our present age. Many consider him to be the greatest philosopher of this century; yet his work has not been assimilated within academic philosophy, and outside of it he is virtually unknown.

Wittgenstein was born in Vienna in 1889, the youngest of eight children. His father, Karl Wittgenstein, was a strong-willed, self-made man, who ran away to America at age seventeen. Returning to Vienna after two years, Karl underwent a brief training in engineering before going to work as a draftsman in a steel mill. In ten years' time he was the head of a large steel company and subsequently organized the first cartel of the Austrian steel industry. Ludwig was educated at home until age fourteen, and then studied mathematics and physical sciences in an Austrian school for three years. Thereafter, he studied mechanical engineering in Germany for two years, and then went to England in 1908 to do aeronautical research at the University of Man-

*Ludwig Wittgenstein was forty-eight when this snapshot was taken in Cambridge.*

*By* NORMAN MALCOLM

chester. He designed a jet-reaction engine, supervised its construction, and tested it successfully. His interest shifted to mathematics, then to the foundaions of mathematics. He came upon Bertrand Russell's *Principles of Mathematics* and was excited by it. In 1912 he gave up engineering and went to Cambridge to study with Russell, who was astonished by the rapidity of his progress in logical studies. Soon Wittgenstein was engaged in the research that culminated in the logical ideas of the *Tractatus.*

At Cambridge Wittgenstein began his first reading in philosophy. To his friend David Pinsent, a fellow student, he expressed "naive surprise" that the philosophers whom he had "worshiped in ignorance" were after all "stupid and dishonest and make disgusting mistakes!" He and Pinsent were united by strong musical interests. They had a repertoire of forty of Schubert's songs, whose melodies Wittgenstein would whistle while Pinsent accompanied him on the piano. Wittgenstein had an excellent memory for music, and in addition to his rare gift for whistling, could play the clarinet. He retained a deep interest in music, and in his writings often made comparisons between musical phrases and the sentences of language.

Pinsent found Wittgenstein a difficult companion: irritable, nervously sensitive, often depressed. Sometimes Wittgenstein was convinced that death would overtake him before he perfected his new ideas in logic; sometimes he was depressed by the thought that his logical work might be of no real value. Even so, his frame of mind was less morbid than it had been before he came to Cambridge. He told Pinsent that in previous years hardly a day had passed in which he had not thought of suicide "as a possibility." (Three of his brothers did commit suicide; the fourth, Paul, became a well-known pianist.) Coming to study with Russell had been his "salvation."

Wittgenstein worked with fierce energy at his logical ideas. He submitted to hypnosis in the hope that while in hypnotic trance he could give clear answers to questions about problems of logic. In 1913 he went to Norway to work in seclusion. During this time he originated his famous conception that logical truths are "tautologies" and "say nothing." His frequent letters to Russell were filled with the excitement of his logical discoveries, and also were warmly affectionate. But he expressed the conviction that he and Russell were not suited for true friendship. This would require that both of them be "pure"; a relationship founded on "hypocrisy" was intolerable. Wittgenstein was deeply disturbed about his own moral condition. "My life is *full* of the most hateful and petty thoughts and acts (this is *no* exaggeration)." "Perhaps you think it is a waste of time for me to think about myself; but how can I be a logician if I am not yet a man! *Before everything else* I must become pure."

*Ludwig was the youngest of eight children, the son of a Viennese businessman.*

Upon the outbreak of the First World War Wittgenstein immediately volunteered for service as a private in the Austrian army. He was an artillery observer in a howitzer regiment on the Russian front and won several decorations for bravery. After being commissioned as an officer, he served in a mountain artillery regiment on the Italian front. He was a good officer in the severe mountain fighting, steadying his men by his example. Throughout the war Wittgenstein continued to think hard about problems of logic and philosophy, writing down his thoughts in notebooks carried in his rucksack. When he was taken prisoner in November, 1918, he had a completed manuscript, which he sent to Russell in England. Through Russell's efforts the work was published, first in a German edition in 1921 under the title *Logisch-philosophische Abhandlung,* and in the following year in England, with German text and English translation, under the title by which it is known: *Tractatus Logico-Philosophicus.*

The *Tractatus* is original and profound. Despite its difficulty, it has been widely influential and is regarded on all sides as a classic. The book is organized into a series of remarks that are carefully ordered and numbered in a decimal notation. From the first sentence ("The world is everything that is the case") to the last ("Whereof one cannot speak, thereof one must be silent") the style is frequently aphoristic. Only seventy-five pages in length, the book sweeps over a great range of topics. It treats of the nature of signs and sentences; the limits of language; sense and nonsense; logical form and logical truth; causality and induction; the self and the will; good and evil. The central problem of the *Tractatus* can be put like this: how is language possible? It has struck many thinkers as remarkable that one can, by making noises or marks on paper, *say* something. Wittgenstein wrote in a notebook: "My *whole* task consists in explaining the nature of sentences." What makes it possible for a combination of marks to represent a fact in the world? How can one *inform* another person that such and such is the case? Wittgenstein was impressed by the notion that we learn the meaning of words but not of sentences. "I understand a sentence without having had its sense explained to me." When we encounter a new sentence composed of familiar words, we understand it. How is this to be explained?

Wittgenstein's solution is that a significant sentence (a "proposition") is a *picture* or a *model.* "A proposition is a picture of reality. A proposition is a model of reality as we think it to be." This idea occurred to Wittgenstein when he saw an account of how a motorcar accident was represented in a law court by means of dolls and toy cars. These could be manipulated to depict different ways in which the accident might have taken place, to construct different accounts of it. A proposition composed of words works in the same way. It depicts a situation in the world. If we know the meaning of its components, then we understand the proposition, without further explanation, by virtue of the fact that just like a picture or model, it *shows* how things are if it is true. According to the *Tractatus,* there must be in any picture a one-to-one correspondence between the elements of the picture and the elements of the state of affairs it portrays. The picture-elements are related to one another in a certain way, and this fact portrays that the corresponding reality-elements are related to one another in the same way. Since a sentence is a picture, there must be as many elements to be distinguished in it as in the state of affairs it portrays. This does not *seem* to be true of our ordinary sentences (e.g., "He shook hands with a hundred people"); nonetheless it is so. Our ordinary sentences have a hidden complexity that comes to light only when they are completely analyzed.

The metaphysics of the *Tractatus* requires that the world be composed of *simple* objects, and that language be composed of *names* which stand for the simple objects. An *elementary* proposition is a combination of names that, like the configuration of small models in the law court, depicts a situation in the world. Every genuine proposition is either elementary or else a truth-functional compound out of elementary propositions. The analysis of our ordinary propositions, by taking account of their complicated modes of symbolizing, their various "methods of projection," will make manifest their concealed pictorial nature. A completely analyzed proposition will consist of names; the meaning of each name will be a simple object; the particular way in which the names are combined in the proposition will *say* that the simple objects in the world are related.

Wittgenstein had no criteria for identifying elementary propositions or names or simple objects. His primary intuition was that language pictures reality; from this it seemed to follow that there *must be* simple objects, names, and elementary propositions, even though he was not able to provide any examples.

A striking feature of the *Tractatus* is its conception of the limits of language. Not only must a propositional-picture contain exactly as many elements as the situation it represents, but all pictures and all possible situations in the world must share the same logical form. This form that is common to language and reality cannot itself be represented. "Propositions can represent the whole of reality, but they cannot represent what they must have in common with reality in order to be able to represent it." "What can be said can only be said by means of a proposition, and so nothing that is necessary for the understanding of *all* propositions can be said."

According to the picture theory, a proposition and its negation are both possible. Which one is true is accidental; there is no necessity in the world. One conclusion drawn by Wittgenstein is that there are no genuine propositions of ethics. His thought here was that if anything is good or bad in an ethical sense, this cannot be accidental; what we feel is that the thing *must* have that value. But everything in the world is accidental; hence there is no value in the world. "In the world everything is as it is, and everything happens as it does happen; *in* it no value exists—and if it did, it would have no value." Genuine propositions can state only what is in the world. What belongs to ethics cannot be stated; it is "transcendental." Furthermore, Wittgenstein's own philosophical propositions are finally seen as trying to say what cannot be said. "Anyone who understands me eventually recognizes them [the propositions] as nonsensical, when he has used them—as steps—to climb up beyond them. (He must, so to speak, throw away the ladder after he has climbed up it.) He must transcend these propositions, and then he will see the world aright."

Upon his father's death in 1912 Wittgenstein inherited a fortune. In 1914 he bestowed a large sum of money, anonymously, on a number of Austrian writers and artists. When he returned to civil life in 1919, he gave his fortune to two of his sisters, remarking that they had so much money already that some more would not hurt them. Once he said that he had given up his wealth so that he would not have friends for the sake of his money; but it is also true that both the ease and the attachments of wealth would have been distasteful to him.

The author of the *Tractatus* believed that he had obtained definitive solutions of the problems treated there. He felt that he had no further contribution to make to philosophy, and after his release from the army he sought another vocation. After a period of painfully humiliating attendance at a teachers' training college he became an elementary-school teacher. From 1920 to 1926 he taught in various tiny villages in Lower Austria. During this period he was severely unhappy and frequently thought of suicide. He was helped by his relationship with his young pupils. A letter says: "The one good thing in my life just now is that I sometimes read fairy-tales to the children at school. It pleases them and relieves the strain on me. But otherwise things are in a mess for yours truly." He also found some joy in music. A fellow teacher in one school was a talented pianist, and the two of them devoted many afternoons to music.

Severe friction developed between Wittgenstein and some of the other teachers and villagers. In 1926 he abandoned his career as a schoolteacher. He worked for a few months as a gardener's assistant at a monastery. Meanwhile, one of his sisters had commissioned the architect Paul Engelmann to build a mansion for her in Vienna.

Engelmann, a friend of Wittgenstein's, proposed to him that they undertake it jointly. Wittgenstein agreed and actually became the directing mind in the project, which occupied him for two years. He gave to this work his characteristic concentration, creating a building that in its exactness of proportion, severe simplicity, and freedom from decoration might be called a *Tractatus* in stone.

For a period of ten years after the war Wittgenstein did not engage in philosophical work. Suddenly he felt that once again he could do creative work in philosophy. What produced this change of mind is unknown, but it has been rumored that it was provoked by a lecture on the foundations of mathematics by L. E. J. Brouwer that Wittgenstein heard in Vienna in 1928. He returned to Cambridge in January, 1929. He was given a research fellowship by Trinity College and began to give lectures in January, 1930. He remained at Cambridge until 1926, when he went to live for nearly a year in a hut he built in Norway. There he began the writing of the *Philosophical Investigations*. In 1937 he returned to Cambridge and two years later was appointed to succeed G. E. Moore as professor of philosophy.

Through his lectures and the wide circulation of notes taken by his students, Wittgenstein began to exert a powerful new influence on philosophical thought throughout the English-speaking world. Each lecture was a fresh creation. His only preparation was to spend a few minutes before the class met in recalling the course that the inquiry had taken at the previous meeting. He had once tried to lecture from prepared notes but was disgusted with the result; the words looked like "corpses" when he read them. The extemporaneous procedure he adopted was made possible by the vast amount of thinking and writing he was devoting to the problems under discussion. His class met twice weekly in his rooms at Trinity for two hours at a time. Typically, he would invite questions or comments, and most of each session might be taken up with his reactions to those remarks. His ideas did not come forth easily or fluently. He carried on a visible struggle with his thoughts. There were long silences during which his gaze was concentrated, his expression was stern, and his hands made arresting movements. His face was remarkably mobile and expressive when he talked, and his words came out with great force. His eyes were fierce and his whole personality was commanding, even imperial.

The major problem areas in which he lectured were the philosophy of mathematics and the philosophy of mind; but some other topics were aesthetics; Freud on dreams, jokes, and the unconscious; Frazer's views, in *The Golden Bough,* on primitive ritual and magic; the nature of philosophical confusion and insight. Wittgenstein's lectures were characterized by great richness of illustration and comparison. He attacked philosophical problems energetically, even passionately.

He once exclaimed: "My father was a businessman and I'm a businessman, too!"—meaning that he wanted to clear up the problems in a businesslike way, to settle them, get rid of them. On the other hand, he returned to the same problems again and again, exploring them from different directions, always dissatisfied with his treatment of them. He wrote in a notebook that his own talent for philosophy consisted in continuing to be puzzled when others had let the puzzlement slip away from them and therefore thought they had arrived at clarity.

Wittgenstein's rooms in Trinity College were austerely furnished. There was no easy chair or reading lamp. There was no ornaments, paintings, or photographs. The walls were bare. In his living room were two canvas chairs and a plain wooden chair, and in his bedroom a canvas cot. An old-fashioned iron heating stove was in the center of the living room. There were some flowers in a window box, and one or two flowerpots in the room. There was a metal safe in which he kept his manuscripts, and a card table on which he did his writing. His dress was equally simple. He wore gray flannel trousers, a flannel shirt open at the throat, and a woolen lumber jacket or leather jacket. Out of doors, in wet weather, he wore a tweed cap and a tan raincoat. He walked with a light cane. His clothes, like his rooms, were always clean and neat. He was about five feet six inches in height and slender. His face was lean and brown, his profile aquiline and strikingly beautiful, his head covered with a curly mass of brown hair. He always spoke emphatically, in a resonant voice, with a distinctive intonation and strong gestures.

Bertrand Russell (above) was Wittgenstein's mentor, friend, and "salvation." It was he who arranged for the publication of the Tractatus. G. E. Moore (below) was a teacher and friend at Cambridge. When Moore retired in 1939, Wittgenstein was appointed professor of philosophy in his place.

Friendship was of utmost importance to Wittgenstein. He was enormously appreciative of any simple kindness. With his friends he was warm, loyal, and generous. Yet friendship with him was an exacting relationship. He could not tolerate sloppy or superficial thinking and was suspicious of motives; he could rebuke a friend with extreme harshness. He once said: "Although I cannot *give* affection, I have a great *need* for it." Human kindness—human concern—was for him a far more important attribute in a person than intellectual power or cultivated taste. With his friends he was occasionally lighthearted; he could put on a charming mood in which he talked nonsense with a semblance of utmost gravity. But usually his thoughts were somber. He was dismayed by the insincerity, vanity, and coldness of the human heart. He was troubled about his own failings and often near despair.

Wittgenstein had an extreme dislike of university life. He refused to dine at High Table in Trinity because he detested shallow conversations. He tried to persuade a number of his students to give up their plans to become teachers of philosophy, believing that it was nearly impossible to become an academic philosopher and remain an honest and serious person. He was disgusted by what he observed of the half-understanding of his own ideas, and feared that his influence was positively harmful. At the end of a term of lectures he exclaimed: "The only seed I am likely to sow is a certain jargon!"

From 1929 until his death in 1951 Wittgenstein wrote prodigiously, although none of this work was published in his lifetime. A large number of his notebooks, manuscripts, and typescripts have been preserved. The crowning achievement of this second period is the *Philosophical Investigations (Philosophische Untersuchungen)*, published posthumously in 1953. Since then a number of related writings have been edited and published. One striking aspect of the new work is its repudiation of the basic ideas of the *Tractatus*. This development is probably unique in the history of philosophy—a thinker producing, at different periods, two highly original systems of thought, each system the result of many years of intensive labors, each expressed in a powerful style, each greatly influencing contemporary philosophy, and the second containing a criticism and rejection of the first.

It is impossible to give here anything more than a rough impression of the differences between the two outlooks. Wittgenstein came to renounce such previous assumptions of his as that reality and language are each composed of simple elements, that language and reality must have the same multiplicity, that each proposition has one and only one complete analysis, that there is one universal form of language. According to the *Tractatus*, the huge variety in the uses of language is misleading; in this variety there is concealed a common structure to which a logician tries to penetrate. In the *Investigations* this is held to be an illusion. In the diversity of the uses of language, there is no unifying essence.

A basic conception of this philosophy is that language is composed of "language-games" in which words are connected with various activities or "forms of life." Wittgenstein draws attention to the way we use the word "game." We do not insist that there be a common feature in all games; in fact there are only various similarities, along with various dissimilarities. The things we call "games" have only a "family resemblance." Some but not all games are amusing, or involve competition, or winning and losing. Some involve skill; but "skill" in tennis is very different from "skill" in poker. Wittgenstein's aim is to get us to see that what is true of our use of "game" also holds for the terms that loom so large in philosophy— "proposition," "statement," "knowledge," "thinking," "understanding," "rule," "recognition," and so on. The word "recognition," for example, is applied to many different cases. When learning language, we are encouraged to make various applications of the word "recognize." We then go on to extend the application of the word to new and different situations. "As in spinning a thread," says Wittgenstein, "we twist fibre on fibre. And the strength of the thread does not reside in the fact that some one fibre runs through its whole length, but in the overlapping of many fibres." The various applications of the word "recognize" are so different that it is even misleading to speak of *the* concept of recognition. It is possible to use a number of different words where in fact we use one.

It is typically philosophical to ask "What is knowledge?" "What is love?" "What is justice?" The normal assumption is that there must be some one formula that will cover *all* cases and will give us logically necessary and sufficient conditions of knowledge, or of love, or of justice. We crave an exact definition. But this is a will-o'-the-wisp. Wittgenstein says: "The worst enemy of clear thinking is the impulse toward greater generality." This impulse is characteristic of the mathematical and scientific spirit of our age, to which Wittgenstein felt himself opposed. Partly we are misled by the fact that *one word* (e.g., "knowledge") is used to cover many different cases; we are, as it were, *bewitched* by a word. But we also tend to concentrate our attention on a single kind of case, in which we think we see a law for the whole use of a word. As Wittgensetin remarks: "A main cause of philosophical disease—a one-sided diet: one nourishes one's thinking with only one kind of example." In order to arrive at a clear view of our concepts we have to resist this tendency.

In a notebook Wittgenstein made the following observation about the alleged static nature of philosophy:

Again and again one hears the remark that philosophy really makes no advance, that the same philosophical problems with which the Greeks were occupied still engage us. But whoever says this does not understand the reason why it must be so, which is that our language remains the same and always tempts us to ask the same questions. As long as there is a verb "to be" that appears to function like "to eat" and "to drink"; as long as there are the adjectives "identical," "true," "false," "possible"; as long as we speak of a flow of time and of an extension of space; and so on—so long will men thrust against the same enigmatic difficulties, and stare at something that no explanation seems to be able to remove.

When we think philosophically, we are constantly deceived or bewildered by the expressions of language. Wittgenstein believed that the only remedy is to *describe the use* of those expressions; only this will relieve our mental cramp. Instead of letting our gaze be fixed on the surface structures of language, we must look to their use. This use is not hidden; it lies open to view. One might suppose that philosophy, so conceived, ought to be easy—one just describes how words are used. Yet, in fact, philosophy is enormously difficult. Wittgenstein sought to explain why this is so by the following metaphor: "Philosophy loosens the knots in our thinking, which we have in a senseless way put there; to this end it must make movements that are just as complicated as those knots are." Philosophy should be purely descriptive; it ought not to formulate hypotheses or give reasons. We ought to see *what* is there, and not ask *why* it is there. Wittgenstein remarked that "People who always ask 'Why?' are like tourists reading in their Baedeker, who stand before a structure and because of reading the history of its origin, etc., are prevented from *seeing* the structure." If we observe in detail the various ways in which we employ such a word as "know" or "intend" or "recognize," arranging the different uses in a spectrum, accepting the variety and the individuality that we see there, not yielding to our obsessive, unwarranted belief that there must be a common nature concealed in the variety, resisting our compulsion to ask "Why?"—then our perplexities about knowledge, intention, recognition, and so on may be dissolved. But all of this requires us to struggle against our inclinations. "A philosopher is one who must heal in himself many illnesses of understanding, before he can arrive at the notion of a sound human understanding."

An outstanding feature of Wittgenstein's second philosophy is his concern in showing how concepts are linked to actions and activities, to responses and reactions, to the expression of the concepts in human life. In a sense his conceptual investigations are anthropological studies; as he put it, they are "remarks on the nature history of human beings." One's puzzlement about the meaning of a form of words may be removed if one asks oneself: "On what occasion, for what purposes, do we say this? What kinds of actions accompany these words? (Think of a greeting.) In what scenes will they be used; and what for?" We should observe the role of words *within* the language games, *within* the living practices where our doubts, questions, inquiries, proofs, certainties, have their home. Philosophers are constantly tempted to ignore the life setting of a form of words. One of Wittgenstein's favorite illustrations is the following: "A philosopher says that he understands the sentence 'I am here,' that he means something by it, thinks something—even if he doesn't consider at all how, on what occasions, this sentence is employed." If we abstract a sequence of words from the context of its employment in the "rough ground" of actual language, no wonder that we do not understand its meaning, for then it has none! As Wittgenstein puts it: "Only in the stream of thought and life do words have meaning."

In the Second World War Wittgenstein could not remain a spectator. He obtained a porter's job at Guy's Hospital in London. Later he worked as a laboratory assistant in the Royal Victoria Infirmary in Newcastle. In the fall of 1944 he returned to Cambridge to resume his lectures and discussions. But he grew more and more restive in the "absurd job" of a professor of philosophy. ("It is a kind of living death.") At the end of 1947 he finally resigned his chair, even though his professorial salary was his sole income. He wanted to devote his time and strength to completing the *Investigations;* but he also felt a need for "thinking *alone,* without having to talk to anybody." In the last years of his life he was frequently ill, and in the fall of 1949 he learned that he had cancer. This discovery did not disturb him, for he had "*no* wish to live on." He continued to work with intensity and power until overcome by the final violence of the cancer. He died in Cambridge on April 29, 1951.

It is not easy to characterize Wittgenstein's attitude toward the philosophical work of his second period. He knew that he had created a new method and a new outlook. On the other hand, he regarded his work as imperfect. He strove with unceasing energy and concentration to perfect it, yet despaired of success. To a friend he quoted the dedication that Bach wrote on the title page of his *Little Organ Book* ("To honor the most high God, and to benefit my fellow man"), and he remarked that he would have liked to have been able to say that about his *Philosophical Investigations.* He was uncertain of the fate of his work, but he inclined toward pessimism. In the preface to the *Investigations* he wrote: "That this work, in its poverty and in the darkness of this time, should bring light into one brain or another, is not impossible; but certainly it is not probable."

It could not be said that Wittgenstein's life was happy. There was the restlessness, the deep pessimism, the intensity of his mental and moral suffering, the relentless way in which he drove his intellect, his need for love together with a harshness that repelled love. Yet there was also the excitement, the freshness and strength, the shattering insights of his thinking. In a notebook he wrote: "The joy of my thoughts is the joy of my own strange life." So there was joy. And the last words he uttered were, "Tell them I've had a wonderful life!" Not happy—but wonderful.

*Wittgenstein lived, taught, and wrote in Trinity College, Cambridge.*

# NORBERT WIENER
## 1894-1964

# WARREN McCULLOCH
## 1898-1969

T he curtain has only just fallen and we can still hear their footfall in the wings. Norbert Wiener took his last bow in 1964; Warren McCulloch followed him five years later. Given a Newton, a Darwin, even a Freud, we can view both the thinker's work and the man's personality in a certain historical perspective. In the case of Wiener and McCulloch, it is too soon to do this, for we are still under the spell of their actual presence. Yet already legend is beginning to take over, and recollection is taking on a definite shape. As we gather up our belongings and file out into the everyday world, the memory forms of an ill-assorted but entirely complementary pair. McCulloch, the gaunt, bearded romantic, with the air of an Old Testament prophet; Wiener, the tubby, fussy, thick-lensed mathematician, displaying the public self-confidence of a Beecham or a Diaghilev—it is hard to think of two men more clearly contrasted in style or in personality. Yet what they achieved between them was something that required them both. They might bicker, disagree, have doubts about each other's approaches, results, even motives. But they were a team. Jointly, they brought off the kind of intellectual transformation that neither could have managed singlehanded. They were as indispensable to one another's success as—yes, that's it—as Sancho Panza and Don Quixote.

Both men were great masters of the word, and their phrases linger on in our ears. They were preoccupied (as McCulloch put it) with *The Embodiment of Mind,* and they were concerned that the results of

*Fathers of the cybernetic revolution: Norbert Wiener, top, and Warren McCulloch.*

their work should (in Wiener's phrase) contribute to *The Human Use of Human Beings*. Perhaps the analytic theory of "control and communication in the animal and machine"—for which Wiener invented the name "cybernetics"—might be laying intellectual foundations for the whole technological world of automation and the computer that raises goose flesh nowadays among all paid-up members of the Counter Culture; but in their eyes, all these methods and instruments were our servants, not our masters. And in any case, the crucial importance of these developments was not practical but intellectual; for they could liberate man from old myths and return him to a proper understanding of his own place within the world of nature, from which his theories had for so long been cutting him off.

Perhaps, again, their arguments might sometimes lead them into "the den of the metaphysician"; but their metaphysics was directed, not by an old-style mechanistic materialism, but toward a new humanism. Man the knower and agent could no longer be divided off from, and set over against, nature, the object of his knowledge and actions. The working dichotomies on which three centuries of Cartesian natural philosophy had been founded were at last outgrown. Mind is embodied: matter is capable of mentality. Views that caused a scandal two centuries earlier, as expounded in Julien de La Mettrie's *L'Homme machine* (1747), could at last have detailed mathematical substance conferred on them. The knower and the known both operated from within a common nature. From now on, each could be understood only in terms of the other. The questions that McCulloch himself posed about number, in particular, we must now ask also about the objects of mental activity generally:

> What is Man, that he may know a Number?
> And what is a Number, that a Man may know it?

So, despite any distaste we may have for the physical machinery of the modern world, we should take care not to overlook the contributions that Norbert Wiener and Warren McCulloch and the whole cybernetic movement have made to the shaping of modern thought as well.

Before we pin down the nature of these contributions, two preliminary points of social history are worth noticing. When we consider the thought of earlier centuries, our picture of the "thinker" is an essentially solitary, individual one. René Descartes, sitting over his winter stove, meditates on the necessity of his own clearest and most distinct ideas; Isaac Newton, shut away in his rooms at Trinity College, Cambridge, confides a jumble of alchemical, Scriptural, and mathematical speculations to the secrecy of his private notebooks; Charles Darwin, sequestered at Downe, refashions the whole of natural history in his own mind. It is a partial, but in the context, a relevant picture. Before the twentieth century the major transformations in men's ideas were, in the first place, the achievement of individuals, and they became the common property of mankind only later.

At the same time, this picture can mislead us, by distracting us from the collective character of our intellectual enterprises, and of the intellectual traditions they embody. And there are times and places at which the scale, subtlety, or sheer technicality of the outstanding problems makes intellectual invention itself a task, not for one man alone, but for the co-operation of two, three, or even more. In the twentieth century, in fact, we are learning to live with the phenomenon of multiple authorship. There is, for instance, a fertile, distinguished, and highly original French writer on pure mathematics called Bourbaki; on investigation, Bourbaki turns out to be not a single mathematician but a group of mathematicians working in collaboration. In high-energy physics, similarly, more and more papers are being published under the names of four, six, or even a dozen research scientists. So there need be nothing paradoxical in the way that the original ideas of Wiener and McCulloch—with other men such as Walter Pitts and Claude E. Shannon in the background—interacted as they did to produce the "cybernetic revolution" in our thought. This cross-fertilization is just a sign of the times.

*Julien de La Mettrie had shocked his readers in 1747 with the views he set forth in* L'Homme machine *(the title page is shown below), views on which cybernetics at last conferred mathematical substance.*

It is also a sign of the times that both the chief architects of this new approach to human nature should have spent the mature part of their professional careers at the Massachusetts Institute of Technology. For the key step in the transition from the Cartesian to the cybernetic method was that of bringing "thinking machines" into the center of the philosophical debate. It involved recognizing that thinking—the central source of puzzlement in the whole Cartesian world-view—is not itself an *argument* so much as an *activity*, and that, as such, it is something we may come to understand much better if we consider how an artifact might be constructed that could simulate it. The switch to cybernetics, that is, took epistemology out of the hands of the logicians and pure mathematicians and handed it over to the physiologists and applied mathematicians. And the motives for this switch were philosophical rather than technological. From this new point of view, the computer was an intellectual "model" to be explored for mental profit, not a tool to be exploited for material gain. If we want to make sense of human thought processes, and of the part played in them by the brain, the computer may, after all, provide us with a better template, or object of comparison, than Descartes's preferred model of a geometric proof.

Nor was it an accident that this cybernetic approach had affiliations with the theory of information transfer and transmission networks, as developed by Shannon and his associates at Bell Telephone Laboratories. The two theories were, in fact, based on some common general concepts. Still, the practical application of those concepts was, above all, the concern of Bell Laboratories. To the scientists at M.I.T. the interest and importance have been strictly theoretical: the question has been what light they could throw on philosophical and physiological questions inherited from Descartes and Locke, Leibnitz and Helmholtz—questions about the nature of perception, about the formation of concepts in the life of the human individual, and about the structure of the brain, regarded as the organ of higher mental function.

As with so many of the fundamental steps in the making of modern thought, the new view of mind and brain developed by Wiener and McCulloch called for a certain sophisticated innocence and simplicity of mind. For it meant acknowledging and setting aside a confusion that had dominated much of European thinking for some three hundred years. The men who founded physical science as we know it, in the seventeenth century, had created the modern mind-body problem almost inadvertently; after Descartes and Newton, that problem was far more acute and insoluble than it had ever been for, say, Aristotle. In retrospect, the reason is clear enough. They ended in insuperable difficulties over mind, just because they were so sure they understood matter—and matter, as they defined it, could certainly not display mentality.

The "new mathematical philosophers" of the seventeenth century had no real doubt in their minds what matter was. It was a passive, extended substratum, whose essential properties were purely geometric—with or without certain physical accidents, such as inertia and gravitational mass, thrown in—and it served only to carry, and pass on, that motion with which constituent parts of the universe had been endowed at the Creation. Bits of material substance could push up against, collide, or become entangled with one another, but they were incapable of displaying spontaneous, still less intelligent, activities. How were the physicists of the seventeenth century so sure about this? That is no longer clear. True, they had to take some such working definition of matter for granted if they were to go ahead and construct the kinds of cosmological theories (or systems of "natural philosophy") at which both Descartes and Newton were aiming; and the spectacular intellectual successes of Newton's theory of universal gravitation certainly appeared to reflect credit retrospectively onto all the assumptions he had made en route to that result. But this view of matter soon became much more than a working definition and acquired the status of an unquestioned axiom.

To Descartes, for example, it was a manifestly "clear" truth about his "distinct" idea of matter that its essence existed in extension and nothing but extension; and few of his seventeenth-century successors in theoretical physics were prepared to challenge that axiom. Once this initial assumption was safely made, however, a great many further questions were prejudged. If that was what matter was like, for instance, then all material operations were necessarily "causal," in a very crude sense of the term, while "rational" thought, mentality, and consciousness were evidently quite foreign to matter and to mechanical processes. Once this way of defining terms like "matter" and "material," "mechanical" and "machine," was accepted, the phrase "thinking machine" became a contradiction in terms. And this is just the conclusion that most philosophers drew, from the time of Descartes right up to the time of Bertrand Russell.

During the eighteenth century a few anti-Cartesians insisted that this conclusion was invalid because the definitions of matter and machine on which it rested were arbitrary and had not been shown to have universal application to actual experience. Here, for instance, is Julien de La Mettrie:

No, there is nothing gross about Matter, except to those coarse eyes which cannot recognize it in its most brilliant Works; and Nature is in no way an Artist of limited capacities . . . I consider Thought so little incompatible with organized Matter that it seems to be a property of it, exactly like electricity, the Motive Faculty, Impenetrability, Extension, and so on.

But the objections of such men as La Mettrie and Joseph Priestley were either ignored, or more often, shouted down. Any such doubts appeared to be evidence of vile materialism, which was taken as also implying religious infidelity; and all of Priestley's piety and theological subtlety was not enough to rescue him from these accusations.

The trouble was that the accepted physical theories of matter had great and growing explanatory achievements to their credit, whereas men like Priestley, however justified their hesitation might be, could produce no comparable counterdemonstrations to lend weight to their skepticism. It was one thing to point out what was the simple truth; namely, that the mind-body problem, in its accepted form, was the immediate consequence of arbitrary a priori assumptions about what matter and/or machines were and were not in principle capable of doing. But it was quite another thing to make this objection stick, or to persuade philosophers in general that the notion of a thinking machine was anything other than an illegitimate *façon de parler.* Until that could be done, such supporters of psychological materialism as La Mettrie and Priestley, Charles Darwin and William Lawrence, merely exposed themselves to the charge that they were degrading man—with all his rational powers—to the level of a machine, which, as everybody knew, was incapable of anything going by the name of thought. *Quod erat refutandum.*

In the long run, the only satisfactory way of countering the influence of this Cartesian axiom was to recover a pre-Cartesian innocence of approach. It was no longer good enough to deal with the question, what matter and machines can or cannot do, simply as a question of principle—to be settled by appeal to axioms and definitions—as Descartes himself had done. Instead, it was time to investigate what limits the capacity of the machines had in actual fact, and so to establish by empirical and practical means, quite aside from all a priori preconceptions, what scope the idea of mechanical explanation truly has. If the whole picture of the mind as a secret chamber mysteriously lodged in the depths of the brain has taken such firm hold on the philosophical and scientific thought of Europeans since 1650, this is because they had lost the ability to look at matter, man, and machine with an unprejudiced and empirical eye. Rather than giving way to polemical rhetoric about degrading men to the level of machines, we should be looking at the whole relationship between material systems and higher mental functions the other way around, that is, we should be asking how far, and in what respects, the capacities of machines might conceivably be raised to the level of human thought and intelligence, or even beyond. To the unvarnished question "Are men machines?" we can give only the plain answer "Certainly not!" But, if that question is rephrased to read "Could machines become like men?" the answer is not so self-evident. It calls, on the contrary, for some complex and abstruse analysis, and also for a subtle and delicate understanding of the features that have made human behavior itself appear so puzzling and unique.

*M.I.T., above, was the birthplace of cybernetics.*

That was the scene onto which Norbert Wiener and Warren McCulloch made their separate entrances at the close of the Second World War. Yet, in the years since 1900, one major obstacle had already been cleared off the stage. Right through the nineteenth century, the Cartesian axioms about matter had retained their unchallenged authority. Between 1900 and 1930 they had been swept away. If the men of the 1890's still thought they understood the essential nature of matter well enough, by 1925 they were thrown back into doubt and confusion. Was matter composed of waves or of particles? Did it consist fundamentally of electromagnetic energy, of kinks in the space-time continuum, or of probabilities? Just because they had previously been so exaggeratedly confident about their knowledge of matter, their skepticism and perplexity were now correspondingly complete. In the new quantum physics one could still give powerful explanations of physical and chemical phenomena—never more so—but whether matter itself could be said to have any essential properties at all, and whether one could accordingly draw any a priori limits to the capacities of material or mechanical systems, who could say? From being the "clearest," the most "distinct," and therefore the most fundamental idea in the whole of natural philosophy, the physicist's concept of matter seemed suddenly to have become entirely obscure and hazy. In this way, the dethronement of Cartesian matter had cleared the ground for a fresh attack on the philosophical and scientific problems of mind also.

To this task, Wiener and McCulloch brought complementary talents and personalities. Both were nearing fifty and had full careers behind them, but their professional preparation and backgrounds were entirely different. Wiener was a Cambridge man born and bred, an academic of the academics. His father had been Professor of Slavic Languages at Harvard, and he himself had grown up within a purely intellectual environment, to become something of an educational prodigy, going through his undergraduate courses at Tufts in his early teens and graduating with a Ph.D. in mathematics at Harvard well before the age of twenty. But it is a hard fate to be a child prodigy; like other prodigies, Norbert Wiener looked back later with some regret on the aftereffects of his own upbringing and continued to bear the hallmarks of his kind. Publicly he could be dogmatic, self-confident, even cocky. But he was also prickly and easily offended, and inwardly, he was much less at ease than he appeared. How difficult it was to establish warm or equal relations with those fellow men who—it seemed—so rarely shared his preoccupations or appreciated his achievements!

In this, as in so many other ways, Warren McCulloch was Wiener's opposite: a warm and loving man, who did not so much dominate his academic colleagues by the force of his arguments as command their affectionate loyalty by the magnetism of his personality and the speculative fertility of his imagination. After his Yale B.A., he had studied medicine at Columbia, and he had worked for some twenty-five years as a practicing psychiatrist and medical researcher before joining the M.I.T. laboratory in 1952. So, by a curious reversal of roles, Warren McCulloch combined the physiognomy and intellectual temperament of Don Quixote with an outward-turning personality, while in Norbert Wiener the physical tubbiness and bustling precision of Sancho Panza overlay an inner anxiety and melancholy.

Still, for all their differences of temperament and background, the two men's qualifications dovetailed, in just the way that the needs of their joint problem required. The task of imagining how a machine might be devised that could match the mental performances of a man was a task of exact mathematical analysis, demanding formal ingenuity and precision of a positively baroque order. The task of seeing how the formal analysis of such mechanisms might then be used to throw light on the actual working of the human brain—in particular, upon its role in regulating human behavior—was one for clinical understanding, philosophical reflectiveness, and speculative imagination. At this point, the respective skills of Wiener the mathematician and McCulloch the psychiatrist and neurologist matched one another admirably. Norbert Wiener had the formal virtuosity to transform the mathematical analysis of the electronic control and communication systems developed during the Second World War into a general and abstract theory of self-correcting, quasi-intelligent mechanisms and interconnecting systems. The idea of "negative feedback"—already implicit in the original design for the steam-engine governor and used by Claude Bernard in the 1860's as the crucial element in a new style of physiological explanation—could thus be extended to yield a general account of self-controlling, or cybernetic, mechanisms. Meanwhile, all Warren McCulloch's empirical familiarity with the actual relations between brain and behavior—ranging from neuroanatomical studies on the structure and interconnections of the cerebral cortex in the higher apes to the accumulated clinical experience of human neurological disorders during his years as a psychiatrist—put him in a special position to judge how these new styles of mathematical and physiological analysis could be used to unravel the actual neurophysiological interactions within the brain.

For traditional Cartesians the deepest mysteries about human behavior had been those connected with its reflexive, self-governing character. Considering the flight of birds, for instance, mechanistically-minded physiologists like Giovanni Birelli had been able to see how sensory stimuli could be transmitted by mechanical chains of causes to the brain, and also how motor impulses could be transmitted similarly to the muscles that directly activate the limbs or wings. But it was self-evident to these men that the ultimate source of motor impulses, by which flight was redirected so as to capture a recognized prey or evade a recognized predator, could not have a mechanistic character. Between the incoming causal chain from the sensory "receptors" and the outgoing causal chain to the muscular "effectors," there was a gap that could be bridged only by some nonmechanical agency.

It was this gap that the novel wartime developments had at last given scientists the means to bridge, at least in theory. First on a semi-empirical basis, later on a more abstract theoretical foundation, the development of "auto-following" for gun laying and similar applications had made possible the production of electromechanical systems capable of doing many of the things that a Borelli would have found mechanistically unintelligible in the behavior of birds or animals. The crucial principle was the one already familiar, in much simpler applications, to James Watt and Claude Bernard. A mechanically steerable radar mirror, pointed in the general direction of a target, was designed to pick up pairs of signals that remained equal as long as the target remained in dead center, but became unequal if the target moved away in one direction or another; the resulting inequality was then made the source of an "error signal" and used to direct the steering of the mirror until equality was restored and the target was once again in dead center. This use of the error signal made the device a feedback mechanism, and because the signal was used to cancel out the inequality that was its original source, it was a negative feedback device.

When made the core of a complete abstract theory, the principle of negative feedback could, as Norbert Wiener saw, be used to dismantle the Cartesian barriers, not just to a mechanical account of self-correcting and self-steering devices, but to a neurophysiology of intelligent, reflexive behavior generally. The new theories of cybernetics were primarily designed with that scientific aim in view. Once formulated, they turned out to have more practical dividends. Those thinking machines, which Descartes and his philosophical successors could never admit to the realm of possibilities, rapidly became tangible realities; and the whole manner in which electronic computers today apply programs to the analysis of new input data finds physical realization as a result of twenty-five years of rapid extrapolation of those same general ideas.

Meanwhile, Warren McCulloch and his associates were pursuing parallel sets of questions. It was not enough to dismantle the Cartesian barriers in abstract, theoretical terms. It was not enough, that is, merely to show that electronic machines having suitable kinds of organization and complexity would be capable, in principle, of reproducing all the modes of behavior that Descartes had declared to be unintelligible in terms of the mechanistic properties of matter, and therefore had to be the concern of the other independent substance, mind. One had to go on to demonstrate that the central nervous system does, in fact, have the kind of "connectivity" that cybernetic theory presupposes. Alongside Wiener's formal analysis of control and communication, therefore, it was necessary to consider also what the structure and interconnections of the human brain and central nervous system must be like if it is to be capable of serving the physiological organ of higher mental functions and activities. Suppose that all our thinking, perception, and learning, all our choices, resolutions, and changes of mind, call into play corresponding neural networks or systems, and suppose that our continued capacity to perform these functions depends on the integrity and continuing operation of those neurological systems; just what kinds and degrees of physiological complexity do our actual mental capacities compel us to presuppose, and just how will one or another sort of damage to the systems concerned make itself apparent, in the form of sensory, intellectual, and other psychological deficits?

At this point, we are on the threshold of a highly technical and difficult field of study. A great deal of exploratory work has led to preliminary insights. McCulloch and his associates at M.I.T., for instance, did some extremely revealing work on vision in the frog, both on how the organs of sight in a frog operate physiologically and on the way in which that operation fits into the frog's own characteristic pattern of life. The result is to reinforce the suspicion that the older habit of calling the eye, the ear, and so on, "sensory receptors" is itself gravely misleading. The eye does not simply "receive." The entire visual system —comprising the eye itself, the visual centers in the cortex, together with the entire bundle of efferent and afferent fibers we call the optic nerve and the muscles by which the scanning movements of the eye are controlled—is called into play *as a whole.* The eye is thus no simple television camera, but rather, an integral part of a complete "cognizing" apparatus. Parallel work on the other systems, by a hundred other teams, is beginning at last to lead to other significant results, especially when set alongside the clinical discoveries of neurologists and work in related fields of biology and medicine. Still, little has yet been achieved by way of explaining, in full and detailed terms, just which neural systems the chief higher mental functions call into play, and just how those systems are involved in such operations as adding two and two, recognizing a friend or the letter A, or understanding a sentence. We have a large number of clues; men like Wiener and McCulloch have given us a great many highly suggestive ideas; there are dozens of promising lines of inquiry to be followed up. But there is not yet much to point to in the way of definitive achievements.

Should this make us any less confident about the value of cybernetics and associated ideas? For myself, I think not. The Cartesian dichotomies—between matter and mind, between mechanical causality and logical rationality, between brain and thought—were justified, not by empirical demonstrations, but by seemingly unanswerable arguments. Correspondingly, the first, indispensable step toward circumventing them must be to show that those arguments were, despite appearances, fallacious and that intellectual bridges can be built for going to and fro across the gulfs between Descartes's "incommensurable" terms. Until that is done, all attempts to construct compre-

*Walter Pitts, above, a brilliant young scientist, assisted Wiener and McCulloch in most of their later work. The theory of information transfer and transmission networks developed at the Bell Telephone Laboratories by Claude E. Shannon, shown below, was quite close to the cybernetic approach.*

hensive theories relating, say, brain structure to higher mental function, must appear to most philosophers and scientists to have only dubious value and validity. Once it is done, however, these attempts would, at any rate, be rescued from a priori or blind prejudices. No doubt it will take decades, even centuries, to develop anything like an adequate neurophysiology of the brain processes involved in higher mental functioning. For the moment, it is enough to know that this enterprise is only *difficult,* and not, as the traditional approach would have it, *downright ridiculous.*

I t will soon be twenty-five years since the appearance of Norbert Wiener's *Cybernetics,* and we are already becoming used to living in the world of new possibilities his ideas opened up. So much is this so that a discussion of the implications of computers will nowadays focus, more likely than not, on the social, political, and economic problems that they are supposed to have created, or to be creating. (Many of these problems are, arguably, no more than the administrative problems of mass industrialization and overpopulation, which the use of computers only enables us to *half* solve.) Yet it is already clear that when the history of cybernetics comes to be written, this will prove to be one further classic illustration of the standing cross-purposes between working scientists and their public. Again and again during the past century, the solution of purely intellectual (Newtonian) problems has made possible practical (Baconian) inventions that were previously unforeseen, and unforeseeable. What could have been more abstract or theoretical than James Clerk Maxwell's puzzlement over the proper relations between the phenomena of electricity and magneticism and between the electromagnetic and electrostatic systems of measurement? And how little could he, or anyone else at the time, have foreseen the work of Marconi, still less the twentieth-century impact of radio and television, of which Maxwell's theory of electromagnetic radiation was the seed? (Even Jules Verne, despite his uncanny previsions of the American moon flights, never went so far as that.) Again and again, the Newtonian impulses of scientists have thus been the source of Baconian possibilities that the scientists themselves did not forecast, let alone intend.

The cybernetic revolution is, at most, a *partial* exception to this. In the work of Wiener and McCulloch, ideas once again came first, gadgets a long way behind. From the beginning, it is true, Norbert Wiener saw something of the way in which his general ideas might eventually find application in the human sciences; for are not socio-economic groups and institutions linked together in feedback systems of their own? Yet, despite all his concern with the new understanding that cybernetic analysis could bring, even Wiener did not foresee the full splendors, and miseries, of the "techtronic age" that our social prophets are acclaiming or denouncing today. In this respect, the founders of cybernetics were almost as shortsighted in their time as Maxwell had been in his. They were basic scientists, and their central concerns were, as ever, strictly scientific. Or—to use the older and more illuminating term—they were "natural philosophers," just as Descartes and Newton, Darwin and Maxwell, had been before them. Picking up Wiener's *Cybernetics,* we do not find him discussing the political problems created by the use of information-storage systems for the collection of data about individual citizens; instead, he discusses at length the circumstances, and the sense, in which a thinking machine might be said to have formed a "universal," or acquired a "concept." (John Locke would have got more out of reading Wiener's book than Marconi would have.) And it would have been asking too much of anyone in 1948 to foresee that by 1970 the latest idiocy of the credit-card company's computer—that "high-speed moron"—would have become as much a topic of everyday conversation as the latest idiocy of the scullery maid had been for an earlier generation.

The belief that the fruits of better knowledge will always be good, on the whole, is not a popular one today. Jeremiahs are in fashion, and the darker side of science and technology gets all the publicity. Still, we are increasingly compelled to accept the hazards involved in that belief, both for good and for ill. The gap between the ostensible topics of intellectual debate in science, and the practical points of impact of their eventual social and technological consequences, is getting progressively wider; and—short of a total system of thought control— any hope of curbing social and technological change at the scientific end is becoming increasingly unrealistic. So let us look at the positive goal that the work of Wiener and McCulloch was intended to achieve, and view it as they did themselves, seeing it not as an instrument of social change but as the means of dispelling an intellectual miasma.

A century and a half ago William Lawrence incurred great hostility for arguing what now seems obvious to almost everyone: that the brain is the organ of thought, as much as the lungs are of respiration, or the legs are of walking. In the orthodox view, Lawrence complained, the very location and complexity of the brain were a paradox. If its sole function in the activity of thinking were to provide a locus for the operation of a totally independent, nonmaterial agency, why then was it so delicately organized, so completely protected in the skull, and so generously supplied with one-fifth of all the blood from the heart? Of this account of the brain, Lawrence declared:

Its office, only one remove above a sinecure, is not a very honorable one: it is a kind of porter, entrusted to open the door, and introduce newcomers to Mind—the master of the house—who takes upon himself the entire charge of receiving, entertaining and employing them.

The view that Lawrence defended ironically, Wiener and Mc-Culloch have substantiated. There is nothing in twentieth-century physiology or physics to warrant Cartesian embarrassments. It is, after all, possible to analyze the physiological systems involved in thinking in mathematical and neurophysiological terms, quite as much as it is those involved in, say, digestion or respiration; and the reflexive functions of self-control and self-correction characteristic of conscious, self-monitoring human beings can be simulated mechanically, quite as much as the more obvious phenomena of sensory stimulation and motor activity. To say this is not to dethrone mental activity, or to reduce it to some lower, brute-mechanical level. It is to say, rather, that we previously underestimated the ingenuity of humans in thinking up more nearly human machines—that is, in raising their machines to their own level. It is not that the brain *is* a computer; on the contrary, it is that progressively more ingenious computers can be devised—apparently without limit—to do all the things that human brains can do. The existence of mental capacities, activities, and disorders remains what it has always been, a familiar feature of human life and behavior. But this fact need no longer be, and is already ceasing to be, the source of puzzlement, obscurantism, and alarm that it was for so long. As so often, the first fruit of a better understanding is a new intellectual and emotional liberation. What we shall do with that new freedom is, as always, quite another question.

*At the 1951 Paris Cybernetic Congress, Wiener, right, took on a chess-playing automaton. It is not recorded which of them won.*

# SUGGESTIONS FOR FURTHER READING

*These reading lists were compiled from information supplied by the authors of the respective essays.*

LEONARDO DA VINCI: There are three editions of the Renaissance genius's *Notebooks* to choose from: the so-called Definitive Edition (translated and edited by Edward McCurdy, New York, Braziller, 1955); a Modern Library edition (New York, no date); and, perhaps most convenient, a paperback edition (edited by Jean P. Richter, New York, Dover, 1970). Also available are *Selections from the Notebooks* (edited by Irma A. Richter, New York, Oxford University Press, 1952) and *The Notebooks: A New Selection* (edited by Pamela Taylor, New York, New American Library, Mentor paperback, 1960). Leonardo's art is covered in *The Complete Paintings of Leonardo Da Vinci* (New York, Abrams, 1969); *Drawings by Leonardo Da Vinci* (edited by Giorgio Castelfranco, translated by Florence H. Phillips, New York, Dover, paperback, 1968); and *Drawings of Leonardo da Vinci* (New York, Harcourt, Brace, paperback, no date). Two somewhat more expensive works are Leonardo's *Treatise on Painting* (translated by A. Philip McMahon, Princeton, Princeton University Press, 1956) and his *On the Human Body* (edited by C. D. O'Malley and J. B. Saunders, Boston, Boston Book and Art, no date).

In co-operation with the Spanish Government McGraw–Hill will publish, tentatively in 1973, five codices of lost manuscript pages of Leonardo's that were discovered in 1965 in the National Library in Madrid. At the same time, McGraw–Hill also plans to publish an edition of the drawings and texts under the title *The Unknown Leonardo*.

Leonardo's many-sided genius awed his contemporaries and has fascinated succeeding generations; the literature on him is extensive and still growing. A classic text is *Leonardo da Vinci: Life and Work, Paintings and Drawings* (with the 1568 biography by Vasari, newly annotated, edited by Ludwig Goldscheider, New York, Praeger, Phaidon, 8th edition, 1967). Sir Kenneth Clark's *Leonardo da Vinci: An Account of His Development as An Artist* (Baltimore, Penguin, revised edition, paperback, no date)

has been called "the best single book on Leonardo." Finally, Sigmund Freud's *Leonardo Da Vinci and a Memory of His Childhood* (New York, Norton, 1964) is a classic, and a controversial one, of speculative psychoanalysis.

NICCOLÒ MACHIAVELLI: The most comprehensive edition of Machiavelli's works is *The Chief Works of Machiavelli and Others* (translated and edited by Allan H. Gilbert, 3 volumes, Durham, N.C., Duke University Press, 1964); his nonpolitical works are collected in *The Literary Works of Machiavelli* (translated and edited by J. R. Hale, New York, Oxford University Press, 1961). The writer's masterpiece, *The Prince*, is available alone or with *The Discourses* in a dozen editions by as many translators, mostly in paperback: Modern Library, Everyman's, Mentor, and Penguin all have editions. Three more available books by Machiavelli are *The Art of War* (translated by Ellis Farneworth, New York, Liberal Arts Press, revised edition, 1965); *The Letters of Machiavelli* (edited by Allan H. Gilbert (New York, Putnam's, Capricorn paperback, 1961); and *The History of Florence and of the Affairs of Italy* (New York, Harper and Row, paperback, 1960).

Two useful studies are John H. Whitfield, *Machiavelli* (New York, Russell and Russell, 1947, reprinted 1965), and John R. Hale, *Machiavelli and Renaissance Italy* (New York, Collier, paperback, 1963). Roberto Ridolfi's *The Life of Niccolò Machiavelli* (translated by Cecile Grayson, Chicago, University of Chicago Press, 1963) is an unusual work of scholarship: written by a direct descendant of Lorenzo de' Medici's, it hardly mentions Machiavelli's writings but gives a detailed account of his last years, when he occupied minor posts in the service of Medicis and popes.

DESIDERIUS ERASMUS: Two easy-to-find paperback collections of the great humanist's writings are *The Essential Erasmus* (edited by John P. Dolan, New York, New American Library, Mentor, 1964) and

Christian Humanism and the Reformation: Selected Writings (edited by J. C. Olin, New York, Harper and Row, 1967). *Erasmus on His Times* (translated and edited by Margaret Mann Phillips, New York, Cambridge University Press, paperback, 1967) consists of his *Adages*, first printed in 1500, which was reprinted many times in its author's lifetime. There are four American editions of *The Praise of Folly* in print, including a Modern Library edition translated by T. Chaloner. Erasmus's attack on Martin Luther and the latter's reply can be found in *Discourse on Free Will* (translated by Ernst F. Winter, New York, Frederick Ungar, paperback, 1961).

Still a valuable source is Percy S. Allen's *The Age of Erasmus* (1914, reprinted New York, Russell and Russell, 1963). An excellent study by a distinguished Dutch scholar is Johan Huizinga, *Erasmus and the Age of Reformation* (New York, Harper and Row, paperback, 1957), while Roland H. Bainton in *Erasmus of Christendom* (New York, Scribner's, paperback, 1970) studies him as a Christian humanist. The most eminently readable biography is surely Stefan Zweig's *Erasmus of Rotterdam* (translated by Eden and Cedar Paul, New York, Viking, paperback, 1956). Finally, two books by the historian Preserved Smith are recommended: *Erasmus: A Study of His Life, Ideals, and Place in History* (New York, Frederick Ungar, 1960) and *A Key to the Colloquies of Erasmus* (New York, Kraus Reprint Company, paperback, no date).

NICOLAUS COPERNICUS: The great astronomer's *De revolutionibus* can be read in a facsimile reprint of the 1543 edition published in New York in 1965 by the Johnson Reprint Corporation, but the only complete English translation is in a volume of *The Great Books of the Western World*, published by Encyclopedia Britannica, Inc. However, the Preface and Book I are available in many translations. The *Commentariolus* and the *Letter Against Werner* were translated by Edward Rosen in *Three Copernican Treatises* (New York, Dover, 2nd edition, paperback, 1959).

Angus Armitage has written several biographies of Copernicus. The best for the general reader is probably *Copernicus: The Founder of Modern Astronomy* (Cranbury, N.J., A. S. Barnes, paperback, 1962), which is simple and accurate. For the general scientific and intellectual background, see Marie Boas, *The Scientific Renaissance* (New York, Harper and Row, paperback, no date). An excellent analysis of the astronomical aspects is Thomas S. Kuhn's *The Copernican Revolution* (Cambridge, Harvard University Press, 1957), which includes much of Book I of *De revolutionibus* in translation. Arthur Koestler's *The Sleepwalkers* (New York, Macmillan, 1968) is a brilliant tour de force but not reliable; the author's hostility to Copernicus leads him to make a manifestly unjust appraisal of the astronomer's character and actions.

MARTIN LUTHER: Since 1955 the publishing houses of Concordia in St. Louis and Fortress in Philadelphia have between them published all of Luther's collected works in English translation, in fifty-six volumes. Samplings of Luther's immense *oeuvre* can be found, however, in *Martin Luther: Selections from His Writings* (edited by John Dillinberger, New York, Doubleday, Anchor paperback, no date) and in *Selected Writings of Martin Luther* (edited by Theodore G. Tappert, 4 volumes, Philadelphia, Fortress, paperback, 1957).

Among biographies of Luther, the most comprehensive on his life and theological development is Roland H. Bainton's *Here I Stand* (Nashville, Abingdon Press, 1951), while the one that integrates him most successfully with his times and circumstances is Edith Simon's *Luther Alive: Martin Luther and the Making of the Reformation* (New York, Doubleday, 1968). Some other useful books about Luther are: Heinrich Boehmer, *Martin Luther: Road to Reformation* (Philadelphia, Fortress, 1946); Robert H. Fife, *The Revolt of Martin Luther* (New York, Columbia University Press, 1957); and Gordon Rupp, *Luther's Progress to the Diet of Worms* (New York, Harper and Row, paperback, 1964).

JOHN CALVIN: There is no lack of translations of Calvin's *Institutes*, but the most helpful of them is probably *The Institutes of the Christian Religion* (translated by F. L. Battle, edited by John T. McNeill, 2 volumes, Philadelphia, Westminster Press, 1960). Another useful primary source is *On the Christian Faith: Selections from The Institutes, Commentaries and Tracts* (edited by John T. McNeill, New York, Liberal Arts Press, paperback, 1958).

The most monumental work on Calvin, Emile Doumergue's *Jean Calvin, les hommes et les choses de son temps*, has never been translated, but the most judicious account of Calvin in English, first published in 1906, is available in paperback: Williston Walker, *John Calvin: The Organiser of Reformed Protestantism, 1509–1564* (New York, Schocken Books, 1969). E. William Monter, *Calvin's Geneva* (New York, Wiley, 1967), gives the city background. A classic interpretation of the significance of Calvin's work is Max Weber's *The Protestant Ethic and the Spirit of Capitalism* (translated by Talcott Parsons, New York, Scribner's, paperback, 1948)—an interpretation to which there are many answers, the best being R. H. Tawney's *Religion and the Rise of Capitalism* (New York, New American Library, paperback, no date).

FRANCIS BACON: Bacon's complete works are available in a fourteen-volume set translated from the Latin by James Spedding and others during the past century, but at a prohibitive cost. The most complete and satisfactory one-volume edition of Bacon is *The Philosophical Works of Francis Bacon* (edited by John M. Robertson, 1905); unfortunately, it is out of print, but it still turns up in secondhand bookstores. There is, on the other hand, no lack of good selections, including: *Francis Bacon: Selection of His Works* (edited by Sidney Warhaft, New York, Odyssey Press, paperback, 1970); *Francis Bacon: Selections from His Writings* (edited by Arthur Johnston, New York, Schocken Books, paperback, 1965); and the Modern Library's *Selected Writings* (New York, 1955).

Fulton H. Anderson, himself a philosopher, has written sympathetic treatments of *The Philosophy of Francis Bacon* (New York, Octagon Books, 1970), and of *Francis Bacon: His Career and His Thought* (Los Angeles, 1962). Other useful sources are James G. Crowther, *Francis Bacon: The First Statesman of Science* (Chester Springs, Pa., Dufour Editions, 1960); Benjamin Farrington, *Philosophy of Francis Bacon* (Chicago, University of Chicago Press, Phoenix paperback, 1967); and Charles Williams, *Bacon* (New York, no date), a beautifully written and penetrating study by a novelist and poet.

THOMAS HOBBES: The standard edition of Hobbes's works is still the one prepared in the nineteenth century by Sir William Molesworth (11 volumes, London, 1839–45, reprinted New York, 1961–66). Useful recent editions of *Leviathan* include those edited by Michael Oakeshott (New York, Collier, paperback, 1962) and Crawford B. Macpherson (Baltimore, Penguin, 1969). *Body, Man, and Citizen* (edited by Richard S. Peters, New York, Collier, paperback, 1962) is a valuable collection of Hobbes's relatively lesser-known writings on philosophy and politics.

The best short commentary on Hobbes's thought is Richard S. Peters, *Hobbes* (Baltimore, Penguin, paperback, 1968). More sophisticated critiques may be found in Howard Warrender's *The Political Philosophy of Hobbes* (New York, Oxford University Press, 1957) and J. W. N. Watkins's *Hobbes's System of Ideas* (New York, Barnes and Noble, paperback, 1968). Leo Strauss's *The Political Philosophy of Hobbes* (translated by Elsa M. Sinclair, Chicago, University of Chicago Press, Phoenix paperback, 1963) has been very influential. Useful collections of recent writings on Hobbes are *Hobbes Studies* (edited by Keith C. Brown, Cambridge, Harvard University Press, 1965) and Richard S. Peters and Maurice Cranston, *Hobbes and Rousseau* (New York, 1971).

RENÉ DESCARTES: The best and most readily available sampler of Descartes's thought is his *Philosophical Writings* (edited and translated by Norman Kemp Smith, Modern Library, New York, no date). There is also an Everyman's edition of the philosopher's *Discourse on Method; Meditations on the First Philosophy; Principles of Philosophy* (translated by J. Veitch, New York, no date). *The Discourse on Method* (translated by Laurence J. Lafleur, Indianapolis, Bobbs–Merrill, no date) is available in paperback. Descartes's complete works and letters were published in Paris from 1897 to 1913 in twelve volumes by Charles Adam and Paul Tannery, but have still not been translated into English, although the final volume of the set, edited by Adam, which was reprinted in 1937 under the title *Descartes, sa vie et son oeuvre*, is still considered the best biography available.

The standard work of exposition in English is Stanley V. Keeling's *Descartes* (New York, Oxford University Press, 2nd edition, paperback, 1968). Also useful are Albert G. Balz, *Descartes and the Modern Mind* (Hamden, Conn., Shoe String Press, 1967), and Norman Kemp Smith, *New Studies in the Philosophy of Descartes* (1938, reprinted New York, Russell and Russell, 1963).

BLAISE PASCAL: Three excellent translations of Pascal's *Pensées* are available—those of A. J. Krailsheimer (Baltimore, Penguin, paperback, 1961); H. F. Stewart (New York, Pantheon Books, 1965); and Martin Turnell (New York, Harper and Row, paperback, 1969). The *Provincial Letters*, translated by A. J. Krailsheimer, appeared in a Penguin edition in 1968. The minor works can be found in *Great Shorter Works of Pascal* (edited by Emile Cailliet and John C. Blankenagel, Philadelphia, 1948).

A brief, authoritative biography by an outstanding scholar is *Pascal* by Jean Mesnard (translated by Claude and Marcia Abraham, University, Ala., University of Alabama Press, 1969). Jack H. Broome's

*Pascal* (New York, Barnes and Noble, 1965) is sound and engaging. Ernest Mortimer's *Blaise Pascal* (New York, Humanities Press, 1959) is well written and philosophically competent. Emile Cailliet's *Pascal: The Emergence of Genius* (Westport, Conn., Greenwood Press, 2nd edition, 1961) is the work of an ardent disciple, and none the worse for that. Morris Bishop's *Pascal: The Life of Genius* (Westport, Conn., Greenwood Press, 1968), originally published in 1936, is a delightful and highly readable book, although its author (and ours) claims that some of its contentions have been undermined by recent research.

JOHN LOCKE: The best editions available of Locke's *Essay Concerning Human Understanding* are those of Alexander C. Fraser (Oxford, 1894, reprinted New York, Dover, paperback, 1959) and John W. Yolton (New York, Everyman, 1961). A recent abridgment edited by Maurice Cranston is available in paperback (New York, Collier, 1965). *An Early Draft of Locke's Essay* (edited by Richard I. Aaron and J. Gibb, Oxford, 1936) is of great interest as evidence of the growth of Locke's thinking. *Two Treatises of Government* (edited by Peter Laslett, New York, Cambridge University Press, 1960) contains both text and commentary. The earlier writings on political theory, which have only been available to scholars since World War II, include *Essays on the Law of Nature* (edited by Wolfgang von Leyden, New York, Oxford University Press, 1954) and *Two Tracts on Government* (edited by Philip Abrams, New York, Cambridge University Press, 1967). *On Politics, Religion and Education* (edited by Maurice Cranston, New York, Collier, paperback, 1965) contains selections of most of Locke's mature writings on political and social theory.

Commentaries on Locke that will interest the general reader include Daniel J. O'Connor, *John Locke* (New York, Dover, paperback, 1952); Martin Seliger, *The Liberal Politics of John Locke* (New York, Praeger, 1969); Richard I. Aaron, *John Locke* (New York, Oxford University Press, 2nd edition, 1955); John W. Yolton, *Locke and the Compass of Human Understanding* (New York, Cambridge University Press, 1970); and J. W. Gough, *John Locke's Political Philosophy* (New York, Oxford University Press, 1950). Maurice Cranston's *John Locke: A Biography* (London, British Book Center, 1961, and New York, Macmillan, 1957) is the most up-to-date account of Locke's life.

ISAAC NEWTON: Newton's masterwork, the great book that ushered in the modern scientific age, is available in a convenient two-volume paperback edition: *Sir Isaac Newton's Mathematical Principles of Natural Philosophy and His System of the World* (Andrew Motte's translation of circa 1729, edited by Florian Cajori in 1930, and by R. T. Crawford; Volume I, *The Motion of Bodies*, Berkeley, University of California Press, 1962; Volume II, *The System of the World*, Berkeley, University of California Press, 1966).

Among biographies, the best is still Louis Trenchard More's *Isaac Newton: A Biography* (New York, Dover, paperback, 1934). Frank E. Manuel, *A Portrait of Isaac Newton* (Cambridge, Harvard University Press, 1968), is an intriguing psychological study of Newton's strange personality. The best general accounts of the scientific revolution that culminated in Sir Isaac Newton are I. Bernard Cohen, *The Birth of a New Physics* (New York, Doubleday, 1960); A. Rupert Hall, *From Galileo to Newton, 1630–1720* (New York, Harper and Row, 1963); and the late Alexander Koyré's *From the Closed World to the Infinite Universe* (Baltimore, Johns Hopkins Press, 1956). Interest in Newton is so great at this writing, and Newton scholars, led by Professor Cohen, so active, that it seems likely that new books will soon be forthcoming that will either supersede some of those listed above or serve as indispensable supplements to them.

VOLTAIRE: There are no good complete editions of Voltaire in English. The reader unacquainted with Voltaire might do well to start with either *Candide and Other Tales* (translated by T. Smollett, New York, Everyman, no date) or *Candide and Other Writings* (edited by Haskell M. Block, New York, Modern Library, 1956); both contain good selections of the philosopher's writings, starting with his most famous work. Voltaire's *Correspondence* (edited by Theodore Besterman, 2 volumes, Toronto, University of Toronto Press, 1969) illuminates Voltaire's character as only private letters can. *The Philosophical Dictionary* (edited and translated by Peter Gay, New York, Basic Books, 1962) is a modern and complete version of Voltaire's famous polemic.

Although it was first published as long ago as 1906, Gustave Lanson's *Voltaire* (translated by Robert A. Wagoner, New York, Wiley, 1966) is still an excellent introduction to the subject. Norman L. Torrey, *The Spirit of Voltaire* (1938, reprinted New York, Russell and Russell, 1968), is a lucid defense of the man and his work. Finally, Peter Gay's *Voltaire's Politics: The Poet as Realist* (New York, Vintage, paperback, 1959) establishes the man firmly in his time and place.

JEAN JACQUES ROUSSEAU: There is no lack of translations of Rousseau's major works. One of the more comprehensive of these is his *Political Writings* (translated and edited by Frederick Watkins, Camden, N.J., Thomas Nelson, 1953), including *The Social Contract*, "Considerations on the Government of Poland," and Part 1 of "The Constitutional Project for Corsica." Easier to find, perhaps, is the Everyman's edition of *The Social Contract and Other Discourses* (translated by G. D. H. Cole, New York, 1950) . Everyman's also offers an edition of Rousseau's *Confessions*, as do Modern Library (New York, 1945) and Penguin (translated by J. H. Cohen, Baltimore, no date).

A scholarly but readable work on Rousseau is Frederick C. Green, *Jean-Jacques Rousseau: A Critical Study of His Life and Writings* (New York, Barnes and Noble, 1970). Also useful is Frances Winwar, *Jean-Jacques Rousseau: Conscience of an Era* (New York, Random House, 1961). Two first-rate studies by eminent European scholars are Ernst Cassirer, *The Question of Jean-Jacques Rousseau* (translated and edited by Peter Gay, Bloomington, Ind., Indiana University Press, paperback, 1963), and Jean Guéhenno, *Jean-Jacques Rousseau* (translated by John and Doreen Weightman, 2 volumes, New York, Columbia University Press, 1966).

ADAM SMITH: The great Scottish professor's most famous work, *The Wealth of Nations,* is available in several editions, including an Everyman's (2 volumes, New York, 1910) and a Modern Library one (New York, 1937). Also available, though harder to find, are compilations entitled *Early Writings of Adam Smith* (edited by J. R. Lindgren, New York, Kelley, 1967) and *Thoughts from Adam Smith* (edited by Clyde E. Dankert, New York, Kelley, 1963), as well as *The Theory of Moral Sentiments, 1759* (New York, Kelley, no date).

A good summary of Smith's inquiry into the workings of the economy is to be found in Robert L. Heilbroner's *The Worldly Philosophers* (New York, Simon and Schuster, revised edition, paperback, 1967). Analyses of Smith's theories and their impact that date from a generation or two ago are: Glen R. Morrow, *The Ethical and Economic Theories of Adam Smith* (New York, Kelley, 1923); John M. Clark and others, *Adam Smith, 1776–1926* (New York, Kelley, 1928); and Arthur H. Jenkins, *Adam Smith Today* (Port Washington, N.Y., Kennikat Press, 1948). Two more recent studies are Eli Ginzberg, *The House of Adam Smith* (New York, Octagon Books, 1964), and A. L. Macfie, *The Individual in Society: Papers on Adam Smith* (New York, Humanities Press, 1967).

IMMANUEL KANT: Readers new to Kant are advised to approach him through two shorter works—*Prolegomena to any Future Metaphysics* (translated by Paul Carus and Lewis W. Beck, New York, Liberal Arts Press) and *Foundations of the Metaphysics of Morals* (translated by Lewis W. Beck, New York, Liberal Arts Press, paperback, 1959)—after which they may feel ready to tackle the *Critique of Pure Reason* (translated by Norman Kemp Smith, New York, St. Martin's Press, New York, 1952).

Among the numerous available commentaries on Kant, three are particularly rewarding: John Kemp's *The Philosophy of Kant* (New York, Oxford University Press, paperback, 1968); Richard Kroner's *Kant's Weltanschauung* (translated by John E. Smith, Chicago, University of Chicago Press, 1956); and on a slightly more advanced level, Stephan Korner's *Kant* (Baltimore, Penguin, 2nd edition, paperback, 1955). The philosopher's place in the history of philosophy is examined in Lewis W. Beck's *Early German Philosophy: Kant and His Predecessors* (Cambridge, Harvard University Press, 1969).

JEREMY BENTHAM: Compiled in the past century under the editorship of John Bowring, *The Complete Works of Jeremy Bentham* are available in a reprint edition (11 volumes, New York, Russell and Russell, 1962). Also relatively easy to find are *Bentham's Economic Writings* (edited by W. Stark, 3 volumes, New York, Burt Franklin, 1952–54) and the important *Introduction to the Principles of Morals and Legislation* (edited by Laurence J. Lafleur, New York, Hofner, 1948). Many readers, however, will be content to sample the contents of the extraordinary Englishman's far-ranging mind in *A Bentham Reader* (edited by Mary P. Mack, New York, Pegasus, 1968).

For a sympathetic appraisal by a brilliant near-contemporary, the reader should consult John Stuart Mill's *On Bentham and Coleridge* (New York, Harper and Row, paperback, 1962). The whole field of utilitarian thought is covered in depth in Elie Halévy's classic study *The Growth of Philosophic Radicalism* (translated by Mary Morris, Boston, Beacon, paperback, 1955). There is an illuminating essay on Bentham's panopticon scheme in Gertrude Himmelfarb's *Victorian Minds* (New York, Harper and Row, paperback, 1970). A good all-around study of the man and his works is D. J. Manning, *The Mind of Jeremy Bentham* (New York, Barnes and Noble, 1968).

MARY WOLLSTONECRAFT: The most recent edition of the crusading writer's major work is *A Vindication* of the Rights of Woman (edited by Charles W. Hagelman, Jr., New York, Norton, paperback, 1967); it includes the introduction to the first edition, addressed to Talleyrand, and a scholarly introduction by the editor.

William Godwin's *Memoirs of the Author of a Vindication of the Rights of Woman* (New York, Haskell House, 1969) is the first biography of Mary and the chief source of the others. Of these, the best is Ralph M. Wardle's *Mary Wollstonecraft: A Critical Biography* (Lincoln, Neb., University of Nebraska Press, Bison paperback, 1966), a scholarly, readable, and complete study. Margaret George, *One Woman's Situation* (Urbana, Ill., University of Illinois Press, 1970), is a well-written biography with a psychoanalytical and feminist point of view. Margaret Crompton, *Shelley's Dream Women* (Cranbury, N.J., A. S. Barnes, 1967), contains an excellent account of the poet's relationships with Mary Wollstonecraft's daughters.

THOMAS ROBERT MALTHUS: Malthus's key essay on population, first published in 1798 and republished in revised form in 1803, is available in *First Essay on the Principles of Population* (New York, 1966), and in both versions in the two-volume *An Essay on the Principle of Population* (New York, Everyman, 1958). Also available are the *Pamphlets of Thomas Robert Malthus* (New York, Kelley, 1970) and Malthus's major work, first published in 1820, *Principles of Political Economy* (New York, Kelley, 2nd edition, no date).

The standard life of Malthus is still James Bonar's *Malthus and His Work* (New York, Kelley, 2nd edition, 1924). Another useful source is Samuel M. Levin, *Malthus and the Conduct of Life* (New York, Twayne Publishers, no date). Of historical interest is a recently-issued book giving the views of Marx and Engels on Malthusian theory, under the title *Malthus: Selections Dealing with the Theories of Thomas Robert Malthus* (edited by Ronald L. Meek, New York, International Publishers, 1970).

GEORG WILHELM FRIEDRICH HEGEL: Among the many English translations of the philosopher's works, four are especially useful. *The Philosophy of Right* (translated by T. M. Knox, New York, Oxford University Press, 1942) is well annotated, while the same translator's *On Christianity: Early Theological Writings* (edited by Richard Kroner and T. M. Knox, Gloucester, Mass., Peter Smith, 1962) includes the most substantial of Hegel's manuscripts; the introduction by Richard Kroner is lucid and informed. Walter Kaufmann's *Hegel* (New York, Dou-

bleday, 1966), a breezy biography-cum-commentary, includes an excellent translation of Hegel's preface to the *Phenomenology of Spirit*. Finally, *Lectures on the History of Philosophy* (translated by E. S. Haldane and F. H. Simson, 3 volumes, New York, Humanities Press, 1965) is basic to understanding Hegel's conception of philosophy.

Among helpful books about Hegel, in addition to Kaufmann's, four may be cited. J. N. Findlay's *Hegel: A Re-Examination* (1958, reprinted New York, Humanities Press, 1964) is one of the early products of the recent renewal of interest in Hegel in English-speaking countries. Alexandre Kojeve, *Introduction to the Reading of Hegel* (edited by Allan Bloom, translated by James H. Nichols, Jr., New York, Basic Books, 1969), is a translation of an influential French work that helped inspire Hegel's radical image. Herbert Marcuse, *Reason and Revolution* (Boston, Beacon, paperback, 1960), is the classic treatment of Hegel in pre-Marxist social thought; and Geoffrey R. G. Mure, *The Philosophy of Hegel* (New York, Oxford University Press, 1965), is the clearest short introduction to Hegel's philosophical method.

ROBERT OWEN: The most interesting of Owen's writings is *The Life of Robert Owen* (2 volumes, New York, Kelley, 1969). It contains liberal "Selections from His Writings and Correspondence." One of his key books, *A New View of Society and Other Writings*, is available in an Everyman's edition (New York, 1927). Other recent reprints include *The Book of the New Moral World* (New York, Kelley, no date) and *Selected Writings of Robert Owen* (New York, Kelley, 1969).

Owen's own *Life*—written with great lucidity while he was in his eighties—is excellent but egocentrically limited. Of the many biographies, the must succinct is Margaret Cole, *Robert Owen of New Lanark* (New York, Kelley, 1969), while the most complete is still Frank Podmore's *Robert Owen*, first published in 1906 and reprinted in New York in 1968 (2 volumes, Kelley). Of the vast literature on Owen and Owenism, the best work from a scholarly standpoint is John F. C. Harrison, *The Quest for the New Moral World: Robert Owen and the Owenites in Britain and America* (New York, Scribner's, 1969), but a more entertaining account of Owenism in action is William E. Wilson, *The Angel and the Serpent: The Story of New Harmony* (Bloomington, Ind., Indiana University Press, 1964).

KARL MARIA VON CLAUSEWITZ: The great military theorist's classic *On War* is available in a three-volume edition (translated by Col. J. J. Graham, edited by Col. F. N. Maude, New York, Barnes and Noble, 1961). Also still in print is his *Principles of War* (translated by Hans W. Gatzke, Harrisburg, Pa., Stackpole Books, 1942).

The single most helpful book on Clausewitz's thought is Roger A. Leonard's *A Short Guide to Clausewitz on War* (New York, Putnam, paperback, 1968). Also useful are Maj. Gen. F. F. C. Fuller, *The Conduct of War* (New Brunswick, N.J., Rutgers University Press, 1961), and *Makers of Modern Strategy* (edited by Edward M. Earle and others, New York, Atheneum, paperback, 1966).

GEORGE PERKINS MARSH: The best edition by far of Marsh's chief work is the one edited by David Lowenthal: *Man and Nature; or, Physical Geography as Modified by Human Action* (Cambridge, Harvard University Press, 1965). Originally published in 1864, it represents, as Stewart Udall has said, "the beginning of land wisdom in this country." A man of wide-ranging interests, Marsh also wrote books on the camel, on the origin of the English language, and on good and evil.

David Lowenthal's *George Perkins Marsh: Versatile Vermonter* (New York, Columbia University Press, 1958) gives details of Marsh's life and work by a geographer competent to assess his importance. Caroline C. Marsh's *Life and Letters of George Perkins Marsh* (New York, Benjamin Blom, 1969) was first published in 1888; it faithfully mirrors the great naturalist's time.

CHARLES ROBERT DARWIN: Of the numerous paperback editions of Darwin's central work, one of the best from the standpoint of the general reader is *The Origin of Species* (edited by J. W. Burrow, Baltimore, Penguin, paperback, 1969). Another readily available primary source is *The Origin of Species and Descent of Man* (New York, Modern Library, 1949). *Darwin* (selected and edited by Philip Appleman, New York, 1970) provides excerpts from some of Darwin's other works as well as critical essays on him. Darwin's *Autobiography* (edited by Nora Barlow, New York, Norton, paperback, 1969) is highly readable, as is his *Voyage of the Beagle* (edited by Millicent E. Selsam, New York, Harper and Row, 1959). Finally, *The Darwin Reader* (edited by Marston Bates and Philip S. Humphrey, New York, Scribner's, paperback, 1968) contains a good representative selection of Darwin's writings.

A very useful introduction to Darwin's life and ideas by a distinguished biologist is Sir Gavin de Beer's *Charles Darwin: Evolution by Natural Selec-tion* (New York, Doubleday, 1964). Darwin's epochal voyage is stirringly re-created in Alan Moorehead's beautifully illustrated *Darwin and the Beagle* (New York, Harper and Row, 1969). Gertrude Himmelfarb's *Darwin and the Darwinian Revolution* (New York, Norton, 1968) is a substantial work, but the author's hostility to Darwin prevents it from being altogether satisfactory. For a simplified exposition of Darwin's thought, the reader is referred to Benjamin Farrington, *What Darwin Really Said* (New York, Schocken Books, 1967).

KARL MARX: There is no edition in English of the complete works of Marx—or of Marx and Engels. The best available edition of selections is *Karl Marx and Friedrich Engels: Basic Writings on Politics and Philosophy* (edited by Lewis S. Feuer, New York, Doubleday, Anchor paperback, 1959). Other useful collections are *The Essential Writings of Karl Marx* (edited by David Caute, New York, Macmillan, 1968) and *Living Thoughts of Karl Marx* (edited by Leon Trotsky, New York, Fawcett World, paperback, 1970). His classic economic work, *Capital*, can be found in both Modern Library and Everyman editions, while there are as many as a dozen paperback editions of *The Communist Manifesto* on the market.

A good introduction to Marx and Marxism in their nineteenth-century context is Edmund Wilson's *To the Finland Station* (New York, Doubleday, Anchor paperback, 1953); the title refers to Lenin's arrival in St. Petersburg in 1917. The weighty Communist biography by Franz Mehring is available in English (translated by Edward Fitzgerald, Ann Arbor, Mich., University of Michigan Press, paperback, 1962). Robert Payne's *Marx* (New York, Simon and Schuster, 1968) is strongly hostile. A simple introduction to the subject is Harry B. Acton, *What Marx Really Said* (New York, Schocken Books, 1967). Among other helpful books on Marx and his ideas are Sir Isaiah Berlin, *Karl Marx: His Life and Environment* (New York, Oxford University Press, Galaxy paperback, 3rd edition, 1963); Joel Carmichael, *Karl Marx* (New York, Scribner's, 1970); and Lewis S. Feuer, *Marx and the Intellectuals* (Garden City, New York, Doubleday, Anchor paperback, 1969).

MICHAEL BAKUNIN: The fullest and most balanced selection of extracts from Bakunin's writings available in the United States is G. P. Maximoff's *Political Philosophy of Bakunin* (New York, The Free Press, paperback, 1964), which includes a biographical essay by Max Nettlau. (Bakunin's major doctrinal writings are so diffuse and poorly organized that a good compendium, like Maximoff's, gives the student a better idea of his thought than any single work of his own does.)

Edward H. Carr's *Michael Bakunin* (New York, Random House, 1961, reprinted from the 1937 British edition) is a bit superficial in dealing with Bakunin's philosophy but is nevertheless the best biography in English. Other helpful books are Irving L. Horowitz, *The Anarchists* (New York, Dell, paperback, 1964); James Joll, *The Anarchists* (New York, Grosset and Dunlap, no date); and George Woodcock, *Anarchism* (New York, World, paperback, 1962).

WILLIAM JAMES: All of the philosopher's major works are still in print. The *Principles of Psychology* (2 volumes, New York, Dover, paperback, 1950) is a reprint of the 1890 edition, while *Psychology: The Briefer Course* (edited by Gordon Allport, New York, Harper and Row, paperback, 1961) is a reprint of James's one-volume abridgment of the *Principles*. Reprints of James's subsequent works include *The Will to Believe, and Other Essays in Popular Philosophy* (New York, Dover, paperback, 1955); *Talks to Teachers on Psychology and to Students on Some of Life's Ideals* (New York, Dover, paperback, 1962); *Pragmatism and Other Essays* (edited by Ralph Barton Perry, New York, World, paperback, 1965); *The Meaning of Truth* (Westport, Conn., Greenwood Press, 1968); and *The Varieties of Religious Experience* (New York, Macmillan, paperback, 1961).

Selections of James's writings include *The Selected Letters of William James* (edited and with an introduction by Elizabeth Hardwick, New York, Farrar, Straus, 1961); *The Moral Philosophy of William James* (edited by John K. Roth, New York, Apollo Editions, 1969); and *A William James Reader* (edited and with an introduction by Gay Wilson Allen, Boston, 1971).

The fullest biography of James is Gay Wilson Allen's *William James: A Biography* (New York, Viking, paperback, 1969). Two other useful works of criticism are Theodore Flournoy, *The Philosophy of William James* (translated by Edwin B. Holt and William James, Jr., Freeport, N.Y., Books for Libraries, 1917); and Ralph Barton Perry, *In the Spirit of William James* (Bloomington, Ind., Indiana University Press, paperback, 1958)—a reprint of the 1938 edition.

FRIEDRICH WILHELM NIETZSCHE: The best introduction to Nietzsche's works are two books edited and translated by Walter Kaufmann: *The Portable Nietzsche* (New York, Viking, paperback, 1954) and *Basic Writings of Nietzsche* (New York, Modern Library, 1968). With R. J. Hollingdale, Kaufmann has also translated and arranged *The Will to Power* (New York, 1968), freeing the text of the distortions imposed by Nietzsche's meddling sister, Elisabeth.

Illuminating secondary sources on Nietzsche include: Walter Kaufmann, *Nietzsche: Philosopher, Psychologist, Antichrist* (New York, Vintage, revised edition, paperback, 1968); Rudolph Binion, *Frau Lou: Nietzsche's Wayward Disciple* (Princeton, N.J., Princeton University Press, 1968); R. J. Hollingdale, *Nietzsche: The Man and His Philosophy* (Baton Rouge, La., Louisiana State University, 1965); and George A. Morgan, Jr., *What Nietzsche Means* (New York, Harper and Row, paperback, 1965).

IVAN PETROVICH PAVLOV: All of Pavlov's books in English are, of course, technical. Those most readily available are: *Conditioned Reflexes* (edited and translated by G. V. Anrep, New York, Dover, paperback, 1927); *Lectures on Conditioned Reflexes* (translated by W. Horsley Gantt, New York, International Publishers, 1963); and *Conditioned Reflexes and Psychiatry* (translated by W. Horsley Gantt, New York, International Publishers, paperback, 1963).

There are at present three available books about Pavlov that will amply repay the reader's attention. Harry K. Wells's *Ivan P. Pavlov: Toward a Scientific Psychology and Psychiatry* (New York, International Publishers, 1956) is the first of two books under the general title *Pavlov and Freud*; it contains a brief biographical sketch of Pavlov and explains his work in terms that a layman can understand. Boris P. Babkin, *Pavlov: A Biography* (Chicago, University of Chicago Press, 1949), is the definitive biography in English, written by a former student of Pavlov's. Finally, *Rape of the Mind* by Joost A. Meerloo, M.D. (New York, Grosset and Dunlap, 1961), analyzes in nonscientific language the methods by which men are turned into what the author calls "Pavlovian puppets."

JAMES GEORGE FRAZER: While Sir James's monumental *Golden Bough: A Study in Magic and Religion* is available in thirteen volumes (New York, St. Martin's Press, 3rd edition, 1955), there is also a good one-volume abridged edition (New York, Macmillan, paperback, 1960). A number of Frazer's other works—and parts of his masterpiece—can be found in recently-published paperback editions.

There are interesting essays on Frazer in Bronislaw Malinowski, *A Scientific Theory of Culture and Other Essays* (Chapel Hill, N.C., University of North Carolina Press, 1944); in Stanley Edgar Hyman, *The Tangled Bank: Darwin, Marx, Frazer and Freud as Imaginative Writers* (New York, Atheneum, 1962); and in Abram Kardiner and Edward Preble, *They Studied Man* (New York, New American Library, paperback, 1965).

SIGMUND FREUD: The great psychoanalyst's complete works, *The Standard Edition of the Complete Psychological Works of Sigmund Freud* (edited by James Strachey, 24 volumes, New York, Macmillan, 1964), are available in English—for $175; on the other hand, *The Collected Papers of Sigmund Freud* (10 volumes, New York, Collier, 1963) are considerably less expensive, being in paperback. Virtually all Freud's major works—and most minor ones as well—can be found in paperback editions. Among these, all translated by James Strachey, are the *Complete Introductory Lectures on Psychoanalysis* (New York, Norton, 1966); *The Interpretation of Dreams* (New York, Avon, paperback, 1965); *On Dreams* (New York, Norton, 1963); *An Outline of Psychoanalysis* (New York, Norton, 1949); and *Totem and Taboo* (New York, Norton, paperback, 1952). The best one-volume compendium is the Modern Library's *The Basic Writings of Sigmund Freud* (translated by A. A. Brill, New York, 1938).

The standard biography of Freud is Ernest Jones's three-volume *The Life and Works of Sigmund Freud* (Hogarth Press, 1954); it is now available in paperback in an abridged edition edited by Lionel Trilling (New York, Doubleday, Anchor paperback, 1963). A simple introduction to the subject is David Stafford–Clark's *What Freud Really Said* (New York, Schocken Books, 1967). Another very useful book is Philip Rieff, *Freud: The Mind of the Moralist* (New York, Doubleday, Anchor paperback, 1961). Paul Roazen's *Freud: Political and Social Thought* (New York, Knopf, 1968) is a penetrating study of the application of Freudian thought to politics.

MOHANDAS KARAMCHAND GANDHI: Gandhi's collected works are being chronologically published, in some sixty volumes, by the Government of India. Meanwhile, his early *Autobiography: The Story of My Experiments With Truth* (translated by Mahadev Desai, Boston, Beacon, paperback, 1957) is available, as is his *All Men Are Brothers* (New York, Columbia University Press, 1969). Two useful compendiums of Gandhi's pronouncements are *The Essential Gandhi* (edited by Louis Fischer, New York, Vintage, 1962) and *The Gandhi Reader* (edited by

Homer A. Jack, New York, AMS Press, 1970).

The best-known biography of Gandhi is Louis Fischer's *The Life of Mahatma Gandhi* (New York, New American Library, paperback, 1960). Bal Ram Nanda's *Mahatma Gandhi* (Woodbury, N.Y., Barron's Educational Series, 1965) contains more recent material, however, and Geoffrey Ashe's *Gandhi: A Study in Revolution* (New York, Stein and Day, 1968) discusses Gandhi's contemporary relevance more fully. Erik H. Erikson has written an absorbing psychoanalytical study in *Gandhi's Truth* (New York, Norton, 1969). Finally, for a straightforward political assessment, there is Penderel Moon's *Gandhi and Modern India* (New York, Norton, 1968).

ALBERT EINSTEIN: The great mathematician's *Relativity: The Special and General Theory* (translated by Robert W. Lawson, New York, Crown, paperback, 1961) is lucidly written but highly detailed, with some mathematics. His *Evolution of Physics* (with Leopold Infeld, New York, Simon and Schuster, 1938) describes the growth of man's understanding of the physical universe from early concepts to relativity and quantum theory.

Ronald W. Clark's massive *Einstein: The Life and Times* (New York, World, 1971) is the most thorough biography to date and is unlikely to be superseded for many years to come. A shorter biographical work, Philipp Frank's *Einstein: His Life and Times* (New York, Knopf, 1953), written by a former colleague and eminent physicist, is also useful. Lincoln Barnett's *The Universe and Dr. Einstein* (New York, New American Library, revised edition, paperback, 1957), with a foreword by Einstein himself, is a popular and easy-to-follow exposition of Einstein's central ideas.

JOHN MAYNARD KEYNES: Like most economists, Keynes is, in print, too technical to be accessible to a wide public. After consulting the secondary sources given below, however, a determined reader may nevertheless find profit in reading Keynes's *General Theory of Employment, Interest, and Money* (New York, Harcourt, Brace, 1936), which contains the core of his work. Keynes was a superb stylist, and his *Essays in Biography* and *Essays in Persuasion* (both, New York, Norton, paperback, 1963) repay reading with much delight.

The standard, if rather stuffy, biography of Keynes is Roy F. Harrod's *The Life of John Maynard Keynes* (New York, Avon, paperback, 1971); as an authorized work, however, it glosses over such matters as Keynes's homosexuality. Robert Lekachman's *The Age of Keynes* (New York, Random House, 1966) provides a good description of his thought. Finally, Michael Stewart's book *Keynes and After* (Baltimore, Penguin, paperback, 1968) offers a particularly lucid exposition, in small compass, of Keynesian economics.

LUDWIG WITTGENSTEIN: The classic of Wittgenstein's first philosophical period, published in 1921, is the *Tractatus Logico-Philosophicus* (translated by D. F. Pears and B. F. McGuinness, New York, Humanities Press, 1961). The single greatest work of the philosopher's second period, composed of material written between 1931 and 1949, is *Philosophical Investigations* (translated by G. E. M. Anscombe, New York, Macmillan, 1953). *The Blue and Brown Books* (New York, Barnes and Noble, 1969) consists of dictations to Cambridge students between 1933 and 1935, while *Zettel* (translated by G. E. M. Anscombe, Berkeley, University of California Press, 1967) is a collection of philosophical remarks mostly composed from 1945 to 1948.

Among biographical works, Paul Engelmann, *Letters from Ludwig Wittgenstein: With a Memoir* (translated by L. Furtmuller, New York, Horizon Press, 1968), covers the period from 1916 to 1937; it is especially valuable for information on Wittgenstein's relationships with some Austrian writers and artists, and includes a biographical sketch by B. F. McGuinness. Norman Malcolm's *Ludwig Wittgenstein: A Memoir* (New York, Oxford University Press, 1958) covers 1938 to 1951; with it is printed an excellent biographical sketch by Georg Henrik von Wright. K. T. Fann's *Wittgenstein's Conception of Philosophy* (Berkeley, University of California Press, 1970) is an informative and readable account of Wittgenstein's two philosophical periods.

NORBERT WIENER and WARREN McCULLOCH: Wiener's classic, *Cybernetics: or Control and Communication in the Animal and the Machine*, first published in 1948, is currently available in a second edition (Cambridge, M.I.T. Press, 1961). Its philosophical character is at once obvious, and while it contains mathematical equations, these passages can be skipped without serious loss. In addition, Wiener wrote several technical books and two more popular ones: *The Human Use of Human Beings* (New York, Avon, paperback, 1969) and *God and Golem, Inc.* (Cambridge, M.I.T. Press, 1964), the latter dealing with "certain points where cybernetics impinges on religion."

McCulloch's essays on human mentality and its neurophysiological basis are collected in two volumes—*Finality and Form* (1952, now out of print) and *Embodiments of Mind* (Cambridge, M.I.T. Press, 1965).

For other related discussions the reader can profitably consult Dean E. Wooldridge, *The Machinery of the Brain* (New York, McGraw–Hill, paperback, 1963), and a useful collection of essays and papers entitled *Perspectives on the Computer Revolution* (edited by Z. Pylyshyn, Englewood Cliffs, N.J. Prentice–Hall, 1970).

# NOTES ON CONTRIBUTORS

JACOB BRONOWSKI is a mathematician and writer associated with the Salk Institute for Biological Studies in San Diego, California. He is co-author, with Bruce Mazlish, of *The Western Intellectual Tradition* and has also written *The Abacus and the Rose: A New Dialogue on the Two World System*, *The Identity of Man*, and *Nature and Knowledge*.

BRUCE MAZLISH, professor of history at Massachusetts Institute of Technology, served as consultant on this book and wrote the introduction to it. He is the author of *The Riddle of History* and *Psychoanalysis and History* and co-author of *The Western Intellectual Tradition*.

GARRETT MATTINGLY, who died in 1963, was William R. Sheperd Professor of European History at Columbia University. Among his numerous books are *The Armada*, *Catherine of Aragon*, *The Invincible Armada and Elizabethan England*, and *Renaissance Diplomacy*.

MARIE BOAS HALL teaches at the Imperial College of Science and Technology in London. She is the author of *Robert Boyle on Natural Philosophy* and the editor of *Nature and Nature's Laws: Documents of the Scientific Revolution*.

EDITH SIMON lives in Edinburgh. She is the author of *Luther Alive: Martin Luther and the Making of the Reformation* and *Saints*, as well as the *Life* Great Ages of Man book on the Reformation.

LACEY BALDWIN SMITH, a professor of history at Northwestern University, is the author of *The Horizon Book of the Elizabethan World*, *The Elizabethan World*, and *Henry VIII: The Mask of Royalty*. In addition, he has edited a four-volume history of England and written, with his wife, Jean R. Smith, *Essentials of World History*.

LOREN EISELEY, professor of anthropology at the University Museum, University of Pennsylvania, is well known both as a scholar and as a writer of scientific articles and verse. His books include *The Immense Journey*, *Darwin's Century: Evolution and the Men Who Discovered It*, *The Firmament of Time*, *The Unexpected Universe*, *The Invisible Pyramid*, and *Night Country*.

MAURICE CRANSTON, professor of political science at the London School of Economics, is the author of numerous books and articles on political and philosophical themes. Among his most recent books are *Political Dialogues*, *Freedom Now: The Civil Rights Struggle in America*, *Western Political Philosophers*, and *The Quintessence of Sartrism*.

CURTIS CATE is an American journalist and freelance writer who has lived in France most of his life. He is the author of the biography *Antoine de Saint-Exupéry*. Long the European correspondent of *The Atlantic*, he has written several articles for *Horizon* magazine.

MORRIS BISHOP, professor emeritus of Romance languages at Cornell University, is a frequent contributor to *Horizon*. In 1968 he wrote *The Horizon Book of the Middle Ages*. He has written a number of books, including *Pascal, the Life of Genius*, and has recently produced a four-volume series: *Classical Storybook*, *Medieval Storybook*, *Renaissance Storybook*, and *Romantic Storybook*.

WALTER KARP, a contributing editor on the staff of *Horizon*, is the author of a biography of Charles Darwin. He has also written extensively on politics, and is presently completing a study of the structure of contemporary politics, tentatively entitled *Power in America*.

PETER GAY, professor of history at Yale, is the author of a two-volume work on the Enlightenment and *The Bridge of Criticism: Dialogues Among Lucian, Erasmus and Voltaire on the Enlightenment*, *The Party of Humanity: Essays in the French Enlightenment*, and *Voltaire's Politics*.

J. CHRISTOPHER HEROLD, who died in 1964, was born in Czechoslovakia and educated in Geneva. He later became an American citizen and continued to write history in three languages. He was an editor of the Columbia University Press and the Stanford University Press and the author of *Bonaparte in Egypt*, *The Horizon Book of the Age of Napoleon*, and, with Gordon Wright, *The Battle of Waterloo*.

LEWIS W. BECK, professor of philosophy at the University of Rochester, has devoted many years to the study of Kant. His works include *A Commentary of Kant's Critique of Practical Reason, Studies in the Philosophy of Kant, Eighteenth-Century Philosophy,* and *Early German Philosophy: Kant and His Predecessors.*

J. W. BURROW is professor of history at the University of Sussex and the author of *Evolution and Society: A Study of Victorian Social Theory.* He has contributed many articles to *Horizon* on men and issues of the nineteenth century.

SHIRLEY TOMKIEVICZ is an associate editor of *Horizon.* She has written a number of articles for the magazine, including "Flaubert's Madame Bovary" in the Winter, 1971, issue and "Hans Memling's Christmas Pageant" in the Winter, 1972, issue.

ANTHONY BURGESS, one of the most prolific writers of this or any other era, has published some twenty-seven books since 1956, mostly novels and works of criticism, together with articles on a wide range of subjects for various periodicals. Among his novels are *A Clockwork Orange* and *M/F;* his latest critical works are *The Novel Now: A Guide to American Fiction* and *Shakespeare.*

GEORGE ARMSTRONG KELLY is a member of the Department of Politics at Brandeis University. He is the author of *Lost Soldiers: The French Army and Empire in Crisis* and *Idealism, Politics and History: Sources of Hegelian Thought.* With Linda B. Miller he wrote *Internal War and International Systems,* and with C. W. Brown, *Struggles in the State: Sources and Patterns of World Revolution.*

BERNARD A. WEISBERGER, an associate editor of *American Heritage,* taught history for eighteen years at such universities as Wayne State, Chicago, and Rochester. He has written numerous articles and ten books, his latest being *The American Heritage History of the American People.*

CORRELLI BARNETT, a distinguished military historian and a member of Britain's Institute for Strategic Studies, is the author of *Swordbearers: Supreme Command in the First World War* and *Britain and Her Army: A Military, Political and Social Survey.*

FRANKLIN RUSSELL, a well-known writer on ecological subjects, is the author of *Secret Islands* and *Searchers at the Gulf.* He has also written many books for young adults, including *Watchers at the Pond, Argen the Gull, Hawk in the Sky,* and *Frightened Hare.*

EDMOND TAYLOR, a European correspondent for American newspapers and magazines since the 1930's, has been an eyewitness to four turbulent decades of history. He is the author of *The Fall of the Dynasties, Richer by Asia,* and a book of memoirs, *Awakening from History.*

GAY WILSON ALLEN, professor emeritus of English at New York University, is the author of *American Prosody, William James: A Biography,* and *The Reader's Guide to Walt Whitman* and the editor of *The William James Reader.*

FRANCIS RUSSELL, a historian and critic, wrote *The American Heritage History of the Making of the Nation* and has contributed a number of articles to *Horizon.* His other books include *The World of Dürer, The Shadow of Blooming Grove,* and *Three Studies in Twentieth-Century Obscurity: Joyce, Kafka, Gertrude Stein.*

ANTHONY STORR, a practicing psychotherapist in London, has contributed three books to the literature of psychology: *Integrity of the Personality, Sexual Deviation,* and *Human Aggression.*

JAMES MORRIS, a native of Wales, is an indefatigable world traveler and a prolific writer. He is the author of *The Road to Huddersfield: A Journey to Five Continents, Pax Britannica: The Climax of an Empire,* and *The Great Port: A Passage through New York.* At present, he is working on the first and third volumes of a three-volume history of the British Empire (*Pax Britannica* is the second volume).

LINCOLN BARNETT, a former associate editor of *Life,* is the author of *The Universe and Dr. Einstein* and *The Treasure of Our Tongue: The Story of English from Its Obscure Beginnings to Its Present Eminence as the Most Widely Spoken Language on Earth.*

LAWRENCE MALKIN, a journalist who specializes in reporting on the world of business, is at present attached to the Washington bureau of *Time.* During the 1960's he spent seven years in London covering the British economy for the Associated Press.

NORMAN MALCOLM, professor of philosophy at the Sage School of Philosophy, Cornell, is the author of *Ludwig Wittgenstein: A Memoir.* He also wrote *Dreaming, Knowledge and Certainty* and *Problems of Mind: Descartes to Wittgenstein.*

STEPHEN TOULMIN, currently a professor of philosophy at Michigan State University, is a British educator and writer and the author of *Foresight and Understanding: An Enquiry Into the Aims of Science, Philosophy of Science, Reason in Ethics, 1950–1960,* and *The Uses of Argument, 1958–1964* and is the editor of *Physical Reality.*

# CREDITS

This book was prepared under the editorial direction of Joseph J. Thorndike with the following staff: Associate Editor, Ormonde de Kay, Jr.; Art Director, Kenneth Munowitz; Assistant Editors, Kaethe Ellis, W. Jeffrey Simpson; Pictorial Research, Peggy Buckwalter; Editorial Assistant, Pamela Wilson.

## PICTURE CREDITS

**10** Biblioteca Reale, Turin—Alinari. **13** Biblioteca Ambrosian, Milan. **15** top: Institut de France, Ms. B, f. 74 r.; center: Institut de France, Ms. B, f. 83 v.; bottom: IBM. **16** top: Royal Collection, Windsor Castle, copyright reserved; bottom: New York Public Library, Art Division. **18, 19** (both) Royal Collection, Windsor Castle, copyright reserved. **20** Institut de France, Ms. 2037—Giraudon. **23** British Museum. **24** Palazzo Vecchio, Florence—Alinari. **27** Palazzo Venezio, Rome—Scala. **28** Duomo, Florence—photo Instituto Geografico de Agostini, Novara. **30** *Mer des Histoires*, Paris, circa 1503. **34** Scala. **37** British Museum. **38** Louvre—Giraudon. **40** New York Public Library, Rare Book Division. **41** (both), **45** Kupferstichkabinett, Basel. **46** Universtatsbibliothek, Basel. **48** From *Du.* **49** By H. Leys, 1834. **50** Art Institute of Chicago. **53** L. Prowe, *Nicolaus Coppernicus*, 1883, 1884. **54** top: The Huntington Library, San Marino, Calif.; bottom: Burndy Library, Norwalk, Conn. **57** Polish Library, Paris—Guiley-Lagache. **59** top: Museo Storia della Scienza; bottom: British Museum. **60** top: Royal Society, London; center: Bibliothèque Nationale—Giraudon; bottom: Cabinet des Dessins, Musée du Louvre. **63** Burndy Library, Norwalk, Conn. **64** Nationalmuseum, Stockholm. **66** both: Lutherhalle, Wittenberg. **69** Wittenberg Stadtkirche—Deutsche Fotothek, Dresden. **70** Collection of Dr. Schleifenbaum, Weidenau—Foto Marburg. **73, 74** Lutherhalle, Wittenberg. **75** Günther Beyer, Weimar. **76** Foto Marburg. **77** Alinari. **79** Staatliche Museen, Berlin. **80** Bibliothèque Publique et Universitaire, Geneva—Arlaud. **83** Bibliothèque Nationale—Giraudon. **85** Editions du Seuil. **88** Emile Dourmerque, *Iconographie Calvienne*. **91, 92** top: Bibliothèque Nationale—Giraudon. **92** bottom: Theodore Beza, *Icones*, 1580. **93** Bibliothèque de l'Ecole des Beaux Arts, Paris—Giraudon. **94** National Portrait Gallery, London. **96, 97** (both), **98** The Gorhambury Collection, courtesy the Earl of Verulam. **101** British Museum. **105** top: Robertson, *History of Scotland during the Reigns of Queen Mary and James VI*, 1771; bottom: National Portrait Gallery, London. **108** Robertson, *History of Scotland during the Reigns of Queen Mary and James VI*, 1771. **111** Burndy Library, Norwalk, Conn. **112** National Portrait Gallery, London. **115** all: British Museum. **118** National Gallery of Scotland. **121** British Museum. **122** Hälsingborgs Museum. **125** Braun, *Civitates Orbis*, 1576; New York Public Library, Rare Book Division. **126** Erik Ritsche International, Geneva. **130** Crombie, *Augustine to Galileo*; New York Public Library. **133** The American Museum of Natural History. **134** Bibliothèque Nationale—Roger-Viollet. **139** Musée National de Versailles. **140** Giraudon. **143** Musée Conservatoire Arts de Metiers—Giraudon. **144** Robert Boyle, *Works*, 1744. **147** Bibliothèque Nationale—Giraudon. **148** National Portrait Gallery, London. **150** Culver Pictures, Inc. **152** British Museum. **154, 155** National Portrait Gallery, London. **159** The New-York Historical Society. **160** National Portrait Gallery, London. **163** Bodleian Library, Oxford. **165** David Loggan, *Cantabrigia Illustrata*, 1905; New York Public Library. **168** Fitzwilliam Museum, Cambridge. **172** New College, Oxford. **175** Tate Gallery, London. **176** Trinity College, Cambridge. **179** University Library, Cambridge. **180** Les Delices, Geneva; photograph, Robert Descharnes. **182** top: The New-York Historical Society; bottom: Private collection—Bulloz. **183** Bibliothèque Nationale Service Photographique. **184, 186** top: Institut Voltaire, Geneva. **186** bottom: Giraudon. **189** Bulloz. **190** National Gallery of Scotland—Giraudon. **195** Bibliothèque Nationale—Roger-Viollet. **196** Public Archives of Canada. **201** *Revue Française*. **202** Musée Carnavalet, Paris. **205** Bulloz. **206** National Por-